The Encyclopaedia Logic

G. W. F. Hegel

The Encyclopaedia Logic
(with the Zusätze)

Part I of the
Encyclopaedia of Philosophical Sciences
with the Zusätze

A new translation with Introduction and notes by
T. F. Geraets, W. A. Suchting, and H. S. Harris

Hackett Publishing Company, Inc.

Indianapolis / Cambridge

G. W. F. Hegel: 1770–1831
Copyright ©1991 by Theodore F. Geraets, W. A. Suchting, H. S. Harris
All rights reserved
Printed in the United States of America
02 01 00 99 98 97 96   2 3 4 5 6 7 8
Cover design by Listenberger Design & Associates
Interior design by Carol Sowell, Elizabeth Shaw Editorial Services
For further information, please address
HACKETT PUBLISHING COMPANY, INC.
P.O. Box 44937
Indianapolis, Indiana 46244-0937

Library of Congress Cataloging-in-Publication Data

Hegel, Georg Wilhelm Friedrich, 1770–1831.
    [Wissenschaft der Logik. English]
    The encyclopaedia logic, with the Zusätze: Part I of the
Encyclopaedia of philosophical sciences with the Zusätze /
G. W. F. Hegel; a new translation with introduction and notes by
T. F. Geraets, W. A. Suchting, H. S. Harris.
      p.   cm.
    Translation of Encyklopädie der philosophischen Wissenschaften.
Teil I, Wissenschaft der Logik. 3rd ed.
    Includes bibliographical references and indexes.
    ISBN 0-87220-071-X (cloth: alk. paper).
    ISBN 0-87220-070-1 (pbk.: alk. paper).
    1. Logic. I. Geraets, Theodore F. II. Suchting, W. A. (Wallis
Arthur). III. Harris, H. S. (Henry Silton), 1926- . IV. Title.
V. Title: Encyclopaedia logic, with the Zusätze. VI. Title:
Encyclopaedia logic.
B2918.E5H37 1991
160–dc20
                                          90–29023
                                             CIP

The paper used in this publication meets the minimum requirements of American National
Standard for Information Sciences — Permanence of Paper for Printed Library Materials,
ANSI Z39.48–1984.

∞

CONTENTS

TRANSLATORS' PREFACE

This book contains a collaborative translation of Hegel's *Encyclopaedia Logic*. The text is that of the third edition (1830) with the *Zusätze* (Additions) added posthumously by the editorial committee that published the first edition of Hegel's *Werke*; the editor responsible for the *Logic* was L. von Henning. We have worked mainly from the *Philosophische Bibliothek* edition (edited by F. Nicolin and O. Pöggeler) for the text of 1830, and from volume 8 of the *Theorie Werkausgabe* (edited by E. Moldenhauer and K.-M. Michel) for the *Zusätze*, first published in 1840.

Our text went through a considerable evolution even before Hegel's editors added the lecture commentary. The first edition of the *Encyclopaedia of the Philosophical Sciences in Outline* (of which our *Logic* is just the first part) was a slim volume that appeared in 1817. The second edition of 1827 was greatly enlarged, and included a lengthy historical preamble on the relation of Hegel's logical standpoint to the rationalist tradition, the empiricists Kant and Jacobi. This second edition was somewhat revised[1] and augmented in the final edition that appeared in 1830.

The *Encyclopaedia* as a whole is a compendious presentation of the foundations of Hegel's entire philosophical system, meant, above all, for the use of those attending his lectures ("Zum Gebrauch seiner Vorlesungen," as it says on the title page). It is essentially a set of propositions and arguments for discussion and explanation in the lectures, set forth in numbered sections. The numbered paragraphs are usually fairly brief, and as a general rule they are supplemented by a Remark (*Anmerkung*). In the present translation the Remarks are indented from the left margin to distinguish them from the main paragraph. The editors of the first collected edition of Hegel's works (which began appearing in 1832, just one year after his death) published the whole *Encyclopaedia* in three volumes with Additions (*Zusätze*) to a great many of the sections; the volumes were put together by the editors from notes taken by themselves and other auditors of the lectures. These Additions are included here, printed in smaller type than the main text.

Just as some paragraphs have no Remark by Hegel, so some were not furnished with a lecture commentary by the first editors. But many of the Additions are quite lengthy, and, where several Additions are given, we can generally see that they came from different courses. Hegel spoke haltingly and some students (notably the redoubtable Captain von Gries-heim in the period 1823–26) managed to transcribe practically everything he said. Of course, their understanding of what they heard was not always perfect, and their records were subject to errors of many kinds. But the editors had several sets of notes available for each course; and although they were quite willing to conflate the scripts of courses given in different years, there is no serious doubt that we have a generally reliable record of what Hegel said.

Of course, not even Hegel's very own spoken words (supposing that we had them) could have the authority of the long-pondered and carefully revised text that Hegel himself published. That is what is indicated by the use of reduced type. But we have followed the example set by the first editors, who inserted the lecture-commentary into Hegel's text, because Hegel himself made clear, in his successive prefaces to every edition, that the printed text was *not* meant to stand alone, but to be supplemented by the lectures. It is always important to remember that the "science of logic" in the *Encyclopaedia* is only an "outline." The truly complete and indepen-dent statement of his *Science of Logic* was given to the world by Hegel in three volumes published between 1812 and 1816. The "outline" published here is often much easier to understand (especially with its less authorita-tive Additions to help us). But anyone seriously interested in Hegel's logic should realise that the *Encyclopaedia* is only a stepping stone to the even-tual study of the larger work. (Hegel was working on a revision of the *Science of Logic* when he died. The first volume of it exists in a second edition that is almost exactly contemporary with our text.)

Our own collaborative translation came into existence gradually. T. F. Geraets began work on a new translation of Hegel's text in 1984, and he enlisted the aid of H. S. Harris soon after he began. Then, through the kind offices of James Hullett of Hackett Publishing Company, the two of us discovered in mid-1987 that W. A. Suchting had been working on a new version of the text for several years. (He actually began in 1984 also.) So, in August 1987, the three of us began to work together, with a general agree-ment that the Geraets draft of Hegel's text (as revised at that time) should be taken as basic. Suchting's draft of the lecture commentary served sim-ilarly as the basis of our translation of the *Zusätze*.

Harris was the "primary" translator only for the three Prefaces. These have never been translated into English before, and the reader should take note that Hegel wrote them as prefaces for the *Encyclopaedia* as a whole. It is also important to remember that the *Encyclopaedia* of 1817 was, to all intents and purposes, a different book from the one that now exists, com-plete in English for the first time.

We have all worked upon the text as a whole; and we have consulted all the previous translations (old and new) that we could find and use, especially the English of Wallace, the French of Bourgeois, and the Italian of Verra. In the main, our standard Glossary was fixed by the Geraets-Harris draft of Hegel's text. There was much agonised debate, and some revisions were made. But Suchting was unable to prevail in many places where we could not agree. Hence the necessity for two introductory statements—an essay by Harris and Geraets outlining the policies that have prevailed, and a set of comments by Suchting explaining how he thinks those policies could have been improved.

Geraets has assumed the primary responsibility for the Glossary, with notes on points that are not covered in either Introduction as well as some that are. The historical and philosophical notes are mainly the work of Harris, though we have all contributed anything useful that we could; and the bibliography (with its notes) is mainly the work of Suchting (though, here again, we have all made suggestions). We hope and believe that, by pooling our knowledge and our thought processes in this way, we have produced a volume that will be of more help to a wider range of readers and students than any of us could have produced working alone.

T. F. G.
W. A. S.
H. S. H.

---

1. At certain points the revisions are quite important. For an example of this see the commentary on § 574–77 by T. F. Geraets, "Les trois lectures philosophiques de l'Encyclopédie ou la réalisation du concept de la philosophie chez Hegel," *Hegel-Studien*, Bd. 10, 1975, pp. 231–54.

ACKNOWLEDGEMENTS

Théodore F. Geraets wishes to thank the Humanities and Social Sciences Research Council of Canada for release time part of which he devoted to the completion of this translation. Special thanks are due to Denise Thérien, the departmental secretary, who undertook most of the arduous, and seemingly unending, task of typing, correcting, and processing the present text. Without her patience and good humour, my work would have been a real nightmare.

H. S. Harris gratefully acknowledges the assistance of James Devin in compiling the Index of References; and the help of Giacomina, Carol, and David Harris in the making of the Analytical Index.

W. A. Suchting thanks V. Leahy for the typing up of his scripts.

INTRODUCTION:
TRANSLATING
HEGEL'S *LOGIC*

The *Encyclopaedia Logic* was the first of Hegel's logical works to be translated as a whole into English (indeed, one of the first of his books altogether). Rendered by William Wallace as *The Logic of Hegel*, it appeared in 1873 in the context of the movement of absolute idealism and the associated interest in Hegel that began in England (and to some extent in the United States) in the last third of the nineteenth century.[1] It was published with an extensive commentary, which was shed in a revised second edition of the translation in 1892.[2] The translation itself was subsequently reprinted no less than eight times by the time the work went into a third edition, differing from the second only in a few insignificant points, in 1975. It has continued to be in demand, being without a competitor (though there have been two complete and independent versions of the *Science of Logic*, a much larger work, within this century).

One of the most striking features of Wallace's rendering is that it reads so well: At least among the translations that appeared before 1939, say, no other has such fluency that it can often make readers forget that they are engaged with a translation and spare them that feeling, familiar to those who use such, of perusing a palimpsest. Those who know little else about Hegel know that he is a notoriously "difficult" writer, as regards both thought and style. He is found to be such, not only by native Anglophones (perhaps spoiled by the generally conversational style of the English philosophical classics), but even by those whose mother tongue is Hegel's. The young Marx, for instance, who was an enthusiastic admirer of Hegel, speaks of his "grotesque craggy melody."[3]

What is generally uninviting about so much of Hegel's work is probably more clearly displayed in the *Encyclopaedia* than anywhere else. It is a long road of brief, dry sections, containing none of the sometimes baroque exuberance of the *Phenomenology of Spirit*, and next to none of the more unbuttoned touches to be met with in the works later put together by other hands from lecture notes, such as those on the philosophy of history, of art, of religion, and so on. Many a sentence, "like a wounded snake, drags its slow length along."[4] Then there is Hegel's unique vocabulary, which involved giving ordinary German words new or at least specialised meanings, inventing new expressions, and deliberately exploiting the special capacity of the German language for neologisms.[5] Even Wallace's translation does not read like the normal English of most native philosophers, but generations of students have regarded his version as a lesser evil in comparison with the original. Perhaps only someone who has struggled with the task of putting Hegel into English can really appreciate Wallace's very many felicitous, and often apparently serendipitous, renderings.

This having been said, it must immediately be added that Wallace paid a high price for the sake of readability. Anyone who compares his version with the German must often be tempted to say, "C'est magnifique, mais ce n'est pas Hegel." All too frequently, Wallace achieves his relatively smooth surface, not just by occasionally supplementing the original, but by taking immense liberties with Hegel's syntax (going well beyond the necessary adjustment to English sentence structures), and by showing little regard for a consistent rendering of Hegel's technical vocabulary. The overall result is frequently more a paraphrase than a translation.[6] So, though Wallace's version sometimes illuminates the sense of the original, and will certainly continue to have a place in the history of philosophical literature in English, it cannot be relied upon by anyone seriously concerned with Hegel's text who must depend solely or for the most part on an English translation of it.*

* * *

Hegel showed his first visible interest in philosophical logic when he obtained his license to teach at Jena. He gave a course on logic and metaphysics at once (winter term 1801), probably at the instance of Schelling and some of Schelling's pupils. For several years he was the recognised "logician" of the Schelling party. But all the time he was becoming increasingly unhappy, both about the "formalism" that was evident among Schelling's imitators and followers, and about the "high academic" character of their terminology. By the end of 1804 he was convinced that logic must be expressed in the plain German of ordinary, unacademic consciousness, and with the most ordinary words for its basic concepts. Rosenkranz cites his first proclamation of a new programme (probably delivered at the beginning of his winter course in October 1804). The introduction to this course, says Rosenkranz,

*These four introductory paragraphs were drafted by W.A. Suchting (and slightly revised by us).

contains important declarations about [philosophical] *terminology* generally—to wit, that as far as possible it should be wholly brought back to the *mother tongue*. Hegel speaks first of how we make the study of philosophy more difficult, partly because we make demands on it that ought not to be made, and partly because we terrify ourselves with pictures of the demands that philosophy makes on us and which are too hard for us to meet. The truth should present itself to us in religion, of course, but for our culture faith is altogether a thing of the past; Reason, with its demand that we should not believe, but know what the truth is, has grown strong, that we should not merely have intuitive consciousness of the truth, but should comprehend it. The truth of his individuality, which the path of his existence traces precisely for him, the single individual is well aware of, but the consciousness of the universal life he expects from philosophy. Here his hope seems to be disappointed when instead of the fullness of life there appear concepts, and in contrast to the riches contained in the world of immediate experience the poorest abstractions are offered. But the concept is itself the *mediator between itself and life*, in that it teaches us how to find life in it and the concept in life. But, of course, only science itself can convince us of this.

What Hegel himself said, so Rosenkranz reports, was:

> For the *fixation* of concepts there is a means at hand which achieves its end, on the one side, but can also become more dangerous than the evil of being without concepts even, namely, *philosophical terminology*, the vocabulary established for this purpose from foreign languages, [specifically] Latin and Greek. I do not know, for example, what there is to the idea that the expression *"quantitative Unterschied"* is more definite than *"Grössenunterschied"*. Properly speaking, it belongs to the highest cultural development of the people *to say everything in their own language*. The concepts that we mark with foreign words seem to us to be themselves something *foreign* and not to belong to us immediately as our very own. The elements of things appear to us not to be the *present* concepts with which we are environed and have to deal with all the time and in which the most ordinary man expresses himself. *Being, Not-Being, One, Many, Quality, Size* and so on, are pure essences of this kind with which we *keep house* all the time in ordinary life. Such forms as these appear to us to be not worthy enough, as it were, for the grasping of those high *other-worldly* things, the Idea, the Absolute, in them; and something foreign is

more apt for it, since the Absolute, the *supersensible world* itself, is foreign to the common round of daily life in which we employ those concepts. But that which is *in itself* must just not have this foreignness *for us*, and we must *not give it this foreign look by using a foreign terminology*, but must count ourselves really convinced that the spirit itself is alive *everywhere* and that it expresses its forms in our own spontaneous natural language. They come up in the speech of everyday, *mingled and wrapped in crude concrete* [instances], for example, in "The tree is green." "Tree" and "green" are what controls our representation. We do not in ordinary life reflect on the "is," we do not set this *pure being* in relief, make it our ob-ject, as philosophy does. But this being is here present and expressed. It is, of course, necessary to have recourse to foreign terminology if we cannot find the determinate characteristics of the concept before us in our own language. It is not customary for us to do violence to language and to mold *new forms out of old words*. Our thought is still not properly at home in our language, it does not dominate the language, as it should, and we cherish in this regard, a blind reverence for what is brought from abroad.

But this foreign terminology, which is used partly in a futile and partly in a perverse way, becomes a great evil because it reduces concepts which are implicitly *movement* to something *stable* and *fixated*, so that the spirit and life of the matter itself disappears and philosophy degenerates into an empty *formalism*, which is very easily supplied for social chat; yet to those who do not understand the terminology it seems very difficult and deep. That is precisely what is *seductive* in a terminology of this kind, that it is in fact very easy to master it. It is all the easier to speak in it, because if I have no sense of personal shame, I can permit myself to utter every possible nonsense and triviality when I am talking to people in a language that they do not understand.[7] [emphasis probably added by Rosenkranz]

When he made this pronouncement, Hegel was still struggling with the problem of how systematic philosophy ought to be shaped, and what the place and function of pure logic were in a philosophical system. He solved this problem (more or less to his own final satisfaction) only at the end of that academic year. So it is crucially significant that he repeats the slogan of his new programme in his letter to J. H. Voss of May 1805:

Luther has made the Bible speak German; you, Homer—the greatest present that can be given to a people; for a people is barbarous and does not consider the excellent things it knows as its own property until it gets to know them in its own language;—if you would forget these two examples, I should like to say of my aspirations that I shall try to teach philosophy to speak German. Once that is accomplished, it will be infinitely more difficult to give shallowness the appearance of profound speech.[8]

The attempt to teach philosophy to speak German, upon which Hegel was just then embarking, involved first an arduous struggle on the part of ordinary consciousness to overcome its own standpoint and assumptions in order to reach the level of "pure thinking." This logic of "the experience of consciousness" was set out in the *Phenomenology of Spirit* (1807). Only after an immensely hard labour of self-purification is the student ready for the discipline of "pure thinking" in his/her "own language"; and the "possession of philosophy in one's own language" is by no means as simple as the reading of Homer in translation (or even of the Bible). As Hegel said in his lectures about twenty years later, it is more nearly comparable to the understanding of his creed achieved by someone who has tried to be a good Christian all his life.[9]

For although the philosophical logic of our own rational being is expressed with the most ordinary words of our ordinary lives, those words are not used in any ordinary way.[10] They are names of the concept of "pure thinking" (and its moments). That "Concept" moves toward full *self*-consciousness through use of these words. The most remarkable aspect of the way that Hegel does logic is his methodical insistence upon the self-reference of the "pure concept." The Concept is made to refer to itself at every stage, because there is nothing else available for its words to characterise. The whole standpoint of "consciousness," which has a world of "things" that its thoughts naturally refer to, has been transcended and put behind us. We are asked first to think what the concept of "pure being" *is*; and we go on from there in what is, or should be, an unbroken chain of "necessary" reflections until we finally comprehend what the logical thinking that has been doing all this self-reflection and self-determining is.

The stages on the way, or the links in the chain, are represented by ordinary words; and we must depend upon our previous familiarity with them, and with how they are used in ordinary life, to guide us to our comprehension of the motion of "pure thinking." But all of the "concept-words" in the chain have been lifted out of the great complex web of their ordinary meanings and uses. Logically, they mean only what the movement of "pure thinking" allows them to mean, at the point where they are introduced; and the destiny of that initial meaning is always to develop until it reaches a breaking point, and becomes a new "concept."[11]

In his own oral commentary, Hegel does quite a lot of picking and choosing among the ordinary uses of his German words. He is very conscious that the most familiar words for the categories and relations that structure our shared universe of discourse and experience, have many uses. Sometimes he tells us that this or that use (or family of uses) is "subordinate"—and then we are meant to disregard it; on the other hand, he also points to what may look like a very "subordinate" use as peculiarly illuminating or instructive. Occasionally he even points out that one of his "concept-names" has a *logical* meaning that diverges seriously from its ordinary use.

What then are we to do when we want to make Hegel's logical concept "speak English"? Obviously we must choose the best equivalents that we can in our natural language for the words that Hegel isolated from his own natural German. But no word in English will have quite the same complex of ordinary uses as a German word. So when we try to render the systematic movement of "the Concept," the words that we choose to isolate must come under strain at times; and the points of serious strain will usually be different from the points where Hegel himself was (or perhaps should have been) conscious of strain in his German.

What are we to do when this happens? To take one of the most elementary examples, philosophers in English (and French) are used to speaking of God as "the supreme *being*" (or *l'Etre suprême*); and of man as "the rational *being*." But Hegel's *German* gives him "das höchste Wesen" and "das vernünftige Wesen"; and for his *logic*, the distinctions between "being" (*Sein*), "essence" (*Wesen*), and "concept" (*Begriff*) are fundamental.

Now, "essence" is the proper *logical* equivalent of *Wesen*. So, if we want to render Hegel's logical thinking clearly and consistently, we must render the German expressions *logically*. This means that we must break radically with "ordinary usage" and speak of "the supreme essence," and the like. To do this is to violate one of the most sacred taboos of the English philosophical tradition. But it is the logical structure of "pure thinking" that is our topic, not the use-structures of two natural languages.

When three translators, with different backgrounds, and differing relations to and experiences of English and German, seek to collaborate in rendering Hegel's *Logic* in English, even a decision as elementary as the consistent rendering of *Wesen* by "essence" causes different degrees of strain. For Harris it causes no strain at all, and is even welcome, because it drives home two fundamental truths: First, that "pure thinking" must be distinguished sharply from the "experience of consciousness" (as we share it in ordinary language); and second, that Hegel's "essences" are real beings, not the mental entities of native English nominalism. Geraets accepts the violation of normal usage because the use of "essence" stresses that we are dealing with beings that are recognised as mediated, as inwardly relational, as having their raison d'être or ground, and therefore as not simply given or "there" any more.

Of course, even when one accepts the principle that the logical relations of the concept-names are what is crucial, there are places where ordinary usage must be respected in the interest of simple intelligibility. Thus, when the decision to render *Beziehung* as "relation" and *Verhältnis* as "relationship" has been painfully arrived at, the difficulty that in the sphere of quantity a *Verhältnis* is properly a "ratio" will not go away. English readers cannot be relied upon to identify "quantitative relationships" as "ratios". So the translator must make this identity explicit, and rely upon the reader to remember that this time the German word has *two* meanings which are *both* essential to the conceptual structure of the *Logic*. (Here, for once, we are all three quite happily agreed.)

As a rule, both the general philosophical tradition and the tradition of English Hegel translation must be respected as far as possible in order that there may be no *avoidable* obstacles in the way of our "possessing philosophy in English." But the English Hegel tradition is loose and various;[12] and the arguments we have had about what precedents should be followed, and what departures are unavoidably necessary, have been as eloquent as they are (in some cases) seemingly interminable. The decision to follow the lonely precedent provided by H. S. Macran,[13] who translated the three "moments" of the Concept (*Allgemeine, Besondere, Einzelne*) as "universal, particular, and singular", was determined by the insistence of Harris that "individuality" is what belongs to the concrete thinking of the logician, who unites the moments and comprehends them in their unity. In this view, the distinction between the "individual" and the "singular" is absolutely fundamental, and no translation that would permit even the accidental possibility of a confusion between them should be considered at all. Geraets agrees, mainly because "individual" and "the individual" have to be used to translate *individual* and *Individuum* (WL 2:571ss. 417ss). Hegel even speaks of "das *einzelne* Individuum" (*Enc.* § 344).

Wallace, Johnston and Struthers, and Miller (together with almost all the commentators) use "individual" for *Einzelne*. But ever since the triumph of nominalism in the fourteenth century, English thinkers have spoken of singular entities as "particulars". When the general tradition has been so radically corrupted, a fresh start is clearly necessary; and, since we have four German terms to render, we should utilise the resources of our logical vocabulary to the full. We do, in fact, have four words available, and there is one place in the logic books where even the nominalists needed them, so that our purely logical tradition was not corrupted by oversimplification.

In the classification of "judgments" the traditional logicians have spoken always of "universal, particular, and singular judgments."[14] This is the usage to which Hegel translators must return, both because it enables us to use "individual(ity)" in exactly the ways that Hegel uses its German cognates, *and* because it belongs to our own properly *logical* tradition. The fact that—because of the nominalist degradation of "particular" in reference to "things", and the implicitly rational tendency of ordinary discourse to speak of singular living organisms as "individuals"—the logical words "single" and "singular" now fall upon the eye and ear somewhat unexpectedly in reference to *real* things, both organic and inorganic, should be looked upon as an advantage in this case, too, because it reminds us that, although philosophical logic is the living spirit of language, the spirit of pure thinking is not directly identical to the spirit of everyday life.[15]

The need to distinguish between the language of logic and the language of experience brings us to one of the most vexing problems in Hegel's logical chain—the word *Daseyn*.[16] Language, as Hegel says in the *Phenomenology*, is the *Daseyn* of the Spirit.[17] In the *Logic* he adds the clarification that, as the element of free subjective spiritual *Daseyn*, ordinary language is the perfect paradigm of the necessary place of contingency in the total scheme of things.[18] Logic itself, on the other hand, is the determination *in* language of the "necessary" structure of the Concept, i.e., of thinking as self-knowing freedom. There can be nothing random in it. Philosophical logic must be a perfectly determinate linguistic structure.

Hegel himself says, at the very beginning of his discussion of *Daseyn*, "Daseyn ist *bestimmtes* Seyn."[19] This looks like a definition, so the earlier translators, faced with a word for which they had no proper equivalent—since they needed "existence" for the directly cognate *Existenz*, which is a much higher "determination of thought"—felt that they were directly authorised here to use "determinate being" for *Daseyn*.

This was a disastrous decision, which has had nothing but misleading consequences. Hegel's opening statement is not a definition; it only tells us that *Daseyn* is the first and most primitive "determination" following pure being (which is *completely* indeterminate). *Daseyn* is, in fact, the most general and, as such, the most *indeterminate* form of "finite" being. It is "determinacy that simply is, quality" (WL 1:95). It is "determinacy as such" (op. cit., p. 96), determinacy in the determination of being. In the *Phenomenology*, §§ 506 and 793, Hegel speaks of *bestimmtes Daseyn*. These are both crucial moments, and if *Daseyn* logically needs to be qualified in this way *specifically*, it is easy to see why a competent translator must not build the qualification into the *universal* rendering of the category. *Daseyn* is, on one side (looking back), "becoming," that which both is and is not; and on the other side (looking forward) it is "something"—a "something" that is not logically distinguishable from "the other".

Anyone who wants to direct the mind of an English reader to the intermediate point in just *this* logical progression (from "becoming" to "something") is bound to recognise that in this instance we must go a little way on the road with J. H. Stirling (who is, in general, the worst possible model for a Hegel translator, because his attempt to use English as if it were a German dialect denies the living genius of *our* native language altogether). Stirling calls *Dasein* "There-being". We must be literal too; but we can at least allow the hyphenated English words their natural order and speak of "being-there" instead. Or we can make a logical universal in the normal way (which is not confined to the schoolroom) and speak of "thereness".[20]

Logic is the "being for itself" of rational knowing, or the absoluteness of *Wissen*. Everything that can properly be called "experience" must have a cognitive aspect; and in that aspect it is a mode of *Wissen*. So *Wissen* must comprehend even our "errors"; and its absolute self-concept must embrace the comprehension of how and why "error" is necessary as relative truth in the process of the very coming-to-be of truth.[21] In his oral commentary on the *Logic*, Hegel illustrates this necessity several times when he discusses how the different stages of the Concept apply to God, or the human spirit.

The development of immediate *wissen* (the extremely fallible "certainties" of our sense and feeling) into absolute (or philosophical) *wissen* is set forth in the *Phenomenology of Spirit* as the discursive theory of the coming-to-be of *erkennen* ("cognition"). When it is fully explicated, and the whole map and compass of the journey are available to us, then cognition as cognition is comprehended and *wissen* has become *Wissenschaft* ("science"). In that perspective, the ordinary common sense *wissen*, from which we began, is mere *kennen* (or unscientific cognition).

The English word "know" is, of course, a blood relation of *kennen*. But the blood relations of *wissen* vanished with the demise of Anglo-Saxon. If we had a verb derived from the Latin *scire* as well as a noun, we should be better off, because we could use that for *wissen*, and so preserve the link between *wissen* and *Wissenschaft*. Then we could use "know" for *erkennen* (which is the normal recourse of all translators of German philosophical works). But as things are, the Hegel translator must take a different route—and it seems that only a rather stony road is available. We must use "know" and "knowledge"—our one surviving general term—for the comprehensive concept, *wissen*; and we must do the best we can with "cognition" and all its cognates for the rendering of *erkennen* and its cognates. *Kennen* is not logically important, and we have a ready supply of appropriate renderings for it.[22] But Hegel's *erkennen* and related terms should always be recognisable to the reader; and since almost any use of the verb "cognize" creates a strained effect, we have frequently replaced it with phrases that involve "cognizance" or "cognizant" as well as "[re]cognise". We are well aware that the results are still somewhat unnatural in places, but we are at least confident that the desired goal has been attained; and one valuable side effect is that the connection between *erkennen* and *anerkennen* ("recognise") is never lost to sight.

Languages, as the *Daseyn* of the Spirit, grow up freely, and reflect the contingency of experience, with its incidental needs and its accidental contrivances. But logic (we can now say clearly) is the linguistic "being-for-self" of thinking Spirit as such, its perfected determinateness; and when someone uses the resources of his or her native language to distinguish the objective "necessity" of thought-thinking-itself from the subjective freedom of experience, then he or she is bound to use those resources in ways that can only be matched artificially in other languages.

Thus, Hegel has two words for "object" available to him. He uses *Objekt* for the logical concept of the object (the one-sided counterpart of the still one-sided logical "subject", or "subjective concept"), and *Gegenstand* for the ordinary object of experience, in all its modes—the object of "consciousness" (and the complement of *Bewusstseyn*). As we would expect, the two words often occur in near proximity. We might well be tempted to think—as Knox did about most of Hegel's vocabulary, and as almost all translators have felt about *Objekt* and *Gegenstand*—that Hegel's usage is determined only by the fact that he recognised (or was taught) very early that frequent repetition of the same word is tedious and inelegant, and should be avoided where possible. But a translator who has grasped the crucial importance of the distinction between "consciousness" (or experience) and "pure thinking" (or logic) must see that any variation upon a word that has an unmistakably logical function (such as *Objekt*) has to be rendered faithfully, because there *may* be a logical distinction involved; and if nothing but a stylistic contingency is actually discoverable, that fact itself must be made visible.

So, we are here obligated to provide the reader with an accurate picture of how Hegel used two words, when we have only one word ourselves. In this case, we have made our one word into two by hyphenating it ("object") whenever it represents *Gegenstand*, the clumsier compound of Hegel's native *Volk*. *Gegenstand* occurs more frequently than *Objekt*, but it is good to remind the reader that it is not the proper counterpart of *Subjekt*; and because it belongs (as we think) to Hegel's "ordinary" vocabulary, we have felt justified in avoiding our artificial expedient wherever "subject matter" or "topic" is an appropriate rendering for *Gegenstand* in ordinary parlance.

A somewhat similar case is the one involving *Unterschied* and *Differenz*, except that here both are specifically logical terms. *Unterschied* belongs properly to the doctrine of essence and has to be distinguished from the otherness of *Daseyn*.[23] It is the distinction of reflection; in absolute distinction (A and non-A) the terms are distinct in virtue of "the *simple not*." Hegel stresses the importance of grasping absolute distinction as simple, i.e., as relating to itself, as self-distinction. "But what is distinct from the distinction is the identity. It [distinction] is therefore itself [i.e., distinction] and identity." Both distinction and identity are at the same time the whole and one of its moments. Although distinction develops into "diversity" which implies comparison by a third and is a moment that "repeats" the otherness of *Daseyn*, and further into the "antithesis" and "opposition" of what is positive and what is negative, it must always be understood in its essential opposition to (or distinction from) identity. *Identität* and *Unterschied* are opposed by virtue of the *Scheidung*, or separation, that negates the unseparatedness of identity. In making our terminological choice we should, as is often the case, take our cue from the verb: *unterscheiden* means "to distinguish". We must not forget, however, that Hegel frequently speaks of *sich unterscheiden* ("to distinguish itself"). Indeed, the logical distinctions are not just *our* work; they are produced by the logical "subject," i.e., the Concept, itself. *Unterschied* is more akin to the *distinctio realis* than to the *distinctio rationis tantum* of traditional metaphysics. It is in no way due to a purely subjective act. "Reason" in the Hegelian sense does, of course, produce (and overcome) distinction, but then, for Hegel, logic is metaphysics; *distinctio rationis* is *distinctio realis*.[24]

Although we recognise that *Unterschied can* mean "difference", this happens because "distinction" itself can and must sometimes be understood in this way. But *Unterschied* does not always, or even principally, mean "difference". The more fundamental meaning is "distinction". And since there is great advantage in using only one English word to translate a logical term of such capital importance and its cognates, we have chosen to translate *Unterschied* always by "distinction".[25] This terminological choice gives us the additional bonus of freeing "difference" for the translation of *Differenz*.

For Hegel, *Differenz* characterises the second moment that follows the first simple and undeveloped unity of determination, and that precedes the third moment of "return from *Differenz* into simple self-relation" (§ 85). This intermediate position gives the term a double meaning. On the one hand, what is *different* is more developed than what remains in its simple, initial unity. *Different* thus means "differentiated" (§§ 196, 199, 200, 201), and *Differentiierung* "differentiation" (§§ 202, 203). These terms are akin to "particular" and "particularisation" (*Besonderung*, § 201). On the other hand, what is *different* can resist the return to self-relation. Under this aspect, *Differenz* does not mean a finitude waiting to be transcended, but a dualism (WL 1:47) that attempts to prevent its assumption into a new, articulated unity and tries to absolutise itself. We then have something quite close to the radical *différence* (or *différance*) of some postmodernists.

The most apt translation for *Differenz* is simply "difference", a term to be interpreted, like the German term itself, in a more positive, developmental, or a more rigid or even absolute way, according to the context in which it occurs.

Quantitative Differenz is Schelling's term to express the difference in degree of either subjectivity or objectivity that characterises subject and object.[26] Each side is a relative Totality in which one of the two outweighs the other, while both sides remain nevertheless absolute identity. Hegel's key criticism of this position is: "Die quantitative Verschiedenheit ist nicht wahrhafter Unterschied; das Verhältnis ist ganz äußerlich" ("The quantitative diversity is no genuine distinction; the relationship is entirely external"). Moreover, the outweighing of one or the other is just "sense determination" (*sinnliche Bestimmung*). For Schelling the Absolute is not only absolute identity; but, more specifically, "*quantitative Indifferenz* des Subjektiven und Objektiven." Hegel uses *Indifferenz* in our text, not only to refer to the middle between the two poles of the magnet (*Indifferenzpunkt*), but also with reference to the Absolute (§ 86). We have decided to translate it as "Indifference", using the initial capital to distinguish it from "indifference", which stands for *Gleichgültigkeit*.

In a number of cases we have had to use *two* English words for one German term. In the case of *Verhältnis*, which has been discussed already, there is an idiomatic use of *Verhalten* or *Verhältnisse* which makes "situation" necessary as a third rendering. The reader will find all such cases in the Glossary; and she or he can rest assured that, whether the Glossary gives one, two, or, in desperate cases, three, renderings for a German word, any overlapping in the rendering of different German words in English has been clearly shown. We believe that all important logical words have been successfully distinguished. The only exception to this rule is that the English idiom "for this reason" (or "for the same reason", etc.) renders words like *darum* and *ebendarum*, and does not indicate the presence of *Vernunft*. (This exception, too, is absolutely reliable, and we think that it will cause no difficulty.)

In another set of cases, we have been forced by the copiousness of German to use the same English word for two different words in German.

In these cases (the couplets *formell/formal*, *ideell/ideal*, *reell/real* are the most obvious, but not the only ones), we have marked the distinction clearly by inserting the German word itself for the less frequent members of the German pair.

After much agonised debate we have managed to rescue the German words *Ding* and *Sache* from this category. *Ding* is the most ordinary word for "thing". In its perfectly determinate logical use it means a complex universal object of perceptual consciousness: an "essence" that "has properties". This is a familiar meaning of "thing" in philosophical English. A *Sache* is a "thing" in another sense. It is an object of theoretical or practical concern, the thing in question; and although it may be a physical thing—for instance, the objects of sense-certainty in the *Phenomenology* ("tree" and "house") are as such *Sachen*, not *Dinge*—it is also, quite typically, a goal of human practical concern, a "cause" that we strive to serve, as well as what our effort of cognition is concerned with.

The two words became connected in German philosophical logic, because both the common sense philosophers and the sceptics who can be loosely classified as "influenced" by Kant, began speaking of his *Ding-an-sich* ("thing-in-itself") as *die Sache selbst* ("the Thing itself"). When Hegel developed his speculative concept of "absolute knowing" as the knowing of "what truly is," this suited his logical need, because it provided him with a perfect bridge in ordinary consciousness between the strictly unknowable and the absolutely known. His *Sache* is a Greek *pragma*—one of those "things" of which Protagoras said that "man is the measure." Hence, the English translators have gone all over the linguistic map in rendering it (and all of them need four or five terms for it). But in logic it is essential to maintain the awareness that *die Sache selbst* is the right answer to the "problem" of the *Ding an sich*; and, of course, we must have *one* word for it. In the *Logic* we do not have to deal with the concrete *Sachen* of sense-certainty, so we have finally settled upon "the matter itself" for *die Sache selbst*. It is true that we also need "matter" as one of the complements of "form"; and that physical "matters" play an important role in the dialectic of *das Ding*; but these uses of "matter" are confined to restricted contexts where the meaning is readily distinguished. So we do not think that any confusion will occur. The "matter" of the discussion will always be readily apparent.

Detailed discussion of other terms seems hardly necessary at this point, except for two that pose special problems: *Schein* (*scheinen*) and *Aufhebung* (*aufheben*). The first is peculiarly obscure, and the second is systematically ambiguous. With *Schein* and *scheinen* we must start from three fixed points, two provided by the context, and one provided by ordinary usage. First, *Erscheinung*, which means "appearance", is a higher development, and contains or expresses the "truth" of *Schein* in a fuller measure. Second, the use of *scheinen* is determined by the physical analogy that is basic to the logic of "reflection". Finally, ordinary usage tells us that *Schein* is deceptive; it is what *seems* to be, but is not really so. This fact of ordinary usage harmonises with our first logical guide, and conflicts with the second. For the "light" of "essence" that "shines" inwardly expresses the inner articulation that makes "being" into "essence", which is "the truth of being."

The reader must be left here with a puzzle. We have used "seem" and "semblance" in the contexts where the negative aspect is clearly dominant; and "shine" (verb and noun) most of the time. The previous tradition favours "show", but nothing in Hegel's discussion is made any clearer by it. It seems wiser—where the interpretation is problematic in any case—to stay as close to Hegel's language (with its implicit metaphor) as possible.[27]

With *aufheben*, there is no problem about the meaning, because Hegel explains the term (in its systematically ambiguous use) as clearly as it can be explained.[28] But there has always been controversy about how it should be rendered. One tradition allows the translator to decide whether the "cancelling" or the "preserving" moment is dominant, and to use a battery of words to render different supposed shades of meaning. But the perfect determinacy of Hegel's logical concept forbids us to take this route (which, being the road of subjective arbitrariness, is a thoroughly bad one in any event). So, for this fundamental name of the logical movement of the Concept, we have had to decide between "sublation", an artificial logical word that has virtually *no* meaning, except what Hegel's explanation and its own context give it, and "suspension", which is the ordinary word that comes closest to being systematically ambiguous in the right way. *Aufheben* is a very ordinary word in German; the English "put by" has most of the same ambiguity, though without the element of "raising up". But "put by" would be as alien in logical discourse as "sublate" is in vernacular speech (and about as empty of all obvious meaning). In the end, our majority has decided that even "suspend" is out of place in pure logic. So only "sublate" will be found in our translation.

Hegel uses *übergreifen* to express the positive aspect of the process of *Aufhebung*. The concept that results from speculative "comprehension" (*begreifen*) reaches back and "overgrasps" the opposition of the moments produced by thought in its dialectical stage. The metaphor comes from Stoic tradition. Zeno used the five fingers to represent the differing "apprehensions" of the five senses; then, closing his fist, he called that gesture "comprehensive sensation". To express the comprehensive power of thought, he grasped the closed fist in his other hand. "Overgrasp" is not to be found in our dictionaries. But anyone who reflects upon Zeno's metaphor will see why we need it, and how different the meaning is from any of the current uses of "overreach".

English is a language with a distinctly mongrel ancestry. But by and large, it will be seen that we have adopted a word of Anglo-Saxon origin in preference to one of Latinate descent where we appeared to have a choice; and where the *Fürsichseyn* of the logical Concept was not at issue, we have exploited the full resources of all the English that we jointly possessed. In the case of some German expressions of which Hegel was fond (*überhaupt*, for example), we were often burdened with an *embarras de richesses* in choosing the best English equivalent. At other times it is a matter for very nice judgment as to whether the use of different words to render the same German word may not produce a misleading impression of the style of the original. In general, we have striven to mimic, where possible and appropriate, the etymology of the foreign words. To take an example largely at random, the verbs "change" and "alter" are pretty much synonyms, but we have often chosen the second to render *verändern*, because the (Latin) root meaning of *alter* mirrors the *ander* root of the German verb. (This is an example of a conflict of criteria, too, since "change" is an Anglo-Norman product.)

Apart from *Daseyn*, there is just one place where we have resorted to Stirling's artificial mimicry of German. Hegel's *schließen* is directly cognate with *Schluß* (which is his regular word for "the syllogism"). There are many verbal plays upon this relationship in German which cannot be reproduced because the corresponding words are *not* cognate in English. But where Hegel uses *mit sich zusammenschließen* to express the "closure of the Concept with itself" (as a "syllogism"), we have concluded that an artificial echo of the process of syllogistic reasoning was not more opaque or obscure than more "normal" expressions like "closing with itself." So we have allowed the Concept to "con-clude with itself." It is our hope that, by reminding the reader of syllogistic inference, this may even be more helpful than the use of more ordinary (but nonlogical) words.

There is one logically significant way in which Hegel violates the normal grammatical conventions. He sometimes gives us a singular verb after two subject terms. This seems to be meant to indicate that the subjects are really identical. Often this is easy to grasp (see, for instance, "vanity and superficiality" on p. 22). But occasionally it is quite unexpected and paradoxical, as in § 149. If his usage were not preserved in such cases, his meaning would be quite lost. So we have elected to follow him consistently in all instances.

Two disconnected points, broadly relating to vocabulary, should be added here. One relates to Hegel's use of emphasis (italics). In some cases this simply reflects different typographical conventions, and as English translators, we have felt free to choose to follow the conventions of our own community and time. For example, Hegel regularly emphasises the names of philosophers, but we have not followed him here. He often uses emphasis where today we would use quotation marks. We have occasionally replaced emphasis by quotation marks where they seemed more appropriate. But wherever Hegel chose to emphasise words and phrases, for some reason that was not apparent to us, we have followed him faithfully.

The other point concerns *our* capitalisation of the initial letter. The reader should understand that we cannot be guided by Hegel's usage here, since *all* German nouns normally have an initial capital. We decided to limit the use of initial capitals to the Concept and the Idea, where these are used in the singular and absolute sense. Being and Essence are capitalised where they stand for the entire first and second "sphere" of the *Logic*.

****

One final remark. No translation is produced in a linguistic vacuum. Even if translators were to work entirely for themselves, rendering a foreign text for self-clarification, for fun, or for some private reason, and not showing the result to anyone else, they would necessarily have to work within a tradition, however much they were to transform it. Those who expect their work to be used by others (whatever the determining motives for embarking on the project) must function even more completely in the context of a tradition, since all readers inevitably have sets of expectations formed by previous, related renderings. Sometimes the translator may judge it essential to depart from the tradition, perhaps radically, in order to achieve, broadly, greater fidelity to the original. But such steps must not be taken lightly if one wants the important innovations to be given a hearing. Any hint of change for its own sake in one place can easily lead the reader to a prejudice against the whole. Here the motto must be: "Hasten slowly!" None of us wanted to go too fast; and if some readers feel that we have done so (or agree with Suchting that we have sometimes gone in the wrong direction), we have at least tried to give a clear account, both here and in the following essay, of what our relation to the tradition is.*

H. S. Harris
T. F. Geraets

*Like our opening paragraphs, this last one was first drafted for us by W.A. Suchting.

NOTES

1. For details about the English scene, see J. Muirhead (1927).

2. A revised text of the commentary was published separately in 1894 as *Prolegomena to the Study of Hegel's Philosophy and Especially of His Logic*.

3. Marx, letter to his father, November 1837, Marx-Engels, *Collected Works*, vol. 1, 18.

4. Alexander Pope, *An Essay on Criticism*, line 357.

5. For the relation of Hegel's "philosophical language" to "ordinary" language, see first John McCumber (1979). For general discussions of Hegel's philosophy of language see further A. Koyré (1931), J. Simon (1966), T. Bodammer (1969), D. Cook (1971), M. Clark (1971), and M. Züfle's detailed study, *Prosa der Welt*, which tends, however, to be oriented more to Hegel's *Aesthetics* and *Phenomenology of Spirit* than to his *Logic* (for which see particularly 71ff, 289ff).

6. See also the criticisms of Wallace's translation of the third part of the *Encyclopaedia* (*Philosophy of Mind*) by M. J. Petry in his translation of Hegel's *Philosophy of Subjective Spirit* (1979), 1:cxxi–xxiii. Wallace himself was very modest about his translation. In the *Prolegomena*, he writes, "With a subject so abstruse and complicated as Hegel's Logic, and a style so abrupt and condensed as that adopted in the *Encyclopaedia*, a satisfactory translation can hardly fall within the range of possibilities." The task of such a translation, he goes on, has "come to seem nearly insuperable." And he notes later: "The translator has tried to keep as closely as possible to the meaning, without always adhering very rigorously to the words of the original. It is, however, much more literal in the later and systematic part, than in the earlier chapters" (op. cit., vii, xvi).

7. K. Rosenkranz, *Das Leben Hegels* (Berlin, 1844), 183–84; Harris and Knox, 256–58 (with some slight modifications).

8. Hegel, *Briefe*, vol. 1:99–100; Butler and Seiler, p. 107.

9. See below, § 237, Addition.

10. "Philosophy has the right to select from the language of common life which is made for the world of representational thinking, such expressions as *seem to come close* to the determinations of the Concept. For a word selected from the language of common life, too, there cannot be any question of *demonstration*; one associates it with the same concept for which philosophy employs it; for common life has no concepts, but [only] notions, and to [re]cognize the concept of what is else a mere notion is philosophy itself. It must suffice therefore if representational thinking, in the use of its expressions that are employed for philosophical determinations, has only a faint notion of their distinctive meanings; just as it may be the case that one [re]cognizes in these expressions nuances of representation that are more closely related to the corresponding concepts." *Wissenschaft der Logik*, ed. G. Lasson, 2:357, *Gesammelte Werke*, 12:130, Miller, 708 (translation amended). Our use of "Concept" or "concepts" for *Begriff(e)*, and of "representational thinking" or "representation" as well as "notion" for *Vorstellung*, is discussed in the Notes to the Glossary. The above quotation shows, we think, how the word "notion" is much more appropriate for translating *Vorstellung* than for *Begriff* (as Miller has done). This departure was initiated by W. Kaufmann in his rendering of the Preface to the *Phenomenology* (1966).

11. Compare further J. McCumber, *Hegel-Studien* 14 (1979): 183–96.

12. See M. J. Inwood, *Hegel Selections*, Glossary, 68–70.

13. In *Hegel's Doctrine of Formal Logic* (Oxford, 1912) and *Hegel's Logic of World and Idea* (Oxford, 1929). Among the commentators, Stace followed this sound precedent. Stirling also

uses these terms for the "forms of the Notion"—see, for instance, *The Secret of Hegel* (1898), 159. But Stirling's habit as a translator was to reproduce the German terms of Hegel with English semantic elements (as if German were the *only* language in which philosophical logic could be written); and his use of the simple antithesis between "universals" and "particulars" in his own English discourse about Hegel illustrates very vividly the nominalist decadence of ordinary English usage.

14. For once we are logically richer than the Germans, so that we can make one necessary logical distinction that drove Hegel himself back to the dog-Latin of the schools. When *he* comes to the classification of judgments he simply uses the traditional terminology (§ 75). Partly this is because he wants the gulf between the "traditional logic" and his own philosophical logic to be quite plain. But partly it is because German did not give him the distinction that he needed. If he *had* used his own terminology here he would be in difficulties. An *einzelne Urteil* would be what we call "a single judgment" rather than what we call "a singular judgment".

15. Although we have called this a "fresh start"—and have mentioned only Macran as a forerunner—the reader should realise that our translation already belongs to a new "tradition" in this matter. The "Trinity Hegel Translation Group" followed the Macran convention in its rendering of the *Jena Logic*; and it has been adopted uniformly, so far, in the translations of Hegel's *Vorlesungen* for which Peter Hodgson is the general editor. (See his Glossary for the *Lectures on the Philosophy of Religion*, University of California Press, 1984–87). The convention also holds for the *Lectures on the History of Philosophy*, which is already in preparation; and Leo Rauch has adopted it in his translation of "Reason in History" (he marks his few departures from it quite carefully; see *Introduction to the Philosophy of History*, Hackett, 1988).

16. We use the spelling of Hegel's own time deliberately, to remind those who think that *Dasein* belongs by right of philosophical conquest to Heidegger and his adherents, that the most ordinary words in a language belong to the people, and not to philosophers (whether collectively or individually).

17. *Gesammelte Werke* 9:276–78; Miller, §§ 508–11.

18. *Encyclopaedia* § 145, Addition.

19. This is the first sentence of Chapter II of the *Science of Logic*, and those who think that it authorises the translation of *Daseyn* as "determinate being" are forced to paraphrase it. But see also *Encyclopaedia* § 90 below.

20. The modern Italian and French translators have seen the necessity to go this far with Stirling too. De Negri began it with *esserci* in 1931; and Bourgeois has followed suit with *Etre-là*. It is ironic to notice that in 1898 Stirling was moved to add a footnote (p. 243) apologising for the "irredeemable ugliness" of "There-being"; for this footnote graces a page upon which we find "be-ënt" (for *seiend*) and "There-beënt-ity" (for *Daseiendes*). Only the hyphen needs any apology in "being-there"; and Stirling himself hoped that "thereness" would join "whereness" in the dictionary. (It is obvious that he did not think that "be-ënt" would do so!)

21. See *Phenomenology*, *Gesammelte Werke* 9:30; Miller, § 39.

22. The expressions actually used are recorded in the Glossary.

23. For this and what follows see WL II, 32ss.

24. Even the most recent French translators have chosen to translate *Unterschied* by *différence*, mainly because the term *différence* has taken on such an important and strongly nonsubjective sense in recent French philosophy. *Distinction* has in French become a close equivalent to *distinctio rationis* in the traditional sense. Our assessment of the situation in English usage is

that this has not (yet) happened. "To be distinct" draws the term "distinction" away from its purely subjective sense. Valerio Verra has also chosen to use *distinzione* for *Unterschied*; so have the Italian translators of the 1817 *Encyclopaedia*.

25. Miller uses "difference" in the section dealing specifically with *Unterschied*. So the sentence quoted above, "Das Unterschiedene aber vom Unterschiede ist die Identität," is translated as "But that which is different from difference is identity" (Hegel's *Science of Logic*, p. 417). One page earlier, however, *die Unterschiedene* is rendered as "distinct terms", *unterschieden sein* as "are distinguished", and *die Unterschiedenheit* as "the distinguishedness". The confusion is made worse by the fact that "difference" is also used to translate *Verschiedenheit* (p. 413).

26. For this and what follows see *Vorlesungen über die Geschichte der Philosophie*, vol. 3, TWA 20: 440–41.

27. Of course, we do not all agree that the interpretation *is* problematic; but the problems arise quickly enough when we start comparing what we think Hegel means.

28. See the Remark to § 96; and compare the Remark at the end of Chapter I of the *Science of Logic* (Lasson 1:93–95; Miller, 106–8).

TRANSLATING HEGEL'S *LOGIC*: SOME MINORITY COMMENTS ON TERMINOLOGY

> What is so much in the power of men as language, will very often be capriciously conducted. . . . The chief rule which I propose to follow, is to make no innovation, without a reason sufficient to balance the inconvenience of change. . . . This . . . will give occasion to many curious disquisitions, and sometimes perhaps to conjectures, which, to readers unacquainted with this kind of study, cannot but appear improbable and capricious. But . . . they are not to be considered altogether as wanton sports of wit, or vain shews of learning.
>
> Samuel Johnson,
> *The Plan of a Dictionary of the English Language*

When people come together to produce a translation disagreements are to be expected, and when the text is Hegel's *Logic* they are inevitable. Many of the differences within the present *troika* have been resolved in the course of long discussions: through persuasion, compromise, or just plain exhaustion. However, a number of problems could not be ironed out thus. In this regard, it has happened that I have been, more often than either of my colleagues, the odd man out. So it was finally decided that we would handle the situation in the following way. As regards comparatively minor issues of terminology and broadly "stylistic" questions, final responsibility would rest with the translator who had produced the original working draft translation—specifically, as regards Hegel's own text, with my two colleagues, and, as regards the "Additions," with me. As to more basic questions of terminology, the majority view would prevail, and the Glossary lists the renderings canonical for the translation. We all contributed a great deal to it, and we all concur on the majority of choices. However, it was agreed that I would have the right to state dissident views in a separate place, and so the most significant of these are presented in the following pages.

What is said there should not obscure the fact that I agree with much of my colleagues' Introduction. I have tried to take account of what positive arguments they offer for their alternative views, even if not always in explicitly polemical form. Informed readers must be the ultimate judges of the strengths and weaknesses of the various cases. They should, we believe, gain from this opportunity to consider differing views about difficult matters.

I do not offer any general theory of translation underlying my approach to the problems of rendering Hegel's *Logic* in particular. In any case, the problems in question cannot be resolved just by appeal to broad principles relating to translation as such or to Hegel's texts in particular; rather, they require detailed, highly contextualised argument. Hence I beg indulgence in advance from readers for many of the following discussions which may sometimes seem at first reading too finely drawn. Nevertheless, some general pointers have emerged in the course of actually working on the translation, and a couple of them may be worth recording here, if only to give the reader some idea of assumptions underlying the following discussions of specific questions.

I take very seriously a passage from one of Hegel's letters which is cited (with fuller context) in my colleagues' Introduction: "I wish to try to teach philosophy to speak German." Hegel here alludes to his program of presenting his philosophy in the words and syntax of his native language rather in those of Latin and Greek in their various derived forms. Now, this is a less clear-cut goal in English, where the influence of the classical tongues, especially via their Romance descendants, is much deeper, much more bone of the bone, flesh of the flesh of the language than is the case in German. But it means at least that the translator should strive for a maximum of linguistic "naturalness," consistent, of course, with fidelity to the meaning of the text in a narrower, so to speak "semantic" sense.

Furthermore, Hegel tried to achieve the aim set out in the sentence quoted above by various means, probably the most important of which was the use of ordinary German words and phrases (either as such or in cognate forms) in special senses. One result is that he often uses the same expression in both technical and nontechnical senses, in different contexts. It is not always easy to decide which is which. However, the translator must try to do so. To say (as it has been put to me) that the translator should render the text "consistently," leaving it up to the reader to decide how a certain expression is being used, is to abdicate the translator's proper role, and, anyway, this rule already breaks down even in the simplest cases.

Finally, the point may be made that it is not by any means always clear when it is correct to say that a "mistranslation" has occurred. When, for example, they render *Entäußerung* as "uttering" or (applied to God) "self-emptying", disagreement may well reduce in the end to a matter of taste.

W. A. Suchting

Specific Disagreements

All otherwise unattributed § references are to the *Encyclopaedia Logic*. The § sign followed by a number signifies Hegel's own major statement, which comprises the initial paragraph of a section; an R after the number means Hegel's own Remark, and an A after the number means the editorial Addition, itself followed by a number if there is more than one such to a section. References to Hegel's *Werke* (see following list) specify volume number followed by a colon and then page number(s).

Abbreviations of titles used are

EL   *Encyclopaedia Logic* (that is, the work of which the present is a translation)

I:THL   "Introduction: Translating Hegel's Logic" (earlier in this book)

OED   *Oxford English Dictionary*

SL   *Science of Logic* (translated by A. V. Miller, London: Allen & Unwin, 1969)

W   Hegel's *Werke in zwanzig Bänden* (Theorie Werkausgabe, Frankfurt a.M.: Suhrkamp Verlag, 1969ff)

(1) *Anzahl*

This is an ordinary German word, meaning "number" or "quantity". Hegel uses it as a purely technical term to signify one of the two conceptual constituents of number, the other being *Einheit*, "unit" (§ 102). *Anzahl* means the number of units contained in a given number. It is important to remember that the notion of *Anzahl* becomes properly applicable only at the stage of multiplication (factorisation) where the units involved are homogeneous, as distinct from addition. This is clear enough from a reasonably close reading of § 102 R, especially paragraph five, but it is made perfectly explicit in SL, 210, line 5 (W 5:240, bottom of page). Thus in, for example, the number 6, if 2 is taken as the unit, then the *Anzahl* is 3; if 3 is the unit, the *Anzahl* is 2.

Wallace rendered the term by the old word "annumeration". This has the considerable merit of similarity in etymology to *Anzahl*. But it may well suggest that an *Anzahl* is the *result* of a process (of counting) (like Miller's "amount") rather than its being more accurately describable as the "index" of a number. This can be captured, retaining the etymological point of Wallace's word, at the expense of a step in the direction of neologism, by rendering *Anzahl* as "annumerator".

The reader should realise that the present translation renders *Anzahl* sometimes as "annumeration" and sometimes as "annumerator", thus suggesting to the unwary reader that there are two concepts, whereas in fact there is just one.

(2) *aufheben, (das) Aufheben, Aufhebung*

Aufheben (the discussion may be confined to the verb) is an ordinary German word, which (as Hegel explains in § 96 A) has the double meaning of "do away with" and "preserve". He uses the word in both nontechnical and technical senses. As to the former, the first of the two meanings just listed (e.g., § 119 R) is the usual one. As to the latter, he makes use of both meanings to mark his conception of the way in which one logical category successively does away with and also includes an immediately preceding one.

The present translation does not clearly recognise the distinction between Hegel's nontechnical and technical uses, rendering *aufheben* as if he always uses it in the second way. If the distinction were to be respected, there would be no difficulty at all about the first, for there are many English words ("cancel", "abolish", and so on) that would do the job quite satisfactorily. It is the second, technical use that gives trouble. Since the publication of J. H. Stirling's *The Secret of Hegel* (1865), the standard English rendering has been "sublate". Now, according to the OED, the term appears first in English about the mid-sixteenth century, with the meaning "remove", including removing by destroying. It appears again in nineteenth-century logic books (as early as 1838), where it means "deny", "contradict". Stirling simply imposed on it the extra semantic dimension of "include", "preserve", for the sole purpose of having an English word with a meaning to match the dual meaning of *aufheben*. So it is clear that this involves the rendering of an ordinary German word by a quite extraordinary English one that by the nineteenth century lived on only in manuals of logic and that as a translation of *aufheben* was completely factitious.

Is there an English word which is both ordinary and also possessed of the dual meaning of the German one? I suggest that "suspend" fills the bill: it is perfectly ordinary and has the dual sense of something's being put out of action whilst continuing to exist. In addition, it has strong etymological similarities to *aufheben: sus-* is a form of *sub-,* which can signify "from below" and consequently "on", and *pend* is the stem of the verb *pendere,* "hang", whilst *aufheben* is formed from *auf,* meaning "on", and *heben,* "lift". These etymologies reflect logical features of the operation of *aufheben.* A category that is *aufgehoben* "hangs" from the next higher one in the sense of being dependent upon it, having been "lifted" into that position by the dialectical process. The only objection I have heard against this suggestion is that "suspend" has an overtone of temporariness, which *aufheben,* at least in Hegel's technical use of it, does not. But, on the one hand, there is nothing incoherent in the idea of something's being suspended indefinitely, and, on the other hand, a category that is *aufgehoben* in Hegel's logic is once more in play when it is abstracted from the larger context in which it has been shown to be a mere "moment", as it regularly is by the "understanding". Even if the objection were judged to be sound, still, taking everything into account, a very good case can be made that "suspend" comes incomparably closer to *aufheben* than "sublate" does, and therefore should be employed in the absence of a better rendering.

(3) *dasein, Dasein* (or *daseyn, Daseyn*)

This is an ordinary German word which Hegel uses both technically and nontechnically. Nontechnically it means, as a noun, "existence" (with a certain bias to what is living) and, as a verb, "to be there" (as its etymology indicates), "to be present", "attend", "exist". The following discussion will be restricted to the nominal form, because this is of most relevance in the context of Hegel's logic. Its technical meaning is explained in the "Doctrine of Being," specifically in the second stage of the initial triad of categories comprising "Quality," and is stated very succinctly in the opening words of the relevant section of the larger *Science of Logic:* "Daseyn ist bestimmtes Sein" (SL, 109 = W 5:115).

(i) Taking the technical meaning first, it is probably true that, as I:THL suggests, the passage just cited is what has been considered by translators and commentators in the main line of the Anglophone tradition to be the authority for rendering *Dasein* as "Determinate Being". In brief, the latter is what Hegel himself says that *Dasein* means. Why change the traditional rendering? I:THL says that the passage in question is not a definition and that in fact *"Daseyn* is . . . the most . . . *indeterminate* form of 'finite' being." So, when Hegel writes "determinate", we are told in effect that he really means "indeterminate"! It is also stated in the same place that rendering the word as "determinate being" is "a disastrous decision, which has nothing but misleading consequences." However, the argument advanced for this claim rests upon a couple of passages in the *Phenomenology of Spirit*, a work that was published a good five years before the first volume of Hegel's logical magnum opus, the *Science of Logic*, and that lacks the rigorous terminology first systematically developed in the latter. An examination in particular of the two passages adduced shows Hegel is there simply using *Dasein* in an "ordinary language" way.

What of the main term used in the present version, namely, "Thereness"? This has the advantage of etymological mimicry of the original (*da* = "there" and *sein* = "ness", as in, for example, *Bewußtsein* = "consciousness"). But I can see no other advantages, and I do see several serious disadvantages, which include the following. (a) "Thereness" renders an ordinary German word by an English expression that is even more remote from ordinary English than "sublate". (The three examples of its use given in the OED include one from the seventeenth century and two (both philosophical texts) from the nineteenth century. (b) This rendering of *Dasein* destroys the verbal continuity with the other two members of the triad (*Sein* and *Fürsichsein*) as well as with others introduced in that first section, like *Ansichsein*. (Of course, continuity could be partly restored by rendering *Fürsichsein* as "foritselfness", and so on. But what, then, becomes of *Sein*? Is it to be rendered "Ness"?) (c) Last but not least, proceeding in this way cannot but cause confusion among readers of Hegel, old and new, in view of the entrenched character of "Determinate Being" in standard translations and secondary literature. This is certainly not a common English expression, but it is not by any means a weird one, and, all things taken into consideration, I believe it should be retained.

(ii) Hegel also uses *Dasein* nontechnically. See, for example, the way in which he uses this and *Sein* interchangeably in §§ 36 and R, 51 R, W 8:103, 157, and its use in combinations such as "Gott hat Dasein" (§ 28 R), or "hat Gott *Dasein*?" (§ 28 A), or "Beweise vom Dasein Gottes" (§ 68 R). The remark about the

alleged logical significance, for Hegel, of *Dasein* in "Dasein
Gottes" is not underpinned with any argument and so cannot
be discussed here.

The present translation, making as it does no distinction
between technical and nontechnical uses of *Dasein*, grips tight
the nettle and renders these, respectively, as "God is there,"
"Does *thereness* belong to God?", and "proofs that God is
there". I rest my case! (Note that the day cannot be saved by
rendering the expressions as "there is a God" and "proofs that
there is a God", for this would be cheating: "there is" would
here be rendered "es gibt".)

In such cases the right path is to render the passages
straightforwardly as "God exists" and "proofs of the existence
of God"; there is no problem in such contexts of a confusion
between Hegel's *Dasein* and *Existenz*.

(4) *Differenz, different*. See *Unterschied*.

(5) *Eines, Einheit*. See *Eins* (*das*).

(6) *Eins*

Some remarks on this term are in order here, both to outline a case for
rendering it slightly differently from the way it is in the present translation
and also to indicate its relations to various other terms which are flagged at
various places in the text but not explicated.

Das Eins has a place and a different meaning in the first two major
subdivisions of the "Doctrine of Being," namely, those under the rubrics
"Quality" and "Quantity." The "bad" or "spurious" infinite involved in
Something's going over into Other, and this, *qua* Something, going over
into a further Other has been terminated by the reflection that the series is
a totality which is self-contained by virtue of the fact that what is contained
in it is determined by itself and which is thus infinite in the sense of not
being limited by anything outside it. This self-enclosed whole is called
"Being-for-itself". Insofar as this is regarded purely in terms of its character as a self-determining whole, abstracting from the reference to otherness
which the preceding section on *Dasein* has shown to be necessary for
determinateness, Being-for-itself is immediate (not mediated), but, as including this necessary reference to otherness (negativity), it is determinate,
"a" Being-for-itself (not *Fürsichsein* but *Fürsichseiendes*), excluding others.
As such, it falls under the category *das Eins*.

Translators of Hegel have usually rendered *das Eins* as "the One", and the present version is no exception. But this is not *dictated* by the expression itself, for the indefinite article in German (as also in, for example, French) is part of a specific noun in a way that is not the case in English. (Thus Marx's main work, *Das Kapital*, is rendered in English *Capital*, not *The Capital*.) My argument for rendering *das Eins* as "One" rather than "the One" is twofold. It is not intended as decisive (insofar as any argument in this area can pretend to be so), but to be at least worth serious consideration. The first takes its point of departure from Hegel's remarks in § 96 A that the most familiar example of Being-for-itself is "I". (Cf. also § 24 A1.) On the one hand, "I" can be looked at from the point of view of pure self-relation as such, and here "I" does not refer to any specific individual. On the other hand, "I" is necessarily some specific "I", though unspecified, as against other specific "I"'s, similarly unspecified. From this second point of view, "I" as Being-for-itself is *a* Being-for-itself.

Now, there is arguably a similar situation in regard to the English "one" in a sentence like "One doesn't eat one's peas from the blade of a knife." "One" refers simultaneously to anyone at all, *any*one, and also to specific individuals, any*one*(s). (It is worth remarking how the language seems to have within it the idea of the correlativeness of otherness with oneness in this sense—"you" can be substituted for "one" in the above example.) This suggests that *das Eins* be rendered simply as "One". The second part of the argument for proceeding thus is that this would be an especially appropriate way of rendering *das Eins* when the latter expression is used in a quantitative (rather than, as so far, a qualitative) context. This is introduced in § 97 in (briefly) the following way. Being-for-itself considered mediately, excluding other "Beings-for-themselves", that is, Being-for-itself as *das Eins*, is one-among-many. This is what Hegel refers to as "repulsion". But, as has been seen, Being-for-itself can also be looked at as immediate, and this Hegel calls "attraction". What is grasped as this oscillation between the two aspects of Being-for-itself is "Quantity". *Das Eins* in the new quantitative context refers to the "moment" of "attraction" or, as it comes to be called in § 100, "continuity", characterised there as "that in which the many ones are *the same*, [namely] *unit*". (Unfortunately, the present translation renders the final word here, *die Einheit*, as "unity", thus destroying the sense of the passage. This is in spite of the fact that the word is correctly rendered in a passage of identical sense in § 102, first paragraph, *ad fin.*) The plural of *das Eins* in the quantitative sense (see §§ 97, 102 R) is very naturally rendered by "Ones", rather than by "the Ones". (It may be remarked, by the way, that Hegel also uses the term *Eines*, § 97 A, which seems to mean one *qua* one-among-many.)

As correlatives of the quantitative *das Eins*, we have the following: (a) *viel/Viele* as in "Setzen *vieler Eins*" and "diese Viele *Seiende* [*sc. Eins*]" (§ 97), as well as *die Vielen* (§ 97 A), which would seem to refer to the quantitative *Eins* taken distributively. (b) *das Viele* (§§ 97 A, 98 A), which would seem to designate manyness-as-such. (c) *ein Vieles* (§ 97 A), which apparently means a particular manyness, so to speak, a particular group of ones.

(7) *erkennen*, (*das*) *Erkennen*, *Erkenntnis*

Hegel uses three groups of words, all from ordinary German, in interconnected ways: (1) *erkennen*, (*das*) *Erkennen*, *Erkenntnis*, (2) *wissen*, (*das*) *Wissen*, (3) *kennen*, (*das*) *Kennen*, *Kenntnis(se)*. In the final analysis, they cannot be considered, especially in Hegel's usage, apart from one another. But this is especially true of (1) and (2), so the discussion will start here; (3) will prove to be relatively easy to sort out. (For the sake of simplicity and brevity, the discussion will mainly concern only the first, verbal form of each.)

The problems in the present context flow from various conjunctions of the following facts: (a) as already indicated, (1) and (2) are all ordinary German words; (b) Hegel sometimes uses them nontechnically (indeed even synonymously so—see, for example, § 24 A3 at W 8:89); (c) he also uses them in technical senses; and (d) they would both be normally rendered by "know". Before considering the problems raised by the conjunction of (a), (c), and (d), let us survey the relevant technical uses. We can then consider questions connected with (b).

> (i) As I:THL correctly points out, *wissen* is the more inclusive, the general concept of knowledge (using the last word in a provisional way at least). As Hegel says in Part III of the *Encyclopaedia*, "*Consciousness* is already knowledge [*Wissen*]" (*Encyclopaedia*, § 445 A at W 10:244 = *Philosophy of Mind*, Wallace-Miller translation, p. 191 [heavily revised here]). But he distinguishes two grades of *Wissen*. The lower he calls in the passage from which I have just cited "*mere* [bloßen] *Wissen*", knowledge "*that* an object *is* . . . what it is *in general* and with respect to its *contingent, external* determinations." Now, this lower grade of *Wissen* is to be distinguished from the next (higher) step, which is achieved by the procedure of knowing in the sense of *erkennen*. In EL this is characterised as follows (translating in an amplified if awkward way in order to bring out the terminological points): "Knowing in the sense of *erkennen* means nothing other than to know [*wissen*] an object [*Gegenstand*] in terms of [*nach*] its *definite*

[bestimmten] content" (§ 46). Knowing an object in the sense of *erkennen* is to *wissen* in a "mediated" way (§ 112 A at W 8:232). All this is in perfect accord with what is said further in the passage from Part III of the *Encyclopaedia* already cited, where it is said further that to know in the sense of *erkennen* is to *wissen* "in what the object's *specific, substantial nature* consists." (For other passages of similar tenor, see for example *Encyclopaedia* § 445 at W 10:240, translation cited, p. 188; W 16:156ff; W 17:334, 335, 379f; W 19:422; W 20:383.) So *wissen* in the first, "lower" sense refers to immediate knowledge, where "immediate" contrasts with explicitly mediated knowledge, which is the province of *erkennen*. (Cf. Kant's distinction between *Wissen* and *eigentliche Wissenschaft* in the Preface to the *Metaphysische Anfangsgründe der Naturwissenschaft*, Suhrkamp Werkausgabe, 9:12.) Now, above this is *Wissen* in the "higher" sense, indeed knowledge in its highest development, absolute philosophical knowledge. (The connection between the two sorts of *Wissen* is presumably that in the second we return to immediacy, only this time with mediation *aufgehoben*.) *Wissen* is used in this way in the present work at § 237 A, but can be found in other places like the last section of the *Phenomenology of Spirit*, entitled *"Das absolute Wissen"*, and the *Philosophy of Religion* at W 17:533: "The concept of spirit is the concept that is in and for itself, *knowledge [das Wissen]*."

(ii) Now, (c) having been cleared up, what is to be done about the problems created by it in conjunction with (a) and (d)? The present translation consistently uses "know" for *wissen* and "cognise" or (sometimes) "[re]cognise" for *erkennen*. The central and very serious problem with this is that it involves rendering an ordinary German word (*erkennen*)—and, moreover, one used many more times than *wissen*—by one that is used in English by no one but a few scholars.

My alternative suggestion is as follows. Since, as just noted, *erkennen* occurs much more frequently than *wissen*, it should be rendered by "know". How, then, is *wissen* in both its senses to be distinguished (where, of course, this is necessary—the question of what is to be done when it is not necessary will be taken up later)? As regards the first, "lower" sense of *wissen*, the OED comes to our aid. This (vol. 3:745, col. 2, 3:8) ties "know" in the sense of "to be aware or apprised of" with *wissen*. So the latter has a natural rendering in "to be aware of" where it is used in its first sense. As regards the comparatively rare use of *wissen* in its second, "higher" sense, it can be rendered as "know absolutely" (taking a clue from the *Phenomenology of Spirit*—see above) or as "know" with appropriate flagging of some sort (for example, the German word in brackets after it or in a footnote).

(iii) Now, what is to be done when the two words in question are used nontechnically? The problem does not arise for the present translation, which does not recognise (b), that is, non-technical uses of them in Hegel's text. This, combined with the choices made of words with which to render the two terms, results in some *bizarreries*. For example, the Biblical phrase we know in English as "tree of knowledge of good and evil", which appears in German as "Baum der Erkenntnis des Guten und Bosen", meets us back in the present translation as "tree of cognition of good and evil" (§ 24 A3). (The remark about the alleged logical significance, for Hegel, of *Erkenntnis* in "Baum der Erkenntnis des Guten und Bösen", like that of similar tenor regarding *Dasein* in "Dasein Gottes" above, is, as simple assertion, not discussible here.) My own suggestion, in line with what has already been said, is, when nothing hangs on it, simply to render them both by "know".

(iv) Finally, the third term in the initial triptych involves no serious difficulty. Hegel does not use words in this set much, in the present work anyway, and does not give any explicit account of the meanings involved. But its everyday use has the sense of personal knowledge (e.g., *kennenlernen*, to meet) or practical knowledge, including information (e.g., *Menschenkenner*, a good judge of people, or *in Kenntnis setzen*, to inform or notify someone of something). Once more the OED provides what is wanted, expressly tying "known" in the sense of "to be acquainted with . . . to be familiar with by experience, or through information or report" with *kennen* (vol. 3:745, col. 1, 2:5). It is true that this does not bring out the etymological continuity with *erkennen*, but, then, no alternative does either.

(8) *formal*

Formal, most accurately and naturally rendered by "formal", or "formally", is the adjective corresponding to *Form*, which is correlative with *Inhalt*, "content" (§§ 133, 134). Roughly, *Form* signifies a state of affairs considered from the point of view of its structure. *Form* and *Inhalt* are two aspects of the same thing, and nothing pejorative attaches to "formal" or "formally" as such.

But this is certainly the case with what is *formell, das Formelle*. Here form is abstracted from content altogether (see, for example, §§ 24 A 2, 63 R, 133 A, 145 A, 160 A, 162 R, 164 R, 172 A, 213 A, 214 at W 8:84, 152, 266, 284, 307, 310, 314, 323f, 369, 372), signifying predominance of subjectivity (§§ 25 R, 162, 192 A at W 9:92, 309, 345), arbitrariness (§ 122 R at W 8:253), the operation of the "understanding" (§ 115 R at W 8:236).

Thus it is obvious that the two terms cannot be satisfactorily translated into English by using the same term (namely, "formal") for both, as the present translation does. *Formell* might be generally rendered by "only formal" or "merely formal", were it not that Hegel more often than not qualifies *formell* with *nur* or *bloß*. When he does not, it may be so rendered. When he does, "formalistic" seems to be the best choice, suggested indeed by what is said in §§ 54 and 231 (at W 8:138, 383). One major exception is *formelle Logik*: "formal logic" is so strongly entrenched in English as to be untouchable. *Formell* is also used in § 140 A in a way which can be understood only in the light of the foregoing comments, but needs a different rendering from any of those so far suggested. For further remarks on this, see the editorial note to that §. Distinguished both from *formal* and *formell* is *förmlich* (§ 183 A), which signifies as much as "observing the correct forms", "by the book", and is probably best rendered by "official". (The English "formalised", meaning something like "formally arranged", does not correspond to any of the above meanings.)

(9) *formell, (das) Formelle, förmlich*. See *formal*.

(10) *Gegenstand*

This is an ordinary German word, which Hegel uses in both untechnical and technical senses.

> (i) In the technical sense, *Gegenstand* contrasts with *Objekt*, which designates objectivity in general, independence of the subject, *Gegenstand* signifying (as its etymology suggests) an object of consciousness, mediated by and thus changing in relation to it. (See §§ 193 and R, 194, *Encyclopaedia*, §§ 413 A, 418 A at W 10:200, 207.)
>
> Now, the problem is that English does not have two appropriate words corresponding to these two German ones, the natural renderings of both, other things being equal, being "object". (The problem is similar in this respect to that with *erkennen* and *wissen*, on which see [7] [i].) So how is the distinction to be marked? The path followed by the present

translation is to do it typographically, using "ob-ject" for *Gegenstand* and "object" for *Objekt*. Now, if this general direction were the one to be taken, then it would be better to reverse the English renderings, as *Gegenstand* is used very much more frequently than *Objekt*, whilst "ob-ject" is not only not an ordinary word but not a word at all in the dictionary sense, and visually awkward, as a neologism. As an alternative I suggest that, for reasons already indicated, *Gegenstand* simply be rendered "object", and *Objekt* in the same way, but flagged somehow (for example, by the German after it in parentheses or in a footnote) or translated by a slight paraphrase, like "object-in-general."

(ii) In its untechnical sense, *Gegenstand* would be naturally rendered by "object" (unbroken) or "subject matter", according to context. The present translation recognises only to an extremely limited extent the difference between the technical and untechnical senses of *Gegenstand*. (Here is a piquant tidbit, *Dasein*—see previous remarks—being there too: 'The object of Cosmology was being-there generally' for 'Die Kosmologie hatte . . . überhaupt das Dasein . . . zum Gegenstand'!) So the work is strewn with broken "ob-jects".

(11) *Gehalt*

The noun "import", when not used as a pompous synonym for "meaning" in general, is centrally employed to signify the *gist* of some utterance (in a certain context), where "gist" means "the substance or pith of a matter, the essence" (OED). So *Gehalt*. In this regard "basic import" is either a pleonasm or so close to one that the difference does not matter. (Cf. "basic essence", which results from substituting for "import" one formulation in the dictionary definition just transcribed.) Of course, "import" can properly accept certain qualifying adjectives (for example, "natural", "ascribed", "surprising") but these do not relate to the *meaning* of "import" (the import of "import").

(12) *gleich, Gleichheit*

The present translation renders these uniformly as "equal" and "equality" respectively. These renderings are sometimes but by no means always correct. Thus a translation of the very important §§ 117, 118 makes sense only if the words in question are translated as "like" and "likeness" (or "unlike" and "unlikeness"), as is standard in the English Hegel literature, or by "similar"/"similarity" ("dissimilar"/"dissimilarity"), which would be equally satisfactory.

(13) *indifferent, Indifferenz.* See *Unterschied.*

(14) *kennen, (das) Kennen, Kenntnis(se).* See *erkennen, (das) Erkennen, Erkenntnis.*

(15) *Objekt.* See *Gegenstand.*

(16) *ungleich, Ungleichheit.* See *gleich, Gleichheit.*

(17) *Unterschied*

The natural rendering of this word, which someone sufficiently familiar with both German and English would come up with spontaneously, is "difference", that being a sufficient explanation of the fact that this has been the standard choice of translators of Hegel into English. Another consideration in favour of this option is that Hegel holds that there is a general correspondence between, on the one hand, the sequence of categories as they are derived from one another in the system of logic and, on the other, the temporal sequence of positions in the history of philosophy. Now, "identity" and "difference" are a traditional couple, and to replace "difference" with anything else (as the present translation does with "distinction") is to obscure the historical dimension of Hegel's system of logic.

Are there any arguments for replacing "difference"? Although I have been unable to follow much of what is said in I:THL in defence of "distinction" over "difference", I have been able to pick out two. One is that we should start from the cognate verb of *Unterschied,* namely, *(sich) unterscheiden,* and this is properly rendered "distinguish", wherefore *Unterschied* should be translated as "distinction". But this begs the question at issue, for the verb may just as well be rendered "differentiate", and in this case the substantival cognate would be "difference". Moreover, even if the two arguments were not parallel, it would have to be shown that the advantage of having a cognate noun and verb was worth sacrificing the two advantages indicated in the first paragraph. The second argument in favour of rendering *Unterschied* by "distinction" rather than "difference" is that by proceeding thus we free the latter for translating *Differenz.* To evaluate this argument, we shall have to look at this term and related matters.

To start with, it is crucial to note that Hegel uses *Differenz* in two senses. (The two are systematically related, but the explanation of this point would take us too far afield.) (a) *Differenz* is used to designate the stage at which the initial apparent simplicity, unity, immediacy of a category is ruptured, when its implicit complexity becomes explicit and it shows itself to be mediated. The newly "posited" moments attain apparent independence. It is the stage of "particularity". (It is followed by a third stage, where the various moments of the category, thus revealed in the stage of *Differenz*, exhibit themselves as aspects of a unified whole.) For all this, see §§ 85, 171 A, 215 A (at W 8:181, 322, 373, 388—also, in other works, *Philosophy of Right* § 181 [W 7:338]; *Philosophy of Religion*, Introduction, C,I, Secs. 2,3 [W 16:68ff], and Part III, II [W 17:241ff]; *History of Philosophy*, Part III, Sec. 3, D [W 20:440ff]). (b) *Differenz* is also used in a way best approached through the adjective *different*. In EL the key passage in this regard is § 194 A. Here *different* is introduced through its negative, *indifferent*. Hegel writes that something is *indifferent* if it "contains difference [*Unterschied*], but the diverse items behave indifferently [*gleichgültig*] towards one another, and their combination is only external to them." Conversely, items are *different* if they "are what they are only through their relation to one another." (On this sense of *Differenz*, via its negative, *Indifferenz*, see also SL, 330, 374ff = W 5:392, 445ff, and *Encyclopaedia*, Part II: *Philosophy* of Nature, §§ 323, 324, 334.) Now, what is to be made of all this in English? To start with, there seems no alternative to translating *indifferent* by "indifferent". ("Neutral" would be a serious alternative except that Hegel also uses the equivalent German word.) The disadvantage of this is that the same word must surely be used for *gleichgültig*. But this is not a serious drawback, if only because *indifferent* is used comparatively seldom and can be flagged in some way (for example, by supplying the German word) if it is necessary to distinguish it. *Different* can then be rendered "nonindifferent", effectively distinguishing it from any cognate of "difference". (For suggestions here I am indebted to the French translation of EL by Bernard Bourgeois, p. 260, note on § 150.) These terms having been tied down thus, *Indifferenz* (as the negative of the second sense of *Differenz*) naturally can be translated as "indifference", and its negative as "nonindifference". Finally, *Differenz* in sense (1) most naturally becomes "differentiation" (or, much less desirably, aesthetically speaking, "differentiatedness"), and *Indifferenz* (as the negative of sense (1) of *Differenz*) becomes "lack [or absence] of differentiation [or differentiatedness]".

All this may seem egregiously laborious, but the distinctions made are unavoidable if sense is to be made of Hegel's text at a number of points. Decisive proof of this may be gained by an attempt to understand, for example, §§ 194 A, 200 A, or 203 in the present translation.

(18) *Viele* (*das*), *Vielen* (*die*), *Vieles* (*ein*). See *Eins* (*das*).

(19) *vorstellen*, (*die*) *Vorstellung*

These are very common words indeed in ordinary German, and Hegel uses both of them in ordinary, untechnical senses as well as in a technical way. In ordinary senses, there are many English words appropriate for translating the German ones in various contexts. Thus *vorstellen* may, according to the particular use, be rendered by, for example, "imagine", "have in mind", "have/frame/form an idea". The most commonly suitable rending of *Vorstellung* is "idea". This was, in fact, the word used by German translators to render the English "idea" in the works of eighteenth-century empiricists. So what more natural procedure than to reverse the exchange? One drawback is that "idea" has no natural cognate verb with which to translate *vorstellen*. But this is not a severe disadvantage, given the wide variety of English verbs available to translate it in different contexts. There is no danger of its being confused with the English equivalent of *Idee* either, because that always has an initial capital. In the technical context, the realm of *vorstellen/Vorstellung* is between *anschauen/Anschauung* (intuiting/intuition), on the one hand, and thought proper, involving concepts (*Begriffe*) proper, on the other. (See especially *Encyclopaedia*, § 451, and cf. EL, § 3 R.) Roughly, it is thinking at the level of everyday life, involving mental contents that are not very "clear and distinct", that are comparatively unanalysed, ill-defined, "pictorial". It is thinking, all right, using universals, but thinking in which the universals are not brought into systematic relation to one another. For this special sense, "present"/"presentation" (less desirably, "represent"/"representation") are probably best. This translation allows only a very few untechnical uses of the words in question and, since Hegel uses them mostly untechnically, becomes rather artificial and stiff.

(20) *wissen*, (*das*) *Wissen*. See *erkennen*, (*das*) *Erkennen*, *Erkenntnis*.

(21) *Zusammenschließen*

This is an ordinary German word meaning to unite or amalgamate. Hegel uses its etymology to express the way in which, on his account, the inferring (*schließen*), which is the syllogism (*Schluß* from *schließen*), locks (*schließen* in another sense) together (*zusammen*) the "moments" of the Concept (universality, particularity, singularity).

In the present translation, the Concept is said to "con-clude with itself." Having in mind "conclude", one at first is probably led to say that yoking the Concept with "with itself" simply makes no English sense. But, since "con-clude" is not an English word (in the dictionary sense), its creators presumably can do as they please with it. However, this freedom is purchased at the price of matching an ordinary German word with one which not only is not an ordinary English one but is not English at all.

My alternative suggestion is to use the phrase "close with itself" which (a) is perfectly good, ordinary English, (b) mimics the German etymologically in large part, and (c) captures much of the meaning of the original, since the phrase means not only "grapple" (hook or fasten on to something) but also "come to terms". (Another possibility is "close on itself", which captures the main thrust of the meaning of *zusammenschließen*, though it loses the etymological mimicry of *zusammen*.)

G. W. F. Hegel

ENCYCLOPAEDIA OF THE PHILOSOPHICAL SCIENCES

PART 1

PREFACE TO THE FIRST
EDITION (1817)

The need to supply my listeners with a guiding thread for my philosophical lectures is the most immediate occasion for letting this survey of the whole range of philosophy see the light of day sooner than I was otherwise minded to do.

The nature of an outline not only rules out any exhaustive discussion of ideas in respect of their *content*, but also particularly cramps the tracing out of their systematic derivation. This derivation must embrace what was formerly understood by the "proof," i.e., the very thing that is quite indispensable for a scientific philosophy. My title for this outline is partly meant to indicate the total range of the work; and partly, it makes plain my intention of reserving the single details for my oral presentation.

Moreover, in an "outline," where the content is one that is already presupposed and familiar and has to be presented in a short space already decided upon, what is aimed at is that the order and arrangement of the topics should be *externally suitable*. The present exposition is not like that; on the contrary, it sets out a new elaboration of philosophy, according to a method that will, I hope, be recognised eventually as the only genuine one, the only method that is identical with the content. So I might well have considered it to be of more advantage to the public—if only my circumstances had permitted this—to publish a book in which the other parts of philosophy were more fully discussed, on the model of the *Logic* that I have already delivered to the public as my treatment of the first part of the whole. But in any case, I believe that, although the side on which the content is closer to *representative awareness*[a] and to what is empirically familiar necessarily had to be restricted in the present exposition, I have still managed to make it evident enough (with respect to the transitions that can only be a mediation taking place through the *Concept*) that the method of the forward movement is quite distinct, both from the merely *external order* that the other sciences require, and from a certain *mannerism* in dealing with philosophical topics that has become quite usual.[1] This fashionable procedure *presupposes a schema*, and uses it to establish paral-

---

a. Vorstellung

lels in the material just as externally and even more arbitrarily than the external procedure of the other sciences; and, through a misunderstanding that is really quite remarkable, it claims to have given every satisfaction to the necessity of the Concept with accidents and arbitrary associations.[a]

We have seen this same arbitrariness take charge of the content of philosophy too, marching out upon adventures of thought, and imposing for a while upon the striving of honest and sincere minds, even though in other quarters it was regarded as a craziness that had risen to the pitch of madness.[2] But instead of being either impressive or crazy, [its] import allowed us more often, and more properly, to [re]cognise familiar *clichés*, just as the form was merely a mannerism, a deliberate methodical trick that is easily acquired, a talent for baroque associations, and a strained complexity. Generally speaking, there was only self-deception, and deception of the public behind the serious air. On the other side, in contrast, we have seen shallow minds give their *lack of thoughts* the stamp of a scepticism that was wise in its own eyes, and of a critical philosophy that is modest in its claims for reason;[3] they let their vanity and conceit advance in step, as their ideas grew ever more vacuous.—For a considerable period these two tendencies in our culture[b] have aped our German seriousness, wearing down its deeper philosophical need. The consequence has been indifference, and even such an outright contempt for philosophy as a science, that nowadays a self-styled modesty even imagines it can join in the discussion of the deepest problems of philosophy, that it may presume to pass judgment about them, and deny to philosophy the rational cognition that used to be comprehended under the form of "proof."

The first of the phenomena touched upon here can in some measure be regarded as the youthful exuberance of the new age that has dawned in the realm of science just as it has in that of politics. If this exuberance greeted the sunrise of the rejuvenated spirit with revelling, and began enjoying the Idea at once without any hard labour, luxuriating for a while in the hopes and prospects that that sunrise offered, it also reconciles [us] more readily to its excesses because there is a kernel [of truth] at the bottom of it, and the morning mist that covers its surface is bound to clear spontaneously.[4] But the other phenomenon is more repellent because we can [re]cognise exhaustion and impotence in it, and it strives to mask them under the conceit of a schoolmaster thinking to give lessons to the philosophical spirits of all the centuries, mistaking what they are, and most of all what it is itself.

This makes it all the more pleasant, however, to perceive and to conclude by pointing out how the concern with philosophy and the earnest love for the *higher cognition* [that it produces] has maintained itself candidly and

a. *mit Zufälligkeit und Willkür der Verknüpfungen*
b. *Richtungen des Geistes*

quite without vanity. Although this concern has sometimes cast itself too much in the form of an *immediate knowing* and of *feeling*, still it does attest to the continuing inner drive of rational insight, which alone gives man his dignity. It attests to it, above all, because man reaches that standpoint of immediate knowing only as the *result* of philosophical knowledge, so that the philosophical knowing that it seems to despise is at least recognised by it as a *condition*.[5]—To this concern with the *cognition of the truth*, I dedicate my effort to supply an introduction, or a contribution to the satisfaction of this concern. May its purpose secure it a kindly reception.

Heidelberg, May 1817

PREFACE TO
THE SECOND
EDITION (1827)

The well-disposed reader of this new edition will find many parts re-
worked in it, and developed into more detailed determinations. In my
revision I have tried to moderate and also to reduce the formal [aspect] of
the presentation; and I have also tried through more extended Remarks of
a generally accessible kind to bring abstract concepts closer to the ordinary
understanding and the more concrete notions of them. But the brevity and
compression that an outline makes necessary, with materials that are in
any case abstruse, will only permit this second edition to have the same vocation[a] as the first one: it serves as a textbook that has to receive the eluci-
dation it needs through an oral commentary. On the face of it, of course,
the title *Encyclopaedia* could leave room for a lesser degree of rigour in the
scientific method, and for the compilation of external parts. But the nature
of the matter entails that logical coherence must remain fundamental.

There could be all too many inducements and stimuli present that seem to
require that I should declare myself about the external bearing of my philosophical activity upon the cultural concerns of our time, some of which are
rich and others poor in spirit; and this can only be done in an exoteric way,
as for instance in a Preface. For although these cultural concerns claim
some relationship with philosophy for themselves, they do not permit of
scientific discussion; so they do not enter into philosophy at all, but carry
on their chatter-wars from outside and stay outside it. It is inappropriate
and even risky to betake oneself to a field that is quite alien to science,
since explanations and discussions of that sort do not advance the scientific understanding which is all that matters for genuine cognition. But a
discussion of some cultural phenomena may be useful or even mandatory.

The scientific cognition of truth is what I have laboured upon, and still
do labour upon always, in all of my philosophical endeavours. This is the
hardest road to travel, but it is the only one that can be of interest and
value for the spirit, once the spirit embarks upon the way of thought,

a. *Bestimmung*

4

without tumbling into vanity upon that road, but maintaining the will and
the courage for the truth. It soon finds that only method can tie thought
down, lead it to the matter, and maintain it there. A methodical pursuit of
this kind proves to be nothing else but the reestablishing of that absolute
import beyond which thought initially strove to go, and above which it
posited itself; but it is a reestablishment in the element of the spirit, which
is most proper to this content, and most free.

There is a more naïve state with a happier aspect—and one that is still
not long gone by—in which philosophy went hand in hand with the
sciences and with culture. The enlightened understanding was content in a
measured way, balancing the needs of insight together with its religion,
and similarly conciliating its natural law theory with state authority and
politics; and its empirical physics bore the title of "natural philosophy." But
the peace was superficial enough, and specifically there was in fact an
inward contradiction between that pure insight and religion, just as there
was between the natural law theory and the State. Then the parting of the
ways came, and the contradiction developed to maturity; but in philosophy
the spirit has celebrated its own reconciliation with itself, so that phi-
losophic science only contradicts that contradiction itself, and the effort to
gloss over it. It is only an ill-minded prejudice to assume that philosophy
stands antithetically opposed to any sensible appreciation of experience, or
to the rational actuality of legal right and to simple-hearted religion and
piety. These shapes [of consciousness] are themselves recognised by philosophy, and even justified by it. Rather than opposing them, the thinking
mind[a] steeps itself in their basic import; it learns from them and grows
strong, just as it does from the great intuitions of nature, history, and art;
for this solid content, once it has been thought, is the speculative Idea
itself. The collision with philosophy only occurs because this soil moves
out of the character that is proper to it when its content is supposed to be
grasped in categories, and is made dependent upon them, without the
categories being led up to the Concept and brought to completion in the
Idea.

When the understanding of our universal scientific culture arrives at the
discovery that no mediation with the truth is possible by the route of its
finite concept, this important negative result usually has precisely the opposite consequence from the one that is immediately implicit in it. What I
mean is that, instead of causing the finite relationships to be removed from
[our theory of] cognition, this conviction has sublated the concern with the
investigation of the categories along with all attentiveness and prudence in
their use. The use of these finite relationships has only become more
barefaced, less conscious, and less critical, as if we had fallen into a state of

a. *denkende Sinn*

despair. From the mistaken view that the inadequacy of finite categories to express truth entails the impossibility of objective cognition, we derive a justification for pronouncing and denouncing according to our feelings and subjective opinions. Assurances present themselves in place of proofs, along with stories about all the "facts" that are to be found in "consciousness"; and the more uncritical they are, the more they count as "pure."[1] Without any further investigation of it, the highest needs of the spirit are to be established upon the category of *immediacy*—and arid as it is, they are to be decided by it.[2] Especially where religious topics are being dealt with, we can soon discover that philosophising is expressly set aside in this way—as if every harm would be banished along with it, and security against error and deception would be achieved. Then the quest for truth is to be instituted by arguing on the basis of assumptions drawn from anywhere. In other words, we employ the ordinary thought-determinations of essence and appearance, ground and consequence, cause and effect, and so on; and we reason in the usual syllogistic fashion either from one relationship of finitude or from the other. "From the Evil One they are free, but the evil still remains";[3] and the evil is ten times worse than before, because they entrust themselves to it without any distrust or criticism. As if philosophy—the very source of all harm that is kept at a distance—were anything else but the quest for truth, but with the consciousness of the nature and worth of the thought-relationships that bind together and determine every content.

But philosophy itself experiences its worst fate at the hands of those enemies when they deal with it directly themselves, both interpreting it and passing judgment on it. It is the *factum*[4] of the physical or spiritual, but especially of religious vitality too, that is misshaped through the reflection that is incapable of grasping it. For itself, however, this interpreting has the sense of raising the *factum* for the first time into something-known, and the difficulty lies in this passage from the matter to cognition that is produced by meditating upon it.[5] In science itself, this difficulty is no longer present. For the *factum* of philosophy is cognition already elaborated; so the interpreting can only be a "thinking-over" in the sense that it is a *further* thinking that *comes later*. Only critical evaluation would require a "thinking-over" in the ordinary meaning[a] of the word. But the uncritical understanding that we are discussing proves to be just as unfaithful in its naked apprehension of the Idea determinately expressed [i.e., in the expression of its immediate knowledge of God]. It has so little difficulty or doubt about the fixed presuppositions that it contains that it is even incapable of repeating what the bare *factum* of the philosophical Idea is. This

---

a. *Bedeutung*

understanding unites the following double perspective within itself in a quite marvelous way: it is struck by the complete divergence, and even by the express contradiction in the Idea against its own employment of the categories; yet at the same time it has no suspicion that there may be another way of thinking than its own, both present and in active use, so that it must here behave in another way than it does in its usual thinking. This is how it happens that the Idea of speculative philosophy is simply kept fixed in its abstract definition;—in the opinion that a definition must appear to be clear and definitive on its own account, and must have its methodic rule and touchstone only in presupposed notions; or at least without knowing that the sense of the definition, like its necessary proof, lies in its development alone—and precisely in its emergence as the result of the development. Now since, more precisely, the Idea is, quite generally, ⅹ the *concrete spiritual* unity, whilst the understanding consists in the interpretation of the Concept's determinations only in their *abstraction*, that is to say, in their one-sidedness and finitude, the spiritual unity is in this way made into an abstract spiritless identity. The result is that distinction is not present in this identity, but the *All is One*—and even Good and Evil are of one kind among all the rest. That is why the name *Identity-System*, or *Philosophy of Identity*, has already become the established one for speculative philosophy. If someone makes his profession of faith by saying, "I believe in God the Father, the maker of Heaven and Earth," one would marvel if someone else could already bring forth from this first part of the Creed the *consequence* that the confessor of God the creator of Heaven held that the Earth was *not* created, and matter was eternal. It is a *factum*, and quite correct, that the first speaker declared in his confession that he believes in God the creator of Heaven, and yet this *factum*, as it is interpreted by others, is completely false; this is so absurd that the example must be regarded as incredible and trivial. And yet in the interpretation of the philosophical Idea, this violent splitting in half is what happens; and what follows is that, in order to avoid all misunderstandings about how the identity is constituted that is asserted to be the principle of speculative philosophy, the corresponding refutation is given; we are expressly instructed, for instance, that the subject is *diverse* from the object, likewise the finite from the infinite, etc.—as if the concrete spiritual unity lacked all inward determination, and did not itself *contain* distinction *within it*. As if any one of us did not know that the subject is diverse from the object, and the infinite diverse from the finite, and philosophy was so drowned in its school-wisdom that it needed the reminder that, outside the schoolroom, there is a wisdom to which that diversity is quite familiar.

With reference to the diversity that it is supposedly unfamiliar with, philosophy is more specifically run down on that account for dropping the distinction between good and evil too; so its critics are usually fair-minded and magnanimous enough to concede "that in their presentation the philosophers do not always develop the ruinous consequences that are *bound up* with their thesis[a] (and perhaps they do not do it because these conclusions are not germane to it)."* Philosophy must disdain the merciful compassion that is here bestowed on it, for it is no more in need of mercy for its moral justification, than it lacks insight into the actual consequences of its principles, or than it falls short in drawing those consequences in express terms. I will briefly elucidate here the alleged consequence according to which the diversity of good and evil has to be made into a mere semblance—more as an example of the hollowness of the interpretation of philosophy that is involved, than as a justification of philosophy itself. To illustrate this we shall consider only Spinozism, the philosophy in which God is determined only as *substance*, and not as subject and spirit. This distinction concerns the *determination* of the unity; the *determination* is all that matters, but although this determination is a *factum*, those who are accustomed to call this philosophy "the Identity-System" know nothing

---

a. *Satz*

*The words are those of F. A. G. Tholuck in his *Florilegium of Eastern Mysticism*, p. 13. Tholuck, too, being a man of deep feeling, allows himself to be misled into following the customary highway of philosophical interpretation. The understanding (he says) can only draw conclusions in the following two ways: either there is a primal ground that conditions everything, and then the ultimate ground of my own self lies in that, so that my being and my free action are only illusory; or I am actually an essence diverse from the primal ground, one whose action is not conditioned and caused by the primal ground, and then the primal ground is not an absolute, all-conditioning essence, so that there is no infinite God but a multitude of Gods, etc. All philosophers who think more profoundly and acutely are supposed to profess the first of these theses (though I do not know why the first one-sidedness should be any more profound and acute than the second); the consequences (which, of course, they do not always develop, as we said above) are "that even man's ethical standard has no absolute truth, but *properly speaking* [the author himself underlines this] good and evil are the same and are only diverse in their semblance." One would always do better, not to talk about philosophy at all as long as, in spite of one's depth of feeling, one is still so deeply entangled in the one-sidedness of the understanding, that one knows nothing better than the *Either/Or*: of a primal ground in which the individual's being and freedom is only an illusion, or of the absolute independence of the individuals; in other words, as long as no inkling of the *Neither/Nor* of these two one-sided views (of this "perilous" dilemma, as Tholuck calls it) has entered into one's experience at all. On page 14, to be sure, he does speak of those spirits—and they are said to be the authentic philosophers—who accept the second thesis (but this is now, it seems, the same as what was previously called the first thesis) and sublate the antithesis of *unconditioned* and conditioned being through the *undifferentiated primal being* in which all antitheses of a relative kind are mutually interfused. But when Tholuck speaks in this way, has he not noticed that the undifferentiated primal being, in which the antithesis is to be interfused, is altogether the same as that unconditioned being, whose one-sidedness was to be sublated? So that in the very same breath he is speaking of the sublation of that

about it. They may even employ the expression that according to this philosophy *everything is one and the same*, that good and evil are *equal* too. All of this is the most spurious type of unity; it cannot be what is talked of in speculative philosophy, and only a thinking that is still barbaric can employ these thoughts in reference to Ideas. As for the allegation that in Spinoza's philosophy the diversity of good and evil is not valid *in-itself* or according to its *authentic* meaning, the question to be asked is: What does *"authentic"* mean here? If it refers to the nature of God, then no one will want evil to be located there; that substantial unity is the good itself; evil is only the splitting in two. So nothing is further from that unity than good and evil being of one kind; on the contrary, evil is excluded. Hence, the distinction between good and evil is not in God as such either; for this distinction is found only in what is split in two—i.e., in that in which evil itself is. Moreover, in Spinozism distinction occurs as well: *man is diverse from God.* In this respect, the system may not be theoretically satisfactory; for although man (and the finite in general) may later be downgraded to a "mode," he only *finds* himself *side by side* with substance in the earlier

one-sided being in a being that is exactly this same one-sided being; and hence he is express-ing the continued subsistence of the one-sidedness instead of its sublation. If one is going to say what *spirits* do, then one must be able to apprehend the *factum* [deed] spiritually; other-wise that *factum* has become falsified under one's hand.—I note, moreover, though somewhat redundantly, that what I have said, both here and further on, about Tholuck's notion of philosophy, cannot and should not be applied just to him *individually*, so to speak. We find the same statements in hundreds of books, and especially in the prefaces of theology books (among all the others). I have cited Tholuck's exposition, first because it chances to be what I have at hand; and secondly because the profound feeling that seems to set his writings in complete opposition to the theology of the understanding comes very near to true profundity of sense. For the fundamental determination of this feeling is *reconciliation*, which is not the unconditioned primal being, or any abstraction of that kind, but the basic import itself, which is the speculative Idea, and which the Idea expresses in thought—an import which that profound sense must on no account fail to recognise in the Idea.

But what happens here (as much as everywhere else in his writings) is that Tholuck allows himself to fall into the currently fashionable talk about *pantheism*—about which I have spoken at greater length in one of the final remarks of my *Encyclopaedia* (§ 573). Here I shall only remark on the peculiar ineptitude and inversion into which Tholuck himself falls. He puts the primal ground on one side of his supposedly philosophical dilemma, and designates this side later on as pantheistic (pp. 33, 38). Similarly, he characterises the other side as that of the Socinians, Pelagians, and popular philosophers; and about this side he says that "there is no infinite God, but a *great number* of gods, namely the number of *all* the essences that are diverse from the so-called primal ground, and have a *being* and action of their own, alongside that so-called primal ground." So, in fact, we have on this side not merely a great number of gods, but *all* [things] *are* gods (since everything finite counts in this context as having a *being* of its own). Hence, it is on this side in fact that Tholuck has his *omnideism* [*Allesgotterei*], or his *pantheism* fully expressed; not on the first side, where he expressly makes the *one* primal ground into its God—the first side, consequently, is only *monotheism*.[6]

discussion. It is here, then, in man, where distinction exists, that it exists essentially as the distinction between good and evil too; and this is where it *authentically* is, for only here is the determination that is proper to it. When we are studying Spinoza, if we have only the substance in mind, then there is of course no distinction between good and evil in it; but that is because—from this point of view—evil has no being at all, just as the finite, and the *world* in general have none—(see the Remark to § 50, below). But when what we have in mind is the standpoint from which man, and the relationship of man to the substance, also occur in this system—the only standpoint where evil can have its place in its distinction from the good—then we must have read through the parts of the *Ethics* that deal with good and evil, or with the passions, human bondage, and human freedom; *then* we can tell the tale of the moral consequences of the system. We can convince ourselves beyond question regarding the high purity of this moral theory whose principle is the unalloyed love of God, just as readily as we can convince ourselves that this purity is the moral consequence of the system. Lessing said in his time that people dealt with Spinoza like a dead dog;[7] and we cannot say that Spinozism, or indeed speculative philosophy generally, has been any better treated in more recent times. For it is clear that those who discuss it and make judgments about it, do not ever make any effort to grasp the facts rightly, or to report and relate them correctly. This is the least that justice requires, and philosophy can demand this much in any case.

The history of philosophy is the story of the discovery of the *thoughts* about the Absolute which is their subject matter. Thus, for example, we can say that Socrates discovered the determination of *purpose* that was filled out as a determinate cognition by Plato, and more particularly by Aristotle. Brucker's history of philosophy[8] is so uncritical, not only with respect to external historical data, but with respect to the reporting of thoughts, that one can find twenty, thirty, or more theses cited from the earlier Greek philosophers as their philosophical dicta, of which not one belongs to them. They are conclusions that Brucker draws after the manner of the bad metaphysics of his time, and falsely ascribes to those philosophers as their own assertions. Conclusions are of two kinds: some are simply the result of following out a principle into greater detail, and others are a regression toward deeper principles. To write history is precisely to record those individuals to whom a further deepening of thought in this way, and an unveiling of it, properly belongs. But Brucker's procedure is not simply improper because the early philosophers did not themselves draw the consequences that are supposed to lie in their principles, and hence merely failed to express them in so many words; but rather because his reasoning involves the direct ascription of validity to finite thought-relationships, and the readiness to use them, [in spite of the fact that] these thought-relationships are directly contrary to the sense of those philosophers (who were speculative in spirit); and (what is more) they only pollute and falsify the philosophical Idea. And if, in the case of ancient philosophers, only a few of whose statements have come down to us, this falsification has the excuse of being supposedly correct reasoning, this excuse falls away in the case of a philosophy that has both grasped its own Idea in determinate thoughts and has expressly investigated and determined the value of the categories as well. There can be no excuse when the Idea is interpreted in a mangled way in spite of that, and only One moment ("identity," for instance) is extracted from the exposition and given out to be the totality; or when the categories are introduced quite naïvely, and just as they come, the very way that they run through everyday consciousness in all their one-sidedness and untruth. Educated cognition of thought-relationships is the primary condition for the correct interpretation of a philosophical *factum*. But crudity of thought is not only justified expressly by the principle of immediate knowing; it is made the law. The cognition of thoughts, and the cultural formation of subjective thinking along with it, is no more a [matter of] immediate knowing than any science or art and skill are.

Religion is the mode, the type of consciousness, in which the truth is present for all men, or for all levels of education; but scientific cognition is a particular type of the consciousness of truth, and not everyone, indeed only a few men, undertake the labour of it. *The basic import is the same*, but just as Homer says about certain things that they have two names,[9] one in the language of Gods, and the other on the tongues of us men, the creatures of a day, so, too, there are two tongues for that import: the tongue of feeling, of representation, and of the thinking that nests in the finite categories and one-sided abstractions of understanding, and the tongue of the concrete Concept. And when we want to discuss and pass judgments about philosophy in a religious perspective, more is required than our just being quite accustomed to the language of the consciousness of our day. The foundation of scientific cognition is the inner basic import, the Idea that dwells in it, and the vitality of that Idea which is stirring in the spirit; just as religion involves no less a thoroughly disciplined heart and mind,[a] a spirit awakened to awareness,[b] and a fully formed import. In the most recent times religion has contracted the cultured expanse of its content more and more, and withdrawn itself into the intensity of piety, i.e., of feeling. Often, indeed, this feeling is one that manifests a very impoverished and barren import. But as long as religion has a creed, a doc-

a. *durchgearbeitetes Gemüt*
b. *Besinnung*

trine, and a dogmatics, philosophy can concern itself with that, and can in that way unite itself as such with religion. But here again, this claim is not to be taken up in the manner of the wrongly separative understanding in which our modern religious attitude is caught up. This attitude represents religion and philosophy as mutually exclusive, or as being generally separable to such a degree that they consequently only link up in an external way. Instead, what is implied by all that we have said so far is that there may be religion without philosophy, but there cannot be philosophy without religion, because philosophy includes religion within it. Genuine religion, the religion of the spirit, must have a creed, a content of this sort. The spirit is essentially consciousness, and hence [consciousness] of the content made into an ob-ject. As feeling, the spirit is just the not yet objective content itself (only a *quale*, to use an expression of Jakob Boehme);[10] it is just the lowest stage of consciousness, in the form of the soul, which we have in common with the lower animals. It is *thinking* that first makes the soul—with which the lower animals are endowed too—into spirit; and philosophy is only a consciousness concerning that content, the spirit and its truth; i.e., concerning spirit in the shape and mode of the essentiality that is its own, which distinguishes it from the lower animals, and makes it capable of religion. The concentrated religious attitude that focuses strictly on the heart must make its contrition and mortification into the essential moment of its rebirth; but it must at the same time recollect that it is dealing with the heart of a spirit, and that the spirit is appointed as the power over the heart, and it can only be this power insofar as it is itself born again. This rebirth of the spirit out of the natural lack of knowledge, and equally out of natural error, happens through instruction, and through faith *in the objective truth*, the faith in the content that arises from the witness of the Spirit. This rebirth of the spirit is also an immediate rebirth of the heart (among other things) out of the vanity of the one-sided understanding, which leads it to boast of its knowledge of such [assumptions] as the diversity of the finite from the infinite, or that philosophy must either be polytheism, or—in the spirits that think most acutely—pantheism. It is a rebirth that liberates us from such lamentable insights as those, insights that enable pious humility to ride its high horse over both philosophy and theological cognition alike. When the religious attitude abides by its intense feeling without any expansion, and hence without any spirit, it does, of course, only know of the antithesis between its narrowed and narrowing form of mind and the spiritual expansion of doctrine, whether religious as such or philosophical.* However, the thinking spirit does not just restrict itself to finding its satisfaction in the "purer," i.e., the simple-hearted religious attitude; on the contrary, that standpoint is itself a result which has emerged from reflection and argument. It is by the aid of the superficial understanding that the religious attitude has given itself this fine liberation from virtually all doctrines; and it is by using the thinking with which it is infected for its zealous attack on philosophy that it maintains itself by force on the rarefied peak of an abstract state of feeling without any content.—I cannot refrain from citing here some excerpts from the "Exhortation" of Franz von Baader about a configuration of piety of that kind, in the fifth volume of his *Fermenta Cognitionis* (Preface, p. ixff).[13]

*To return once more to Herr Tholuck, who can be regarded as the enthusiastic representative of the pietist current of thought, the lack of any *doctrine* in his essay "On the doctrine of Sin" (second edition [anonymous, Hamburg, 1825]), which has just come to my notice, is quite marked. I was struck by his treatment of the dogma of the Trinity in his essay *The Speculative Doctrine of the Trinity in the Later Orient* [Berlin, 1826]. I am deeply grateful to him for the historical notes that he has drawn from his sources with such industry. But he calls the doctrine a *scholastic doctrine*; and in any case it is much older than anything that we call "scholastic." He treats it only on its external side as being supposedly only a doctrine that arose historically from speculation about biblical passages under the influence of Platonic and Aristotelian philosophy (p. 41). Then, in his essay about sin, he dismisses the dogma in cavalier fashion, one might say, declaring that it can only be an artificial framework in which the doctrines of the faith (but which ones?) can be put in order (p. 220). Indeed, we must even say about this dogma, that to one standing on the bank (in the sand of the spirit perhaps?) it appears as a Fata Morgana (p. 219).[11] The doctrine of the Trinity is not "a foundation" (Tholuck calls it the "tripod," ibid., p. 221) "upon which *our faith can be grounded* ever again." But has not this doctrine (as the most sacred one) always—or from time immemorial anyway—been, as our Creed, the main content of the faith itself? And has not this Creed always been the foundation of subjective faith? How can the doctrine of reconciliation— which Tholuck seeks so energetically to bring to our feelings in the essay under discussion— have more than a moral sense (or, if you like, a pagan sense), how can it have a Christian sense without the dogma of the Trinity? There is nothing in this essay about other specific dogmas either. For instance, Tholuck leads the reader always to the passion and death of Christ, but no further; not to his resurrection and ascension to the right hand of the Father [nor yet to the pouring forth of the Spirit—1830]. One of the main determinations in the doctrine of reconciliation is the *punishment for sin*; in Tholuck's essay (pp. 119ff) this is the self-conscious burden (and the damnation bound up with it) that all must carry, who live *apart from* God, the one and only source of blessedness and holiness alike. This means that sin, the consciousness of guilt, and damnation cannot be *thought* separately from one another (so this is a place where even some thinking occurs, just as on p. 120 it is also demonstrated that the determinations flow out of the *nature* of God). This determination of the punishment for sin is what has been called the *natural* punishment of sin; and (like indifference about the doctrine of the Trinity) it is the result of the teaching of that reason and enlightenment that Tholuck decries so much.—Some time ago in the Upper House of the English Parliament, a bill concerning the sect of the Unitarians failed to pass; at this juncture, an English newspaper published a report about the great number of Unitarians in Europe and America. Then it added this comment: "At present Protestantism and Unitarianism are mostly synonymous on the continent of Europe."[12] Theologians may be left to decide whether Tholuck's dogmatics is distinct from the ordinary theology of the Enlightenment in anything save one or two points—and not even in those respects when it is closely examined.

"For as long as religion and its doctrines have not regained in the eyes of science, a respect that is grounded upon free research, and hence upon genuine conviction" he says. " . . . For so long all of you, the pious and the impious, with all of your do's and don't's, and all your talk and action, will have no remedy against evil, and for so long will this unrespected religion not be loved; because only what is seen to be sincerely respected and [re]cognised to be indubitably worthy of respect can be wholeheartedly and sincerely loved, just as religion can only be served with an *amor generosus* [generous love] of the same kind. . . . In other words: If you want the practice of religion to flourish again, then you must make sure that we achieve a rational theory of it once more, and not leave your enemies (the atheists) in complete possession of the field with their *irrational* and *blasphemous* assertion that no such theory of religion is to be thought of at all, that such a thing[a] is impossible because religion is a matter of the heart only, a region where one quite conveniently can, and indeed one must, divest oneself of one's head."*

Regarding poverty of content we can remark further that this can only be talked of as the way in which the external state of religion appears at a particular time. A time of that kind may be lamented, because such an effort is needed just to bring forth the mere faith in God—a need that weighed so heavily on the noble Jacobi—and further to awaken only a concentrated Christianity of feeling. All the same, we cannot fail to recognise the higher principles that announce themselves even here (see the Introduction to the *Logic*, § 64 Remark). But what lies before science is the rich content that hundreds and thousands of years of cognitive activity have brought forth for itself; and this content does not lie before it as historical information that only *others* possess. Then it would be something-dead-and-gone for us, just an occupation to exercise our memories and our acuteness in the critical evaluation of reports, not [a topic] for the cognition of the spirit and the [rational] concern with truth. What is most sublime, most profound, and most inward has been called forth into the light of day in the religions, philosophies, and works of art, in more or less pure, in clearer or more obscure shapes, often in very repulsive ones. We

a. *Sache*

*Tholuck quotes several passages from Anselm's treatise *Cur Deus homo*, and celebrates "the profound humility of this great thinker" (p. 127).[14] But he is not mindful of, and does not cite, the passage from this same treatise that I have quoted below (at § 77 of the *Encyclopaedia*): Negligentiae mihi videtur si . . . non studemus quod credimus *intelligere* [It seems to me to be negligence if . . . we do not study to *understand* what we believe].—Certainly when the Creed is shrivelled up into just a few articles, there is not much stuff left for cognitive effort, and little can come from the cognition of it.

can count it as a particular merit of Franz von Baader that he not only goes on bringing such forms to our recollection, but also with a profoundly speculative spirit he brings their basic import expressly into scientific honour because on that basis he expounds and confirms the philosophical Idea. The depth of Jakob Boehme, in particular, offers the occasion and the forms for this. The name "Teutonic Philosopher" has rightly been conferred upon this mighty spirit.[15] On the one hand, he has enlarged the basic import of religion, [taken] on its own account, to the universal Idea; within that basic import he formulated the highest problems of reason and tried to grasp spirit and nature in their determinate spheres and configurations. [All this was possible] because he took as his foundation [the thesis] that the spirit of man and all things else are created in the image of God— and, of course, of God as the Trinity; their life is just the process of their reintegration into that original image after the loss of it. On the other hand (and conversely), he forcibly misappropriated the forms of natural things (sulphur, saltpeter, etc.; the sharp, the bitter, etc.) as spiritual forms and forms of thought.[16] The gnostic interpretation that von Baader attaches to configurations of this kind is his own special way of kindling and advancing the philosophical concern; it sets itself forcefully against any coming to rest in the barren void of enlightened polemics[a]—and equally against the piety that wants simply to remain intense. In all of his writings von Baader shows, incidentally, that he is far from taking this gnostic interpretation to be the exclusive mode of cognition. It has its inconveniences on its own account: its metaphysics does not push on to deal with the categories themselves, or with the methodical development of the content. Its weakness is that the Concept is not well adapted to the wildness and spontaneous spirit of forms and configurations of this kind; just as its general weakness is that it has the absolute content as its *presupposition*, and that it offers explanations, arguments, and refutations on the basis of this presupposition.*

It might be said that we have *enough* configurations of the truth, and *all too many* of them, some purer and others more cloudy, in the religions and mythologies, or in the gnostic and mystery-making philosophies of ancient

---

a. *Aufklärerei*

*I am certainly delighted to learn that Herr von Baader agrees with many of my propositions—as is evident both from the content of several of his more recent writings and from his references to me by name. About most of what he contests—and even quite easily about everything—it would not be difficult for me to come to an understanding with him, that is to say, to show that there is, in fact, no departure from his views in it. There is only one complaint that I want to touch on. It occurs in the "Comments upon some anti-religious philosophical dicta of our time" [Leipzig], 1824, p. 5, cf. pp. 56ff. There he discusses a dictum

and modern times. One may delight in the *uncovering* of the Idea in these configurations, and one may in this way satisfy oneself that the philosophical truth is not something merely solitary, but that, on the contrary, its effective action has been present—at least as a ferment—in these configurations. But when the conceit of immaturity undertakes a rehashing of these productions of the fermentation—as was the case with one imitator of von Baader—that conceit, in all its laziness and incapacity for scientific thinking, can easily exalt a gnosis of this kind into the exclusive mode of cognition. For it is less of a strain to let oneself go in these [symbolic] patterns,[a] and tie one's philosophical dicta onto them, than to take up the development of the Concept, and submit one's thinking, indeed, one's whole heart and mind, to the logical necessity of the Concept. Also, a conceited person will easily attribute to himself what he has learned from others, and he will believe this all the more easily when he is attacking or belittling those others; the truth is, rather, that he is irritated with them precisely because he has derived his insights from them.

Although deformed, the impulse of thought announces itself in the very phenomena of the time that we have taken note of in this foreword; and that is why, for the thought that is cultivated to the high level of the spirit,

which "having emerged from the school of the philosophy of nature, establishes a false concept of matter, in that it affirms regarding the transient essence of this world—which contains corruption within it—that it is *immediately* and eternally emergent and emerging from God, as the eternal outgoing ([self]-emptying)[b] of God which *conditions* his eternal re-entry [into himself] (as spirit)" [Hegel's emphases]. As far as the first part of this representation is concerned—the *emerging* of matter from God—"emergence" is, in any case, a category that I do not use, because it is a picturing expression, and no category. But I do not see how to avoid admitting that this proposition is implied in the determination that God is the creator of the world. As far as the other part is concerned—that the eternal outgoing *conditions* the re-entry of God as spirit—for one thing, von Baader posits the category of "condition" at this point where it is in and for itself out of place; hence I never use it to express this relation either. Please recollect the comments I made earlier about the uncritical exchanging of the determinations of thought. In what von Baader himself offers us about the concept of matter (pp. 54ff), I see nothing that departs from my own determinations concerning it. Nor do I understand what help there is for the absolute task of grasping the creation of the world as a concept, in what von Baader offers us on page 58, to wit, that matter "is not the immediate product of the unity, but of those *principles* (the empowered ones, the Elohim) *which the unity* calls forth, for this purpose." Whether the sense of this is that matter is the product of the principles—the grammatical structure does not make this completely clear—or alternatively that it is matter which has called forth these Elohim for itself, and that it has let itself be produced by them; [but in any case] the Elohim, or even the whole circle together [of matter and Elohim], must be posited in a relation to God. And this relation is not clarified at all by the insertion of the Elohim here.[17]

a. *Gebilde*
b. *Entäußerung*

it is in and for itself a need (both for the thinker and for the time) that what was revealed as a mystery in earlier times should now be revealed for thinking itself. (The mystery remains a complete secret for formal thought, even in the purer configurations of its revelation, and still more in the cloudier ones.) This task alone is therefore worthy of our science, and in the absolute right of its freedom, thinking affirms the stubborn determination only to be reconciled with the solid content so far as that content has, at the same time, been able to give itself the shape that is most worthy of it. This is the shape of the Concept, the shape of the necessity that binds all, content and thoughts alike, and precisely thereby makes them free. If we are to renew what is old—and I speak only of the configuration as being old, because the basic import itself is ever young—then perhaps the configuration of the Idea as Plato, and much more deeply Aristotle, gave it to us is infinitely more worthy of recollection [than any mysteries]. This is also because the unveiling of the Idea through its adaptation to our intellectual culture[a] is at once not merely an understanding of that Idea, but an advance of science itself. But, of course, the understanding of such forms of the Idea as theirs does not lie so ready on the surface as the grasping of gnostic and cabalistic phantasmagorias; and the further development of those forms for our time happens even less spontaneously than the discovery and identification of echoes of the Idea in those gnostic dreams.

Just as it was rightly said of the true that it is *index sui et falsi* [index both of itself and of the false][18] but that the true is not known by starting from the false, so the Concept is the understanding both of itself and of the shape without Concept, but the latter does not from its own inner truth understand the Concept. Science understands feeling and faith, but science itself can only be assessed through the Concept (as that on which it rests); and since science is the self-development of the Concept, an assessment of science through the Concept is not so much a judgment upon it as an advancing together with it. That is the sort of judgment that I cannot but desire for this present endeavour, and it is only a judgment of that sort that I can be both respectful and responsive to.

Berlin, 25 May 1827

---

a. *Gedankenbildung*

FOREWORD TO THE THIRD EDITION (1830)

In this third edition improvements of many kinds have been made throughout, and a particular attempt has been made to increase the clarity and determinacy of the exposition. All the same, because of the purpose of the manual as a compendium, the style had to remain condensed, formal, and abstract. The book retains its [original] vocation: it is to receive the necessary commentary only in my lectures.

Since the second edition, a variety of assessments of my method of doing philosophy have appeared—and for the most part they have shown little or no calling for the task. Such careless responses to works that were thought through for many years, and worked over with all the seriousness that the subject matter and scientific discussion require, can bring no joy to the mind in view of all the evil passions that crowd upon you there: conceit, pride, envy, scorn, and the rest. Still less is anything to be learned from them. In the second book of his *Tusculans* [2.4] Cicero says: "Est philosophia paucis contenta judicibus, *multitudinem* consulto ipsa fugiens, eique ipsi et *invisa* et *suspecta*; ut, si quis universam velit vituperare, *secundo* id *populo* facere possit." [Philosophy is content to have but few judges, and flies from the *mob* deliberately; by the mob itself philosophy is both *envied* and *distrusted*. So that if someone wanted to cry down philosophy as a whole, they could do it with the *support of the people*.] To run philosophy down is all the more popular, when one does it without insight or seriousness. How petty the adverse passion is can be grasped from the echo that comes back to it from others; and the absence of knowledge keeps it company just as naturally. Other ob-jects strike the senses, or are given to representation in global intuitions; if we are to converse about them, we feel the necessity of some acquaintance with them, however slight it may be; and they are more easily recollected by our common sense because they are there in their familiar, firm presence. But the fact that philosophy lacks all this is brought up against it without shame, or rather it is brought up against some fantastic empty image of philosophy that the ignorance of it dreams up and talks into being. This ignorance has nothing before it by which it can orient itself, so it runs loose completely in an indeterminate, empty, and senseless talk. I have undertaken elsewhere the ungrateful and fruitless task of exposing some of these phenomena woven out of passion and ignorance in all their obvious nakedness.[1]

A little while ago it may have looked as if a more serious inquiry about God, divine things, and reason, in a broader range of scientific endeavour, would be called forth from the basis of theology and even of religious experience.[2] But even the way that that movement began allowed no hope of such an outcome; for the impulse sprang from *personalities*, and neither the pretensions of piety nor the pretensions of free reason—neither the accuser nor the accused—rose up to the *matter* [itself], still less to the consciousness that the territory of philosophy must be entered upon if the matter was to be discussed. That personal attack, grounded upon very specific external details of religion, showed itself in the appalling presumption of those who were ready to excommunicate certain individuals from Christianity upon their own full authority, and thereby put upon them the seal of damnation in this world and in eternity. Dante arrogated to himself the power of Peter's keys under the forceful inspiration of his divine poetry, and condemned many of his contemporaries to damnation in Hell by name—even Popes and Emperors—but they were dead already.[3] One of the defamatory complaints made against a certain modern philosophy has been that in it [the][4] human individual posits himself as God; but compared with this complaint based on a false inference, the presumption in which one assumes the role of the World's Judge, gives one's verdict against the Christianity of individuals, and utters the sentence of inmost damnation upon them, is an actual presumption of quite another sort. The shibboleth of this absolute authority is the *name of the Lord Christ* and the *assurance* that the Lord dwells in the hearts of these judges. Christ says (Matt. 7:20), "By their fruits ye shall [re]cognise them," but the appalling insolence of condemnation and casting into outer darkness is no good fruit. Christ continues: "Not all that say unto me, 'Lord, Lord' shall enter into the Kingdom of Heaven. Many will say unto me on that day: 'Lord, Lord, have we not prophesied in thy name? Have we not *in thy name* cast out devils? Have we not done many deeds *in thy name?*' Then shall I profess unto them: 'I have never [re]cognised you, *depart ye all from me, ye evildoers.'* " Those who assure us that they are in exclusive possession of Christianity, and demand this same faith from others, have not carried their faith so far as to cast out devils. Instead, many of them, like those who have faith in the medium of Prevorst,[5] are inclined to congratulate themselves about being on good terms with a mob of ghosts, of whom they stand in awe, instead of driving out and banishing these lies that belong to a servile and anti-Christian superstition. They are equally incapable of speaking words of wisdom, and are completely unable to do great deeds of cognition and science, though that ought to be their vocation and their duty; mere erudition is not yet science. They busy themselves at great length with the mass of indifferent external matters of the faith; but then in contrast they stand by the name of the Lord Christ in a completely barren fashion as far as the basic import and intellectual content of the faith itself is concerned; and they deliberately and scornfully disdain the elaboration of doctrine that is the foundation of the faith of the Christian church. For the spiritual, fully thoughtful, and scientific expansion [of the doctrine] would upset, and even forbid or wipe out, the self-conceit of their subjective boasting which relies on the spiritless and fruitless assurance—rich only in evil fruits—that they are in possession of Christianity, and have it exclusively for their very own.—In the scriptures, the "spiritual expansion" that I mentioned is distinguished from mere "faith" in the most determinate and conscious way. Faith only comes to be *truth* through its expansion. "He who *has faith* in me altogether," says Christ (John 7:38), "out of his belly shall *rivers of living water* flow." Then, at once, this is elucidated and determined in verse 39: it is not the simple faith in the temporally sensible, present personality of Christ that works this wonder, for he is not yet the truth as such. In verse 39 the faith meant is determined thus: that Christ spoke here about the *Spirit* which they that believed in him *should receive*; for the Holy Spirit *was not yet there*, because Jesus was *not yet glorified*. The still unglorified shape of Christ is the personality that was then sensibly present in time, or afterwards represented so (which is the same content). This is the immediate ob-ject of the faith. In this [historical] presence Christ himself revealed his external nature to his disciples by word of mouth. He revealed his own vocation to reconcile God with himself, and man with him—the order of salvation and the doctrine of ethics. And the faith that the disciples had in him embraced all this within it. Notwithstanding all that, this faith which lacked not an atom of the strongest certainty, is declared to be only the beginning and the fundamental condition for what was still incomplete. Those who believed in that way still did not have the Spirit; they were still to *receive* it. The Spirit, the truth itself, the Spirit that leads us into all truth, comes only later than that faith. But our new disciples stand fast in the certainty which is only the condition; and that certainty, being itself only subjective, brings forth only the subjective fruit of formal *assurances*, and thereby further that of pride, calumny, and anathema. In defiance of Scripture, they hold fast only to the certainty, and against the spirit, which is the expansion of cognition, and only then the truth.

The new piety shares this barrenness of scientific and of spiritual import generally, with what it immediately makes into the ob-ject of its accusation and damnation: the enlightenment of the understanding. Through its formal and abstract thinking, [which is] lacking all basic import, this enlightenment has emptied all content out of religion, just as the new piety has done, by its reduction of the faith to the shibboleth of the "Lord, Lord." In this respect, neither has any advantage over the other; and because they collide in simple antagonism, there is no stuff present within which they are in contact, and could reach a common soil and the possibility of entering into an inquiry, and finally reaching cognition and truth. For its own part, the enlightened theology[6] has stood stock still in its own formalism: i.e., its appeal to *freedom* of conscience, *freedom* of thought, *freedom* of teaching, and even to reason and science. To be sure, this freedom is the category of the *infinite right* of the spirit; and as such, it is the other *particular condition* of the truth, which goes with faith as the first one. But *what* the free and genuine conscience *contains* as rational determinations and laws, *what* the free faith and thought has and teaches as its *content*, this material question they have refrained from broaching. They have taken their stand upon their formalism of the negative, and upon the freedom to fill out their freedom according to their own opinion and liking, so that the content itself is, in principle, indifferent. Another reason why this party cannot come near to any content is that the Christian community must be, and always ought to be, united by the bond of a doctrinal concept, or confession of faith, whilst the lifeless water of the understanding, with its generalities and its abstract rationalism,[a] cannot tolerate the specificity of an inwardly determinate, expressly formed Christian content and doctrinal concept. The other party, in contrast, relying on the formula "Lord, Lord" as their "Open Sesame," quite frankly disdains the fulfilling of the faith as spirit, import, and truth.

In this way a great dust cloud of pride, malice, and personal abuse has certainly been raised—with empty generalities too. But the faith was stricken with unfruitfulness; it could not contain the matter, it could not lead to import and cognition.—Philosophy could well be content to be left out of the game. Its place is outside the terrain of those pretensions—both of personalities and of abstract generalities; and had it been drawn onto a field of that sort, only unpleasant and unprofitable results were to be expected.

---

a. *Die Allgemeinheiten und Abstraktionen des abgestandenen, nicht lebendigen rationalistischen Verstandeswassers.*

Because the rich and deep import has rotted out of the supreme interest, or unconditional concern, of human nature, and the religious attitude—both the pious and the reflecting attitude together—has reached the point where it finds the highest contentment in being without content, philosophy has become a contingent and subjective need. In both types of religious attitudes these unconditional concerns have been arranged (by [finite] argument and nothing else) in such a way that philosophy is no longer needed to satisfy those interests. On the contrary, it is rightly held that philosophy will only upset this newly created sufficiency and a contentment that is so narrowly based.[a] Philosophy, therefore, is left altogether to the freely felt need of the subject. No pressing invitation at all is addressed to the subject; on the contrary, where the need is present, it has to be steadfast against insinuations and dire warnings. It exists only as an inner necessity that is stronger than the subject, by which his spirit is then driven without rest "that he may overcome,"[7] and may create the gratification that the impulse of reason deserves. Thus, without the encouragement of any authority, even that of the religious authority (it is regarded, in fact, as a superfluity, and as a dangerous or at least doubtful luxury), our occupation with this science stands all the more freely upon our concern with the matter and with the truth alone. If, as Aristotle says, *theoria* is the most *blessed*, and among goods the *best*,[8] then those who participate in this gratification know what they have in it: the satisfaction of the necessity of their spiritual nature. They can refrain from making demands on others with respect to it, and can leave them to their own needs, and to the satisfactions that they themselves find for those needs. What is to be thought about the urge to do the business of philosophy without a calling we have said above: that the more noise it makes, the less fitted it is to take part in the work. The deeper and more serious participation is lonelier at home, and more silent abroad. Vanity and superficiality is quickly ready, and feels driven to a hasty meddling; but serious concern about an inwardly great matter—one for which only the long and difficult labour of a complete development suffices—submerges itself in it in quiet pursuit for a long time.

The rapid exhaustion of the second edition of this encyclopaedic guiding thread (which, in accord with the way it was determined above, does not make the study of philosophy easy) has given me the satisfaction of seeing that, quite apart from the noise made by superficiality and vanity, a quieter

---

a. *ins Enge gezogen*

and more rewarding participation in philosophy has taken place. I wish now that, for this new edition too, it may continue.

Berlin, 19 September 1830

INTRODUCTION

§ 1

Philosophy lacks the advantage, which the other sciences enjoy, of being able to *presuppose* its *ob-jects* as given immediately by representation. And, with regard to its beginning and advance, it cannot *presuppose* the *method* of cognition as one that is already accepted. It is true that it does, initially, have its ob-jects in common with religion. Both of them have the *truth* in the highest sense of the word as their ob-ject, for both hold that *God* and God *alone* is the truth. Both of them also go on to deal with the realm of the finite, with *nature* and the *human spirit*, and with their relation to each other and to God as to their truth. Hence, philosophy can, of course, presuppose some *familiarity* with its ob-jects; in fact it *must* presuppose this, as well as an interest in these ob-jects. The reason is that in the order of time consciousness produces *representations* of ob-jects before it produces *concepts* of them; and that the *thinking* spirit only advances to thinking cognition and comprehension by going *through* representation and by converting itself *to* it.

But when we consider something in thought, we soon become aware that thoughtful consideration implies the requirement that the *necessity* of its content should be shown, and the very being, as well as the determinations, of its ob-jects should be proved. As a result, the familiarity with these ob-jects that was mentioned above is seen[a] to be insufficient, and making— or granting the validity of—*presuppositions* and *assurances*, is seen to be inadmissible. The difficulty of making a beginning arises immediately, because a beginning (being something *immediate*) does make a presupposition or, rather, it is itself just that.

§ 2

To begin with, philosophy can be determined in general terms as a *thinking consideration* of ob-jects. But if it is correct (as indeed it is), that the *human*

object of experience

a. *erscheint*

24

being distinguishes itself from the *animals* by thinking, then everything human is human because it is brought about through thinking, and for that reason alone. Now, since philosophy is a peculiar mode of thinking—a mode by which thinking becomes cognition, and conceptually comprehensive cognition at that—philosophical thinking will also be *diverse* from the thinking that is active in everything human and brings about the very humanity of what is human, even though it is also identical with this thinking, and *in-itself* there is only *One* thinking. This distinction is connected with the fact that the human import of consciousness, which is based on thinking, does not *appear in the form of thought* straightaway, but as feeling, intuition, representation—which are *forms* that have to be distinguished from thinking *itself as form.*

> It is an old prejudice, a saying that is now a cliché, that man is distinguished from the lower animals by thinking; it may seem to be a cliché, but it must also seem remarkable that there is need to recall this old belief. Yet one can hold that the need is there, in view of the prejudice of our day and age, which separates *feeling* and *thinking* from each other in such a way that they are supposedly opposed to each other, and are even so hostile that feeling—religious feeling in particular—is contaminated, perverted, or even totally destroyed by thinking, and that religion and religiosity essentially do not have their root and their place in thinking.[1] Making a separation of this kind means forgetting that only man is capable of religion, and that the lower animals have no religion, any more than right and morality belong to them.
>
> When this separation between religion and thinking is asserted, one has in mind the thinking that can be called "*thinking-over*"— the *reflective* thought that has *thoughts* as such as its *content* and brings them to consciousness. Because the distinction with regard to thinking that is clearly indicated by philosophy is neglected, the crudest notions and complaints against philosophy are brought forth. Religion, right, and ethical life belong to man alone, and that only because he is a thinking essence. For that reason *thinking* in its broad sense has not been inactive in these spheres, even at the level of feeling and belief, or of representation; the activity and productions of thinking are *present* in them and are *included* in them. But it is one thing to have feelings and representations that are *determined* and *permeated* by *thinking*, and another to have *thoughts about them.* The thoughts *about* these modes of consciousness— generated by *thinking them over*—are what reflection, argumentation, and the like, as well as philosophy, are comprehended under.

In this context it has happened—and the misunderstanding has prevailed quite often—that *meditation* of this kind [or "*thinking-over*"][a] was alleged to be the condition, or even the only way for us, to arrive at the representation of what is eternal and true and the belief that it is so. For instance, the (now rather *obsolete*) *metaphysical proofs that there is a God* were passed off in this way, as if it were essentially and exclusively through our being acquainted with them, and being convinced [of their validity], that the belief and conviction that there is a God could be brought about. This sort of assertion is like saying that we can only eat after we have become acquainted with the chemical, botanical, or zoological determinations of our food, and that we should delay our digestion until we have completed the study of anatomy and physiology. If that were so, these sciences would certainly gain greatly in usefulness in their field, just as philosophy would in its field. Indeed their usefulness would be raised into an absolute and universal indispensability. But then too, instead of being indispensable, they would not exist at all.

§3

Whatever kind it may be, the *content* that fills our consciousness is what makes up the *determinacy* of our feelings, intuitions, images, and representations, of our purposes, duties, etc., and of our thoughts and concepts. Hence feeling, intuition, image, etc., are *the forms* of this content, a content that remains *one and the same*, whether it be felt, intuited, represented, or willed, and whether it be *only* felt, or felt, intuited, etc., with an admixture of thought, or whether it is thought quite *without any admixture*.[2] In any one of these forms or in a mixture of several of them, the content is *ob-ject* of our consciousness. But in this ob-jectivity the *determinacies of these forms join themselves onto the content*;[b] with the result that each of these forms seems to give rise to a particular ob-ject, and that what is in-itself the same can look like a diverse content.

Since the determinacies of feeling, of intuition, of desire, of willing, etc., are generally called *representations*, inasmuch as we have *knowledge* of them, it can be said in general that philosophy puts *thoughts* and *categories*, but more precisely *concepts*, in the place of representations. Representations in general [or "notions"] can be

---

a. Nachdenken
b. schlagen sich zum Inhalte

regarded as *metaphors* of thoughts and concepts. But that we have these notions does not mean that we are aware of their significance for thinking, i.e., that we have the thoughts and concepts of them. Conversely, it is one thing to have thoughts and concepts, and another to know what the representations, intuitions, and feelings are that correspond to them.—One side of what is called *the unintelligibility of philosophy* is related to this. The difficulty lies partly in the inability (which in-itself is just a *lack of practice*) to think abstractly, i.e., to hold on to pure thoughts and to move about in them. In our ordinary consciousness thoughts are affected by and united with the sensible and spiritual material with which we are familiar; and in thinking about something, in reflecting and arguing about it, we *mix* feelings, intuitions, and representations with thoughts. (Categories, like *being*, or *singularity*, are already mingled into every proposition, even when it has a completely sensible content: "This leaf *is* green.") But it is a very different thing to make the thoughts themselves, unmixed with anything else, into ob-jects.⫽—The other aspect of the unintelligibility of philosophy is an impatient wish to have before us, in the mode of representation, what is in our consciousness as thought and concept. There is a saying that, when we have grasped a concept, we still do not know what to *think* with it. But there is nothing to be thought with a concept save the concept itself. What this saying means, however, is that we long for an *ordinary notion*, one that we are already *familiar* with; consciousness feels as if, together with the mode of representation, the very ground, where it stands solidly and is at home, has been pulled from under it. Finding itself displaced into the pure realm of the concept, it does not know *where* in the world it is.⫽—Hence the writers, preachers, orators, etc., who tell their readers or listeners things that they already knew by heart, things that are familiar to them and even *self-explanatory*, are the ones that are most readily "understood."

§ 4

In its relation to our ordinary consciousness, philosophy would first have to show *the need* for its *peculiar mode of cognition*, or even to awaken this need. But in relation to the ob-jects of religion, i.e., to *truth* altogether, it would have to prove that we have the *ability* to reach their cognition on our own; and in relation to any *diversity* that comes to light between *religious* notions and its own diverging determinations, it would have to *justify* the latter.

§ 5

In order to reach a provisional agreement about the distinction that has been mentioned and the insight connected with it, namely, that the genuine *content* of our consciousness is *preserved* when it is translated into the form of thought and the concept, and even that it is not placed in its proper light until then, we can conveniently call to mind another *old prejudice*. This prejudgment holds that, when we want to experience what is *true* in ob-jects and occurrences, as well as in feelings, intuitions, opinions, notions, etc., then we must *think them over*. And the very least that this thinking-over does in any case is to change our feelings, and notions, etc. into *thoughts*.

> But since philosophy claims that it is *thinking* that is the proper *form* of its business, and since every human is by nature able to think, what happens as a result of this abstraction, which leaves out the distinction that was indicated in § 3, is just the opposite of what we have mentioned already as the complaint about the *unintelligibility* of philosophy. Philosophic science is often treated with contempt by those who imagine and say—although they have not made any effort to come to grips with it—that they already understand what philosophy is all about quite spontaneously,[a] and that they are able to do philosophy and to judge it just by holding on to what they have learnt at a very ordinary level, in particular from their religious feelings. In the case of the other sciences, we admit that one has to have studied them in order to know about them, and that one is only entitled to judge them in virtue of a studied acquaintance. We admit that in order to make a shoe, one has to have learnt and practiced how to do it, even though everyone of us has the required measure in his own feet, and we all have hands with a natural aptitude for the trade in question. It is only for doing philosophy that study, learning, and effort of this kind is supposedly not needed.—Of late, this convenient opinion has received its confirmation through the doctrine of immediate knowing, [i.e.,] of knowing through intuition.

§ 6

It is equally important, on the other hand, that philosophy should be quite clear about the fact that its content is nothing other than the basic import that is originally produced and produces itself in the domain of the living

---

a. *von Haus aus*

spirit, the content that is made into the *world*, the outer and inner world of consciousness; in other words, the content of philosophy is *actuality*. The first consciousness of this content is called *experience*. Within the broad realm of outer and inner thereness, a judicious consideration of the world already distinguishes that which is only *appearance*, transient and insignificant, from that which truly and in itself merits the name of *actuality*. Since philosophy is distinguished only in form from other ways of becoming conscious of this same identical import, its accord with actuality and experience is necessary. Indeed, this accord can be viewed as an outward touchstone, at least, for the truth of a philosophy; just as it has to be seen as the supreme and ultimate purpose of science to bring about the reconciliation of the reason that is conscious of itself with the reason that *is*, or actuality, through the cognition of this accord.

In the *Preface* to my *Philosophy of Right* p. xix[3] the following propositions will be found:

> *What is rational, is actual,*
> *and what is actual, is rational.*

These simple propositions have seemed shocking to many and they have been attacked, even by those who are not ready to renounce the possession of philosophy, and certainly not that of religion. In the present context, we do not need to discuss religion, since the doctrines of the divine governance of the world express these propositions quite definitely. But as far as their philosophical meaning is concerned, we have to presuppose that the reader has enough education to know, not just that God is actual—that he is what is most actual, that he alone is genuinely actual—but also (with regard to the formal aspect) that quite generally, what is there is partly *appearance* and only partly actuality. In common life people may happen to call every brainwave, error, evil, and suchlike "actual," as well as every existence, however wilted and transient it may be. But even for our ordinary feeling, a contingent existence does not deserve to be called something-actual in the emphatic sense of the word; what contingently exists has no greater value than that which something-*possible* has; it is an existence which (although it is) can just as well *not be*. But when I speak of actuality, one should, of course, think about the sense in which I use this expression, given the fact that I dealt with actuality too in a quite elaborate *Logic*, and I distinguished it quite clearly and directly, not just from what is contingent, even though it has existence too, but also, more precisely, from being-there, from existence, and from other determinations.[4]

The notion that ideas and ideals are nothing but chimeras, and that philosophy is a system of pure phantasms, sets itself at once against the *actuality of what is rational*; but, conversely, the notion that ideas and ideals are something far too excellent to have actuality, or equally something too impotent to achieve actuality, is opposed to it as well. However, the severing of actuality from the Idea is particularly dear to the understanding, which regards its dreams (i.e., its abstractions) as something genuine, and is puffed up about the "ought" that it likes to prescribe, especially in the political field—as if the world had had to wait for it, in order to learn how it ought to be, but is not. If the world were the way it ought to be, what then would become of the pedantic wisdom of the understanding's "ought to be"? When the understanding turns against trivial, external, and perishable ob-jects, institutions, situations, etc., with its "ought"—ob-jects that may have a great relative importance for a certain time, and for particular circles—it may very well be in the right; and in such cases it may find much that does not correspond to correct universal determinations. Who is not smart enough to be able to see around him quite a lot that is not, in fact, how it ought to be? But this smartness is wrong when it has the illusion that, in its dealings with ob-jects of this kind and with their "ought," it is operating within the [true] concerns of philosophical science. This science deals only with the Idea— which is not so impotent that it merely ought to be, and is not actual—and further with an actuality of which those ob-jects, institutions, and situations are only the superficial outer rind.

§ 7

It is, quite generally, *meditative thinking*[a] that initially contains the principle of philosophy (also in the sense of "beginning"); and now that (since the times of the Lutheran Reformation) it has once more come into bloom in its [proper] *independence*, the name of *philosophy* has been given a wider significance. This is because, right from the start, our meditative thinking did not confine itself to its merely abstract mode (as it did in the philosophical beginnings made by the Greeks), but threw itself at the same time upon the material of the world of appearance—a material that seems to be measureless. Hence, the name "philosophy" was given to all of the know-

a. *Nachdenken*

ing that deals with the cognition of fixed measure and of *what is universal* in the sea of singular empirical data, and with *what is necessary*, with the *laws*, in the seeming disorder of the infinite mass of what is contingent. In consequence, "philosophy" has at the same time taken its *content* from its *own* intuiting and perceiving of the outward and the inward, from the *presence* of nature as much as from the *presence* of spirit and from the human heart.[a]

> The principle of *experience* contains the infinitely important deter-mination that, for a content to be accepted and held to be true, man must himself *be* actively involved *with it*,[b] more precisely, that he must find any such content to be at one and in unity with *the certainty of his own self*. He must himself be involved with it, whether only with his external senses, or with his deeper spirit, with his essential consciousness of self as well.—This is the same principle that is today called faith, immediate knowing, revelation in the outer [world], and above all in one's *own* inner [world]. We call the sciences that have the name "philosophy" *empirical* sciences, because of their point of departure. But their essential purpose and results are *laws, universal principles*, a *theory*; i.e., the *thoughts* of what is present. Thus, the *Newtonian* physics has been called philosophy of nature, whereas *Hugo Grotius*, for instance, established a theory that can be called philosophy of international law,[5] by classifying the modes of conduct of peoples toward each other, and by establishing universal principles on the basis of ordi-nary argumentation.—The name "philosophy" still generally has this determination in England; and Newton continues to be cele-brated as the greatest of philosophers. Even in the catalogues of instrument makers, the instruments, such as the thermometer, the barometer, etc., that are not classified under the heading of mag-netic or electrical apparatus are called "philosophical instruments." But, surely, it is only *thinking* that ought to be called the instru-ment of philosophy, and not some contraption of wood, iron, etc.*—Our most recently emergent science of political economy, in

a. *aus dem* präsenten *Geiste und der Brust des Menschen*

b. *selbst* dabei sein *müsse*

*Even the journal that Thomson edits is called "Annals of *Philosophy* or Magazine of *Chemistry, Mineralogy, Mechanics, Natural History, Agriculture*, and *Arts*."—This title gives us automat-ically a fair notion of what sort of materials are here called "philosophical."—Among the anouncements of newly published books I recently found the following in an English news-paper: The Art of Preserving the Hair, on *Philosophical Principles*, neatly printed in post octavo, price 7 sh.—What is meant by "philosophical" principles of the preservation of the hair is probably chemical or physiological principles and the like.[6]

particular, is also called philosophy—the science that we usually call *rational* or *intellectual* political economy.*

§ 8

This cognition may be satisfactory enough within its own field. But, *first of all*, another circle of *ob-jects* shows up that are not part of this field: *freedom, spirit, God*. The reason that these are not to be found upon that soil is not because they ought not to belong to experience. It is true that they are not experienced by the senses, but everything that is in consciousness at all is experienced. (This is even a tautological proposition.) The reason is that these ob-jects present themselves directly as infinite with regard to their *content*.

> There is an old saying that is usually (but falsely) attributed to *Aristotle*—as if it were supposed to express the standpoint of his philosophy: "Nihil est in intellectu, quod non fuerit in sensu."[8] (There is nothing in the intellect that has not been in sense-experience.)[a] If speculative philosophy refused to admit this principle, that would have to be considered a misunderstanding. But conversely, philosophy will equally affirm: "Nihil est in sensu, quod non fuerit in intellectu"—in the most general sense that the *nous*, and more profoundly *the spirit*, is the cause of the world, and more precisely (see § 2) that feelings concerning right, ethical life, and religion are feelings—and hence an experience—of the kind of content that has its root and its seat in thinking alone.

---

*When referring to the universal principles of political economy, English politicians often use the expression "*philosophical* principles", even in public speeches. In the House of Commons, on Feb. 2, 1825, Brougham, in his reply to the Speech from the Throne, talked of "the statesman-like and *philosophical* principles of Free Trade—for they are undoubtedly philosophical—upon the acceptance of which His Majesty has this day congratulated Parliament."—But it is not just this member of the opposition [who talks like that]. The annual dinner of the Shipowner's Society took place the same month, with the prime minister (the Earl of Liverpool) presiding; Lord Canning (the secretary of state) and Sir Charles Long (the paymaster-general of the army) were at his side. Here Lord Canning, in reply to the toast that was drunk to him, said: "a period has lately commenced when Ministers have had it in their power to apply to the state of the country the just maxims of *profound philosophy*."— However great the difference between English and German philosophy may be, it is in any case a matter for rejoicing that the name of philosophy is still honoured in the mouth of an English cabinet minister, while elsewhere it is used only as a nickname and an insult, or as something to be hated.[7]

a. *im Sinne, in der Erfahrung*

§ 9

Secondly, subjective reason wants further satisfaction *with regard to form*; this form is *necessity* in general (see § 1). In the kind of science mentioned above [see § 7], the *universal* (the genus, etc.) contained in it is not determined on its own account, nor is it intrinsically[a] connected with what is *particular*; but universal and particular are mutually external and contingent, just as much as the particularities that are combined are, on their own account, external to each other and contingent. Moreover, the beginnings are immediate, found, or presupposed. In both respects, the form of necessity fails to get its due. Insofar as it aims at satisfying this need, meditative thinking is the thinking that is philosophical in the proper sense, [i.e., it is] *speculative thinking*. Hence, as a meditation, which in all its *community* with that first [empirically scientific] meditation is at the same time *diverse* from it, philosophical thinking has its own *peculiar forms*, apart from the forms that they have in common. The universal form of it is the *Concept*.

> Hence the relationship of speculative science to the other sciences is simply the following: speculative science does not leave the empirical content of the other sciences aside, but recognises and uses it, and in the same way recognises and employs what is universal in these sciences, [i.e.,] the laws, the classifications,[b] etc., for its own content; but also it introduces other categories into these universals and gives them currency. So the distinction between speculative and empirical science relates only to this alteration of the categories. Speculative Logic contains the older logic and metaphysics; it preserves the same forms of thought, laws, and ob-jects, but it develops and transforms them with further categories.
>
> What has usually been called a "concept" has to be distinguished from the *Concept* in the speculative sense. The assertion, repeated many thousands of times, until it became a prejudice, that the Infinite cannot be grasped through concepts, is made only in the customary, or one-sided sense.

§ 10

This thinking itself in the philosophical mode of cognition needs to be grasped in its necessity, as well as justified in respect of its ability to become cognizant of the absolute ob-jects. But any insight of this kind is

a. *für sich*
b. die Gattungen

itself philosophical cognition, and therefore it can only fall *within* philosophy. So any *preliminary* explanation would have to be an unphilosophical one, and it could not be more than a tissue of presuppositions, assurances, and argumentations, i.e., of contingent asssertions, against which the opposite assurances could be made with the same right.

> One of the main points of view in the *Critical* Philosophy is the following: before we embark upon the cognition of God, or of the essence of things, etc., we should first investigate our *faculty of cognition* itself, to see whether it is capable of achieving this. We should first get to know about the *instrument*, before undertaking the task[a] that is supposed to be accomplished by means of it; for, otherwise, if the instrument is inadequate, then all further effort would have been expended in vain.[9]—This thought seemed to be so *plausible* that it has elicited the greatest admiration and assent; and it led our cognition, from its concern with *ob-jects* and its dealings with them, back to itself, back to the formal aspect [of cognition itself]. But if we are not going to deceive ourselves with words, then it is obvious that other instruments can, of course, be investigated and judged in other ways than through the undertaking of the peculiar task for which they are meant to be used. But the investigation of cognition cannot take place in any other way than *cognitively*; in the case of this so-called tool, the "investigation" of it means nothing but the cognition of it. But to want to have cognition *before* we have any is as absurd as the wise resolve of Scholasticus to learn to *swim before he ventured into the water*.[10]
>
> *Reinhold*, who recognised the confusion that prevails in beginnings of this kind, has proposed as the remedy for it, that we should commence provisionally with a *hypothetical* and *problematic* philosophising, and continue with this—Heaven knows how—until somehow we happen, further along this road, to reach the *original truth*.[b] When we look at it more closely, we can see that it leads to the usual procedure, namely the analysis of an empirical foundation, or of a provisional assumption that has been transformed into a definition. We should not overlook the correct consciousness involved in Reinhold's proposal that the usual course of presuppositions and provisional statements is a hypothetical and problematic procedure. But his correct insight does not alter the way that this procedure is constituted; on the contrary, it directly expresses the inadequacy of it.[11]

a. *Arbeit*
b. *das Urwahre*

§ 11

The need for philosophy can be determined more precisely in the following manner. As feeling and intuition the spirit has what is sensible for its ob-ject; as fantasy, it has images; and as will, purposes, etc. But the spirit needs also, in *antithesis to*, or merely in *distinction from these forms* of its thereness and of its ob-jects, to give satisfaction to its highest inwardness, *to thinking*, and to make thinking into its ob-ject. In this way, spirit comes *to itself*, in the deepest sense of the word; for its principle, its unadulterated selfhood, is thinking. But when it goes about its business in this way, what happens is that thinking gets entangled in contradictions; that is to say, it loses itself in the fixed nonidentity between thoughts, and therefore it does not reach itself, but rather stays stuck in its counterpart [in the world of ob-jects]. The higher need goes against this result reached by a thinking that belongs to the understanding alone; it is grounded in the fact that thinking will not give up, but remains faithful to itself even in this conscious loss of its being at home with itself, *"so that it may overcome,"*[12] and may accomplish in thinking itself the resolution of its own contradictions.

> The insight that the very nature of thinking is the dialectic, that, as understanding, it must fall into the negative of itself, into contradictions, is an aspect of capital importance in the Logic. When thinking despairs of being able to bring about, *from its own re-sources*,[a] the resolution of the contradiction in which it has put itself, then it returns to the solutions and appeasements in which the spirit has participated in its other modes and forms. But it was not necessary to let this return degenerate into *misology*, an experience which *Plato* already confronted;[13] thinking does not need to conduct itself polemically against itself, which is what happens when a so-called *immediate knowing* is asserted to be the *exclusive* form of the consciousness of truth.

§ 12

The *coming into being* of philosophy out of the need that has been mentioned has *experience*, the immediate and argumentative consciousness, as its *starting point*. With these needs as its stimulus, thinking conducts itself essentially so as to *raise* itself above the natural, sensible, and argumentative consciousness into its own unadulterated element; and it gives itself initially a self-distancing *negative relationship* to this beginning. Thus,

a. aus sich

thinking finds its first satisfaction in itself—in the Idea of the universal essence of these appearances; this Idea (the Absolute, God) can be either more or less abstract. Conversely, the experiential sciences carry with them the stimulus to vanquish *the form* in which the wealth of their content is offered only as something that is merely immediate and simply found, as a manifold of *juxtaposition*, and hence as something altogether *contingent*. They are stimulated to elevate this content to [the level of] necessity: this stimulus pulls thinking out of its abstract universality, and out of the satisfaction that is only warranted *implicitly*; and it drives thinking on to *develop* itself *by its own means*.[a] On the one hand, this development is just a taking up of the content and of the determinations that it displays; but, on the other hand, it also gives these determinations the shape of coming forth freely (in the sense of original thinking) in accordance with the necessity of the matter itself alone.

 We shall have to speak more explicitly, and at greater length, below about the relationship of *immediacy* and *mediation* within consciousness. At this point it is only necessary to draw attention, in a preliminary way, to the fact that, whilst each of these moments does also *appear* as distinct, *neither of them* can *be wanting*, and they are *inseparably* bound together.—In this way, our knowing of God, like our knowledge of all that is *super*sensible in general, essentially involves an *elevation* above sensible feeling or intuition; hence, it involves a *negative* attitude toward the latter as first and in that sense it involves *mediation*. For mediation is a beginning, and a having advanced to a second, in such a way that this second is only there because one has come to it from something that is other vis-à-vis this second. But the knowing of God is nonetheless independent of that empirical side; it even gives itself *its* independence essentially through this negation and elevation.—If mediation is one-sidedly stressed and made into a condition, then we can say that philosophy owes its first beginning[b] to experience (to what is a posteriori).—But that is not saying very much, for thinking is in fact essentially the negation of something immediately given[c]— just as we owe our eating to food because without it we could not eat. It is true that, in this context, eating is represented as ungrateful, since it is the digesting of that to which it is supposed to owe itself. In this sense, thinking is no less ungrateful.

a. von sich aus
b. *Entstehen*
c. *Vorhandenes*

But thinking's own *immediacy (that which is a priori)* is inwardly reflected and hence inwardly mediated; it is *universality,* the overall being-at-home-with-itself of thinking. In this universality, thinking is inwardly contented, and for that reason it has inherited an indifference towards *particularisation,* and hence toward its development. Just as religion possesses the same intensive nature of contentment and bliss, whether it is more developed or less cultivated, developed into scientific consciousness, or held in naïve faith and in the heart. When thinking stops at the *universality* of the ideas—as was necessarily the case with the first philosophies (for instance, with the *Being* of the Eleatic school, the *Becoming* of Heraclitus, and so on)—then it is rightly accused of *formalism.* It can happen, even in a developed philosophy, that only abstract principles or determinations are apprehended (for instance, "That in the Absolute all is one," "The identity of the subjective and the objective"), and that with regard to what is particular these same principles and determinations are simply repeated.[14] With reference to the first abstract universality of thinking, there is a correct and more fundamental sense in which the *development* of philosophy is due to experience. On the one hand, the empirical sciences do not stop at the perception of *single instances* of appearance; but through thinking they have prepared[a] the material for philosophy by finding universal determinations, genera, and laws. In this way they prepare the content of what is particular so that it can be taken up into philosophy. And, on the other hand, they contain the invitation for thinking, to advance to these concrete determinations. The assumption of this content, through which the immediacy that still clings to it, and its givenness, are sublated by thinking, is at the same time a *developing* of thinking out of itself. Thus, philosophy does owe its development to the empirical sciences, but it gives to their content the fully essential shape of the *freedom* of thinking (or of what is a priori) as well as the *validation* of *necessity* (instead of the content being warranted because it is simply found to be present, and because it is a fact of experience). In its necessity the fact becomes the presentation and imitation of the activity of thinking that is original and completely independent.

§ 13

In the peculiar shape of *external history,* the coming to be of philosophy and its development is represented as the *history of this science.* This shape

a. *entgegen gearbeitet*

gives the form of a *contingent* succession to the stages of the Idea's development, and it gives a kind of mere *diversity* to the principles and their
exposition in the various philosophies of these stages. But the master
workman of this labour of thousands of years is the One living Spirit,
whose thinking nature is to bring to consciousness *what it is*; and when
what it is has become ob-ject in this way, it is at once raised above this, and
it is inwardly a higher stage. With regard to philosophies that appear
diverse, the *history of philosophy*[15] shows, on the one hand, that there is
only One philosophy at diverse stages of its formation, and, on the other,
that the particular *principles* on which each system is grounded one by one
are only *branches* of one and the same whole. The philosophy that is the
latest in time is the result of all the preceding philosophies; and it must
therefore contain the principles of all of them; for this reason, it is the most
unfolded, the richest, and the most concrete one—provided that it does
deserve the name of philosophy.

> When we are faced with so many *diverse* philosophies, the *univer-
> sal* must be distinguished from the *particular* according to its
> proper determination. Taken formally, and put *side by side* with the
> particular, the universal itself becomes something particular too.
> In dealing with the ob-jects of ordinary life, this juxtaposition
> would automatically strike us as inappropriate and awkward; as if
> someone who wants fruit, for instance, were to reject cherries,
> pears, raisins, etc., because they are cherries, pears, raisins, but *not*
> fruit. But in the case of philosophy we allow ourselves to justify
> the rejection of it by pointing out that philosophies are so diverse,
> and that each of them is only *one* philosophy, not *the* philosophy,[16]
> just as if cherries were not fruit. It also happens that a philosophy
> whose principle is the universal is put *side by side* with one whose
> principle is something-particular, or even next to doctrines that
> assert that there is no philosophy at all, in the sense that both are
> *only diverse* views of philosophy—rather as if light and darkness
> were said to be just two *diverse* kinds of light.

§ 14

The same development of thinking that is presented in the history of
philosophy is presented in philosophy itself, but freed from that historical
outwardness, i.e., purely in the element of thinking. Free and genuine
thought is inwardly *concrete*; hence it is *Idea*, and in all its universality it is
the Idea or *the Absolute*. The science of it is essentially a *system*, since what
is *concretely* true is so only in its inward self-unfolding and in taking and

holding itself together in unity, i.e., as *totality*. Only through the distinguishing, and determination of its distinctions, can what is concretely true be the necessity of these distinctions and the freedom of the whole.

A philosophising *without system* cannot be scientific at all; apart from the fact that philosophising of this kind expresses on its own account a more subjective disposition, it is contingent with regard to its content. A content has its justification only as a moment of the whole, outside of which it is only an unfounded presupposition or a subjective certainty. Many philosophical writings restrict themselves like this—to the mere utterance of *dispositions* and *opinions*.—It is erroneous to understand by "system" a philosophy whose principle is restricted and [kept] distinct from other principles; on the contrary, it is the principle of genuine philosophy to contain all particular principles within itself.

§ 15

Each of the parts of philosophy is a philosophical whole, a circle that closes upon itself; but in each of them the philosophical Idea is in a particular determinacy or element. Every single circle also breaks through the restriction of its element as well, precisely because it is inwardly [the] totality, and it grounds a further sphere. The whole presents itself therefore as a circle of circles, each of which is a necessary moment, so that the system of its peculiar elements constitutes the whole Idea—which equally appears in each single one of them.

§ 16

As an *Encyclopaedia*, science is not presented in the detailed development of its particularisation; instead, it has to be restricted to the beginnings and the fundamental concepts of the particular sciences.

How much of each particular part is required to constitute a particular science is undetermined, insofar as the part must not be just an isolated moment, but in order to be something-true it must itself be a totality. The whole of philosophy genuinely forms *One* science; but it can also be considered as a whole made up of several particular sciences.—The philosophical encyclopaedia distinguishes itself from the other, ordinary encyclopaedia because the latter has to be some sort of *aggregate* of sciences, which are taken up contingently and empirically; and among them there are also some that are "sciences" only in name, since they are themselves no more than a mere collection of bits of information. In the case of such an aggregate, since the sciences in it are taken up externally, the unity in which the sciences are brought together is itself an *external* unity—*an order*. For the same reason, as well as because the materials are of a contingent nature too, this order has to remain *tentative*. It must always display aspects that do not really fit in.

The philosophical encyclopaedia excludes, first of all, mere aggregates of information, such as philology at first sight appears to be. Secondly, it also (just as decisively) excludes learning that is based on mere arbitrariness, such as heraldry, for instance. Sciences of this kind are *positive* through and through. Thirdly, there are other sciences that are called "positive," too, in spite of the fact that they have a rational basis and beginning. Here the rational component belongs to philosophy; but the *positive side* is peculiar to each one of them. And what is positive in the sciences is of diverse kinds:

1. The implicitly rational beginning of the sciences passes over into what is contingent, because they have to bring the universal down to *empirical singularity* and *actuality*. In this field of alterability and contingency, it is not the *Concept* that can be made to count, but only *grounds*. The science of jurisprudence, for instance, or the system of direct and indirect taxation, require *ultimate and precise* decisions. These lie outside the *determinateness-in-and-for-itself of the Concept*, so that they leave a latitude for their determination—which can be grasped in one way upon one ground, and in another way on another ground, and which admits of no certain and ultimate ground. In the same way the Idea of *nature* loses itself in its dispersion of isolated contingencies; and *natural history, geography, medicine*, etc., fall into determinations of existence, species, and distinctions, etc., that are determined externally, by chance and by a play [of circumstances], not by reason. *History*, too, belongs here, inasmuch as, although the Idea is its essence, the appearing of this Idea takes place in contingency and in the field of freedom of choice.

2. Sciences of this kind are also *positive* inasmuch as they do not recognise their determinations as *finite*, or show the passage of these and of their entire sphere into a higher one, but take these same determinations to be *absolutely valid* ones.

3. The finitude of the *ground of cognition* is connected with this second finitude (which is the finitude of the *form*, just as the first

was the finitude of the *material*). This cognitive ground is partly argumentation; partly feeling, belief, the authority of others; and, in general, the authority of inner or outer intuition. The philosophy that wants to base itself on anthropology, on facts of consciousness,[17] on inward intuition or outward experience, belongs here too.

4. It is also possible that only the *form of the scientific presentation* may be empirical, but that an insightful intuition orders what are only phenomena in a way that corresponds to the inner sequence of the Concept. In an empirical presentation of this kind the *external, contingent circumstances* of the conditions are sublated through the opposition and manifoldness of the appearances that are put together; and the universal comes before the mind[a] as a result.— An experimental physics, or a history, etc., that makes sense will present the rational science of nature and of human events and actions in this way, as an external image that mirrors the Concept.[18]

§ 17

With regard to the *beginning* that philosophy has to make, it seems, like the other sciences, to start in general with a subjective presupposition, i.e., to have to make a particular ob-ject, in this case *thinking*, into the ob-ject of thinking, just like space, number, etc., in the other sciences. But what we have here is the free act of thinking putting itself at the standpoint where it is for its own self, *producing its own ob-ject for itself* thereby, and *giving it to itself*. Within the Science this standpoint, which in this first act appears as *immediate*, must make itself into the *result*, and (what is more) into its last result, in which it reaches its beginning again and returns into itself. In this way, philosophy shows itself as a circle that goes back into itself; it does not have a beginning in the same sense as the other sciences, so that the beginning only has a relation to the subject who takes the decision to philosophise, but not to the science as such.[19]—Or, to put the same thing another way, the concept of the Science and therefore the first concept— which, since it is the first one, contains the severance that thinking is ob-ject for an (as it were external) philosophising subject—must be grasped by the Science itself. This is even its unique purpose, deed, and goal: to arrive at the Concept of its concept and so to arrive at its return [into itself] and contentment.

a. *vor den Sinn*

§ 18

Just as a provisional, or a general, notion of a philosophy cannot be given, because only the *whole* of the Science is the presentation of the Idea, so the *division* of it, too, can be comprehended only from the whole presentation; [at this point] the division is only something anticipated, like the [coming] presentation from which it has to be taken. But the Idea shows itself as the thinking that is strictly identical with itself, and this at once shows itself to be the activity of positing itself over against itself, in order to be for-itself, and to be, in this other, only at home with itself. Hence, the science falls into three parts:

  I. The *Logic*, the science of the Idea in and for itself.

 II. The *Philosophy of Nature*, as the science of the Idea in its otherness.

III. The *Philosophy of Spirit*, as of the Idea that returns into itself out of its otherness.

> In § 15 above, it was remarked that what distinguishes the particular philosophical sciences are only determinations of the Idea itself, and that it is only this Idea that presents itself in these diverse elements. In nature, it is not something-other than the Idea that is [re]cognised, but the Idea is in the form of [its] uttering,[a] just as in the spirit we have the same Idea *as being for-itself,* and *coming to be in and for itself.* A determination of this kind, in which the Idea appears, is at the same time a moment *that flows*; hence, the single science is just as much the cognition of its content as an ob-ject *that is,* as it is the immediate cognition in that content of its passage into its higher circle. The *representation* of *division* is therefore incorrect inasmuch as it puts the particular parts or sciences *side by side,* as if they were only immobile parts and substantial in their distinction, the way that *species* are.

a. *Entäußerung*

FIRST PART:

THE SCIENCE OF LOGIC

PRELIMINARY CONCEPTION

The Logic is the science of *the pure Idea*, that is, of the Idea in the abstract element of *thinking*.

What holds for all anticipatory concepts about philosophy applies to this determination just as it does to all the others contained in this Preliminary Conception; i.e., that they are determinations drawn *from* and *subsequent* to the survey of the whole.

It can, of course, be said that logic is the science of *thinking*, of its *determinations* and *laws*, but thinking as such constitutes only the *universal determinacy* or the *element* in which the Idea is [simply] logical. The Idea is thinking, not as formal[a] thinking, but as the self-developing totality of its own peculiar determinations and laws, which thinking does not already *have* and find given within itself, but which it gives to itself.

The Logic is the *most difficult* science, inasmuch as it has to do, not with [sensible] intuitions nor even, like geometry, with abstract sense-representations, but with pure abstractions, and inasmuch as it requires a trained ability at withdrawing into pure thought, holding onto it and moving within it. It could, on the other hand, be viewed as the *easiest* science, because its content is nothing but our own thinking and its ordinary determinations, and because these are both the *simplest* and *what is elementary*. They are also what we are *most familiar* with: being, nothing, etc.; determinacy, magnitude, etc.; being-in-itself, being-for-itself, one, many, and so on. But this familiarity only tends to make the study of the Logic more difficult. For one thing, we are prone to believe that it is not worthwhile to occupy oneself any further with what is so familiar. On the other hand, what we have to do is to become familiar with it in a way that is quite other than, and even opposed to, the one in which we are already used to it.

a. *formal*

The *usefulness* of logic is a matter of its relationship to the subject, insofar as one gives oneself a certain formation for other purposes. The formation of the subject through logic consists in one's becoming proficient in thinking (since this science is the thinking of thinking) and in one's coming to have thoughts in one's head and to know them also as thoughts.—However, since the logical is the absolute form of the truth and, even more than that, also the pure truth itself, it is really something quite other than anything merely *useful*. But, just as that which is most excellent, most free, and independent is what is most useful, so the logical can be grasped as useful too. But in this case its usefulness is to be measured on quite another scale than as being just the formal exercise of our thinking [capacity].

Addition 1. The first question is: What is the subject matter of our science? The simplest and most intelligible answer to this question is that it is the *truth*. "Truth" is an elevated word and the thing itself still more so. As long as man's mind and spirit are healthy, his heart must begin at once to beat more quickly when it [truth] is mentioned. But very soon a reservation appears: can we also know the truth? There seems to be a lack of proportion between us men, limited as we are, and the truth as it is in and for itself; and the question arises of the bridge between the finite and the infinite. God is the Truth; how then are we to be cognizant of him? There seems to be a contradiction between any such project and the virtues of humility and modesty.

But we also ask whether there could be any cognition of the truth in order to justify our continuing to be content with the coarseness of our finite purposes. So humility of this sort is not worth very much. Language such as: "How should a poor worm like me be able to discover what is true?" is a thing of the past; in its place has come self-assurance and presumption, and men imagine that they are in immediate contact with what is true.[a]—They have made the young believe that they already possess what is true (in religion and ethics), just as they stand. In particular, it has been said, from the same point of view, that the whole adult world is sunk, petrified, and ossified in untruth. A new dawn has appeared to youth, but the older world still lies in the slough and the morass of common day.[1] The special sciences have been pointed to as what we must in any case acquire, but simply as the means for the external purposes of life. Here it is not modesty that holds us back from the study and cognition of the truth, but rather the conviction that we possess the truth in and for itself already. Older people certainly pin their hopes on the young, for it is the young who are to make progress for the world and in science.[2] But we can only repose this hope in the young inasmuch as they do not just stay as they are, but take upon themselves the bitter labour of the spirit.

There is still another shape assumed by modesty regarding truth. This is the sort of refined superiority toward truth that we see in Pilate when he confronts Christ.

a. *unmittelbar im Wahren zu sein*

Pilate asked, "What is truth?" with the attitude of someone who has settled accounts with everything, someone for whom nothing has a meaning any more—in the same sense in which Solomon says that "All is vanity" [Eccles. 1:2]. All that remains at this point is subjective vanity.

Then again, timidity hampers the cognition of the truth, too. It comes so easily to the slothful mind to say: "We do not mean to be serious about philosophising. We go to hear the logic lectures, too, of course, but they have to leave us unchanged." We are of the opinion that if thinking goes beyond the circle of our familiar notions it must be going wrong; we are then entrusting ourselves to a sea on which we are beaten back and forth by the billows of thought, and in the end we land once more "upon this bank and shoal of time"[3] which we left behind for nothing and in vain. What comes of such a view we can see in the world. One can acquire all manner of skills and all kinds of learning, become an official well versed in one's routine, and in every way train oneself for one's particular purposes. But it is quite another thing to cultivate one's spirit for higher things and to make efforts on behalf of that. We may hope that in our time a longing for something better has sprung up in the young, and that they will not be content with the mere straw of a cognition that remains on the outside of things.

Addition 2. That *thinking* is the subject matter of logic, we are all agreed. But about thinking we can have a very low and also a very high opinion. Thus, we say on the one hand, "That is *only* a thought," and we mean thereby that thought is only subjective, arbitrary, and contingent, and not the matter that really counts, not what is true and actual. But, on the other hand, people can also have a high opinion of thought and take it in the sense that only thought attains to what is highest, God's nature, and that there is no cognition of God by means of the senses. We say that God is Spirit and that it is his will that we should worship him in spirit and in truth [John 4: 24]. But, we concede that the merely felt and sensible is not the spiritual; on the contrary, the inmost heart of the latter is thought, and only spirit can [re]cognise spirit. Of course, spirit can also behave as something that feels (e.g., in religion), but feeling as such, the *mode* of feeling, is one thing, while the *content* of feeling is another. Feeling as such is the general form of what is sensible; we have it in common with the animals. This form can indeed take hold of the concrete content, but the content does not belong to this form; feeling is the lowest form that the spiritual content can assume. It is only in thinking, and as thinking, that this content, God himself, is in its truth. In this sense, therefore, thought is not just *mere* thought; on the contrary, it is what is highest and, considered strictly, it is the one and only way in which what is eternal, and what is in and for itself can be grasped.

People can have a high or a low opinion of the science of thought, just as they can of thought itself. Everybody can think without logic—so we say—just as we can digest without studying physiology. Even if you have studied logic, you still think afterwards the way you did before, perhaps more methodically, but with little change. If logic had nothing else to do than make us acquainted with the activity of merely formal thinking, it would not have brought forth anything that we could not have done just as well without studying logic. In fact, the traditional logic did no more than that. Still, to be acquainted with thinking as a merely subjective activity already does man honour, and has an interest for him; by knowing what he is and what he does, man distinguishes himself from the animals.

But now, on the other hand, logic as the science of thinking also has a higher standpoint inasmuch as thought alone is able to experience what is highest, or what is true. Thus, if the Science of Logic considers thinking in its activity and its production (and thinking is not an activity without content, for it produces thoughts and Thought itself),[a] its content is in any event the supersensible world; and to be occupied with that world is to sojourn in it. Mathematics has to do with the abstractions of number and of space; but these are still something sensible, though in an abstract way and not as really being there.[b] Thought says farewell even to this last element of the sensible, and is free, at home with itself; it renounces external and internal sensibility, and distances itself from all particular concerns and inclinations. Insofar as this is the terrain of logic, we must think more worthily of it than people are in the habit of doing.

Addition 3. The need to understand logic in a deeper sense than that of the science of merely formal thinking is sparked by the interests of religion, of the State, of law, and of ethical life. In earlier times people saw no harm in thinking and happily used their own heads. They thought about God, nature, and the State, and were convinced that only by thinking would they become cognizant of what the truth is, not through the senses or through some chance notion or opinion. But, because they pushed on with thinking in this way, it turned out that the highest relationships in life were compromised by it. Thinking deprived what was positive of its power. Political constitutions fell victim to thought; religion was attacked by thought; firm religious notions that counted as totally genuine revelations were undermined, and in many minds the old faith was overthrown. For example, the Greek philosophers set themselves against the old religion and destroyed its representations. Consequently, philosophers were banished and killed[4] for seeking to overthrow religion and the State (which essentially belonged together). In this way thinking asserted its validity in the actual world and exerted the most tremendous influence. Being thereby made aware of the power of thinking, people began to investigate its claims more closely, and professed to have discovered that it was presumptuous and could not accomplish what it had undertaken. Instead of arriving at the cognition of the essence of God, of Nature, and of Spirit or, in sum, of truth itself, this thinking overturned the State and religion. For this reason, a justification of thinking with regard to its results was demanded; and the inquiry into the nature and competence of thinking is just what has very largely constituted the concern of modern philosophy.

a. *das Denken . . . produziert Gedanken und den Gedanken*
b. *obschon das abstrakt Sinnliche und Daseinslose*

§ 20

If we take thinking according to the most obvious notion of it, then it appears (α) first in its ordinary subjective significance, as one spiritual activity or faculty *side by side* with others such as sensation, intuition, imagination, etc., desire, volition, etc. What it *produces*, the determinacy or form of thought, is the *universal*, the abstract in general. Thus, *thinking* as an *activity* is the *active* universal, and indeed the *self*-actuating universal, since the act, or what is brought forth, is precisely the universal. Thinking represented as a *subject* is *that which thinks*, and the simple expression for the existing subject as thinker is "*I*".

> The determinations indicated here and in the coming paragraphs should not be taken as assertions or as my *opinions* about thinking; but since in this preliminary discussion no deduction or proof can take place, they can be counted as *facta* in the sense that, when anyone has thoughts and considers them, it is empirically given in his consciousness that universality, as well as the determinations that follow in its train, is found in them. Of course, the presence of a trained capacity for attention and abstraction is required for the observation of the *facta* of one's consciousness and of one's representations.
>
> Already in this preliminary exposition, we are speaking of the distinction between the sensible, representation, and thought; this distinction is altogether decisive for our grasp of the nature and the kinds of cognition; so it will clarify matters if we call attention to this distinction already at this point.—To elucidate the *sensible* we refer first to its external origin, to the senses of sense organs. But simply naming the organ does not give us the determination of what we apprehend with it. The distinction of the *sensible* from thought is to be located in the fact that the determination of the sensible is *singularity*, and since the singular (in quite abstract terms, the atom) stands also within a context, the sensible is a [realm of] mutual *externality* whose proximate abstract forms are *juxtaposition* and *succession*.—*Representation* has sensible material of this kind as its content; but it is posited in the determination of its being *mine*—that the represented content is in *me*—and of its *universality*, of its self-relation, or of its *simplicity*.—Apart from the sensible, however, representation also has material that has sprung from self-conscious thinking as its content, such as the notion of what is right, of what is ethical or religious, and also of thinking itself; and it is not very easy to see where the distinction between these *representations* and the *thoughts* of those contents is to be

located. Here the content is a thought, and the form of universality is present too, for that form already belongs to a content as being in *me*, or, quite generally, as being a representation. The peculiarity of representation, however, is in general to be located in this fact also—that the content in it stands at the same time in isolation. "Right" and juridical and other similar determinations certainly do not stand in the sensible mutual externality of *space*. They do appear somehow in time, one after the other; but their content is not itself represented as affected by time, as passing away and changing in it. Nevertheless, these determinations, which are in themselves spiritual, stand at the same time *in isolation* upon the broad field of the inner, abstract universality of representation in general. In this isolation they are *simple*: right, duty, God. Representation either sticks to the claim that right is right, God is God, or, (at a more cultivated level) it points out determinations, such as that God is the Creator of the world, that he is all-wise, almighty, etc. Here, too, several isolated and simple determinations are strung together; but they remain external to each other, in spite of the link that is allotted to them in their subject. In this respect, representation agrees with the *understanding*, which is only distinct from it because it posits relationships of universal and particular, or of cause and effect, etc., and therefore necessary relations between the isolated determinations of representation—whereas representation leaves them *side by side*, in its undetermined space, linked only by the simple "and."—The distinction between representation and thought is all the more important because we can say in general that philosophy does nothing but transform representations into thoughts—although, of course, it does go on to transform the mere thought into the Concept.

Moreover, when the determinations *of singularity and of mutual externality* have been earmarked for the sensible, we can add that these determinations themselves are again thoughts and universals. It will be seen in the Logic that this is just what thought and the universal are: that thought is itself and its other, that it overgrasps its other and that nothing escapes it. And because *language* is the work of thought, nothing can be said in language that is not universal. What I only *mean*[a] is *mine*;[b] it belongs to me as this particular individual. But if language expresses only what is universal, then I cannot say what I only *mean*. And *what cannot be said*

a. meine
b. mein

—feeling, sensation—is not what is most important, most true, but what is most insignificant, most untrue. When I say "*the singular,*" "*this* singular," "here," "now," all of these expressions are universalities; *each* and *every* thing is a singular, a this, even when it is sensible—here, now. Similarly when I say "I," I *mean* me *as this one* excluding all others; but what I say ("I") is precisely everyone, an "I" that excludes all others from itself.—Kant[5] employed the awkward expression, that I "accompany" all my representations—and my sensations, desires, actions, etc., too. "I" is the universal in and for itself, and communality is one more form—although an external one—of universality. All other humans have this in common with me, to be "I," just as all *my* sensations, representations, etc., have in common that they are *mine*. But, taken abstractly as such, "I" is pure relation to itself, in which abstraction is made from representation and sensation, from every state as well as from every peculiarity of nature, of talent, of experience, and so on. To this extent, "I" is the existence of the entirely *abstract* universality, the abstractly *free*. Therefore "I" is *thinking* as the *subject*, and since I am at the same time in all my sensations, notions, states, etc., thought is present everywhere and pervades all these determinations as [their] category.[6]

Addition. When we talk about "thinking," it appears at first to be a subjective activity, one faculty among many others, e.g., memory, representation, volition, and the like. If thinking were merely a subjective activity and, as such, the subject matter of the Logic, then the Logic would, like other sciences, have a determinate subject matter. It could then appear to be an arbitrary choice to make thinking—and not willing, imagination, etc.—the subject matter of a particular science. The reason why thinking is accorded this honour might well be the fact that we concede a certain authority to it, and that we regard it as what constitutes man's genuine nature, as that wherein his difference from animals consists.

And it is interesting to become acquainted with thinking even as a merely subjective activity. Its more precise determinations would in that case be rules and laws that we become acquainted with through experience. Thinking considered in this perspective, with regard to its laws, is what used formerly to constitute the content of logic. Aristotle is the founder of this science. He had the force of mind to assign to thinking what properly belongs to it. Our thinking is very concrete, but in its multiform content we must distinguish what belongs to thinking, to the abstract form of the activity. The activity of thinking is the gentle spiritual bond that connects this entire content; and this bond, this form as such, is what Aristotle brought into relief and determined. Right up to the present day, this logic of Aristotle is still the content of logic, which has simply been spun out further, mainly by the mediaeval Scholastics.[7] These still did not increase the material, but just developed it further. The work on logic that has been done in modern times has principally consisted in the simple omission of many logical determinations elaborated by Aristotle and the Scholastics, on the one hand, and in stuffing logic with a lot of psychological material, on the other. The point of this science is to become familiar with how finite thinking proceeds, and the science is correct when it corresponds to its presupposed subject matter. There is no doubt that working on this formal logic has its use. Through it, as people say, we sharpen our wits; we learn to collect our thoughts, and to abstract. For in ordinary consciousness we deal with sensible representations, which cut across one another and cause confusion; but in abstraction what happens is that the mind concentrates on *one* point, and we acquire in that way the habit of occupying ourselves with what is inward. Acquaintance with the forms of finite thinking can be used as a means of training in the empirical sciences, which proceed according to these forms, and it is in this sense that people have called logic "instrumental." We can, of course, speak in a more liberal way, and say that logic should be studied not for its usefulness, but for its own sake, because what is excellent should not be pursued for the sake of mere advantage. And, on the one hand, this is quite correct, to be sure; but, on the other, what is excellent is also what is the most advantageous. For it is what is substantial, what stands most firmly on its own, so that it is what sustains our particular purposes, which it furthers and brings to fulfillment. We must not regard these particular purposes as what comes first, but what is excellent furthers them nevertheless. Religion, for example, has its absolute value within itself, but other purposes are supported and upheld by it at the same time. Christ said, "Seek ye first the kingdom of God, and all these things shall be added unto you" [Matt. 6:33].—Our particular purposes can be attained only insofar as what is in and for itself is attained.

§ 21

(ß) When thinking is taken as active with regard to ob-jects, as the *thinking-over of* something, then the universal—as the product of this activity—contains the value of the *matter*, what is *essential, inner, true.*

> In §5 we mentioned the old belief that what is genuine in ob-jects, [their] constitutions, or what happens to them, [i.e.,] what is inner, what is essential, and the matter that counts, is not to be found in consciousness immediately; that it cannot be what the first look or impression already offers us, but that we must first *think it over* in order to arrive at the genuine constitution of the ob-ject, and that by thinking it over this [goal] is indeed achieved.

Addition. Even the *child* is enjoined to think about things. For instance, we set children to connect adjectives with substantives.[8] Here, they have to pay attention and to distinguish; they have to remember a rule and apply it to the particular case.

The rule is nothing but a universal, and the child must make the particular conform to this universal.

Furthermore, in life we have *purposes* which we think about to see how we can attain them. Here the purpose is the universal, the governing factor, and we have means and instruments, the action of which we direct in accordance with the purpose.—In a similar way we actively think about *moral situations*. Here, to think about them means to be mindful of right and duty, or, in other words, of the universal to which we must conform our particular behaviour in given cases as to the fixed rule. The universal determination should be recognisably contained in our particular way of acting.

We find the same thing, too, in our behaviour with regard to *natural phenomena*. For example, we take note of thunder and lightning. We are acquainted with this phenomenon and we often observe it. But man is not satisfied with this mere acquaintance, with the simple sensible phenomenon; he wants to look behind it; he wants to know what it is, wants to comprehend it. We think about it, therefore; we want to know the cause as something distinct from the phenomenon as such; we want to know what is inward as distinct from what is merely outward. So we reduplicate the phenomenon; we break it in two, the inward and the outward, force and its utterance, cause and effect. Here again, the inner side, or force, is the universal, that which persists; it is not this or that lightning, this or that plant, but what remains the same in all. What is sensible is something singular and transitory; it is by thinking about it that we get to know what persists in it. Nature offers us an infinite mass of singular shapes and appearances. We feel the need to bring unity into this manifold; therefore, we compare them and seek to [re]cognise what is universal in each of them. Individuals are born and pass away; in them their kind is what abides, what recurs in all of them; and it is only present for us when we think about them. This is where laws, e.g., the laws of the motion of heavenly bodies, belong too. We see the stars in one place today and in another tomorrow; this disorder is for the spirit something incongruous, and not to be trusted, since the spirit believes in an order, a simple, constant, and universal determination [of things]. This is the faith in which the spirit has directed its [reflective] thinking upon the phenomena, and has come to know their laws, establishing the motion of the heavenly bodies in a universal manner, so that every change of position can be determined and [re]cognised on the basis of this law.—It is the same with regard to the powers that govern human action in its infinite diversity. Here, too, man believes in a ruling universal.—From all these examples we may gather how, in thinking about things, we always seek what is fixed, persisting, and inwardly determined, and what governs the particular. This universal cannot be grasped by means of the senses, and it counts as what is essential and true. Duties and rights, for example, are what is essential in actions, and the truth of actions consists in their conforming with those *universal* determinations.

When we determine the universal in this way, we find that it forms the antithesis of something else, namely, the merely immediate, external, and singular, as against the mediated, the inward, and the universal. This universal does not exist externally as universal: the kind as such cannot be perceived; the laws of the motion of the heavenly bodies are not inscribed in the sky. So we do not see and hear the universal; only for the spirit is it present. Religion leads us to a universal, which embraces everything else within itself, to an Absolute by which everything else is brought forth, and this Absolute is not [there] for the senses but only for the spirit and for thought.

§ 22

(γ) Thinking it over *changes* something in the way in which the content is at first [given] in sensation, intuition, or representation; thus, it is only *through the mediation* of an alteration that the *true* nature of the *ob-ject* comes into consciousness.

Addition. When we think about something, what results is a product of our think-ing. For instance, the laws that Solon gave to the Athenians he produced from his own head.[9] On the other side of the coin, however, there is the fact that we also view the universal, the laws, as the opposite of something merely subjective, and we [re]cognise in them what is essential, genuine, and objective about things. In order to experience what is true in things, mere attention is not enough; on the contrary, our subjective activity, which transforms what is immediately before us, is involved. At first glance, to be sure, this seems to stand things on their heads, and to run counter to the proper purpose of cognition. But we can say, too, that it has been the conviction of every age that what is substantial is only reached through the reworking of the immediate by our thinking about it. It has most notably been only in modern times, on the other hand, that doubts have been raised and the distinction between the products of our thinking and what things are in them-selves has been insisted on. It has been said that the In-itself of things is quite different from what we make of them. This separateness is the standpoint that has been maintained especially by the Critical Philosophy, against the conviction of the whole world previously in which the agreement between the matter [itself] and thought was taken for granted. The central concern of modern philosophy turns on this antithesis. But it is the natural belief of mankind that this antithesis has no truth. In ordinary life we think about things without the special reflection that that is how what is true comes forth; we think without hesitation, in the firm belief that our thought agrees with its matter, and this belief is of the highest importance. The sickness of our time, which has arrived at the point of despair, is the assumption that our cognition is only subjective and that this is the last word about it. But the truth is what is objective, and this truth ought to be the rule governing everyone's convictions, so that the convictions of a single mind are bad insofar as they do not correspond with this rule. But, according to the modern view, conviction as such, the mere form of being convinced, is already good (whatever its contents may be), since no criterion is available for its truth.

We said earlier that it has been man's ancient faith that it is the vocation of the spirit to know the truth. This has the further implication that the ob-jects, both the outer and the inner nature, the object in general, is in-itself just as it is in thought, and that thinking is therefore the truth of what is ob-jective. The business of philosophy consists only in bringing into consciousness explicitly what people have held to be valid about thought from time immemorial. Thus, philosophy establishes nothing new; what we have brought forth by our reflection here is what everyone already takes for granted without reflection.[a]

§ 23

Because it is equally the case that in this thinking-over the genuine nature [of the ob-ject] comes to light, and that this thinking is *my* activity, this true nature is also the *product of my* spirit, [of me] as thinking subject. It is mine according to my simple universality as [universality] of the "I" *being* simply *at home with itself*, or it is the product of my *freedom*.

> We often hear the expression "thinking for oneself,"[10] as if it meant something important. But in fact one cannot think for someone else, any more than one can eat or drink for him; this expression is therefore a pleonasm.—Thinking immediately involves *freedom*, because it is the activity of the universal, a self-relating that is therefore abstract, a being-with-itself that is undetermined in respect of subjectivity, and which in respect of its *content* is, at the same time, only in the *matter* [itself] and in its determinations. So when one speaks of humility or modesty, and of arrogance, with reference to the doing of philosophy, and when this humility or modesty consists in not attributing any *particularity* of feature or agency to one's subjectivity, then philosophising has to be absolved from arrogance at least, since thinking is only genuine with respect to its content insofar as it is immersed in the *matter*, and with respect to its form insofar so it is not a *particular* being or doing of the subject, but consists precisely in this, that consciousness conducts itself as an abstract "I," as *freed* from *all particularity*[b] of features, states, etc., and does only what is universal, in which it is identical with all individuals.—When Aristotle[11] summons us to consider ourselves as *worthy* of conduct of this sort, then the worthiness that consciousness ascribes to itself consists precisely in the giving up of our *particular* opinions and beliefs and in allowing the *matter* [itself] to hold sway over us.

a. *ist schon unmittelbares Vorurteil eines jeden*
b. Partikularität

§ 24

In accordance with these determinations, thoughts can be called *objective* thoughts; and among them the forms which are considered initially in ordinary logic and which are usually taken to be only forms of *conscious* thinking have to be counted too. Thus *logic* coincides with *metaphysics*, with the science of *things* grasped in *thoughts* that used to be taken to express the *essentialities* of the *things*.

> The relationship of forms such as concept, judgment, and syllogism to others like causality, etc., can only establish itself within the Logic itself. But one can see already, though only in a preliminary way, that, since thought seeks to form a *concept* of things, this concept (along with judgment and syllogism as its most immediate forms) cannot consist in determinations and relationships that are alien and external to the things. As we said above, thinking things over leads to what is *universal* in them; but the universal is itself one of the moments of the Concept. To say that there is understanding, or reason, in the world is exactly what is contained in the expression "objective thought." But this expression is inconvenient precisely because "thought" is all too commonly used as if it belonged only to spirit, or consciousness, while "objective" is used primarily just with reference to what is unspiritual.

Addition 1. If we say that thought, *qua* objective, is the inwardness of the world, it may seem as if consciousness is being ascribed to natural things. But we feel a repugnance against conceiving the inner activity of things to be thinking, since we say that man is distinguished from what is merely natural by virtue of thinking. In this view we would have to talk about nature as a system of thought without consciousness, or an intelligence which, as Schelling says, is petrified.[12] So in order to avoid misunderstanding, it is better to speak of "thought-determinations" instead of using the expression "thoughts".

In line with what has been said so far, then, the Logical is to be sought in a system of thought-determinations in which the antithesis between subjective and objective (in its usual meaning) disappears. This meaning of thinking and of its determinations is more precisely expressed by the Ancients when they say that *nous* governs the world, or by our own saying that there is reason in the world, by which we mean that reason is the soul of the world, inhabits it, and is immanent in it, as its own, innermost nature, its universal. An example closer at hand is that, in speaking of a definite animal, we say that it is [an] "animal." "Animal as such" cannot be pointed out; only a definite animal can ever be pointed at. "The animal" does not exist; on the contrary, this expression refers to the universal nature of single animals, and each existing animal is something that is much more concretely determinate, something particularised. But "to be animal," the kind considered as the universal, pertains to the determinate animal and constitutes its determinate essentiality. If we were to deprive a dog of its animality we could not say what it is. Things as such have a persisting, inner nature, and an external thereness. They live and die, come to be and pass away; their essentiality, their universality, is the kind, and this cannot be interpreted merely as something held in common.

Just as thinking constitutes the substance of external things, so it is also the universal substance of what is spiritual. In all human intuiting there is thinking; similarly, thinking is what is universal in all representations, recollections, and in every spiritual activity whatsoever, in all willing, wishing, etc. These are all of them just further specifications of thinking. When thinking is interpreted in this way, it appears in quite a different light than when we simply say that, along with and beside other faculties such as intuiting, representing, willing, and the like, we have a faculty of thinking. If we regard thinking as what is genuinely universal in everything natural and everything spiritual, too, then it overgrasps all of them and is the foundation of them all. As the next step, we can add to this interpretation of thinking in its objective meaning (as *nous*) [our account of] what thinking is in its subjective sense. First of all, we say that man thinks, but, at the same time, we say too that he intuits, wills, etc. Man thinks and is something universal, but he thinks only insofar as the universal is [present] *for* him. The animal is also *in-itself* something universal, but the universal as such is not [present] *for* it; instead only the singular is ever [there] for it. The animal sees something singular, for instance, its food, a man, etc. But all these are only something singular for it. In the same way our sense experience always has to do only with something singular (*this* pain, *this* pleasant taste, etc.). Nature does not bring the *nous* to consciousness for itself; only man reduplicates himself in such a way that he is the universal that is [present] *for* the universal. This is the case for the first time when man knows himself to be an "I." When I say "I," I mean myself as this singular, quite determinate person. But when I say "I," I do not in fact express anything particular about myself. Anyone else is also "I," and although in calling myself "I," I certainly mean me, this single [person], what I say is still something completely universal.

"I" is pure being-for-itself, in which everything particular is negated and sublated—consciousness as ultimate, simple, and pure. We can say that "I" and thinking are the same, or, more specifically, that "I" is thinking as what thinks. What I have in my consciousness, that is for me. "I" is this void, this receptacle for anything and everything, that for which everything is and which preserves everything within itself. Everyone is a whole world of representations, which are buried in the night of the "I." Thus, "I" is the universal, in which abstraction is made from everything particular, but in which at the same time everything is present, though veiled. It is not merely abstract universality therefore, but the universality that contains everything within itself. We start by using "I" in a wholly trivial manner, and it is only our philosophical reflection that makes it a subject matter of inquiry. In the "I," we have thought present in its complete purity. Animals cannot say "I"; no, only man can do so, because he *is* thinking itself. In the "I" there is a manifold inner and outer content, and, according to the way in which this content is constituted, we behave as sensing, representing, remembering, [beings], etc. But the "I" is there in all of these, or, in other words, thinking is present everywhere. Thus man is always thinking, even when he simply intuits; if he considers something or other he always considers it as something universal, he fixes on something singular, and makes it stand out, thus withdrawing his attention from something else, and he takes it as something abstract and universal, even though it is universal in a merely formal way.

With our representations, two cases are possible: either the *content* is something thought but the *form* is not, or, conversely, the form belongs to thought but the content does not. If I say, e.g., "anger," "rose," "hope," I am familiar with all this through feeling,[a] but I express this content in a universal way, in the form of thought; I have left out a good deal of what is particular about it, and given only the content as universal, but that content remains sensible. Conversely, if I represent God to myself, then certainly the content is purely something thought, but the form is still sensible, just as I already find it immediately within me. In these representations, therefore, the content is not merely sensible, as when I simply look at something: either the content is sensible, while the form belongs to thinking, or conversely. In the first case, the material is given and the form belongs to thinking; in the other case, thinking is the source of the content, but through the form the content becomes something given, which therefore comes to the spirit from outside.

ϗ *Addition 2.* In the Logic we have to do with pure thought or with the pure thought-determinations. In the case of thought in the ordinary sense, we always represent to ourselves something that is not merely pure thought, for we intend by it something that is thought of, but which has an empirical content. In the Logic, thoughts are grasped in such a way that they have no content other than one that belongs to thinking itself, and is brought forth by thinking. So these thoughts are *pure* thoughts. Spirit is here purely at home with itself, and thereby free, for that is just what freedom is: being at home with oneself in one's other, depending upon oneself, and being one's own determinant. In all drives I begin with an other, with what is for me something external. Hence, we speak of dependence in this case. Freedom is only present where there is no other for me that is not myself. The natural man, who is determined only by his drives, is not at home with himself; however self-willed he may be, the *content* of his willing and opining is not his own, and his freedom is only a *formal*[b] one. When I think, I give up my subjective particularity, sink myself in the matter, let thought follow its own course; and I think badly whenever I add something of my own.

When, in accordance with what has been said so far, we consider the Logic as the system of *pure* thought-determinations, the other philosophical sciences—the Philosophy of Nature, and the Philosophy of Spirit—appear, in contrast, as applied logic, so to speak, for the Logic is their animating soul. Thus, the concern of those other sciences is only to [re]cognise the logical forms in the shapes of nature and spirit, shapes that are only a particular mode of expression of the forms of pure thinking. If we take the *syllogism*, for instance (not in the sense of the older formal logic, but in its truth), then it is that [thought-] determination in which the particu-

a. *Empfindung*
b. formelle

lar is the middle that con-cludes[13] the extremes of the universal and the singular. This syllogistic form is a universal form of all things. All of them are particulars that con-clude themselves as something universal with the singular. But it is a consequence of the impotence of nature that it cannot present the logical forms in their purity. The magnet, for instance, is an impotent presentation of the syllogism; it brings its poles together[14] in the middle, at its point of Indifference,[a] and, as a result, the poles, though distinct, are immediately one. In physics, too, we become acquainted with the universal, the essence, and the distinction is only that the Philosophy of Nature makes us conscious of the genuine forms of the Concept in natural things.

In this way the Logic is the all-animating spirit of all sciences, and the thought-determinations contained in the Logic are the pure spirits;[15] they are what is most inward, but, at the same time, they are always on our lips, and consequently they seem to be something thoroughly well known. But what is well known in this manner is usually what is most unknown. Thus, *Being*, for example, is a pure thought-determination; but it never occurs to us to make "is" the subject matter of our inquiry. We usually suppose that the Absolute must lie far beyond; but it is precisely what is wholly present, what we, as thinkers, always carry with us and employ, even though we have no express consciousness of it. It is in language that these thought-determinations are primarily deposited.[16] Hence, the instruction in grammar that is imparted to children has the useful role of making them unconsciously attentive to distinctions that occur in thinking.

It is usually said that logic deals only with *forms* and that their *content* must be taken from elsewhere. It is not logical thoughts, however, that are "only" so-and-so, in comparison with all other content; on the contrary, it is all other content that is an "only" in comparison with them. Logical thoughts are the ground that is in and for itself of everything.—Concern with such pure determinations does, to be sure, presuppose a superior level of education. Studying them in and for themselves signifies further that we deduce them from thinking itself, and see from their own [development] whether they are *genuine*. We do not take them up in an external way, and then define them or exhibit their value and validity by comparing them with how they actually occur in consciousness. If we did that we would be starting from observation and experience. We would say, for example, "We normally use 'force' in such and such a way." We call a definition of that sort correct if it agrees with what is found to be the case with its ob-ject in our ordinary consciousness of it. In this way, however, a concept is not determined in and for itself but according to a presupposition, which then becomes the criterion, the standard of correctness. We do not have to use such a standard, however; we can simply let the inherently living determinations take their own course instead. The question about the truth of thought-determininations is bound to sound strange to our ordinary consciousness, for the determinations of thought seem to acquire truth only in their application to given ob-jects, and on this assumption it makes no sense to question their truth apart from this application. But this question is precisely the point at issue. Certainly, when we raise it, we must know what is to be

a. *Indifferenzpunkt*

understood by "truth." In the ordinary way, what we call "truth" is the agreement of an ob-ject with our representation of it. We are then presupposing an ob-ject to which our representation is supposed to conform.

In the philosophical sense, on the contrary, "truth," expressed abstractly and in general, means the agreement of a content with itself. This is therefore a meaning of "truth" quite different from the one mentioned above. Besides, the deeper (philosophical) meaning of "truth" is also partly found in ordinary linguistic usage already. We speak, for instance, of a "true" friend, and by that we understand one whose way of acting conforms with the concept of friendship; and in the same way we speak also of a "true" work of art. To say of something that it is "untrue" is as much as to say that it is bad, that it involves an inner inadequacy. A bad State, in this sense, is an "untrue" State; and what is bad and untrue consists always in a contradiction between the ob-ject's determination or concept and its existence. We can form a correct representation of a bad ob-ject of this sort, but the content of this representation is something inwardly "untrue." We may have many examples of such things in our heads, examples that are correct and at the same time "untrue."

God alone is the genuine agreement between Concept and reality; all finite things, however, are affected with untruth; they have a concept, but their existence is not adequate to it. For this reason they must go to the ground, and this manifests the inadequacy between their concept and their existence. The animal as something singular has its concept in its kind, and the kind frees itself from singularity through death.

The consideration of truth in the sense explained here, that of agreement with itself, constitutes the proper concern of logical thinking. The question of the truth of the thought-determinations does not arise in our ordinary consciousness. The business of the Logic can also be expressed by saying that it considers how far the thought-determinations are capable of grasping what is true. So the central question becomes: which of them are the forms of the Infinite, and which are the forms of the finite? In ordinary consciousness we see nothing wrong with the finite determinations of thought; they are held to be valid without further question. But all our illusions arise from thinking and acting according to finite determinations.

Addition 3. We become cognizant of what is true in various modes, and the modes of cognition must be considered only as forms. Thus, we can certainly become cognizant of what is true through experience, but this experience is only a form. With experiences everything depends on the mind with which we approach actuality. A great mind[a] has great experiences, and in the motley play of appearance spots the crucial point.[b] The Idea is present and actual, not something over the hills and far away. A great mind, the mind of a Goethe, for instance, has great experiences, when it looks[c] into nature or history; it sees what is rational and expresses it. Furthermore, we can also become cognizant of what is true through reflection; we are then determining it through relationships of thought. But what is true in and for itself is not present in its proper form in either of these cognitive modes.

a. *Sinn*
b. *erblickt das, worauf es ankommt*
c. *blickt*

The most perfect mode of cognition is that which takes place in the pure form of thinking. Here, man behaves in a way that is thoroughly free. That the form of thinking is the absolute one, and that the truth appears within it as it is in and for itself—this is what philosophy in general asserts. Proving this means, to start with, showing that those other forms of cognition are finite. The high scepticism of antiquity accomplished this by showing that every one of those forms contained a contradiction within itself.[17] When this scepticism was applied to the forms of reason also, it first foisted something finite onto them in order to have something to lay hold of. All the forms of finite thinking will come before us in the course of their logical development, and, what is more, they will come forth in their necessary order of appearance: here (in the introduction) they have had to be taken up first in an unscientific way, as something given. In the logical treatise itself, not only the negative but also the positive side of these forms will be exhibited.

When we are comparing the various forms of cognition with one another, it can easily appear that the first one, that of immediate knowledge, is the most adequate, the finest, and the highest. It includes everything that is called innocence in the moral sphere, as well as religious feeling, simple trust, love, fidelity, and natural faith. Both of the other forms, first reflective cognition and then philosophical cognition too, step out of that immediate natural unity. Insofar as they have this in common with one another, the mode of cognition that consists in wanting to grasp the truth through thinking can easily appear as the human conceit that wants to recognise the true by its own strength. This standpoint of universal separation can certainly be looked on as the origin of all wickedness and evil, as the original transgression; and on this view it seems that thinking and cognition must be given up in order to return [to unity] and become reconciled again. As for the abandonment of natural unity here, this marvellous inward schism of the spiritual has been something of which all peoples from time immemorial have been conscious.[a] An inner schism like this does not occur in nature, and natural things do not do evil. We have an old account of the origin and consequences of this schism in the Mosaic myth of the Fall.[18] The content of this myth forms the foundation of an essential doctrine of faith, the doctrine of the natural sinfulness of man, and his need of help to overcome it. It appears appropriate to consider the myth of the Fall at the very beginning of the Logic, because the Logic is concerned with cognition, and the myth too deals with cognition, with its origin and significance. Philosophy should not shy away from religion, and adopt the attitude that it must be content if religion simply tolerates it. And, on the other hand, we must equally reject the view that myths and religious accounts of this kind are something obsolete, for they have been venerated for millenia by the peoples of the world.

Let us now consider the myth of the Fall more closely. As we remarked earlier, what is expressed here is the general relationship of cognition to the spiritual life. In its immediate shape spiritual life appears first as innocence and simple trust; but it is of the essence of spirit to sublate this immediate state, since spiritual life distinguishes itself from natural life, and more precisely from the life of animals, by the fact that it does not abide in its being-in-itself, but is *for itself*. In like manner, however, this stage of schism must itself be sublated in turn, and spirit must return

a. *von alters her ein Gegenstand des Bewußtseins der Völker gewesen*

through its own agency to union with itself. This resulting union is a spiritual one, and the guiding principle of that return lies in thinking itself. It is thinking that both inflicts the wound and heals it again.

Now, it says in our myth that Adam and Eve, the first human beings, or human-kind as such, found themselves in a garden, in which there were both a tree of life and a tree of cognition of good and evil. We are told that God had forbidden this human pair to eat of the fruits of the latter tree; at this point there is no more talk of the tree of life. So what this means is that humanity should not come to cogni-tion, but remain in a state of innocence. We also find this representation of the original state of humanity as one of innocence and of union, among other peoples that have reached a deeper consciousness. What is correct in it is the implication that the schism in which we find everything human involved can certainly not be the last word; but, on the other hand, it is not correct to regard the immediate, natural unity as the right state either. Spirit is not something merely immediate; on the contrary, it essentially contains the moment of mediation within itself. Child-like innocence does certainly have something attractive and touching about it, but only insofar as it reminds us of what must be brought forth by the spirit. The harmonious union that we see in children as something natural is to be the result of the labour and culture of the spirit.—Christ says, "Except ye *become* as little children," etc. [Matt. 18:3]; but that does not say that we must remain children.

In our Mosaic myth, moreover, we find that the occasion for stepping out of the unity [of innocence] was provided for humanity by external instigation (by the serpent). But in fact, the entry into the antithesis, the awakening of consciousness, lies within human beings themselves, and this is the story that repeats itself in every human being. The serpent expounds divinity as consisting in the knowledge of good and evil, and it is this cognition that was in fact imparted to man when he broke with the unity of his immediate being and ate of the forbidden fruit. The first reflection of awakening consciousness was that the human beings became aware that they were naked. This is a very naïve and profound trait. For shame does testify to the severance of human beings from their natural and sensible being. Hence animals, which do not get as far as this severance, are without shame. So the spiritual and ethical origin of clothing is to be sought for in the human feeling of shame; the merely physical need, on the contrary, is something only secondary.

At this point there follows the so-called Curse that God laid upon human beings. What this highlights is connected with the antithesis of man and nature. Man must labour in the sweat of his brow, and woman must bring forth in sorrow. What is said about labour is, more precisely, that it is both the result of the schism and also its overcoming. Animals find what they need for the satisfaction of their wants immediately before them; human beings, by contrast, relate to the means for the satisfaction of their wants as something that they themselves bring forth and shape. Thus, even in what is here external, man is related to himself.

But the myth does not conclude with the expulsion from paradise. It says fur-ther, "God said: Behold Adam is become as one of us, to know good and evil" [Gen. 3:22]. Cognition is now called something divine and not, as earlier, what ought not to be. So in this story there lies also the refutation of the idle chatter about how philosophy belongs only to the finitude of spirit; philosophy is cognition, and the original calling of man, to be an image of God, can be realised only through cognition.—The story now goes on to say that God drove man out of the garden of Eden, so that he should not eat of the tree of life; this means that man is certainly finite and mortal on the side of his nature, but that he is infinite in cognition.

That mankind is by nature evil is a well-known doctrine of the Church, and this natural state of evil is what is called Original Sin. But in this connection, we must give up the superficial notion that Original Sin has its ground only in a contingent action of the first human pair. It is part of the concept of spirit, in fact, that man is by nature evil; and we must not imagine that this could be otherwise. The relationship[a] [of man to nature] in which man is a natural essence, and behaves[b] as such, is one that ought not to be. Spirit is to be free and is to be what it is through itself. Nature is, for man, only the starting point that he ought to transform. The profound doctrine of the Church concerning Original Sin is confronted by the modern Enlightenment doctrine that man is by nature good and should therefore remain true to nature. When man goes beyond his natural being he thereby distinguishes his self-conscious world from an external one. But this standpoint of separation, which belongs to the concept of spirit, is not one that man should remain at either. All the finitude of thinking and willing falls within this standpoint of schism. Here man creates his purposes from himself, and it is from himself that he draws the material of his action. Inasmuch as he takes these purposes to their ultimate limits, knows only himself, and wills in his particularity without reference to the universal, he is evil, and this evil is his subjectivity. At first glance we have a double evil here; but both evils are in fact the same. Insofar as he is spirit, man is not a natural being; insofar as he behaves as a natural essence and follows the purposes of desire, he *wills* to be a natural essence. Thus, man's natural evil is not like the natural being of animals. Man's belonging to nature is further determined by the fact that the natural man is a single [individual] as such, for nature lies everywhere in the bonds of isolation. So, insofar as man wills this state of nature, he wills singularity. But this acting on the basis of drives and inclinations that is characteristic of natural singularity is then, of course, confronted by the law or universal determination too. This law may be an external power or may have the form of divine authority. Man is in servitude to the law so long as he continues his natural behaviour. Among his inclinations and feelings, man does also have benevolent and social inclinations that reach beyond his selfish singularity—sympathy, love, etc. But, insofar as these inclinations are immediate in character, their content, though implicitly universal, still has the form of subjectivity; self-seeking and contingency still have free play here.

§ 25

The expression *objective thoughts* signifies the *truth* which ought to be the absolute *ob-ject*, not just the *goal* of philosophy. But at the same time

a. *Verhältnis*
b. *sich verhält*

this expression indicates in any case an antithesis—indeed, the very one whose determination and validity is the focus of our philosophical interest at the present time, and around which the quest for *truth* and for the cognition of it revolves. If the thought-determinations are afflicted with a fixed antithesis, i.e., if they are only of a *finite* nature, then they are inadequate to the truth which is absolutely in and for itself, and the truth cannot enter into thinking. The thinking that brings forth only *finite* determinations and moves within these alone is called *understanding* (in the more precise sense of the word). The *finitude* of the thought-determinations has further to be taken in two ways: first, they are *only subjective* and are permanently in antithesis to the objective; secondly, being quite generally of *limited content*, they persist both in their antithesis to each other, and (even more) in their antithesis to the Absolute. As a further introduction, we now ought to consider the *positions available to thinking with respect to objectivity*, in order to clarify the meaning of the Logic and to lead into the standpoint that is here given to it.

> In my *Phenomenology of Spirit*,[19] which was for this reason described, when it was published, as the first part of the system of science, the procedure adopted was to begin from the first and simplest appearance of the spirit, from *immediate consciousness*, and to develop its dialectic right up to the standpoint of philosophical science, the necessity of which is shown by the progression. But for this purpose it was not possible to stick to the formal aspect of mere consciousness; for the standpoint of philosophical knowing is at the same time inwardly the richest in basic import and the most concrete one; so when it emerged as the result [of the development], it presupposed also the concrete shapes of consciousness, such as morality, ethical life, art, and religion. Hence, the development of the *content*, or of the subject matters of special parts of philosophical science, falls directly within that development of consciousness which seems at first to be restricted just to what is formal; that development has to take place behind the back of consciousness so to speak, inasmuch as the content is related to consciousness as what is *in-itself*. This makes the presentation more complicated, and what belongs to the concrete parts [of the System] already falls partly within that introduction.—The examination that will be undertaken here has the even greater inconvenience that it can only be conducted descriptively[a] and argumentatively; but its principal aim is to contribute to the insight that the questions about the nature of *cognition*, about *faith* and so on, that

a. *historisch*

confront us in the [realm of] representation, and which we take to be fully *concrete*, are in point of fact reducible to *simple* determinations of thought, which only get their genuine treatment in the Logic.

A
The First Position of Thought with Respect to Objectivity

METAPHYSICS

barriers to philosophy's goal

§ 26

The first position is the *naïve* way of proceeding, which, being still unconscious of the antithesis of thinking within and against itself, contains the *belief* that *truth* is [re]cognised, and what the objects genuinely are is brought before consciousness, through *thinking about* them. In this belief, thinking goes straight to the ob-jects; it reproduces the content of sense-experience and intuition out of itself, as a content of thought, and is satisfied with this as the truth. All philosophy in its beginnings, all of the sciences, even the daily doing and dealing of consciousness, lives in this belief.

§ 27

category

Because it is unconscious of its antithesis, this thinking *can*, in respect of its basic import, equally well be authentic *speculative* philosophising; but it can also dwell within *finite* thought-determinations, i.e., within the *still unresolved* antithesis. Here, in the introduction, our concern can only be to consider this position of thinking with regard to its limit; so we shall begin by taking up this [finite] way of *philosophising*.—In its most determinate development, which is also the one closest to us, this way of thinking was the *metaphysics of the recent past*, the way it was constituted among us before the Kantian philosophy. It is only in relation to the history of philosophy, however, that this metaphysics *belongs to the past*; for, on its own account, it is always present as the way in which the *mere understanding views* the ob-jects of reason. Hence, a closer examination of its procedure[a] and its principal content has this more directly present interest for us too.

---

a. *Manier*

§ 28

This science regarded the thought-determinations as the *fundamental deter-minations of things*; and, in virtue of this presupposition, that the cognition of things as they are *in-themselves* results from the *thinking* of what *is*, it stood at a higher level than the later critical philosophising. But two points should be noted. First, these determinations, in their abstraction, were taken to be valid on their own account, and capable of being *predicates of what is true*. In any case, this metaphysics presupposed that cognition of the Absolute could come about through the *attaching of predicates to it*; and it investigated neither the peculiar content and validity of the determina-tions of the understanding, nor yet this form of determining the Absolute by attaching predicates to it.

> *Being there*, for instance, is a predicate of this kind like in the proposition, "God is there";[a] or *finitude* and *infinity*, in the ques-tion whether the world is finite or infinite; or *simple* and *composite*, in the proposition, "The soul is *simple*";—or, again, "The thing is *one*, a *whole*," etc.—There was no investigation of whether predi-cates of this kind are something true in and for themselves, nor of whether the form of the judgment could be the form of truth.

Addition. The presupposition of the older metaphysics was that of naïve belief generally, namely, that thinking grasps what things are *in-themselves*, that things only are what they genuinely are when they are [captured] in thought. Nature and the mind and heart of man are protean, constantly in a process of transformation, and the reflection that things as they immediately present themselves are not the things in themselves is an obvious one.—The standpoint of the older metaphysics referred to here is the opposite of the one that resulted from the Critical Philoso-phy. We can fairly say that this latter standpoint sends man to feed upon husks and chaff.

But, to be more precise about the procedure of the older metaphysics, we should note that it did not go beyond the thinking of mere *understanding*. It took up the abstract determinations of thought immediately, and let them count in their imme-diacy as predicates of what is true. When we are discussing thinking we must distin-guish *finite* thinking, the thinking of the mere *understanding*, from the *infinite* thinking of *reason*. Taken in isolation, just as they are immediately given, the thought-determinations are *finite* determinations. But what is true is what is in-finite within itself; it cannot be expressed and brought to consciousness through what is finite.

If we adhere to the modern notion that thinking is always restricted, then the expression "infinite thinking" may appear quite astonishing. But, in fact, thinking is inwardly and essentially[b] infinite. To put the point formally, "finite" means what-

a. *Gott hat Daseyn*; literally, "God has thereness"
b. *seinem Wesen nach in sich*

ever comes to an end, what *is*, but ceases to be where it connects with its other, and is thus restricted by it. Hence, the finite subsists in its relation to its other, which is its negation and presents itself as its limit. But thinking is at home with itself, it relates itself to itself, and is its own ob-ject. Insofar as my ob-ject is a thought, I am at home with myself. Thus the I, or thinking, is infinite because it is related in thinking to an ob-ject that is itself. An ob-ject as such is an other, something negative that confronts me. But if thinking thinks itself, then it has an ob-ject that is at the same time not an ob-ject, i.e., an ob-ject that is sublated, ideal. Thus thinking as such, thinking in its purity, does not have any restriction within itself.

Thinking is only finite insofar as it stays within restricted determinations, which it holds to be ultimate. Infinite or speculative thinking, on the contrary, makes determinations likewise, but, in determining, in limiting, it sublates this defect again. Infinity must not be interpreted as an abstract, ever-receding beyond (the way it is in our ordinary notion of it), but in the simple manner specified above.

The thinking of the older metaphysics was *finite*, because that metaphysics moved in thought-determinations whose restrictions counted for it as something fixed, that would not be negated again. Thus, the question was asked, "Does *thereness* belong to God?" and "being-there" was thus treated as something purely positive, something ultimate and excellent. But we shall see later that *being-there* is in no way a merely positive determination, but one that is too lowly for the Idea, and unworthy of God.—Or again, the question of the finitude or infinity of the world was raised. Here infinity is sharply contrasted with finitude, yet it is easy to see that if the two are set against one another, then infinity, which is nevertheless supposed to be the whole, appears as *one* side only, and is limited by the finite.

But a limited infinity is itself only something finite. In the same sense the question was raised whether the soul is simple or composite. Thus simplicity, too, was counted as an ultimate determination, capable of grasping what is true. But "simple" is a determination just as poor, abstract, and one-sided as "being-there." a determination which, as we shall see later, is incapable of grasping what is true because it is itself untrue. If the soul is considered only as simple, then it is determined as one-sided and finite by an abstraction of that kind.[20]

Thus, the older metaphysics was concerned with the cognition of whether predicates of the kind here mentioned could be attached to its ob-jects. However, these predicates are restricted determinations of the understanding which express only a restriction, and not what is true.—We must notice particularly, at this point, that the metaphysical method was to "attach" predicates to the ob-ject of cognition, e.g., to God. This then is an external reflection about the ob-ject, since the determinations (the predicates) are found ready-made in my representation, and are attached to the ob-ject in a merely external way. Genuine cognition of an ob-ject, on the other hand, has to be *such* that the ob-ject determines itself from within itself, and does not acquire its predicates in this external way. If we proceed by way of predication, the spirit gets the feeling that the predicates cannot exhaust what they are attached to.

From this point of view, therefore, the Orientals are quite right to call God the being who is Many-Named or Infinitely Named.[21] Our mind and heart find no satisfaction in any of those finite determinations, so that the Oriental cognition consists in a restless seeking out of such predicates. In the case of finite things it is certainly true that they must be determined by means of finite predicates, and here the understanding with its activity has its proper place. Being itself finite, the understanding is cognizant only of the nature of the finite. Thus, if I call an action a "theft," for instance, the action is thereby determined with regard to its essential content, and to [re]cognise this is sufficient for the judge. In the same way, finite things behave as "cause" and "effect," as "force" and "utterance"; and when they are grasped according to these determinations, they are known in their finitude. But the ob-jects of reason cannot be determined through such finite predicates, and the attempt to do this was the defect of the older metaphysics.

§ 29

Predicates of this kind are, on their own account, a *restricted* content, and they show themselves to be inappropriate to the *fullness* of the *representation* (of God, nature, spirit, etc.) which they do not at all exhaust. Moreover, although they are connected with each other because they are predicates of One subject, they are nevertheless diverse through their content, so that they are taken up from *outside* and *in opposition to one another*.[a]

> The Orientals sought to correct the first defect; for instance, in the case of the determination of God, through the many *names* they attach to him; but at the same time, the names had to be *infinitely many*.[22]

§ 30

Secondly, the ob-jects of this metaphysics were, it is true, totalities that belong in and for themselves to *reason*, to the thinking of the inwardly *concrete* universal: the *soul*, the *world*, God. But this metaphysics took them from *representation*, and when it applied the determinations-of-the-understanding to them, it grounded itself upon them, as *ready-made or given subjects*, and its only *criterion* of whether the predicates fitted, and were satisfactory or not, was that representation.

§ 31

The representations of the soul, of the world, of God, seem at first to provide thinking with a *firm hold*. But apart from the fact that the character of a particular subjectivity is mingled with them, and that therefore they

a. gegeneinander

can have a most diverse significance, what they need all the more is to receive their firm determination only through thinking. Every proposition expresses this need, because in it *what* the subject, i.e., the initial representation, is ought only to be indicated by the *predicate* (that is to say, in philosophy, by the thought-determination).

> In the proposition "God *is* eternal, etc.," we begin with the representation "God"; but what he *is*, is not yet *known*; only the predicate states expressly what he *is*. In logical thinking, therefore, where the content is only and exclusively determined in the form of thought, it is first of all superfluous to make these determinations into predicates of propositions whose *subject* is God, or more vaguely the Absolute, and in addition there is the disadvantage that doing this sends us back to a criterion other than the nature of thought itself.—In any case, the form of the proposition, or more precisely that of the judgment, is incapable of expressing what is concrete (and what is true is concrete) and speculative; because of its form, the judgment is one-sided and to that extent false.[23]

Addition. This metaphysics was not a free and objective thinking, for it did not allow the ob-ject to determine itself freely from within, but presupposed it as ready-made.—As for free thinking, Greek philosophy thought freely, but Scholasticism did not, since, like this metaphysics, it adopted its content as something given, and indeed given by the Church.—We moderns are initiated, through our whole education, into representations that it is in the highest degree difficult to transcend, because they have a content of the deepest sort. We must imagine the ancient philosophers as men who stand right in the middle of sensory intuition, and presuppose nothing except the heavens above and the earth beneath, since mythological representations had been thrown aside. In this simply factual environment, thought is free and withdrawn into itself, free of all [given] material, purely at home with itself. When we think freely, voyaging on the open sea, with nothing under us and nothing over us, in solitude, alone by ourselves—then we are purely at home with ourselves.

§ 32

Thirdly, this metaphysics became *dogmatism* because, given the nature of finite determinations, it had to assume that of *two opposed assertions* (of the kind that those propositions were) one must be *true,* and the other *false.*

Addition. Dogmatism has its first antithesis in *scepticism.* The ancient Sceptics gave the general name of "dogmatism" to any philosophy that sets up definite theses.[24]

In this wider sense scepticism also counted properly speculative philosophy as dogmatic. But in the narrower sense dogmatism consists in adhering to one-sided determinations of the understanding whilst excluding their opposites. This is just the strict "either-or," according to which (for instance) the world is *either* finite *or* infinite, but *not both*. On the contrary, what is genuine and speculative is precisely what does not have any such one-sided determination in it, and is therefore not exhausted by it; on the contrary, being a totality, it contains the determinations that dogmatism holds to be fixed and true in a state of separation from one another united within itself.

It often happens in philosophy that a one-sided view sets itself up beside the totality, claiming to be something particular and fixed vis-à-vis the latter. But, in fact, what is one-sided is not fixed and does not subsist on its own account; instead, it is contained within the whole as sublated. The dogmatism of the metaphysics of the understanding consists in its adherence to one-sided thought-determinations in their isolation, whereas the idealism of speculative philosophy involves the principle of totality and shows itself able to overgrasp the one-sidedness of the abstract determinations of the understanding. Thus, idealism will say, "The soul is neither *just* finite nor *just* infinite, but is essentially *both* the one *and* the other, and hence *neither* the one *nor* the other." In other words, these determinations are not valid when they are isolated from one another but only when sublated.

This idealism occurs even in our ordinary consciousness too. Accordingly, we say of sensible things that they are alterable, i.e., that they are and that they are not.—Regarding the determinations of the understanding we are more stubborn. As thought-determinations they count as more fixed, and indeed as fixed absolutely. We regard them as separated from one another by an infinite abyss, so that determinations that stand opposed to one another are never able to reach each other. The struggle of reason consists precisely in overcoming what the understanding has made rigid.

§ 33

In its orderly shape this metaphysics had, as its *first part*, *Ontology*,[25] the doctrine of the *abstract determinations of essence*. In their manifoldness and finite validity, these determinations lack a principle; they must therefore be enumerated *empirically* and *contingently*, and their more precise *content* can only be based upon *representation*, [i.e.,] based upon the *assurance* that by one word one thinks precisely this, or perhaps also upon the word's etymology. What can be at issue in this context is merely the *correctness* of the analysis as it corresponds with the usage of language, and the empirical *exhaustiveness*, not the *truth* and *necessity* of these determinations in and for themselves.

The question whether being, being-there, or finitude, simplicity, compositeness, etc., are *concepts that are in and for themselves true,* must be surprising, if one is of the opinion that one can speak only of the truth *of a proposition*, and that the only question that can be raised with regard to a *concept* is whether (as people say) it can be truthfully *"attached"* to a subject or not. Untruth would depend on the contradiction to be found between the subject of the representation and the concept to be predicated of it. But since the Concept is something-concrete, and since it is itself every determinacy without exception, it is essentially, and within itself, a unity of distinct determinations. So, if truth were nothing more than lack of contradiction, one would have to examine first of all, with regard to each concept, whether it does not, on its own account, contain an inner contradiction of this kind.

§ 34

The *second part* was *Rational Psychology* or *Pneumatology*. This is concerned with the metaphysical nature of the *soul*, that is to say, of the spirit [taken] as a *thing*.

Immortality was looked for in the sphere where *compositeness, time, qualitative alteration, quantitative increase* or *decrease* have their place.

Addition. Psychology was called "rational" in antithesis to the empirical mode of observing the manifestations of the soul. Rational Psychology considered the soul according to its metaphysical nature, as it was determined by abstract thinking. It wanted to recognise the inner nature of the soul, as it is in-itself, as it is for thought.—Nowadays, "the soul" is not often mentioned in philosophy; we speak rather of "the spirit." But spirit is distinct from the soul (which is, so to speak, the middle term between corporeity and the spirit, or what forms the bond between the two). As soul, the spirit is sunk in corporeity, and the soul is what animates the body.

The older metaphysics considered the soul as a thing. But "thing" is a very ambiguous expression. By a thing we understand first of all something that exists immediately, so that we have a sensible representation of it, and people have spoken of the soul in this way. The question has been raised therefore of where the soul has its seat. But if the soul has a seat, then it is in space, and is represented in a sensible way. And when we ask whether the soul is simple or composite, the same way of interpreting it as a thing is involved. This was a specially important question in connection with the immortality of the soul, which was considered to be conditional upon the simplicity of the soul. But, in fact, abstract simplicity is a determination that no more corresponds to the essence of the soul than compositeness.

As for the relationship between rational and empirical psychology, the first stands higher than the second in virtue of the fact that it sets itself the task of

achieving the cognition of spirit through thought and of proving what it thinks as
well; whereas empirical psychology starts from perception, and simply enumerates
and describes what lies to hand there. If we want to grasp the spirit in thought,
however, we must not be so coy about its particular characteristics. Spirit is activity
in the sense in which the Schoolmen already said of God that he is absolute
actuosity.[26] The spirit's being active implies, however, that it manifests itself outwardly. Accordingly, it is not to be considered as an *ens* lacking all process, the way
it was regarded in the older metaphysics, which separated a spirit's inwardness that
lacked process from its outwardness. It is essential that the spirit be considered in
its concrete actuality, in its energy, and more precisely in such a way that its
utterances are recognised as being determined through its inwardness.

§ 35

The *third part, Cosmology,* dealt with the *world,* with its contingency, necessity, and eternity, with its being limited in space and time, with the formal
laws and their modifications, and further with the freedom of man and the
origin of evil.

> In this context, the following were taken to be absolute antitheses:
> contingency and necessity; external and internal necessity; effi-
> cient and final causes, or causality in general and purpose; es-
> sence, or substance, and appearance; form and matter; freedom
> and necessity; happiness and suffering; good and evil.

Addition. The ob-ject of cosmology was both nature and also spirit in its external
entanglements, or its appearance; in short, the ob-ject of cosmology was being-
there generally, the comprehensive sum of the finite. It did not treat its ob-ject as a
concrete whole, however, but only according to abstract determinations. It dealt, for
instance, with questions such as whether chance or necessity ruled the world, and
whether the world is eternal or created. It was therefore one main concern of this
discipline to establish what were called universal cosmological laws, such as the
one that says that "nature makes no leaps," for example. "Leap" means here
qualitative distinction and qualitative alteration, which appear to take place without
mediation, whilst, on the contrary, what is (quantitatively) gradual presents itself
as something mediated.

With regard to the way spirit appears in the world, the main questions raised in
this cosmology were those concerning the freedom of man and the origin of evil.
These are certainly questions of the highest interest; but to answer them in a
satisfactory way, it is above all necessary not to cling to the abstract determinations
of the understanding as if they were ultimate—as if each of the two terms of an
antithesis could stand on its own, and were to be considered as something substantial and genuine in its isolation. This, however, was the standpoint of the older
metaphysics, and also the general framework of these cosmological discussions.

Because of this, they could not attain their purpose, namely, a comprehension of the phenomena of the world. The distinction between freedom and necessity was subjected to inquiry, for example, and these determinations were applied to nature and spirit in such a way that the operations of nature were considered to be subject to necessity, while those of spirit were free. This distinction is certainly essential, and it is grounded in the very core of spirit; but considered as abstractly confronting one another, freedom and necessity pertain to finitude only and are valid only on its soil. A freedom that had no necessity within it, and a mere necessity without freedom, are determinations that are abstract and hence untrue. Freedom is essentially concrete, eternally determinate within itself, and thus necessary at the same time. When people speak of necessity, it is usually initially understood as just determination from without; for instance, in finite mechanics, a body moves only when another body collides with it, and precisely in the direction imparted to it by this collision. This is a merely external necessity, however, not a genuinely inner necessity, for that is freedom.

The situation is the same with the antithesis between *good* and *evil*—one that is typical of the modern world, self-absorbed as it is. It is quite correct to consider evil as something that has a fixed character of its own, as something that is not the good—giving the antithesis its due—but only because its merely apparent and relative character should not be taken to mean that evil and good are all one in the Absolute, or, as it has lately been said, that evil is only something in the eye of the beholder. What is wrong here is that evil is looked on as something fixed and positive, whereas it is the negative that does not subsist on its own account, but only *wants* to be on its own account, and is in fact only the absolute semblance of inward negativity.[a]

§ 36

The *fourth part*, *Natural* or *Rational Theology*, considered the concept of God or its possibility, the proof of his being-there and his attributes.

> (a) In this account of God from the point of view of the understanding, what counts above all is which predicates agree or not with what *we represent* to ourselves as "God." The antithesis of reality and negation is here absolute; hence, what remains for the *concept*, as it is taken to be by the understanding, is, in the end, only the empty abstraction of indeterminate *essence*, of pure reality or positivity, the dead product of the modern Enlightenment. (b) In any case, the procedure of finite cognition in *proving* something stands things on their heads by requiring that an objective ground should be specified for God's being—which, on that score, presents itself as *something that is mediated* by something else. This

a. Emphasis added

mode of proof, which follows the rule of the identity that belongs to the understanding, labours under the difficulty that it must make a transition from the *finite* to the *infinite*. Thus, it is either unable to free God from the abidingly positive finitude of the world that is there, so that he would have to be determined as the immediate substance of his world (Pantheism); or God remains as an object vis-à-vis the subject, and in this way, and for that reason, he is something-*finite* (Dualism). (c) After all, the *attributes* are supposed to be determinate and diverse ones, but, strictly speaking, they have disappeared in the abstract concept of pure reality, or indeterminate essence. But insofar as the finite world remains a *true* being, and God is represented as facing it, the representation of diverse relationships that are determined as attributes comes into focus; and on the one hand, as relationships to finite situations,[a] these attributes must themselves be of a finite kind (for instance, justice, benevolence, might, wisdom, etc.), but on the other hand, they are at the same time supposed to be infinite. From this point of view, the only solution that this contradiction allows for is a quite obscure one: to push these attributes through quantitative enhancement into indeterminacy, into the *sensus eminentior*.[27] But in fact this nullifies the attribute, and what is left of it is merely a name.

Addition. The concern of this part of the older metaphysics was to establish how far reason could take us on its own account in the cognition of God. To have cognition of God through reason is certainly the highest task of science. Religion initially contains representations of God; these representations are communicated to us from our youth up as the doctrines of our religion, compiled in the Creed; and, insofar as the individual has faith in these teachings, and they are the truth for him, he has what he needs as a Christian. Theology, however, is the science of this faith. If theology provides a merely external enumeration and compilation of religious teachings, then it is not yet science. Even the merely historical treatment of its subject matter that is in favour nowadays (for instance, the reporting of what this or that Church Father said) does not give theology a scientific character. Science comes only when we advance to the business of philosophy, i.e., the mode of thinking that involves comprehension. Thus, genuine theology is essentially, at the same time, Philosophy of Religion, and that is what it was in the Middle Ages too.

When we look more closely at the *Rational Theology* of the older metaphysics, we can see that it was a science of God that rested not upon *reason* but on the *understanding*, and its thinking moved only in abstract thought-determinations.

a. *Zustände*

Whilst what was treated was the *concept* of God, it was the *representation* of God that formed the criterion for cognition. Thinking, however, must move freely within itself; all the same, it must be remarked at once that the result of this free thinking agrees with the content of the Christian religion, for the Christian religion is a revelation of reason. The rational theology of the older metaphysics, however, did not achieve any such agreement. Since it set out to determine the notion of God by means of thinking, what emerged as the concept of God was only the abstraction of positivity or reality in general, to the exclusion of negation, and God was accordingly defined as the *Supremely Real Essence*.[28] But it is easy to see that, since negation was excluded from it, this Supremely Real Essence is precisely the opposite of what it should be and of what the understanding intended it to be. Instead of being what is richest, and utter fullness, it is instead rather the poorest, and utter emptiness—all on account of this abstract apprehension of it. The mind and heart rightly long for a concrete content, but concreteness is only present if the content contains within it determinacy, i.e., negation. When the concept of God is apprehended merely as that of the abstract or Supremely Real Essence, then God becomes for us a mere Beyond, and there can be no further talk of a cognition of God; for where there is no determinacy, no cognition is possible either. Pure light is pure darkness.

In the second place, this rational theology was concerned to prove that God is there. The main thing here is that a proof, as it is envisaged by the understanding, is the dependence of one determination on another. In this sort of proof something fixed is presupposed and from it something else follows. Thus, what is exhibited here is the dependence of a determination upon a presupposition. But, if we suppose that it can be proved in this way that God is there, this means that the being of God must depend upon other determinations, which therefore constitute the ground of the being of God. So we can see at once that what must emerge is something distorted, since God is supposed to be precisely the sole ground of everything, and thus not to depend on anything else. In this connection, modern theologians have said that God's being-there cannot be proved, but that we must have immediate cognition of this. But reason understands by proof something quite different than the understanding and common sense do. Certainly the process of proof characteristic of reason also has something other than God as its starting point, but its progress does not leave this other in the status of something immediate which merely is; instead, because the process of proof exhibits the other as mediated and posited, this has the simultaneous result that God must be considered to contain mediation sublated within himself, hence to be genuinely immediate, original, and resting upon himself.—When we say, "Consider nature, for it will lead you to God, and you will find an absolute final purpose," this does not mean that God is mediated, but only that *we* make the journey from an other to God, in the sense that God, being the consequence, is at the same time the absolute ground of what we started with, so that the position of the two is reversed: what appears as the consequence also shows itself to be the ground, while what presented itself as ground to start with is reduced to [the status of] consequence. And that is precisely the path of rational proof.

If we cast another glance at the general procedure of this metaphysics in the light of our explanation, we find that it consisted in grasping the ob-jects of reason in abstract, finite determinations of the understanding, and making abstract identity into the [main] principle.[29] But this infinity of the understanding, this pure Essence, is itself only something finite, for particularity is excluded from it, and this exclusion restricts and negates it. Instead of achieving concrete identity, this metaphysics held onto abstract identity; but what was good about it was the consciousness that thought alone constitutes the essentiality of what is. The material of this metaphysics was furnished by the earlier philosophers, and especially by the Scholastics. The understanding is, of course, one moment of speculative philosophy, but it is a moment at which we should not stop. Plato is not a metaphysician of this sort, and Aristotle still less so, although people usually believe the contrary.

B
The Second Position of Thought with Respect to Objectivity

I. EMPIRICISM
§ 37

Empiricism[30] was the initial result of a double need: there was the need first for a *concrete* content, as opposed to the abstract theories of the understanding that cannot advance from its universal generalisations to particularisation and determination on its own, and secondly for a *firm hold* against the possibility of proving any claim at all in the field, and with the method, of the finite determinations. Instead of seeking what is true in thought itself, Empiricism proceeds to draw it from *experience*, from what is outwardly or inwardly present.

Addition. Empiricism owes its origin to the need, indicated in the preceding paragraph, for a *concrete content* and a *firm footing*, a need which cannot be satisfied by the abstract metaphysics of the understanding. As for this concreteness of content, it simply means that the ob-jects of consciousness are known as inwardly determined, and as a unity of distinct determinations. As we have seen, however, this is in no way the case with any metaphysics based upon the principle of the understanding. As mere understanding, thinking is restricted to the form of the abstract universal, and is unable to advance to the particularisation of this universal. For example, the older metaphysics made the attempt to bring out, through thinking, what the essence or the basic determination of the soul is, and it was decided that the soul is *simple*. This simplicity ascribed to the soul has here the significance of abstract simplicity, excluding all distinction, which, as compositedness, was considered the basic determination of the body and then further of matter generally. Abstract simplicity, however, is a very poor determination, in which it is completely impossible to capture the wealth of the soul and of the spirit as well. Since abstract metaphysical thinking thus proved itself to be inadequate, the need was felt to take refuge in empirical psychology. The same situation arose in rational physics. To say, for instance, that space is infinite, and that nature makes no leaps, etc., is completely unsatisfactory in view of the fullness and life of nature.

§ 38

In one respect, Empiricism has this source in common with metaphysics itself, which likewise has representations—i.e., the content that comes originally from experience—as the guarantee for the authentication of its definitions (its presuppositions as well as its more determinate content). But on the other side, this or that single perception is distinct from experience, and Empiricism elevates the content that belongs to perception, feeling, and intuition into the *form of universal notions*, *principles*, and *laws*, etc. This only happens, however, in the sense that these universal determinations (for instance, "force") are not supposed to have any more significance and validity on their own account than that which is taken from perception, and no justification save the connection that can be demonstrated in experience. On its *subjective* side, empirical cognition gets a firm hold from the fact that in perception consciousness has its *own immediate presence* and *certainty*.

> In Empiricism there lies this great principle, that what is true must be in actuality and must be there for our perception. This principle is opposed to the "ought" through which reflection inflates itself, and looks down upon what is actual and present in the name of a *beyond* that can only have its place and thereness in the subjective understanding. Philosophy, like Empiricism, is cognizant (§ 7) only of what *is*; it does not know that which only *ought* to be, and for that reason *is not there*.—On the subjective side we must recognise also the important principle of *freedom* that lies in Empiricism; namely, that what ought to count in our human knowing, we ought to see *for ourselves*, and to know *ourselves* as *present* in it.— But inasmuch as, so far as content is concerned, Empiricism restricts itself to what is finite, the *consistent* carrying through of its programme denies the supersensible altogether or at least its cognition and determinacy, and it leaves thinking with abstraction only, [i.e.,] with formal universality and identity.—The fundamental illusion in scientific empiricism is always that it uses the metaphysical categories of matter, force, as well as those of one, many,

universality, and the infinite, etc., and it goes on to draw *conclu-sions*, guided by categories of this sort, presupposing and applying the forms of syllogising in the process. It does all this without knowing that it thereby itself contains a metaphysics and is engaged in it, and that it is using those categories and their connections in a totally uncritical and unconscious manner.

Addition. From Empiricism the call went out: "Stop chasing about among empty abstractions, look at what is there for the taking,[a] grasp *the here and now*, human and natural, as it is *here* before us, and enjoy it!" And there is no denying that this contains an essentially justified moment. This world, the *here and now*, the present, was to be substituted for the empty Beyond, for the spiderwebs and cloudy shapes of the abstract understanding. That is precisely how the firm footing, i.e., the infinite determination, that was missing in the older metaphysics was gained. The understanding only picks out finite determinations; these by themselves are shaky and without footing, and the building erected on them collapses upon itself. To find an infinite determination was always the impulse of reason; but the time was not yet ripe to find it in thinking [itself]. Thus, this drive took hold of the present, the "Here," the "This," which has the infinite form in it, even though this form does not have its genuine existence. What is external is *implicitly* what is true, for the true is actual and must exist. Thus the infinite determinacy which reason seeks is in the world, although it is there in a sensible, singular shape, and not in its truth.—More precisely, *perception* is the form in which comprehension was supposed to take place, and this is the defect of Empiricism. Perception as such is always something singular that passes away, but cognition does not stop at this stage. On the contrary, in the perceived singular it seeks what is universal and abides; and this is the advance from mere perception to experience.[b]

In order to find things out,[c] Empiricism makes use, especially, of the form of *analysis*. In perception we have something multifariously concrete, whose determinations must be pulled apart from one another, like an onion whose skins we peel off. So this dismembering means that we loosen up, and take apart, the determinations that have coalesced,[d] and we add nothing except the subjective activity of taking them apart. Analysis, however, is the advance from the immediacy of perception to thought, inasmuch as the determinations that the analysed ob-ject contains united within it acquire the form of universality by being separated. Empiricism falls into error in analysing ob-jects if it supposes that it leaves them as they are, for, in fact, it transforms what is concrete into something abstract. As a result it also happens that the living thing is killed, for only what is concrete, what is One, is alive. Nevertheless, the division has to happen in order for com-

a. *schaut auf eure Hände*
b. *Erfahrung*
c. *Um Erfahrungen zu machen*
d. *zusammengewachsen*

prehension to take place, and spirit itself is inward division. But this is only *one* side, and the main issue is the unification of what has been divided. Insofar as analysis remains at the standpoint of division, we can apply to it the words of the poet:

> *Encheiresin naturae*, says Chemistry now,
> Mocking itself without knowing how.
> Then they have the parts and they've lost the whole,
> For the link that's missing was the living soul.[31]

Analysis starts with the concrete, and in this material it has a great advantage over the abstract thinking of the older metaphysics. Analysis itself fixes the distinctions, and this is of great importance; but these distinctions are themselves only abstract determinations once more, i.e., *thoughts*. And since these thoughts count as what the ob-jects are in-themselves, we meet again the presupposition of the older metaphysics, namely, that what is genuine in things lies in thought.

Let us now push the comparison of the standpoint of Empiricism with that of the older metaphysics a bit further with respect to content. As we saw earlier, the content of this last was the universal ob-jects of reason, God, the soul, and the world generally; this content was adopted from representation, and the business of philosophy consisted in tracing it back to the form of thoughts. The situation was much the same in Scholastic philosophy, for which the dogmas of the Christian church formed the presupposed content, and the issue was to determine and systematise this content more precisely through thought.

The presupposed content of Empiricism is of quite another sort. It is the sensible content of Nature and the content of finite spirit. Here we have before us a material that is finite, while in the older metaphysics we had one that was infinite (and that then was made finite through the finite form of the understanding). In Empiricism we have the same finitude of form; in addition, the content is now finite too. Besides, the method is the same in both ways of philosophising, inasmuch as both begin from presuppositions that are taken to be something fixed. For Empiricism, what is true is quite generally what is external, and even if it concedes something supersensible, no cognition of it is supposed to be possible. We have to confine ourselves to what belongs to perception. The full working out of this principle, however, has produced what was later called "Materialism"—the view in which matter as such counts as what is genuinely objective. But matter is itself already something abstract, something which cannot be perceived as such. We can therefore say that there is no "matter"; for whenever it exists it is always something determinate and concrete. Yet this abstract "matter" is supposed to be the foundation of everything sensible, i.e., the sensible in general, the realm of absolute isolation into oneself, and where everything is external to everything else. Since for Empiricism this sensible domain is and remains something given, this is a doctrine of unfreedom, for freedom consists precisely in my not having any absolute other over against me, but in my being dependent upon a content that is just myself. From this point of view, moreover, reason and unreason are only subjective, in other words, we have to accept the given as it is, and we have no right to ask whether, and to what extent, it is rational within itself.

§ 39

In reflecting upon this principle it has been observed, to begin with, that
in what is called "experience" and what has to be distinguished from
merely singular perceptions of single facts, there are *two* elements; one of
them is the infinitely *manifold material* that isolates itself into single [bits]
that stand on their own,[a] the other is the *form*, the determinations of
universality and *necessity*. It is true that empirical observation does show
many perceptions of the same kind, even more than we can count; but
universality is altogether something other than a great number. It is true
that empirical observation also provides perceptions of alterations *that
follow one after the other*, and of ob-jects that *lie side by side*; but it does not
provide any *necessary* connection.[b] Since, however, perception is to remain
the foundation of what counts as truth, universality and necessity appear
to be something *unjustified*, a subjective contingency, a mere habit, the
content of which may be constituted the way it is or in some other way.

> An important consequence of this is that in this empirical ap-
> proach juridical and ethical determinations and laws, as well as the
> content of religion, appear to be something contingent, and that
> their objectivity and inner truth have been given up.
>
> *Hume*'s scepticism,[32] from which this reflective observation
> mainly starts, should be very carefully distinguished from *Greek
> scepticism*. In Humean scepticism, the *truth* of the empirical, the
> truth of feeling and intuition is taken as basic; and, on that basis,
> he attacks all universal determinations and laws, precisely because
> they have no justification by way of sense-perception. The old
> scepticism was so far removed from making feeling, or intuition,
> into the principle of truth that it turned itself against the sensible
> in the very first place instead. (Concerning modern scepticism as
> compared with ancient, see *Kritisches Journal der Philosophie*.
> Schelling and Hegel, eds., 1802, vol. 1, no. 2.)[33]

II. CRITICAL PHILOSOPHY

§ 40

Critical Philosophy has in common with Empiricism that it accepts experience as the *only* basis for our cognitions; but it will not let them count as
truths, but only as cognitions of appearances.

a. *der für sich vereinzelte, unendlich* mannigfaltige Stoff
b. *einen Zusammenhang* der Notwendigkeit

The distinction between the elements found in the analysis of experience—the *sensible material* and its *universal relations*—serves as the first starting point. Combined with this we have the reflection (mentioned in the preceding paragraph [§ 39]) that only *what is singular* and only *what happens* are contained in perception [taken] on its own account. But at the same time, Critical Philosophy *holds on to the factum* that *universality* and *necessity*, being also essential determinations, are found to be present in what is called experience. And, because this element does not stem from the empirical as such, it belongs to the spontaneity of *thinking*, or is a priori.—The thought-determinations or *concepts of the understanding* make up *the objectivity* of the cognitions of experience. In general they contain *relations*, and hence *synthetic* a priori judgments[34] (i.e., original relations of opposed terms) are formed by means of them.

> The Humean scepticism does not deny the fact that the determinations of universality and necessity are found in cognition. But in the Kantian philosophy, too, this is nothing else but a presupposed fact; in the ordinary language of the sciences, we can say that this philosophy has only advanced another *explanation* of that fact.

§ 41

First of all, the Critical Philosophy subjects to investigation the validity of the *concepts of the understanding* that are used in metaphysics, but also in the other sciences and in ordinary representation. This critique does not involve itself with the *content*, however, or with the determinate mutual relationship of these thought-determinations to each other; instead, it considers them according to the antithesis of *subjectivity* and *objectivity* in general. In the way that it is taken here, this antithesis relates to the distinction of the elements *within* experience (see the preceding paragraph [§ 40]). In this context "objectivity" means the element of *universality* and *necessity*, i.e., of the thought-determinations themselves—the so-called a priori.[35] But the Critical Philosophy extends the antithesis in such a way that experience *in its entirety* falls within *subjectivity*; i.e., both of these elements together are subjective, and nothing remains in contrast with subjectivity except the *thing-in-itself*.

The more detailed *forms* of the a priori, i.e., of thinking which, in spite of its objectivity, is interpreted as a merely subjective activity, are presented as follows—in a systematic order which, it may be remarked, rests only upon psychological-historical foundations.

Addition 1. Subjecting the determinations of the older metaphysics to investigation was without doubt a very important step. Naïve thinking went about unsuspectingly in the thought-determinations that were formed directly and spontaneously. No one asked, at that stage, to what extent these determinations would have value and validity [if taken] on their own account. We have already remarked earlier that thinking that is free is without presuppositions. By this standard, the thinking of the older metaphysics was not free, because, without further ado, it let its determinations count as something given in advance, or as an a priori, although reflection had not put them to the test.

By contrast, the Critical Philosophy set itself the task of investigating just how far the forms of thinking are in general capable of helping us reach the cognition of truth. More precisely, the faculty of cognition was to be investigated before cognition began. This certainly involves the correct insight that the forms of thinking themselves must be made the ob-ject of cognition; but there soon creeps in, too, the mistaken project of wanting to have cognition before we have any cognition, or of not wanting to go into the water before we have learned to swim. Certainly, the forms of thinking should not be used without investigation; but this process of investigation is itself a process of cognition. So the activity of the forms of thinking, and the critique of them, must be united within the process of cognition. The forms of thinking must be considered in and for themselves; they are the ob-ject and the activity of the ob-ject itself; they investigate themselves, [and] they must determine their own limits and point out their own defects. This is the same activity of thinking that will soon be taken into particular consideration under the name "dialectic"; and we can only remark here, in a preliminary way, that it is not brought to bear on the thought-determinations from outside; on the contrary, it must be considered as dwelling within them.

The very first [task] in the Kantian philosophy, therefore, is for thinking to investigate how far it is capable of cognition. Nowadays we have gone beyond the Kantian philosophy, and everyone wants to go further. There are two ways of going further, however: one can go forward or backward. Looked at in the clear light of day, many of our philosophical endeavours are nothing but the (mistaken) procedure of the older metaphysics, an uncritical thinking on and on, of the kind that anyone can do.

Addition 2. Kant's investigation of the thought-determinations suffers essentially from the defect that he did not consider them in and for themselves, but only to see whether they were *subjective* or *objective*. In ordinary language, to be "objective" is to be present outside us and to come to us from outside through perception. Kant denied that the thought-determinations (cause and effect, for instance) were "objective" in this sense, i.e., that they were given in perception; instead he regarded them as pertaining to our thinking itself or to the spontaneity of thinking, and so in *this* sense as subjective.

But all the same Kant calls the thought-product[36]—and, to be precise, the universal and the necessary—"objective," and what is only sensed, he calls "subjective." As a result, the linguistic usage mentioned above appears to have been stood on its head, and for that reason Kant has been charged with linguistic confusion. This, however, is a great injustice. More precisely, the situation is as follows: What ordinary consciousness is confronted with, what can be perceived by the senses (e.g., this animal, this star, etc.), appears to it as what subsists on its own account, or as what is independent. Thoughts, on the other hand, count for it as what is not self-standing, but rather dependent upon an other. In fact, however, what can be perceived by the senses is really secondary and not self-standing, while thoughts, on the contrary, are what is genuinely independent and primitive. It is in this sense that Kant called what measures up to thought (the universal and the necessary) "objective"; and he was certainly quite right to do this. On the other hand, what is sensibly perceptible is certainly "subjective," in that it does not have its footing within itself, and is as fleeting and transient as thought is enduring and inwardly stable. Nowadays we find this same determination of the distinction between the "objective" and "subjective," which Kant validated in the linguistic usage of the more highly educated consciousness. For example, people demand that the judgment of a work of art should be "objective" and not "subjective," and this is understood to mean that it should not be based on a contingent, particular feeling or mood of the moment, but should keep in mind the points of view that are universal and grounded in the essence of art. When dealing with something scientifically, we can distinguish between an "objective" and a "subjective" concern in the same sense.

Moreover, even the objectivity of thinking in Kant's sense is itself again only subjective in its form, because, according to Kant, thoughts, although they are universal and necessary determinations, are still *only our* thoughts, and are cut off from what the thing is *in-itself* by an impassable gulf. On the contrary, the true objectivity of thinking consists in this: that thoughts are not merely our thoughts, but at the same time the *In-itself* of things and of whatever else is ob-jective.

"Objective" and "subjective" are convenient expressions which we employ currently; but their use can very easily give rise to confusion too. So far our explanation has shown that "objectivity" has a threefold significance. *To start with*, it has the significance of what is externally present, as distinct from what is *only* subjective, meant, dreamed, etc.; *secondly*, it has the significance, established by Kant, of what is universal and necessary as distinct from the contingent, particular, and subjective that we find in our sensation; and *thirdly*, it has the last-mentioned significance of the *In-itself* as thought-product, the significance of what is there, as distinct from what is only thought by us, and hence still distinct from the matter itself, or from the matter *in-itself*.

§ 42

(a) *The theoretical faculty*, cognition as such.

This philosophy points to the *original identity* of the "I" within thinking (the transcendental unity of self-consciousness)[37] as the determinate *ground* of the concepts of the understanding. The representations that are given through feeling and intuition are a *manifold* with regard to their *content*. They are equally manifold through their form, [i.e.,] through the *mutual externality* of sensibility in its two forms, space and time,[38] which as forms of intuiting (as what is universal in it) are themselves a priori. Since the "I" relates this manifold of sense-experience and intuiting to itself and unites it inwardly as within One consciousness (pure apperception), this manifold is brought into an identity, into an original combination. The determinate modes of this relating are the pure concepts of the under-standing, the *categories*.[39]

> We are all well aware that Kant's philosophy took the easy way in its *finding* of the categories. "I," the unity of self-consciousness, is totally abstract and completely undetermined. So how are we to arrive at the *determinations* of the I, or at the categories? For-tunately, we can find the *various kinds of judgment* already specified empirically in the traditional logic. To judge, however, is to *think* a determinate ob-ject. So, the various modes of judgment that have already been enumerated give us the various *determinations of thinking*.—It remains the profound and enduring merit of *Fichte's* philosophy[40] to have reminded us that the *thought-determinations* must be exhibited in their *necessity*, and that it is essential for them to be *deduced*.—Fichte's philosophy ought to have had at least this effect upon the method of presenting a treatise on logic: that the thought-determinations in general, or the usual logical material, the species of concepts, judgments, and syllogisms, are no longer just taken from observation and thus apprehended only em-pirically, but are deduced from thinking itself. If thinking has to be able to prove anything at all, if logic must require that *proofs* are given, and if it wants to teach us how to prove [something], then it must above all be capable of proving its very own peculiar content, and able to gain insight into the necessity of this content.

Addition 1. Thus Kant's assertion is that the thought-determinations have their source in the Ego, and that the Ego therefore furnishes the determinations of universality and necessity.—If we consider what we have before us to begin with, we find that, in general terms, it is a manifold; the categories, then, are simple terms with respect to which this manifold is related. The sensible, by contrast, consists of what is mutually external as well as external to itself; this is the proper and basic determination of it. Thus "now," for instance, only has being in relation to a "before" and an "after." Similarly, red is only present because yellow or blue stands against it. But this other is outside this or that sensible [thing] which only is because it is not the other, and only because the other is.—The situation of think-ing, or the Ego, is precisely the contrary of what holds for the sensible, which is mutually external as well as external to itself. The Ego is what is originally identical, at one with itself, and utterly at home with itself. If I say "I," this is the abstract self-relation, and what is posited in this unity is infected by it, and transformed into it. Thus the Ego is, so to speak, the crucible and the fire through which the indifferent multiplicity is consumed and reduced to unity. This, then, is what Kant calls "pure apperception," as distinct from ordinary apperception; the latter takes up the manifold into itself, as a manifold, whereas pure apperception must be considered the activity of making [the ob-ject] mine.

Now this certainly expresses correctly the nature of all consciousness. What human beings strive for in general is cognition of the world; we strive to appropriate it and to conquer it. To this end the reality of the world must be crushed as it were; i.e., it must be made ideal. At the same time, however, it must be remarked that it is not the subjective activity of self-consciousness that introduces absolute unity into the multiplicity in question; rather, this identity is the Absolute, genuineness itself. Thus it is the goodness of the Absolute, so to speak, that lets singular [beings] enjoy their own selves, and it is just this that drives them back into absolute unity.

Addition 2. Expressions like "transcendental unity of self-consciousness" look very difficult, as if something monstrous were concealed there; but what is really in question[a] is simpler than that. What Kant understands by "transcendental" is clear from the distinction between "transcendental" and "transcendent."[41] The "transcendent" here is (quite generally) whatever goes beyond the determinacy of the understanding, and in this sense it occurs first in mathematics. For instance, it is said in geometry that one must imagine the circumference of a circle to consist of an infinite number of infinitely small straight lines. Determinations that count as utterly diverse for the understanding (straight line and curve) are expressly posited here as identical. Another example of something that is transcendent in this sense is the self-consciousness that is self-identical and inwardly infinite, as distinct from the ordinary consciousness, that is determined by finite material. However, Kant called that unity of self-consciousness "transcendental" only, and by this he understood that it is only subjective, and does not also pertain to ob-jects themselves as they are in-themselves.

Addition 3. That the *categories* are to be regarded as belonging only to *us* (or as "subjective") must seem very bizarre to the ordinary consciousness, and there is certainly something awry here. This much is correct about it, however: that the categories are not contained in immediate sensation. Consider, for example, a piece of sugar. It is hard, white, sweet, etc. We say that all these properties are united in *one* ob-ject, and this *unity* is not found in sensation. The situation is the same when we regard two events as standing to one another in the relationship of cause and effect; what is perceived here is the two isolated events, which succeed one another in time. But that one is the cause and the other the effect (the causal nexus between them) is not perceived; on the contrary, it is present merely for our thinking. Now, although the categories (e.g., unity, cause and effect, etc.) pertain to thinking as such, it does not at all follow from this that they must therefore be merely some-

a. *die Sache*

thing of ours, and not also determinations of ob-jects themselves. But, according to Kant's view, this is what is supposed to be the case, and his philosophy is *subjective idealism*, inasmuch as the Ego (the knowing subject) furnishes both the *form* and also the *material* of knowing—the former as *thinking* and the latter as *sensing* subject.

Regarding the content of this subjective idealism we do not have to lift a finger. One might perhaps think, at first, that ob-jects are deprived of reality because their unity has been transferred to the subject. But neither we nor the ob-jects would gain anything merely because *being* pertained to them. What matters is the *content*, and whether the content is a *true* one. The fact that things merely *are* is of no help to them. Time catches up with *what is*, and so what is will soon be *what is not* as well.—You could also say that, according to subjective idealism, man is entitled to have a high opinion of *himself*. But if his world is a mass of sense-intuitions he has no cause to be proud of it. So nothing at all hangs upon the distinction between subjectivity and objectivity in this sense; instead, everything hangs upon the content, and that is both subjective and objective. Even a crime is objective in the sense that it merely exists, but its existence is inwardly null—and it is precisely this nullity that comes to be there in the punishment.

§ 43

On the one hand, it is the categories that elevate mere perception into objectivity, into *experience*; but, on the other hand, these concepts, which are unities merely of subjective consciousness, are conditioned by the given material. They are empty on their own account[42] and have their application and use only in experience, whose other component, the determinations of feeling and intuition, is equally something merely subjective.

Addition. To assert that, by themselves, the categories are empty is unfounded, because they have a content in any case, just by being *determinate*. But, of course, the content of the categories is not one that is perceptible to the senses. Nor is it spatiotemporal; but this is not to be regarded as a defect, since it is really a merit. That is why this is already recognised even in ordinary life, specifically, for example, when people say that a book or a speech is the *richer in content* because more thoughts, general conclusions, etc., are to be found in it; while they will not, conversely, count a book (perhaps more specifically a novel) as rich in content just because a great crowd of isolated incidents, situations, and the like are thrown together in it. In this way even ordinary consciousness recognises that there is *more* to "content" than the sensible material; but this "more" consists of thoughts, and here in the first place the *categories*.

In this regard it must also be remarked that the assertion that the categories by themselves are empty is certainly correct in the sense that we ought not to rest content with them and the totality which they form (the logical Idea), but to advance to the real[a] domains of Nature and Spirit. This advance, however, should not be interpreted as meaning that the logical Idea comes to receive an alien content that stems from outside it; on the contrary, it is the proper activity of the logical Idea to determine itself further and to unfold itself into Nature and Spirit.

§ 44

The categories, therefore, are unfit to be determinations of the Absolute, which is not given in perception; hence the understanding, or cognition through the categories, cannot become cognizant of *things-in-themselves*.

> The *thing-in-itself* (and here "thing" embraces God, or the spirit, as well)[44] expresses the ob-ject, inasmuch as *abstraction* is made of all that it is for consciousness, of all determinations of feeling, as well as of all determinate thoughts about it. It is easy to see what is left, namely, what is *completely abstract*, or totally *empty*, and determined only as what is "beyond"; the *negative* of representation, of feeling, of determinate thinking, etc. But it is just as simple to reflect that this *caput mortuum*[45] is itself only *the product* of thinking, and precisely of the thinking that has gone to the extreme of pure abstraction, the product of the empty "I" that makes its own empty self-*identity* into its *ob-ject*. The *negative* determination that contains this abstract identity as [its] *ob-ject* is likewise entered among the Kantian categories,[46] and, like that empty identity, it is something quite familiar.—We must be quite surprised, therefore, to read so often that one does not know what the *thing-in-itself* is; for nothing is easier to know than this.

§ 45

Now, it is *reason*, the faculty of the *unconditioned*, that sees what is conditioned in all this empirical awareness[b] of things. What is here called object of reason, the *unconditioned* or *infinite*, is nothing but the self-equivalent; in other words, it is that *original identity* of the I in *thinking* which was mentioned in § 42. This *abstract* "I," or the thinking that makes this pure *identity* into its ob-ject or purpose, is called "reason." (See the remark to the preceding paragraph.) Our empirical cognitions[c] are not

---

a. *real*[43]
b. *Erfahrungskenntnisse*
c. *Erfahrungs-Erkenntnisse*

appropriate for this identity that *lacks determinations* altogether, because they are always *determinate* in content. When an unconditioned of this sort is accepted as the Absolute and the Truth[a] of reason (or as the *Idea*), then, of course, our empirical awareness is declared to be untrue, to be [only] *appearances*.

Addition. Kant was the first to emphasise the distinction between understanding and reason[47] in a definite way, establishing the finite and conditioned as the subject matter of the former, and the infinite and unconditioned as that of the latter. It must be recognised that to have established the finitude of the cognition that is based merely on experience and belongs to the understanding, and to have termed its content "appearance," was a very important result of the Kantian philosophy. But we ought not to stop at this negative result, or to reduce the unconditioned character of reason to the merely abstract identity that excludes distinction. Since, upon this view, reason is regarded as simply going beyond the finite and conditioned character of the understanding, it is thereby itself degraded into something finite and conditioned, for the genuine infinite is not merely a realm beyond the finite: on the contrary, it contains the finite sublated within itself. The same holds for the *Idea* too, which Kant did indeed restore to honour, in that he vindicated it for reason, distinguishing it from the abstract determinations of the understanding and from merely sensible representations (all of which, even the latter, being habitually called "ideas" in ordinary life). But, with regard to the Idea too, he halted at the negative aspect and at a mere "ought."

As for the interpretation of the ob-jects of our immediate consciousness, which form the content of empirical cognition, as mere *appearances*, this anyway must be regarded as a very important result of the Kantian philosophy. For our ordinary consciousness (i.e., the consciousness at the level of sense-perception and under-standing) the ob-jects that it[b] knows count as self-standing and self-founded in their isolation from one another; and when they prove to be related to each other, and conditioned by one another, their mutual dependence upon one another is regarded as something external to the ob-ject, and not as belonging to their nature. It must certainly be maintained against this that the ob-jects of which we have immediate knowledge are mere appearances, i.e., they do not have the ground of their being within themselves, but within something else. The further question, then, is how this other is determined. According to the Kantian philosophy, the things that we know about are only appearances for *us*, and what they are *in-themselves* remains for us an inaccessible beyond.

The naïve consciousness has rightly taken exception to this subjective idealism, according to which the content of our consciousness is something that is *only* ours, something posited only through *us.* In fact, the true situation is that the things of which we have immediate knowledge are mere appearances, not only *for us,* but also *in-themselves,* and that the proper determination of these things, which are in

a. *das Absolute und Wahre*
b. reading *es* not *er*

this sense "finite", consists in having the ground of their being not within themselves but in the universal divine Idea. This interpretation must also be called idealism, but, as distinct from the subjective idealism of the Critical Philosophy, it is *absolute idealism*. Although it transcends the ordinary realistic consciousness, still, this absolute idealism can hardly be regarded as the private property of philosophy in actual fact, because, on the contrary, it forms the basis of all religious consciousness. This is because religion, too, regards the sum total of everything that is there, in short, the world before us, as created and governed by God.

§ 46

But the need arises to be cognizant of this identity or of the empty *thing-in-itself*. *To be cognizant*, however, means nothing else but the knowing of an ob-ject according to its *determinate* content. A determinate content, however, contains a manifold *connection* within itself and is the basis for connections with many other ob-jects. So, this [Kantian] reason has nothing but the *categories* for its determination of the *thing-in-itself*, or of that infinite; and when it wants to use them for this purpose, it *flies off* (and becomes "transcendent").[a]

> This is where the second side of the *critique of reason* comes in, and this second side is more important than the first one. The first one, to be precise, is the view discussed above, that the *categories* have their source in the unity of self-consciousness; hence it is the view that in fact cognition through the categories contains nothing objective, and that the objectivity that is ascribed to them (§§ 40, 41) is itself only something *subjective*. If this is all that is taken into account, then the Kantian critique is only a *subjective* (vulgar) *idealism*, one which has nothing to do with the *content*, and has before it only the abstract forms of subjectivity and objectivity; and on top of that it sticks one-sidedly with the former, i.e., subjectivity, as the ultimate, and thoroughy affirmative, determination. But when we consider the so-called *application* of the categories by reason in the cognition of its ob-jects, then the content of the categories becomes a topic of discussion, at least with regard to some of their determinations—or at any rate we have here an occasion for some discussion to occur. It is especially interesting to see how Kant judges this *application of the categories to the Unconditioned*; in other words, metaphysics itself. His procedure will be briefly described and criticised here.

a. *wird sie* überfliegend *(transzendent)*

§ 47

(1) The *first unconditioned* that he considers is the *soul*[48] (see § 34).—In my consciousness I always find myself (α) as the *determining subject,* (β) as a *singular* or as something abstractly simple, (γ) as what is *One* and *the same* in everything manifold of which I am conscious—as *something-identical,* (δ) as something *that distinguishes me* as thinking from *everything outside me.*

The procedure of the traditional metaphysics is correctly specified [by saying] that it sets the corresponding *categories,* or *thought-determinations,* in the place of these *empirical* determinations. This gives rise to four propositions: (α) the *soul is a substance;* (β) it is a *simple* substance; (γ) it is *numerically identical* with respect to the various times of its being-there; (δ) it stands in *relationship* to *what is spatial.*

Kant draws attention to the flaw involved in this transition: that two types of determination are confounded (*paralogism*), namely, empirical determinations with categories; *concluding* from the former to the latter, or in general replacing the first with the second, is quite unjustified.

It is obvious that this criticism expresses nothing other than the comment of Hume that we referred to above (§ 39): that thought-determinations in general—universality and necessity—are not found in perception, and that, both in its content and in its form, the empirical is diverse from the determination of thought.

> If the empirical were to authenticate our thought, then it would certainly be requisite that the thought can be precisely exhibited in our perceptions.—In Kant's critique of metaphysical psychology, the only reason that substantiality, simplicity, self-identity, and the independence that maintains itself in its community with the material world cannot be attributed to the soul, is that the determinations which the consciousness of the soul lets us *experience* are not exactly those that are produced by *thinking* in the same context. But, according to our presentation here, Kant himself makes cognition in general, and even *experience,* consist in the fact that our *perceptions* are thought; i.e., that the determinations which first belong to perception are *transformed* into thought-determinations.— But it must be counted as one good result of the Kantian critique in any case that philosophising about the spirit has been freed from the soul-*things* and their categories; and hence from questions about whether the soul is *simple* or *composite,* whether it is *material,* and so on.—Even for ordinary human understanding, after all, the genuine point of view about the *inadmissibility* of such forms is not the fact that they are *thoughts,* but rather that in and for themselves these thoughts do not contain the truth.—If thought and

appearance do not completely correspond with each other, we have a choice, initially, of which of them to regard as the deficient one. In Kant's idealism, so far as it concerns the rational, the defect is shifted onto the thoughts; they are found to be unsatisfactory because they do not match up with what is perceived, or with a consciousness that restricts itself to the range of perception, [so that] these thoughts are not to be found in a consciousness of this sort. The content of the thought, on its own account, does not come under discussion here.

Addition. "Paralogisms" are basically defective syllogisms, whose defect consists, more precisely, in the fact that one and the same word is used in the two premises in diverse senses. According to Kant, the procedure of the older metaphysics in Rational Psychology is supposed to rest upon paralogisms of this kind; to be precise, merely empirical determinations of the soul are regarded by this psychology as pertaining to the soul in and for itself.

For that matter, it is quite correct to say that predicates like "simplicity," "unalterableness," etc., cannot be applied to the soul. This is not for the reason that Kant gives, however (viz., that reason would thereby overstep the limit assigned to it), but because the abstract determinations of the understanding are not good enough for the soul, which is something quite other than the merely simple, unalterable, etc. For instance, the soul is certainly simple self-identity; but at the same time, because it is active, it distinguishes itself inwardly, whereas what is *only* simple, i.e., simple in an abstract way, is (for that very reason) also dead at the same time.—The fact that, through his polemic against the older metaphysics, Kant removed those predicates from the soul and the spirit must be regarded a great result, but the reason that he gives for doing this is quite wrong.

§ 48

(2) In reason's attempt to be cognizant of the unconditioned [aspect] of the *second ob-ject* (§ 35), i.e., of *the world*,[49] it gets involved in *antinomies*, i.e., in the assertion of two *opposed* propositions about *the same* ob-ject; and it finds, moreover, that each of the propositions must be affirmed with equal necessity. What follows from this is that the content of this "world," whose determinations give rise to contradictions of this sort, cannot be *in-itself*, but can only be appearance. The *solution* is that the contradiction does not fall in the ob-ject in and for itself, but is only attributable to reason and to its cognition of the ob-ject.

What is made explicit here is that it is the content itself, namely, the categories on their own account, that bring about the contradiction. This thought, that the contradiction which is posited by the determinations of the understanding in what is rational is *essential* and *necessary*, has to be considered one of the most important and profound advances of the philosophy of modern times. But the solution is as trivial as the viewpoint is profound; it consists merely in a tenderness for the things of this world. The stain of contradiction ought not to be in the essence of what is in the world; it has to belong *only* to thinking reason, to the *essence* of the *spirit*. It is not considered at all objectionable that the world *as it appears* shows contradictions to the spirit that observes it; the way the world is for subjective spirit, for *sensibility*, and for the *understanding*, is the world as it appears. But when the *essence* of what is in the world is compared with the *essence* of spirit, it may surprise us to see how naïvely the humble affirmation has been advanced, and repeated, that what is inwardly contradictory is not the essence of the world, but belongs to reason, the thinking essence. It does not help at all to express this by saying that reason *only* falls into contradiction through *the application of the categories*.[50] For it is also asserted that this application is *necessary*, and that, for the purpose of cognition, reason has no determinations other than the categories. Cognition really is *determining* and *determinate* thinking; if reason is only empty, indeterminate thinking, then it thinks *nothing*. But if reason is ultimately reduced to that *empty identity* (see the following paragraph), then it is, in the end, lucky to be freed from contradiction after all—through the easy sacrifice of all import and content.

It may also be remarked that, as a result of his failure to study the antinomy in more depth, Kant brings forward only *four* antinomies. He arrived at them by presupposing the table of categories just as he did in the case of the so-called paralogisms. While doing this he followed the procedure,[a] which became so popular afterwards, of simply subsuming the determinations of an ob-ject under a ready-made *schema*, instead of deducing them from the Concept. I have pointed out further deficiencies in the treatment of the antinomies at appropriate points in my *Science of Logic*.[51]—The main point that has to be made is that antinomy is found not only in the four particular ob-jects taken from cosmology, but rather in *all* objects of all kinds, in *all* representations, concepts, and ideas. To know this, and to be cognizant of this property of ob-jects, belongs to what is essential in philosophical study; this is the

---

a. *Manier*

property that constitutes what will determine itself in due course as the *dialectical* moment of logical thinking.

Addition. In the perspective of the older metaphysics it was assumed that, where cognition falls into contradictions, this is just an accidental aberration and rests on a subjective error in inferring and arguing. For Kant, on the contrary, it lies in the very nature of thinking to lapse into contradictions ("antinomies") when it aims at cognition of the infinite. In the remark to the above paragraph we have mentioned that the pointing out of the antinomies should be regarded as a very important advance for philosophical cognition, because in that way the rigid dogmatism of the metaphysics of the understanding is set aside and attention is directed to the dialectical movement of thinking. But, at the same time, it must be noted that here again Kant stopped at the merely negative result (that how things are in-themselves is unknowable), and did not penetrate to the cognition of the true and positive significance of the antinomies. This true and positive significance (expressed generally) is that everything actual contains opposed determinations within it, and in consequence the cognition and, more exactly, the comprehension of an ob-ject amounts precisely to our becoming conscious of it as a concrete unity of opposed determinations. As we showed earlier, in dealing with the metaphysical cognition of the ob-jects it was concerned with, the older metaphysics went to work by employing one set of abstract determinations of the understanding, and excluding those opposed to them; Kant, on the contrary, sought to demonstrate that other assertions of opposite content can, with equal justification and equal necessity, be set against the assertions that result from this procedure. In exhibiting these anti-nomies Kant confined himself to the cosmology of the older metaphysics; and in his polemic against it, taking the schema of the categories as a basis, he produced four antinomies.

The *first* of these concerns the question of whether or not the world should be thought of as limited in space and time. The *second* antinomy deals with the dilemma of whether matter is to be regarded as infinitely divisible or as consisting of atoms. The *third* antinomy relates to the antithesis between freedom and necessity; more precisely, the question is raised of whether everything in the world is to be regarded as conditioned by the causal nexus or whether free beings, i.e., absolute starting points of action in the world, must also be assumed. Finally, Kant adds, as the *fourth* antinomy, the dilemma of whether the world as a whole has a cause or not.

The procedure that he employs in his discussion of these antinomies is as follows: he first sets up the opposing determinations contained in them as thesis and anti-thesis,[52] and proves both (that is, he seeks to present them as necessary results of reflection). In doing this he expressly defends himself against the accusa-tion that he has sought out tricks in order to support what is only a lawyer's "proof." But, in fact, the proofs that Kant brings forward for his theses and anti-theses must be regarded as mere pseudoproofs, because what is supposed to be proved is always already contained in the presuppositions that form the starting point, and the semblance of a mediation is produced only through Kant's prolix, apagogic procedure.

Nevertheless, the setting-up of the antinomies remains a very important result of the Critical Philosophy, and one that is worthy of recognition: for what is brought out in this way (even if it is only done in the first instance [i.e., by Kant himself] in a subjective and immediate manner) is the factual unity of the determinations which the understanding clings to in their separation from one another. For instance, it is implied in the first of the cosmological antinomies listed above that space and time are to be considered not only as continuous, but also as discrete, whereas the older metaphysics stood firm at mere continuity, and as a result the world was considered to be unlimited in space and time. It is quite correct to say that we can go beyond any *determinate* space and similarly beyond any *determinate* time; but it is no less correct to say that space and time are only actual in virtue of their determinacy (i.e., as "here" and "now"), and that this determinacy lies in their very concept. The same holds for the other antinomies adduced above, too; for instance, when the antinomy of *freedom* and *necessity* is more closely considered, the situation is that what the understanding takes to be freedom and necessity are in fact only ideal moments of true freedom and true necessity; neither of them has any truth if separated from the other.

§ 49

(3) The *third* object of reason is *God*[53] (§ 36); he has to be cognised, i.e., *determined by thinking*. But as opposed to simple *identity*, all determination is for the understanding only a *restriction*, i.e., a negation as such. Hence, all reality is to be taken only without restriction, i.e., as *indeterminate*, and God, as the essential sum of all realities or as the supremely real Essence, becomes the *simple abstraction*; while the only determination that remains available for him is the just as strictly abstract determinacy of *being*. Abstract *identity* (which is what is here also is called "concept") and *being* are the two moments that reason seeks to unify; this unification is the *Ideal* of reason.

§ 50

Two ways or forms are admissible for this unification: we can begin with *being* and pass on from there to the *abstraction of thinking*; or, conversely, we can effect the passage from the *abstraction* to *being*.

As far as beginning with being is concerned, this being, as what is immediate, presents itself as determined as an infinite manifold, as a world in all its fullness. This world can be determined more precisely as a collection of whatever infinitely many contingencies [there are] (in the *cosmological* proof); or as a collection of infinitely many *purposes* and *purposive* relationships (in the *physico-theological* proof).[54]—*Thinking* of this fullness of being means stripping it of the form of the singularities and contingencies, and grasping it as a universal being, necessary in and for itself, one that is self-determining and active in accordance with universal purposes, one that is diverse from that contingent and singular collection: [i.e.,] grasping it as *God*.—The critique of this procedure is directed mainly against its being a syllogising, a passage [from one being to another]. As such and in themselves, our *perceptions*, and their aggregate "the world," do not show the universality that results from the purification of that content by thinking; so this universality is not justified by that empirical notion of the world. This elevation of thought from the empirical notion of the world to God is countered with the *Humean* standpoint[55] (as was the case with the paralogisms; see § 47), the standpoint that proclaims the *thinking* of our perceptions to be inadmissible; i.e., the eliciting of the universal and necessary out of these perceptions.

> Since man is a thinking being, neither sound common sense nor philosophy will ever give up raising itself *out of* the empirical worldview to God. This elevation has the *thinking* consideration of the world as its only foundation, not the merely sensory one that we have in common with the animals. It is for thinking, and for thinking *alone*, that the *essence*, the *substance*, the *universal might*, and *purposive determination* of the world are [present]. The so-called proofs that God is there have to be seen simply as the *descriptions* and analyses of the inward *journey*ᵃ *of the spirit*. It is a *thinking* journey and it thinks what is sensory. The *elevation* of thinking above the sensible, its *going out* above the finite to the infinite, the *leap* that is made into the supersensible when the sequences of the sensible are broken off, all this is thinking itself; this transition is *only thinking*. To say that this passage ought not to take place means that there is to be no thinking. And in fact, animals do not make this transition; *they* stay with sense-experience and intuition; for that reason they do not have any religion either.[56] Both generally and in particular, two remarks have to be made about this critique of the elevation of thinking. *First of all*, where this elevation is given the form of *syllogisms* (the so-called *proofs* that God is there), the *starting point* is always the view of the world determined somehow or other as an aggregate of contingencies, or of purposes and purposive relations. It may seem that in thinking, where it constructs *syllogisms*, this starting point may seem to *remain* and to be *left there* as a *fixed foundation*— one that is just as empirical as the material is to begin with. In this

a. Gang

way, the relation of the starting point to the point of arrival is represented as *affirmative* only, as a concluding from *one* [reality] that *is*, and *remains*, to an *other* that equally *is as well*. But this is the great mistake: wanting cognition of the nature of thinking only in this form that is proper to the understanding. On the contrary, thinking the empirical world essentially means altering its empirical form, and transforming it into something-universal; so thinking exercises a *negative* activity with regard to that foundation as well: when the perceived material is determined by universality, it does *not remain* in its first, empirical shape. With the removal and *negation* of the shell, the inner *import* of what is perceived is brought out (cf. §§ 13, 23). The metaphysical proofs that God is there are deficient explanations and descriptions of the elevation of the spirit from the world to God, because they do not express, or rather they do not bring out, the moment *of negation* that is contained in this elevation—for the very fact that the world is *contingent* implies that it is only something *incidental*, phenomenal, and in and for itself *null and void*.[a] This elevation of the spirit means that although being certainly does pertain to the world, it is only semblance, not genuine being, not absolute truth; for, on the contrary, the truth is beyond that appearance, in God alone, and only God is genuine being. And while this elevation is a *passage* and *mediation*, it is also the *sublating* of the *passage* and the *mediation*, since that through which God could seem to be mediated, i.e., the world, is, on the contrary, shown up as what is null and void. It is only the *nullity* of the being of the world that is the bond of the elevation; so that what does mediate vanishes, and in this mediation, the mediation itself is sublated.—In his attack upon the way that the understanding conducts its proofs, *Jacobi* concentrates mainly on the relationship [between the world and God] that is grasped only as affirmative, as a relationship between two beings; he rightly objects that in this procedure *conditions* (i.e., the world) are sought and found for the *Unconditioned*, and that in this way the *Infinite* (God) is represented as *grounded* and *dependent*. However, the way that the elevation itself takes place in the spirit corrects this semblance; indeed, its whole import is the correction of this semblance. But Jacobi did not [re]cognise this as the genuine nature of essential thinking: that, in its mediation, it sublates mediation itself. Hence, he wrongly regarded the objection, which he makes quite correctly against the mere reflecting of the under-

a. *ein* Fallendes, *Erscheinendes, an und für sich* Nichtiges standing, as an objection against thinking in general—and hence as one that strikes against the thinking of reason as well.

The objection that is made against *Spinozism*—that it is a pantheism and an atheism—can be used as an example to elucidate the overlooking of the *negative* moment. It is true that the *absolute substance* of Spinoza is not yet the absolute *spirit*, and it is rightly required that God must be determined as absolute spirit. But if Spinoza's determination [of God] is represented as the confusing of God with nature or with the finite world, and he is said to have made the world into God, what is presupposed is that the finite world possesses genuine actuality, *affirmative reality*. Upon this assumption the unity of God with the world implies that God, too, becomes radically finite, and is degraded into the merely finite, external manifoldness of existence. Apart from the fact that Spinoza does not define God as the unity of God and the world, but as the unity of *thinking* and extension[57] (the material world), this unity does already imply—even when it is taken in that first very clumsy way—that, on the contrary, the world is determined in the Spinozist system as a mere phenomenon without genuine reality, so that this system must rather be seen as *acosmism*.[58] At the very least, a philosophy that maintains that God, and *only* God, *is*, should not be passed off as atheism. We ascribe religion even to peoples who worship apes, the cow, statues of stone or iron, etc., as God. But within this representational mode[a] it goes even more against the grain to give up the presupposition that is peculiar to it,[59] namely that this aggregate of finitude which they call the "world" has actual reality. That *there is no world*, as it might be put in this mode, to assume something like that is easily dismissed as quite impossible, or at least much less possible than that it might come into a man's head that *there is no God*. People believe much more easily (and this is certainly not to their credit) that a system rejects God than that it rejects the world; they find it much more comprehensible that God should be rejected than that the world should be.

The *second* remark concerns the critique of the *basic import* that this thinking elevation initially acquires. If this content consists only in the determinations of the *substance* of the world, of its *necessary essence*, of a cause that *disposes* and *directs it according to purpose*, etc., then it is surely not proportionate to what is under-

---

a. *Aber im Sinne der Vorstellung*

stood, or ought to be understood, by "God." But, setting aside this way of presupposing a certain notion of God, and judging the result by the standard of that presupposition, these determinations are already of great value and are necessary moments in the Idea of God. But in this line of thought, if we want[a] to bring the import before thinking in its genuine determination, i.e., the genuine Idea of God, then we must not take our starting point from a subordinate content. The *merely contingent* things of the world are a very abstract determination. The organic formations and their purposive determinations belong to a higher circle, to *life*. But apart from the fact that the study of living nature, and of the general relation of given things to *purposes*, can be vitiated by the triviality of the purposes, or even by imputations of purposes and their relations that are outright childish. So, nature itself as merely alive is still not really that in terms of which the genuine *determination* of the Idea of God can be grasped; God is more than living, he is spirit. Insofar as thinking adopts a starting point and wants to adopt the closest one, *spiritual* nature alone is the worthiest and most genuine *starting point* for the thinking of the Absolute.

§ 51

The *other way of unification*, through which the *Ideal* is to be established, starts from the *abstraction of thinking* and goes *on to* the determination for which *being* alone remains; this is the *ontological proof* that *God is there*. The antithesis that occurs here is the one between *thinking* and *being*, whereas in the first way *being* is common to both sides, and the antithesis concerns only the distinction between what is singularised and what is universal. What the understanding sets against this second way is in-itself the same as was alleged before, namely that, just as the universal is not found to be present in the empirical, so, conversely, the determinate is not contained in the universal—and the determinate here is "being." In other words, "being" cannot be deduced from the concept or analysed out of it.

> One reason why Kant's critique of the ontological proof has been taken up, and accepted with so much unconditional acclaim, is undoubtedly that, in order to make quite clear what sort of distinction there is between thinking and being, Kant used the example of the *hundred dollars*.[60] With respect to their *concept*, these are

a. *Um in diesem Wege*

equally one hundred, whether they are merely possible or actual; whereas, for the state of my fortune, this distinction is an essential one.—Nothing can be more obvious than that what I think or represent to myself is not yet *actual* because of that: nothing is more obvious than the thought that representing, or even the concept, falls short of being.—Calling such things as one hundred dollars a "concept" can rightly be called a barbarism; but quite apart from that, those who repeat over and over again in their objections to the philosophical Idea, that *thinking and being* are *diverse*, surely ought to presuppose from the first that philosophers are familiar with this fact too. Can there in fact be a more trivial point of information than this? But then, too, we have to bear in mind that when we speak of "God," we are referring to an ob-ject of quite another kind than one hundred dollars, or *any* other particular concept, notion, or whatever other name you want to give it. In fact what makes everything *finite* is this and *only* this: that *its being-there is diverse from its concept*. But God has to be expressly that which can only be "*thought as existing*,"[61] where the Concept includes being within itself. It is this unity of the Concept and of being that constitutes the concept of God.—It is true that this is still a formal[a] determination of God, and one which, for that reason, only in fact contains the nature of the *Concept* itself. But it is easy to see that, even if it is taken in its totally abstract sense, the Concept includes *being* within itself. For however the Concept may be further determined, it is itself minimally the *immediate relation* to itself that emerges through the sublation of its mediation, and being is nothing else but that.—We might well say that it would be very odd if spirit's innermost core, the Concept, or even if I, or above all the concrete totality that God is, were not rich enough to contain within itself even so poor a determination as *being* is—for being is the poorest and the most abstract one of all. For thought, nothing can have less import than *being*. Only the notion that we have when we hear the word "being",[b] namely an *external, sensible* existence (like that of the paper which I have here in front of me), may be even poorer; but [at this point] we do not want to speak of the sensible existence of a restricted, perishable thing at all.— Besides, the trivial remark that thought and being are diverse may, at the most, hinder, but not abolish, the movement of man's spirit from the *thought* of God to the certainty that God *is*. Moreover, it is

a. *formal*

b. *was man sich etwa beim Sein zunächst vorstellt*

this passage, the absolute inseparability of the thought of God from his being, that has been restored to its rightful position by the theory[a] of "immediate knowing" or "faith," which will be considered later.

§ 52

For the *thinking* that goes on in this way, even when it reaches its highest point, *determinacy* remains something *external*; what is still meant by "reason" then is just a radically *abstract thinking*. It follows as a result that this "reason" provides nothing but the *formal unity* for the simplification and systematisation of experiences; it is a *canon*, not an *organon* of *truth*; it cannot provide a *doctrine* of the Infinite, but only a *critique* of cognition.[62] In the last analysis, this critique consists in the *assertion* that within itself thinking is only *indeterminate unity*, and the *activity* of this *indeterminate* unity.

Addition. Kant did, of course, interpret reason as the faculty of the unconditioned; but his exclusive reduction of reason to abstract identity directly involves the renunciation of its unconditionedness, so that reason is in fact nothing but empty understanding. Reason is unconditioned only because it is not externally determined by a content that is alien to it; on the contrary, it determines itself, and is therefore at home with itself in its content. For Kant, however, the activity of reason expressly consists only in systematising the material furnished by perception, through the application of the categories, i.e., it consists in bringing that material into an external order, and hence its principle is merely that of noncontradiction.

§ 53

(b) *Practical reason* is grasped as the will that determines itself—and it does so, of course, in a *universal* way—i.e., as the will that is *thinking*. It has to give imperative, objective laws of freedom, i.e., laws of the kind that say what *ought to happen*.[63] The justification for accepting that thinking is here an activity that is *objectively determining* (as a "reason" in the true sense of the word) is supposed to be that practical freedom is *proven through experience*; i.e., it can be shown to appear within self-consciousness. Against this experience within consciousness there recurs everything that determinism can bring forward against it (from experience likewise). In particular there

a. *Ansicht*

is the sceptical (as well as the Humean) induction of the *infinite diversity* of what counts as right and duty among mankind,[64] i.e., of the laws of freedom which ought to be objective.

§ 54

Once more, there is nothing available for what practical thinking makes into its law, as the criterion of its inward self-*determining*, except the same *abstract identity* of the understanding, i.e., that in this determining there should be no contradiction; hence *practical* reason does not get beyond the formalism that was supposed to be the last word of *theoretical* reason.

> But this practical reason not only posits the univeral determination, i.e., *the good, within itself*;[65] on the contrary, it is only "practical" in the more proper sense, when it requires that the good should be there in the world,[a] that it should have external objectivity; in other words, that thought should not be merely *subjective*, but altogether objective. More later about this postulate of practical reason.

Addition. The free self-determination that Kant denied to theoretical reason, he expressly vindicated for practical reason. It is this aspect of the Kantian philosophy especially that has won great favour for it, and that is, of course, perfectly justified. To appreciate what we owe to Kant in this regard, we have first to recall the shape of the practical philosophy, and more precisely of the moral philosophy, that prevailed when Kant came on the scene. This prevalent moral theory was, generally speaking, the system of *Eudaemonism*[66] which, in response to the question of the vocation of man, imparted the answer that he must posit his *happiness* as his aim. Insofar as happiness was understood to be the satisfaction of man's particular inclinations, wishes, needs, etc., what is accidental and personal was made into the principle of his willing and its exercise. In reaction against this Eudaemonism, which lacked any firm footing, and opened the door to every sort of caprice and whim, Kant set up practical reason; and by so doing he expressed the demand for a determination of the will that is universal and equally binding upon all.

As we have remarked in the preceding paragraphs, theoretical reason is for Kant merely the negative faculty of the infinite, and, being without a positive content of its own, it ought to be restricted to insight into the finite aspect of empirical cognition; in contrast with this restriction, he expressly recognised the positive infinity of practical reason, specifically by ascribing to *willing* the faculty of determining itself in a universal manner, that is to say, through *thinking*. Of course, the will certainly possesses this faculty, and it is of great importance to know that man is only free insofar as he possesses that will and employs it when he acts; but the

---

a. *weltliches Dasein habe*

recognition of this faculty does not yet answer the question of what the *content* of willing or of practical reason is. If it is said that man should make the *Good* the content of his willing, the question of the content, i.e., of the determinacy of this content, immediately recurs; reference to the mere principle that willing should be self-consistent, and the demand that people should do their duty for the sake of duty, do not advance things a single step.

§ 55

(c) The principle of an *intuitive understanding*[67] is ascribed to *the reflecting faculty of judgment*; i.e., an understanding in which the *particular*, which is *contingent* for the *universal* ([i.e., the] abstract identity) and cannot be deduced from it, would be determined through this universal itself; and this is experienced in the products of *art* and of *organic* nature.

> The outstanding merit of the *Critique of Judgment* is that Kant has expressed in it the notion and even the thought *of the Idea*. The notion of an *intuitive understanding*, of *inner* purposiveness, etc., is the *universal* concurrently thought of as *concrete* in itself. It is only in these notions that Kant's philosophy shows itself to be *speculative*. Many, and Schiller[68] in particular, have found in the Idea of *artistic beauty*, or of the *concrete* unity between thought and sense-representations, a way of escape from the *abstractions* of the separative understanding; others have found it in the intuition and consciousness of *living vitality*[a] in general, whether it be natural or intellectual.[69]—Both the product of art and the living individuality are, of course, restricted in their content; but the Idea that is all-embracing even with respect to content is set up by Kant as the postulated harmony between nature (or necessity) and the purpose of freedom; i.e., as the final purpose of the world thought of as realised. In dealing with this highest Idea, however, the laziness of *thought*, as we may call it, finds in the "ought" an all too easy way out, since, in contrast to the actual realisation of the final purpose, it is allowed to hold on to the divorce between concept and reality. But the *presence*[b] of living organisations and of artistic beauty shows the *actuality* of the *Ideal*[70] even for the senses and for intuition. That is why Kant's reflections about these ob-jects were particularly well adapted to introduce consciousness to the grasping and thinking of the *concrete* Idea.

a. Lebendigkeit
b. Gegenwart

§ 56

What is here established is the thought of a relationship between the *universal* of the understanding and the *particular* of intuition other than the one that is fundamental in the doctrine of theoretical and practical reason. But the insight that this universal *is* what is *genuine*, and is even the *truth* itself, is not linked with this thought. On the contrary, this unity is merely taken up, just as it comes into existence in finite appearances, and is exhibited within *experience*. First then, within the *subject*, experience of this sort is secured in one way by *genius*,[71] or by the ability to produce aesthetic ideas, i.e., representations produced by the free *imagination*, which serve an idea and provide food for *thought*, without this content's being expressed in a *concept*, or being capable of such expression; it is also provided in another way by the *judgment of taste*, by the feeling of the *agreement* between the *intuitions* or representations (in all their freedom) and the *understanding* (in its law-abiding character).

§ 57

Moreover, the principle of the reflecting faculty of judgment is determined, with respect to *the living products of nature*, as *purpose*,[72] as the active *Concept*, as the universal that is inwardly determined and determining. At the same time, what is discarded is the representation of *external* or *finite purposiveness*, where the purpose is only an external form for the means and the material in which it realises itself. On the contrary, within the *living* [being], the purpose is a determination and an activity that is immanent in its [bodily] matter, and all of its members are means for each other as well as ends.[a]

§ 58

The relationship between ends[b] and means, between subjectivity and objectivity, as determined by the understanding, is sublated in an idea of this kind; but all the same (and in contradiction to this) the purpose is again explained as a cause that exists and is active *only as representation*, i.e., as *something-subjective*; and hence the purposive determination, too, is declared to be a principle of judging that belongs only to *our* understanding.[73]

a. *Zweck*
b. *Zweck*

Even after the Critical Philosophy had arrived at the final view that reason could only be cognizant of *appearances*, there was still, regarding living nature, a choice between two *equally subjective* modes of thought, as well as the obligation, according to the Kantian presentation itself, not to restrict the cognition of the products of nature to the categories of quality, cause and effect, composition, constituents, etc. If the principle of *inner purposiveness* had been adhered to and developed in its scientific application, it would have brought about a completely different, much higher way of envisaging this purposiveness.

§ 59

If this principle were followed without any restriction at all, the Idea would be that the universality that is determined by reason—the absolute final purpose, *the good*—is made actual in the world, and this through a third, through the might that itself posits this final purpose and realises it—i.e., it is made actual by *God*, in whom, since he is the absolute truth, those antitheses of universality and singularity, of subjectivity and objectivity, are resolved and declared to be not self-standing[a] and untrue.

§ 60

However, the *good*—which is posited as the final purpose of the world—is determined, from the very beginning, simply as *our* good, or as the moral law of *our* practical reason; so that the unity does not go beyond the correspondence of the state of the world, and of what happens in it, with our morality.* Moreover—even with this restriction—the *final purpose*, or the good, is an abstraction lacking all determination, and the same applies to what is supposed to be *duty*. More precisely, the antithesis, which is posited in its content as *untrue*, is here revived and reasserted against this harmony, so that the harmony is determined as something merely *subjective*—as what only *ought* to be; i.e., what does *not* at the same time have

---

a. *unselbständig*

*In Kant's own words: "Final purpose is merely a concept of our practical reason. It cannot be deduced *from any data of experience* for the making of theoretical judgments about nature nor even related to its cognition. The only possible use of this concept is for practical reason according to moral laws; and the *final purpose of creation* is that constitution of the world which agrees with the only purpose that we can specify as determined according to laws, i.e., with the final purpose of *our pure practical reason*—and that [only] insofar as it ought to be practical." *Critique of Judgment*, § 88[74] [our translation; Hegel's emphasis].

reality. It is something *believed* that can only claim subjective certainty, not truth; i.e., *not* that objectivity which corresponds to the Idea.—If this contradiction seems to be palliated by transferring the Idea into *time*, into a future where the Idea also *is*, [we must say that] any such sensible condition, as time, is really the opposite of a solution of the contradiction; and the representation of the understanding that corresponds to this, i.e., the *infinite progress*,[75] is simply[a] nothing but the contradiction itself, posited as forever recurring.

> Another general remark can be made about the result that the Critical Philosophy has yielded regarding the nature of *cognition*; this result has grown into one of the prejudices, i.e., one of the general presuppositions, of our time.
>
> In any dualistic system, but especially in the Kantian system, the fundamental defect reveals itself through the inconsistency of *uniting* what, a moment earlier, was declared to be independent, and therefore *incompatible*. Just as, a moment before, what is united was declared to be what is genuine, so now it is said that *both moments* (whose subsisting-on-their-own was denied by [asserting] that their unification is their truth) have truth and actuality only by being separate—and this, therefore, is what is genuine instead. What is lacking in a philosophising of this kind is the simple consciousness that, in this very to-ing and fro-ing, each of the simple determinations is declared to be unsatisfactory; and the defect consists in the simple incapacity to bring two thoughts together—and in respect of form there are only *two* thoughts present. Hence, it is the supreme inconsistency to admit, on the one hand, that the understanding is cognizant only of appearances, and to assert, on the other, that this cognition is *something absolute* —by saying: cognition *cannot* go any further, this is the *natural*, absolute *restriction* of human knowing. Natural things are restricted, and they are just natural things inasmuch as they *know nothing* of their universal *restriction*, inasmuch as their determinacy is a restriction only *for us*, not *for them*. Something is only known, or even felt, to be a restriction, or a defect, if one is at the same time *beyond* it. Living things have the privilege of pain compared with the lifeless; even for them, a single determinacy becomes the feeling of something-*negative*, because as living things they do have, within them, the *universality* of *living vitality*[b] which is

a. *unmittelbar*
b. Lebendigkeit

beyond the singular, and because they maintain themselves even in the negative of themselves, and are sensible of this *contradiction* as existing within them. This contradiction is in them only because both the universality of its sense of vitality,[a] and the singularity that is negative with regard to it, are [found] in the One subject. In cognition, too, restriction and defect are only determined as restriction and defect by *comparison* with the Idea that is *present*—the Idea of the universal, of something-whole and perfect. It is only lack of consciousness, therefore, if we do not see that it is precisely the designation of something as finite or restricted that contains the proof of the *actual presence* of the Infinite, or Unrestricted, and that there can be no knowledge of limit unless the Unlimited is *on this side* within consciousness.

There is *this further* remark that can be added about the result reached by Kant's philosophy regarding cognition: that this philosophy cannot have had any influence on the way we deal with the sciences. *It leaves the categories and the usual method of cognition totally uncontested.* Although scientific writings of that period sometimes began with propositions taken from the Kantian philosophy, it becomes clear in the course of the treatise itself that those propositions were only a superfluous ornament, and that the same empirical content would have come out even if all these initial pages had been left out.*

As far as the more precise comparison of Kant's philosophy with *metaphysical empiricism*[77] is concerned, [it should be noticed that] although *naïve* empiricism attaches itself to sensible perception, it also concedes that there is a spiritual actuality, a supersensible world—no matter how its *content* is constituted, whether it comes from thought or from fantasy, etc. In respect of *form*, this content has its attestation in spiritual authority,[78] just as the other content of empirical knowing has its own attestation in the authority of outward perception. But the *empiricism* that *reflects*, and makes *consistency* its principle, attacks this dualism with respect to the ultimate, highest content; it negates the independence of the thinking principle and of a self-developing spiritual world within it. The

---

a. *Lebensgefühl*

*Even Hermann's *Handbook of Prosody*[76] begins with some paragraphs taken from Kant's philosophy. In § 8 the conclusion is reached that the law of rhythm must be (1) an *objective*, (2) a *formal*, (3) an a priori *determinate* law. With these requirements and the principles of causality and reciprocal action that follow later, we should compare the treatment of the verse-measures themselves, upon which these formal principles do not exercise the slightest influence.

consistent system of empiricism is *materialism,* or *naturalism.*—
Kant's philosophy sets the principle of thinking and of freedom in
strict opposition to this empiricism, and allies itself with naïve
empiricism without derogating in the least from the universal
principle of empiricism. The world of perception and of the understanding that reflects upon it remains on one side of its dualism.
This world is passed off as a world of *appearances,* to be sure; but
that is just a title, a merely formal determination, since the source,
the basic import, and the method of study remain exactly the
same. The other side, in contrast, is the independence of the thinking that grasps itself, the principle of freedom, which this philosophy has in common with the metaphysics of the older tradition;
but it empties all the content out of it, and is not able to put any
back into it. Being thus robbed of all determination, this thinking,
now called "reason," is set free from all *authority.* The main effect
of Kant's philosophy has been that it has revived the consciousness
of this absolute inwardness. Although, because of its abstraction,
this inwardness cannot develop itself into anything, and cannot
produce by its own means any determinations, either cognitions or
moral laws, still it altogether refuses to allow something that has
the character of *outwardness* to have full play in it, and be valid for
it. From now on the principle of the *independence of reason,* of its
absolute inward autonomy,[a] has to be regarded as the universal
principle of philosophy, and as one of the assumptions[b] of our
times.

Addition 1. The Critical Philosophy deserves great credit, negatively speaking, for
establishing the conviction that the determinations of the understanding are finite,
and that the cognition that moves within them falls short of the truth. But the one-
sidedness of this philosophy consists all the same in the fact that the finitude of
those determinations of the understanding is identified with their belonging
merely to our subjective thinking, while the thing-in-itself is supposed to remain
an absolute beyond. In fact, however, the finitude of the determinations of the
understanding does not lie in their subjectivity; on the contrary, they are finite in
themselves, and their finitude should be exhibited in these determinations themselves. For Kant, by contrast, what we think is false just because *we* think it.

It should be regarded as a further defect of this philosophy that it provides only
an informative description[80] of thinking, and a mere inventory of the moments of
consciousness. To be sure, this inventory is mainly correct; but the necessity of
what is thus empirically apprehended is not discussed in the process. The result of

a. *Selbständigkeit*
b. *Vorurteile*[79]

the reflections about the various stages of consciousness is then said to be that the content of all that we know about is only appearance. We must agree with this conclusion up to a point: finite thinking certainly has to do only with appearances. But this stage of appearance is not the end of it. On the contrary, there is still a higher land; but for the Kantian philosophy it remains an inaccessible beyond.

Addition 2. Initially, the principle that thinking determines itself from within[a] was established in a merely formal way in the Kantian philosophy; Kant did not demonstrate the *manner* and *extent* of this self-determination of thinking. On the contrary, it was Fichte who recognised this defect; and when he made his demand for a deduction of the categories, he also tried at the same time to furnish an actual deduction too. Fichte's philosophy makes the Ego the starting point for the development of philosophical thinking; and the categories are supposed to result from its activity. But the Ego does not genuinely appear as free, spontaneous activity here, since it is regarded as having been aroused only by a shock[81] from outside; the Ego is then supposed to react to this shock, and to achieve consciousness of itself through this reaction.

On this view, the nature of the shock remains something outside of cognition, and the Ego is always something conditioned which is confronted by an other. So, in this way Fichte, too, comes to a halt at Kant's conclusion that there is cognition only of the finite, and the infinite transcends thinking. What Kant calls "the thing-in-itself" is for Fichte the shock from outside, this abstraction of something other than the Ego, which has no determination other than that it is negative; it is the Non-Ego in general. So the Ego is regarded as standing in relation to the Non-Ego. It is only the Non-Ego that arouses its self-determining activity, and it does this in such a way that the Ego is only the continuous activity of self-liberation from the shock. But it never achieves actual liberation, since the cessation of the shock would mean the cessation of the Ego, whose being is simply its activity. Moreover, the content that the activity of the Ego brings forth is nothing else but the usual content of experience, with the added proviso that this content is merely appearance.

C
The Third Position of Thought with Respect to Objectivity

IMMEDIATE KNOWING[82]

§ 61

In the Critical Philosophy, thinking is interpreted as being *subjective*, and its *ultimate*, unsurpassable determination is *abstract universality*, or formal

a. *aus sich selbst*

identity; thus, thinking is set in opposition to the truth, which is inwardly concrete universality. In this highest determination of thinking, which is reason, the categories are left out of account.—From the opposed stand-point thinking is interpreted as an activity *of the particular*, and in that way, too, it is declared to be incapable of grasping truth.

§ 62

As an activity of the particular, thinking has the *categories* as its only product and content. The way the understanding fixes them, these catego-ries are *restricted* determinations, forms of what is *conditioned, dependent,* and *mediated*. The Infinite, or the true, is not [present] for a thinking that is restricted in this way. Unlike the proofs that God is there,[a] Critical Philoso-phy cannot make the passage to the Infinite. These thought-determinations are also called "concepts"; and hence to "comprehend" an ob-ject means nothing more than to grasp it in the form of something conditioned and mediated; so that inasmuch as it is what is true, infinite, or unconditioned, it is transformed into something conditioned and medi-ated, and, instead of what is true being grasped in thinking, it is perverted into untruth.

> This is the simple, one and only polemic that is advanced by the standpoint which asserts that God and the true can only be known immediately. In earlier times, every type of so-called an-thropomorphic representation was banished from God as finite, and hence unworthy of the Infinite; and as a result he had already grown into something remarkably empty. But the thought-determinations were not generally considered anthropomorphic; on the contrary, thinking counted as what stripped the representa-tions of the Absolute of their finitude—in accordance with the prejudice of all times, mentioned above, that it is only through [reflective] thinking that we arrive at the truth. But now, finally, even the thought-determinations in general are declared to be an-thropomorphic, and thinking is explained as the activity of *just making* [the ob-ject] *finite*.[84]—In Appendix VII of his *Letters on Spinoza*,[85] Jacobi has expounded this polemic in the most determi-nate way, deriving it indeed from Spinoza's philosophy itself, and then using it to attack cognition in general. In this polemic, cogni-tion is interpreted only as cognition of the finite, as the thinking progression through *sequences*, from one *conditioned* item to an-other *conditioned* one, where each condition is itself just something-conditioned once more. In other words, cognition is a

---

a. *(gegen die Beweise vom Dasein Gottes)*[83]

progression through *conditioned conditions*. To explain and to comprehend, therefore, means to show that something is *mediated* through something *else*. Hence, every content is only a *particular*, *dependent*, and *finite* one. God, or what is infinite and true, lies outside the mechanism of a connection of this kind to which cognition is supposed to be restricted.—Since Kant's philosophy posited the finitude of the categories most notably in the formal determination of their *subjectivity* alone, it is important that, in this polemic, the categories are dealt with in their determinacy, and the category as such is [re]cognised as being finite.—Jacobi had in view particularly the splendid successes of the natural sciences (the *sciences exactes*)[86] in the cognition of the forces and laws of nature. But, of course, the Infinite does not allow itself to be found immanent in this domain of the finite;[87] *Lalande*[88] could say that he had searched all through the heavens, but he had not found God (cf. the Remark to § 60). The final result arising from investigations conducted in this domain was the *universal* as the *indeterminate* aggregate of finite outwardness[a]—*matter*; and Jacobi saw, quite rightly, that this path of a mere progression by way of mediations can have no other issue.

§ 63

At the same time, it is asserted that the *truth is for the spirit*—so much so that it is through reason alone that man subsists, and this reason is *the knowledge of God*.[89] But since mediated knowledge is supposed to be restricted simply to a finite content, it follows that reason is *immediate knowing, faith*.

> *Knowing, believing, thinking, intuiting* are the categories that occur at this standpoint; and since these categories are *presupposed* as already *familiar*, they are often employed in accordance with merely psychological notions and distinctions. What their nature and concept is, is not investigated—though that is what everything depends on. Thus, we find *knowing* commonly opposed to *believing*, even though believing is at the same time determined as immediate knowing, and hence directly recognised as a [kind of] knowing, too. Indeed, it is found to be an empirical fact that what we believe is in our consciousness, so that we do at least *know about it*;

a. *des äußerlichen Endlichen*

also that what we believe is in our consciousness as something *certain*, and hence that we know *it*.—Most notably, *thinking* is set in opposition to immediate knowing and believing, and particularly to intuiting. [But] when intuiting is determined as "intellectual," this can only mean an intuiting that is *thinking*—unless, even here where God is the ob-ject, we still want to understand by "intellectual" only the images and representations of our fantasy. In the language used by those who philosophise in this way, it happens that "believing" is also used in relation to the common things which are *sensibly* present. We *believe*, says Jacobi, that we have a *body*,[90] we believe in the *existence* of *sensible things*. But, when we talk about faith in what is true and eternal, or about God being revealed, or given, in immediate knowing and intuition, these are not sensible things at all, but a content that is *inwardly universal*, i.e., ob-jects that are [present] only for the *thinking* spirit. Also, when *singularity* is understood as I, when *personality* itself— not an empirical I, a *particular* personality—is meant, above all when the personality of God is present to consciousness, then what is at issue is *pure*—i.e., *inwardly universal*—personality; and this is a thought and pertains only to thinking.—Pure *intuiting*, moreover, is altogether the same as pure thinking. "Intuiting" and "believing" express initially the determinate representations that we associate with these words in our ordinary consciousness; it is true that in this usage, they are diverse from thinking, and just about everyone is able to understand the distinction. But at this point believing and intuiting ought to be taken in a higher sense, as faith in God, as intellectual intuition of God; and this means that abstraction is to be made precisely from what constitutes the distinction between intuiting, or believing, and thinking. When they are promoted to this higher region, we cannot say how believing and intuiting are still diverse from thinking. One may think that with distinctions of this sort that have become empty, one is saying and asserting something very important; the determinations that one intends to attack are the same as the ones that one is asserting.—The expression "believing", however, carries with it the particular advantage that it calls *Christian religious* faith to mind, and seems to include it; it may quite easily even seem to be the same. Hence, this fideistic philosophising looks essentially pious and Christian; and on the ground of this piety it claims for itself the freedom to make its assurances with even more pretension and authority. But we must not let ourselves be deceived by a semblance that can only sneak in because the same words are

used. We must maintain the distinction firmly. The Christian faith
implies an authority that belongs to the church, while, on the
contrary, the faith of this philosophising standpoint is just the
authority of one's own subjective revelation. Moreover, the Christian faith is an objective content that is inwardly rich, a system of
doctrine and cognition; whereas the content of this [philosophical]
faith is inwardly so indeterminate that it may perhaps admit that
content too—but equally it may embrace within it the belief that
the Dalaï-Lama, the bull, the ape, etc., is God, or it may, for its own
part, restrict itself to *God in general*, to the "highest essence."[91]
Faith itself, in that would-be philosophical sense, is nothing but the
dry abstraction of immediate knowing—a totally formal determination, which should not be mistaken for, or confounded with,
the spiritual fullness of the Christian faith, either on the side of the
faithful heart and the Holy Spirit that inhabits it, or on the side of
the doctrine that is so rich in content.

Besides, what is called believing and immediate knowing here is
just the same as what others have called inspiration, revelation of
the heart, a content implanted in man by nature, and in particular
sane human understanding (or "common sense")[a] as well. All of
these forms similarly make immediacy—i.e., the way that a content
is found within consciousness, and is a fact in it—into their
principle.

§ 64

What this immediate knowing knows is that the Infinite, the Eternal or
God, that is [present] in our *representation* also *is*—that within our consciousness the certainty of its *being* is immediately and inseparably combined with our *representation* of it.

The last thing philosophy would want to do is to contradict these
propositions of immediate knowing; on the contrary, it can congratulate itself upon the fact that *its own* old propositions, which
even express its entire universal content, have somehow become
also the general prejudices of the times—though in a quite unphilosophical way, to be sure. All there is to be surprised about,
rather, is the fact that anyone could be of the opinion that these
propositions are opposed to philosophy: namely, the propositions
that what is held to be true is immanent in the spirit (§ 63), and

a. English in Hegel's text

that truth is [present] for the spirit (ibid.). In a formal perspective, the proposition that God's *being* is immediately and inseparably linked with the *thought* of God and that *objectivity* inseparably goes with the *subjectivity* that thought initially has, is particularly interesting. Indeed, the philosophy of immediate knowing goes so far in its abstraction that the determination "existence" is inseparably linked, not only with the thought of God alone, but just as much (in intuition) with the *representation* of my *body* and of *external* things.—When philosophy attempts to prove a unity of this sort, i.e., when it wants to show that the nature of thought or of subjectivity implies that they are inseparable from being or from objectivity, then (whatever the status of such proofs may be) philosophy must in any case rest entirely content with the assertion and demonstration that its propositions are also *facts of consciousness* and hence that they are in agreement with *experience*.—The distinction between the assertions of immediate knowing and philosophy simply comes down in the end to this: that immediate knowing adopts an *excluding* posture or, in other words, it sets itself against the doing of philosophy.—But the proposition "Cogito, ergo sum," which stands at the very centre, so to speak, of the entire concern of modern philosophy, was also uttered by its author in the mode of immediacy. Anyone who takes this proposition as a syllogism must know little more about the nature of the syllogism than that "ergo" occurs in it. For where can the middle term be here? Yet the middle term belongs much more essentially to the syllogism than the word "ergo". But if, in order to justify the name, we want to call the linkage in Descartes an *un-mediated*[a] syllogism, then this redundant form designates nothing but a *connection* of *distinct* determinations *that is mediated by nothing*. And in that case, the connection of being with our representations, which is expressed in the proposition of immediate knowing, is a syllogism too, neither more nor less.—I take the following citations in which Descartes himself expressly declares that the proposition "Cogito, ergo sum" is not a syllogism from Mr. Hotho's dissertation about the Cartesian philosophy that was published in 1825.[92] The passages are the responses to the Second Objections; *De Methodo IV*; and *Ep.* I.118.[93] I quote the more precise statements from the first passage. That we are thinking essences, says Descartes, is "prima quaedam notio quae ex nullo syllogismo concluditur" ["a certain primary concept that is not concluded from any syllogism"], and

a. unmittel-baren

he continues: "neque cum quis dicit: ego cogito, ergo sum sive existo, *existentiam ex cogitatione per syllogismum* deducit" ["and when someone says 'I am thinking; therefore I am, or I exist,' he does not deduce *existence from thought by* means of a syllogism"]. Since Descartes knows what belongs to a syllogism, he adds that if with this proposition there had to be a deduction through a syllogism, then the required major premise would be: "illud omne, quod cogitat, est sive existit" ["everything that thinks is, or exists"]. But, on the contrary, this last proposition is one that is only deduced from the first one.

What Descartes says about the proposition that my being is inseparable from my thinking is that this connection is contained and indicated in the *simple intuition* of consciousness, that this connection is what is absolutely first; i.e., it is the principle, or what is most certain and evident, so that we cannot imagine any scepticism so extravagant[a] [94] as not to admit it. These statements are so eloquent and precise that the modern theses of Jacobi and others about this immediate connection can only count as useless repetitions.

§ 65

This standpoint is not content when it has shown that *mediate* knowing, taken *in isolation*, is inadequate for the [cognition of] truth; its peculiarity is that *immediate* knowing can only have the truth as its content when it is taken *in isolation*, to the *exclusion* of mediation.—Exclusions of this kind betray that this standpoint is a relapse into the metaphysical understanding, with its *Either-Or*; and hence it is really a relapse into the relationship of external mediation based upon clinging to the finite; i.e., to one-sided determinations beyond which this view mistakenly thinks that it has risen. But let us not push this point; exclusively immediate knowing is only asserted as *a fact*, and here, in the introduction, it only has to be taken up under the aspect of this external reflection. The important issue in-itself is the logical thinking of the antithesis of immediacy and mediation. But the standpoint of immediate knowing rejects the study of the nature of the matter, i.e., of the Concept, as one that leads to mediation and even to cognition. The genuine treatment of this topic, that of logical thinking,[b] must find its own place within the Science itself.

a. *kein Skeptizismus so enorm vorgestellt werden könne*
b. *die des Logischen*

The entire second part of the *Logic*, the doctrine of *Essence*, deals with the essential self-positing unity of immediacy and mediation.

§ 66

So we stand by the position that immediate knowing has to be taken *as a fact*. But this means that our study is directed at the field of *experience*, and toward a *psychological* phenomenon.—In this connection we should point out, as one of the most common experiences, that truths, which we know very well to be the result of the most complicated, highly mediated studies, can present themselves immediately in the consciousness of those who are well versed in that kind of cognition. Like anyone who has been instructed in a science, a mathematician has solutions at his fingertips that were arrived at by a very complicated analysis; every educated human being has a host of general points of view and principles immediately present in his knowing, which have only emerged from his meditation on many things, and from the life experience of many years. The facility that we achieve in any kind of knowing, and also in art and technical skill, consists precisely in the fact that, when the occasion arises, we have this know-how, these ways of handling things, *immediately* in our consciousness, and even in our outwardly directed activity and in the limbs of our body.—Not only does the immediacy of knowing not exclude its mediation in all of these cases, but they are so far connected that the immediate knowing is even the product and result of the mediated knowing.

> The connection of immediate *existence* with its mediation is just as trivial an insight; the seed and the parents are an immediate, orig- inating existence with regard to the children, etc., which are the offspring. But, for all that the seed and the parents (in virtue of their just existing) are *immediate*, they are offspring as well; and, in spite of the mediation of their existence, the children, etc., are now immediate, for they *are* too. That I *am* in Berlin, which is my *immediate* present, is *mediated* by the journey I made to come here, etc.

§ 67

As far as the *immediate knowing* of God, or *what is right*, or *what is ethical* is concerned—and all the other determinations of instinct, of implanted or innate ideas, of common sense, of natural reason, etc., fall in this same category—whatever form may be given to this primordial [element], the universal experience is that (even for *Platonic reminiscence*)[95] *education* or development is required to bring what is contained in it to consciousness. Although Christian baptism is a sacrament, it implies, of itself, the further responsibility of providing a Christian education. This means that, for all that religion and ethical life are a matter of *believing*, or *immediate* knowing, they are radically conditioned by mediation, which is called development, education, and culture.

> Both those who assert that there are *innate* ideas and those who deny it have been dominated by an antithesis of [mutually] exclusive determinations, similar to the one that we have just been considering; namely, the antithesis between what may be formulated as the essential, *immediate* combination of certain universal determinations with the *soul*, and another combination that would take place in an external way and would be mediated by *given* objects and representations. The empirical objection to the assertion of *innate ideas* was that all humans would have to have these ideas. For instance, they would have to have the principle of contradiction in their consciousness, and to know it, since this principle, and the others like it, were counted among the innate ideas. This objection can be said to depend upon a misunderstanding, because, although the determinations in question may be innate, they do not, just for that reason, have to be already in the *form* of ideas, of representations, or of what is known. But this objection is quite appropriate when it is directed against immediate knowing, since the former explicitly asserts that its determinations are within consciousness.—If the standpoint of immediate knowing does perhaps grant that, for religious faith in particular, a development and a Christian or religious education are *necessary*,[96] then it is quite arbitrary to want to ignore this when we come to talk about believing; and it is sheer mindlessness not to know that when the necessity of education is granted, it is just the essential requirement of mediation that is expressed.

Addition. The claim in the Platonic philosophy that we *remember* the Ideas means that the Ideas are implicitly in the human mind[a] and are not (as the Sophists maintained) something alien that comes to the mind from outside. In any case, this interpretation of cognition as "reminiscence" does not exclude the development of what is *implicit* in the human mind, and this development is nothing but mediation. The situation is the same with the "innate ideas" that occur in Descartes and the Scottish philosophers; these ideas are also initially only *implicit* and must be considered as present in the mind by way of an aptitude.[97]

a. *im Menschen*

§ 68

In the experiences that we have mentioned, there is an appeal to what shows itself to be *bound up* with immediate knowing. Although this bond may be taken initially to be just an *external*, or empirical, connection, it does show itself to be essential and inseparable, even when it is studied only empirically, because it is constant. But moreover, if according to experience this immediate knowing is taken on its own account, then inasmuch as it is the knowing of God and of the divine, a consciousness of this kind is universally described as an *elevation above* the sensible and the finite, as well as above the immediate desires and inclinations of the natural heart. This elevation passes over into faith in God and in the divine, and it ends there, so that this faith is an immediate knowing and persuasion,[a] although it does, nonetheless, have this process of mediation as its presupposition and condition.

> We have noted already that the so-called "proofs that God is there," which start from finite being, express this elevation and are not inventions of an artificial reflection, but the necessary mediations that belong to spirit—although they do not have their correct and complete expression in the traditional form of those proofs.

§ 69

It is the transition, mentioned in § 64, from the subjective Idea to being that constitutes the main focus of interest for the standpoint of immediate knowing; this passage is what is essentially asserted as an original connection without mediation. Taken entirely without regard to seemingly empirical[b] associations, this central point exhibits within itself the mediation, which is determined the way it truly is, not as a mediation with and through something-external, but as one that comes to its own inward resolve.[c]

§ 70

For what is asserted from this standpoint is that neither the *Idea*, as a merely *subjective* thought, nor a mere *being* on its own account, is what is true; for being on its own account, any being that is not that of the Idea, is the sensible, finite being of the world. But what is immediately asserted by

a. *Fürwahrhalten*
b. *empirisch scheinende Verbindungen*
c. *als sich in sich selbst beschließend*

this is that the Idea *is what is true* only *as mediated* by being, and, conversely, that being is *what is true* only *as mediated* by the Idea. What the
principle of immediate knowing rightly insists on is not an indeterminate,
empty immediacy, abstract being, or pure unity on its own account, but the
unity of *the Idea* with being. But it is quite mindless not to see that the
unity of *distinct* determinations is not just a purely immediate, i.e., a totally
indeterminate and empty unity, but that what is posited in it is precisely
that one of the determinations has truth only through its mediation by the
other; or, in other words, that each of them is mediated with the truth only
through the other.—It is thereby shown to be *a factum*, that the determination of mediation is contained in that very immediacy, against which the
understanding (in accordance with its own fundamental principle of immediate knowing) is not allowed to have any objections. It is only the ordinary abstract understanding that takes the determinations of immediacy
and mediation to be absolute, each on its own account, and thinks that it
has an example of a *firm* distinction[a] in them; in this way, it engenders for
itself the unsurmountable difficulty of uniting them—a difficulty which, as
we have shown, is not present in the *factum*, while within the speculative
Concept it vanishes too.

§ 71

The one-sidedness of this standpoint brings determinations and consequences with it whose main features have still to be highlighted, now
that the explanation of their very foundation has been given. *In the first
place*, since it is not the *nature of the content*, but the *factum of consciousness*,
that has been made into the criterion of truth, therefore it is *subjective*
knowing, and the *assertion* that I find a certain content to be present within
my consciousness, that are the foundation of what is alleged to be the
truth. What I find to be present in *my* consciousness is thereby promoted
into something present in the consciousness of *everyone*, and given out as
the *nature* of consciousness itself.

> In the past, the *consensus gentium* to which Cicero[98] already ap-
> pealed was cited among the so-called proofs that God is there. The
> *consensus gentium* is an authority of significance, and it is very
> easy[b] to pass from [the fact] that a content can be found in *every-
> one*'s consciousness to [the conclusion] that it lies in the nature of
> consciousness itself and is necessary to it. Implicit in this category

a. *etwas* Festes *von Unterscheidung*
b. *es liegt nahe bei der Hand*

of *universal* agreement was the essential consciousness, which does not escape even the least cultivated mind, that any single consciousness is always something-particular or *contingent*. If the nature of this consciousness itself is not investigated, i.e., if what is particular or contingent in it is not separated out—an operation of laborious meditation, which is the only way to find out what is universal in and for itself in this consciousness—then it is only when *everyone* agrees about a content that the prejudice that this content belongs to the nature of consciousness itself is respectably grounded. But the need of thinking to know that what shows itself as *universally* present is *necessary* is still not satisfied by the *consensus gentium*. For even if it were accepted that the universality of the factum was a satisfactory proof, the *consensus gentium* has been abandoned as a proof for the belief in God because experience shows that there are individuals and peoples in or among whom no belief in God is found.* But there is nothing quicker and easier than making the simple *assertion* that I find a content in my consciousness, together with the certainty of its truth, and therefore that this certainty does not belong to me, as this particular subject, but to the nature of spirit itself.

---

*Whether we find atheism or faith in God spread more or less widely in experience depends on whether we are content with the determination of a God *in general*, or require a more determinate cognition of God. In the Christian world, at least, it is not conceded that idols like those of China and India, or the fetishes of Africa, or even the gods of Greece are God. Those who believe in them therefore do not believe in God. But if we consider, on the other hand, that *implicitly* the *general* belief in God is present in any such belief in idols, just as the kind is implicit in the particular individual, then the idolatry also counts as belief, not just in an idol, but in God. Conversely, the Athenians[99] treated the poets and philosophers who held that Zeus, and so on, were only clouds, and asserted perhaps [that there is] only a *God in general*, as atheists.—What counts is not what is contained in an ob-ject *in-itself*, but what part of it *stands out*[a] for consciousness. If we could accept the interchange of these determinations as valid then every human sense-intuition, even the most ordinary one, would be religion, since in every one of them, in everything spiritual, the principle is at least *implicitly* contained, which, when developed and purified, enhances itself into religion. But *to be capable* of religion is one thing (and our "contained in-itself" expresses the capacity and possibility); but *to have* religion is something else.—In modern times, travelers (for instance, the captains Ross and Parry)[100] have again found tribes (the Esquimaux), which they claim have no religion at all, not even the tiny trace of it that may still be found in African *sorcerers* (the "wonder-workers" of Herodotus).[101] On the other hand, the Englishman who spent the first months of the last Jubilee year in Rome, says in the account of his travels that among the Romans of today the common people are bigots, while those who can read and write are all atheists.—The main reason why the accusation of atheism has become less frequent in modern times is that the basic import and requirements in the matter of religion have been reduced to a minimum (see § 73).

a. *heraus ist*

§ 72

In the *second* place, it follows from the supposition that *immediate knowing* is the criterion of truth, that all superstition and idolatry is proclaimed as truth, and the most unjust and unethical content of the will is justified. It is not because of so-called mediated knowing, argumentation, and syllogising that the Indian looks on the cow or the ape, the Brahmin or the Lama, as God, but he *believes* in it. The natural desires and inclinations automatically deposit their interests in consciousness, and immoral purposes are found in it quite immediately. A good or evil character expresses the *determinate being* of the will, which is known in its interests and purposes, and therefore in the most immediate way.

§ 73

Finally, the immediate knowing of God is only supposed to extend to [the affirmation] *that* God is, not *what* God is; for the latter would be a cognition and would lead to mediated knowing. Hence God, as the ob-ject of religion, is expressly restricted to *God in general*, to the indeterminate supersensible, and the content of religion is reduced to a minimum.

> If it were actually necessary to bring about just the maintenance of the belief *that there is a God*[a] or even the establishment of this belief, then the only matter for surprise would be the poverty of the times, which lets us count the most indigent [form] of religious knowing as a gain, and has reached the point of returning in its church to the altar dedicated *to the unknown God* [Acts 17:23] that was long ago found in *Athens*.

§ 74

The general nature of the *form of immediacy* has still to be indicated briefly. For it is this form itself which, because it is *one-sided*, makes its very content one-sided and hence *finite*. It gives the *universal* the one-sidedness of an *abstraction*, so that God becomes an essence lacking all determination; but God can only be called spirit inasmuch as he is known as inwardly *mediating himself with himself*. Only in this way is he *concrete*, living, and spirit; and that is just why the *knowing* of God as spirit contains mediation within it.—The form of immediacy gives to the *particular* the determination of *being*, or of relating *itself to itself*. But the particular is

a. es sei ein Gott

precisely the relating of itself to *another* outside it; through that form the *finite* is posited as absolute. Being totally abstract, this form is *indifferent* to *every content* and, just for that reason, it is receptive to any content; so it can sanction an idolatrous and immoral content just as easily as the reverse. Only the insight that the content is not independent, but is *mediated through an other*, reduces it to its finitude and untruth. And since the content brings mediation with it, this insight [too] is a knowing that contains mediation. But a content can only be [re]cognised as what is true, inasmuch as it is not mediated with an other, i.e., is not finite, so that it mediates itself with itself, and is in this way both mediation and immediate self-relation all in one.—That same understanding, which thinks that it has emancipated itself from finite knowing, and from the *the understanding's identity* [which is the principle] of metaphysics and of the Enlightenment, immediately makes this *immediacy, i.e., the abstract self-relation*, or the abstract identity, into the principle and criterion of truth once more. *Abstract thinking* (the form of reflective metaphysics) and *abstract intuiting* (the form of immediate knowing) are one and the same.

Addition. When the form of immediacy is held onto as firmly opposed to the form of mediation, then it becomes one-sided, and this one-sidedness is imparted to any content that is traced back to this form alone. In general, immediacy is abstract self-relation, and hence it is abstract identity or abstract universality at the same time. So if the universal in and for itself is taken only in the form of immediacy, it becomes just abstractly universal, and God acquires from this standpoint the significance of an Essence that is utterly indeterminate. To go on speaking of God as "spirit" is simply to use an empty word, for, being both consciousness and self-consciousness, spirit is in any case a distinguishing of itself from itself and from an other, so that it is at once mediation.

§ 75

The *evaluation* of this third position, that has been assigned to thinking with regard to the truth, can only be undertaken in the way that is immediately and inwardly indicated by this very standpoint, and allowed by it. That *there is*[a] an immediate knowing, i.e., a knowing without mediation (either with another, or inwardly with itself), is hereby shown to be *factually* false. Likewise, it has been shown up as factually untrue that thinking only proceeds by way of finite and conditioned determinations that are *mediated* by *something else*—and untrue that this mediation does not also sublate itself in the mediation. But for the *factum* that there is a cognition

a. es gebe

of this kind, which proceeds neither in one-sided immediacy nor in one-sided mediation, the *Logic* itself and the *whole of philosophy* is the *example*.

§ 76

If we consider the principle of immediate knowing in relation to our starting point, which was the metaphysics that we have called "naïve," then the comparison shows that this principle is *a return* to the beginning which this metaphysics made in modern times as the *Cartesian* philosophy. Both of them assert the following:

> (1) The simple inseparability of the *thinking* and the *being* of the thinker: *cogito ergo sum* is exactly the same as the fact that the being, reality, and existence of the I are immediately revealed to me within consciousness (Descartes explains at once and explicitly that by "thinking" he understands *consciousness* in general and as such; *Princ. Phil.* 1.9);[102] and that this inseparability is the very *first* cognition, which is not mediated, or proven, as well as the *most certain* one.

> (2) Likewise the inseparability of the notion of *God* from his *existence*; so that this existence is contained in the very notion of God, which cannot be without that determination—an existence that is therefore necessary and external.*

> (3) With regard to the equally immediate consciousness of the existence of *external* things, this is nothing else than *sensible* consciousness; that we have a consciousness of this kind is the least of all cognitions. All that is of interest here is to know that this immediate knowing of the *being* of external things is deception and error, and that there is no truth in the sensible as such, but that the *being* of these external things is rather something-

---

*Descartes, *Princ. Phil.* 1.15: "Magis hoc (ens summe perfectum existere) *credet*, si attendat, nullius alterius rei ideam apud se inveniri, in qua eodem modo necessariam existentiam contineri animadvertat; . . . intelliget, illam ideam exhibere veram et immutabilem naturam, quaeque *non potest non existere*, cum necessaria existentia *in ea contineatur*" ["The mind will be even more ready to accept this (i.e., that a supremely perfect being exists) if it considers that it cannot find within itself an idea of any other thing such that necessary existence is seen to be contained in the idea in this way. And from this it understands that the idea of a supremely perfect being is not an idea which was invented by the mind, or which represents some chimera, but that it represents a true and immutable nature which cannot but exist, since necessary existence is contained within it"].[103] A phrase that follows, and which sounds like a mediation and a proof, does not prejudice this first fundamental claim. Exactly the same is found in Spinoza: that God's *essence*, i.e., the abstract notion, includes existence. The first definition of Spinoza is that of the *causa sui*: it is that "cujus *essentia* involvit existentiam; sive id, cujus *natura non potest concipi* nisi existens" ["that whose essence involves existence, or

contingent, something that passes away, or a *semblance*; they are essentially this: to have only an existence that is separable from their concept, or their essence.

§ 77

The two standpoints are, however, distinct in the following ways: (1) The philosophy of Descartes *proceeds* from these unproven and unprovable presuppositions *to a further* developed cognition, and in this way it has given rise to the sciences of modern times. But the more recent standpoint, in contrast, has reached the result—which is important on its own account (§ 62)—that a cognition that proceeds by way of *finite* mediations is only cognizant of what is finite and contains no truth; and it also demands that our consciousness of God should stand fast upon that [immediate] faith— which is a wholly abstract belief.*

(2) On the one hand, this modern standpoint changes nothing in the method of ordinary scientific cognition that was initiated by Descartes, and the sciences of what is empirical and finite that have originated from that method are carried on by it in exactly the same way. But, on the other hand, it rejects this method, and hence *all* methods, since it does not know of any other method [appropriate] for the knowing of what is infinite in import. Therefore it surrenders itself to the untamed arbitrariness of imaginations and assurances, to moral conceit and haughtiness of feeling, or to opinions and arguments without norm or rule[a]—all of which declare themselves to be most strongly opposed to philosophy and philosophical theses. For philosophy will not tolerate any mere assurances or imaginings, nor does it allow thinking to swing back and forth while using this type of arbitrary reasoning.[b]

---

that whose nature cannot be conceived except as existing"]; the inseparability of the Concept from being is the fundamental determination and presupposition. But what Concept is it to which this inseparability from being belongs? Not the concept of *finite* things, for these are precisely such that their existence is *contingent* and created.—That the eleventh proposition of Spinoza: "That God necessarily exists," and likewise the twentieth: "That God's existence and his essence are one and the same," are both followed by a proof—is a redundant relic of the formalism of [geometric] demonstration. God is the Substance (and the only one at that), but the Substance is *causa sui, therefore* God necessarily exists—this only means that God is the one whose Concept and Being are inseparable.[104]

*Anselm, on the contrary, says: "*Negligentiae* mihi videtur, si postquam confirmati sumus in fide, non *studemus*, quod *credimus*, *intelligere*" ["Once we are confirmed in the faith, I would consider it negligence not to strive to understand what we believe."] (*Tractat. Cur Deus Homo*).[105]—Given the concrete content of the Christian doctrine, Anselm faced a cognitive problem of quite another [order of] difficulty, than the one contained in this modern "faith."

a. *einem maßlosen Gutdünken und Räsonnement*

b. *beliebiges Hin-und Herdenken des Räsonnements*

§ 78

The *antithesis* between an independent immediacy of the content or of knowing, and, on the other side, an equally independent mediation that is irreconcilable with it, must be put aside, first of all, because it is a mere *presupposition* and an arbitrary *assurance*. All other presuppositions or assumptions[a] must equally be given up when we enter into the Science, whether they are taken from representation or from thinking; for it is this Science, in which all determinations of this sort must first be investigated, and in which their meaning and validity like that of their antitheses must be [re]cognised.

> Being a negative science that has gone through all forms of cognition, *scepticism* might offer itself as an introduction in which the nullity of such presuppositions would be exposed. But it would not only be a sad way, but also a redundant one, because, as we shall soon see, the dialectical moment itself is an essential one in the affirmative Science. Besides, scepticism would only have to find the finite forms empirically and unscientifically, and to take them up as given. To require a consummate scepticism of this kind, is the same as the demand that the Science should be preceded by *universal doubt*, i.e., by total *presuppositionlessness*. Strictly speaking, this requirement is fulfilled by the freedom that abstracts from everything, and grasps its own pure abstraction, the simplicity of thinking—in the resolve of *the will to think purely*.

a. *Vorurteile*[106]

MORE PRECISE CONCEPTION AND DIVISION OF THE *LOGIC*

§ 79

With regard to its form, the *logical* has three sides: (α) *the side of abstraction* or *of the understanding*, (β) *the dialectical* or *negatively rational side*, [and] (γ) *the speculative* or *positively rational* one.

These three sides do not constitute three *parts* of the Logic, but are *moments of everything logically real*; i.e., of every concept or of everything true in general. All of them together can be put under the first moment, that *of the understanding*; and in this way they can be kept separate from each other, but then they are not considered in their truth.—Like the division itself, the remarks made here concerning the determinations of the logical are only descriptive anticipations[a] at this point.

§ 80

(α) Thinking as *understanding* stops short at the fixed determinacy and its distinctness vis-à-vis other determinacies; such a restricted abstraction counts for the understanding as one that subsists on its own account, and [simply] is.[b]

Addition. When we talk about "thinking" in general or, more precisely, about "comprehension," we often have merely the activity of the understanding in mind. Of course, thinking is certainly an activity of the understanding to begin with, but it must not stop there and the Concept is not just a determination of the

a. *antizipiert und historisch*
b. *als für sich bestehend und seiend*

125

understanding.—The activity of the understanding consists generally in the bestowing of the form of universality on its content; and the universal posited by the
understanding is, of course, an abstract one, which is held onto in firm opposition
to the particular. But as a result, it is itself determined also as a particular again.
Since the understanding behaves toward its ob-jects in a way that separates and
abstracts them, it is thereby the opposite of immediate intuition and feeling,[a]
which, as such, deal entirely with the concrete and stick to that.

The oft-repeated complaints that are regularly made against thinking in general
are connected with this antithesis between understanding and sense-experience.
The burden of the complaints is that thinking is hard and one-sided and, if pursued consistently, leads to ruinous and destructive results. The first answer to these
charges, insofar as they are justified in content, is that they do not apply to all
thinking, and specifically not to rational thinking, but only to the thinking of the
understanding.

But it should be added that even the thinking of the understanding must un-
questionably be conceded its right and merit, which generally consists in the fact
that without the understanding there is no fixity or determinacy in the domains
either of theory or of practice. First, with regard to cognition, it begins by apprehending given ob-jects in their determinate distinctions. Thus, in the consideration of nature, for example, distinctions are drawn between matters, forces, kinds,
etc., and they are marked off, each on its own account, in isolation one from
another. In doing all this, thinking functions as understanding, and its principle
here is identity, simple self-relation. So it is first of all this identity by which the
advance from one determination to another is conditioned in cognition. Thus, for
instance, in mathematics, magnitude is *the* one determination with respect to which
a progression happens, all others being left out. In the same way we compare
figures with one another in geometry, bringing out what is identical in them. In
other areas of cognition, too, for instance, in jurisprudence, it is identity that is the
primary means of progress. For, since we here infer one determination from another, our inferring is nothing but an advance in accordance with the principle of
identity.

Understanding is just as indispensable in the practical sphere as it is in that of
theory. Character is an essential factor in conduct, and a man of character is a man
of understanding who (for that reason) has definite purposes in mind and pursues
them with firm intent. As Goethe says,[107] someone who wants to do great things
must know how to restrict himself. In contrast, someone who wants to do everything really wants to do nothing, and brings nothing off. There is a host of interesting things in the world; Spanish poetry, chemistry, politics, music are all very
interesting, and we cannot blame a person who is interested in them. But if an
individual in a definite situation is to bring something about, he must stick to
something determinate and not dissipate his powers in a great many directions.
Similarly, in the case of any profession, the main thing is to pursue it with understanding. For instance, the judge must stick to the law and give his verdict in
accordance with it; he must not let himself be sidetracked by this or that; he must

a. *Empfindung*

admit no excuse, and look neither to right nor left.—Furthermore, the understanding is an essential moment in culture generally. A cultivated person is not satisfied with what is cloudy and indeterminate; indeed, he grasps subject matters in their fixed determinacy, whilst someone who is uncultivated sways uncertainly hither and thither, and it often takes much effort to come to an understanding with such a person as to what is under discussion, and get him to keep the precise point at issue steadily in view.

Our earlier explanation showed that logical thinking in general must not be interpreted merely in terms of a subjective activity, but rather as what is strictly universal and hence objective at the same time. It should be added that this applies to the understanding as well, which is the first form of logical thinking. The understanding must therefore be regarded as corresponding to what people call the *goodness* of God,[108] where this is understood to mean that finite things *are*, that they subsist. For instance, we recognise the goodness of God in nature by the fact that the various kinds and classes, of both animals and plants, are provided with everything they need in order to preserve themselves and prosper. The situation is the same with man, too, both for individuals and for whole peoples, who similarly possess what is required for their subsistence and their development. In part this is given to them as something that is immediately present (like climate, for example, or the character and products of the country, etc.); and in part they possess it in the form of aptitudes, talents, etc. Interpreted in this way, then, the understanding manifests itself everywhere in all the domains of the ob-jective world, and the "perfection" of an ob-ject essentially implies that the principle of the understanding gets its due therein. For example, a State is imperfect if a definite distinction between estates and professions has not yet been achieved in it, and, similarly, if the conceptually diverse political and governmental functions have not yet formed themselves into particular organs—just like the various functions of sensation, motion, digestion, etc., in the developed animal organism.

From the discussion so far, we can also gather that even in the domains and spheres of activity which, in our ordinary way of looking at things, seem to lie furthest from the understanding, it should still not be absent, and that, to the degree that it is absent, its absence must be considered a defect. This holds especially for art, religion, and philosophy. In art, for example, the understanding manifests itself in the fact that the forms of the beautiful, which are conceptually diverse, are maintained in their conceptual distinctness and are presented distinctly. The same holds for single works of art, too. It is a feature of the beauty and perfection of a dramatic work, therefore, that the characters of the various persons should be sustained in their purity and determinacy, and, similarly, that the various purposes and interests that are involved should be presented clearly and decisively.—As to what follows next, the domain of religion, the superiority of Greek over Nordic mythology, for instance, essentially consists (apart from any further diversity of content and interpretation) in the fact that in the former each figure of the Gods is developed into a sculptural determinacy, whilst in the latter they flow into one another in a fog of murky indeterminacy.—And finally, after what has been said already, it scarcely requires special mention that philosophy cannot do without the understanding either. Philosophising requires, above all, that each thought should be grasped in its full precision and that nothing should remain vague and indeterminate.

But again, it is usually said also that the understanding must not go too far. This contains the valid point that the understanding cannot have the last word. On the contrary, it is finite, and, more precisely, it is such that when it is pushed to an extreme it overturns into its opposite. It is the way of youth to toss about in abstractions, whereas the man of experience does not get caught up in the abstract *either-or*, but holds onto the concrete.

§ 81

(β) The *dialectical* moment is the self-sublation of these finite determinations on their own part, and their passing into their opposites.

> (1) The dialectical, taken separately on its own by the understanding, constitutes *scepticism*, especially when it is exhibited in scientific concepts. Scepticism contains the mere negation that results from the dialectic. (2) Dialectic is usually considered as an external art, which arbitrarily produces a confusion and a mere *semblance* of *contradictions* in determinate concepts, in such a way that it is this semblance, and not these determinations, that is supposed to be null and void, whereas on the contrary what is understandable would be true. Dialectic is often no more than a subjective seesaw of arguments that sway back and forth, where basic import is lacking and the [resulting] nakedness is covered by the astuteness that gives birth to such argumentations.—According to its proper determinacy, however, the dialectic is the genuine nature that properly belongs to the determinations of the understanding, to things, and to the finite in general. Reflection is initially the transcending of the isolated determinacy and a relating of it, whereby it is posited in relationship but is nevertheless maintained in its isolated validity. The dialectic, on the contrary, is the *immanent* transcending, in which the one-sidedness and restrictedness of the determinations of the understanding displays itself as what it is, i.e., as their negation.[109] That is what everything finite is: its own sublation. Hence, the dialectical constitutes the moving soul of scientific progression, and it is the principle through which alone *immanent coherence and necessity* enter into the content of science, just as all genuine, nonexternal elevation above the finite is to be found in this principle.

Addition 1. It is of the highest importance to interpret the dialectical [moment] properly, and to [re]cognise it. It is in general the principle of all motion, of all life, and of all activation in the actual world. Equally, the dialectical is also the soul of all genuinely scientific cognition. In our ordinary consciousness, not stopping at the abstract determinations of the understanding appears as simple fairness, in accordance with the proverb "live and let live", so that one thing holds and the other does *also*. But a closer look shows that the finite is not restricted merely from the outside; rather, it sublates itself by virtue of its own nature, and passes over, of itself, into its opposite. Thus we say, for instance, that man is mortal; and we regard dying as having its ground only in external circumstances. In this way of looking at things, a man has two specific properties, namely, he is alive and *also* mortal. But the proper interpretation is that life as such bears the germ of death within itself, and that the finite sublates itself because it contradicts itself inwardly.

Or again, the dialectic is not to be confused with mere *sophistry*, whose essence consists precisely in making one-sided and abstract determinations valid in their isolation, each on its own account, in accord with the individual's interest of the moment and his particular situation. For instance, it is an essential moment of my action that I exist and that I have the means to exist. But if I consider this aspect, this principle of my well-being, on its own, and derive the consequence from it that I may steal, or that I may betray my country, then we have a piece of sophistry.—In the same way, my subjective freedom is an essential principle of my action, in the sense that in my doing what I do, I am [there] with my insights and convictions. But if I argue abstractly from this principle *alone*, then my argument is likewise a piece of sophistry, and all the principles of ethical life are thrown overboard in arguments like that.—The dialectic diverges essentially from that procedure, since it is concerned precisely with considering things [as they are] in and for themselves, so that the finitude of the one-sided determinations of the understanding becomes evident.

Besides, the dialectic is not a new thing in philosophy. Among the Ancients, Plato is called the inventor of the dialectic,[110] and that is quite correct in that it is in the Platonic philosophy that dialectic first occurs in a form which is freely scientific, and hence also objective. With Socrates, dialectical thinking still has a predominantly subjective shape, consistent with the general character of his philosophising, namely, that of *irony*. Socrates directed his dialectic first against ordinary consciousness in general, and then, more particularly, against the Sophists. He was accustomed to pretend in his conversations that he wanted to be instructed more precisely about the matter under discussion; and in this connection he raised all manner of questions, so that the people with whom he conversed were led on to say the opposite of what had appeared to them at the beginning to be correct. When the Sophists called themselves teachers, for instance, Socrates, by a series of questions, brought the Sophist Protagoras[111] to the point where he had to admit that all learning is merely recollection.

And by means of a dialectical treatment, Plato shows in his strictly scientific dialogues the general finitude of all fixed determinations of the understanding. Thus, for example, in the *Parmenides*,[112] he deduces the Many from the One, and, notwithstanding that, he shows that the nature of the Many is simply to determine itself as the One. This was the grand manner in which Plato handled the dialectic.—In modern times it has mainly been Kant who reminded people of the dialectic again and reinstated it in its place of honour; as we have already seen (§ 48), he did this by working out the so-called antinomies of reason, which in no way involve a simple seesawing between [opposite] grounds as a merely subjective activity, but rather exhibit how each abstract determination of the understanding, taken simply on its own terms, overturns immediately into its opposite.

And, however much the understanding may, as a matter of habit, bristle at the dialectic, still the latter must in no way be regarded as present only for philosophical consciousness; on the contrary, what is in question here is found already in all other forms of consciousness, too, and in everyone's experience. Everything around us can be regarded an example of dialectic. For we know that, instead of being fixed and ultimate, everything finite is alterable and perishable, and this is nothing but the dialectic of the finite, through which the latter, being implicitly the other of itself, is driven beyond what it immediately is and overturns into its opposite. We said earlier (§ 80) that the understanding must be regarded as what is contained in the notion of the *goodness* of God. We must now add that the principle of the dialectic in the same (objective) sense corresponds to the notion of God's *might*. We say that all things (i.e., everything finite as such) come to judgment, and in that saying we catch sight of the dialectic as the universal, irresistible might before which nothing can subsist, however firm and secure it may deem itself to be. This determination certainly does not exhaust the depth of the divine essence, the concept of God; but it still forms an essential moment in all religious consciousness.

Furthermore, the dialectic also asserts itself in all the particular domains and formations of the natural and spiritual world. In the motion of the heavenly bodies, for example, a planet is now in this position, but it also has it in-itself to be in another position, and, through its motion, brings this, its otherness, into existence. Similarly, the physical elements prove themselves to be dialectical, and the meteorological process makes their dialectic apparent. The same principle is the foundation of all other natural processes, and it is just this principle by virtue of which nature is driven beyond itself. As to the occurrence of the dialectic in the spiritual world, and, more precisely, in the domain of law and ethical life, we need only to recall at this point how, as universal experience confirms, the extreme of a state or action tends to overturn into its opposite.

This dialectic is therefore recognised in many proverbs. The legal proverb, for instance, says, "Summum ius summa iniuria", which means that if abstract justice is driven to the extreme, it overturns into injustice. Similarly, in politics, it is well known how prone the extremes of anarchy and despotism are to lead to one another. In the domain of individual ethics, we find the consciousness of dialectic in those universally familiar proverbs: "Pride goes before a fall", "Too much wit outwits itself", etc.—Feeling, too, both bodily and spiritual, has its dialectic. It is well known how the extremes of pain and joy pass into one another; the heart filled with joy relieves itself in tears, and the deepest melancholy tends in certain circumstances to make itself known by a smile.

Addition 2. Scepticism should not be regarded merely as a doctrine of doubt; rather, it is completely certain about its central point,[a] i.e., the nullity of everything finite.

a. *Sache*

The person who simply doubts still has the hope that his doubt can be resolved, and that one or other of the determinate [views] between which he wavers back and forth will turn out to be a firm and genuine one. Scepticism proper, on the contrary, is complete despair about everything that the understanding holds to be firm, and the disposition that results is imperturbability and inward repose. This is the high ancient scepticism, as we find it presented specifically in Sextus Empiricus,[113] and as it was developed in the later Roman period as a complement to the dogmatic systems of the Stoics and the Epicureans. This ancient high scepticism must not be confused with the modern one that was mentioned earlier (§ 39), which partly preceded the Critical Philosophy and partly grew out of it. This consists simply in denying that anything true and certain can be said about the supersensible, and in designating, on the contrary, the sensible and what is present in immediate sense-experience as what we have to hold onto._ *the end of the philosophical road*

Even nowadays, of course, scepticism is often regarded as an irresistible foe of any positive knowledge, and hence of philosophy too, so far as the latter deals with positive cognition. In response to this it needs to be remarked that in fact it is only the finite and abstract thinking of the understanding that has anything to fear from scepticism, and that cannot resist it; philosophy, on the other hand, contains the sceptical as a moment within itself—specifically as the dialectical moment. But then philosophy does not stop at the merely negative result of the dialectic, as is the case with scepticism. The latter mistakes its result, insofar as it holds fast to it as mere, i.e., abstract, negation. When the dialectic has the negative as its result, then, precisely as a result, this negative is at the same time the positive, for it contains what it resulted from sublated within itself, and it cannot be without it. This, however, is the basic determination of the third form of the Logical, namely, the *speculative* or positively rational [moment].

§ 82

(γ) The *speculative* or *positively rational* apprehends the unity of the determinations in their opposition, the *affirmative* that is contained in their dissolution and in their transition.

> (1) The dialectic has a *positive* result, because it has a *determinate content*, or because its result is truly not *empty, abstract nothing*, but the negation of *certain determinations*, which are contained in the result precisely because it is not an *immediate nothing*, but a result. (2) Hence this rational [result], although it is something-thought and something-abstract, is at the same time *something-concrete*, because it is not *simple, formal* unity, but a *unity of distinct determinations*. For this reason philosophy does not deal with mere abstractions or formal thoughts at all, but only with concrete thoughts. (3) The mere *logic of the understanding* is contained in the speculative Logic and can easily be made out of the latter; nothing more is needed for this than the omission of the dialectical and the ra-

tional; in this way it becomes *what is usually called logic*, a *descriptive collection*[a] of determinations of thought put together in various ways, which in their finitude count for something infinite.

Addition. In respect of its *content*, what is rational is so far from being just the property of philosophy that we must rather say that it is there for all people, whatever level of culture and spiritual development they possess. That is the sense in which, from time immemorial, man has been called, quite correctly, a rational essence. The empirically universal way of knowing about what is rational is that of prejudgment and presupposition; and, as we explained earlier (§ 45), the general character of what is rational consists in being something unconditioned which therefore contains its determinacy within itself. In this sense, we know about the rational above all, because we know about God, and we know him as [the one] who is utterly self-determined. But also, the knowledge of a citizen about his country and its laws is a knowledge about what is rational, inasmuch as these things count for him as something unconditioned, and at the same time as a universal, to which he must subject his individual will; and in the same sense, even the knowing and willing of a child is already rational, when it knows its parents' will, and wills that.

To continue then, the *speculative* is in general nothing but the rational (and indeed the positively rational), inasmuch as it is something *thought*. The term "speculation" tends to be used in ordinary life in a very vague, and at the same time, secondary sense—as, for instance, when people talk about a matrimonial or commercial speculation. All that it is taken to mean here is that, on the one hand, what is immediately present must be transcended, and, on the other, that whatever the content of these speculations may be, although it is initially only something subjective, it ought not to remain so, but is to be realised or translated into objectivity.

The comment made earlier about the Idea holds for this ordinary linguistic usage in respect of "speculations," too. And this connects with the further remark that very often those who rank themselves among the more cultivated also speak of "speculation" in the express sense of something *merely* subjective. What they say is that a certain interpretation of natural or spiritual states of affairs or situations may certainly be quite right and proper, if taken in a merely "speculative" way, but that experience does not agree with it, and nothing of the sort is admissible in actuality. Against these views, what must be said is that, with respect to its true significance, the speculative is, neither provisionally nor in the end either, something merely subjective; instead, it expressly contains the very antitheses at which the understanding stops short (including therefore that of the subjective and objective, too), sublated within itself; and precisely for this reason it proves to be concrete and a totality. For this reason, too, a speculative content cannot be expressed in a one-sided proposition. If, for example, we say that "the Absolute is the unity of the subjective and the objective," that is certainly correct; but it is still one-sided, in that it expresses only the aspect of *unity* and puts the emphasis on that, whereas in fact, of course, the subjective and the objective are not only identical but also distinct.

a. *eine Historie*

It should also be mentioned here that the meaning of the speculative is to be understood as being the same as what used in earlier times to be called "mystical", especially with regard to the religious consciousness and its content. When we speak of the "mystical" nowadays, it is taken as a rule to be synonymous with what is mysterious and incomprehensible; and, depending on the ways their culture and mentality vary in other respects, some people treat the mysterious and in-comprehensible as what is authentic and genuine, whilst others regard it as belong-ing to the domain of superstition and deception. About this we must remark first that "the mystical" is certainly something mysterious, but only for the understand-ing, and then only because abstract identity is the principle of the understanding. But when it is regarded as synonymous with the speculative, the mystical is the concrete unity of just those determinations that count as true for the understanding only in their separation and opposition. So if those who recognise the mystical as what is genuine say that it is something utterly mysterious, and just leave it at that, they are only declaring that for them, too, thinking has only the significance of an abstract positing of identity, and that in order to attain the truth we must renounce thinking, or, as they frequently put it, that we must "take reason captive." As we have seen, however, the abstract thinking of the understanding is so far from being something firm and ultimate that it proves itself, on the contrary, to be a constant sublating of itself and an overturning into its opposite, whereas the rational as such is rational precisely because it contains both of the opposites as ideal moments within itself. Thus, everything rational can equally be called "mystical"; but this only amounts to saying that it transcends the understanding. It does not at all imply that what is so spoken of must be considered inaccessible to thinking and incomprehensible.

§ 83

The Logic falls into three parts:
  I. *The Doctrine of Being*
 II. *The Doctrine of Essence*
III. *The Doctrine of the Concept and [of the] Idea*
In other words [it is divided] into the doctrine of thought:
  I. In its *immediacy*—the doctrine of the *Concept in-itself*
 II. In its *reflection* and *mediation*—[the doctrine of] the *being-for-itself* and *shine [or semblance]* of the Concept
III. In its *being-returned-into-itself* and *its developed being-with-itself*—[the doctrine of] the Concept *in-* and *for-itself*

Addition. Like our whole explanation of thinking so far, the division of the Logic that has here been given must be regarded simply as an anticipation; and its justification or proof can only result from the completed treatment of thinking, since, in philosophy, "proving" amounts to exhibiting how the ob-ject makes itself what it is through and of itself.—The relationship in which the three main stages of thought or of the logical Idea that we have mentioned here stand to one another must be interpreted in the following general terms. Only the *Concept* is what is true, and, more precisely, it is the truth of *Being* and of *Essence*. So each of these, if they are clung to in their isolation, or by themselves, must be considered at the same time as untrue—*Being* because it is still only what is *immediate*, and *Essence* because it is still only what is *mediated*. At this point, we could at once raise the question why, if that is the case, we should begin with what is untrue and why we do not straightaway begin with what is true. The answer is that the truth must, precisely as such, *validate* itself and here, within logical thinking itself, validation consists in the Concept's showing itself to be what is mediated through and with itself, so that it shows itself to be at the same time the genuinely immediate. This same relationship of the three stages of the logical Idea is exhibited in a more real[a] and concrete shape in the fact that we achieve cognition of God, who is truth, in this his truth, i.e., as absolute spirit, only when we recognise that the world created by him—nature and finite spirit—is not true in its distinction from God.

---

a. *real* [not: *reell*]

FIRST SUBDIVISION OF THE
LOGIC
THE DOCTRINE OF BEING

§ 84

Being is the Concept only *in-itself*; its determinations [simply] *are;*[a] in their distinction they are *others* vis-à-vis each other, and their further determination (the form of the dialectical) is a *passing-over into another*. This process of further determination is both a *setting-forth*, and thus an unfolding, of the Concept that is *in-itself*, and at the same time the *going-into-itself* of being, its own deepening into itself. The explication of the Concept in the sphere of Being becomes the totality of being, just as the immediacy of being, or the form of being as such, is sublated by it.

§ 85

Being itself, as well as the following determinations (the logical determinations in general, not just those of Being), may be looked upon as definitions of the Absolute, as the *metaphysical definitions of God*; more precisely, however, it is always just the first simple determination of a sphere that can be so regarded and again the third, the one which is the return from difference[b] to simple self-relation. For to define God metaphysically means to express his nature in *thoughts* as such; but the Logic embraces all thoughts while they are still in the form of thoughts. The *second* determinations, on the other hand, which constitute a sphere in its *difference*, are the definition of the *finite*. But if the form of definitions were used, then this form would entail the hovering of a substrate of representation before the mind; for even *the Absolute*,[3] as what is supposed to express God in the sense and form of thought, remains in its relationship to the predicate (which is its determinate and actual expression in thought) only

a. *sind* seiende[1]
b. *Differenz*[2]

what is *meant* to be a thought,[a] a substrate that is not determined on its own account. Because the thought, the matter which is all that we are here concerned about, is contained only in the predicate, the propositional form, as well as the subject [of the proposition], is something completely superfluous (cf. § 31, and the chapter on judgment below [i.e., §§ 166–80]).

Addition. Each sphere of the logical Idea proves to be a totality of determinations and a presentation of the Absolute. In particular, this is the case with Being too, which contains within it the three stages of *quality*, *quantity*, and *measure*. Quality is, to begin with, the determinacy that is identical with being, in such a way that something ceases to be what it is if it loses its quality. *Quantity*, on the contrary, is the determinacy that is external to being, indifferent for it. For example, a house remains red whether it be bigger or smaller, and red remains red, whether it be brighter or darker. The third stage of Being, *measure*, is the unity of the first two, it is qualitative quantity. Everything has its measure; i.e., things are quantitatively determinate, and their being of this or that magnitude is indifferent for them; but at the same time, there is a limit to this indifference, the overstepping of which by a further increase or decrease means that the things cease to be what they were. From measure there follows then the advance to the second major sphere of the Idea, to *Essence*.

Precisely because they come first, the three forms of Being that have been mentioned here are also the poorest in content, i.e., the most abstract. Insofar as it also involves thinking, our immediate, sensible consciousness is mainly limited to the abstract determinations of quality and quantity. This sense-consciousness is usually considered to be the most concrete and therefore at the same time the richest; but this is the case only with regard to its material, whereas in respect of its thought-content, on the other hand, it is in fact the poorest and most abstract.

A
Quality

A. BEING

§ 86

Pure being makes the beginning, because it is pure thought as well as the undetermined, simple immediate, [and because] the first beginning cannot be anything mediated and further determined.

a. gemeiner *Gedanke*

All of the doubts and objections [*Erinnerungen*] that can be brought against beginning the science with abstract empty *being* are disposed of by the simple consciousness of what the nature of the beginning implies. Being can be determined as I = I, as *absolute Indifference* or *Identity*, and so on. Where there is the need to begin, either with something strictly *certain*, i.e., with the certainty of oneself, or with a definition or intuition of *what is absolutely true*, these and other similar forms can be looked upon as the ones that must come first. But since there is already *mediation* within each of these forms, they are not truly the first; [for] mediation consists in having already left a first behind, to go on to a second, and in a going forth from moments that are distinct. When I = I, or even intellectual intuition, is truly taken just as the first, then in this pure immediacy it is nothing else but *being*; just as, conversely, pure being, when it is no longer taken as this abstract being, but as being that contains mediation within itself, is pure thinking or intuiting.

If *being* is enunciated as a predicate of the Absolute, then we have as its first definition: "The Absolute is being". This is the definition that is (in thought) absolutely initial, the most abstract and the poorest. It is the definition given by the *Eleatics*, but at the same time it is the familiar [assertion] that *God* is *the essential sum of all realities*.ª That is to say, one has to abstract from the restrictedness which is [there] in every reality, so that God is only what is *real*ᵇ in all reality, the *Supremely Real*. Since "reality" already contains a reflection, this is expressed more immediately in what Jacobi says of Spinoza's God, that he is the "*principium* of being in all that is there."[4]

Addition 1. When thinking is to begin, we have nothing but thought in its pure lack of determination, for determination requires both one and another; but at the beginning we have as yet no other. That which lacks determination, as we have it here, is the immediate, not a mediated lack of determination, not the sublation of all determinacy, but the lack of determination in all its immediacy, what lacks determination prior to all determinacy, what lacks determinacy because it stands at the very beginning. But this is what we call "being". Being cannot be felt, it cannot be directly perceived nor can it be represented; instead, it is pure thought, and as such it constitutes the starting point. Essence lacks determination too, but, because it has already passed through mediation, it already contains determination as sublated within itself.

a. der Inbegriff aller Realitäten
b. *das* Reale

Addition 2. We find the various stages of the logical Idea in the history of philosophy in the shape of a succession of emerging philosophical systems, each of which has a particular definition of the Absolute as its foundation. Just as the unfolding of the logical Idea proves to be an advance from the abstract to the concrete, so the earliest systems in the history of philosophy are the most abstract and therefore at the same time the poorest. But the relationship of the earlier to the later philosophical systems is in general the same as the relationship of the earlier to the later stages of the logical Idea; that is to say, the earlier systems are contained sublated within the later ones. This is the true significance of the fact (which is so often misunderstood) that in the history of philosophy one philosophical system refutes another, or, more precisely, that an earlier philosophy is refuted by a later one.

When people talk about a philosophy's being refuted, they usually take this first in a merely abstract, negative sense—in other words, as meaning that the refuted philosophy is simply no longer valid at all, that it is set aside and done with. If this were the case, then the study of the history of philosophy would have to be considered an utterly mournful affair indeed, since it only shows how all the philosophical systems that have emerged in the course of time have met their refutations. But, although it must certainly be conceded that all philosophies have been refuted, it must also equally be affirmed that no philosophy has ever been refuted, nor can it be. This is the case in two ways. First, every philosophy worthy of the name always has the Idea as its content, and second, every philosophical system should be regarded as the presentation of a particular moment, or a particular stage, in the process of development of the Idea. So, the "refuting" of a philosophy means only that its restricting boundary has been overstepped and its determinate principle has been reduced to an ideal moment.

Consequently, so far as its essential content is concerned, the history of philosophy does not deal with the past, but with what is eternal and strictly present; it does not result in a gallery of aberrations of the human spirit, but must instead be compared with a pantheon of divine shapes. These divine shapes are the various stages of the Idea, as they emerge successively in their dialectical development. It must be left to the history of philosophy to show more precisely the extent to which the unfolding of its content coincides with the dialectical unfolding of the pure logical Idea on the one hand, and deviates from it on the other; but we must at least point out here that the starting point of the Logic is the same as the starting point of the history of philosophy in the proper sense of the word. This starting point is to be found in Eleatic philosophy, and, more precisely, in the philosophy of Parmenides, who apprehends the Absolute as being. For he says that, "Only being is, and nothing is not."[5] This must be taken as the proper starting point of philosophy, because philosophy as such is cognition by means of thinking, and here pure thinking was firmly adhered to for the first time and became ob-jective for itself.

Of course, humans have been thinkers from the first, for it is only by thinking that they distinguish themselves from the animals; but it has taken millennia for them to grasp thinking in its purity, and, at the same time, as what is wholly objective. The Eleatics are famous as daring thinkers; but this abstract admiration is often coupled with the remark that, all the same, these philosophers surely went too far, because they recognised only being as what is true, and denied truth to every other ob-ject of our consciousness. And, of course, it is quite correct that we must not stop at mere being; but it shows only lack of thought to treat the further content of our consciousness as discoverable somewhere "beside" and "outside" being, or as something that is just given "also." On the contrary, the true situation is that being as such is not firm and ultimate, but rather something that overturns dialectically into its opposite—which, taken in the same immediate way, is *nothing*. So, when all is said and done, being is the first pure thought; and whatever else may be made the starting point (I = I, absolute Indifference, or God himself)[6] is initially only something which is represented, rather than thought. With regard to its thought-content, it is quite simply being.

§ 87

But this pure being is the *pure abstraction*, and hence it is the *absolutely negative*, which when taken immediately, is *nothing*.[7]

> (1) From this the second definition of the Absolute followed, that it is *nothing*; in fact, this definition is implied when it is said that the thing-in-itself is that which is indeterminate, absolutely without form and therefore without content—or again when it is said that God *is just* the *supreme essence* and no more than that, for to call him that expresses precisely the same negativity; the nothing, which the *Buddhists*[8] make into the principle of everything (and into the ultimate end[a] and goal of everything too), is this same abstraction.—(2) When the antithesis is expressed in this immediacy, as *being* and *nothing*, then it seems too obvious that it is null and void, for people not to try to fix being and to preserve it against the passage [into nothing]. In this situation, we are bound, as we think it over, to start searching for a stable determination for being by which it would be distinguished from nothing. For example, being is taken as what persists through all variation as the infinitely determinable [prime] *matter*, and so on; or even without thinking it over at all, as any *single* existence whatever, anything readily available, be it sensible or spiritual. But none of these additional and more concrete determinations of this kind leave us with being as *pure being*, the way it is here in the beginning, in its immediacy. Only in this pure indeterminacy, and because of it, is being *nothing*—something *that cannot be said*; what distinguishes it from nothing is something merely *meant*.—All that really matters here is consciousness about these beginnings: that they are nothing but these empty abstractions, and that each of them is as

a. *letzten Endzweck*

empty as the other; the *drive* to find in being or in both [being and nothing] a stable meaning is this very *necessity*, which leads being and nothing further along and endows them with a true, i.e., concrete meaning. This progression is the logical exposition and course [of thought] that presents itself in what follows. The *thinking them over* that *finds* deeper determinations for them is the logical thinking by which these determinations produce themselves, not in a contingent but in a necessary way.

Every subsequent meaning that they acquire must therefore be regarded as only a *more articulate determination*[a] and a *truer definition* of the *Absolute*; hence, any such determination or definition is no longer an empty abstraction like being and nothing, but is, instead, something concrete within which both being and nothing are moments.—In its highest form of explicitation[b] nothing would be *freedom*. But this highest form is negativity insofar as it inwardly deepens itself to its highest intensity; and in this way it is itself affirmation—indeed absolute affirmation.[9]

Addition. Being and nothing are at first only *supposed* to be distinguished, i.e., the distinction between them is initially only *in-itself*, but not yet *posited*. Whenever we speak about a distinction we have in mind *two* items, each of which possesses a determination that the other does not have. But being is precisely what strictly lacks determination, and nothing is this same lack of determination also. So the distinction between these two [terms] is only meant to be such, a completely abstract distinction, one that is at the same time no distinction. In all other cases of distinguishing we are always dealing also with something common, which embraces the things that are distinguished. For example, if we speak of two diverse kinds, then being a kind is what is common to both. Similarly, we say that there are natural and spiritual essences. Here, being an essence is what they have in common. By contrast, in the case of being and nothing, distinction has no basis,[c] and, precisely because of this, it is no distinction, since neither determination has any basis.[d] Someone might want to say that being and nothing are still both thoughts, and so to be a thought is what is common to them both. But this would be overlooking the fact that being is not a particular, determinate thought, but is the still quite undetermined thought which, precisely for this reason, cannot be distinguished from nothing.

We certainly also represent being as absolute riches, and nothing, on the contrary, as absolute poverty. But, when we consider the entire world, and say simply that everything is, and nothing further, we leave out everything determinate, and,

a. *nähere Bestimmung*
b. *Die höchste Form des Nichts für sich*
c. *in seiner Bodenlosigkeit*
d. *dieselbe Bodenlosigkeit*

in consequence, have only absolute emptiness instead of absolute fullness. The same applies to the definition of *God* as mere being. Against it there stands, with equal justification, the definition of the Buddhists that God is nothing—from which it follows that man becomes God by annihilating himself.

§ 88

And similarly, but conversely, *nothing*, as this immediate [term] that is equal to itself, is *the same* as *being*. Hence, the truth of being and nothing alike is the *unity* of both of them; this unity is *becoming*.

> (1) In *representation*, or for the understanding, the proposition: *"Being and nothing is the same,"* appears to be such a paradoxical proposition that it may perhaps be taken as not seriously meant. And it really is one of the hardest propositions that thinking dares to formulate, for being and nothing are the antithesis in all its *immediacy*, i.e., without the prior *positing* of any determination in one of the two which would contain its relation to the other. But as was shown in the preceding paragraph, they *do contain* this determination; i.e., the one that is precisely the same in both. The deduction of their unity is to this extent entirely *analytic*; just as, quite generally, the whole course of philosophising, being methodical, i.e., *necessary*, is nothing else but the mere *positing* of what is already contained in a concept.—But correct as it is to affirm the unity of being and nothing, it is *equally* correct to say that *they are absolutely diverse too*—that the one is *not* what the other is. But because this distinction has here not yet determined itself, precisely because being and nothing are still the immediate—it is, as belonging to them, *what cannot be said*, what is merely *meant*.
>
> (2) No great expense of wit is needed to ridicule the proposition that being and nothing are the same, or rather to produce absurdities which are falsely asserted to be consequences and applications of this proposition; e.g., that, on that view, it is all the same whether my house, my fortune, the air to breathe, this city, the sun, the law, the spirit, God, *are* or *are not*. In examples of this kind, it is partly a matter of *particular purposes*, the *utility* that something has for *me*, being sneaked in. One then asks whether it matters *to me* that the useful thing is or that it is not. But philosophy is in fact the very discipline that aims at liberating man from an infinite crowd of finite purposes and intentions and at making him indifferent with regard to them, so that it is all the same to him whether such matters are the case or not. But wherever and as

soon as one speaks about a *content*, a connection is already posited with *other* existences, purposes, etc., that are *presupposed* as valid, and whether the being or nonbeing *of a determinate content* is *the same* or *not* has now become dependent on *these presuppositions*. A distinction that is *full of content* has been sneaked into the empty distinction of being and nothing.—In part, however, it is purposes that are in themselves essential, absolute existences and Ideas, that are just posited under the determination of *being* or nonbeing. Concrete ob-jects of this kind are something much more than what only *is* or *is not*. Poor abstractions, like being and nothing—which, precisely because they are only the determinations of the begin-ning, are the poorest of all—are quite inadequate to the nature of these ob-jects; genuine content has already left these abstractions themselves and their antithesis far behind.—Whenever something concrete is sneaked into being and nothing, it is just business as usual for the unthinking [mind]:[a] something else altogether ap-pears before it and it speaks about that as if it were what is at issue, whereas at the moment only abstract being and nothing are at issue.

(3) It is easy to say that we do not *comprehend* the unity of being and nothing. But the concept of both has been indicated in the preceding paragraphs, and it is nothing more than what has been indicated; to comprehend their unity means no more than to grasp this. But what is understood by "comprehension" is often some-thing more than the concept in the proper sense; what is desired is a more diversified, a richer consciousness, a notion such that this sort of "concept" can be presented as a concrete case of it, with which thinking in its ordinary practice would be more familiar. Insofar as the inability to comprehend only expresses the fact that one is not used to holding onto abstract thoughts without any sensible admixture or to the grasping of speculative propositions, all we can say is that philosophical knowing is indeed quite diverse in kind from the knowing that we are used to in everyday life, just as it is diverse from what prevails in the other sciences too. But if noncomprehension only means that one cannot *represent* the unity of being and nothing, this is really so far from being the case, that on the contrary everyone has an infinite supply of notions of this unity; saying that one has none can only mean that one does not [re]cognise the present concept in any of those notions, and one

a. *die Gedankenlosigkeit*

does not know them to be examples of it. The readiest example of it is *becoming*. Everyone has a notion of becoming and will also admit moreover that it is *One* notion; and further that, if it is analysed, the determination of *being*, but also that of *nothing*, the stark Other of being, is found to be contained in it; further, that these two determinations are undivided in this *One* notion; hence that becoming is the unity of being and nothing.—Another example that is equally ready to hand is the *beginning*; the matter [itself] *is not yet* in its beginning, but the beginning is not merely its *nothing*: on the contrary, its *being* is already there, too. The beginning itself is also becoming, but it expresses already the reference to the further progression.—In conformity with the most usual procedure of the sciences, one could begin the Logic with the notion of "beginning" thought purely, i.e., with the notion of beginning as beginning, and one could analyse this notion; and then it would perhaps be more readily conceded, as a result of the analysis, that being and nothing show themselves to be undivided within a unity.[a]

(4) It remains to be noted, however, that the expression: "Being and nothing is *the same*," or "*the unity* of being and nothing"—like all other *unities* of this kind (the unity of subject and object, etc.)— can fairly be objected to, because it is misleading and incorrect insofar as it makes the *unity* stand out; and although diversity is contained in it (because it is, for instance, being and nothing whose unity is posited), this diversity is not expressed and recognised along with the unity. So we seem only to have abstracted quite improperly from this diversity, and to have given no thought to it. The fact is that no speculative determination can be expressed correctly in the form of such a proposition; what has to be grasped is the unity *in* the diversity that is both *given* and *posited* at the same time. As their unity, *becoming* is the true expression of the result of being and nothing; it is not just the *unity* of being and nothing, but it is inward *unrest*—a unity which in its self-relation is not simply motionless, but which, in virtue of the diversity of being and nothing which it contains, is inwardly turned against itself.—*Being-there*, on the contrary, is this *unity* or becoming in this form of unity; that is why it is *one-sided* and *finite*. It is, as if the antithesis had disappeared; it is contained in the unity, but only *in-itself*, not as *posited* in the unity.

a. *als in Einem ungetrennt*

(5) To the proposition that being is the passing into nothing and that nothing is the passing into being—to the proposition of *becoming*, is opposed the proposition: *"From nothing, nothing comes,"* "Something only comes from something," the proposition of the eternity of matter, or of pantheism. The Ancients[10] made the simple reflection that the proposition: "Something comes from something," or "From nothing, nothing comes," does indeed sublate becoming; for that from which there is becoming and that which comes to be are one and the same; all we have here is the proposition of the abstract identity of the understanding. But it must strike one as amazing to see the propositions: "From nothing, nothing comes," or "Something comes only from something," advanced quite naïvely, without any consciousness that they are the foundation of pantheism; and equally without any awareness that the Ancients have already dealt with these propositions exhaustively.

Addition. Becoming is the first concrete thought and hence the first concept, whereas being and nothing, in contrast, are empty abstractions. If we speak of the concept of being, this can only consist in becoming, for as being it is the empty nothing, but as the latter it is empty being. So, in being we have nothing, and in nothing being; but this being which abides with itself in nothing is becoming. The unity of becoming cannot leave out the distinction, for without that we would return once more to abstract being. Becoming is simply the positedness of what being is in its truth.

We often hear it asserted that thinking is opposed to being. Regarding such an assertion the first thing to ask is what is understood here by "being". If we take "being" in the way that reflection determines it, we can only assert of it that it is what is thoroughly identical and affirmative; and if we then consider "thinking", it cannot escape us that thinking is, at least, in like manner, what is thoroughly self-identical. So the same determination accrues to both "being" and "thinking". But this identity of being and thinking is not to be taken concretely; it must not be taken as saying that a stone, insofar as it is, is the same as a human thinker. Something concrete is always quite different from the abstract determination as such. But, in the case of being, we are not speaking of anything concrete, for being is precisely just what is wholly abstract. In consequence, the question of the being of God, i.e., [of the being of] what is infinitely concrete within itself,[11] is also of very little interest.

As the first concrete determination of thought, becoming is also the first genuine one. In the history of philosophy it is the system of Heraclitus that corresponds to this stage of the logical Idea. When Heraclitus says, "Everything flows" (*panta hrei*), then it is *becoming* that is thereby pronounced to be the basic determination of everything that is there; whereas on the contrary, as we said earlier, the Eleatics took being, rigid being without process, to be what is uniquely true. In connection with the principle of the Eleatics Heraclitus[12] says further, "Being is no more than not-being" (*ouden mallon to on tou me ontos esti*); what this expresses is precisely the negativity of abstract being, and the identity, posited in becoming, between it and nothing, which, in its abstraction, is equally unstable.—We have here, too, an example of the genuine refutation of one philosophical system by another. The refutation consists precisely in the fact that the principle of the refuted philosophy is exhibited in its dialectic and reduced to an ideal moment of a higher concrete form of the Idea.

But now, furthermore, even becoming is, by itself, still a very poor determination; and it must inwardly deepen itself a lot more, and fill itself out.[13] An inward deepening of becoming is what we have, for example, in *life*. This is a becoming, but its concept is not exhausted by that. We find becoming in a still higher form in *spirit*. This, too, is a becoming, but one that is more intensive, richer than the merely logical becoming. The moments whose unity is Spirit are not those mere abstractions, being and nothing, but the system of the logical Idea and of Nature.

B. BEING-THERE

§ 89

In becoming, being, as one with nothing, and nothing as one with being, are only vanishing [terms]; because of its contradiction becoming collapses inwardly, into the unity within which both are sublated; in this way its *result* is *being-there*.

> In this first example we have to recall once and for all what was indicated in § 82 and the Remark there: the only way that a progression and a development in knowing can be grounded is to hold firmly onto the results in their truth.—There is *nothing at all* anywhere, in which contradiction—i.e., opposed determinations—cannot and should not be exhibited. The abstracting activity of the understanding is a clinging on to One determinacy by force, an effort to obscure and to remove the consciousness of the other one that is contained in it.—But if the contradiction is exhibited and recognised in any ob-ject or concept whatever, then the conclusion that is usually drawn is: "*Therefore* this ob-ject is *nothing*." Thus Zeno first showed that movement contradicts itself, and that it therefore *is* not;[14] likewise the Ancients recognised *coming to be* and *passing away*, the two kinds of becoming, as untrue determinations, by saying that the *One*, i.e., the Absolute, does not come into being or pass away. This dialectic does not go beyond the negative

side of the result, and abstracts from what is effectively given at the same time: a determinate result, which here is not a pure *nothing* but a *nothing* which includes *being* within itself, and equally a being, which includes nothing. It follows that (1) being-there is the unity of being and nothing, in which the immediacy of these determinations, and therewith their contradiction, has disappeared in their relation—a unity in which they are only *moments*. (2) Because the result is the sublated contradiction, it is in the form of *simple* unity with itself or even as a *being*, but [as] a being with its negation or determinacy; it is becoming posited in the *form* of *one* of its moments, of being.

Addition. Even our representation of it implies that, if there is a becoming, something comes forth and that becoming therefore has a result. But at this point the question arises of why becoming does not remain mere becoming but has a result. The answer to this question follows from what becoming has previously shown itself to be. That is to say, becoming contains being and nothing within itself and it does this in such a way that they simply overturn into one another and reciprocally sublate one another as well as themselves. In that way becoming proves itself to be what is thoroughly restless, but unable to maintain itself in this abstract restlessness; for, insofar as being and nothing vanish in becoming—and just this is its concept—becoming is thereby itself something that vanishes, like a fire, that dies out within itself by consuming its material. But the result of this process is not empty nothing; instead it is being that is identical with negation, which we call *being-there*—and its significance proves to be, first of all, this: that it is *what has become*.[a]

§ 90

(α) *Being-there* is being with a *determinacy*, that is [given] as immediate determinacy or as a determinacy that [simply] is: *quality*. As reflected *into itself* in this its determinacy, being-there is *that which is there*,[b] *something*.— The categories that develop in respect of being-there only need to be indicated in a summary way.

Addition. Quality is, in general, the determinacy that is immediate, identical with being, as distinct from *quantity* (which will be considered next). Of course, quantity is likewise [a] determinacy of being, though it is a determinacy that is not immediately identical with being, but rather one that is indifferent with respect to being and external to it.—Something is what it is by virtue of its quality, and if it loses its quality it ceases to be what it is. Furthermore, quality is essentially only a category of the finite—and for that reason it has its proper place only in nature and not in

a. geworden *zu sein*
b. Daseiendes

the spiritual world. Thus, for instance, the so-called simple matters,[a] oxygen, nitrogen, etc., must be considered as existent qualities within nature.

Within the sphere of spirit, on the other hand, quality occurs only in a secondary way, and never so that it exhausts the content of any determinate shape of spirit. For example, if we consider subjective spirit, which forms the subject matter of psychology, we can certainly say that the logical significance of what people call "character" is that of quality. But this is not to be understood as if character were a determinacy that pervades the soul and is immediately identical with it, as is the case in nature with the simple matters referred to above. Nevertheless, quality shows itself in a more determinate way in spirit, too, where the latter is found in an unfree, morbid state. This is the case in states of passion, and especially where passion has risen to the height of derangement. We can properly say of a deranged person whose consciousness is completely pervaded by jealousy, fear, etc., that his consciousness is determined in the manner of quality.

§ 91

As determinacy that [simply] *is* vis-à-vis the *negation* which it contains but which is distinct from it, quality is *reality*. The negation is no longer abstract nothing, but as a being-there and as *something*, it is only a form of the something: it is as *otherness*. Since this otherness is quality's own determination, though at first distinct from it, quality *is being-for-another*—an expanse of being-there, of something. The *being* of quality as such, vis-à-vis this relation to another, is *being-in-itself*.[b]

Addition. The basis of all determinacy is negation (*omnis determinatio est negatio*, as Spinoza says).[15] Unthinking opinion considers determinate things to be merely positive and holds them fast in the form of being. Mere being is not the end of the matter, however, for, as we saw earlier, that is something utterly empty and at the same time unstable. Still, this confusion of being-there (as determinate being) with abstract being implies the correct insight that the moment of negation is certainly already contained in being-there, but only shrouded as it were; it emerges freely and comes into its own only in being-for-itself.

If we now go on to consider being-there as determinacy that *is*, we have the same as what is generally understood by "reality". We speak, for instance, of the reality of a plan or of an intention, and we understand by this that such things are no longer merely something inner and subjective, but have moved out into being-there. In the same sense the body can be called the reality of the soul, and this [or that] law[c] can be called the reality of freedom; or, quite universally, the world is the reality of the divine Concept. But, in addition, we often speak of "reality" in still

a. *Stoffe*
b. *An-sich-sein*
c. *dies Recht*[16]

another sense, understanding by it that something behaves in accordance with its essential determination or its concept. For example, someone may say: "This is a real occupation," or: "This is a real person." Here it is not a question of what is immediately and externally there, but rather of the correspondence between what is there and its concept. Interpreted in this way, however, reality is not distinct from ideality, which we shall first become acquainted with as being-for-itself.

§ 92

(β) The being that is kept firmly distinct from the determinacy, *being-in-itself*, would be only the empty abstraction of being. In being-there the determinacy is one with being and is at the same time posited as negation; this determinacy is *limit, restriction*.[17] Thus, otherness is not something-indifferent outside it, but its own moment. In virtue of its quality, *something* is first *finite* and secondly *alterable*, so that the finitude and alterability belong to its being.

Addition. In being-there negation is still immediately identical with being, and this negation is what we call "limit". Something only is what it is *within* its limit and *by virtue* of its limit. We cannot regard limit, therefore, as merely external to being-there; on the contrary, limit totally permeates everything that is there. The interpretation of limit as a merely external determination of being-there is based on a confusion of quantitative with qualitative limit. Here we are dealing first with qualitative limit. When we are considering a piece of land three acres in area, for example, that is its quantitative limit. But, in addition, this piece of land is also a meadow and not a wood or a pond, and this is its qualitative limit.—Humans who want to be actual must be *there*, and to this end they must limit themselves. Those who are too squeamish toward the finite achieve nothing real at all, but remain in the realm of the abstract and peter out.

Let us now consider more closely what a limit implies. We find that it contains a contradiction within itself, and so proves itself to be dialectical. That is to say, limit constitutes the reality of being-there, and, on the other hand, it is the negation of it. But, furthermore, as the negation of the something, limit is not an abstract nothing in general, but a nothing that *is*, or what we call an "other". In something we at once hit upon the other, and we know that there is not only something, but also something else. But the other is not such that we just happen upon it; it is not as if something could be thought without that other; rather, something is *in* itself the other of itself, and the limit of a something becomes objective to it in the other. When we ask what the distinction between the something and the other is, then it turns out that both are the same; and this identity is expressed in Latin by calling the pair *aliud-aliud*. The other, as opposed to the something, is itself a something and accordingly we call it "*something* else".[18] On the other hand, the first something opposed to an other that is similarly determined as a something is itself something else. When we say "something else" we think initially that something taken by itself is only something, and the determination of being something else only accrues to it in virtue of a merely external point of view. Thus we suppose, for instance, that the moon, which is something else than the sun, could quite well exist if the sun did not. But, in fact, the moon (as something) has its other in itself, and this constitutes its finitude.

Plato says: "God made the world from the nature of the One and the Other (*tou heterou*); he brought them together and formed a Third out of them, which is of the nature of the One and the Other."[19]—This expresses the general nature of the finite which, being something, does not stand over against the other indifferently, but in such a way that it is in-itself the other of itself and hence it alters. Alteration exhibits the inner contradiction with which being-there is burdened from the start, and which drives it beyond itself. In representation, being-there appears initially to be simply positive and to be quietly persisting within its limit as well; but, of course, we also know that everything finite (and being-there is finite) is subject to alteration. But this alterability of being-there appears in our representation as a mere possibility, whose realisation is not grounded within being-there itself. In fact, however, self-alteration is involved in the concept of being-there, and is only the manifestation of what being-there is in-itself. The living die, and they do so simply because, insofar as they live, they bear the germ of death within themselves.

§ 93

Something becomes an other, but the other is itself a something, so it likewise becomes an other, and so on *ad infinitum*.

§ 94

This *infinity* is *spurious or negative* infinity,[20] since it is nothing but the negation of the finite, but the finite arises again in the same way, so that it is no more sublated than not. In other words, this infinity expresses only the requirement that the finite *ought* to be sublated. This progress ad infinitum does not go beyond the expression of the contradiction, which the finite contains, [i.e.,] that it is just as much *something* as its *other*, and [this progress] is the perpetual continuation of the alternation between these determinations, each bringing in the other one.

Addition. If we let something and other, the moments of being-there, fall asunder, the result is that something becomes an other, and this other is itself a something, which, as such, then alters itself in the same way, and so on without end. Reflection takes itself to have arrived here at something very elevated, indeed the most elevated [truth] of all. But this infinite progression is not the genuine Infinite, which consists rather in remaining at home with itself in its other, or (when it is expressed as a process) in coming to itself in its other. It is of great importance to grasp the concept of true Infinity in an adequate way, and not just to stop at the spurious infinity of the infinite progress. When the infinity of space and time are spoken of, it is first the infinite progression that we usually stop at. So we say, for example, "*this* time," "*now*," and then we keep continually going beyond this limit, backward and forward. It is the same with space, about whose infinity astronomers with a taste for edification have preached many empty sermons.

Of course, it is also usually maintained that thinking must surrender as soon as it begins to deal with this infinity. Well, one thing is certainly correct, and that is that we must ultimately abandon the attempt to pursue this consideration further and further; but we do so not because of the sublimity, but rather because of the tedium of this occupation. It is tedious to go on and on in the consideration of this infinite progression because the same thing is continually repeated. A limit is set, it is exceeded, then there is another limit, and so on without end. So we have nothing here but a superficial alternation, which stays forever within the sphere of the finite. If we suppose that we can liberate ourselves from the finite by stepping out into that infinitude, this is in fact only a liberation through flight. And the person who flees is not yet free, for in fleeing, he is still determined by the very thing from which he is fleeing. So if people then add that the infinite cannot be attained, what they say is quite correct, but only because the determination of being something abstractly negative is being lodged in the infinite. Philosophy does not waste time with such empty and otherworldly stuff. What philosophy has to do with is always something concrete and strictly present.

The task of philosophy has, indeed, also been formulated in such a way that it has to answer the question of how the Infinite comes to the resolve to go out of itself. This question, which presupposes a rigid antithesis between infinite and finite, can only be answered by saying that the antithesis is something untrue, and that the Infinite is in fact eternally gone from itself, and also eternally not gone from itself.—Besides, if we say that the infinite is the "*non*finite," then by saying that we have already expressed what is true: for, since the finite itself is the first negative, the nonfinite is the negative of the negation, the negation that is identical with itself, so that it is at the same time true affirmation.

The infinity of reflection discussed here is merely the attempt to attain true Infinity; it is a wretched intermediate thing. Generally speaking, this is the philosophical standpoint that has recently prevailed in Germany. In this view, the finite only *ought* to be sublated; and the infinite ought not to be merely something negative but something positive as well. This "ought" always implies impotence: the fact that something is recognised as justified, and yet can never make itself prevail. With regard to the ethical domain, the Kantian and the Fichtean philosophies got stuck at this standpoint of the "ought." Perpetual approximation to the law of reason is the utmost that can be attained on this path; and even the immortality of the soul has been based on this postulate.

§ 95

(γ) What is indeed given is that something becomes another, and the other becomes another quite generally. In its relationship to an other, something is already an other itself vis-à-vis the latter; and therefore, since what it passes into is entirely the same as what passes into it—neither having any further determination than this identical one of being an *other*—in its passing into another, something only comes together *with itself*; and this relation to itself in the passing and in the other is *genuine Infinity*.[21] Or, if we look at it negatively: what is changed is the *other*, it becomes the *other* of the *other*. In this way being is reestablished, but as negation of the negation. It is now *being-for-itself*.

> Dualism, which makes the opposition of finite and infinite insuperable, fails to make the simple observation that in this way the infinite itself is also just *one of the two*, [and] that it is therefore reduced to one *particular*, in addition to which the finite is the other one. Such an infinite, which is just one particular, *beside* the finite, so that it has precisely its restriction, its limit, in the latter, is *not* what it ought to be. It is not the Infinite, but is only *finite*. In this relationship, where one is situated *here*, and the other over *there*, the finite *in this world* and the infinite *in the other world*, an *equal dignity* of *subsistence* and independence is attributed to the finite and to the infinite; the being of the finite is made into an absolute being; in this Dualism it stands solidly on its own feet. If it were touched by the infinite, so to speak, it would be annihilated; but it is supposed to be not capable of being touched by the infinite; there is supposed to be an abyss, an impassable gulf, between the two; the infinite has to *remain* absolutely on the other side and the finite on this side. This assertion of the solid persistence of the finite vis-à-vis the infinite supposes itself to be beyond all metaphysics, but it stands simply and solely on the ground of the most vulgar metaphysics of the understanding. What happens at this point is just what the infinite progress expresses; it is first admitted that the finite *is not in and for itself*, that it has *no* title to independent actuality, or to *absolute* being, but that it is only something that passes; then in the *next* moment, this is forgotten, and the finite is represented as merely facing the infinite, radically separate from it and rescued from annihilation, [i.e., represented] as independent, and persisting on its own.— Although thinking means in this way to elevate itself to the Infinite, what happens to it is just the opposite—it arrives at an infinite which is only a finite, and the finite which it had left behind is, on the contrary, just what it always maintains and makes into an absolute.
>
> After the above consideration of the nullity of the antithesis set up by the understanding between the finite and the infinite (with which it would be useful to compare Plato's *Philebus* [23–38]), one

can easily fall back upon the expression that the finite and the infinite are therefore *One*, that the True, or the genuine Infinity, is determined and expressed as the *unity* of the infinite and the finite. And this expression does indeed contain something correct, but it is equally misleading and false, just as we said earlier in the case of the *unity* of being and nothing. It leads, moreover, to the justified complaint about the Infinite having been made finite, about a finite infinite. For in the above expression ("The Infinite is the *unity* of the infinite and the finite"), the finite appears to be left as it was; it is not explicitly expressed as *sublated*.—Or, if we were to reflect upon this fact that the finite, when posited as one with the infinite, could surely not remain what it was outside of this unity, and would at the every least be somewhat affected in its determination (just as an alkali when combined with an acid loses some of its properties), then the same would happen to the infinite, which as the negative would, for its part, also be blunted upon the other. And this is, indeed, what does happen to the abstract, one-sided infinite of the understanding. But the genuine Infinite does not merely behave like the one-sided acid; on the contrary it preserves itself; the negation of the negation is not a neutralisation; the Infinite is the affirmative, and it is only the finite which is sublated.

In being-for-itself the determination of *ideality* has entered. *Being-there*, taken at first only according to its being or its affirmation, has *reality* (§ 91); and hence finitude, too, is under the determination of reality at first. But the truth of the finite is rather its *ideality*. In the same way the infinite of the understanding, which is put *beside* the finite, is itself also only one of two finites, something-untrue, something-ideal. This ideality of the finite is the most important proposition of philosophy, and for that reason every genuine philosophy is *Idealism*.[22] Everything depends on not mistaking for the Infinite that which is at once reduced in its determination to what is particular and finite.—That is why we have here drawn attention to this distinction at some length; the basic concept of philosophy, the genuine Infinite, depends on it. This distinction is established by the reflections contained in the paragraph. They may seem to be unimportant, because they are quite simple, but they are irrefutable.

C. BEING-FOR-ITSELF

§ 96

(α) As relation to itself, being-for-itself is *immediacy*, and as relation of the negative to itself it is what-is-for-itself, the *One*—that which lacks inward distinction, thereby *excluding* the *Other* from itself.

Addition. Being-for-itself is quality completed, and as such it contains being and being-there within itself as its ideal moments. As *being*, being-for-itself is simple self-relation, and as *being-there* it is determined; but this determinacy is no longer the finite determinacy of the something in its distinction from the other, but the infinite determinacy that contains distinction within it as sublated.

The most familiar example of being-for-itself is the "I." We know ourselves to be beings who are there, first of all distinct from other such beings, and related to them. But secondly, we also know that this expanse of being-there is, so to speak, focused into the simple form of being-for-itself. When we say "I," that is the expression of the infinite self-relation that is at the same time negative. It may be said that man distinguishes himself from the animals, and so from nature generally, because he knows himself as "I"; what this says, at the same time, is that natural things never attain to free being-for-oneself, but, being restricted to being-there, are always just being-for-another.

But again, being-for-itself has to be interpreted generally as *ideality*,[23] just as, in contrast, being-there was earlier designated as *reality*. *Reality* and *ideality* are frequently considered as a pair of determinations that confront one another with equal independence, and therefore people say that apart from reality, there is "also" an ideality. But ideality is not something that is given outside of and apart from reality. On the contrary, the concept of ideality expressly consists in its being the *truth* of reality, or in other words, reality posited as what it is in-itself proves itself to be ideality. So we must not believe that we have given to ideality all the honour that is due to it, if we simply allow that reality is not all, but that we have to recognise an ideality outside it as well. An ideality of this kind, set beside or even above reality, would in fact be only an empty name. Ideality has a content only because it is the ideality of something: and this "something" is not merely an indeterminate this or that—on the contrary, it is being-there characterised as "reality"—to which, when it is maintained on its own, no truth pertains.

The distinction between nature and spirit has been interpreted quite correctly as meaning that we must trace nature back to "reality" as its basic determination, and spirit to "ideality." But nature is not just something fixed and complete on its own account, which could therefore subsist even without spirit; rather, it is only in spirit that nature attains to its goal and its truth. Similarly, spirit, for its part, is not just an abstract world beyond nature; on the contrary, it only genuinely *is*, and proves to be spirit, insofar as it contains nature sublated within itself.

At this point we should remember the double meaning of the German expression *"aufheben"*. On the one hand, we understand it to mean "clear away" or "cancel", and in that sense we say that a law or regulation is cancelled (*aufgehoben*). But the word also means "to preserve", and we say in this sense that something is well taken care of (*wohl aufgehoben*). This ambiguity in linguistic usage, through which the same word has a negative and a positive meaning, cannot be regarded as an accident nor yet as a reason to reproach language as if it were a source of confusion. We ought rather to recognise here the speculative spirit of our language, which transcends the "either-or" of mere understanding.

§ 97

(β) The relation of the negative to itself is *negative* relation, and therefore distinguishing of the One from itself, the *repulsion* of the One, i.e., the positing of *many Ones*. In keeping with the *immediacy* of what-is-for-itself, these many [simply] *are*,[a] and as a result the repulsion of the ones that [simply] are becomes their repulsion *against each other* as given, or their reciprocal *exclusion*.

Addition. When we speak of the One, the *many*[b] usually come to mind at the same time. So the question arises here as to where the many come from. Within representational thinking there is no answer to this question, because the many is there regarded as immediately present, and the One counts only as one among the many.[c] But in accordance with its concept, the One forms the presupposition of the many, and it lies in the thought of the One to posit itself as what is many. In other words, the One which is for-itself is under that aspect not something that lacks relation, like being; instead it is relation, just as being-there is. But now it is not related as something to something else; being the unity of the something and the other, it is relation to itself instead, and, of course, this relation is a negative one. In consequence, the One proves to be what is strictly incompatible with itself, it expels itself out of itself, and what it posits itself as is what is *many*.[d] We can designate this side of the process of being-for-itself by the figurative expression "repulsion". The term "repulsion" is primarily used with reference to matter; and what is understood by it is precisely that matter, as a many,[e] behaves, in each of these many ones, as exclusive of all the others. Besides, we must not interpret this process of repulsion to mean that One[f] is *what repels* while the many[g] are *what is repelled*; instead, as we said earlier, it is the One that is just what excludes itself from itself and posits

a. *sind diese Viele Seiende*
b. *die Vielen*
c. *das Viele*
d. *das Viele*
e. *ein Vieles*
f. *Eins*
g. *die Vielen*

itself as what is many;[a] each of the many, however, is itself One, and because it behaves as such, this all-round repulsion turns over forthwith into its opposite—*attraction*.

§ 98

But the *many* are each one what the other is, each of them is one or also one of the many; they are therefore one and the same. Or, when the repulsion is considered in itself then, as the negative *behaviour* of the many ones against each other, it is just as essentially their *relation* to each other; and since those to which the One relates itself in its repelling are ones, in relating to them it relates itself to itself. Thus, repulsion is just as essentially *attraction*; and the excluding One or being-for-itself sublates itself. Qualitative determinacy, which in the One has reached its determinateness-in-and-for-itself, has thus passed over into determinacy *as sublated*, i.e., into being as *quantity*.

The *atomistic* philosophy is the standpoint from which the Absolute determines itself as being-for-itself, as One, and as many Ones. The repulsion which shows itself in the concept of the One was assumed to be its fundamental force; it is not attraction, however, but *chance*, i.e., what is without thought, that is supposed to bring them together. Since the One is fixed as One, its coming together with others does, indeed, have to be considered as something quite external.—The *void*, which is assumed to be the other principle [added] to the atoms, is repulsion itself, represented as the nothingness *that is* between the atoms.[24] Modern Atomism— and physics still maintains this principle—has abandoned the atoms, in that it just holds onto small parts or molecules; by doing that it has come closer to sensible representation, but has abandoned the determination by thought.—And since a force of attraction is put beside the force of repulsion, the antithesis has indeed been made *complete*, and the discovery of this so-called force of nature has occasioned much pride. But the relation of both forces with one another, which constitutes what is concrete and genuine in them, needs to be rescued from the muddy confusion in which it is left, even in Kant's *Metaphysical Foundations of Natural Science*.[25]—In modern times, the atomistic view has become even more important in the *political* [realm] than in the physical [one]. According to this view, the will of the *single* [individuals] as such is

a. *das Viele*

the principle of the State; what produces the attraction is the particularity[a] of needs [and] inclinations; and the universal, the State
itself, is the external relationship of a contract.

Addition 1. The philosophy of Atomism forms an essential stage in the historical
development of the Idea, and the overall principle of this philosophy is being-for-
itself in the shape of what is many.[b] Since Atomism is still held in high esteem
nowadays among those natural scientists who do not want anything to do with
metaphysics, it should be remembered in this connection that we do not escape
metaphysics (or, more precisely, the tracing back of nature to thoughts) by
throwing ourselves into the arms of Atomism, because, of course, the atom is itself
a thought, and so the interpretation of matter as consisting of atoms is a metaphysical one.

It is true that Newton expressly warned physics to beware of metaphysics;[26] but,
to his honour, let it be said that he did not conduct himself in accordance with this
warning at all. Only the animals are true blue physicists by this standard, since
they do not think; whereas humans, in contrast, are thinking beings, and born
metaphysicians. All that matters here is whether the metaphysics that is employed
is of the right kind; and specifically whether, instead of the concrete logical Idea,
we hold on to one-sided thought-determinations fixed by the understanding, so
that they form the basis both of our theoretical and of our practical action. This is
the reproach that strikes down the philosophy of Atomism.

Like many thinkers nowadays, the ancient atomists regarded everything as a
many; and it was supposed to be chance that brings the atoms together, as they
float about in the void. But the relation of the many to one another is not a merely
accidental one at all; instead their relation is grounded in the many themselves (as
we said before). It is Kant who deserves the credit for having perfected the theory[c]
of matter by considering it as the unity of repulsion and attraction. This involves
the correct insight that attraction should certainly be recognised as the other of the
two moments in the concept of being-for-itself, and hence attraction belongs to
matter just as essentially as repulsion. But Kant's so-called dynamic construction of
matter suffers from the defect that repulsion and attraction are postulated as present without further ado, rather than being deduced. The "how" and the "why" of
this merely asserted unity would have followed logically from a proper deduction.
Besides, Kant expressly insisted that we must not regard matter as present on its
own account, and only fitted out afterwards ("on the side" as it were) with the two
forces of repulsion and attraction here referred to; on the contrary, matter consists
in nothing else but their unity.

German physicists were satisfied with this pure dynamics for a time, but in more
recent times the majority of them have found that it suited them better to return
once more to the standpoint of Atomism; and, in spite of the warning of their
colleague, the late lamented Kästner,[27] they regard matter as then consisting of
infinitely small particles, called atoms. They suppose these atoms to be set in

a. *die Partikularität*

b. *des Vielen*

c. *Auffassung*

relation with each other through the play of the forces (attractive, repulsive, or whatever) that attach to them. This is a "metaphysics," too; and there is certainly a sufficient ground to beware of it, because there is so little thought in it.

Addition 2. The passage from quality to quantity indicated in the preceding paragraph is not found in our ordinary consciousness. In the ordinary way, quality and quantity count as a pair of determinations standing independently side by side; and we say, therefore, that things are not only qualitatively, but "also" quantitatively, determined. We make no further inquiry as to where these determinations come from, or what relationship they have to one another. We have seen, however, that quantity is nothing but sublated quality, and it is through the dialectic of quality considered here that this sublation comes about.

Initially we had *being*, and its truth turned out to be becoming; this formed the passage to being-there, whose truth we saw to be alteration. But alteration showed itself in its result to be being-for-itself, that is exempt from relation to another and passage into another. And finally, being-for-itself (in the two sides of its process, repulsion and attraction) has proved itself to be the sublating of itself, and hence of quality altogether, in the totality of its moments. This sublated quality, however, is neither an abstract nothing nor the similarly abstract being (lacking all determination), but only a being that is indifferent with regard to determinacy; and this is the shape of being that occurs, even in our ordinary representation, as *quantity*. Accordingly, we consider things first from the point of view of their quality—and this means for us the determinacy that is identical with their being. When we move on to the consideration of quantity, this gives us at once the representation of an indifferent, external determinacy, such that a thing still remains what it is, even when its quantity alters and it becomes greater or smaller.

B
Quantity

A. PURE QUANTITY

§ 99

Quantity is pure being in which determinacy is no longer posited as one with being itself, but as *sublated* or *indifferent*.

> (1) *Magnitude* is not an apt expression for quantity insofar as it especially designates *determinate* quantity. (2) In mathematics magnitude is usually defined as what can be *increased* or *decreased*. This definition is faulty, since it still contains what is to be defined; but it does at least imply that the determination of magnitude is such

that it is posited as *alterable* and *indifferent*, so that, notwithstanding a change of this determination (whether it be an extensive or an intensive increase), the thing in question,[a] for instance a house, or red, would not cease to be a house, or red. (3) "The Absolute is pure quantity"—this standpoint coincides in general with the attribution of the determination of *matter*[b] to the Absolute, [a matter] in which, it is true, form would be present, but only as an indifferent determination. Quantity also constitutes the fundamental determination of the Absolute, if it is so grasped that, being what is absolutely-undifferentiated, distinctions in it are only quantitative.—Pure space, time, etc., may also be taken as examples of quantity, insofar as the real is supposed to be grasped as an *indifferent* filling for space or time.

Addition. The usual definition of magnitude in mathematics, as "what can be increased or decreased", seems at first sight to be more illuminating and more plausible than the conceptual determination contained in the present paragraph. When we look at it more closely, however, it contains, in the form of presupposition and representation, the same [content] that has emerged as the concept of quantity simply by pursuing the path of logical development. In other words, when it is said of magnitude that its concept consists in the possibility of being increased or decreased, what is meant by that is just that magnitude (or, more correctly, quantity)—in distinction from quality—is a determination with respect to whose alteration this or that thing[c] is indifferent. As for the defect in the usual definition of quantity which was the subject of a reproach made above, this, when examined more closely, turns out to consist in the fact that to increase and to decrease means precisely to determine the magnitude differently. Consequently, quantity would basically be just something alterable as such. But quality is alterable, too, and the distinction between quantity and quality that was previously mentioned is here expressed by the reference to "increasing *or* decreasing." This implies that, in whatever direction the determination of magnitude is changed, the thing in question remains what it is.

We should, moreover, take note here that philosophy has absolutely nothing at all to do with merely correct definitions and even less with merely plausible ones, i.e., definitions whose correctness is immediately evident to the representing consciousness; it is concerned, instead, with definitions that have been *validated*, i.e., definitions whose content is not accepted merely as something that we come across, but is recognised as grounded in free thinking, and hence at the same time as grounded within itself. This applies to the present case. For, however correct and immediately evident the usual definition of quantity in mathematics may be, the requirement that we should know how far this particular thought is

a. *die Sache*
b. Materie
c. *Sache*

grounded in universal thinking, and is therefore necessary, still remains quite unsatisfied.

There is another relevant consideration here too. If quantity is adopted directly from our representational consciousness without being mediated by [pure] thinking, it can happen very easily that its range of validity is exaggerated, and indeed that quantity is elevated to the rank of an absolute category. This is what does happen in fact when only those sciences whose ob-ject can be submitted to a mathematical calculus are recognised as *exact* sciences. Here the bad metaphysics mentioned above (§ 98 Addition) appears once more—the metaphysics that substitutes one-sided and abstract determinations of the understanding for the concrete Idea. There would indeed be something badly amiss with our cognition if we had to renounce the possibility of exact cognition of ob-jects such as freedom, law, ethical life, and even God himself, because they cannot be measured and computed or expressed in a mathematical formula.

It is immediately obvious what pernicious practical consequences would follow if we had in general to be satisfied with a quite indeterminate representation of these ob-jects and to abandon them, as far as their more precise or particular character is concerned, to the pleasure of every single [person] to make of them what he will. For that matter, when we look closely at the exclusively mathematical standpoint that is here referred to (according to which quantity, which is a definite stage of the logical Idea, is identified with the Idea itself) we see that it is none other than the standpoint of *Materialism*. This can be confirmed completely in the history of the scientific consciousness, especially in France since the middle of the last century. "Matter" is an abstraction precisely because form is present in it, to be sure, but only as an indifferent and external determination.

Besides, it would be a serious mistake to interpret the above discussion as disparaging the dignity of mathematics, or as supplying a clear conscience for inertia and superficiality, because it designates the quantitative determination as a merely external and indifferent one. We are not maintaining that quantitative determinations can be left to take care of themselves, or even that they do not have to be treated as precisely as possible. Quantity is, in any case, a stage of the Idea, and it must be accorded its due as such, first as a logical category, and then in the world of ob-jects, both natural and spiritual.

But here again a distinction shows up at once, namely, that determinations of magnitude do not have the same importance in the ob-jects of the natural world as in those of the spiritual world. In nature, specifically, where the Idea has the form both of otherness and of self-externality, quantity also has—precisely for this reason—greater importance than in the world of the spirit, which is a world of free inwardness. It is true that we consider spiritual content, too, from the point of view of quantity. But it is evident at once that, when we consider God as the Trinity, the number "three" has a much more subordinate significance here than when we are considering, for example, the three dimensions of space or even the three sides of a triangle, for which the basic determination is precisely to be just a surface limited by three lines.

Even within nature this same distinction between a greater and a lesser importance of quantitative determination has its place; for it is certainly the case that quantity plays what we may call a more important role in inorganic nature than in organic. And if we make a further distinction, within inorganic nature, between the mechanical domain, and the physical and chemical domain in the narrower sense, then again the same distinction shows up, since mechanics is generally recognised as the scientific discipline that can least do without the help of mathematics. For in mechanics, of course, hardly any step can be taken without it, and mechanics is for that reason regarded, next to mathematics, as the exact science *par excellence*. At this point, we should recall our earlier comment about the coincidence of the exclusively mathematical standpoint with materialism.

Moreover, in the light of all that we have said here, we must designate the highly popular effort to find all distinction and all determinacy in the world of ob-jects merely in what is quantitative, as one of the most obstructive prejudices that stand in the way of any exact and thorough cognition. For example, spirit is in any case more than nature, and animals are more than plants; but we know very little about these things and the distinction between them, if we simply stick to a "more or less" of this kind, and do not advance to some grasp of specific determinacy, which is here in the first place qualitative.

§ 100

To begin with, in its immediate relation to itself, or in the determination of self-equivalence posited by attraction, quantity is *continuous* magnitude; in the other determination which it contains—that of the *One*—it is *discrete* magnitude. But continuous quantity is also discrete, for it is only continuity *of the many*; and discrete quantity is also continuous, for its continuity is the One as that in which the many ones are *the same, unity*.[a]

> (1) Hence, continuous and discrete magnitude should not be looked upon as *species*, as if the determination of the one did not belong to the other, but they distinguish themselves only in this, that *the same whole* is posited first under one of its determinations, and then under the other. (2) The antinomy of space, of time, or of matter (with regard to its divisibility ad infinitum or, conversely, with regard to its being composed of indivisibles) is nothing but the affirmation of quantity, first as continuous, then as discrete. If space, time, etc., are posited only with the determination of contin-uous quantity, then they are *divisible* ad infinitum; but under the determination of discrete magnitude they are in-themselves *divided* and consist of indivisible ones; each affirmation is as one-sided as the other.

Addition. As the proximate result of being-for-itself, quantity contains within itself as ideal elements both sides of its process (repulsion and attraction). Hence it is both continuous and discrete. Each of these two moments contains the other

a. die Einheit—See also p. xxxix above.

within itself, so that there *is* no such thing as a merely continuous or a merely discrete magnitude. If we happen to speak of them as two particular and contrasting species of magnitude, that is just the result of our abstractive reflection. In the consideration of determinate magnitudes, this reflection prescinds now from the one and then from the other of the two moments that are contained in the concept of quantity in inseparable unity. So we say, for instance, that the space that this room takes up is a continuous magnitude, whilst the hundred people who are gathered in it form a discrete magnitude. But the space is both continuous and discrete at once, so that we also speak of spatial points and subdivide every space— e.g., a certain length into so and so many feet, inches, etc., which can only occur on the presupposition that space is *in-itself* discrete too. On the other hand, the discrete magnitude consisting of a hundred people is equally and at the same time continuous; and what is common to them, the species mankind, which pervades all of the single instances and unites them with each other, is that wherein the continuity of this magnitude is grounded.

B. QUANTUM

§ 101

Quantity, *posited* essentially with the excluding determinacy that it contains, is *quantum* or limited quantity.

Addition. Quantum is the way that quantity *is there*, whereas pure quantity corresponds to *being*, and degree (which will come next) corresponds to *being-for-itself*. —As for the details of the advance from pure quantity to quantum, this progress is grounded in the fact that, whereas distinction is initially present in pure quantity only implicitly (as the distinction between continuity and discreteness), in quantum, on the other hand, distinction is posited. It is, indeed, posited in such a way that from now on quantity appears always as distinguished or limited. But as a result quantum also breaks up at the same time into an indeterminate multitude of quanta or determinate magnitudes. Each of these determinate magnitudes, as distinct from the others, forms a unit, just as, on the other hand, considered all by itself, it is a many. And in this way quantum is determined as *number*.

§ 102

Quantum has its development and perfect determinacy in *number*, which contains the One within itself as its element. As its qualitative moments, number contains according to its moment of discreteness, *annumeration*,[a] and according to its moment of continuity, *unit*.

a. Anzahl

In arithmetic the *kinds of calculation* are usually presented as contingent ways of treating numbers. If a necessity and hence a [matter for] understanding is to be found in them, then it has to lie in a principle; and this [in turn] can only be found in the determinations that are contained within the concept of number itself. This principle must be briefly expounded at this point.—The determinations of the concept of number are *annumeration* and *unit*; and number itself is the unity of the two. But unity, when applied to empirical numbers, is only their *equality*; hence, the principle of the kinds of calculation has to be the positing of numbers in the relationship of unit and annumeration and the production of the equality of these determinations.

Since the ones, or the numbers, are themselves indifferent toward each other, the unity into which they are transposed appears to be an external combination. To calculate, therefore, is quite generally to *count*; the distinction between the kinds of calculation lies only in the qualitative character of the numbers which are counted together, and the principle of that character[a] is the determination of unit and annumeration.

Numbering comes first: the making of numbers *generally*, which is the combining of as many *ones* as we want.—But it is the counting together of what are no longer merely ones but already numbers that is a *kind* of calculation.

Immediately and *to begin with*, numbers are just numbers in general without any [further] determination, and hence they are generally unequal too; the combination or counting of such numbers is *addition*.

The *next* determination is that the numbers [to be calculated] are *equal* throughout, so that they form One *unit*, and there is an *annumeration* of them; the counting of these numbers is *multiplication*—in this case it does not matter[b] how the determinations of annumeration and unit are distributed between the two numbers that are the factors (which of them is taken as the annumerator[28] and which as the unit).

The *third* and last determinacy is the *equality* of the *annumerator* and the *unit*. The counting together of numbers thus determined is the *raising of the power*—and first of all *squaring*.—Raising the power further is the continued multiplication of the number with itself, a continuation which is [a] formal continuation that leads

a. *Beschaffenheit*
b. *est ist gleichgültig*

once more to the indefinite annumeration.—Since the complete equality of the only distinction that is available—that of annumeration and of unit—is reached in this third determination, there cannot be more than these three kinds of calculation.—To [each form of] counting together there corresponds the dissolution of the numbers according to the same determinations. There are therefore three *negative* kinds of calculation beside the three that have been indicated (which are on that account called the *positive* ones).

Addition. Since number is just quantum in its completed determinacy, we can employ it not only for the determination of so-called discrete magnitudes but equally for so-called continuous ones as well. And hence, number must also be utilised in geometry, wherever there is a question of specifying determinate figurations of space and their relationships.

C. DEGREE

§ 103

The *limit* is identical with the whole of the quantum itself; as multiple *within itself* it is *extensive* magnitude, but as determinacy that is *simple* within itself, it is *intensive* magnitude or *degree*.

Hence, the distinction between continuous and discrete magnitude and extensive and intensive magnitude consists in this: that the former concerns *quantity in general*, whereas the latter concerns the *limit* or determinacy of quantity as such.—Like continuous and discrete magnitude, extensive and intensive magnitude are not two species (each of which would contain a determinacy that would be lacking in the other); whatever has extensive magnitude has intensive magnitude as well, and vice versa.

Addition. Intensive magnitude or *degree* is conceptually diverse from *extensive magnitude* or *quantum*; we must therefore label as a mistake the frequent failure to recognise this distinction, and to identify the two forms of magnitude without further ado. This is notably the case in physics, where a distinction in specific gravity, for instance, is explained by saying that a body whose specific gravity is twice that of another contains within the same space twice as many material parts (atoms) as the other. It would be the same with heat and light, if the various degrees of temperature and brightness were to be explained in terms of a greater or lesser number of heat or light particles (or molecules). When physicists who employ such explanations are reproached with the untenability of this procedure they usually try, of course, to wriggle out of it by saying that they do not at all mean to decide about the (admittedly unknowable) character of these phenomena in-themselves, and that they use these expressions only because they are more *convenient*.

First then, this greater convenience is supposed to be connected with the easier application of the methods of calculation; but it is hard to see why intensive magnitudes, which do, of course, equally have their determinate expression in number, should not be just as convenient for calculation as extensive magnitudes. Surely, it would be even more convenient to give up calculation altogether, and thinking as well. Another comment that should be made against this excuse is that when physicists engage in explanations of this sort, they are, in any case, overstepping the domain of perception and experience; they are taking refuge in the domain of metaphysics and speculation (which they declare on other occasions to be idle, and even pernicious). We do find by experience, to be sure, that if one of two purses filled with dollars is twice as heavy as the other, it is because the first purse contains two hundred dollars and the second only one hundred. We can see these pieces of money, and can always perceive them with our senses; but, atoms, molecules, and the like lie outside the domain of sense-perception, and it is the task of thinking to decide about their admissibility and significance.

As we said earlier (in the Addition to § 98), it is the abstract understanding that fixes the moment of the many contained in the concept of being-for-itself in the shape of atoms, and sticks to this moment as to something ultimate; and it is the same abstract understanding which, in the present case, contradicts both unprejudiced perception and genuinely concrete thinking, by considering extensive magnitude to be the one and only form of quantity. So, where intensive magnitudes are found, it fails to recognise them in their own determinacy, and tries to reduce them to extensive magnitudes by force instead, on the basis of an hypothesis which is in itself untenable.

Among the reproaches that have been levelled against recent philosophy, the one that is heard very frequently is the claim that it reduces everything to identity; and hence it has even been given the nickname "Philosophy of Identity".[29] But the argumentation that we have just presented shows that it is precisely philosophy that insists on distinguishing between what is, both conceptually and experimentally, diverse; on the contrary, it is the professed empiricists who elevate abstract identity to the highest principle of cognition, and whose philosophy should therefore more properly be called the "Philosophy of Identity".

For the rest, it is quite correct that there are no merely intensive and merely extensive magnitudes, any more than there are merely continuous and merely discrete ones; and hence, these two determinations of quantity are not independent species that confront one another. Any intensive magnitude is also extensive, and conversely. So, a certain degree of temperature, for instance, is an intensive magnitude, to which, as such, there corresponds a wholly simple sensation; and if we then go to the thermometer we find that a certain expansion of the column of mercury corresponds to this degree of temperature, and this extensive magnitude changes together with the temperature taken as an intensive magnitude. It is the same in the domain of spirit, too; a more intense character exerts influence over a wider range than a less intense one.

§ 104

In degree, the *concept* of quantum is *posited*. Degree is magnitude as indifferent *for-itself* and simple, but in such a way that the magnitude has the determinacy in virtue of which it is quantum, strictly *outside of it* in other magnitudes. In this contradiction—that although it *is for-itself*, the indifferent limit is absolute *externality*—the *infinite* quantitative *progress* is posited. This is an *immediacy* that immediately turns over into its opposite, into its *being mediated* (a going beyond the just posited quantum), and vice versa.

> *Number* is thought, but it is thought as a being that is completely external to itself. Number does not belong to intuition, because it is thought, but it is thought that has the externality of intuition as its determination.—Hence, it is not only the case that quantum *can* be increased or decreased ad infinitum; by its very concept, quantum is just this expulsion beyond itself. Similarly the infinite quantitative progress is that unthinking repetition of that one and the same contradiction, which is quantum in general and (when posited in its determinacy) degree. It is superfluous to express this contradiction in the form of an infinite progress; on this topic *Zeno* rightly says (in Aristotle's report)[30] that it is the same to say something *once* and to say it *over and over again*.

Addition 1. According to the usual definition of it in mathematics (discussed in § 99), magnitude is what can be increased or decreased; and there is nothing against the correctness of the intuition that underlies this. But the prior question still remains of how we come to assume this *capacity for increase* or *decrease*. A simple appeal to experience does not suffice to answer this question, because, quite apart from the fact that in experience we have only the representation of magnitude and not the thought of it, this capacity would prove to be just a possibility (of increasing and decreasing), and we should lack all insight into the necessity of this state of affairs. By contrast, the path of our logical development has not only brought us to quantity as a stage of self-determining thinking, but has shown us also that it lies strictly in the *concept* of quantity to project beyond itself, so that what we have to do with here is not merely possible but necessary also.

Addition 2. It is mainly the quantitative infinite progression that the reflective understanding usually relies upon when it has to deal with infinity in general. But, to begin with, what we said earlier about the qualitatively infinite progress holds good for the quantitative form of the infinite progress too, namely, that it is the expression not of true Infinity but only of the spurious infinity that never gets beyond what merely *ought* to be the case, so that in fact it gets stuck in the finite. As for the specifically quantitative form of this finite progession, which Spinoza rightly calls a merely imaginary infinity (*infinitum imaginationis*),[31] the poets, too, (Haller and Klopstock are good examples) have quite often availed themselves of this representation in order to depict not only the infinity of nature but also that of God himself. There is a famous description of the infinity of God in Haller, for example:

> I heap up monstrous numbers,
> Mountains of millions,
> Time I pile on time
> And world on top of world;
> And when from the awful height
> I cast a dizzy look on Thee:
> Then all the might of number,
> Numbered itself a thousand times,
> Is not yet a simple part of Thee.[32]

Here we have at once the perpetual projection of quantity—or more precisely, number—beyond itself, which Kant describes as "terrible," though the only really terrible thing about it would be the tedium of continually positing a limit which is again done away with, so that one stays forever at the same spot. But then, the same poet ends his description of that spurious infinity with the very relevant conclusion:

> These I remove, and thou liest all before me.

This expresses precisely the fact that the genuine Infinite is not to be considered merely as what is beyond the finite, and that we must renounce that *progressus in infinitum* in order to reach the consciousness of the genuine Infinite.

Addition 3. It is well known that Pythagoras[33] philosophised with numbers, and conceived number to be the basic determination of things. To the ordinary mind this interpretation must at first sight appear to be thoroughly paradoxical, and indeed quite mad. So the question arises, what we are to make of it. To answer this question we must first remember that the task of philosophy consists just in tracing things back to thoughts, and to determinate thoughts at that. Now, number is certainly a thought, and indeed it is the thought which stands closest to the sensible world; more precisely, it expresses the thought of the sense-world itself, because we understand generally by that what is mutually external and what is many.[a] So we can recognise in the attempt to interpret the universe as Number the first step toward metaphysics.

a. *das Viele*

It is also well known that in the history of philosophy Pythagoras stands between the Ionian philosophers and the Eleatics. As Aristotle already remarked, the Ionians went no further than to regard the essence of things as something material (as a *hule*); the Eleatics, however, and in particular Parmenides, advanced to pure thinking in the form of being. Thus, the principle of the Pythagorean philosophy forms as it were the bridge between the sensible and the supersensible. This tells us how we should assess the view of those who hold that Pythagoras obviously went too *far* in interpreting the essence of things as consisting in pure numbers, and who comment that, whilst there is nothing objectionable in the view that things are certainly countable, still, things are *more* than mere numbers. As for the "more" that is here ascribed to things, we must, of course, willingly concede that things are more than mere numbers; but the real question concerns how this "more" is to be understood. Consistently with its own standpoint, the ordinary sensible consciousness will not hesitate to answer the question by referring to what is sensibly perceptible; hence, it will remark that things are not merely countable but also visible, odorous, palpable, etc.

So, putting this in our modern way, the reproach levelled against the Pythagorean philosophy reduces to the claim that it is too idealistic. In fact, however, the situation is quite the opposite, as can already be inferred from what we have just said about the historical position of the Pythagorean philosophy. In other words, the concession that things are "more" than mere numbers must be understood as meaning that the mere thought of *number* does not suffice to express the determinate essence or concept of things. So, instead of maintaining that Pythagoras went too *far* with his philosophy of numbers, we ought to say, on the contrary, that he did not go *far enough*; and, of course, it was the Eleatics who already took the next step toward pure thinking.

Moreover, even if there are no things whose determinacy rests essentially on definite numbers and relationships of numbers, still there are states of things, and all sorts of natural phenomena that rest on them. This is especially the case with the differences of tone and their harmonic concord; everyone knows the story that it was the perception of this phenomenon that prompted Pythagoras to apprehend the essence of things as numbers. Now it is certainly an important scientific concern to trace back the phenomena that rest on determinate numbers to the right ratios; but, by the same token, it is quite inadmissible to regard the determinacy of thought generally as a merely numerical one.

We may, of course, be prompted at first to connect the most general determinations of thought with the first numbers, and to say therefore that *one* is what is simple and immediate, *two* is distinction and mediation, and *three* the unity of both. But these combinations are completely external, and there is nothing in these numbers as such to make them the expression of precisely these determinate thoughts. Besides, the further we advance in applying this method, the more obvious becomes the sheer arbitrariness of combining determinate numbers with determinate thoughts. For instance, [the number] 4 can be considered the unity of 1 and 3, and of the thoughts connected with them; but 4 is also just as much twice 2, and, similarly, 9 is not only the square of 3, but also the sum of 8 and 1, of 7 and 2, etc. Even today some secret societies place great weight on all manner of numbers and figures; but this can only be regarded a harmless game, on the one hand, and as a sign of ineptitude in thinking, on the other. Of course, it is also claimed that there is a deep meaning concealed in all this, and that one could find a lot to think about here. But what is important in philosophy is not that we *can* think about something, but that we *really* do think, and the genuine element of thought must be sought not in arbitrarily chosen symbols but only in thinking itself.

§ 105

In its determinacy of *being on its own account* quantum *is external* to itself. This self-externality constitutes its *quality*; it is in this very self-externality that it is itself and is related to itself. In this way, the externality, i.e., the quantitative, and the being-for-itself, the qualitative, are united.—Posited *upon itself*[a] in this way, quantum is quantitative *relationship* [or *ratio*], [i.e., the] determinacy that is both an *immediate* quantum (the exponent), and *mediation* (namely the *relation* of any quantum to another)—the two terms of the ratio, which do not count according to their immediate value, since their value is only [determined] in this relation.

Addition. The quantitative infinite progress appears at first as a perpetual projection of numbers beyond themselves. However, when we look more closely, it turns out that in this progression quantity returns to itself, for the thought that is contained in it is in any event the determination of number by number, and this gives us *quantitative ratio*. If we speak of the ratio 2:4, for example, then we have two magnitudes whose significance does not lie in their immediate character as such, but only in their reciprocal relation to one another. But this relation (the exponent of the ratio) is itself a magnitude, which is distinguished from the magnitudes that stand in relation to one another by virtue of the fact that altering them changes the ratio, whereas the ratio remains indifferent to the alteration of its two sides and stays the same, just as long as the exponent is not altered. So we can substitute 3:6 for 2:4, without altering the ratio, because the exponent, 2, remains the same in both cases.

a. an ihm selbst

§ 106

The *terms* of the ratio are still immediate quanta, and the qualitative and quantitative determinations are still external to each other. But according to their truth—that, even in its externality, the quantitative itself is relation to itself, or that the being-for-itself and the indifference of the determinacy are united—the ratio is *measure*.

Addition. In virtue of the dialectical movement of quantity through its moments which we have considered so far, quantity has turned out to be a return to quality. Initially, we had the concept of quantity as sublated quality, that is, as determinacy which is not identical with being, but, on the contrary, indifferent to it, and only external with regard to it. This is also the concept which (as we said earlier) underlies the usual definition of magnitude in mathematics, as what can be increased or decreased. Now, it may seem at first sight that according to this definition magnitude is simply what is alterable as such—for both increasing and decreasing mean just determining the magnitude differently. But by this definition, magnitude would not be distinct from *being-there* (the second stage of quality) which, according to its concept, is alterable in like manner. So the content of that definition of magnitude would have to be completed by adding that in quantity we have something which is alterable, but which still remains the same in spite of its alteration. As a result, the concept of quantity turns out to contain a contradiction, and it is this contradiction that constitutes the dialectic of quantity. But the result of this dialectic is not a mere return to quality, as if the latter were what is true, and quantity[34] on the contrary what is untrue. Instead, the result is the unity and truth of the two of them: it is qualitative quantity or *measure*.

One more comment in place at this point is that when we are concerned with quantitative determinations in the study of the world of ob-jects, it is in fact always measure that we have in mind as the goal of our endeavours. This is indeed indicated in our language by the fact that we call the ascertaining of quantitative determinations and ratios "measuring". For instance, we measure the length of various strings that have been made to vibrate, with an eye to the corresponding distinction between the sounds that are brought about by the vibration. Likewise, in chemistry, we calculate the quantity of the substances that have been brought into combination, so as to be cognizant of the measure by which these combinations are conditioned—in other words, to discover the quantities that underlie determinate qualities. And in statistics, too, the numbers with which we are occupied have an interest only on account of the qualitative results which are conditioned by them. By contrast, mere numerical findings as such, apart from the guiding interest which we have discussed here, rightly count as empty curiosities that satisfy neither a theoretical nor a practical concern.

C
Measure

§ 107

Measure is qualitative quantum; at first, as *immediate* [measure], it is a quantum, with which a being-there or a quality is bound up.

Addition. As the unity of quality and quantity, measure is thus also completed being. When we speak of being, it appears initially to be what is entirely abstract and lacking all determination; but being is essentially what determines itself, and it reaches its completed determinacy in measure. We can also consider measure as a definition of the Absolute, and it has been said accordingly that God is the measure of all things.[35] That is also why this intuition forms the keynote of many ancient Hebrew psalms,[36] where the glorification of God essentially comes down to saying that it is *he* who has appointed for everything its limit, for the sea and the dry land, the rivers and the mountains, and equally for the various kinds of plants and animals.—In the religious consciousness of the Greeks we find the divinity of measure represented, with special reference to the ethical order, by *Nemesis*. Nemesis involves the general notion that everything human—wealth, honour, power, and similarly joy, sorrow, etc.—has its definite measure, the transgression of which leads to undoing and ruin.

As for the occurrence of measure in the world of ob-jects, we find first that in nature things exist whose essential content is measure. This is especially the case with the solar system, which we have to regard generally as the realm of free measure. As we advance further in the consideration of inorganic nature, measure retreats into the background, so to speak, because the qualitative and quantitative determinations that we have here prove to be largely indifferent to one another. For example, the qualitative character of a rock or a river is not bound up with a determinate magnitude. Still, a closer study shows that even ob-jects like these are not utterly without measure, since chemical investigation reveals that the water in a river, and the single constituents of a rock, are again qualities that are conditioned by quantitative ratios between the substances they contain. But then, measure emerges again in organic nature, falling now more decisively into the domain of immediate intuition. The various kinds of plants and animals have a certain measure, both as a whole and also in their single parts. We should notice here that the more imperfect organic formations, those that stand closer to inorganic nature, are distinguished in part from the higher organisms through the greater indeterminacy of their measure. Thus, we find among fossils, for example, some so-called ammonites, of which we are cognizant only through the microscope, and others which reach the size of a coach wheel. The same indeterminacy of measure is also shown by many plants which stand on a lower stage of organic development. This is the case with ferns, for example.

§ 108

Insofar as in measure quality and quantity are only in *immediate* unity, their distinction shows itself in them in an equally immediate way. Under this aspect the specific quantum is in some cases mere quantum, and what is there[a] is capable of increase and decrease without the sublation of measure, which to that extent is a *rule*; but in other cases the alteration of the quantum is also an alteration of the quality.

Addition. The identity of quality and quantity present in measure is only *implicit* at first, and not yet *posited*. This implies that each of the two determinations, whose unity is measure, also claims validity on its own account. In this way, on the one hand, quantitative determinations of what is there can be altered, without its quality being affected thereby, but, on the other, this indifferent increase and decrease also has a limit, the transgression of which alters the quality. Thus, for instance, the temperature of water is, up to a point, indifferent in relation to its liquid state; but there comes a point in the increasing or decreasing of the temperature of liquid water where this state of cohesion changes qualitatively, and the water is transformed into steam, on the one hand, and ice, on the other. When a quantitative alteration takes place it appears, to start with, to be something quite innocent; but something quite different lurks behind it, and this seemingly innocent alteration of the quantitative is like a ruse with which to catch the qualitative.

The antinomy of measure that is involved here was already depicted by the Greeks under many guises. They raised the question, for instance, [of] whether *one* grain of wheat can make a heap of wheat, or whether the plucking of *one* hair from the tail of a horse makes it a bald-tail.[37] Regarding the nature of quantity as an indifferent and external determinacy of being, we are, at first, inclined to answer those questions in the negative. Nevertheless, we must soon concede that this indifferent increasing or decreasing also has a limit, and that a point in the process is finally reached where, through the continued adding of just *one* grain of wheat at a time, a heap of wheat results, and through the continued plucking of just *one* hair at a time we have a bald-tail. It is the same with these examples as with the story of a farmer who, as his ass cheerfully strode along, increased its load *one* ounce at a time, until at last it sank down under the burden that had become unbearable. It would be very wrong to treat considerations of this sort as idle academic twaddle, for in fact we are dealing with thoughts that it is also very important to be familiar with in our practical and especially in our ethical life. With regard to the outlays that we make, for instance, there is initially a certain latitude within which a bit more or a bit less does not matter; but if we exceed, on one side or the other, the measure determined by the individual circumstances of the situation, then the qualitative nature of the measure comes into play (just as it does in the above example of the various temperatures of the water), and what could be considered good management of resources a moment ago now becomes avarice or waste.

a. *das Dasein*

The same applies in the political sphere as well—for, of course, it is the case that the constitution of a State must be regarded both as independent of, and also as dependent upon, the size of its territory, the number of its inhabitants, and other such quantitative determinations. For instance, if we consider a State with a territory of a thousand square miles, and a population of four million inhabitants, we would at first admit without hesitation that a few square miles of territory or a few thousand inhabitants more or less would not have an essential influence on its constitution. In contrast, however, we could not deny either that in the continual increase or decrease of the State a point is finally reached where, simply because of the quantitative change (quite apart from all other circumstances), the qualitative aspects of the constitution cannot remain unaltered. The constitution of a small Swiss canton will not do for a great empire, and the constitution of the Roman republic was equally unsuitable when it was transferred to the small "free cities" of the German empire.

§ 109

The *measureless* occurs initially when a measure, in virtue of its quantitative nature, goes beyond its qualitative determinacy. But since the new quantitative ratio, which is measureless with regard to the first, is just as qualitative, the measureless is also a measure; both of these transitions, from quality to quantity and vice versa, can once more be represented as *infinite progress*—as the self-sublation and restoration of measure in the measureless.

Addition. As we have seen, quantity is not merely *capable* of alteration, i.e., of increase and decrease; rather, it is, generally and as such, the process of going beyond itself. And in measure, quantity does indeed confirm this nature. But now, when the quantity that is present in measure exceeds a certain limit, the corresponding quality is thereby sublated, too. What is negated in this way, however, is not quality in general, but only this determinate quality, whose place is immediately taken again by another one. This process of measure, which proves to be alternately a mere alteration of quantity and an overturning of quantity into quality, can be visualised in the image of a knotted line.[38] We find these knotted lines first in nature, in a variety of forms. We have already given the example of water's qualitatively various states of aggregation, conditioned by increase and decrease [of temperature]. The various stages of oxidation of metals are a similar case. The distinctions of musical notes can also be regarded as an example of the overturning of what is initially a merely quantitative into a qualitative alteration that takes place in the process of measure.

§ 110

What actually happens here is that the *immediacy*, which still belongs to measure as such, is sublated; quality and quantity themselves are initially in measure as *immediate,* and measure is only their *relational identity.* But although measure sublates itself in the measureless, it shows itself equally to be only going together *with itself* in the measureless, which is its negation, but is itself a unity of quantity and quality.

§ 111

Instead of the more abstract sides (of being and nothing, of something and an other, etc.) the Infinite, the affirmation as the negation of the negation, now has quality and quantity for its sides. These sides (α) *have passed over* into one another: quality into quantity (§ 98) and quantity into quality (§ 105), and they have thus exhibited themselves to be *negations.* (β) But in their *unity* (in measure) they are at first distinct, and each is only *through the mediation* of the other; and (γ) after the immediacy of this unity has proven to be self-sublating, this unity is now *posited* as what it is *in-itself,* as simple self-relation that contains within it being in general and its forms as sublated.—Being or immediacy which, through self-negation, is mediation *with itself* and relation to itself, and which is therefore equally mediation that sublates itself into relation to itself or into immediacy—this being or immediacy is *Essence.*

Addition. The process of measure is not just the spurious infinity of the infinite progression in the shape of a perpetual overturning of quality into quantity and of quantity into quality; rather, it is, at the same time, the true Infinity which consists in the going together with oneself in one's other. Quality and quantity do initially confront one another in measure like something and other. But quality is indeed *in-itself* quantity, and conversely, quantity is *in-itself* quality, too. Hence, in that the two determinations pass over into one another in the process of measure, each of them only becomes what it already is *in-itself,* and we now obtain the being that is negated in its determinations, in general terms the sublated being that is *Essence.* Essence was already implicit within measure, and its process consists simply in its positing itself as what it is in-itself.

Ordinary consciousness interprets things as [simply] being, and considers them in terms of quality, quantity, and measure. But these immediate determinations then prove not to be fixed, but to pass into something else, and Essence is the result of their dialectic. In Essence no passing-over takes place any more; instead, there is only relation. In Being, the relational form is only [due to] our reflection; in Essence, by contrast, the relation belongs to it as its own determination. When something becomes other (in the sphere of Being) the something has thereby vanished. Not so in Essence: here we do not have a genuine other, but only diversity, relation between the One and *its* other. Thus, in Essence passing-over is at the same time not passing-over. For in the passing of what is diverse into another diversity, the first one does not vanish; instead, both remain within this relation. For instance, if we say "being" and "nothing," then being is by itself and nothing is by itself too. The situation is not at all the same with the "positive" and the "negative." Certainly, these contain the determination of being and nothing. But the positive makes no sense by itself; rather, it is strictly related to the negative. And the situation is the same with the negative. In the sphere of Being, relatedness is only *implicit*; in Essence, on the contrary, relatedness is posited. This then is in general what distinguishes the form of Being from that of Essence. In Being, everything is immediate; in Essence, by contrast, everything is relational.

SECOND SUBDIVISION
OF THE *LOGIC*
THE DOCTRINE OF ESSENCE

§ 112

Essence is the Concept as *posited* Concept. In Essence the determinations are only *relational*, not yet as reflected strictly within themselves; that is why the Concept is not yet *for-itself*. Essence—as Being that mediates itself with itself through its own negativity—is relation to itself only by being relation to another; but this other is immediately, not as what *is* but as *something-posited* and *mediated*.—Being has not vanished; but, in the first place, essence as simple relation to itself is being; while on the other hand, being, according to its one-sided determination of being *something-immediate*, is *degraded* to something merely negative, to a *shine* [or *semblance*].ª—As a result, essence is being as *shining* within itself.

> The Absolute is the *essence*.—Inasmuch as being is also simple self-relation, this definition is the same as the one that says it is *being*, but at the same time it is a higher definition, because essence is being that has gone *into itself*; i.e., its simple self-relation is this relation, posited as the negation of the negative, or as inward mediation of itself with itself.—But when the Absolute is determined as *essence*, the negativity is often taken only in the sense of an *abstraction* from all determinate predicates. In that case the negative activity, the abstracting, falls outside essence, and consequently essence is taken only as a result, *without this premise that belongs to it*; it is the *caput mortuum*[2] of abstraction. But because this negativity is not external to being, but is its own dialectic, its truth is essence, as being that has gone *into itself* or is *self*-contained; this *reflection*, its shining within itself, is what distinguishes it from immediate being, and it is the proper determination of essence itself.

a. *zu einem* Scheine[1]

Addition. When we speak of "essence", we distinguish it from being, i.e., from what is immediate. In comparison with essence, we regard being as a mere *semblance*. But this semblance is not simply "not"; it is not an utter nothing;[a] rather, it is being as sublated.—The standpoint of essence is in general the standpoint of reflection. The term "reflection" is primarily used of light, when, propagated rectilinearly, it strikes a mirrored surface and is thrown back by it. So we have here something twofold: first, something immediate, something that is, and second, the same as mediated or posited. And this is just the case when we reflect on an ob-ject or "think it over" (as we also say very often). For here we are not concerned with the ob-ject in its immediate form, but want to know it as mediated. And our usual view of the task or purpose of philosophy is that it consists in the cognition of the essence of things. By this we understand no more than that things are not to be left in their immediate state, but are rather to be exhibited as mediated or grounded by something else. The immediate being of things is here represented as a sort of rind or curtain behind which the essence is concealed.

Now, when we say further that all things have an essence, what we mean is that they are not truly what they immediately show themselves to be. A mere rushing about from one quality to another, and a mere advance from the qualitative to the quantitative and back again, is not the last word; on the contrary, there is something that abides in things, and this is, in the first instance, their essence. As for the further significance and use of the category of essence, we can recall first at this point how the term "Wesen" is employed to designate the past for the German auxiliary verb "sein" [to be]; for we designate the being that is past as "gewesen". This irregularity in linguistic usage rests upon a correct view of the relation of being and essence, because we can certainly consider essence to be being that has gone by, whilst still remarking that what is past is not for that reason abstractly negated, but only sublated and so at the same time conserved. If we say in German, e.g., "Cäsar ist in Gallien *gewesen*" ["Caesar *was* in Gaul"], what is negated by that is just the immediacy of what is asserted about Caesar, but not his sojourn in Gaul altogether, for indeed it is just that which forms the content of this assertion—only it is here represented as having been sublated.

When a "Wesen" is spoken of in ordinary life, it frequently only means a comprehensive whole or an essential sum; we speak in this way, for instance, of a "Zeitungswesen" [the press], of the "Postwesen" [the postal service], or of the "Steuerwesen" [the taxation system], etc., which simply amounts to saying that the things that are part of these are not to be taken singly in their immediacy, but as a complex, and then further in their various relations as well. So this linguistic use involves just about the same content as essence has turned out to have for us.

We speak also about *finite* essences,[3] and we call man a finite essence. But, in speaking of essence, we have, strictly speaking, gone beyond finitude, so that to designate man as a finite essence is inaccurate. When we add that "es gibt"[b] [there is] a "highest essence," and that God ought to be designated by that name, two things should be noted. First, the expression "geben" [to give] refers to something

a. *Dieser Schein ist nun aber nicht gar nicht, nicht ein Nichts*
b. Literally "it gives," from *geben*, "to give"

finite, as when we say, for instance, that "*Es gibt* so-and-so many planets," or "*Es gibt* plants with this constitution, and others with that one." The things that are "given" in this way are such that others are "given" outside and beside them. But God, as the Infinite itself, is not something that is "given" whilst *outside* and *beside* him there are also other essences. Whatever else is "given" outside of God has no essentiality in its separateness from God; on the contrary, any such thing lacks internal stability and essence in its isolation, and must be considered as a mere semblance.

And this implies a *second* point too: namely, that all talk of God merely as the "*highest*" essence" must be called unsatisfactory. For the category of quantity that is applied here has its place only in the domain of the finite. For instance, when we say, "This is the highest mountain on earth," we have the notion that, apart from this highest mountain, there are also other mountains that are high. The situation is the same when we say that someone is the richest or the most learned man in his country. But God is not merely *an* essence and not even merely the *highest* essence either. He is *the* essence. In this connection also, we should notice at once that, although this interpretation of God forms an important and necessary stage in the development of the religious consciousness, it in no way exhausts the depth of the Christian representation of God. When we just regard God purely and simply as the essence and stop at that, then we know him only as the universal, irresistible Might, or, to put it another way, as the *Lord*. Well, of course, the fear of the Lord is the beginning of wisdom, but it is only the beginning of it.

It was first in the Jewish and then later in the Mohammedan religions that God was interpreted as the Lord and essentially *only* as the Lord. The defect of these religions consists generally in their not giving the finite its due; whereas holding fast to the finite on its own account (be it something natural or something finite in the spiritual realm) is what is characteristic of the heathen (and thereby at the same time polytheistic) religions.

Another position that has frequently been maintained is that there can be no cognition of God as the "highest essence." This is the general standpoint of the modern Enlightenment, which is content to say, "Il y a un être suprême,"[4] and lets the matter rest there. When people talk like this, and regard God only as the "highest essence" in the beyond, then they have the world in view as something firm and positive in its immediacy. They are forgetting, then, that essence is precisely the sublation of everything immediate. As the abstract essence in the beyond, outside of which all distinction and determinacy must fall, God is in fact a mere name, a mere *caput mortuum* of the abstractive understanding. The true cognition of God begins with our knowing that things in their immediate being have no truth.

It frequently happens, not only in relation to God but in other contexts too, that the category of essence is employed in an abstract way, and that in the study of things their essence is fixed as something indifferent to the determinate content of their appearance, as something that subsists on its own account. Thus, we often say specifically that the main thing about people is their essence, and not what they do or how they behave. What is quite right in this claim is that what someone does must be considered not just in its immediacy, but only as mediated by his inwardness and as a manifestation of it. But it should not be overlooked either that essence, and inwardness as well, only prove themselves to be what they are by moving out into the domain of appearance; whereas, what underlies the appeal to an essence that is different from the content of what people do is often just the aim of making their mere subjectivity count, and of evading what holds in and for itself.

§ 113

In Essence, relation-to-self is the form of *identity*, of *inward reflection*. This form has here taken the place of the *immediacy* of being; both are the same abstractions of relation-to-self.

> The absence of thought in sense-knowledge, which takes everything limited and finite for something *that [simply] is,*[a] passes over into the stubbornness of the understanding, which grasps everything finite as *something-identical-with-itself, [and] not inwardly contradicting itself.*

§ 114

As it emerges from being, this identity appears at first to be burdened only with the determinations of being, and related to being as to *something-external*. When being is taken separately from essence in this way, it is called the "*inessential*." But essence is being-within-self,[b] it is *essential* only insofar as it has the negative of itself, [i.e.,] the relation-to-another, or mediation, within itself. It has the inessential, therefore, as its own shine within itself. But there is a distinguishing contained in the shining or mediation, and what is distinct does itself acquire the form of identity, in its distinction from the identity from which it emerges, and in which it is not or lies [only] as semblance. Hence, what is distinct is itself in the mode of self-relating immediacy or of being. And for this reason the sphere of Essence becomes a still imperfect connection of *immediacy* and *mediation*. Everything is posited in it in such a way that it relates itself to itself, while at the same time [the movement] has already gone beyond it. [It is posited] as a *being of reflection*, a being within which an other shines and which shines within an other.—Hence, the sphere of Essence is also the sphere of *posited contradiction*, whereas, in the sphere of Being, contradiction is only *implicit*.

a. *ein* Seiendes
b. *In-sich-sein*

Because the One Concept is what is substantial in everything, the same determinations occur in the development of Essence as in the development of being—but they occur in *reflected* form. Instead of *being* and *nothing*, the forms of the *positive* and *negative* present themselves; initially the positive corresponds, as *identity*, to the being that lacks antithesis, while the negative (shining within itself) develops as *distinction*. Then, *becoming* presents itself in the same way as the very *ground* of *being-there*, which, as reflected upon the ground, is *existence*, and so on.—This part of the Logic, which is the most difficult one, contains most notably the categories of metaphysics and of the sciences generally;—it contains them as products of the reflecting understanding, which both assumes the distinctions as *independent* and at the same time posits their relationality *as well*. But it only ties the two assumptions together—and it links the two of them only in contiguity or succession, by means of an "also"; it does not bring these thoughts together; it does not unite them into the Concept.

A
Essence as Ground of Existence[5]

A. THE PURE DETERMINATIONS OF REFLECTION

(α) IDENTITY

§ 115

Essence shines *within itself* or is pure reflection. In this way it is only relation to self (though not as immediate but as reflected relation): *identity with itself*.

Formal identity or identity-of-the-understanding is this identity, insofar as one holds onto it firmly and *abstracts* from distinction. Or rather, *abstraction* is the positing of this formal identity, the transformation of something that is inwardly concrete into this form of simplicity—whether it be the case that a part of the manifold that is present in the concrete is *left out* (by means of what is called *analysis*) and that only *one* of these [elements] is selected, or that, by leaving out their diversity, the manifold determinacies are *drawn together* into One.

When identity is linked with the Absolute, as the subject of a proposition, then the proposition reads: "The Absolute is what is identical with itself."—This proposition is true enough, but it is quite unclear whether it is meant in its true sense. So it is at best incomplete in its expression, for it remains undecided whether it is the abstract *identity*-of-the-understanding that is meant—i.e., [identity] in antithesis to the other determinations of Essence—or rather the identity that is inwardly *concrete*. The latter (as will be seen later) is first the *ground* and then, in its higher truth, the *Concept*.—The very word *"absolute"* itself often has no other meaning than that of *"abstract"*; thus, *absolute* space and *absolute* time do not mean anything more than abstract space and abstract time.

Taken as *essential* determinations, the determinations of Essence become predicates of a presupposed subject, which, because they are essential, is *everything*. The propositions that arise in this way have been expressed as *the universal laws of thought*. Thus *the principle of identity* reads: "Everything is identical with itself,[6] A = A"; and negatively: "A cannot be both A and non-A at the same time."—Instead of being a true law of thinking, this principle is nothing but the law of the *abstract understanding*. The *propositional form* itself already contradicts it, since a proposition promises a distinction between subject and predicate as well as identity; and the identity-proposition does not furnish what its form demands. Specifically, however, it is sublated by the so-called laws of thought that follow it; for these make the contrary of this law into laws.— If someone says that this proposition cannot be proven, but that *every* consciousness proceeds in accordance with it and, as experience shows agrees with it at once, as soon as it takes it in, then against this alleged experience of the Schools we have to set the universal experience that no consciousness thinks, has notions, or speaks, according to this law, and no existence of any kind at all exists in accordance with it. Speaking in accordance with this supposed law of truth (a planet is—a planet, magnetism is— magnetism, the spirit is—a spirit) is rightly regarded as silly; that is indeed a universal experience. The Schoolroom, which is the only place where these laws are valid, along with its logic which propounds them in earnest, has long since lost all credit with sound common sense as well as with reason.

Addition. Identity is in the first place the repetition of what we had before us earlier as being, but now as what has come to be through the sublation of immediate determinacy; hence, it is being as ideality.—It is of great importance to reach an adequate understanding of the true significance of identity, and this means above all that it must not be interpreted merely as abstract identity, i.e., as identity that excludes distinction. This is the point that distinguishes all bad philosophy from what alone deserves the name of philosophy. In its truth, as the ideality of what immediately is, identity is a lofty determination both for our religious consciousness and for the rest of our thinking and consciousness in general. It can be said that the true knowledge of God begins at the point where he is known as Identity, i.e., as absolute identity; and this implies, at the same time, that all the power and the glory of the world sinks into nothing before God and can subsist only as the shining [forth] of *his* power and *his* glory.

Similarly, it is his identity as consciousness of himself that distinguishes man from nature in general, and particularly from animals, which do not achieve a grasp of themselves as "I," i.e, as their pure self-unity.—As for the significance of identity in relation to thinking, this is above all a matter of not confusing true identity, which contains being and its determinations sublated within itself, with abstract, merely formal identity. All the charges of one-sidedness, harshness, lack of content, etc., which are so often levelled at thinking (especially from the standpoint of feeling and immediate intuition), have their basis in the perverse assumption that the activity of thinking is only an abstract positing of identity, and it is formal logic itself that confirms this assumption, by setting up the supposedly highest law of thought that has been elucidated in the above paragraph. If thinking were no more than that abstract identity it would have to be declared the most otiose and boring business in the world. Certainly the Concept, and furthermore the Idea, are self-identical, but they are self-identical only insofar as they at the same time contain distinction within themselves.

(β) Distinction
§ 116

Essence is pure identity and inward shine only because it is negativity relating itself to itself, and hence by being self-repulsion from itself; thus it contains the determination of *distinction* essentially.

> At this point otherness is no longer *qualitative*, i.e., no longer determinacy, or limit; but within the self-relating of essence, negation, being also relation, is at the same time *distinction, positedness, mediatedness.*

Addition. The question, "How does identity arrive at distinction?" presupposes that identity, taken as mere (i.e., abstract) identity is something on its own account, and that distinction, too, is something else that is equally something on its own account. But this presupposition makes it impossible to answer the question raised, for when identity and distinction are regarded as diverse, then what we have in fact is only distinction; and for that reason the advance to distinction cannot be demonstrated, because what the advance is supposed to start from is not present at all for the one who is asking about the "how" of the advance. So when we look more closely, the question proves to be a completely unthinking one and whoever raises it should be asked first of all what he understands by "identity". It would then turn out that no thought underlies the word he uses and that identity is just an empty name for him. Moreover, as we have seen, identity is certainly something negative, though not just abstract, empty nothing; instead, it is the negation of being and of its determinations. But as this negation, identity is at the same time relation; indeed, it is negative relation to itself or a distinguishing of itself from itself.

§ 117

Distinction is (1) *immediate* distinction, *diversity*, in which each of the distinct [terms] *is* what it is *on its own account* and each is indifferent vis-à-vis its relation to the other, so that the relation is an external one for it. Because of the indifference of the diverse [terms] with regard to their distinction, the distinction falls outside of them in a third, that *makes the comparison*. As identity of those that are related, this external distinction is *equality*, as their nonidentity it is *inequality*.

> The understanding lets these determinations themselves fall outside of each other in such a way that, although the comparison has one and the same substratum for the equality and the inequality, these are supposed to be diverse *sides* and *aspects* of it; but equality on its own is just the preceding [term], identity, and inequality on its own is distinction.
>
> Diversity has also been transformed into a principle: "Everything is diverse," or "There are no two things that are perfectly equal to each other." Here *everything* is given the predicate opposed to the identity which was attributed to it in the first principle—and thus a law that contradicts the first one is proclaimed. All the same, inasmuch as diversity only belongs to external comparison, something *by itself is supposed* to be only *identical* with itself; and in this way the second principle is supposed not to contradict the first. But in this case the diversity does *not belong* to the something or to everything, it does not constitute an essential determination of this subject; so, the second principle cannot be proclaimed at all.—But if, in accordance with the [second] principle, the something is *itself* diverse, then it is so in virtue of *its own* determinacy; but in this case it is no longer diversity as such that is meant, but *determinate* distinction.—This is the meaning of Leibniz's principle, too.[7]

Addition. When it sets itself to consider identity, the understanding is in fact already beyond it, and has distinction before it in the shape of mere diversity. In other words, if we follow the so-called law of identity, and say: "The sea is the sea," "The air is the air," "The moon is the moon," etc., we are regarding these ob-jects as being indifferent to one another; and hence it is not identity but distinction that we have before us. But, of course, we do not simply stop at the point of considering things as merely diverse; we *compare* them with one another instead, and in that way we obtain the determinations *equality* and *inequality*.

The business of the finite sciences consists for the most part in the application of these determinations; and when we speak of a scientific treatment nowadays, we usually and principally understand by that the procedure of comparing the ob-jects which have been chosen for investigation. It is obvious that many very important results have been achieved by this procedure and in this connection we may recall especially the great achievements of modern times in the fields of comparative anatomy and comparative linguistics. But it must also be noted in this regard that those who think that this comparative procedure can be applied in all fields of knowledge with the same success are going too far; on the contrary, it must be particularly emphasised that the needs of science cannot ultimately be satisfied by mere comparison, and that results like those we have just recalled must be considered only as preliminary (though quite indispensable) steps toward genuinely comprehending cognition.—Besides, insofar as comparison aims at tracing back given distinctions to identity, mathematics must be regarded as the science in which this goal is most perfectly attained, and that is because distinctions of quantity are completely external distinctions. In geometry, for example, a triangle and a rectangle, which are qualitatively diverse, are equated to one another with respect to their magnitude by abstracting from this qualitative distinction. We have already said earlier (§ 99 Addition) that neither the empirical sciences nor philosophy need to be envious of this advantage of mathematics; and this follows also from the remark made earlier about the mere identity that belongs to the understanding.

We are told that on one occasion Leibniz propounded the principle of diversity [i.e., of the identity of indiscernibles] when he was at court; and the ladies and gentlemen who were strolling in the garden tried to find two leaves that could not be distinguished from one another, in order, by exhibiting them, to refute the philosopher's law of thought. This is doubtless a convenient way to busy oneself with metaphysics and one that is still popular today; but with regard to Leibniz's principle it must be noted that being distinct must not be conceived as external and indifferent diversity, but as inner distinction,[a] and that to be distinct pertains to things in themselves.

§ 118

Equality is only an identity of [terms] that are *not the same*, not identical with one another—and inequality is the *relation* between unequal [terms].

---

a. *Unterschied an sich*

So equality and inequality do not indifferently fall apart into diverse sides or aspects but each is a shining into the other. Hence diversity is distinction of reflection, or *distinction that is in its own self, determinate* distinction.

Addition. Whereas what is merely diverse proves to be mutually indifferent, equality and inequality, on the contrary, are a pair of determinations that are strictly related to one another, and such that neither of them can be thought without the other. This advance from mere diversity to opposition can already be found in our ordinary consciousness, too, since we admit that comparing has meaning only on the assumption that there is a distinction, and conversely, likewise, that distinguishing has a meaning only on the assumption that there is some equality. So, too, when the problem is to indicate a distinction, we do not ascribe a great degree of acuity to someone who only distinguishes ob-jects from one another that are immediately and obviously distinct (e.g., a pen and a camel); just as we would say, on the other hand, that someone who can only compare things that are obviously alike—a beech with an oak, a temple with a church—has not advanced very far in the business of comparison.

So, where there is distinction, we require identity and, where there is identity, distinction. It frequently happens in the domain of the empirical sciences, however, that one of the two determinations diverts attention from the other, and that scientific interest is directed toward the tracing back of given distinctions to identity in one instance, and, in a similarly one-sided way, toward the discovery of new distinctions in the other. This is especially the case in the natural sciences. Natural scientists are primarily concerned with the discovery of new and ever newer substances, forces, genera, species, etc., or, in another direction, with the demonstration that bodies which had previously been taken to be simple are compound; modern physicists and chemists do indeed smile at the Ancients who were satisfied with four elements that were not even simple. But then, on the other hand, mere identity is made the centre of attention once more, and so electricity and chemical affinity are not only considered to be the same, for example, but even the organic processes of digestion and assimilation are taken to be merely chemical processes. We have noticed (§ 103 Addition) that although recent philosophy has frequently been nicknamed "Philosophy of Identity", it is precisely philosophy, and above all speculative logic, which exhibits the nullity of the mere identity that belongs to understanding, the identity that abstracts from distinction. This philosophy then also insists, to be sure, that we should not rest content with mere diversity but become cognizant of the inner unity of everything there is.

§ 119

(2) Distinction *in its own self* is the *essential* [distinction], the *positive* and the *negative*: the positive is the identical relation to self in such a way that it is *not* the negative, while the negative is what is distinct on its own account

in such a way that it is *not* the positive. Since each of them is on its own account only in virtue of *not being the other one*, each *shines* within the other, and is only insofar as the other is. Hence, the distinction of essence is *opposition* through which what is distinct does not have an *other in general*, but *its own* other facing it; that is to say, each has its own determination only in its relation to the other: it is only inwardly reflected insofar as it is reflected into the other, and the other likewise; thus each is the other's *own* other.

> Distinction in itself gives us the principle: "Everything is something essentially distinct"—or (as it also has been expressed): "Of two opposed predicates, only one belongs to something," and "There is no third."—This principle of antithesis[a] contradicts the principle of identity most explicitly, since according to the latter something is supposed to be only *relation to self*, while according to the former it is supposed to be an *opposite*, or *the relation to its other*. It is the peculiar absence of thought in abstraction to put two such contradictory principles side by side, without even comparing them.—The principle *of the excluded third* is the principle of the determinate understanding, which tries to avoid the contradiction and by doing so commits it. A must be either +A or −A; thus the third [term], the A which is *neither + nor −* and which is posited *also equally* as +A and as −A, is already expressed. If +W means 6 miles in the westerly direction, but −W 6 miles in the easterly direction, and + and − sublate each other, then 6 miles of road or of space remain what they were, with or without the antithesis. Even the mere plus and minus of number or of abstract direction have, if one pleases, zero for their third [term]; but one ought not to deny that the empty antithesis of the understanding between + and − also has its place, precisely in the context of such abstractions as number, direction, etc.
>
> In the doctrine of contradictory concepts, one concept is, for instance, called *blue* (for in a doctrine of this kind even something like the sense-representation of a colour is called a concept), the other *not-blue*, so that this other would not be an affirmative (like, for instance, *yellow*), but is just the abstractly negative that has to be held fast.—That the negative is also positive within itself is shown in the following paragraph [§ 120]; but this is already implied in the determination that that which is opposed to an other is

---

a. *Satz der Gegensatzes*

its other.—The emptiness of the antithesis between so-called contradictory concepts had its full presentation in the grandiose expression (as we may call it) of a universal law, that of *all* such opposed predicates one applies to *each* thing and the other not—so that spirit would be either white or not white, yellow or not yellow, and so on ad infinitum.

Since it is forgotten that identity and opposition are themselves opposed, the principle of opposition is taken also for the principle of identity in the form of the principle of contradiction; and a *concept* to which neither (see above) or both of two mutually contradictory characteristics apply, is declared to be logically false, like, for instance, a square circle.[8] Now, although a polygonal circle or a rectilinear arc contradicts this principle just as much, geometers do not hesitate to consider and to treat the circle as a polygon with rectilinear sides. But something like a circle (its mere determinacy) is not yet a *concept*; in the concept of circle, centre and periphery are equally essential, both characteristics belong to it; and yet periphery and centre are opposed to and contradict each other.

The notion of *polarity*, which is so generally current in physics, contains within itself a more correct determination of opposition; but if physics holds onto ordinary logic as far as its thoughts are concerned, it would easily get scared, if it were to develop polarity for itself, and would thus come to the thoughts that are implied in it.

Addition 1. The positive is identity once more, but now in its higher truth, as identical relation to itself, and at the same time in such a way that it is not the negative. The negative on its own account is nothing but distinction itself. The identical as such is, to begin with, what lacks determination; the positive, in contrast, is what is identical with itself, but determined against an other, and the negative is distinction as such, determined as not being identity. This is the inward distinction of distinction itself.

In the positive and the negative we think we have an absolute distinction. Both terms, however, are implicitly the same, and therefore we could call the positive "the negative" if we liked, and conversely we could call the negative "the positive" as well. Consequently, assets and debts are not two particular, independently subsisting species of assets. What is something negative for the debtor is something positive for the creditor. The same applies to a road to the East: it is equally a road to the West. Thus, what is positive and what is negative are essentially conditioned by one another, and are [what they are] only in their relation to one another. There cannot be the north pole of a magnet without the south pole nor the south pole without the north pole. If we cut a magnet in two we do not have the north pole in one piece and the south pole in the other. And in the same way, positive and negative electricity are not two diverse, independently subsisting fluids.

Quite generally, what is distinct in an opposition confronts not only *an* other, but *its* other. Ordinary consciousness treats the distinct terms as indifferent to one another. Thus we say, "I am a human being, and I am surrounded by air, water, animals, and everything else." In this ordinary consciousness everything falls outside everything else. The purpose of philosophy is, in contrast, to banish indifference and to become cognizant of the necessity of things, so that the other is seen to confront *its* other. And so, for instance, inorganic nature must be considered not merely as something other than organic nature, but as its necessary other. The two are in essential relation to one another, and each of them is [what it is], only insofar as it excludes the other from itself, and is related to it precisely by that exclusion. Or in the same way again, there is no nature without spirit, or spirit without nature. In any case, it is an important step in thinking, when we cease to say, "Well, something else is possible, too." When we say that, we are burdened with the contingent, whereas, as we remarked earlier, true thinking is the thinking of necessity.

In the natural science of the recent past, opposition that was first perceived as polarity in magnetism has come to be recognised as running through the whole of nature, or as a universal law of nature. This must without doubt be regarded as an essential step forward in science, as long as we are careful from now on not to let mere diversity take its place again beside opposition, as if nothing had happened. Colours, for instance, are rightly treated as confronting one another in polar opposition (as so-called complementary colours), on the one hand, and then, on the other hand, they are also regarded as the indifferent and merely quantitative distinction of red, yellow, green, etc.

Addition 2. Instead of speaking in accordance with the law of excluded middle (which is a law of the abstract understanding), it would be better to say, "Everything stands in opposition." There is in fact nothing, either in heaven or on earth, either in the spiritual or the natural world, that exhibits the abstract "either-or" as it is maintained by the understanding. Everything that is at all is concrete, and hence it is inwardly distinguished and self-opposed. The finitude of things consists in the fact that their immediate way of being does not correspond with what they are in-themselves. For instance, in inorganic nature, acid is at same time in-itself base, i.e., its being is totally and solely in its relatedness to its other. Hence also, however, acid is not something that persists quietly in the antithesis, but is rather what strives to posit itself as what it is in-itself. Generally speaking, it is contradiction that moves the world, and it is ridiculous to say that contradiction cannot be thought. What is correct in this assertion is just that contradiction is not all there is to it, and that contradiction sublates itself by its own doing. Sublated contradiction, however, is not abstract identity, for that is itself only one side of the antithesis. The proximate result of opposition posited as contradiction is the *ground*, which contains within itself both identity and distinction as sublated and reduced to merely ideal moments.

§ 120

The *positive* is that *diverse* [term], which has to be on its own account and at the same time *not* indifferent vis-à-vis its relation *to its other*. The *negative*, as negative relation *to self*, has to be equally independent. It has *to be on its own account* but at the same time, as strictly negative, it has to have its positive, this relation to self that belongs to it, only in the other. Both of them, therefore, are the posited contradiction, both are *in-themselves* the same. And both are the same *for-themselves*, too, since each is the sublating of the other and of itself. As a result they go to the *ground*.ª—In other words, essential distinction, as distinction in and for itself, is immediately only distinction of itself from itself; it therefore contains the identical; so essential distinction itself belongs, together with identity, to the whole distinction that is in and for itself.—*As relating itself to itself*, essential distinction is already expressed equally *as what is identical with itself*; and *what is opposed* is precisely that which contains *the One* and *its Other*, both *itself* and *its opposite* within itself. The being-within-self of essence, determined in this way, is *ground*.

(γ) GROUND
§ 121

Ground is the unity of identity and distinction; the truth of what distinction and identity have shown themselves to be, the inward reflection which is just as much reflection-into-another and vice versa. It is *essence* posited as *totality*.

> The *principle of ground* reads, "Everything has its sufficient *ground*,"⁹ i.e., the true essentiality of something is not the determination of it as identical with itself or as diverse, as merely positive or as merely negative, but the fact that it has its being in an other, which (as the identical-with-itself that belongs to it)ᵇ is its essence. The latter also is not abstract reflection *into self*, but reflection *into another*. Ground is the essence that is *within itself*, the latter is essentially ground, and it is ground only insofar as it is the ground of something, of an other.

Addition. When we say that ground is the *unity* of identity and distinction, this unity must not be understood as abstract identity, for then we would just have another name for a thought that is once more just that identity of the understand-

a. *gehen zu* Grunde
b. *als dessen Identisches-mit-sich*

ing which we have recognised to be untrue. So, in order to counter this misunderstanding, we can also say that ground is not only the unity but equally the distinction of identity and distinction, too. Ground, which we encountered first as the sublation of contradiction, therefore makes its appearance as a new contradiction. But, as such, it is not what abides peacefully within itself, but is rather the expulsion of itself from itself. Ground is ground only insofar as it grounds; but what has come forth from the ground is the ground itself, and herein lies the formalism of ground. The ground and what is grounded are one and the same content; and the distinction between them is the mere distinction of form between simple relation to self and mediation or positedness.

When we ask about the grounds of things, this is precisely the standpoint of reflection that we mentioned earlier (§ 112 Addition); we want to see the thing in question duplicated as it were: first in its immediacy and secondly in its ground, where it is no longer immediate. This is indeed the simple meaning of the so-called principle of sufficient reason or ground. This principle only asserts that things must essentially be regarded as mediated. Moreover, in setting up this law of thought, formal logic gives the other sciences a bad example, since it asks them not to take their content as valid in its immediacy; while, for its own part, it sets up this law of thought without deducing it and exhibiting its process of mediation. With the same right that the logician asserts when he maintains that our faculty of thinking happens to be so constituted that we must always ask for a ground, the doctor could answer that people are so organised that they cannot live under water when he is asked why a person who falls into the water drowns; and in the same way a jurist who is asked why a criminal is punished could answer that civil society is so constituted that crime cannot be allowed to go unpunished.

But even if we prescind from the demand, addressed to logic, that it should furnish a grounding for the principle of sufficient reason or ground, still it must at least answer the question of what is to be understood by "ground". The usual explanation, that a ground is what has a consequence, appears at first sight to be more illuminating and accessible than the determination of this concept that was given above. But if we go on to ask what a consequence is, and we get the answer that a consequence is what has a ground, then it is clear that the accessibility of this explanation consists only in the fact that what in our case has been reached as the result of a preceding movement of thought is simply presupposed in that explanation. It is precisely the business of the Logic, however, to exhibit the thoughts that are merely represented, and which as such are not comprehended nor demonstrated, as stages of self-determining thinking, so that these thoughts come to be both comprehended and demonstrated.

In ordinary life, and equally in the finite sciences, we very frequently employ this form of reflection with the aim of finding out, by its use, what the situation of the ob-jects under examination really is. And although there is nothing wrong with this way of looking at things, so long as it is only a matter of the immediate housekeeping needs of cognition, so to speak, still it should be noted at once that this method cannot provide definitive satisfaction, either in a theoretical or in a practical regard. This is because the ground still has no content that is determined in and for itself; and in consequence of that, when we consider something as grounded, we obtain only the mere distinction of form between immediacy and mediation. Thus, for instance, when we see an electrical phenomenon and ask for its ground, we receive the answer that the ground of this phenomenon is electricity; but this is simply the same content that we had before us immediately, translated into the form of something internal.

Now, of course, the ground is also not just what is simply identical with itself; it is also distinct, and for that reason various grounds can be offered for one and the same content. So, in accordance with the concept of distinction, that diversity of grounds now leads to opposition in the form of grounds *for* and *against* the same content.—Suppose, for example, that we consider an action, let us say, for argument's sake, a theft. This is a content in which a number of aspects can be distinguished. Property has been violated by the theft; while the thief, who was in need, has obtained the means for the satisfaction of his wants. It may be the case, too, that the person from whom the theft was made did not make good use of his property. Well, it is certainly correct that the violation of property which has taken place is the decisive point of view before which the others must give way; but this decision is not entailed by the principle of thought according to which everything must have a ground.

It is certainly the case that according to the usual version of this law of thought, what is meant is not merely any ground but a *sufficient* one; and one might think therefore that, in the case of the action that has been mentioned as an example, the points of view brought forward, other than violation of property, are grounds, to be sure, although they are not sufficient grounds. But what has to be said about that is that when people speak of a sufficient ground, the predicate is either otiose, or else it is one which transcends the category of ground as such. The predicate "sufficient" is otiose and tautological if it is supposed to express only the capacity to ground something, since a ground only is a ground to the extent that it possesses this capacity. If a soldier runs away from a battle in order to save his life, he acts in a way that is contrary to his duty, of course; but it cannot be maintained that the ground which has determined him to act in this way was insufficient, for if it was he would have stayed at his post.

However, it must also be said that, just as on the one hand, all grounds are sufficient, so, on the other hand, no ground is sufficient as such. This is because, as we have already remarked, the ground does not yet have a content that is determinate in and for itself; and consequently it does not act of itself and bring forth. It is the *Concept* that will soon show itself to be a content of this kind, one that is determinate in and for itself, and hence acts on its own; and that is what *Leibniz* is concerned with when he speaks of a *"sufficient* reason" or "ground" and insists on considering things from this point of view. What Leibniz primarily had in mind here was the merely mechanical approach that many people are still so attached to even now; and he rightly declared that it is inadequate. For instance, when the organic process of circulation of the blood is traced back to the contraction of the heart, this is a merely mechanical interpretation; and the theories of criminal law that consider the purpose of punishment to be to render the criminal harmless, or to deter, or to lie in other such external grounds are similarly mechanical. It is very unjust to Leibniz to suppose that he contented himself with something so lame as the formal principle of reason or ground. The mode of consideration that he asserted as valid is precisely the reverse of the formalism that lets the matter rest with mere "grounds"—where what is at issue is a cognition that comprehends. In this regard, Leibniz contrasted *causae efficientes* and *causae finales*, and required that we should not stop at the former but press on to the latter. According to this distinction, light, heat, and moisture, for example, must certainly be considered as *causae efficientes*, but not as the *causa finalis* of the growth of plants—the *causa finalis* being nothing else but the concept of the plant itself.

We may also remark at this point that to go no further than mere grounds, especially in the domain of law and ethics, is the general standpoint and principle of the Sophists. When people speak of "sophistry" they frequently understand by it just a mode of consideration which aims to distort what is correct and true, and quite generally to present things in a false light. But this tendency is not what is immediately involved in sophistry, the standpoint of which is primarily nothing but that of abstract argumentation. The Sophists came on the scene among the Greeks at a time when they were no longer satisfied with mere authority and tradition in the domain of religion and ethics. They felt the need at that time to become conscious of what was to be valid for them as a content mediated by thought. This demand was met by the Sophists because they taught people how to seek out the various points of view from which things can be considered; and these points of view are, in the first instance, simply nothing else but grounds. As we remarked earlier, however, since a ground does not yet have a content that is determined in and for itself, and grounds can be found for what is unethical and contrary to law no less than for what is ethical and lawful, the decision as to what grounds are to count as valid falls to the subject. The ground of the subject's decision becomes a matter of his individual disposition and aims. In this way the objective basis of what is valid in and for itself, and recognised by all, was undermined, and it is this negative side of sophistry that has deservedly given it the bad name referred to above.

As is well known, Socrates fought the Sophists[10] on all fronts; but he did not do so just by setting authority and tradition against their abstract argumentation, but rather by exhibiting the untenability of mere grounds dialectically, and by vindicating against them the validity of what is just and good, the validity of the universal generally, or of the concept of willing. We prefer to go to work only in an abstractly argumentative way nowadays, not only in discussions about secular things, but also in sermons. Thus, for example, all possible grounds for gratitude to God are brought forward. Socrates, and Plato, too, would not have scrupled to declare all this to be sophistry, since sophistry is primarily a matter not of content, which may well be true, but of the form of [arguing about] grounds, an argumentation by which everything can be defended, but also everything can be attacked. In our time, rich as we are in reflection, and given to abstract argumentation, someone who does not know how to advance a good ground for everything, even for the worst and most perverse views, cannot have come far. Everything in the world that has been corrupted, has been corrupted on good grounds. When an appeal is made to "grounds" people are at first inclined to give way to them; but if they have had experience of this procedure, they will turn a deaf ear and not let themselves be imposed upon any further.

§ 122

At first, essence is shining and mediation *within itself*; but as totality of mediation, its unity with itself is now *posited* as the self-sublation of distinction, and so of mediation. This, therefore, is the restoration of *immediacy* or of *being*, but of being inasmuch as it *is mediated through the sublation of mediation:—existence*.

> Ground does not yet have any *content* that is determined in and for itself, nor is it *purpose*. So it is neither *active* nor *productive*; instead, an existence simply *emerges* from the ground. The *determinate* ground is therefore something formal; it is any determinacy at all, insofar as it is posited as *related to itself* (i.e., as affirmation) in its relationship to the immediate existence that is connected with it. Precisely because it is *ground*, it is also a *good* ground [or reason]: for "good", in its entirely abstract use, means no more than something affirmative, and every determinacy is good which can be expressed in any way at all as something admitted to be affirmative. Hence, it is possible to find and to indicate a ground for everything; and a *good ground* (for instance, a good motive to act) may be effective or *not*, it may have a consequence or have *none*. It becomes a motive that produces something, for instance, by being taken up by someone's will, which is what first makes it active and a cause.

B. EXISTENCE

§ 123

Existence is the immediate unity of inward reflection and reflection-into-another. Therefore, it is the indeterminate multitude of existents as inwardly reflected, which are at the same time, and just as much, shining-into-another, or *relational*; and they form a *world* of interdependence and of an infinite connectedness of grounds with what is grounded. The grounds are themselves existences, and the existents are also in many ways grounds as well as grounded.

Addition. The term "existence" (derived from *existere*) points to a state of emergence,[a] and existence is being that has emerged from the ground and become reestablished through the sublation of mediation. As sublated being, essence has proved in the first place to be shining within itself, and the determinations of this shining are identity, distinction, and ground. Ground is the unity of identity and distinction, and as such it is at the same time the distinguishing of itself from itself. But what is distinct from the ground is not mere distinction anymore than the ground itself is abstract identity. The ground is self-sublating and what it sublates itself toward, the result of its negation, is existence. Existence, therefore, which is what has emerged from the ground, contains the latter within itself, and the ground does not remain behind existence; instead, it is precisely this process of self-sublation and translation into existence.

What we have here is therefore also to be found in the ordinary consciousness: when we consider the ground of something, this ground is not something abstractly inward, but is instead itself an existent again. So, for instance, we consider the ground of a conflagration to be a lightning flash that set a building on fire, and, similarly, the ground of the constitution of a people is their customs and circumstances of life. This is the general shape in which the existing world is presented initially to reflection, namely, as an indeterminate multitude of existents which, being reflected simultaneously into themselves and into something else, are in the mutual relationship of ground and grounded with regard to each other. In this motley play of the world, taken as the sum total of all existents, a stable footing cannot be found anywhere at first, and everything appears at this stage to be merely relative, to be conditioned by something else, and similarly as conditioning something else. The reflective understanding makes it its business to discover and to pursue these all-sided relations; but this leaves the question of a final purpose unanswered, and, with the further development of the logical Idea, the reason that is in need of comprehension therefore strikes out beyond this standpoint of mere relativity.

§ 124

But the reflection-into-another of what exists is not separate from its inward reflection; the ground is the unity of these two, out of which existence has gone forth. Hence, what exists contains relationality and its own manifold connectedness with other existents in itself; and it is *reflected* within itself as *ground*. Thus what exists is *thing*.

a. *deutet auf ein Hervorgegangensein*

The *thing-in-itself*,[11] which has become so famous in the Kantian philosophy, shows itself here in its genesis, i.e., as the abstract reflection-into-itself that is clung to, as against reflection-into-another and against distinct determinations in general, as the empty *basis* of all of them.

Addition. If we are to understand by "cognition" the apprehending of an ob-ject in its concrete determinacy, then the assertion that the "thing-in-itself" is beyond cognition must be admitted to be correct, since the thing-in-itself is nothing but the completely abstract and indeterminate thing in general. But, with the same right that we speak of the "thing-in-itself," we could also speak of "quality-in-itself," "quantity-in-itself," and similarly of all the other categories, and this would be understood to mean these categories in their abstract immediacy, i.e., apart from their development and inner determinacy. So we must consider the fixating of the thing as the only "in-itself" to be a whim of the understanding. But we also have the habit of applying the term "in-itself" to the content both of the natural and of the spiritual world. Hence we speak, for example, of electricity "in-itself" or a plant "in-itself," and similarly of man or the State "in-itself;" and by the "in-itself" of these ob-jects we understand what they rightly and properly are.

The situation here is no different than it is in respect to the thing-in-itself generally; that situation is, more precisely, that if we halt at ob-jects as they are merely in-themselves, then we do not apprehend them in their truth, but in the one-sided form of mere abstraction. Thus, for instance, "man-in-himself" is the child, whose task is not to remain in this abstract and undeveloped [state of being] "in-itself," but to become *for-himself* what he is initially only *in-himself*, namely, a free and rational essence. Similarly, the State-in-itself is the still undeveloped, patriarchal State, in which the various political functions implied by the concept of the State have not yet become "constitutionalised" in a way that is adequate to its concept. In the same sense the germ, too, can be regarded as the plant-in-itself. We can see from these examples that all who suppose that what things are in-themselves, or the thing-in-itself in general, is something that is inaccessible to our cognition are very much mistaken. Everything is initially "in-itself," but this is not the end of the matter, and just as the germ, which is the plant-in-itself, is simply the activity of self-development, so the thing generally also progresses beyond its mere in-itself (understood as abstract reflection-into-itself) to reveal itself to be also reflection-into-another, and *as a result it has properties*.

C. THING

§ 125

The *thing* is the totality as the development of the determinations of ground and of existence posited all in One. According to one of its moments, that of *reflection-into-another*, it has in it the distinctions according to which it is a *determinate* and concrete thing.

(α) These determinations are diverse *from each other*; they have their inward reflection not in themselves, but in the thing. They are *properties* of the thing, and their relation to it is [its] *having* [them].

> *Having*, which is a relation, replaces *being*. *Something* does, indeed, also "have" *qualities* in it, but this transference of having to what *is* is inaccurate, since determinacy as quality is immediately one with the something and since something *ceases to be*, when it loses its quality. The *thing*, however, is inward reflection, as the identity which is also distinct from the distinction, i.e., from its determinations.—"Having" is used in many languages to indicate the *past*, and rightly, because the past is *sublated being*, and spirit is the inward reflection of the past. Only in this reflection does the past still have subsistence; though spirit also distinguishes this being that is sublated within it from itself.

Addition. In the thing all the determinations of reflection recur as existent. Thus, the thing is identical with itself initially just as the thing-in-itself. But, as we have seen, there is no identity without distinction, and the properties which the thing has are its existent distinction in the form of diversity. Whereas previously the diverse terms proved themselves to be indifferent to one another, and their relation to one another was posited only through a comparison external to them, we now have, in the thing, a bond that connects the various properties with one another. Moreover, a property is not to be confused with a quality. We do certainly say also that something "has" qualities. But this way of speaking is unsuitable, insofar as "having" indicates an independence which does not yet belong to the something that is immediately identical with its quality. The something is what it is only through its quality; in contrast, although it is true that the thing likewise only exists insofar as it has properties, it is not bound up with this or that determinate property and therefore it can also lose the property without ceasing to be what it is.

§ 126

(β) But in the *ground*, reflection-into-another is in itself immediately inward reflection as well; consequently the properties are likewise self-identical, [i.e., they are] *independent* and freed from their attachment to the thing. Being inwardly reflected they are the determinacies of the thing *that are distinguished from each other*; and therefore they are not themselves things (since things are concrete), but existences reflected into themselves as abstract determinacies: they are *matters*.

The matters—for instance, magnetic, or electric matter[12]—are not called "things".—They are qualities in the proper sense of the term, they are one with their being (the determinacy that has reached immediacy), but they are one with a being that is reflected or is existence.

Addition. The transformation of the properties that the thing "has" into independent matters or stuffs "out of" which the thing "is made up" is certainly grounded in the concept of the thing, and therefore it is found in experience. But it is as much contrary to thought as it is to experience to conclude that, because certain properties of a thing, such as, for example, its colour, its smell, etc., can be presented as a particular colour-stuff or smell-stuff, therefore that is all there is to it, and that in order to get to the bottom of how things really are, nothing more needs to be done than to break them up into the stuffs out of which they are composed.

This breaking up of things into independent stuffs has its proper place only in inorganic nature, and the chemist is within his rights when he breaks up cooking salt or gypsum, for instance, into their stuffs and then says that the former consists of hydrochloric acid and sodium, and the latter of sulphuric acid and calcium. And, in the same way, geology rightly considers granite to be composed of quartz, feldspar, and mica. These stuffs of which the thing consists are partly things themselves, too, which can, in their turn, be broken down again into more abstract stuffs (for example, sulphuric acid is made up of sulphur and oxygen).

But although these stuffs or matters can in fact be presented as subsisting in their own right, it also happens quite often that other properties of things can similarly be considered as particular matters which are not, however, independent in this way. For instance, there is talk of caloric, electrical, and magnetic stuffs and matters; but these have to be regarded as mere fictions of the understanding. This is just how the abstract reflection of the understanding always proceeds, seizing arbitrarily upon single categories which are valid only as determinate stages in the development of the Idea; and then employing them—allegedly in the service of explanation, but in contradiction to unprejudiced intuition and experience—in such a way that every ob-ject investigated is traced back to them. Indeed, the view that things consist of independent stuffs is frequently applied in domains where it has no validity.

Even within nature, this category shows itself to be inadequate in the sphere of organic life. An animal may, of course, be said to "consist of" bones, muscles, nerves, etc., but it is immediately evident that this is a state of affairs quite different from a piece of granite that "consists of" the stuffs that were mentioned. These stuffs behave in a way that is completely indifferent to their union, and they could subsist just as well without it, whereas the various parts and members of the organic body have their subsistence only in their union, and cease to exist as such if they are separated from one another.

§ 127

Thus, a *matter* is the *abstract* or indeterminate reflection-*into-another*. It is inward reflection that is at the same time *determinate*. Hence, it is *thinghood that is there*, or the subsistence of the thing.[a] In this way the thing has its inward reflection in the matters (the contrary of § 125); it does not subsist in itself, but consists *of the matters*[b] and is only their superficial connectedness, i.e., an external combination of them.

§ 128

(γ) As the *immediate unity* of existence with itself, matter is also indifferent with regard to determinacy; the many diverse matters therefore merge into the *One matter* (or existence in the reflective determination of identity). As against this One matter, these distinct determinacies and the external *relation* which they have to each other in the thing are the *form*—the reflective determination of distinction, but as existing and as totality.

> This One matter, without determination, is also the same as the thing-in-itself; but it is the thing-in-itself as inwardly quite abstract,[c] and it is indeterminate matter as being in itself that is also for-another, and first of all for the form.

Addition. The diverse matters of which the thing consists are *in-themselves* [or implicitly] the same as one another. In this way we obtain the *one* general matter with respect to which distinction is posited as something external, i.e., as mere *form*. The interpretation that things are all based upon one and the same matter, and are only externally diverse in respect of their form, occurs frequently in reflective consciousness. On this view, matter counts as something that is completely indeterminate in itself, though susceptible of all determinations, and at the same time as something utterly permanent and self-same in all change and all alteration.

Now this indifference of matter with regard to determinate forms is certainly to be found in finite things; thus, e.g., it is indifferent to a block of marble whether it be given the form of this or that statue or even of a pillar. However, it should not be overlooked in this context that matter, such as a block of marble, is indifferent to form only in a relative way (in relation to the sculptor), but is never without form altogether. Hence, the mineralogist considers this only relatively formless marble as a determinate rock formation quite distinct from other, similarly determinate formations, such as, for example, sandstone, porphyry, and the like. So it is only the abstractive understanding that fixates "matter" in isolation and as formless in itself;

a. *die* daseiende Dingheit, *das Bestehen des Dings*
b. *besteht nicht an ihm selbst, sondern* aus den Materien
c. *als insich ganz abstraktes*

whereas in fact the thought of matter always contains the principle of form within it, and hence no existent matter that is formless is ever met with in experience.

But the interpretation of matter as present from the beginning and as formless in itself is, in any case, very old; we meet it already among the Greeks, initially in the mythical shape of Chaos, which was represented as the formless foundation of the existing world. One consequence of this representation is that God has to be considered, not the creator of the world, but the mere architect of it, the demiurge. The deeper view, in contrast, is that God created the world from nothing. What this expresses in general is that matter as such is not independent, on the one hand, and, on the other hand, that form does not accrue to matter from outside but, being [itself] totality, bears the principle of matter within itself. This free and infinite form will soon emerge for us as the *Concept*.

§ 129

The thing thus falls apart into *matter* and *form*, each of which is the *totality* of thinghood and is independent on its own account. But (*qua* existence) *matter*, which is supposed to be the positive, undetermined existence, involves reflection-into-another just as much as it does being-within-self; as unity of these determinations it is itself the totality of the form. But as totality of the determinations the form already contains inward reflection, or, *as form that relates itself to itself*, it has what ought to constitute the determination of the matter. Both are *in-themselves* the same. Once *posited*, this unity of theirs is quite generally the *relation* of matter and form, which are equally distinct.

§ 130

As this totality, the thing is the contradiction of being (according to its negative unity) the *form*—in which the matter is determined and degraded into *properties* (§ 125)—and of *consisting* at the same time of *matters*—which within the inward reflection of the thing are both independent and negated at the same time. Thus, in being the essential existence (as existence that sublates itself inwardly), the thing is [*shining forth* or] *appearance*.[a]

> The *negation*, also *posited* in the thing as independence of the matters, occurs in physics as *porosity*.[14] Each of the many matters (colour-stuff, odour-stuff, and other stuff, including, according to some, sound-stuff, and further, in any case, heat-stuff, electric matter, etc.) is *also negated*, and in this negation of it—in its pores—the many other independent matters are [found], which are equally

a. Erscheinung[13]

porous and which thus mutually let the others exist within themselves. The pores are nothing *empirical*; they are figments of the
understanding, which represents the negation of the independent
matters in this way, and covers up the further development of
contradictions with that nebulous confusion in which all of them
are *independent* and all of them equally *negated* in one another.—
When the faculties or activities are hypostatised in the same way
in spirit, their living unity becomes equally the confusion of the
influence[a] of the one upon the other.

The pores do not have their verification in observation (for we
are not talking about the organic pores, in wood, or in the skin, but
about the ones in the so-called matters, such as colour-stuff, heat-
stuff, etc., or in metals, crystals, and the like); the same is true of
matter itself, and a fortiori of any form separate from it (either the
thing consisting of matters, or subsisting itself and only having
properties). All of this is a product of the reflecting understanding,
which, while observing and pretending to indicate what it observes, brings forth the contrary, a metaphysics instead, and one
that is contradictory in all directions, though this fact remains
hidden from it.

B
Appearance

§ 131

Essence must *appear*. Its inward shining is the sublating of itself into immediacy, which as inward reflection is *subsistence* (matter) as well as *form*,
reflection-into-another, subsistence *sublating itself*. Shining is the determination, in virtue of which essence is not being, but essence, and the
developed shining is [shining-forth or] appearance. Essence therefore is
not *behind* or *beyond* appearance, but since it is the essence that exists,
existence is appearance.

Addition. Existence, posited in its contradiction, is appearance. The latter must not
be confused with mere semblance. Semblance is the proximate truth of being or
immediacy. The immediate is not what we suppose it to be, not something independent and self-supporting, but only semblance, and as such it is comprehended
in the simplicity of self-contained essence.[b] Essence is initially a totality of inward

---

a. *des Einwirkens*
b. *zusammengefaßt in die Einfachheit des in sich seienden Wesens*

shining, but it does not remain in this inwardness; instead, as ground, it emerges into existence; and existence, since it does not have its ground within itself but in an other, is quite simply appearance. When we speak of "appearance" we associate with it the representation of an indeterminate manifold of existing things, whose being is mediation pure and simple, so that they do not rest upon themselves, but are valid only as moments.

At the same time, however, this implies that the essence does not remain behind or beyond the appearance; instead, it is, so to speak, the infinite goodness that releases its semblance into immediacy and grants it the joy of being-there. When posited in this way appearance does not stand on its own feet, and does not have its being within itself but within an other. Just as God, the essence, is goodness, by virtue of lending existence to the moments of his inward shining in order to create a world, so he proves himself at the same time to be the might that rules it, as well as the justice that shows the content of this existing world to be mere appearance, whenever it wants to exist on its own account.

Appearance, in any case, is a very important stage of the logical Idea, and it may be said that philosophy distinguishes itself from ordinary consciousness by regarding what counts for the latter as having being and independence as mere appearance. But what matters here is to grasp the significance of appearance adequately. For, when we say of something that it is "only" appearance, this can be misunderstood as meaning that (in comparison with this thing that only appears) what *is*, or is *immediate*, is something higher. In fact the situation is precisely the reverse: appearance is higher than mere being. Appearance is precisely the truth of being and a richer determination than the latter, because it contains the moments of inward reflexion and reflexion-into-another united within it, whereas being or immediacy is still what is one-sidedly without relation, and seems to rest upon itself alone. Of course, the "only" that we attach to appearance certainly does indicate a defect, and this consists in the fact that appearance is still this inwardly broken [moment] that does not have any stability of its own. What is higher than mere appearance is, in the first place, *actuality*, which will be treated later, being the third stage of Essence.

In the history of modern philosophy it is Kant who has the merit of having been the first to rehabilitate the distinction between the common and the philosophical consciousness that we have mentioned. Kant stopped halfway, however, inasmuch as he interpreted appearance in a merely subjective sense, and fixated the abstract essence outside it as the "thing-in-itself" that remains inaccessible to our cognition. It is the very nature of the world of immediate ob-jects to be only appearance, and since we do know that world as appearance, we thereby at the same time become cognizant of its essence. The essence does not remain behind or beyond appearance, but manifests itself as essence precisely by reducing the world to mere appearance.

In any case, the naïve consciousness cannot be blamed, if in its desire for totality, it hesitates to acquiesce when subjective idealism asserts that we have to do strictly with mere appearances. But it easily happens that, in trying to save the objectivity of cognition, this naïve consciousness returns to abstract immediacy and, without more ado, holds fast to that, as what is true and actual. Fichte has treated the antithesis between subjective idealism and immediate consciousness in a short work bearing the title *Report, Clear as Daylight, to the Wider Public about the Real Nature of Recent Philosophy; an Attempt to Force the Reader to Understand.*[15] Here we find a conversation in which the author attempts to demonstrate to the reader how the subjective idealist standpoint is justified. During the conversation the reader complains to the author that he, the reader, cannot succeed in putting himself in the idealist position; he is inconsolable about the fact that the things that surround him are supposed not to be real things but merely appearances. The reader is certainly not to be blamed for this distress, since he is required to regard himself as confined within an impenetrable circle of merely subjective representations; but then, quite apart from this merely subjective interpretation of appearance, it must be said that we all have cause to be glad that, in dealing with the things that surround us, we only have to do with appearances and not with firm and independent existences, because in that case we would soon die of hunger, both bodily and mental.

A. THE WORLD OF APPEARANCE

§ 132

What appears exists in such a way that its *subsistence* is immediately sublated, and is only One moment of the form itself; the form contains subsistence or matter within itself as one of its determinations. Thus, what appears has its ground in the form as its essence, or as its inward reflection vis-à-vis its immediacy—but that only means that it has its ground in another determinacy of the form. This ground of what appears is just as much something-that-appears,[a] so that appearance proceeds to an infinite mediation of its subsistence by its form, hence by nonsubsistence as well. This infinite mediation is at the same time a unity of relation to self; and existence is developed into a *totality* and a *world* of appearance, or of reflected finitude.

B. CONTENT AND FORM

§ 133

The mutual externality of the world of appearance is totality and it is entirely contained within its *relation-to-self.* Hence, the relation of ap-

a. *ein Erscheinendes*

pearance to itself is completely determinate, it has the *form* within itself, and, because it has it in this identity, [it has the form] as its essential subsistence. Hence too, the form is *content*; and in its developed determinacy it is the *law* of appearance. The negative of appearance, that which is dependent and alterable, belongs to the form as *not reflected within-itself*: this is the indifferent, *external form*.

> Regarding the antithesis of form and content it is essential to remember that the content is not formless, but that it has the *form within itself* just as much as the form is *something external* to it. We have here the doubling of the form: on the one hand, as inwardly reflected, it is the content; on the other hand, as not reflected inwardly, it is the external existence, that is indifferent to the content. What is here present *in-itself* is the absolute relationship of content and form, i.e., the reciprocal overturning of one into the other, so that "content" is nothing but the *overturning of form* into content, and "form" nothing but *overturning of content* into form. This overturning is one of the most important determinations. But it is not *posited* until we reach *absolute relationship*.

Addition. Form and content are a pair of determinations that are frequently employed by the reflective understanding, and, moreover, mainly in such a way that the content is considered as what is essential and independent, while the form, on the contrary, is inessential and dependent. Against this, however, it must be remarked that in fact both of them are equally essential, and that, whilst there is no more a formless content than there is a formless stuff, still the two of them (content, and stuff or matter) are distinguished from one another precisely because the matter, although it is not in itself without form, shows itself to be indifferent in its way of being with regard to form, while content as such is what it is only in virtue of the fact that it contains developed[a] form within itself. But we find the form, too, has an existence that is indifferent with respect to the content and external to it, and this is the case because appearance in general is still burdened with externality.

If we consider a book, for instance, it certainly makes no difference, as far as its content is concerned, whether it be handwritten or printed, whether it be bound in paper or in leather. But this does not in any way imply that, apart from the external and indifferent form, the content of the book itself is formless. Certainly, there are books enough which may without injustice be said to be formless even with respect to their content; but, as it bears upon content here, this formlessness is synonymous with deformity,[b] which should be understood not as the absence of form altogether, but as the lack of the *right* form. This right form is so far from being indifferent with respect to content, however, that, on the contrary, it is the

a. *ausgebildete*
b. *Unförmlichkeit*

content itself. A work of art that lacks the right form cannot rightly be called a work of art, just for that reason. It is not a true work of art. It is a bad excuse for an artist as such to say that the content of his works is certainly good (or even excellent) but that they lack the right form. The only genuine works of art are precisely the ones whose content and form show themselves to be completely identical. We can say of the *Iliad* that its content is the Trojan War or, more precisely, the wrath of Achilles; in saying this we have said everything, but also only very little, for what makes the *Iliad* into the *Iliad* is the poetic form into which that content is moulded. Similarly, the content of *Romeo and Juliet* is the ruin of two lovers brought about by strife between their families; but by itself this is not yet Shakespeare's immortal tragedy.

Moreover, as far as the relationship of content and form in the domain of science is concerned, we ought to recall here the distinction between philosophy and the other sciences. The finitude of the latter consists altogether in the fact that thinking, which is a merely formal activity in them, adopts its content as something given from outside, and the content is not known to be determined from within by the underlying thought, so that the form and content do not completely permeate one another. In philosophy, on the contrary, this separation falls by the wayside, and hence it must be called infinite cognition. But even philosophical thinking is very frequently regarded as a mere activity of the form; in regard to logic especially, which admittedly has to do only with thoughts as such, its lack of content is taken for granted. If we simply understand by content only what is palpable, what is perceptible by the senses, then it must indeed be conceded willingly that philosophy as such, and the Logic in particular, have *no* content, i.e., they have no content of this sensibly perceptible kind. But with regard to what is understood by content, even our ordinary consciousness and our general linguistic usage do not stop at what is perceptible by the senses at all, nor yet in general at what is merely there. When we speak of a book that lacks content everybody understands that this does not simply mean that the book has empty pages; it means a book whose content is as good as nil; and it will turn out, on closer consideration, that, in the last analysis, what an educated mind refers to primarily as "content" only means what is well thought out. But this means also that we must admit that thoughts are not to be considered as indifferent to their content, or as being in themselves empty forms, and that, just as in art, so too in all other domains, the truth and the solidity of the content rest essentially on the fact that this content shows itself to be identical with the form.

§ 134

Immediate existence, however, is a determinacy of subsistence itself as well as of the form; hence, it is just as much external to the determinacy of content as this externality, which the content has through the moment of its subsistence, is essential to the content. Posited in this way, appearance is *relationship*, in which one and the same, the content, is the developed form; i.e., both the externality and *opposition* of independent existences, and their *identical* relation, within which alone these distinct existences are what they are.

C. RELATIONSHIP

§ 135

(α) The *immediate* relationship is that of the whole and *the parts*; the content is the whole and *consists* of its opposite, i.e., of the parts (of the form). The parts are diverse from each other and they are what is independent. But they are parts only in their identical relation to each other, or insofar as, taken together, they constitute the whole. But *the ensemble*[a] is the opposite and negation of the part.

Addition. Essential relationship is the determinate, quite universal mode of appearing. Everything that exists stands in a relationship, and this relationship is what is genuine in every existence. Consequently, what exists does not do so abstractly, on its own account, but only within an other; within this other, however, it is relation to self, and relationship is the unity of relation to self and relation to another.

The relationship of the whole and its parts is *untrue* inasmuch as its concept and reality do not correspond to one another. It is the very concept of a whole to contain parts; but if the whole is posited as what it is according to its concept, then, when it is divided, it ceases at once to be a whole. There certainly are things that answer to this part-whole relationship, but, just for that reason, they are only inferior and untrue existences. In this connection we should recollect the general point that when we speak of something's being "untrue" in a philosophical discussion, that should not to be understood to mean that the sort of thing spoken of does not exist; a bad State or a sick body may exist all the same, but they are "untrue" because their concept and their reality do not correspond to one another.

The relationship of whole and parts, being relationship in its immediacy, is in any case one that easily recommends itself to the reflective understanding; hence the understanding is frequently content with it where deeper relationships are in fact involved. For instance, the members and organs of a living body should not be considered merely as parts of it, for they are what they are only in their unity and are not indifferent to that unity at all. The members and organs become mere "parts" only under the hands of the anatomist; but for that reason he is dealing with corpses rather than with living bodies. This is not to say that this kind of dissection should not happen at all, but only that the external and mechanical relationship of whole and parts does not suffice for the cognition of organic life in its truth.

a. das Zusammen

The same applies in a much higher degree when the part-whole relationship is applied to spirit and to the configurations of the spiritual world. Even in psychology we do not speak expressly of "parts" of the soul or of the spirit; but still the treatment of this discipline from the point of view of the understanding also presupposes the representation of that finite relationship, because the various forms of spiritual activity are enumerated one after the other and are only described in their isolation, as so-called particular powers and faculties.

§ 136

(β) What is one and the same in this relationship, [i.e.,] the relation to self that is present in it, is thus an immediately *negative* relation to self, namely as the mediation, by virtue of which one and the same *is indifferent* with regard to the distinction and *is* the *negative* relation *to self*—the relation which, as inward reflection, repels itself into distinction, and as reflection-into-another, posits itself [as] existing, and conversely leads this reflection-into-another back into relation to self and into indifference. [This is] *force* and its *utterance*.

The *relationship of the whole and the parts* is the immediate (and therefore the thoughtless) relationship and overturning of self-identity into diversity. We pass from the whole to the parts and from the parts to the whole, forgetting in each the antithesis to the other, because we take each of them by itself—now the whole, and now the parts—as an independent existence. Or, since the parts are supposed to subsist *in* the whole and this [is supposed to consist] *of* the parts, it follows that, in one case, the whole is *what subsists*, in the other case, the parts, and each time the other [term] is correspondingly *what is unessential*. In its superficial form this is just what the *mechanical* relationship consists in: that the parts, as independent, stand over against each other and against the whole.

The *progress ad infinitum* that is involved in the *divisibility* of *matter* can also employ this relationship; and when it does, it becomes the thoughtless alternation of the two sides. First a thing is taken as *a whole*, and then we pass on to the *determination of its parts*; then this determination is forgotten, and we treat what was previously a part as a whole; then the determination of the part comes back, and so on ad infinitum. But when it is taken as the negative that it [really] is, this infinity is the *negative* relation of the relationship to itself; it is *force*, the whole that is identical with itself, as being-within-self—and as sublating this being-within-self and uttering itself—and conversely the utterance which vanishes and returns into the force.

In spite of this infinity, force is also finite; for the content, the *one and the same* of force and its utterance, is still only *in-itself* this identity; the two sides are not yet, each of them on its own account, the concrete identity of the relationship, i.e., the totality. Hence, they are diverse for each other and the relationship is a finite one. The force therefore needs solicitation from outside; it acts blindly, and, because of this defectiveness of the form, the content is restricted and contingent too. It is not yet truly identical with the form, not yet Concept and purpose, which is what is determinate in and for itself.—This distinction is most essential, but it is not easy to grasp; it has to determine itself more precisely in the concept of purpose itself. If we disregard this distinction, we are led into the confusion of grasping God as force—a confusion from which Herder's *God*[16] suffers quite conspicuously.

It is often said that the *nature* of *force* itself is *unknown* and that we are cognizant only of its utterance. But, on the one hand, the whole *determination of the content* of the *force* is just the same as the content-determination of the *utterance*; and because of this the explanation of an appearance through a force is an empty tautology. Thus, what is supposed to remain unknown is in fact nothing but the empty form of inward reflection, which is all that makes the force distinct from its utterance, and this form is likewise something that is quite well known. It adds nothing at all to the content and the law, of which we are supposed to be cognizant just from the appearance alone. We are also assured everywhere that this does not imply any assertion concerning the force [itself]; but in that case it is hard to see why the form of force was introduced into the sciences.—Yet, on the other hand, the nature of force is certainly something unknown, because both the necessity of the internal coherence of its content, and the necessity of the content insofar as it is restricted on its own account and hence has its determinacy through the mediation of an other that is outside it, are still lacking.

Addition 1. In comparison with the preceding immediate relationship of whole and parts, the relationship of force and its utterance should be considered infinite, because in it the identity of the two sides that was present only implicitly in "whole and parts" is now posited. Although it consists implicitly of parts, the whole does cease to be a whole when it is divided; a force, on the other hand, only proves itself to be a force by uttering itself. It returns to itself in its utterance, for the utterance is itself a force once more. But this relationship, too, is again a finite one, and its finitude consists generally in the fact that it is mediated; just as, conversely, the relationship of whole and parts has shown itself to be finite because of its immediacy. The finitude of the mediated relationship of force and its utterance is shown, first, by the fact that any force is conditioned by something else and needs something other than itself in order to subsist. Thus we all know, for instance, that the principal vehicle of magnetic force is iron, whose remaining properties (colour, specific weight, relationship to acids, etc.) are independent of this relation to magnetism. The situation is the same with all the other forces, which show themselves always to be conditioned and mediated by something other than themselves.

The finitude of force is shown further by the fact that it requires solicitation in order to utter itself. What solicits a force is again itself the utterance of a force (which in order to be uttered must similarly be solicited). In this way we get either an infinite progression once more or a reciprocity of soliciting and being solicited; but an absolute beginning of motion is still lacking here. Unlike purpose, force is not yet something that determines itself from within; the content is something determinately given, so that force, in uttering itself, is, as we say, blind in its working; and that is what is to be understood as the difference between the abstract utterance of force and all purposive activity.

Addition 2. The oft-repeated assertion that there can be cognition only of the utterance of a force, and not of the force itself, must be rejected as unfounded, because a force consists precisely in its utterance, so that cognition of the totality of utterance grasped as law is cognition of the force itself. Nevertheless, it should not be overlooked here that the assertion that what forces are in-themselves is beyond cognition, involves a correct hunch about the finitude of this relationship. We first encounter the single utterances of a force as an indeterminate manifold, and in their isolation they are contingent. Then we reduce this manifold to its inner unity, which we designate as "force", and by becoming cognizant of the law that reigns in it we become aware that what seems to be contingent is something necessary. But the various forces themselves are again manifold and, being merely juxtaposed, they appear contingent.

In empirical physics, therefore, we talk about the forces of gravity, of magnetism, of electricity, and so on; and similarly, in empirical psychology, we speak of the force of memory, the force of imagination, the force of will, and all manner of other forces of the soul. Hence, the need to become conscious of these various forces as a similarly unified whole recurs once more; and this need would not be satisfied by the simple reduction of the various forces to one primitive force that is common to them all. In fact, any such primitive force would be only an empty abstraction, as much lacking in content as the abstract thing-in-itself. Moreover, the relationship of force to its utterance is essentially a mediated one, and consequently, if we interpret the force as original or as self-subsistent, this contradicts the very concept of force.

This being the nature of force, we may well be content to let it be said that the existent world is an utterance of divine forces; but we should object to the treatment of God himself as a mere force, because force is still a subordinate and finite determination. It was in this sense therefore that the church declared impious the undertaking of those who (at the time of the so-called reawakening of the sciences) set themselves to trace the singular phenomena of nature back to the same underlying force. For, if it were the forces of gravitation, of vegetation, etc., which occasion the motion of the heavenly bodies, the growth of plants, etc., then nothing would remain for the divine governance of the world to do, and God would thereby be degraded into the idle spectator of this play of forces. Certainly, the natural scientists, and especially Newton,[17] claimed quite expressly that, although they employed the reflective form of force for the explanation of natural phenomena, their doing so was not meant to prejudice the honour of God as the creator and governor of the world. Nevertheless, this explanation by reference to forces has the consequence that the argumentative understanding proceeds to fixate the singular forces, each one on its own account, and cleaves to them in this finitude as something ultimate; so that, over and against this finitised world of independent forces and stuffs, nothing remains for the determination of God but the abstract infinity of a highest essence in a beyond that is unaccessible to our cognition.

This is, indeed, the standpoint of materialism, and of the modern Enlightenment, whose knowledge of God reduces to the fact *that* he is and disclaims all knowledge of *what* he is. So, in the polemic of which we are speaking, the church and the religious consciousness must be said to have been right, inasmuch as the finite forms of the understanding certainly do not suffice for the cognition either of nature or of the configurations of the spiritual world in their truth. All the same, we should not overlook the formal justification of the empirical sciences by the Enlightenment. This justification consists generally in reclaiming the content of this present world in all its determinacy for our thinking cognition—instead of letting the matter end simply with the abstract faith that God created and governs the world. When our religious consciousness, supported by the authority of the church, teaches us that it is God who created the world by his almighty will, and that it is he who guides the stars in their courses, and grants all creatures subsistence and well-being, the question "why?" remains to be answered, and the answering of this question is just what constitutes the common task of science, both empirical and philosophical. Insofar as the religious consciousness does not recognise this task and the right contained it it, but appeals to the impossibility of inquiry into the divine decrees, it adopts the above standpoint of the Enlightenment itself, and does not go beyond the mere understanding. But any such appeal must be regarded as the arbitrary assurance, not of Christian humility at all, but of courtly and fanatical self-debasement, since it contradicts the express command of the Christian religion that we should [re]cognise God in spirit and truth [John 4:24].

§ 137

As the whole which in its own self is negative relation to self, force is this: the repulsion of itself from itself and the *utterance* of itself.[a] But since this

a. *sich zu äußern*

reflection-into-another, or the distinction of the parts, is to the same extent inward reflection, the utterance is the mediation, through which the force, which returns into itself, *is* as force. The utterance itself is the sublation of the diversity (of the two sides) that is present in this relationship, and the positing of the identity, which *in-itself* constitutes the content. Its truth is therefore the relationship whose two sides are distinct only as *what is inner* and *what is outer*.

§ 138

(γ) *What is inner* is the ground, inasmuch as the ground, as mere form, is one *side* of appearance and of the relationship, the empty form of inward reflection; over against it likewise stands existence, the form of the other side of the relationship, with the empty determination of reflection-into-another, or what is *outer*. Its identity is fulfilled, it is the *content*, the *unity* of inward reflection and of reflection-into-another that is posited in the movement of the force; both are the same *one* totality, and this unity makes them into the content.

§ 139

Hence, what is outer is, *first of all*, *the same content* as what is inner. What is internal is also present externally, and vice versa; appearance does not show anything that is not within essence, and there is nothing in essence that is not manifested.

§ 140

Secondly, however, what is inner and what is outer are also *opposed* to each other as determinations of the form; and as abstractions of identity with self and of mere manifoldness or reality they are radically opposed. But since as moments of the One form they are essentially identical, what is first posited *only* in one abstraction is also *immediately only* in the other one. Hence, what is only *something-internal*, is also (by the same token) *only something-external*; and what is *only* something-external is also as yet *only something-internal*.

> The usual error of reflection is to take *essence* as what is merely *inner*. If it is taken only in this way, then this view of it is also a quite *external* one and that "essence" is the empty external abstraction.

> Into the *inwardness*[a] of Nature—says a poet—
> No created spirit penetrates,
> Most fortunate, if it knows but the *outer* shell!*

He should rather have said that, precisely when, for such a spirit, the essence of nature is determined as *what is inner*, then it only knows the *outer* shell.—Because in *being* in general, or even in mere sense-perception, the *concept* is still only what is inner, it is something outer [with regard] to being: both a being and a thinking that are subjective and without truth.—Both in nature and in spirit, too, Concept, purpose, and law, so far as they are still only *inner* dispositions, pure possibilities, are still only an external inorganic nature, what is known by a third, an alien power, etc.—The way a man is externally, i.e., in his actions (not of course just in his merely corporeal externality), that is how he is internally; and if he is *only* internally virtuous or moral, etc., i.e., *only* in his intentions, and dispositions, and his outward [behaviour][b] is not identical with those, then the former is as hollow and empty as the latter.

Addition. As the unity of the two preceding relationships, the relationship of inward and outward is at the same time the sublation of mere relationality and of appearance altogether. But for as long as the understanding holds inward and outward fast in their separation from one another, they are a pair of empty forms, and the one is as null as the other.

Both in the study of nature and in that of the spiritual world, it is of great importance to keep the special character of the relationship between inward and outward properly in view, and to guard against the error of thinking that only what is *inward* is essential, that it is the heart of the matter,[c] whilst, the *outward* side, on the contrary, is what is inessential and indifferent. We first meet this error when, as often happens, the distinction between nature and spirit is traced back to the abstract distinction between outward and inward. As for the interpretation of nature that is involved here, it is certainly true that nature is what is external gener-

---

*See Goethe's "Indignant Outcry" in *Zur Morphologie*, vol. 1:3:

> For sixty years I hear repeated,
> What I curse—be it in secret—:
> Nature has no core nor crust,
> Here everything comes all at once.[18]

a. *Ins* Innere
b. *sein Äußeres*
c. *worauf es eigentlich ankommt*

ally, not only for the spirit but also *in-itself*. But, this "generally" must not be taken in the sense of abstract externality, for there simply is no such thing, but rather in the sense that the Idea, which forms the common content of nature and spirit, is present in nature only in an external way, and yet, precisely for this reason, in a merely internal way too. And, however much the abstract understanding with its "either-or" may baulk at this interpretation of nature, still it is one that is also found in our other modes of consciousness, and in our religious consciousness most distinctly of all. Our religion says that nature, no less than the spiritual world, is a revelation of God, and the two are distinguished from one another by the fact that, whereas nature never gets to the point of being conscious of its divine essence, it is the express task of finite spirit to achieve this. That is just why the spirit is initially finite. So those who regard the essence of nature as something merely inward and therefore inaccessible to us are adopting the standpoint of those Ancients who considered God to be jealous, a position against which Plato and Aristotle have already declared themselves.[19] God imparts and reveals what he is, and he does it, first of all, through nature and in it.

Furthermore, the defect or imperfection of an ob-ject consists generally in its being only something inward, and hence at the same time only something outward, or (what is the same thing) in its being only something external, and hence at the same time only something internal. Thus a child, for instance, [considered] as human in a general sense, is of course a rational essence; but the child's reason as such is present at first only as something inward, i.e., as a disposition or vocation, and this, which is merely internal, has for it equally the form of what is merely external, namely, the will of its parents, the learning of its teachers, and in general the rational world that surrounds it. The education and formation of the child consists therefore in the process by which it becomes *for-itself* also what it is initially only *in-itself* and hence for others (the adults). Reason, which is at first present in the child only as an inner possibility, is made actual by education, and conversely, the child becomes in like manner conscious that the ethics, religion, and science which it regarded initially as external authority are things that belong to its own and inner nature.

In this connection, the situation is the same for the adult as it is for the child, to the extent that, in conflict with his vocation, he remains embroiled in the natural state of his knowing and willing; and similarly, for example, the punishment to which the criminal is subjected has for him the form of an external violence, but in fact it is only the manifestation of his own criminal will.

And from this discussion we can also gather what our attitude should be when someone appeals to his quite different inner self, and his allegedly excellent intentions and sentiments, in the face of his inadequate performances and even of his discreditable acts. There may, of course, be single instances where, through the adversity of external circumstances, well-meant intentions come to nothing and the execution of well–thought out plans is frustrated. But here, too, the essential unity of inward and outward generally holds good; and hence it must be said that a person *is* what he *does*, and the mendacious vanity that warms itself with the consciousness of inner excellence must be confronted with the saying of the Gospels that "By their fruits ye shall cognise them" [Matt. 7:16,20]. Just as it holds good first in an ethical and a religious connection, so that great saying holds for scientific and artistic achievements, too. As far as artistic ability is concerned, a teacher of keen eye may perhaps, when he becomes aware of notable talents in a boy, express the opinion that a Raphael or a Mozart lies hidden in him; and the results will show how far that opinion was well founded. But it is cold comfort for a dauber or a poetaster to console himself with the view that his inner self is full of high ideals; and when he demands that he should be judged by his intentions rather than his achievements, his pretensions are rightly rejected as empty and unfounded. Conversely, it is also very often the case that in judging others, who have brought about something fair, square, and solid, we may employ the false distinction of inward and outward, in order to maintain that what they have done is only something external to them, and that their inner motives were completely different, because they acted to satisfy their vanity or some other discreditable passion. This is the envious disposition which, being itself unable to accomplish anything great, strives to drag greatness down to its own level and to belittle it. As against this, we may recall the fine saying of Goethe, that for the great superiorities of others there is no remedy but love.[20] So if in order to depreciate the praiseworthy achievements of others there is talk of hypocrisy, we must notice, on the contrary, that although a man may certainly dissemble and hide a good deal in single instances, still he cannot hide his inner self altogether; it reveals itself infallibly in the *decursus vitae* [course of life], so that even in this connection it must be said that a man is nothing but the series of his acts.

In our modern era, what we call "pragmatic historiography"[21] has often sinned quite notably with regard to great historical characters through this false separation between inward and outward, dimming and distorting the unprejudiced apprehension of them. Instead of contenting themselves with simply narrating the great deeds that have been accomplished by heroes of world-historical stature, and recognising that their inner selves correspond to the content of these deeds, the pragmatic historians have considered it a right and duty to scent out allegedly secret motives behind what lies open to the light of day; and their opinion has been that historical inquiry is all the deeper the more it succeeds in removing the halo of the hero who has hitherto been celebrated and praised, and degrading him, with regard to his origin and his "real" significance, to the level of common mediocrity. In the interest of this kind of pragmatic historical inquiry, the study of psychology is often recommended, too, because it is supposed to yield information about the "real" motives by which people are generally determined to act. The psychology that is here appealed to, however, is nothing but that petty expertise about human nature[a] which takes as the ob-ject of its study, not what is universal and essential about human nature, but principally just what is peculiar and contingent such as isolated drives, passions, and so on. Besides, although this psychological-pragmatic approach to the motives that underlie great deeds would still leave the historian the choice between the substantial interests of the fatherland, of justice, of religious truth, etc., on the one hand, and the subjective and formal interests of vanity, ambition, avarice, etc., on the other, the latter are considered the "real" moving

a. *Menschenkennerei*

forces, because otherwise the presupposed antithesis between what is inward (the disposition of the person acting) and what is outward (the content of the action) would not be borne out. But since inward and outward have in truth the same content, it must be expressly asserted, against all such schoolmasterly cleverness, that if the historical heroes had been only concerned with subjective and formal[22] interests, they would not have accomplished what they did; and with reference to the unity of inward and outward, it must be recognised that the great men willed what they did and did what they willed.

§ 141

The empty abstractions, because of which the one identical content is still supposed to be in relationship, sublate themselves, through their immediate passing-over, into one another; the content is itself nothing but their identity (§ 138); they are the semblance of essence, posited as semblance. Through the utterance of force, what is inward is *posited* in existence; this *positing* is a *mediation* through empty abstractions; it vanishes within itself into the *immediacy*, in which what is *inner* and what is *outer* are identical *in and for themselves* and where their distinction is determined as mere positedness. This identity is *actuality*.

C
Actuality

§ 142

Actuality is the unity, become immediate, of essence and existence, or of what is inner and what is outer. The utterance of the actual is the actual itself, so that the actual remains still something-essential in this [utterance] and is only something-essential so far as it is in immediate external existence.

> *Being* and *existence* presented themselves earlier as forms of the immediate; *being* is quite generally unreflected immediacy and *passing-over* into another. *Existence* is immediate unity of being and reflection, and hence *appearance*; it comes from the ground and goes to the ground. The actual is the *positedness* of that unity, the relationship that has become identical with itself; hence, it is ex-

empted from *passing-over*, and its *externality* is its energy; in that externality it is inwardly reflected; its being-there is only the *manifestation of itself*, not of an other.

Addition. Actuality and thought—more precisely the Idea—are usually opposed to one another in a trivial way, and hence we often hear it said therefore that, although there is certainly nothing to be said against the correctness and truth of a certain thought, still nothing like it is to be found or can actually be put into effect. Those who talk like this, however, only demonstrate that they have not adequately interpreted the nature either of thought or of actuality. For, on the one hand, in all talk of this kind, thought is assumed to be synonymous with subjective representation, planning, intention, and so on; and, on the other hand, actuality is assumed to be synonymous with external, sensible existence.

These assumptions may be all very well in common life where people are not very precise about categories and their designation; and it may of course happen to be the case that the plan, or the so-called "idea", of a certain method of taxation, for example, is quite good and expedient in itself, but that nothing of the sort can be found in what is called (in the same ordinary usage) "actuality"—and that in the given circumstances it cannot be put into effect. All the same, when the abstract understanding takes control of these categories and exaggerates their distinction to the point of regarding them as a hard and fast antithesis, such that in this actual world we must knock ideas out of our heads, then it is necessary, in the name of science and sound reason, to reject such stuff decisively. For, on the one hand, ideas are not just to be found in our heads, and the Idea is not at all something so impotent that whether it is realised or not depends upon our own sweet will; on the contrary, it is at once what is quite simply effective and actual as well. On the other hand, actuality is not so bad or so irrational as it is imagined to be by "practical men" who are devoid of thoughts or at odds with thinking and intellectually derelict. As distinct from mere appearance, actuality, being initially the unity of inward and outward, is so far from confronting reason as something other than it, that it is, on the contrary, what is rational through and through; and what is not rational must, for that very reason, be considered not to be actual. This agrees, for that matter, with the usage of educated speech, in that, for example, we would object to recognising someone who does not know how to bring about something valid and rational as being "actually" a poet or a statesman.

The ground of a widespread prejudice about the relationship between the philosophies of Aristotle and Plato must also be looked for in the common interpretation of actuality that we are here discussing, and in the confusion of actuality with what is tangible and immediately perceptible. According to this prejudice, the difference between Plato and Aristotle is supposed to be that, whereas the former recognises the Idea and only the Idea as what is true, the latter, in contrast, rejects the Idea, and clings to what is actual; for that reason he should be considered the founder and leader of empiricism. On this head it must be remarked that actuality certainly does form the principle of Aristotle's philosophy, but his actuality is that of the Idea itself, and not the ordinary actuality of what is immediately present.

More precisely, therefore, Aristotle's polemic against Plato consists in his designation of the Platonic Idea as mere *dynamis*, and in urging, on the contrary, that the Idea, which is recognised by both of them equally to be what is alone true, should be regarded essentially as *energeia*, i.e., as the inwardness that is totally to the fore,[a] so that it is the unity of inward and outward. In other words, the Idea should be regarded as Actuality in the emphatic sense that we have given to it here.[23]

§ 143

As this concreteness, actuality contains those determinations [i.e., essence and existence, what is inner and what is outer] and their distinction; and it is therefore their development, too, so that they are at the same time determined in it as semblance, or as merely posited (§ 141). (1) As *identity* in general it is, first, *possibility*—the inward reflection that is posited as the *abstract* and *unessential essentiality*, in contrast to the *concrete* unity of the actual. Possibility is what is *essential* to reality, but in such a way that it is at the same time *only* possibility.

> It was probably the determination of *possibility* that allowed *Kant* to regard it—together with actuality and necessity—as *modalities*, "since these determinations do not in the least enlarge the concept as object, but only express its relationship to the faculty of cognition."[24] Possibility is indeed the empty abstraction of inward reflection—what was earlier called the inner, except that now it is determined as sublated, *merely posited*, external inwardness;[b] and so it is certainly now also *posited* as a mere modality, as an inadequate abstraction, or taken more concretely, as belonging only to subjective thinking. Actuality and necessity, on the contrary, are truly anything but a mere *mode or manner*[c] for something else; they are rather just the opposite, [for] they are posited as the concrete that is not only posited, but inwardly completed.—Since possibility is at first the mere form of *self-identity*, in contrast to the concrete as what is actual, the rule for it is only that something shall not inwardly contradict itself; consequently *everything is possible*, for this form of identity can be given to every content through abstraction. But *everything* is just as much *impossible* too; for in every content, since it is something-concrete, its determinacy can be grasped

a. *heraus*
b. *das . . . äußerliche Innre*
c. *Art und Weise*

as a determinate opposition and hence as a contradiction.—
For this reason there is nothing emptier than the talk about possibilities and impossibilities of this kind. And in particular, there should be no talk in philosophy of proving *that something* is *possible*, or *that something else* is *possible*, too; and that something, as people also say, is "thinkable." And the warning not to use this category which has already been shown up as untrue even on its own account applies just as immediately to the historian. But the subtlety of the empty understanding takes the greatest pleasure in this pointless invention of possibilities, and right many of them at that.

Addition. The notion of possibility appears initially to be the richer and more comprehensive determination, and actuality, in contrast, as the poorer and more restricted one. So we say, "Everything is possible, but not everything that is possible is on that account actual too." But, in fact, i.e., in thought, actuality is what is more comprehensive, because, being the concrete thought, it contains possibility within itself as an abstract moment. We find this accepted in our ordinary consciousness, too: for when we speak of the possible, as distinct from the actual, we call it "merely" possible.

It is usually said that possibility consists generally in thinkability. But thinking is here understood to mean just the apprehending of a content in the form of abstract identity. Now, since any content can be brought into this form, providing only that it is separated from the relations in which it stands, even the most absurd and nonsensical suppositions can be considered possible. It is possible that the moon will fall on the earth this evening, for the moon is a body separate from the earth and therefore can fall downward just as easily as a stone that has been flung into the air; it is possible that the Sultan may become Pope, for he is a human being, and as such he can become a convert to Christianity, and then a priest, and so on. Now in all this talk of possibilities it is especially the principle[a] of "grounding" that is applied in the way discussed earlier: according to this principle, anything for which a ground (or reason) can be specified is possible. The more uneducated a person is, the less he knows about the determinate relations in which the ob-jects that he is considering stand and the more inclined he tends to be to indulge in all manner of empty possibilities; we see this, for example, with so-called pub politicians in the political domain.

Moreover, it happens not infrequently in practical matters that evil will and inertia hide behind the category of possibility, in order to avoid definite obligations in that way; what we said earlier about the use of the principle of "grounding" holds good here, too. Rational, practical people do not let themselves be impressed by what is possible, precisely because it is only possible; instead they hold onto what is actual—and, of course, it is not just what is immediately there that should

a. *Denkgesetz*

be understood as actual. For that matter, there is no shortage of all manner of proverbs in common life in which the justly low estimation of abstract possibility is expressed. For instance, we say that "A bird in the hand is worth two in the bush."

And, furthermore, just as everything can be considered possible, so we can say with equal right that everything can be considered impossible, since any content (which, as such, is always something-concrete) contains not only diverse but also opposite determinations. Thus, for example, nothing is more impossible than the fact that I exist, for "I" is at once simple self-relation as well as, unconditionally, relation to another. The same situation holds for every other content in the natural and spiritual world. We can say that matter is impossible, because it is the unity of repulsion and attraction. The same holds for life, for law, for freedom, and, above all, for God himself as the true, i.e., triune God; indeed the Trinity is a concept that has been rejected by the abstract Enlightenment of the understanding in accordance with its principle, because it is allegedly an expression that cannot be thought without contradiction. In any case it is the empty understanding that roams around in these empty forms, and the business of philosophy with regard to them consists simply in exhibiting their nullity and lack of content. Whether this or that is possible or impossible depends on the content, i.e., on the totality of the moments of actuality, an actuality which, in the unfolding of its moments, proves to be Necessity.

§ 144

(2) But, in its distinction from possibility as inward reflection the actual is itself just the *externally* concrete, i.e., the immediate that is *inessential*. Or immediately, insofar as it is to begin with (§ 142) the simple unity of what is inner and what is outer, a unity which is itself immediate, the actual is [actual] as something-outer that is *inessential*. Thus, it is at the same time (§ 140) what is *only* internal, the abstraction of inward reflection; hence it is itself determined as something *only* possible. When it is given this value of a mere possibility, the actual is *something-contingent*, and conversely, possibility is mere *chance* itself.

§ 145

Possibility and contingency are the moments of actuality, what is inner and what is outer, posited as mere forms that constitute the *externality* of the actual. They have their inward reflection in the actual that is determinate *within-itself*, i.e., in the *content*, as their essential ground of determination. Hence, the finitude of the contingent and the possible consists more precisely in the distinctness of the form-determination from the content, and *for that reason whether something is contingent and possible depends on the content.*

Addition. Being just the inwardness of actuality, possibility is, precisely for that reason, merely external actuality or *contingency* as well. The contingent is generally what has the ground of its being not within itself but elsewhere. This is the shape in which actuality first presents itself to consciousness, and which is frequently confused with actuality itself. But the contingent is only the actual in the one-sided form of reflection-into-another or the actual considered as what is merely possible. We consider the contingent, therefore, as what either can be or can also not be, as what can be thus or otherwise too, i.e., as that whose being or not being, being thus or otherwise, is grounded not within itself but in another. It is, on the one hand, the general task of cognition to overcome the contingent, whilst, on the other hand, in the domain of the practical, the point is not to remain at the stage of the contingency of willing or of [simple] *freedom of choice*.[a] All the same, it has often happened, particularly in modern times, that contingency has been improperly elevated, and a value that it does not have has been ascribed to it, both in reference to nature and to the spiritual world as well. To begin with nature, it is very often admired chiefly on account of the richness and the multiplicity of its configurations alone. But, apart from the unfolding of the Idea that is present in it, that wealth (taken as it stands) offers nothing of higher rational interest; and the great multiplicity of inorganic and organic configurations affords only the intuition of a contingency that loses itself in indeterminateness. In any case, the motley play of single varieties of animals and plants, the ever-changing figures and groupings of clouds and so on, all conditioned by external circumstances, should not be rated higher than the equally contingent brain waves of a spirit that indulges itself in its own arbitrariness; and the admiration devoted to these phenomena is a very abstract mode of behaviour, from which we ought to advance to a closer insight into the inner harmony and lawfulness of nature.

In the next place, it is particularly important to make an adequate evaluation of contingency in respect of the will. When people speak of freedom of the will, they frequently understand by this simply freedom of choice, i.e., will in the form of contingency. Now, freedom of choice, as the capacity to determine oneself in this way or that, is certainly an essential moment of the will, which by its very concept is free. But it is not freedom itself at all; on the contrary, it is still only freedom in the formal sense.[b] The will that is genuinely free, and contains freedom of choice sublated within itself, is conscious of its content as something steadfast in and for itself; and at the same time it knows the content to be utterly its own. In contrast, the will that does not go beyond the level of freedom of choice, even when it decides in favour of what is, as regards its content, true and right, remains infected with the conceit that, had it so pleased, it could also have decided in favour of something else. For the rest, when we look at it more closely, freedom of choice proves to be a contradiction, because the form and content are here still opposed to one another. The content of freedom of choice is something given, and known to be grounded, not within the will itself, but in external circumstances. For this

a. *Willkür*
b. *die formelle Freiheit*

reason, freedom in relation to such content consists only in the form of choosing; and this formal freedom must be regarded as a freedom that is only supposed to be such[a] because it will be found, in the final analysis, that the same external sort of circumstances in which the content given to the will is grounded must also be invoked to explain the fact that the will decides in favour of just this and not that.

Although it follows from discussion so far that contingency is only a one-sided moment of actuality, and must therefore not be confused with it, still as a form of the Idea as a whole it does deserve its due in the world of ob-jects. This holds first for nature, on the surface of which contingency has free rein, so to speak. This free play should be recognised as such, without the pretension (sometimes erroneously ascribed to philosophy) of finding something in it that could only be so and not otherwise. Similarly, as we have already noted in respect to the will, the contingent also asserts itself in the world of spirit, since will contains the contingent within itself in the shape of freedom of choice, though only as a sublated moment. In regard to the spirit and its activity, we also have to be careful that we are not misled by the well-meant striving of rational cognition into trying to show that phe-nomena that have the character of contingency are necessary, or, as people tend to say, into "constructing them a priori."[25] For example, although language is the body of thinking, as it were, still chance indisputably plays a decisive role in it, and the same is true with regard to the configurations of law, art, etc. It is quite correct to say that the task of science and, more precisely, of philosophy, consists generally in coming to know the necessity that is hidden under the semblance of contingency; but this must not be understood to mean that contingency pertains only to our subjective views and that it must therefore be set aside totally if we wish to attain the truth. Scientific endeavours which one-sidedly push in this direction will not escape the justified reproach of being an empty game and a strained pedantry.

§ 146

More precisely, this *externality* of actuality implies that contingency (as immediate actuality) is essentially what is identical with itself only as *positedness*; but this positedness is equally sublated, it is an externality that is there. Thus it is *something-presupposed*, whose immediate way of being is at the same time a *possibility*, and is destined[b] to be sublated—i.e., to be the possibility of an other: the *condition*.

Addition. Being actuality in its immediacy, the contingent is at the same time the possibility of an other. But it is no longer the merely abstract possibility that we began with; instead it is the possibility that *is*; and as such it is *condition*. When we speak of the condition for this or that matter, this has a double implication: namely,

a. *eine bloß gemeinte Freiheit*
b. *die Bestimmung hat*

first, something-there, an existent, or in general something immediate; and secondly, the destination of this immediate being is to be sublated and to serve for the realisation of another one.

Now, immediate actuality as such is quite generally not what it ought to be; on the contrary, it is a finite actuality, inwardly fractured, and its destination is to be used up. But then the other side of actuality is its essentiality. Initially this is what is inward, which, being mere possibility, is similarly destined to be sublated. As sublated possibility it is the emergence of a new actuality, for which the first immediate actuality was the presupposition. This is the alternation that the concept of condition contains within itself. When we consider the conditions of a matter, they appear to be something quite without bias.[a] But, in fact, any such immediate actuality contains within it the germ of something else altogether. Initially, this other is just something possible; but this form then sublates and translates itself into actuality. The new actuality that emerges in this way is the specific inwardness of the immediate actuality, which the new actuality uses up. So what comes to be is quite another shape of things, and yet it is not another one either: for the first actuality is now simply posited in accordance with its essence. The conditions that sacrifice themselves, go under and are used up, only come together with themselves in the other actuality.—This is just what the process of actuality is like. Actuality is not just something that is immediately; but, as the essential being, it is the sublation of its own immediacy, and in this way it mediates itself with itself.

§ 147

(3) When it is developed in this way, this externality is a *circle* of the determinations of possibility and immediate actuality; the reciprocal *mediation* of these determinations is *real possibility* in general. As this circle, moreover, it is the totality, i.e., the *content*, the *matter* [i.e., *thing in question*][b] that is determined in and for itself; and, according to the distinction of the determinations within this unity, it is likewise the concrete *totality of the form* for-itself, the immediate self-translation of the inner into the outer and of the outer into the inner. This self-movement of the form is *activity*, activation[c] of the *matter* [itself], as the *real* ground, which sublates itself into actuality, and the activation of the contingent actuality, i.e., of the conditions: their inward reflection and their self-sublation into another actuality, the actuality of the *matter*. When *all conditions* are present, the matter *must* become actual, and the matter is itself one of the conditions; for, as what is inner, it is at first itself only something-presupposed. *Devel-*

a. *etwas ganz Unbefangenes*
b. *die Sache*[26]
c. *Betätigung*

oped actuality as the coincident[a] alternation of what is inner and what is outer, or the alternation of their opposed movements which are united into One movement, is *necessity*.

> It is true that necessity has been rightly defined as the unity of possibility and actuality. But when it is expressed only in this way, this determination is superficial, and therefore unintelligible. The concept of necessity is very difficult, precisely because it is the Concept itself, but its moments are still actualities, which have to be grasped at the same time only as forms, or as inwardly broken and in passage.[b] For this reason, the exposition of the moments that constitute necessity must be given in more detail in the following two paragraphs.

Addition. When it is said of something that it is necessary, what we ask in the first place is: "Why?". So, what is necessary should prove to be something posited, something mediated. If we stop at simple mediation, however, we do not yet have what is understood by necessity. What is merely mediated is what it is not through itself but through an other, and therefore it is also merely something-contingent. In contrast, we require of what is necessary that it be what it is through itself, and so, although it may be mediated, it must at the same time also contain mediation sublated within itself. We say of what is necessary, therefore, that it *is*, and hence that it counts for us as a simple relation to self, within which its being conditioned by an other falls away.

It is usually said about necessity that it is "blind," and this is quite right, inasmuch as *purpose* is still not present *explicitly* as such in the process of necessity. The process of necessity begins with the existence of dispersed circumstances that seem to have no concern with one another and no inward coherence. These circumstances are an immediate actuality that collapses inwardly; and from this negation a new actuality emerges. We have here a content that has a dual character within it in respect to its form: first, as the content of the matter that is at issue,[c] and secondly, as the content of the dispersed circumstances that appear to be something positive, and initially assert themselves as such. Because of its inward nullity, this content is inverted into its negative, and so becomes the content of the matter. As conditions, the immediate circumstances go under, but at the same time they are also preserved as the content of the matter. We say then that something quite different has emerged from these circumstances and conditions, and hence the necessity that constitutes this process is called "blind." By contrast, if we consider purposive activity, then the content is a purpose of which we knew beforehand, so that this activity is not blind but sighted.

---

a. *in Eins fallende*
b. *übergehende*
c. *als Inhalt der Sache*

When we say that the world is governed by Providence, this implies that, being predetermined in and for itself, purpose is what is at work generally, so that what is to come corresponds to what was previously known and willed. In any case, the interpretation of the world as determined by necessity, and the faith in a divine Providence, do not have to be considered reciprocally exclusive at all. What underlies the divine Providence[27] at the level of thought will soon prove to be the *Concept*. The Concept is the truth of necessity and contains the latter sublated within itself, just as, conversely, necessity is *implicitly* the Concept. Necessity is blind only insofar as it is not comprehended, and hence there is nothing more absurd than the reproach of blind fatalism that is levelled against the Philosophy of History because it regards as its proper task the cognition of the necessity of what has happened. In this perspective, the Philosophy of History takes on the significance of a theodicy; and those who think to honour divine Providence by excluding necessity from it by this abstraction actually degrade Providence to the level of blind, irrational arbitrariness. The naïve religious consciousness speaks of God's eternal and immutable decrees, and in that there lies the express recognition that necessity belongs to the essence of God. As distinct from God, man with his particular opining and willing carries on according to his mood and caprice, and so it happens to him that when he acts, what comes forth is something quite different from what he intended and willed; on the contrary, God knows what he wills, he is not determined in his eternal willing by inward or outward chance, and what he wills he also irresistibly brings about.

In relation to our disposition and behaviour generally, the standpoint of necessity is in any case of great importance. When we consider what happens as necessary, we seem at first sight to be in a completely unfree situation. As we all know, the Ancients viewed necessity as *destiny*, whereas the modern standpoint, on the contrary, is that of *consolation*. The general meaning of this "consolation" is that when we give up our purposes and interests, we do it in the expectation of receiving some compensation for them. Destiny, in contrast, is without consolation. But when we consider the matter more carefully, we find that the disposition of the Ancients with regard to destiny does not bring us face to face with unfreedom at all, but rather with freedom.[28] This is because unfreedom is grounded upon firmly cleaving to the antithesis, in such a way that we consider that what *is* and does happen stands in contradiction with what *ought* to be and to happen. The disposition of the Ancients, on the contrary, was to say: It is so, *because* it is, and it ought to be just *the way* it is. So there is no antithesis here, and hence no unfreedom, no pain, and no suffering.

Of course, as we remarked before, this attitude to destiny is without any consolation; but a disposition of this kind was never in need of consolation either, just because subjectivity had here not yet attained its infinite significance. This is the standpoint that must be kept in view, as what is decisive, when we compare the ancient frame of mind with our modern Christian disposition. Suppose that we first understand by subjectivity just the finite immediate subjectivity with the contingent and arbitrary content of its private inclinations and interests, or, in short, what we call a person, as distinct from the matter[a] in the emphatic sense of the

a. *Sache*

word (in the sense in which we usually say—and rightly so—that it is the "matter" that matters,[a] not the person). When we do that, we cannot but admire the serene submission of the Ancients to destiny, or fail to recognise this disposition as one that is higher and worthier than the modern one, which stubbornly pursues its subjective purposes, and, when it sees itself forced to renounce their attainment after all, can only console itself with the prospect of receiving compensation in another shape. But in addition, subjectivity is not really just that first subjectivity which, as opposed to the matter, is bad and finite; no, in its truth, subjectivity is immanent in the matter, and, being therefore infinite Subjectivity, it is the truth of the matter itself. When we interpret it in this way, the standpoint of consolation acquires quite another and higher significance, and it is in this sense that the Christian religion should be regarded as the religion of consolation and indeed of absolute consolation. As we all know, Christianity contains the doctrine that God wills that all men should be saved [1 Tim. 2:4], and that means that subjectivity has an infinite value. More precisely then, the consoling power of the Christian religion consists in the fact that God himself is known as absolute Subjectivity, and this Subjectivity contains the moment of particularity within itself. Hence, *our* particularity, too, is recognised to be something that is not just to be abstractly negated; it must at the same time be preserved.

Or again the gods of the Ancients were likewise regarded as personal, of course; but the personality of Zeus, or of Apollo and of the others, is not an actual personality but only an imaginary one. Or, to put it in another way, these gods are merely personifications; they do not *know themselves* as such; they are only *known about* instead. We also find this defect and this impotence of the ancient gods in the religious consciousness of the Ancients, in that they regarded the gods themselves, and not only human beings, as subject to destiny (to the *peprōmenon* or *heimarmenē*) —a destiny that had to be represented as unrevealed necessity, and hence as what is thoroughly impersonal, without self, and blind. The Christian God, in contrast, is not merely known, but utterly self-knowing, and not a merely imaginary personality, but rather the absolutely actual one.

For the rest, although we must refer to the Philosophy of Religion for a more developed explanation of the points touched upon here, we can add one more comment on how important it is that everyone should interpret whatever happens to him in the spirit of the old proverb that says, "Everyone is the smith who forges his own fortune." What this means, in general, is that man has the enjoyment only of himself.[b] The opposite view is the one where we shift the blame for what befalls us onto other people, onto unfavourable circumstances, and the like. But that is just the standpoint of unfreedom once more, and the source of discontent as well. By contrast, when we recognise that whatever happens to us is only an evolution of our own selves, and that we carry only the burden of our own debts, we behave as free men, and whatever may befall us, we keep the firm faith that nothing unjust can happen to us. People who live in discord with themselves and their lot get involved in much that is wrong and awry, precisely because of the false opinion

a. *daß es auf die Sache ankommt*
b. *Hierin liegt, daß der Mensch überhaupt nur sich selbst zu genießen bekommt*

that injustice has been done to them by others. Now, certainly, there is much that is contingent in what happens to us. But this contingency is grounded in the natural dimension of man. And, since we also have the consciousness of our freedom, the harmony of our souls and our peace of mind will not be destroyed by the misfortunes that befall us. Thus, it is our own view of necessity that determines our human contentment and discontent, and thereby our very destiny.

§ 148

Among the three moments, *condition*, *matter* [i.e., thing in question], and *activity*:

(a) The *condition* is (α) what is presupposed; as only *posited* it is only in relation to the matter; but as *pre*[supposed] it is by itself: it is a contingent, external circumstance that exists without reference to the matter. What is presupposed here is (in this contingency, but at the same time with reference to the thing in question, which is the totality) a *complete circle of conditions*. (β) The conditions are *passive*; they are used as material for the matter and in that way they enter into the *content* of the matter; they are thus in conformity with this content and already contain its *entire determination* within themselves.

(b) The *matter* [itself] is equally (α) something-presupposed: as *posited* it is still only something-inner and possible, and as *pre*[supposed] it is a content that is independent on its own account; (β) through the employment of the conditions it acquires its external existence, the realisation of its content determinations, which correspond on their side to the conditions, so that it also establishes itself as [the] thing in question on the basis of these conditions and emerges from them.

(c) The *activity* is (α) likewise existent on its own account, independently (a man, a character); and at the same time it has its possibility only in the conditions and in the matter [itself]; (β) it is the movement of translating the conditions into the matter, and the latter into the former as the side of existence; more precisely [it is the movement] to make the matter [itself] go forth from the conditions, in which it is *implicitly* present, and to give existence to the matter by sublating the existence that the conditions have. Insofar as these three moments have the shape of *independent existence* vis-à-vis one another, this process is *external* necessity.—This necessity has a *restricted* content as its matter. For the matter [itself] is this whole in *simple* determinacy; but since the whole is external to itself in its form, it is also inwardly and in its content external to itself, and this externality belonging to the matter is the restriction of its content.

§ 149

Hence, necessity is in-itself the *One essence* that is identical *with itself* but full of content, which shines within itself in such a way that its distinctions have the form of *independent actualities*; and as absolute *form* this identical [essence] is at the same time the *activity* of the sublating [of immediacy] into mediatedness and of mediation into immediacy.—What is necessary is so through an *other* that has fallen apart into the *mediating ground* (the matter and the activity), and an *immediate* actuality, something-contingent which is at the same time [its] condition. As what is through an other, the necessary is not in and for itself, but is something that is merely *posited*. But this mediation is just as immediately the sublating of itself; the ground and the contingent condition is transposed into immediacy,[29] whereby that positedness is sublated into actuality, and the matter has *gone together with itself*. In this return into itself the necessary *simply is*, as [an] unconditioned actuality.—The necessary is so, [because it is] *mediated* by a circle of circumstances: it is so, because the circumstances are so; and at the same time[a] it is so *without mediation*—it is so, because it is.

A. RELATIONSHIP OF SUBSTANTIALITY

§ 150

Inwardly the necessary is *absolute relationship*; i.e., it is the *developed* process (see the preceding paragraphs), in which relationship sublates itself equally into absolute identity.

In its immediate form it is the relationship of *substantiality* and *accidentality*. The absolute identity of this relationship with itself is *substance* as such. As necessity substance is the negativity of this form of inwardness,[b] and therefore it posits itself as *actuality*. But it is equally the *negativity* of this external [side], for through this negativity the actual, as immediate, is only *something-accidental*, which in virtue of this [very status of] mere possibility passes into another actuality; and this *passing-over* is substantial identity as *activity-of-form* (§§ 148, 149).

§ 151

Substance, therefore, is the totality of the accidents; it reveals itself in them as their absolute negativity, i.e., as the *absolute might* and at the same time as the *richness of all content*. The content, however, is *nothing but this manifestation itself*, since the determinacy that is inwardly reflected into

a. *in Einem*
b. *Innerlichkeit*

content is itself only a moment of the form, which passes over into the *might* of the substance. Substantiality is the absolute activity-of-form and the might of necessity, and every content is just a moment that belongs to this process alone—the absolute overturning of form and content into one another.

Addition. In the history of philosophy, we meet with *substance* as the principle of Spinoza's philosophy. About the significance and value of this philosophy, which has been as much praised as decried, there has been from the first much misunderstanding, and much argument pro and con. The charge that is raised as a rule against Spinoza's system is principally that of atheism, and then, on top of that, there is the charge of pantheism. The reason in both cases is that in Spinoza's system God is apprehended as substance and only as substance. What we should think about these charges follows directly from the position that substance occupies in the system of the logical Idea. Substance is an essential stage in the process of development of the Idea, but it is not the Idea itself; it is not the absolute Idea, but only the Idea in the still restricted form of necessity. Now, God is certainly necessity or, as we can also say, he is the *absolute matter*,[a] but at the same time he is the absolute *Person*, too. This is the point that Spinoza never reached, and it must be admitted that in this respect his philosophy fell short of the true concept of God which forms the content of the Christian religious consciousness. Spinoza was by descent a Jew, and on the whole it is the Oriental intuition, according to which everything finite appears as something merely transient and ephemeral, that has found in his philosophy its expression at the level of thought. It is true, of course, that this Oriental intuition of the unity of substance forms the foundation of all genuine further development, but we cannot stop at that; what it still lacks is the Occidental principle of individuality, which first emerged in its philosophical shape in the monadology of Leibniz, at the same time as Spinozism itself.[30]

If we review the charge of atheism levelled at the philosophy of Spinoza from the point of view that we have reached, we must reject it as ungrounded, because not only is God not denied in this philosophy, but, on the contrary, he is recognised as what alone truly *is*. Nor can it be maintained that, although Spinoza certainly speaks of God as the uniquely true, still this God of his is not the true one, and is therefore as good as no God at all. For in that case, if they remained at a subordinate stage of the Idea in their philosophising, we would have to charge all the other philosophers with atheism as well; and we should have to charge not only the Jews and the Mohammedans, because they know of God only as the *Lord*, but all the many Christians, too, who regard God only as the unknowable, the supreme and otherworldly Essence. When we look at it more closely, the charge of atheism levelled against the philosophy of Spinoza reduces to the point that his philosophy does not give the principle of difference (or finitude) its due; and this means that this system should be called, not atheism, but "acosmism" instead. For there is not, properly speaking, any world at all in it (in the sense of something that positively is).

a. *die* absolute Sache

What we ought to hold about the charge of *pantheism* follows from this too. If we accept a view that is widely held, and understand pantheism to be the doctrine that considers finite things as such, and the complex of them, to be God, then we shall be forced to acquit Spinoza's philosophy of the charge of pantheism, because no truth at all is ascribed to finite things or to the world as a whole in that philosophy. Nevertheless, this philosophy is certainly pantheistic, precisely because of its acosmism. Thus, the defect that we have recognised with respect to its *content* does at the same time prove to be a defect with respect to its *form*, in the first place because Spinoza places Substance at the head of his system and defines it as the unity of thinking and extension, without demonstrating how he arrives at this distinction and how he succeeds in tracing it back to the unity of Substance. The further treatment of the content then takes place according to the so-called mathematical method, which involves the initial setting-up of definitions and axioms, from which a series of theorems follow in sequence, the proof of which consists simply in deriving them in the manner of the understanding, from those unproven presuppositions. Spinoza's philosophy is usually praised for the strict consistency of its method, even by those who completely reject its content and its results. But this unconditional recognition of the form is, in fact, just as unjustified as the unconditional rejection of the content. On the side of content, the defect of Spinoza's philosophy consists precisely in the fact that the form is not known to be immanent to that content, and for that reason it supervenes upon it only as an external, subjective form. Substance, as it is apprehended immediately by Spinoza without preceding dialectical mediation—being the universal might of negation—is only the dark, shapeless abyss, so to speak, in which all determinate content is swallowed up as radically null and void, and which produces nothing out of itself that has a positive subsistence of its own.

§ 152

In the first form of necessity substance is [simply] substance. Then, as absolute might, substance is the might that *relates itself to itself* as a merely inner possibility, and hence determines itself to accidentality. According to this moment [of might], from which the externality that is thereby posited is distinguished, substance is *relationship* in the most proper sense: the *relationship of causality*.

B. RELATIONSHIP OF CAUSALITY

§ 153

Substance is *cause*, because—in contrast to its passing-over into accidentality—it is inwardly reflected; and in this way, it is the *original*

Thing.[a] But it is cause also because it equally sublates the inward reflection (or its mere possibility); i.e., because it posits itself as the negative of itself, and in that way produces an *effect*: an actuality which is therefore only a *posited* one, although at the same time it is a necessary one in virtue of the causal process.[b]

> As the *original Thing* the cause has the determination of absolute independence and of a subsistence that preserves itself against the effect; but in the necessity, the identity of which constitutes that originality itself, it has merely passed over into the effect. Inasmuch as we can speak again of a determinate content, there is no content in the effect that is not in the cause. That identity is the absolute content itself; but it is equally the form-determination as well: the originality of the cause is sublated in the effect, where it *makes* itself into a *positedness*. But this does not mean that the cause has vanished, so that only the effect would be actual. For this *positedness* is just as immediately sublated; it is rather the inward self-reflection of the cause, or its originality: it is only in the effect that the cause is actual, and is [truly] cause. In and for itself therefore the cause is *causa sui*.—Holding firmly to the one-sided representation of the *mediation*, Jacobi took this absolute truth of the cause, the *causa sui* (which is the same as the *effectus sui*), to be a mere formalism (*Letters on Spinoza*, 2d ed., 416).[31] He also declared that God must not be determined as ground, but essentially as cause; that this does not establish the point he was concerned about, however, would have become evident through a more thorough meditation on the nature of "cause." Even in the *finite* cause and in its representation this identity with regard to the content is present; the rain, which is the cause, and the wetness, which is the effect, are one and the same existing water. With regard to the form the cause (rain) is lost in the effect (wetness); but by the same token the determination of the effect [as "effect"] is lost, too, for the effect is nothing without the cause; and there remains only the undifferentiated wetness.
>
> In the usual sense of the causal relationship the cause is *finite*, inasmuch as its content is finite (just as it is in the finite substance) and inasmuch as the cause and the effect are represented as two diverse independent existences—but that is only what they are when we abstract from the causal relationship in considering

a. *die* ursprüngliche Sache
b. *Prozess des Wirkens*

them. In the realm of the finite, we do not get beyond the *distinction* of the form-determinations within their relation; hence, it is the turn of the cause to be *also* determined as *something-posited* or as an *effect*; this effect then has yet an *other* cause; and in this way the progress ad infinitum, from effects to causes, arises once more. A *descending* progress arises in the same way, since it follows from the identity of the effect with the cause that the effect is itself determined as a cause and at the same time as an *other* cause, which has again other effects, and so on forever.

Addition. Just as the understanding tends to baulk at substantiality, so, on the contrary, it is quite comfortable with causality, i.e., the relationship of cause and effect. When it is a case of interpreting some content as necessary, the reflective understanding makes a special point of tracing it back to the relationship of causality. This relationship certainly has the character of necessity, but it is itself only one side of the process of necessity. This process is just as much the sublation of the mediation that is contained in causality, and the demonstration that it [i.e., necessity] is simple self-relation. If we stop short at causality as such we do not have causality in its truth, but only a finite causality instead; and the finitude of this relationship then consists in holding fast to cause and effect in their distinction. Cause and effect, however, are not only distinct, but are just as much identical too, and this is even registered in our ordinary consciousness, when we say that the cause is a cause only because it has an effect, and the effect is an effect only because it has a cause. Thus, cause and effect have, both of them, one and the same content, and the distinction between them is primarily just that between *positing* and *being posited*; but then this difference of form sublates itself again, too, since the cause is not only the cause of an other, but is also the cause of itself, and the effect is not only the effect of an other, but also the effect of itself. So, the finitude of things consists in the fact that, although cause and effect are conceptually identical, the two forms occur separated in just *this* way: that although the cause is indeed an effect too and the effect is also a cause, nevertheless, the cause is not an effect in the same relation in which it is cause, and the effect is not a cause in the same relation in which it is an effect. This then gives us once again an infinite progression in the shape of an endless series of causes, which exhibits itself at the same time as an endless series of effects.

§ 154

The effect is *diverse* from the cause; as such the effect is *positedness*. But this positedness is likewise inward reflection and immediacy; and insofar as we hold onto the diversity of the effect from the cause, the effective action of the cause, its positing, is at the same time a *presupposing*. Hence, there is an *other substance* present, upon which the cause happens to work. As *immediate*, this [other] substance is not a negativity relating itself to itself; it is not *active*, but *passive*. Yet as substance it is active, too; it sublates the presupposed immediacy and the effect that is posited in it: it *reacts*, i.e., it sublates the activity of the first substance; but the first substance is likewise this sublation of its immediacy or of the effect posited in it, so that it sublates the activity of the second, too, and reacts. As a result causality has passed over into the relationship of *reciprocal action*.

> Although causality is not yet posited in its genuine determination, the progress, as an infinite progress from causes to effects, is truly sublated as progress in reciprocal action, because the rectilinear progression from causes to effects and from effects to causes is *curved* and *bent back* upon itself. As in every other case, this curving of the infinite progress into a relationship that is self-enclosed is the simple reflection that in all those unthinking repetitions there is only one and the same relation: namely, *this* cause and that *other* one, and their relation to each other. Reciprocal action, however, being the development of this relation, is itself the alternation of the *distinguishing*, not now of causes, but of the moments: *in each of which on its own* (again in accordance with the *identity* that the cause is cause in the effect, and vice versa, i.e., in accordance with this inseparability) *the other* moment, too, is posited equally.

C. RECIPROCAL ACTION

§ 155

The determinations that are maintained firmly as distinct in reciprocal action are (α) *in-themselves* the same; each side is the cause, original, active, passive, etc., just as much as the other one. Similarly, the presupposing of an other and the working upon it, the immediate originality and the positedness through the exchange, are one and the same. In virtue of its immediacy, the cause that is taken as the *first one* is *passive*, *positedness* and *effect*. The distinction between the causes that are said to be *two* is therefore empty, and there is *in-itself* only One cause present, which both sublates itself as substance in its effect and equally gives itself independence only in this effective action.[a]

a. *in diesem Wirken*

§ 156

(β) But this unity is also *for-itself*, since the whole exchange is the cause's own *positing*, and since only this positing of it is its *being*. The nullity of the distinctions is not only in-itself or [due to] our reflection (see the preceding paragraph). On the contrary, the reciprocal action is itself also the sublating-again of each of the posited determinations and its conversion into the opposite one; and hence it is the positing of the nullity (which is [at first] in-itself) of the moments. In the originality there is posited an effect, i.e., the originality is sublated; the action of a cause becomes reaction, and so on.

Addition. Reciprocal action is the relationship of causality posited in its complete development, and hence it is to this relationship that reflection tends to have recourse when the consideration of things from the standpoint of causality proves to be unsatisfactory because of the infinite progression discussed above. In the case of historical studies, for instance, the question discussed first is whether the character and the customs of a people are the cause of its constitution and laws, or whether, conversely, they are the effect of the constitution. Then the discussion moves on to the interpreting of both terms, character and customs on the one hand, and constitution and laws on the other, from the standpoint of reciprocal action, so that the cause is also the effect, in the same relation in which it is cause, and the effect is at the same time the cause, in the same relation in which it is effect. Or again, the same thing happens in the study of nature, and especially in that of the living organism, where single organs and functions likewise turn out to stand to one another in the relationship of reciprocal action.

Of course, reciprocal action certainly is the proximate truth of the relationship of cause and effect, and it stands on the threshold of the Concept, so to speak; but, just for this reason, we must not be satisfied to employ this relationship, when what is at issue is conceptually comprehensive cognition. If we stop at considering a given content just from the point of view of reciprocal action, we are in fact proceeding quite unconceptually; we are then dealing just with a dry fact, and the requirement of mediation, which is what is at issue when we start to use the relationship of causality, still remains unsatisfied. Looked at more closely, the use of the relationship of reciprocal action is unsatisfactory because, instead of being able to count as an equivalent of the Concept, this relationship itself still requires to be comprehended. And comprehension comes when its two sides are not left as something immediately given, but (as we have shown in the two preceding paragraphs) when they are recognised as the moments of a third, a higher [whole], which is, in fact, precisely the Concept. To consider the customs of the Spartans, for example, as the effect of their constitution, and then, conversely, to regard the constitution as the effect of their customs, may be correct so far as it goes. But this interpretation does not give us any ultimate satisfaction, because neither the constitution nor the customs of this people are in fact comprehended by this approach.

Comprehension comes about only when both of them, and similarly all of the other particular aspects that the life and the history of the Spartans display, are recognised as grounded in their concept.

§ 157

(γ) Hence, this pure exchange with itself is *unveiled* or *posited necessity*. The bond of necessity as such is the identity that is still *inner* and hidden; for it is the identity of those [terms] which count as *actual*, although their independence should precisely be the necessity. Hence, the course of substance through causality and reciprocal action is just the *positing* [of the fact] that *independence* is the infinite *negative relation to self*—*negative* indeed [because] distinction and mediation become in it the originality of *actualities* that are *independent* vis-à-vis each other—infinite *relation to itself* because the independence of these [terms] is just nothing but their identity.

§ 158

This *truth* of *necessity* is thereby *freedom*, and the *truth* of *substance* is the *Concept*, i.e., the independence, that is the repulsion of itself from itself into distinct independent [terms], [but] which, as this repulsion, is identical with itself, and which is this movement of exchange *with itself* alone that remains at home *with itself*.

Addition. Necessity is usually called hard, and indeed rightly so, to the extent that we do not go beyond it as such, i.e., beyond it in its immediate shape. We have here a state of things, or in general a content, that subsists on its own account; and necessity implies, in the first place, that this content is overcome by another which brings it to the ground. That is what is hard and sorrowful about immediate or abstract necessity. The identity of the two things which appear as bound to one another in necessity, and which, for that reason, lose their independence, is at first only an inner identity that is not yet present to those who are subject to necessity. And from this point of view, freedom, too, is, initially, just the abstract freedom that can only be saved by renouncing what we immediately have and are.

But again, as we have seen already, the process of necessity is the overcoming of what is present at first as rigid externality, so that its inwardness is revealed. What this process shows is that the terms that appear initially to be bound together are not in fact alien to one another; instead, they are only moments of *one* whole, each of which, being related to the other, is at home with itself, and goes together with itself. This is the transfiguration of necessity into freedom, and "freedom" now is not just the freedom of abstract negation, but concrete and positive freedom instead. From this we can also gather how absurd it is to regard freedom and necessity as mutually exclusive. To be sure, necessity as such is not yet freedom; but freedom presupposes necessity and contains it sublated within itself. The ethical person is conscious of the content of his action as something necessary, something that is valid in and for itself; and this consciousness is so far from diminishing his freedom, that, on the contrary, it is only through this consciousness that his abstract freedom becomes a freedom that is actual and rich in content, as distinct from freedom of choice,[a] a freedom that still lacks content and is merely possible. A criminal who is punished may regard the punishment meted out to him as a restriction of his freedom; in fact, however, the punishment is not an alien violence to which he is subject, but is only the manifestation of his own deed; and it is when he recognises this that he behaves as a free person. Generally speaking, the highest independence of man is to know himself as totally determined by the absolute Idea; this is the consciousness and attitude that Spinoza calls *amor intellectualis Dei* [the intellectual love of God].[32]

§ 159

The *Concept*, therefore, is the *truth of being and essence*, since the shining of reflection within itself is, at the same time, independent immediacy, and this *being* of [a] diverse actuality is immediately just a shining *within itself*.

In that the Concept has proven itself to be the truth of being and essence, which are both *returned* into it as their *ground*, it has also, conversely, *developed* itself out of *being* as out of its *ground*. The first side of the progression can be considered as a *deepening* of being into itself, whose inwardness[b] has been unveiled through this progression; while the second side can be considered as a going forth of *the more perfect from the imperfect*. Where this development has been considered only from the latter side, philosophy has been criticised for it. The more determinate import, which the superficial thoughts about imperfect and more perfect have here, is the distinction of *being*, as *immediate* unity with itself, from the *concept*, as *free mediation* with itself. Since *being* has shown itself to be a *moment* of the Concept, the latter has thereby proven itself to be the truth of being; as its inward reflection and as the sublating of mediation, the Concept is the *presupposing* of the *immediate*—a presupposing which is identical with the return-into-self: the identity that constitutes freedom and the concept. Hence, if the *moment*

a. *Willkür*
b. *Innere*

is called the imperfect, then the Concept, as what is perfect, is more precisely its own self-development from the imperfect, for it is essentially this sublating of its presupposition. But at the same time it is the Concept alone which, by positing itself, makes the presupposition. This has been shown to be the case in causality in general and more precisely in reciprocal action.

Thus, the Concept is determined in relation to being and essence as *essence that has returned* to *being* as *simple immediacy*. Through this return the shining of essence has actuality, while its actuality *is* at the same time a *free shining within itself*. In this way the Concept has being as its simple self-relation or as the immediacy of its unity, *within itself*; being is a determination that is so poor that it is the very least that can be exhibited in the Concept.

The passage from necessity to freedom, or from the actual into the Concept, is the hardest one, since independent actuality has to be thought of as having its substantiality only in its passing into, and its identity with, the independent actuality that is *other* than itself; thus the Concept is also the hardest, because it is itself precisely this identity. Actual substance as such, however (the cause, which in its being-for-itself will not allow anything to penetrate into it), is already subjected to the *necessity*, or to the destiny, of passing-over into positedness, and it is this subjection that is really the hardest. The *thinking* of necessity, on the contrary, is rather the dissolution of this hardness; because it is its[a] going-together with *itself* in the other—the *liberation*, which is not the flight of abstraction, and not the having of itself in that other actuality (with which the actual is bound together through the might of necessity) as something-other, but the having of its very own being and positing in it. As *existing for-itself*, this liberation is called "*I*," as developed into its totality, it is *free spirit*, as feeling, it is *love*, as enjoyment, *beatitude*.—The great intuition of Spinoza's substance *is* the *liberation* from finite being-for-itself, but only *implicitly*; however, it is the Concept itself that is *for-itself* the might of necessity as well as *actual* freedom.

Addition. When the Concept is called the truth of being and of essence (as it is here), we must be prepared for the question of why we did not start with it. A sufficient reply is that, when what is in question is cognition in the mode of thinking, we cannot begin with the truth, because truth, when it forms the beginning, rests on bald assurance, whereas the truth that is thought has to prove itself

---

a. *Seiner*

to be truth at the bar of thinking. If the Concept were posted at the head of the Logic, and defined as the unity of being and essence (which would be quite correct from the point of view of its content), then the question would arise about what is meant by "being" and by "essence", and how the two of them come to be brought together into the unity of the Concept. This would mean that we were beginning with the Concept in name only and not in actual fact. We would then really begin with "being," just as we did here; and the only difference would be that the determinations of being, and likewise those of essence too, would have to be taken up directly from representation, whereas we have here considered being and essence in their own dialectical development and have recognised how they sublate themselves into the unity of the Concept.

THIRD SUBDIVISION
OF THE *LOGIC*
THE DOCTRINE OF
THE CONCEPT

§ 160

As the *substantial might which is for itself* the Concept is what is *free*; and since[1] *each* of its moments is *the whole* that *it* is, and is posited as inseparable unity with it, the Concept is *totality*; thus, in its identity with itself it is what is *in and for itself determinate*.

Addition. The general standpoint of the Concept is indeed that of Absolute Idealism, and philosophy is conceptually comprehensive cognition, insofar as everything which in other forms of consciousness counts as something that is—and because it is immediate, as independent—is known within the Concept simply as an ideal moment. In the logic of the understanding we are accustomed to regard the Concept as a mere form of thinking, and, more precisely, as a general representation; and it is this subordinate interpretation of the Concept that is referred to by the assertion, so often repeated on behalf of feeling and the heart, that "concepts" as such are something dead, empty, and abstract. The situation is in fact quite the reverse: properly speaking, the Concept is the principle of all life, and hence, at the same time, it is what is utterly concrete.

That this is so has emerged as the result of the entire logical movement up to this point; so we do not have to start proving it here. The antithesis between form and content, which is given special validity when the Concept is supposed to be what is only formal, now lies behind us, together with all the other antitheses that reflection keeps fixed. They have been overcome dialectically, i.e., through themselves; and it is precisely the Concept that contains all the earlier determinations of thinking sublated within itself. Certainly the Concept must be considered as a form, but it is a form that is infinite and creative, one that both encloses the plenitude of all content within itself, and at the same time releases it from itself. For all that, the Concept can indeed be called abstract, too, if we understand by "con-

crete" only what is sensibly concrete, and in general what is immediately perceptible; for the Concept as such will not let us grasp it with our hands,[2] and, in
general, when the Concept is in question, hearing and seeing are things of the
past. All the same, as we have said already, the Concept is also what is utterly
concrete, precisely because it contains Being and Essence, and hence all the riches
of both these spheres, within itself in ideal unity.

As we said earlier, the various stages of the logical Idea can be considered as a
series of definitions of the Absolute. Consequently, the definition that results at
this point is that "the Absolute is the *Concept*." For this to be true, we must
certainly apprehend the Concept in another and higher sense than that which
"concept" has in the logic of the understanding, where it is regarded merely as a
form of our subjective thinking, without any content of its own. In this connection,
and because the Concept has a meaning in the speculative Logic that is so different
from the one that we usually associate with this term, we might raise just the
following question: "Why is something that is so completely different nevertheless
called 'concept'?" For the result is that an occasion for misunderstanding and
confusion is created. The answer to this question must be that, however great the
distance between the concept of formal logic and the speculative Concept may be, a
more careful consideration will still show that the deeper significance of the Concept is in no way so alien to general linguistic usage as it might seem to be at first
sight. We do speak of the "deduction" of a content from its concept, for instance, of
the deduction of legal determinations pertaining to property from the concept of
property; and conversely, we speak of tracing a content of this kind back to its
concept. This involves the recognition that the Concept is not merely a form which
is without any content of its own; for, on the one hand, nothing could be deduced
from such a form, and, on the other, tracing a given content back to the empty form
of the concept would only rob the content of its determinacy, instead of securing
the cognition of it.

§ 161

The progression of the Concept is no longer either passing-over or shining
into another, but *development*; for the [moments] that are distinguished are
immediately posited at the same time as identical with one another and
with the whole, and [each] determinacy is as a free being of the whole
Concept.

Addition. In the sphere of *Being* the dialectical process is passing-over into another,
whilst in the sphere of *Essence* it is shining into another. In contrast, the movement
of the *Concept* is *development*, through which only that is posited which is already
implicitly present. What corresponds to the stage of the Concept in nature is
organic life. For example, a plant develops from its germ: the germ already contains
the whole plant within itself, but in an ideal way, so that we must not envisage its

development as if the various parts of the plant—root, stem, leaves, etc.—were already present in the germ *realiter*, though only in a very minute form. This is the so-called Chinese box hypothesis,[3] the defect of which is that what is present initially only in an ideal way is regarded as already existent. What is correct in this hypothesis, however, is just that the Concept remains at home with itself in the course of its process, and that the process does not posit anything new as regards content, but only brings forth an alteration of form. This "nature" of the Concept, which shows itself in its process to be a development of itself, is what people have in view when they speak of the ideas that are innate in man, or when they say, as Plato himself did, that all learning is merely reminiscence; but, all the same, "reminiscence" should not be understood to mean that whatever constitutes the content of a mind that is educated by instruction was already present in that mind previously in its determinate unfolding.

The movement of the Concept must be considered, so to speak, only as a play; the other which is posited by its movement is, in fact, not an other. In the doctrine of the Christian religion this is expressed by the assertion that God not only created a world that confronts him as an other, but also that he has from all eternity begotten a Son in whom he, as Spirit, is at home with himself.

§ 162

The doctrine of the Concept subdivides into: (1) the doctrine of the subjective or *formal* Concept, (2) that of *objectivity* or of the Concept as determined to immediacy, (3) that of the *Idea*, or of the Subject-Object, the unity of the Concept and of objectivity, the absolute Truth.

> *Ordinary logic* embraces only the matters that we here encounter as one *part* of the *third* part of the whole, together with the so-called laws of thinking that we encountered above; and in applied logic there is some discussion of cognition, in combination with psychological, metaphysical, and other empirical material, because those forms of thinking turned out to be no longer sufficient by themselves; but as a result this science has lost its firm orientation.[4]— And those forms, which do at least belong to the proper domain of the Logic, are taken only as determinations of conscious thinking, or more exactly of conscious thinking only at the level of the understanding, not at the level of reason.
>
> The preceding logical determinations, the determinations of being and essence, are (of course) not mere thought-determinations; in the dialectical moment of their passing-over, and in their return into themselves and in their totality, they prove themselves to be *concepts*. But they are (cf. §§ 84 and 112) only *determinate* concepts, concepts in-themselves—or to say the same

thing another way, concepts *for us*. For the *other* (into which each determination *passes over*, or within which it *shines* and therefore is as something-relational) is not determined as *something-particular*, nor is its third moment determined as *something-singular* or as *subject*: the identity of the determination in its opposite, [i.e.,] its freedom, is not *posited*, because it is not *universality*.—What is usually understood by "concepts" are *determinations* of the *understanding*, or even just general *notions*; hence such "concepts" are always *finite* determinations (cf. § 62).

The Logic of the Concept is usually understood as a merely *formal* science, in the sense that what counts for it is the mere *form* of concept, judgment, and syllogism, but not at all whether something is *true*; truth is supposed to depend exclusively on the *content*. If the logical forms of the Concept were really dead, inactive, and indifferent receptacles of representations or thoughts, then, as far as truth is concerned, our information about them would be a completely superfluous and dispensable *description*.[a] In fact, however, being forms of the Concept they are, on the contrary, *the living spirit of what is actual*; and what is true of the actual is only *true in virtue of these forms, through them* and *in them*. Yet the truth of these forms on their very own account has never been considered and investigated until now, any more than the necessary connection between them has.

A
The Subjective Concept

A. THE CONCEPT AS SUCH

§ 163

The *Concept* as such contains the moment of *universality*, as free equality with itself in its determinacy; it contains the moment of *particularity*, or of the determinacy in which the Universal remains serenely equal to itself; and it contains the moment of *singularity*, as the inward reflection of the determinacies of universality and particularity. This singular negative unity with itself is what is *in and for itself determined*, and at the same time identical with itself or universal.

a. Historie

The singular is the same as the actual, except that it has issued from the Concept, and hence is *posited* as something-universal, or as negative identity with itself. Since the *actual* is still only *in-itself* or *immediately* the *unity* of essence and existence, it is *potentially* effective; but the singularity of the Concept is strictly *what is effective*—and of course it no longer works like a cause, with the semblance of producing something else: rather [it is] what produces *itself*.—Singularity, however, is not to be taken in the sense of merely *immediate* singularity—as when we speak of single things, or human beings, etc.; this determinancy of singularity is found only where we have the judgment. Every moment of the Concept is itself the whole Concept (§ 160); but singularity, the subject, is the Concept *posited* as totality.

Addition 1. When people speak of the Concept, they ordinarily have only abstract universality in mind, and consequently the Concept is usually also defined as a general notion. We speak in this way of the "concept" of colour, or of a plant, or of an animal, and so on; and these concepts are supposed to arise by omitting the particularities through which the various colours, plants, animals, etc., are distinguished from one another, and holding fast to what they have in common. This is the way in which the understanding apprehends the Concept, and the feeling that such concepts are hollow and empty, that they are mere schemata and shadows, is justified. What is universal about the Concept is indeed not just something common against which the particular stands on its own; instead the universal is what particularises (specifies) itself, remaining at home with itself in its other, in unclouded clarity.

It is of the greatest importance, both for cognition and for our practical behaviour, too, that we should not confuse what is merely communal with what is truly universal. All the reproaches that are habitually levelled against thinking in general, and, more specifically, against philosophical thinking, from the standpoint of feeling, and the oft-repeated assertion that it is dangerous to pursue thought to what are alleged to be too great lengths have their ground in this confusion. And in any case it must be said that in its true and comprehensive significance the universal is a thought that took millenia to enter into men's consciousness; and it only achieved its full recognition through Christianity. The Greeks, although otherwise so highly cultivated, did not know God, or even man, in their true universality. The Greek gods were only the particular powers of the spirit; and the universal god, the god of all nations, was, for the Athenians, still the hidden god. Consequently, for the Greeks there was an absolute gulf between themselves and the barbarians, and they did not yet recognise man as such in his infinite worth and his infinite justification. The question of why slavery has disappeared in modern Europe has indeed been raised; and this or that circumstance has been offered as the explanation of this phenomenon. But the genuine reason why there are no longer any slaves in Christian Europe is to be sought in nothing but the principle of Christianity itself. The Christian religion is the religion of absolute freedom, and only for

Christians does man count as such, man in his infinity and universality. What the slave lacks is the recognition of his personality; but the principle of personality is universality. The master considers the slave not as a person, but as a thing[a] devoid of self; and the slave himself does not count as an "I", for his master is his "I" instead.[5]

The distinction that we have made above between what is merely held in common and the genuine universal is strikingly expressed in Rousseau's well-known *Contrat social*, when he says that the laws of a State must emerge from the general will (the *volonté générale*), but that they do not at all need on that account to be the will *of all* (*volonté de tous*).[6] With regard to the theory of the State, Rousseau would have achieved something sounder if he had kept this distinction in mind all the time. The general will is the *Concept* of willing, and the laws are the particular determinations of willing as grounded in this Concept.

Addition 2. We must add a remark about the explanation of the origin and formation of concepts that is usually given in the logic of the understanding. It is not *we* who "form" concepts, and in general the Concept should not be considered as something that has come to be at all. Certainly the Concept is not just Being or what is immediate; because, of course, it involves mediation too. But mediation lies in the Concept itself, and the Concept is what is mediated by and with itself. It is a mistake to assume that, first of all, there are ob-jects which form the content of our representations, and then our subjective activity comes in afterwards to form concepts of them, through the operation of abstracting that we spoke of earlier, and by summarising what the ob-jects have in common. Instead, the Concept is what truly comes first, and things are what they are through the activity of the Concept that dwells in them and reveals itself in them. This comes up in our religious consciousness when we say that God created the world out of nothing or, in other words, that all finite things have emerged from the fullness of God's thoughts and from his divine decrees. This involves the recognition that thought, and, more precisely, the Concept, is the infinite form, or the free, creative activity that does not need a material at hand outside it in order to realise itself.

§ 164

The Concept is what is altogether *concrete*, because negative unity with itself as being-determined-in-and-for-itself (which is what singularity is) constitutes its own relation to self, or universality. From this point of view, the moments of the Concept cannot be separated; the determinations of reflection are *supposed* to be grasped and to be valid each on its own, separately from the one opposed to it; but since in the Concept their *identity* is *posited*, each of its moments can only be grasped immediately on the basis of and together with the others.[b]

a. *Sache*
b. *aus und mit den andern*

Taken abstractly, universality, particularity, and singularity are the same as identity, distinction, and ground. But the universal is what is identical with itself *explicitly in the sense* that it contains the particular and the singular at the same time. Furthermore, the particular is what is distinct or the determinacy, but in the sense that it is inwardly universal and is [actual] as something-singular. Similarly, the singular means that it is *subject*, the foundation that contains the genus and species within itself and is itself substantial. This is the *posited* unseparatedness of the moments in their distinction (§ 160)—the *clarity* of the Concept, in which each of the distinctions does not constitute a breach, or blurring, but is transparent precisely as such.

There is no greater commonplace than that the Concept is something *abstract*. This is correct in two ways: inasmuch as the element of the Concept is just thinking, and not the sensible in its empirical concreteness; and inasmuch as the Concept is not yet the *Idea*. From this point of view the subjective Concept is still *formal*, but this in no way means that it has to have or to receive any content other than itself.—As the absolute form itself, it is every *determinacy*, but in the way that it is in its truth. Although it is abstract, therefore, it is also what is concrete, and indeed it is what is altogether concrete, subject as such. What is absolutely concrete is the spirit (see § 159 Remark): the Concept, insofar as it *exists* as Concept, distinguishing itself from its own objectivity (which remains its *own*, however, in spite of the distinguishing). Everything else that is concrete, however rich it may be, is not so intimately identical with itself, and hence not so concrete in itself; and least of all what is commonly understood by "concrete", [i.e.,] a manifold that is externally held together.—What are also called concepts, and indeed determinate concepts, for instance, man, house, animal, etc., are simple determinations and abstract representations; these are abstractions that take only the moment of universality from the Concept, leaving out particularity and singularity, so that they are not developed in themselves and therefore they abstract precisely from the Concept.

§ 165

It is only the moment of *singularity* that *posits* the moments of the Concept as distinctions, inasmuch as singularity is the negative inward reflection of the Concept. Hence, it is *initially* its free distinguishing, as the *first negation*. Hereby the *determinacy* of the Concept is posited, but as particularity; i.e., the distinct [moments] have at first only the determinacy of the moments of the Concept over and against each other, and then secondly their identity (that the one moment is the other) is *posited* likewise. This *posited* particularity of the Concept is the *judgment*.

> The usual classification of concepts as *clear, distinct,* and *adequate*[7] does not apply to the Concept; but so far as it refers to representations it belongs rather to psychology, in that what is meant by a "clear" concept is an abstract, simply determined representation, and by a "distinct" concept a similar one, but in such a way that one *characteristic* in it, i.e., some determinacy, is emphasised as a sign for subjective cognition. There is nothing more characteristic of the superficiality and degradation of logic than the favorite category of the "characteristic" itself. The *adequate* concept comes closer to the Concept, and even to the Idea, but it still expresses only the formal aspect of the correspondence of a concept or a representation with its object, i.e., with an external thing.—The so-called "subordinate" and "coordinate" concepts are founded on the conceptless distinction of the universal and the particular, and on their relational connection[a] in an external reflection. Moreover, an enumeration of the types of *contrary* and *contradictory, affirmative* and *negative* concepts,[8] etc., is nothing but a haphazard recital of determinacies of thought which for their own part belong to the sphere of Being or to that of Essence, where they have already been considered; they have nothing to do with the determinacy of the Concept as such.—Only the genuine distinctions of the Concept, the universal, the particular, and the singular, constitute *types* of the Concept; and even then only so far as they are kept apart by an external reflection.—The immanent distinguishing and determining of the Concept is given in the *judgment*, for to judge is to determine the Concept.

B. THE JUDGMENT

§ 166

The *judgment* is the Concept in its particularity, as the distinguishing *relation* of its moments, which are posited as being-for-themselves and at the same time as identical with themselves, and not with each other.

---

a. *Verhältnis-Beziehung*

When considering the judgment, one usually thinks first of the *independence* of the extremes (the subject and the predicate): that the first is a thing or determination [that stands] on its own, and that the predicate likewise is a universal determination outside that subject (for instance, in my head), which is then brought together with the subject by me, and is thus "judged." But since the copula *"is"* attributes the predicate to the subject, that external, subjective *subsumption* is again sublated, and the judgment is taken as a determination of the *ob-ject* itself.—The *etymological* meaning of *"Urteil"* in our language is more profound and expresses the unity of the Concept as what comes first, and its distinction as the *original* division, which is what the judgment truly is.

The abstract judgment is the proposition: "The *singular* is the *universal*." These are the determinations which *subject* and *predicate* primitively have vis-à-vis each other, where the moments of the Concept are taken in their immediate determinacy or first abstraction. (The propositions: "The *particular* is the *universal*," and: "The *singular* is the *particular*," belong to the further determination of the judgment.) It must be considered a quite amazing lack of observation that we do not find any mention in the logic books of the fact that a proposition of this kind is expressed in *every* judgment: *"The singular is the universal,"* or, more determinately: *"The subject is the predicate"* (e.g., "God is absolute spirit"). It is true that the determinations of singularity and universality, or subject and predicate, are also distinct, but the absolutely universal *fact* remains, nonetheless, that every judgment expresses them as identical.

The copula *"is"* flows from the nature of the Concept: to be identical with itself in its uttering;[a] as moments of the *Concept*, the singular and the universal are the sort of determinacies that cannot be isolated. The preceding determinacies of reflection have among their relationships *also* the relation to each other, but their connection is only one of "having," not of "being"; it is not *identity posited as such* or *universality*. Hence, only the judgment is the genuine *particularity* of the Concept, for it is the determinacy or distinguishing of the Concept which continues to be *universality* all the same.

Addition. The judgment is usually considered to be a combination of concepts, and indeed of concepts of diverse sorts. What is right in this interpretation is that the

---

a. *Entäußerung*

Concept certainly forms the presupposition of the judgment, and that in the judgment it presents itself in the form of distinction. On the contrary, it is false to speak of concepts of diverse sorts, for the Concept as such, although concrete, is still essentially *one*, and the moments contained within it must not be considered to be diverse sorts of concepts; similarly, it is false to speak of a "combination" of the sides of judgment, because, when we speak of a combination, we think of the terms combined as occurring also in their own right outside the combination.

This external interpretation shows up in an even more definite way, when the judgment is said to come about through the "ascription" of a predicate to a subject. In this view, the subject counts as what subsists "out there" on its own account, while the predicate is what is found in our heads. But the copula "is" already contradicts this view. When we say, "This rose *is* red," or "This picture *is* beautiful," what the assertion expresses is that it is not just *we* who, from outside, dress the rose in red, or the picture in beauty, but, rather, that these are the objects' own characteristics. A further defect of the usual interpretation of the judgment in formal logic is the fact that in this perspective the judgment always appears to be something merely contingent, and the advance from the Concept to the judgment is not demonstrated.

But the Concept as such does not abide within itself, without development (as the understanding would have it); on the contrary, being the infinite form, the Concept is totally active. It is the *punctum saliens*[9] of all vitality, so to speak, and for that reason it distinguishes itself from itself. This sundering of the Concept into the distinction of its moments that is posited by its own activity is the *judgment*, the significance of which must accordingly be conceived of as the *particularisation* of the Concept. Indeed the Concept is *in-itself* already the particular, but the particular is not yet *posited* in the Concept as such; it is still in transparent unity with the universal there. So, as we have already noted (§ 160 Addition), the germ of a plant, for instance, already contains the particular: root, branches, leaves, etc., but the particular is here present only *in-itself*, and is posited only when the germ opens up; this opening up should be regarded as the judgment of the plant. Consequently, the same example can also serve to make it obvious that neither the Concept nor the judgment is found only in our heads and that they are not merely formed by us. The Concept dwells within the things themselves, it is that through which they are what they are, and to comprehend an ob-ject means therefore to become conscious of its concept. If we advance from this to the judging of the ob-ject, the judgment is not our subjective doing, by which this or that predicate is ascribed to the ob-ject; on the contrary, we are considering the ob-ject in the determinacy that is posited by its concept.

§ 167

The judgment is usually taken in a *subjective* sense, as an *operation* and a form, which occurs only in thinking that is *conscious of itself*. But this distinction is not yet present in the logical [realm]; [here] the judgment is to be taken as entirely universal: *every thing is a judgment.*—That is, every thing is a *singular* which is inwardly a *universality* or inner nature, in other words, a *universal* that is made singular; universality and singularity distinguish themselves [from each other] within it, but at the same time they are identical.

> The supposedly merely subjective sense of the judgment (as if it were *I* who "ascribe" a predicate to a subject) is contradicted by the expression of the judgment, which is, on the contrary, objective: "The rose *is* red," "Gold *is* a metal," etc. It is not I who first ascribe something to these [subjects].—Judgments are distinct from *propositions*; propositions contain a determination of the subjects which does not stand in a relationship of universality to them—a state, a singular action, and the like. "Caesar was born in Rome in this or that year, waged war in Gaul for 10 years, crossed the Rubicon," etc.—these are propositions, not judgments. Moreover, it is quite vacuous to say that propositions such as, for instance, "I slept well last night," or even "Present arms!" *can* be put in the form of a judgment. A proposition like: "A carriage is passing by," would be a judgment, and a subjective one at that, only if there could be doubt whether what is passing by is a carriage, or whether the ob-ject is moving, and not, on the contrary, the standpoint from which we observe it; for then the concern would be to find the [right] determination for [my] not yet appropriately determined representation.

§ 168

The standpoint of the judgment is *finitude*, and from this point of view the *finitude* of things consists in their being a judgment; [i.e.,] their thereness and their universal nature (their body and their soul) are indeed united (otherwise the things would be nothing), but these moments are already diverse as well as separable in principle.

§ 169

In the abstract judgment: *"The singular is the universal,"* the subject, as what relates itself to itself negatively, is what is immediately *concrete*; the predicate, on the contrary, is what is *abstract* or undetermined—it is the *universal*. But since they are connected by *"is"*, the predicate, too, must contain within its universality the determinacy of the subject; hence this determinacy is *particularity*, and this particularity is the *posited identity* of the subject and the predicate; but as what is therefore indifferent vis-à-vis this distinction of form it [the determinacy of the subject] is the *content*.

> The subject only has its explicit determinacy and content in the predicate;[10] and hence, taken on its own, it is a mere representation or an empty name. In the judgment: "*God* is the most real, etc." or: "The Absolute is identical with itself, etc."—*God*, or the *Absolute*, is a mere name: what the subject *is* is expressed only in the predicate. What else it may be, as something concrete, does not concern *this* judgment (cf. § 31).

Addition. It is quite trivial to say, "The subject is what something is said about, and the predicate is what is said about it"; from this we learn nothing more precise about the distinction between subject and predicate. At the level of its thought, the subject is first of all the singular, and the predicate is the universal. What happens in the further development of the judgment is that the subject does not remain just the immediate singular, nor does the predicate continue to be just the abstract universal; next subject and predicate also acquire the significance of the particular and the universal (in the case of the subject), and of the particular and the singular (in the case of the predicate). This exchange of significance between the two sides of the judgment is what takes place under the designations "subject" and "predicate".

§ 170

With regard to the more precise determinacy of the subject and the predicate, the *first*, as negative relation to itself (§§ 163, 166 Remark), is the solid ground in which the predicate has its subsistence and is ideal (it *inheres* in the subject); and since the subject is altogether and *immediately* concrete, the determinate content of the predicate is only *one* of the *many* determinacies of the subject, and the latter [is] richer and wider than the predicate.

Conversely, the predicate, as what is universal, subsists on its own account, and it is indifferent as to whether this subject is or is not; it reaches beyond the subject, *subsumes* it under itself, and is for its part wider than the subject. It is only the *determinate content* of the predicate (§ 169) that constitutes the identity of the two.

§ 171

In the judgment, subject, predicate, and the determinate content or [their] identity are posited at first precisely in their relation as *diverse*, or as falling outside each other. But *in-themselves* (i.e., according to the Concept) they are *identical*, since the concrete totality of the subject consists, not in being some undeterminate manifold, but in the fact that only it is *singularity*, [i.e.,] it is the particular and the universal within an identity, and precisely this unity is the predicate (§ 170).—In the copula, moreover, the *identity* of the subject and the predicate is *posited*, to be sure, but it is posited at first only as an abstract *is*. According to this *identity*, the subject also has to be *posited* in the determination of the predicate, and therefore the predicate, too, receives the determination of the subject, and the copula *fulfills* itself. This is the *further determination* of the judgment by the fulfilled copula [which leads] to the *syllogism*. But in respect of the judgment there is first the further determination of the judgment itself, the determination of the initially abstract, *sensible universality* to *allness*, *genus*, and *species* and to the developed *universality of the Concept*.

> It is only the cognition of the further determination of the judg-
> ment that gives *coherence* as well as *sense* to what are usually pre-
> sented as the *species* of judgment. Apart from looking quite con-
> tingent, the usual enumeration is superficial, and even confused
> and disorderly, in its indication of the distinctions. How positive,
> categorical, and assertoric judgments are distinguished is some-
> times just a matter of pure conjecture and sometimes it remains
> undetermined. The various judgments have to be looked upon as
> following necessarily from one another and as *a further determina-
> tion of the Concept*, for the judgment itself is nothing but the *deter-
> minate* Concept.
>
> In their relation to the two preceding spheres of *Being* and of
> *Essence*, the *determinate concepts* are, as judgments, reproductions
> of these spheres, but they are posited in the simple relation of the
> Concept.

Addition. The various types of judgment are to be interpreted not just as an empirical multiplicity, but as a totality determined by thinking; and one of Kant's great
achievements was to have been the first to draw our attention to this. Kant's
classification of judgments[11] according to the schema of his table of categories into
the judgments of quality, quantity, relation, and modality, cannot be regarded as
adequate, partly because of the merely formal application of the schema, and partly
because of its content. But all the same, what underlies this classification is the
genuine intuition that the various types of judgment are determined by the universal forms of the logical Idea itself. Thus we obtain, first of all, three main types of
judgment, which correspond to the stages of Being, Essence, and Concept. In
accord with the character of Essence, as the stage of difference, the second of these

main types is again inwardly divided in two. The inner ground of this system of the judgment must be sought in the fact that, since the Concept is the ideal unity of being and essence, the unfolding of it that comes about in the judgment must also, first of all, reproduce these two stages in a conceptual transformation, while the Concept itself shows itself to be what determines the genuine judgment.

The various types of judgment must not be regarded as standing beside one another, each having the same value; instead, they must be seen as forming a sequence of stages, and the distinction between them rests on the logical significance of the predicate. We can indeed find this already in our ordinary consciousness, in that we unhesitatingly ascribe only a very inadequate power of judgment to someone who habitually frames only such judgments as "This wall is green," "This oven is hot," and so on; in contrast, we say that someone genuinely understands how to judge only when his judgments deal with whether a certain work of art is beautiful, whether an action is good, and so on. In the case of judgments of the first kind, the content is only an abstract quality, the presence of which can be adequately decided by immediate perception; whereas, to say of a work of art that it is beautiful, or of an action that it is good, the ob-jects in question must be compared with what they ought to be, i.e., with their concept.

(α) The Qualitative Judgment
§ 172

The immediate judgment is the *judgment* of *thereness*; the subject [is] posited in a universality (as its predicate) which is an immediate (and hence sensible) quality. (1) The *positive* judgment: the singular is something-particular. But the singular is *not* something-particular; more precisely, such a singular quality does not correspond to the concrete nature of the subject: (2) the *negative* judgment.

> It is one of the most fundamental logical prejudices that qualitative judgments such as: "The rose is red," or: "is not red," can contain truth.[12] *Correct* they may be, but only in the restricted confines of perception, finite representation, and thinking; this depends on the content which is just as finite, and untrue on its own account. But the truth rests only on the form, i.e., on the posited Concept and the reality that corresponds to it; truth of this kind is not present in the qualitative judgment, however.

Addition. In ordinary life correctness and truth are very often considered to be synonymous, and hence we often speak of the truth of a content when it is a matter of mere correctness. In general, correctness is only a matter of the formal agreement of our representation with its content, whatever kind this content may otherwise be. Truth, on the contrary, consists in the agreement of the ob-ject with itself, i.e., with its concept. It may certainly be correct that someone is ill, or has stolen something; but a content like this is not "true," for an ill body is not in agreement with the concept of life, and similarly theft is an action that does not correspond to the concept of human action. From these examples it may be gathered that, no matter how correct it may be, an immediate judgment, in which an abstract quality is asserted of something immediately singular, simply cannot contain any truth; for subject and predicate do not stand to one another here in the relationship of reality and concept.

Furthermore, the untruth of the immediate judgment consists in the fact that its form and its content do not correspond to one another. When we say: "This rose is red," the copula "is" implies that subject and predicate agree with one another. But, of course, the rose, being something concrete, is not merely red; on the contrary, it also has a scent, a definite form, and all manner of other features, which are not contained within the predicate "red". On the other hand, this predicate, being something abstractly universal, does not belong merely to this subject. For there are other flowers, too, and other ob-jects altogether that are also red. In an immediate judgment subject and predicate do not coincide with one another, but touch at just *one* point, so to speak. With the judgment of the Concept the situation is different. When we say, "This action is good," we are asserting a judgment of the Concept. We can notice here at once that the subject and predicate do not now have the loose and external relationship that occurs in the immediate judgment. In the latter the predicate consists in some abstract quality or other, which may or may not belong to the subject; in the judgment of the Concept, on the contrary, the predicate is, as it were, the soul of the subject, by which the latter, as the body of this soul, is determined through and through.

§ 173

Since this negation is the *first* one and the *relation* of the subject to the predicate still remains in it; and the predicate is therefore something relatively universal of which only the determinacy is negated. ("The rose is *not* red" implies that it does have some colour—obviously some other colour, which when identified would be just another positive judgment.) But the singular is also *not* a universal. Hence (3) the judgment falls apart into itself as (aa) the empty *identity*-relation: the singular is the singular—the judgment *of identity*; and into itself as (bb) presenting the total incommensurability[a] of the subject and the predicate, the so-called *infinite* judgment.

> Examples of the latter are: "The spirit is not an elephant," "A lion is not a table," etc.—propositions that are correct, but pointless, exactly like the identical propositions: "A lion is a lion," "The spirit is spirit." Propositions like these are indeed the truth of the imme-

a. *Unangemessenheit*

diate, so-called qualitative judgment, but [they are] not really judgments at all; they can only occur in a subjective thinking that is able to hold onto an untrue abstraction as well.—Objectively considered, they express the nature of what [finitely] *is* or of *sensible* things, namely, that they are a falling-apart into an *empty* identity and a *fulfilled* relation, which is, all the same, the *qualitative otherness of the related* [terms], their complete incommensurability.

Addition. The negatively infinite judgment, in which there is no longer any relation between subject and predicate at all, tends to be cited in formal logic only as a meaningless curiosity. But, in fact, this infinite judgment must not be considered merely as a contingent form of subjective thinking; on the contrary, it shows itself to be the proximate dialectical result of the preceding immediate judgments (the positive and the simply negative), whose finitude and untruth come to light explicitly in it. A crime can be considered as an objective example of the negative-infinite judgment. Someone who commits a crime—for argument's sake a theft— does not merely deny the particular right of someone else to this particular thing[a] (as in a suit about civil rights); instead, he denies the rights of that person completely, and therefore he is not merely obliged to return the thing that he stole, but is punished as well, because he has violated right as such, i.e., right in general.

The civil law suit, in contrast, is an example of the simple negative judgment, because it deals with cases where only this particular right is negated, and right in general therefore remains recognised. So the situation is the same as in the case of the negative judgment, "This flower is not red," where what is denied to the flower is merely this particular colour, but not colour in general, for the flower can still be blue, yellow, etc. In the same way, death is a negative-infinite judgment, too, whereas, in contrast, illness is a singular negative judgment. In illness, it is merely this or that particular life-function that is checked or denied, whereas in death—as we normally say—body and soul separate, in other words, they fall apart completely.

(β) The Judgment of Reflection
§ 174

Posited in the judgment, the singular *as* singular (inwardly reflected) has a predicate, against which the subject, as relating itself to itself, remains at the same time an *other*.—In *existence* the subject is no longer immediately qualitative, but in *relationship* and *connectedness with an other* (with an external world). Hence, universality has acquired the significance of this relativity. (For instance, useful, dangerous; weight, acidity; and [at a higher level] drive, and so on.)

a. *Sache*

Addition. The judgment of reflection is basically distinguished from the qualitative judgment by virtue of its predicate's being no longer an immediate, abstract quality, but something through which the subject proves itself to be related to something else. If we say, "This rose is red," for example, we are considering the subject in its immediate singularity, without relation to anything else; while, on the other hand, if we frame the judgment, "This plant is curative," we are considering the subject (the plant) as standing in a relation to something else (the illness to be cured by the plant) in virtue of its predicate, curativeness. The situation is the same with the judgments, "This body is elastic," or "This instrument is useful," or "This punishment is deterrent," and so on. The predicates of these judgments are all of them determinations of reflection, by which the immediate singularity of the subject is, of course, transcended, but where the concept of the subject is still not specified.— This is the manner of judgment that we predominantly practice in our ordinary argumentation. The more concrete the ob-ject, the more points of view it offers to reflection; but reflection never exhausts the ob-ject's own nature, i.e., its concept.[13]

§ 175

(1) The subject, the singular *as* singular (in the *"singular" judgment*[14]), is something-universal. (2) In this relation it is elevated above its "singularity." This extension is an external one; [it is] *subjective* reflection, [resulting] to begin with, [in] an indeterminate *particularity* (in the *particular* judgment, which is immediately negative as well as positive; the singular is inwardly divided, it relates itself to itself on the one hand, and to something else on the other). (3) Some are the universal, and hence particularity is extended to universality; universality determined by the singularity of the subject is *allness* (communality, the ordinary universality of *reflection*).

Addition. When it is determined in the *singular* judgment[14] as a universal, the subject thereby goes beyond itself as this merely single instance.[a] To say, "This plant is curative," implies that it is not merely this single plant that is curative, but that some or many plants are, and this gives us the *particular*[b] judgment ("Some plants are curative," "Some men are inventive," etc.). By virtue of this "particularity"[c] the immediately single instance loses its independence and becomes interconnected with something else. As *this* man, a man is no longer merely this single man; he now stands beside other men instead, and is one of the crowd. But, precisely for this reason, he also belongs to his universal and consequently he is elevated. The particular[d] judgment is just as much positive as negative. If only some bodies are elastic, then the rest are not elastic.

a. *dieses bloß Einzelme*
b. partikulär
c. *Partikularität*
d. *partikulär*

This in its turn implies the advance to the third form of the judgment of reflection, i.e., the judgment of allness ("All men are mortal," "All metals are conductors of electricity"). Allness is the first form of universality upon which reflection normally happens to hit. The singular instances form the foundation here, and it is through our subjective action that they are collected together and determined as "all". The universal appears here only as an external bond that embraces all the singular instances which subsist on their own account and are indifferent to one another. But, in fact, the universal is the ground and soil, the root and substance of the single instance. For instance, if we consider Caius, Titus, Sempronius, together with all the other inhabitants of a city or a country, the fact that they are all men is not something that they simply have in common; on the contrary, it is what is *universal* in them, it is their *kind*, and none of them would be what he is at all without this kind.

The situation is quite different in the case of the superficial, merely so-called "universality", whose status is in fact merely that it pertains to all the single instances in question, and is what they have in common. It has been noticed that one thing that men have in common, as distinct from animals, is that they are furnished with earlobes.[15] But it is obvious that if perhaps someone or other were not to have earlobes, this would not affect the rest of his being, his character, his capacities, etc., whereas it would not make sense to assume that Caius might perhaps be brave, learned, etc., and yet not be a man. The single human is what he is in particular, only insofar as he is, first of all, human as such, and within the universal; and this universal is not just something over and above other abstract qualities or mere determinatins of reflection, but it is rather what permeates all the particulars and embraces them within itself.

§ 176

Because the subject is equally determined as something-universal, its identity with the predicate and consequently the determination of the judgment itself, too, is *posited* as indifferent. This unity of the *content*—as a universality which is identical with the negative inward reflection of the subject—makes the judgmental relation into a *necessary* one.

Addition. The advance from the allness-type of the judgment of reflexion to the judgment of necessity can already be found in our ordinary consciousness when we say that what pertains to all pertains to the kind and is therefore necessary. When we say "all plants," "all men," etc., this is the same as if we had said "the plant *as such*," "man *as such*," etc.

(γ) The Judgment of Necessity
§ 177

The judgment of necessity, as that of the identity of the content in its distinction (1) contains in its predicate first the *substance* or *nature* of the

subject, the *concrete* universal—the *genus*; and secondly (since this universal also contains within itself the determinacy as negative) the predicate
contains the *excluding* essential determinacy—the *species*; [this is] the *categorical* judgment. (2) In accordance with their substantiality both sides
acquire the shape of independent actuality; their identity is only an *inner*
one, so that the actuality of the one is at the same time *not its own*, but is
the being *of the other*; [this is] the *hypothetical* judgment. (3) Since, in this
uttering[a] of the Concept, the inner identity is at the same time *posited*, the
universal is the genus which [even] in its excluding singularity is identical
with itself. The judgment that has this universal as both of its sides—first
as such, and then as the circle of its self-excluding particularisation (of
which the *either-or* as well as *both-and* is the genus)—is the *disjunctive
judgment*. Thus universality, having been posited first as genus and now
also as the range[b] of its [various] species, is hereby determined and posited
as totality.

Addition. The categorical judgment ("Gold is a metal," "The rose is a plant") is the
immediate judgment of necessity, and corresponds to the relationship of substantiality in the sphere of Essence. Everything is a categorical judgment; i.e., things
have their substantial nature, which forms their firm and unchangeable foundation.
It is only when we consider things from the point of view of their kind, and as
necessarily determined by it, that the judgment begins to be a genuine one. To
regard judgments such as "Gold is expensive" and "Gold is a metal" as being on
the same level has to be called a defect in logical training. Gold's being expensive is
a matter of its external relation to our inclinations and wants, to the cost of obtain-
ing it, and so on; and gold remains what it is even if that external relation changes
or disappears. Being a metal, in contrast, constitutes the substantial nature of gold,
without which whatever else there may be in it, or whatever else may be asserted
about it, could not subsist. The situation is the same when we say, "Caius is a man";
by means of this we assert here that whatever else he may be has value and significance only insofar as it corresponds to his substantial nature, that of being a man.
     But, of course, even the categorical judgment is still defective in that it does not
give the moment of particularity its due. Thus, for instance, gold is certainly a
metal; but so are silver, copper, iron, and the rest; and their simply being metals is
indifferent with regard to the particular kinds [of metal] to which they belong. This
is where the advance from the categorical to the *hypothetical* judgment comes in.
The hypothetical judgment can be expressed through the formula, "If A is, then B
is." The advance here is the same as the earlier one from the relationship of
substantiality to the relationship of causality. In the hypothetical judgment the
determinacy of the content shows itself to be mediated, to be dependent upon
another, and this, then, is precisely the relationship of cause and effect. The significance of the hypothetical is generally that the universal is posited through it in its

a. *Entäußerung*
b. *Umkreis*

particularity, and this gives us the *disjunctive* judgment as the third form of the judgment of necessity. "A is either B or C or D"; "A work of poetry is either epic or lyric or dramatic"; "A colour is either red, yellow, or blue,"[16] etc. Both sides of the disjunctive judgment are identical; the genus is the totality of its species, and the totality of the species is the genus. This unity of the universal and the particular is the Concept, and it is the Concept that forms the content of the judgment henceforth.

(δ) The Judgment of the Concept
§ 178

The *judgment* of the *Concept* has the Concept, the totality in simple form, as its content, the universal with its complete determinacy. The subject is first (1) something-singular which has as its predicate the *reflection* of the particular that is thereupon its universal: the agreement or disagreement of these two determinations. This is the *assertoric* judgment about what is good, true, correct, etc.

> This is the first type of judging that is called "judging" in ordinary life as well: whether an object, an act, etc., is good or bad, true, beautiful, etc. We never attribute the "power of judgment" to anyone because he knows how to make positive or negative judgments such as: "This rose is red" or "This painting is red, green, dusty," etc.
>
> Because of the principle of immediate knowledge and faith, the assertoric judgment has been made the sole and essential form of doctrine even in philosophy. Yet in society it is regarded as improper when it pretends that it ought to have validity just as it stands. In the so-called philosophical works that uphold the principle of immediate knowledge and faith one can read hundreds and hundreds of *assurances* about reason, knowing, thinking, etc.; and since external authority does not count for much any more, they seek to gain acceptance for themselves through endless repetitions of one and the same [statement].

§ 179

In its initially immediate subject the assertoric judgment does not contain the relation of the particular and the universal that is expressed in the predicate. Consequently this judgment is only a *subjective* specification[a] and the opposite assertion confronts it with the same right or rather the same lack of right. Hence it is (2) straightaway just a *problematic* judgment.

a. *Partikularität*

But (3) when the objective specification[a] is *posited* in the *subject* or when its particularity is posited—as the special way that its thereness is constituted—then the subject expresses the relation of this way of being constituted to its determination, i.e., to its genus. Thus it expresses what constitutes the content of the predicate (see preceding paragraph). Here we have the *apodeictic* judgment (e.g., "*This*—the immediate singularity— *house*—the genus—*being constituted thus and so*—particularity—is good or bad").—*All things* are a *genus* (which is their determination and purpose) in a *single* actuality with a *particular* constitution; and their finitude consists in the fact that what is their particular [way of being] may (or again may not) conform to the universal.

§ 180

In this way the subject and the predicate themselves are each of them the whole judgment. Initially the immediate constitution of the subject shows itself as the *mediating ground* between the singularity of what is actual and its universality, as the ground of the judgment. What has been posited in fact is the unity of the subject and the predicate as the Concept itself. The Concept is the fulfillment of the empty "*is*" of the copula; and since (as subject and predicate) its moments are at the same time distinct, the Concept is posited as their unity, as the relation mediating between them. [This is] *the Syllogism.*

C. THE SYLLOGISM

§ 181

The syllogism is the unity of the Concept and the judgment; it is the Concept as the simple identity into which the form-distinctions of the judgment have returned, and it is judgment, insofar as it is posited at the same time in reality, i.e., in the distinction of its determinations. The syllogism is what is *rational*, and it is *everything* that is rational.

It is, of course, quite usual for the syllogism to be given out as the *form of what is rational*—but [only] as a subjective form and without any connection being demonstrated between this form and any

a. *Partikularität*

other rational content, for instance, a rational principle, a rational action or idea, etc. There is, in general, much talk of "reason" and it is frequently appealed to; but its *determinacy, what* it is, is not stated—and the last thing anyone thinks of in that context is syllogistic reasoning. *Formal syllogising* is indeed "rational" in a way that is so devoid of reason that it has nothing to do with the rationality of its basic import. But since any such import can only be rational in virtue of the determinacy that makes *thinking* into reason, it can only be rational in virtue of that form, which is the syllogism.—And this last is nothing but the *posited,* (and at first formally) *real Concept,*[a]—just as the above paragraph expresses it. Hence the syllogism is the *essential ground of everything true;* and the *definition of the Absolute* from now on is that it is the syllogism. Expressed as a proposition this determination becomes: "Everything is a syllogism." Everything is a *concept,* and the way that the concept is there is the distinction of its moments, in such a way that its *universal* nature gives itself external reality through *particularity,* and in this way, i.e., as negative inward reflection, the concept makes itself into the *singular.*—Or, conversely: the actual is a *singular* that raises itself by means of *particularity* to *universality* and makes itself identical with itself.—The actual is One, but it is equally the stepping asunder of the moments of the Concept; and the syllogism is the cycle of the mediation of its moments, the cycle through which it posits itself as One.

Addition. Like the Concept and the judgment, the syllogism also is usually considered only as a form of our subjective thinking, and it is said therefore that the syllogism is the grounding of the judgment. Now, it is certainly the case that the judgment refers us to the syllogism, but it is not merely our subjective doing that brings this advance about; on the contrary, it is the judgment itself that posits itself as syllogism and returns in it to the unity of Concept. More precisely, it is the apodeictic judgment which forms the passage to the syllogism. In the apodeictic judgment we have something singular that relates to its universal, i.e., to its concept, in virtue of its constitution. Here the particular appears as the mediating middle[b] between the singular and the universal; and this is the basic form of the syllogism, whose further development, interpreted in a formal way, consists in the fact that the singular and the universal also occupy this position of being the middle. It is this process that forms the passage from subjectivity to objectivity.

a. *reale Begriff*
b. *die vermittelnde Mitte*

§ 182

In the *immediate* syllogism, the determinations of the Concept—being *ab-stract*—stand in a merely external[a] *relationship* to each other; hence the two extremes are *singularity* and *universality*, but in the same way the Concept (as the middle term which con-cludes these two) is only abstract *par-ticularity*. As a result the extremes are posited as subsisting *on their own account*, just as *indifferent* toward each other as toward their middle term. This syllogism, therefore, is the rational that lacks the Concept, it is the formal *syllogism of the understanding*.—Here the subject is con-cluded with an *other* determinacy; or [from the other side] by means of this mediation the universal subsumes a subject that is *external* to it. What happens in the rational syllogism, on the contrary, is that by means of the mediation the subject con-cludes *itself with itself*. Only then is it [truly] subject; or the subject is all by itself the syllogism of reason.

> In the following examination, the syllogism of the understanding
> is expressed in its subjective mode, according to its ordinary cur-
> rent meaning.[17] This mode belongs to it when we say that *we* make
> these syllogisms. And, in fact, the syllogism of the understanding
> is *only* a *subjective* syllogising; but this has also the objective mean-
> ing that this syllogism expresses only the *finitude* of things, albeit
> in the determinate mode that the form has achieved at this point.
> In finite things their subjectivity—as a thinghood that is separable
> from their properties, [i.e.,] from their particularity—is equally
> separable from their universality, not only insofar as this univer-
> sality is the mere quality of the thing and its external connected-
> ness with other things, but also insofar as it is its genus and
> concept.

Addition. In conformity with the above mentioned interpretation of the syllogism as the form of what is rational, reason itself has been defined as the faculty of syllogising, while the understanding, in contrast, has been defined as the faculty of forming concepts. Quite apart from the underlying superficial representation of the spirit as a mere ensemble of forces or faculties subsisting side by side, there is this to be said about the association of the understanding with the concept and of reason with the syllogism: that we ought not to regard the Concept as a mere determination of the understanding any more than we ought to regard the syllog-ism as rational without qualification. For, on the one hand, what is usually dealt with in formal logic as the doctrine of the syllogism is nothing but the simple syllogism of the understanding. It does not deserve the honour of counting as the

---

a. *äussere*

form of the rational, of counting indeed as what is rational purely and simply. Nor yet, on the other hand, is the Concept as such just a mere form of the understanding. On the contrary, it is only the abstractive understanding that depreciates the Concept in this way.

So, although people do habitually distinguish between mere concepts of the understanding and concepts of reason, this distinction should not be understood to mean that there *are* two kinds of concepts; instead, it is *our* choice, whether we stay with the merely negative and abstract form of the Concept or whether we interpret it, in accordance with its true nature, as what is also positive and concrete. For instance, the "concept" of freedom as framed by the mere understanding regards freedom as the abstract antithesis of necessity, whereas the true and rational concept of freedom contains necessity sublated within itself. Similarly, the definition of God set up by what is called Deism is just the understanding's concept of God, whereas the Christian religion, which knows God as the Trinity, contains reason's concept of God.[18]

(α) The Qualitative Syllogism
§ 183

As was indicated in the preceding paragraph, the first syllogism is the *syllogism of thereness* or *qualitative* syllogism, (1) S-P-U: that a subject as something-singular is con-cluded with a *universal determinacy* through *a quality*.

> Only the forms through which subject and predicate constitute a syllogism are considered here—not the fact that the subject (the minor term) has other determinations besides that of singularity, just as the other extreme (the major term, i.e., the predicate of the conclusion) is determined in other ways and is not just something-universal.

Addition. The syllogism of thereness is merely a syllogism of the understanding, because singularity, particularity, and universality confront one another quite abstractly in it. So this syllogism is the last extreme of the process in which the Concept becomes external to itself.[a] Here we have something immediately singular as subject; then some particular aspect or property of this subject is emphasised, and by way of this property the singular proves to be a universal. An example would be, "This rose is red, red is a colour, therefore this rose is something coloured." It is mainly the syllogism in this shape that is usually dealt with in ordinary logic.

In former times the syllogism was regarded as the absolute rule of all cognition, and a scientific assertion was only held to be justified when it had been demonstra-

---

a. *das höchste Außersichkommen des Begriffs*

bly mediated by a syllogism. Nowadays, we meet the various forms of the syllog-ism almost exclusively in the logic manuals, and acquaintance with them counts only as an empty piece of book learning, which is of absolutely no further use, neither in practical life nor in science. The first comment to be made about this is that, although it would be superfluous and pedantic to enter into the whole detail of formalistic syllogising on every occasion, still, the various forms of the syllogism reassert themselves continually in our cognition. For instance, when someone hears the creaking of a cart in the street as he wakes on a winter's morning and is led by that to the conclusion that it must have frozen quite hard, he is performing here the operation of syllogising, and we repeat this operation every day in the most varied and complicated ways. So, at least it should not be less interesting to become expressly conscious of this activity that we perform daily as humans that think, than it is generally acknowledged to be to become acquainted not only with the functions of our organic life, such as that of digestion, or of the formation of the blood, or of respiration, and so on, but also with the processes and formations of the nature that is all around us. But it must be conceded, without hesitation, that drawing correct conclusions no more depends on a previous study of logic than adequate digestion, respiration, etc., requires a preliminary study of anatomy and physiology.

Aristotle was the first to observe and describe the various forms, and the so-called figures, of the syllogism in their subjective significance; indeed, he did this with such sureness and accuracy that, in essentials, there has been no need to add anything further. But, although this achievement does great honour to Aristotle, he himself made no use of the forms of the syllogism of the understanding in his properly philosophical inquiries, nor even of finite thinking in general. (See the Remark to § 187.)[a]

§ 184

This syllogism is (α) entirely *contingent* with regard to its determinations, since, as an abstract particularity, the middle term is *any determinacy* of the subject *whatever*. For—being something-immediate, and hence empirically concrete—the subject has several of these determinacies. So it can be con-cluded *with a variety of other* universalities as well. In the same way, since even a *single* particularity can again have diverse determinacies within it, the subject can be related to *distinct* universals through *one and the same* middle term.

> It is more the case that formalistic syllogising has gone out of fashion, than that people have become aware of its incorrectness and have tried to justify not using it on that account. This para-

a. Not § 189 (our correction)

graph and the one following show that syllogising of this kind is quite pointless for the truth.

Under the aspect that is dealt with in the present paragraph, all sorts of things can, as people say, be *proven* by means of this kind of syllogisms. We only have to choose the middle term from which the passage can be made to the determination that we want. But with another middle term something else can be *proven*—even its opposite.—The more concrete an ob-ject is, the more sides there are that belong to it, and can serve as middle terms. Which of them is more essential than the others must again depend on a syllogising of this kind, which holds onto the single determinacy and can easily find a side and an *aspect* in this determinacy according to which it can be made *important* and *necessarily valid*.

Addition. Although we hardly ever think of the syllogism of the understanding in the daily business of life, still it does continually play its role there. For instance, it is the job of advocates in a civil lawsuit to make the legal titles that are favourable to their clients into the ones that count. But, in its logical aspect, a legal title is nothing but *medius terminus* [a middle term]. The same thing happens in diplomatic negotiations, too, for example, when various powers lay claim to one and the same piece of land. In this case, the right of inheritance, the geographic lie of the land, the descent and language of its inhabitants, or any other ground, can be brought up as a *medius terminus*.

§ 185

(β) This syllogism is equally contingent because of the form of the *relation* that it involves. According to the concept of the syllogism, the true is the relation of distinct [terms], through a middle term which is their unity. But the relations of the extremes to the middle term (the so-called *premises*, *major* and *minor*) are *immediate* relations instead.

This contradiction of the syllogism expresses itself once more through an infinite *progress*—as the requirement that the premises be likewise demonstrated by a syllogism. But since the new syllogism has two equally immediate premises, this requirement—which constantly duplicates itself, of course—is repeated ad infinitum.

§ 186

What has been noted at this point (because of its empirical importance) as a *defect* of the syllogism to which absolute correctness is ascribed in this form, must sublate itself of its own accord as the determination of the syllogism proceeds. Here, within the sphere of the Concept, as well as in the Judgment, the *opposite* determinacy is not merely present *in-itself*, but it is *posited*; and in this way the further determination of the syllogism, too, requires only that we take up what is posited each time by the syllogism itself. Through the immediate syllogism S-P-U, the *singular* is mediated with the universal; and it is posited in this *conclusion* as *something-universal*. Thus the singular, as a subject that is itself something-universal, is now the unity of the two extremes and is what mediates. This gives the *second figure* of the syllogism: (2) U-S-P. This figure expresses the truth of the first— that, since the mediation has taken place in singularity, it is something contingent.

§ 187

The second figure con-cludes the universal with the particular. (Since the universal steps across from the preceding conclusion, it now occupies the place of the immediate subject.) The *universal* is, therefore, posited as something-particular, hence as what mediates between the extremes, whose places are now occupied by the other [terms]. [This is] the *third figure* of the syllogism: (3) P-U-S.

> Aristotle rightly admits only *three* figures of the syllogism; the *fourth* is a superfluous and even absurd addition made by the Moderns. In the usual accounts of these so-called figures[19] they are juxtaposed, without any thought of showing their necessity and still less of showing their significance and their value. It is no wonder, therefore, that these figures later have come to be treated as an empty formalism. But they do have a very fundamental meaning, which rests on the necessity that, as a determination of the Concept, *each moment* becomes itself the *whole* and the *mediating ground*.—Studying how the propositions have to be deter- mined—whether they can be universal, etc., or negative—in order to produce a *correct* syllogism in the various figures: this is a merely *mechanical* inquiry, which has quite justly fallen into obliv- ion, because it is inwardly meaningless and its mechanism lacks the Concept.—To appeal to *Aristotle*, in defence of the importance of such inquiries and of the syllogism of the understanding in general, is quite out of the question. Aristotle did, indeed, describe them just as he did countless other forms of spirit and of nature; and he investigated and indicated their determinacy. But in his metaphysical *concepts*, just as in the *concepts* of the natural and the

spiritual, he was so far from seeking to make the form of the syllogism of the understanding the basis and the criterion, that one might say that not a single one of the metaphysical concepts could have arisen or stood its ground, if it had had to be subjected to the laws of the understanding. Even if, in his own way, Aristotle contributes much that is essentially a product of description and of the understanding, the *speculative* concept is always what is dominant with him; and he does not allow the syllogistic reasoning of the understanding, which he had been the first to expose so definitely, to encroach upon the speculative sphere.[20]

Addition. The objective sense of the figures of the syllogism is generally that everything rational shows itself to be a threefold syllogism, and it does that in such a way that each of its members occupies the position both of an extreme and of the mediating middle. This is the case especially with the three "members" of philosophical science, i.e., the logical Idea, Nature, and Spirit. Here, it is first Nature that stands in the middle as the member that con-cludes the others. As the immediate totality, Nature unfolds itself in the two extremes of logical Idea and Spirit. Spirit, however, is Spirit by being mediated through Nature. In the second place, Spirit which we know as what is individual and actuating is the middle, and Nature and the logical Idea are the extremes. It is Spirit that knows the logical Idea in Nature, and elevates it to its essence. Equally, in the third place, the logical Idea itself is the middle; it is the absolute substance of Spirit and of Nature, that which is universal and all-pervading. These are the members of the absolute syllogism.

§ 188

Since each moment has passed through the place of the middle term and of the extremes, their determinate *distinction* from each other has *sublated* itself; and in this form where its moments are not distinguished,[a] the syllogism has at first the external identity-of-the-understanding, or *equality*, as its relation—this is the *quantitative* or *mathematical* syllogism. If two things are *equal* to a third, they are equal to one another.

Addition. As we all know, the quantitative that is referred to here occurs in mathematics as an axiom, whose content, like that of the other axioms, is normally said to be insusceptible of proof, though it does not require any proof either, being immediately self-evident. But, in fact, these mathematical axioms are nothing but logical propositions which, insofar as they express particular and definite thoughts, must

a. *in dieser Form der Unterschiedslosigkeit seiner Momente* be deduced from universal and self-determining thinking; and this deduction must be considered their proof. This proof is here given for the quantitative syllogism which is set up in mathematics as an axiom, but which shows itself to be the direct result of the qualitative or immediate syllogism.

Incidentally, the quantitative syllogism is the syllogism that lacks form altogether, since the distinction between the terms, determined by the Concept, is sublated within it. External circumstances determine here which propositions are to be the premises, and hence, in using this syllogism, we presuppose what is already established and proven elsewhere.

§ 189

With regard to the form a double result has now been established: (1) Since each of the moments has assumed the determination and the place of the *middle term*, and hence of the whole in general, it has *in-itself* lost the one-sidedness of its abstraction (§§ 182, 184); (2) *the mediation* (§ 185) has been completed, but again only *in-itself*, i.e., only as a *circle* of mediations that reciprocally presuppose each other. In the first figure, S-P-U, the two premises, S-P and P-U, are still unmediated; the former is mediated in the third, the latter in the second figure. But for the mediation of their premises each of these two figures presupposes again both of the other figures.

> Consequently, the mediating unity of the Concept has to be posited as the *developed* unity of singularity and universality and no longer just as abstract particularity. Indeed, it has to be posited first of all as [the] *reflected* unity of these determinations; [i.e., as] the *singularity* that is *at the same time* determined as universality. This kind of middle term gives us the *syllogism of reflection*.

(β) THE SYLLOGISM OF REFLECTION
§ 190

Since, to begin with (1) the middle term is thus not just an abstract, *particular* determinacy of the subject, but at the same time *all singular concrete* subjects, to which that determinacy belongs (though only as one determinacy among others), we have the syllogism *of allness*. But now the major premise itself—which has the particular determinacy, the middle term, as Allness for its subject—really *pre*supposes the *conclusion*, of which it is supposed to be the presupposition. Hence (2) the major premise is based on an *induction*, of which the middle term are all the singular [instances] as such, a, b, c, d, etc. But since immediate, empirical singularity is diverse from universality and therefore unable to provide completeness, the induction is (3) based on *analogy*, the middle term of which is something-singular, but in the sense of its essential universality, of its genus or essential determinacy.—The first syllogism refers to the second for its mediation and the second to the third; but once the forms of the external relation of singularity and universality have been run through in the figures of the syllogism of reflection, the third syllogism also requires a universality that is inwardly determinate, i.e., singularity as genus.

> The defect of the basic form of the syllogism of the understanding, that was indicated in § 184, is corrected by the syllogism of Allness; but only in such a way that a new defect arises, namely, that the major premise itself presupposes what was supposed to be the conclusion, so that the conclusion is [again] an *immediate* proposition.—"All men are mortal, *therefore* Caius is mortal,"—"All metals conduct electricity, *therefore* copper, for instance, does the same." In the affirmation of these majors, which are supposed to express the *immediate* singular [instances] as "all cases" and which ought to be essentially *empirical* propositions—what is involved is that the propositions about the singular [case of] Caius, about the *singular* [case of] copper, have *previously* been ascertained to be correct.—Everyone is struck, not just by the pedantry, but by the empty[a] formalism of syllogisms like: "All men are mortal, but Caius is . . . etc."

Addition. The syllogism of Allness refers us to the syllogism of induction, in which the single instances form the con-cluding middle. If we say, "All metals are conductors of electricity," this is an empirical proposition, which results from the testing of every single metal. In this way we obtain the syllogism of induction, which has the following shape:

$$P \longrightarrow S \longrightarrow U$$
$$S$$
$$S$$
$$\cdot$$
$$\cdot$$
$$\cdot$$

"Gold is a metal, silver is a metal, and so are copper, lead, etc." This is the major premise. Then comes the minor premise: "All these bodies are conductors of electricity," and from this results the conclusion: "All metals are conductors of electricity." So the linkage is effected here by singularity in the form of Allness.

a. *nichtssagende*

Now this syllogism likewise sends us on again to another syllogism. As its middle term it has the complete set of single instances; and this presupposes that observation and experience are complete in a certain domain. But because what is in question here are single instances, there is an infinite progression once more (S,S,S, . . .). The single instances can never be exhausted in an induction. If we say, "All metals, all plants, etc.," this just means, "All the metals, all the plants that we have so far encountered." Consequently, any induction is imperfect. To be sure, we have made this and that observation, lots and lots of them, but not all cases, not all individuals, have been observed. It is this defect of induction that leads us to *analogy*. In the syllogism of analogy it is concluded that because things of a certain kind have a certain property, therefore other things of the same kind have the same property, too. It is an example of a syllogism of analogy when we say: "We have found that all the planets observed so far obey such and such a law of motion, and that therefore any newly discovered planet will probably move according to the same law."

Analogy is rightly held in high esteem in the empirical sciences, and very important results have been arrived at by this path. It is the instinct of reason which surmises that this or that empirically discovered determination is grounded in an ob-ject's inner nature or kind, and which proceeds on that basis.[21] Analogy, it may be added, can be more or less superficial or well grounded. For instance, if someone says, "Caius, who is a man, is a scholar; Titus is a man, too, so he will probably be a scholar also." This is a very bad analogy in any case, because, of course, a man's being a scholar is certainly not grounded just in his being human. Superficial analogies of this kind do, however, occur very often. For example, it is often said that "The earth is a heavenly body and has inhabitants; the moon is also a heavenly body; therefore it will probably be inhabited too." This analogy is in no way better than the one given above. That the earth has inhabitants does not rest merely on the fact that it is a heavenly body; on the contrary, some further conditions are necessary, especially that of being surrounded with an atmosphere, the related presence of water, and so on; and it is precisely these conditions which, as far as we know, the moon lacks. What has been called Philosophy of Nature in modern times consists for the most part in a futile play with empty and external analogies, which are supposed, all the same, to count as profound results. That is why the philosophical study of nature has fallen into deserved discredit.[22]

(γ) THE SYLLOGISM OF NECESSITY
§ 191

According to its merely abstract determinations, this syllogism has *the universal* as its middle term—just as the syllogism of reflection has *singularity* [as its middle]; the latter according to the second figure, the former according to the third. [But in the syllogism of necessity the middle term is] the universal posited as essentially determinate within itself. The mediating determination is initially (1) the *particular* in the sense of the determinate *genus* or *species*; this is the case in the *categorical* syllogism. [Then, it is] (2) the *singular* in the sense of immediate being, so that it is both mediating and mediated—in the *hypothetical* syllogism. (3) The mediating *universal* is also posited as the totality of its *particularisations* and as a *singular* particular [or as] excluding singularity—in the disjunctive syllogism. So that there is one and the same universal in all these determinations, but it is in the forms of distinction.

§ 192

The syllogism has been taken according to the distinctions which it contains, and the universal result of its course is that the self-sublation of these distinctions and of the self-externality of the Concept is produced in it. And indeed, (1) each of the moments has proven itself to be the *totality* of the moments, hence the whole syllogism: in this way, they are *in-themselves* identical. (2) The *negation* of their distinctions, and the mediation of them, constitutes the *being-for-itself* [of the Concept]; so that it is one and the same universal that is in these forms and hence is posited also as their identity. In this ideality of the moments, syllogistic reasoning acquires the determination of essentially containing the *negation* of the determinacies through which it proceeds—and hence that of being a mediation through the sublation of mediation, and a con-cluding of the subject, not with [an] *other*, but with [a] *sublated* other, [i.e.,] *with itself*.

Addition. It is customary in traditional logic to conclude the first part, the so-called doctrine of elements, with a treatment of the doctrine of the syllogism. What follows then, as the second part, is the so-called doctrine of method, in which it is supposed to be shown how a whole body of scientific cognition can be brought into existence by applying the forms of thinking treated in the doctrine of elements to the objects that are present.[23] Where these objects come from and how it stands with the thought of objectivity are questions about which the logic of the understanding gives no information. In that logic thinking is taken to be a merely subjective and formal activity, and the objective world that confronts thinking counts as something fixed and present in its own right. But this dualism is not the true state of affairs, and to take up the determinations of subjectivity and objectivity without further ado, and without examining their origins, is a mindless procedure. Both subjectivity and objectivity are thoughts in any case; and indeed they are determinate thoughts, which have to prove themselves to be grounded in the thinking that is universal and self-determining.

This has been done here, first with regard to subjectivity. We have come to the cognition of subjectivity, or the subjective Concept, which contains the Concept as such, the judgment, and the syllogism within it, as the dialectical result of the first

two principal stages of the logical Idea, namely, being and[a] essence. It is quite
correct to say of the Concept that it is subjective and only subjective, because it is
certainly subjectivity itself. And both the judgment and the syllogism are as subjective as the Concept as such. These, together with the so-called laws of thought (the
laws of identity, of distinction, and of sufficient reason), form the content of the so-
called doctrine of elements in traditional logic. But now, this subjectivity, with the
determinations which have been cited here (the Concept, the judgment, and the
syllogism), is not to be regarded as an empty framework that can only be filled up
from outside, by objects that are present on their own account; on the contrary, it is
subjectivity itself which, being dialectical, breaks through its own barrier, and
opens itself up into objectivity by means of syllogism.

§ 193

This *realisation* of the Concept, in which the universal is this *One* totality
returned into itself, whose distinctions are equally this totality, and which
through the sublation of the mediation has determined itself as *immediate*
unity, is the *object*.

> This passage from the subject, from the Concept in general and
> more precisely from the syllogism, to the object, may seem at first
> sight to be very strange (especially if one thinks only of the syllog-
> ism of the understanding and considers syllogistic reasoning as
> done by consciousness). But all the same, it is not part of our
> concern to make this passage plausible to representation. We can
> only look back to see whether our usual notion of what is called an
> "object" corresponds more or less with what constitutes the deter-
> mination of the object here. Now we do not usually understand by
> an "object" merely something that *is* abstractly, or an existing
> thing, or something-actual in general, but something-independent,
> that is concrete and *complete* within itself; this completeness is the
> *totality of the Concept*. The fact that the *object* is also *ob-ject*, and is
> *something-external*[b] to an other will be established later—insofar as
> it sets itself up in its *antithesis* to what is *subjective*. But at this
> point, the object, as that into which the Concept has passed over
> from its mediation, is initially just *immediate* unaffected object—
> just as the Concept is likewise only determined as what is *subjec-
> tive* in the antithesis that comes later.
>
> Moreover, the *object* is quite generally the *One* whole that is
> inwardly still undetermined; it is the objective world in general,
> God, the absolute object. But equally the object has distinction in

a. Reading *und* (instead of *oder*)
b. *Äusseres*

it; as objective *world* it falls apart inwardly into [an] undetermined manifoldness—and each of these *isolated* [bits] is also an object, or something-there that is inwardly concrete, complete, and independent.

We have compared objectivity with being, existence, and actuality; in the same way the passage to existence and actuality (for being is the first, totally abstract immediacy) has to be compared with the passage to objectivity. The *ground* from which existence emerges, the *relationship* of reflection that sublates itself into actuality, are nothing but the still imperfectly *posited Concept*; i.e., they are only abstract sides of it. The ground is just the unity of the Concept at the level of essence; the relationship is just the relation of *real* sides that are supposed to be only *inwardly reflected*—the Concept is the unity of the two, and the object is a unity which is not just one appropriate to essence, but one that is inwardly universal: it does not merely contain real distinctions, but contains them as totalities within itself.

It is clear, moreover, that what is at issue in all these transitions is more than just showing the inseparability of the Concept (or of thinking) from being. It has often been noted that *being* is nothing more than the simple relation to itself, and that this poor determination is indubitably contained in the Concept (or in thinking). The sense of these transitions is not to take up determinations simply as *contained* [in the Concept] (in the way this happens in the ontological argument for God's being-there, by means of the proposition that being is *one of* the realities). [The task here] is rather to take the Concept, the way it initially *ought* to be determined on its own account as Concept (with which this remote abstraction of being or even of objectivity has still nothing to do); and then, in its determinacy as determinacy of the *Concept* alone, to see whether, and [indeed] that this determinacy passes over into a form that is diverse from determinacy as it belongs to the Concept and appears *in it*.

If the object, as the product of this passage, is put in relation with the Concept (which as far as its proper form is concerned has vanished in this transition), then the result may be *correctly* expressed by saying that the Concept (or even, if one prefers, subjectivity) and the object are *in-themselves the same*. But it is equally correct to say that they are *diverse*. Precisely because each statement is as correct as the other, each of them is as incorrect as the other; expressions of this kind are incapable of presenting the genuine relationship. The "sameness in-themselves" that was mentioned above is something-abstract and even more one-sided than the Concept itself—whose one-sidedness sublates itself, generally speaking, in the fact that the Concept sublates itself into the object, the opposite one-sidedness. That "sameness in-themselves" also must therefore determine itself to *be for itself* through the *negation* of itself. As is always the case, the speculative identity is not the trivial one, that Concept and objectivity are in-themselves identical; this is a remark that has been repeated often enough, yet it cannot be repeated often enough, if the intention is to put an end to the stale and totally malicious misunderstandings about this identity. But, of course, there is no hope of achieving this at the level of the understanding.

Besides, if one takes this unity quite generally, without remem-bering the one-sided form of its *being-in-itself*, then as everyone knows, it is this unity that is *presupposed* in the *ontological* proof that there is a God; it is presupposed precisely as what is the *most perfect*. It is true that *Anselm* (to whom the most remarkable thought of this proof occurs for the first time) simply discusses to begin with whether a content is in *our thinking* only. His words are briefly these: "Certe id, quo majus cogitari nequit, non potest esse in intellectu solo. Si enim vel in solo intellectu est, potest cogitari esse *et in re*: quod maius est. Si ergo id, quo maius cogitari non potest, est in solo intellectu: id ipsum, quo maius cogitari non potest, est, quo maius cogitari potest. Sed certe hoc esse non pot-est." [Assuredly, that than which nothing greater can be thought cannot be in the intellect alone. For suppose it is in the intellect alone—then it can be thought to be *in reality as well*: and that is greater. Therefore, if that than which nothing greater can be thought is in the intellect alone, then precisely that than which nothing greater can be thought is that than which a greater can be thought. But obviously this is impossible.][24] According to the de-terminations which we have now reached, *finite* things are such that their objectivity is not in agreement with the thoughts of them; i.e., not in agreement with their universal determination, their genus, and their purpose. Descartes and Spinoza and others have expressed this unity in a more objective way, but the princi-ple of immediate certainty or of faith takes it more in the subjective way of Anselm; i.e., that *in our consciousness* the determination of God's being is inseparably bound up with our representation of him. And if the principle of this faith also takes the representa-tions of external finite things in the inseparability of the conscious-ness of them and of their being (because they are bound up with the determination of existence *in our intuition*), that too is quite correct. But it would be mindless[a] in the extreme, if this were supposed to mean that in our consciousness existence is bound up with the representation of finite things in the same way as it is with the representation of God. To suppose that would be to forget that finite things are alterable and perishable, i.e., that existence is bound up with them only in a transitory manner, that this bond is not eternal but can be severed. Hence Anselm put aside the sort of linkage that occurs in finite things, and declared rightly that the perfect [being][b] is that which is not merely in a subjective way, but in an objective way as well. Every attempt to look down upon the so-called ontological proof and upon Anselm's determination of what is perfect is futile, since this determination is implicit in every unprejudiced human mind, just as it finds its way back in every philosophy, even against its wit and will (as in the case of the principle of immediate faith).

The defect in Anselm's argumentation, however, which is also shared by Descartes and Spinoza, as well as by the principle of immediate knowing, is that this *unity*, which is proclaimed as what is most perfect (or subjectively as the true knowing), is *presupposed*; i.e., it is assumed as *in-itself* only. Consequently this unity is abstract; and the *diversity* of the two determinations is at once brought up against it, as happened to Anselm long ago. In other words, it is the representation and existence of the *finite* that is actually brought up against the infinite; for, as was remarked above, the finite is the sort of objectivity which is at the same time not adequate to its purpose, to its essence and concept, but diverse from it; or it is the sort of representation, the sort of subjective something, that does not involve existence. This objection and antithesis is only removed by showing that the finite is something-untrue, or that these determinations are on their own account one-sided and null, and that their identity is therefore one into which they pass over by themselves and in which they are reconciled.

a. *Gedankenlosigkeit*
b. *das Vollkommene*

B
The Object

Because of its indifference vis-à-vis the distinction that has sublated itself in it, the object is immediate being, and it is an inward totality.[a] At the same time it is equally indifferent vis-à-vis its own immediate unity, since that identity [i.e., totality] is the identity of its moments *that is only in-itself*. It is a falling apart into distinct [moments], each of which is itself the totality. Hence, the object is the absolute *contradiction* of the complete independence of the [distinct moments] that are manifold and of their equally complete dependency.

> The definition: "*The Absolute is the object*," is contained in its most determinate form in the *Monad* of Leibniz,[25] which is supposed to be an object, but one which *in-itself* represents—and which is indeed—the totality of the representation of the world; in the simple unity of this Monad all distinction is [present] only as something-ideal, or as dependent. Nothing enters into the Monad from outside, it is within itself the whole Concept, and only distinct from it in virtue of the greater or lesser development of the Concept [in it]. This simple totality also falls apart into the absolute plurality of distinctions, in such a way that the distinctions are independent monads. But in the Monad of monads and in the preestablished harmony of their inner development these substances are also again reduced to nonindependence and ideality. Thus the philosophy of Leibniz is the completely developed *contradiction*.

Addition 1. When the Absolute (God) is interpreted as the object and we do not go beyond that, we have the general standpoint of superstition and servile fear. It is Fichte especially who has rightly emphasised this in our modern period.[26] Certainly God is the object, indeed he is the object pure and simple, as against which our particular (subjective) opinions and volitions have neither truth nor validity. But precisely as the absolute object, God does not confront subjectivity as a dark and hostile power; instead, he contains it within himself as an essential moment. In the doctrine of the Christian religion this is expressed by saying that God wills that all men shall be saved and come to blessedness. Men are saved and attain blessed-

---

a. *ist in sich Totalität*

ness by becoming conscious of their unity with God. Then God ceases to be a mere object to them; and ipso facto he ceases to be an ob-ject of fear and terror, as God was especially in the religious consciousness of the Romans. Then later, in the Christian religion, God becomes known as love, precisely because he revealed himself to man in his Son, who is one with him; he revealed himself as this single man, and redeemed mankind by doing that. What this also means is that the antithesis of objectivity and subjectivity is overcome *implicitly*; and it is our business[a] to participate in this redemption by laying aside our immediate subjectivity (putting off the old Adam) and becoming conscious of God as our true and essential Self.

Now, just as religion and religious worship consist in the overcoming of the antithesis between subjectivity and objectivity, so too the task of science, and more precisely of philosophy, is nothing but the overcoming of this antithesis through thinking. In cognition, what has to be done is all a matter of stripping away the alien character of the objective world that confronts us. As we habitually say, it is a matter of "finding ourselves in the world," and what that amounts to is the tracing of what is objective back to the Concept, which is our innermost Self. The explanation we have given shows how absurd it is to consider subjectivity and objectivity as a fixed and abstract antithesis. Both moments are thoroughly dialectical. The Concept, which is initially only subjective, proceeds to objectify itself by virtue of its own activity and without the help of an external material or stuff. And likewise the object is not rigid and without process; instead, its process consists in its proving itself to be that which is at the same time subjective, and this forms the advance to the *Idea*. Anyone who is not familiar with the determinations of subjectivity and objectivity, and who wants to hold fast to them in abstraction from one another, will find that these abstract determinations slip through his fingers before he knows it, and that he says precisely the opposite of what he wanted to say.

Addition 2. Objectivity contains the three forms of *mechanism, chemism,* and *teleology.* The *mechanically* determined object is the immediate, undifferentiated[b] object. This object certainly contains distinction, but its diverse [parts] behave indifferently[c] to each other, and their linkage is only external to them. In *chemism,* by contrast, the object proves to be essentially differentiated,[d] so that the objects are what they are only through their relation to one another, and their difference[e] constitutes their quality. The third form of objectivity, the *relationship of teleology,* is the unity of mechanism and chemism. Like the mechanical object, purpose is once more a self-enclosed totality, but it is enriched by the principle of difference which came forth in chemism, so that it relates itself to the object that confronts it. It is the realisation of purpose, therefore, that forms the passage to the *Idea.*

a. *Sache*
b. *indifferente*
c. *gleichgültig*
d. *different*
e. *Differenz*

A. MECHANISM

§ 195

(1) In its immediacy, the object is only the Concept *in-itself*; initially it has the Concept *outside it*, and every determinacy is [present] as one that is posited externally. Hence, as a unity of distinct [terms], it is *something-composite*; it is an aggregate, and its operation upon another remains an external relation. This is *formal mechanism*.—In this relation and dependence the objects remain equally independent; they offer resistance, and are *external* to each other.

> Just as pressure and impact are mechanical relationships, so we have mechanical knowledge, too: we know things *by rote*, inasmuch as the words remain without meaning for us and are external to sense, representation, and thought; the words are in like manner external to themselves: they form a meaningless sequence. Action, piety, etc., are *mechanical* in the same way, inasmuch as what a man does is determined for him by ritual prescriptions, or by a director of conscience, etc., and his own spirit and will are not in his actions, so that even within himself they remain external.[27]

Addition. As the initial form of objectivity, mechanism is also the first category that presents itself to reflection when it considers the world of ob-jects, and it is the very one at which reflection most often halts. But this is a superficial, intellectually impoverished point of view, inadequate in regard to nature and still more so in regard to spirit. In nature only the wholly abstract relationships of a matter which is still not opened up within itself[28] are subject to mechanism; in contrast, not even the phenomena and processes of the physical domain in the narrower sense of the word (such as the phenomena of light, heat, magnetism, and electricity, for instance) can be explained in a merely mechanical way (i.e., through pressure, collision, displacement of parts and the like). The transference and application of this category into the domain of organic nature is even more unsatisfactory, since the task there is to comprehend what is specific about that domain, in particular, the nutrition and growth of plants or even animal sensation. So we must in any case regard it as a very crucial defect of the modern inquiry into nature—indeed as the main defect—that it holds so stubbornly to the categories of mere mechanism even where quite different and higher categories are really involved. In doing this, it contradicts what offers itself to unprejudiced intuition, and bars the way to an adequate cognition of nature.

In the study of the formations of the world of spirit, too—which comes next—the mechanical view has frequently been adopted in a quite unwarranted manner.

This is the case, for example, when it is said that man "consists" of body and soul. In this view, body and soul are held to subsist each on its own account and to be connected together only in an external way. It is the same, too, when the soul is treated as a mere complex of forces and faculties that subsist independently, one beside the other.

But, although, on the one hand, the mechanical point of view must be rejected quite decisively when it pretends to take the place of conceptually comprehensive cognition altogether, and to establish mechanism as the absolute category, still, on the other hand, we must also vindicate for mechanism the right and the significance of a universal logical category; and therefore we must not restrict it simply to that domain of nature from which it derives its name. So there is no reason for us to object when attention is drawn to mechanical actions outside of the domain of mechanics proper, especially in physics and physiology (e.g., actions like those of weight, the lever, and the like). But it must not be overlooked here that in these domains the laws of mechanism are no longer the decisive ones, but enter only in a subservient position, so to speak.

Another remark that directly follows is that wherever in nature the higher functions suffer some kind of disturbance or check in their normal functioning (and especially the functions of the organism), the otherwise subordinated mechanism immediately advances to a dominating role. For example, someone who suffers from weakness of the stomach feels "pressure" there after having eaten a small quantity of certain foods, whilst others, whose digestive organs are healthy, remain free of this feeling, even though they have eaten the same amount. It is the same with regard to a general feeling of "heaviness" in the limbs in the case of bodily indisposition.

Even in the domain of the spiritual world, mechanism has its place, though again it is only a subordinate one. It is quite right to speak of "mechanical" memory, and of all manner of "mechanical" activities, such as reading, writing, and playing music, for example. As for memory specifically, we may note, in this connection, that a mechanical mode of behaviour belongs even to its essence; this is a circumstance that is not infrequently overlooked by modern pedagogy in a mistaken zeal for the freedom of intelligence—something that has caused great harm to the education of youth. Nevertheless, anyone who has recourse to mechanics in order to explain the nature of memory and wants to apply its laws without further ado to the soul will thereby show himself to be a bad psychologist. The mechanical aspect of memory simply consists in the fact that certain signs, tones, etc., are here apprehended in their merely external combination and are then reproduced in this combination, without there being any need to draw attention expressly to their significance and inner association. To be cognizant of this aspect of mechanical memory requires no further study of mechanics, and the study of mechanics cannot advance psychology as such.

§ 196

The object only has the dependence according to which it suffers *violence*, inasmuch as it is independent (see the preceding paragraph); and as posited Concept-in-itself neither of these determinations sublates itself in its other, but the Object con-cludes itself with itself through its own negation—or its dependence—and only in this way is it independent. This [independence of the object] (in distinction from the externality which it negates in its independence) is *negative unity* with itself, *centrality*, subjectivity—in which the object is itself directed at and related to what is external [to it]. The latter is centered on itself in the same way, and therein it is only related to the other centre likewise; it also has its centrality in the other. [This is] (2) *differentiated* mechanism (fall, desire, urge to socialise, etc.).

§ 197

The development of this relationship forms the syllogism in which the immanent negativity, as the *central* singularity of an object (i.e., the abstract centre), relates itself to objects that are not independent (as to the other extreme) through a middle term (the relative centre) which unites the centrality and the dependence of the objects within itself. [This gives us] (3) *absolute mechanism.*

§ 198

The syllogism we have now reached (S-P-U) is a triad of syllogisms. *Qua* dependence, the spurious *singularity* of the *dependent* objects among which formal mechanism is at home, is just as much external *universality*. These objects, therefore, are also the *middle term* between the *absolute* and the *relative* centre (the form of the syllogism U-S-P); for it is through this dependence that the absolute and relative centres are sundered into extremes, as well as related to each other. Similarly, *absolute centrality* is what mediates between the *relative centre* and the *independent* objects (the form of the syllogism P-U-S). It is the substantial universal—the gravity that remains identical—which (as pure negativity), includes singularity within itself equally; and, of course, it mediates just as essentially in its sundering action (according to its immanent singularity) as it does in its identical cohesion and undisturbed being-within-self (according to its universality).

> In the practical sphere, for instance, the State is a system of three syllogisms just like the solar system. (1) The *singular* (the person) con-cludes himself through his *particularity* (the physical and spiritual needs, which when further developed on their own account give rise to civil society) with the *universal* (society, right, law, government). (2) The will or the activity of the individuals is the mediating [term] that gives satisfaction to their needs in the con-

text of society,[a] right, etc., and provides fulfillment and actualisation to society, right, etc. (3) But it is the universal (State, government, right) that is the substantial middle term within which the individuals and their satisfaction have and preserve their full reality, mediation, and subsistence. Precisely because the mediation con-cludes each of these determinations with the other extreme, each of them con-cludes itself with itself in this way or produces itself; and this production is its self-preservation.—It is only through the nature of this con-cluding, or through this triad of syllogisms with the same terms, that a whole is truly understood in its organisation.

§ 199

The *immediacy* of the existence that the objects have in absolute mechanism is *in-itself* negated by the fact that their independence is mediated through their relations to each other, i.e., through their dependence. Hence the object has to be posited as *differentiated* in its *existence* vis-à-vis *its own* other.

B. CHEMISM

§ 200

The *differentiated object* has an immanent *determinacy* which constitutes its nature and in which it has existence. But as the posited totality of the *Concept*, it is the contradiction between this, its own totality, and the determinacy of its existence: hence, it is the striving to sublate this contradiction and to make its way of being equal to the Concept.

Addition. Chemism is a category of objectivity which as a rule is not particularly emphasised. Instead, it is lumped together with mechanism, and then they are contrasted with the relationship of *purposiveness* under the common name of mechanical relationship. The reason for this must be sought in the fact that *mechanism* and *chemism* do indeed have in common the fact that they are only *implicitly* the existent Concept, whereas *purpose* must be considered the Concept as it exists *for-itself*. But mechanism and chemism are also very definitely distinct from one another; specifically, this is because in the mode of mechanism the object is, initially, only indifferent relation to itself, whereas the chemical object proves to be strictly

a. *an der Gesellschaft*

related to what is other. It is true, of course, that even in the course of development of mechanism, some relations to what is other emerge already; but the relation of mechanical objects to one another is, to start with, only an external one, a relation in which the objects that are related to one another retain the semblance of independence. So, for example, in nature, the various heavenly bodies that form our solar system move in relationship to one another, and thereby show themselves to be related to one another. But as the unity of space and time, motion is only the quite external and abstract relation, and it seems therefore as if the heavenly bodies, being thus externally related to one another, would be what they are, and remain so, even without this relation to one another that they have.

The situation is different with chemism, however. Objects that are chemically differentiated are explicitly what they are only in virtue of their difference. Hence, they are the absolute drive to integrate themselves through and into one another.

§ 201

Hence, the chemical process has as its product the *neutral* [state] between its tensed extremes (which are *in-themselves* this neutral [state]). Through the difference of the objects—their particularising—the Concept, as the concrete universal, con-cludes itself with the singularity, i.e., with the product, and thus only with itself. And the other syllogisms are again contained in this process too; as activity, the singularity is again the mediating [term], just like the concrete universal, the essence of the tensed extremes, which comes to be there in the product.

§ 202

As the reflective relationship of objectivity, chemism still has as its presupposition, not just the differentiated nature of the objects, but also their *immediate* independence. The process is the going back and forth, from one form to the other, while these forms still remain external to each other.—In the neutral product, the determinate properties which the extremes had vis-à-vis each other are sublated. It is in conformity with the Concept, to be sure, but the *inspiriting* principle[a] of differentiation does not exist in it, because it has sunk back into immediacy. Hence, the neutral product is something-separable. But both the judging [or dividing] principle[b] which sunders the neutral into the differentiated extremes and gives the un-

a. *das* begeistende *Prinzip*
b. *das urteilende Prinzip*

differentiated object generally its difference and inspiration[a] vis-à-vis an other—and the process as a separation with tension, fall outside that first process.

Addition. The chemical process is still a finite, conditioned one. The Concept as such is still just the inward aspect of this process, and it does not yet come into existence here in its being-for-itself. In the neutral product the process is extinct, and what stimulated it falls outside of it.

§ 203

But the *externality*, which lets these two processes (the reduction of what is differentiated to the neutral and the differentiating of the undifferentiated or neutral) appear as independent vis-à-vis each other, also shows their finitude when they pass over into products in which they are sublated. And conversely, the process presents the presupposed immediacy of the differentiated objects as null and void.—Through this *negation* of the exteriority and immediacy in which the Concept *qua* object was immersed, it is set *free* and posited *for-itself against* that externality and immediacy. It is posited *as purpose.*

Addition. The passage from chemism to the teleological relationship is contained in the fact that the two forms of the chemical process sublate one another reciprocally. What results from this is that the Concept, which in chemism and in mechanism was still only present *in-itself*, becomes free, and the Concept that now exists for itself is *purpose.*

C. TELEOLOGY

§ 204

Purpose is the Concept that has entered into free existence, and *is-for-itself*, by means of the *negation* of immediate objectivity. It is determined as *subjective*, because this negation is initially *abstract*, and so at first it merely stands opposed to objectivity. But this determinacy of its subjectivity is *one-sided* vis-à-vis the totality of the Concept; and this one-sidedness holds

a. *Begeistung*

for the purpose itself, since all determinacy has posited itself in it as sub-lated. So, for the purpose too, the presupposed object is only an ideal reality, one that is *null and void in-itself*. As this contradiction between its identity with itself and the negation and antithesis that is posited in it, the purpose itself is the sublation, the *activity* which negates the antithesis in such a way that the purpose posits it as identical with itself. This is the *realising of the purpose*, in which the purpose has sublated the distinction between the two, i.e., subjectivity and objectivity, since it makes itself into the other of its subjectivity and objectifies itself. It has con-cluded *itself with itself alone* and has *preserved* itself.

> On the one hand, the concept of purpose is called redundant; but, on the other hand, it is quite rightly called a *concept-of-reason*—and it has been set up in contrast to the abstract universal of the under-standing which relates itself to the particular only by *subsuming* this particular which it does not have in itself.—Moreover, the distinction of the purpose as *final cause* from the merely *efficient cause* (i.e., from what is usually called "cause") is of the highest importance. The cause belongs to the necessity that is not yet unveiled and blind; hence, it appears to pass over into its other and thus to lose its originality in its positedness. Only in-itself (or for us) does the cause return *into itself*—being cause only in the effect. The purpose, on the contrary, is posited as containing *within itself* the determinacy (or what still appears there, in the context of causality, as otherness, i.e., the effect). In this way the purpose does not pass over, but *preserves* itself, in its operation; i.e., it brings only itself about and is at the *end* what it was in the *begin-ning*, or in its originality: what is truly original comes to be only through this self-preservation.—The purpose requires a specula-tive interpretation, as the Concept which itself (in its own *unity* and in the *ideality* of its determinations) contains the *judgment* or negation, i.e., the antithesis of the subjective and objective—and which is just as much their sublation.
>
> In dealing with the purpose, we must not think at once (or merely) of the form in which it occurs in consciousness as a deter-mination that is present in representation. With his concept of *in-ternal* purposiveness, *Kant* has resuscitated the Idea in general and especially the Idea of life. The determination of life by *Aristotle*[29] already contains this internal purposiveness; hence, it stands in-finitely far above the concept of modern teleology which had only *finite*, or *external*, purposiveness in view.

Need and drive are the readiest examples of purpose. They are the *felt* contradiction, as it occurs *within* the living subject itself; and they lead into the activity of negating this negation (which is what mere subjectivity still is). *Satisfaction* establishes peace between the subject and the object, since what is objective, what stands *on the other side* in the contradiction while it is still present (i.e., in the need), is sublated with respect to its one-sidedness by being united with the subjective.—Those who talk so much about the stability and invincibility of the finite (whether subjective or objective) can find an example of the contrary in every drive. Drive is, so to speak, the *certainty* that the subjective is only one-sided and that it has no more truth than the objective. Drive, moreover, is the *carrying out* of the certainty that belongs to it; it accomplishes the sublation of this antithesis ([between] the subjective that is and remains only something-subjective, and the objective that is and remains only something-objective) and of this finitude that belongs to each of them.

Concerning the activity of the purpose, it may be worth noting that in the *syllogism* (which this activity is and which con-cludes the purpose with itself by means of its realisation) the *negation* of the terms is essentially present: this is the negation of the immediate subjectivity present in the purpose as such that was just mentioned, as well as the negation of the *immediate* objectivity (of the means and of the presupposed objects). It is the same negation that is put into practice in the elevation of the spirit to God, above the contingent things of the world as well as above our own subjectivity. As has been mentioned in the *Introduction* and in § 192, this is the moment which is overlooked and left out in the form that is given to this elevation in the so-called proofs that there is a God—i.e., in the form of the syllogisms of the understanding.

§ 205

In its immediacy, the teleological relation is initially *external* purposiveness, and the Concept confronts the object as *something-presupposed*. As a result the purpose is *finite*, partly in respect to its *content*, and partly because it has an external condition in a pre-given[a] object which is the *material* for its realisation; in these respects its self-determination is merely

a. *vorzufindend*

formal. More precisely, its immediacy implies that the *particularity* (which as a *determination of form* is the *subjectivity* of the purpose) appears as inwardly reflected and that the *content* appears as *distinct* from the *totality of the form*, i.e., from the subjectivity *in-itself*, or from the Concept. This diversity is what constitutes the *finitude* of the purpose *within itself*. Because of it the content of the purpose is just as much restricted, contingent, and given as the object is particular and given in advance.

Addition. When people speak of "purpose" they usually have only external purposiveness in mind. From this point of view things are held not to bear their determination within themselves, but to count merely as *means*, which are used and used up in the realisation of a purpose that lies outside them. This is the general viewpoint of *utility*, which once played a great role, even in the sciences, but soon fell into deserved discredit, and was [re]cognised as a viewpoint that does not suffice for a genuine insight into the nature of things. Certainly finite things as such must be given their due by being regarded as not ultimate and as pointing beyond themselves. But this negativity of finite things is their own dialectic, and if we are to [re]cognise this, we must involve ourselves first of all in their positive content. However, since in the teleological approach we also have to deal with the well-intentioned concern to demonstrate the wisdom of God, as it specifically announces itself in nature, it must be remarked that, in all this searching out of the purposes for which things serve as means, we do not get beyond the finite, and we can very easily end up in lame reflections; for example, when it is not only the vine that is considered under the aspect of the well-known utility that it has for men, but the cork tree, too, is considered in its relation to the stoppers cut from its bark in order to seal wine bottles. Whole books used to be written in this spirit, and it is easy to see that neither the true interest of religion nor that of science can be advanced in this way. External purposiveness stands immediately before the Idea, but what stands on the threshold like that is often precisely what is most unsatisfactory.

§ 206

The teleological relation is the syllogism in which the subjective purpose con-cludes itself with the objectivity external to it, through a middle term which is the unity of these two. This unity is both the purposive *activity* and the objectivity posited *immediately* as subservient to the purpose; [in other words] it is the *means*.

Addition. The development of purpose into the Idea proceeds through three stages: *first*, subjective purpose, *secondly*, purpose in the process of accomplishing itself, and *thirdly*, the accomplished purpose.—In the first place, we have the subjective purpose, and this, being the Concept which is for-itself, is itself a totality of conceptual moments. First among these moments is the universality that is identical with itself, as it were the neutral first water,[30] in which everything is contained, but not yet separated out. The second moment then is the particularisation of this universal, through which it acquires a definite content. And when this definite content is posited by the agency of the universal, the latter returns to itself through this content and *con-cludes*[31] itself with itself.

Accordingly, too, when we set ourselves a purpose, we say [in German] that we "beschließen"[32] something, and we consider ourselves therefore initially as "open," so to speak, and as "accessible" to this or that determination. But we say equally that we have "entschlossen" on something, expressing in this way that the subject steps out from his inwardness that is merely on its own and starts to deal with the objectivity that confronts him. This results in the advance from the merely subjective purpose to the purposive activity that is turned outwards.

§ 207

(1) The *subjective* purpose is the syllogism in which the *universal* Concept con-cludes itself with singularity through particularity, in such a way that, as self-determination, singularity *judges*[a]—i.e., it not only particularises the still indeterminate universal and makes it into a determinate *content*, but it also posits the *antithesis* of subjectivity and objectivity. At the same time, singularity is, in itself, the return into itself. For it determines that the subjectivity of the Concept, presupposed as confronting the objectivity, is something-deficient, in comparison with the totality that is con-cluded within itself; and it thereby turns itself *outwards* at once.

§ 208

(2) In the subjective purpose this *outward-directed activity* is the *singularity* that is identical with the particularity in which, together with the content, *external objectivity* is *included* as well. This activity relates itself in the first place immediately to the object, and makes itself master of it as a *means*. The Concept is this immediate *might*, because it is the negativity that is identical with itself, in which the entire *being* of the object is determined only as an *ideal* being.—The *whole middle term* is now this inner might of the Concept, as the *activity* with which the *object* is immediately united as a *means*, and to which it is subservient.

> In finite purposiveness the middle term is *broken apart* into these two moments that are external to each other: the activity and the

a. urteilt

object that serves as a means. The relation of the purpose as *power* to this object, and the latter's subservience to it, is *immediate* (it is the *first premise* of the syllogism) inasmuch as the object is posited as *in-itself* null within the Concept as the ideality that is for-itself. [But] because the purpose con-cludes itself with the objectivity through this relation—the activity in which it is contained and which it continues to dominate—this [immediate] relation or first premise *becomes itself the middle* which *is inwardly* the syllogism at the same time.

Addition. The execution of the purpose is the mediated way of realising it, but immediate realisation is also equally necessary. The purpose seizes upon the object in immediate fashion, because it is the power over the object: particularity is contained within it, and within this particularity objectivity is contained as well.— The living being has a body; the soul takes hold of the body and, in doing so, it has objectified itself immediately. The human soul has much to do in making its corporeal nature into a means. Man must first take possession of his body, as it were, in order for it to be the instrument of his soul.

§ 209

(3) Even in conjunction with its means the purposive activity is still directed outwards, because the purpose is also *not* identical with the object; consequently it, too, must still be mediated with the object. In this *second premise* the means, as object, is *immediately* related with the *other* extreme of the syllogism, the objectivity as presupposed, the material. This relation is the sphere of mechanism and chemism which now *serve* the purpose— which is the truth and free Concept of them both. The fact that the subjective purpose, as the power over these processes (in which the *objective* gets used up through mutual friction and sublates itself), keeps itself *outside of them* and *preserves itself* in them is the *cunning* of reason.[a]

Addition. Reason is as *cunning* as it is *mighty*. Its cunning generally consists in the mediating activity which, while it lets objects act upon one another according to their own nature, and wear each other out, executes only *its* purpose without itself mingling in the process. In this sense we can say that, with regard to the world and its process, divine Providence behaves with absolute cunning. God lets men, who have their particular passions and interests, do as they please, and what results is the accomplishment of *his* intentions, which are something other than those whom he employs were directly concerned about.

a. *die* List *der Vernunft*

§ 210

Thus the realised purpose is the *posited unity* of the subjective and the objective. But this unity is essentially determined in such a way that the subjective and the objective are only neutralised and sublated in their *one-sidedness*, while the objective is subordinated to and brought into conformity with the purpose, which is the free Concept and hence the might over it. The purpose *preserves* itself against and within the objective, since it is not only the *one-sided* subjective [moment], the particular, but also the concrete universal, the identity (of both the subjective and the objective) that is in-itself. As simply reflected inwardly this universal is the *content*, which remains *the same* through all three terms of the syllogism, and throughout their movement.

§ 211

But in finite purposiveness even the accomplished purpose is still something inwardly broken, just as much as the middle term and the initial purpose were. Only a form that is *externally* posited in the pre-given[a] material is established thereby; and because of the restricted content of the purpose, this form is likewise a contingent determination. Hence, the purpose that is attained is merely an object, which is once more a means or a material for other purposes, and so on ad infinitum.

§ 212

But in the realising of the purpose what happens *in-itself* is *that the one-sided subjectivity* is sublated, along with the semblance of an objective independence standing over against it. In taking hold of the means, *the Concept* posits itself as the essence of the object. *In-itself* the independence of the object has already evaporated in the mechanical and chemical processes; and as they take place under the dominion of the purpose, even the *semblance* of this independence—the negative *as against the Concept*—sublates itself. But since the accomplished purpose is determined *only* as means and material, this object is already posited at once as something that is in-itself null and merely ideal. And thereby the opposition of *content* and *form* has vanished as well. For, because the purpose con-cludes itself with itself by sublating the form-determinations, the form is posited as *identical* with itself, and hence as content—so that *the Concept*, as the *activity of the form*, has only *itself* for *content*. Through this whole process, therefore, what was previously the *Concept* of the purpose is now *posited*:

a. *vorgefunden*

the unity *in-itself* of the subjective and the objective is now posited as *being-for-itself*. [This is] the *Idea*.

Addition. The finitude of purpose consists in the fact that, in its realisation, the material used as means is only externally subsumed under it and adapted to it. But in fact the object is *implicitly* the Concept, and when the Concept, as purpose, is realised in the object, this purpose is only the manifestation of the object's own inwardness. So objectivity is, as it were, only a wrapping under which the Concept lies hidden. In the sphere of the finite we can neither experience nor see that the purpose is genuinely attained. The accomplishing of the infinite purpose consists therefore only in sublating the illusion that it has not yet been accomplished. The good, the absolute good, fulfills itself eternally in the world, and the result is that it is already fulfilled in and for itself, and does not need to wait upon us for this to happen. This is the illusion in which we live, and at the same time it is this illusion alone that is the activating element[a] upon which our interest in the world rests. It is within its own process that the Idea produces that illusion for itself; it posits an other confronting itself, and its action consists in sublating that illusion. Only from this error does the truth come forth, and herein lies our reconciliation with error and with finitude. Otherness or error, as sublated, is itself a necessary moment of the truth, which can only be in that it makes itself into its own result.

C
The Idea

§ 213

The Idea is what is true *in and for itself, the absolute unity of Concept and objectivity*. Its ideal content is nothing but the Concept in its determinations; its real content is only the presentation that the Concept gives itself in the form of external thereness; and since this figure is included in the ideality of the Concept, or in its might, the Concept preserves itself in it.

> The definition *of the Absolute* as the *Idea* is now itself absolute. All definitions given previously return into this one.—The Idea is the *Truth*; for truth means that objectivity corresponds with the Concept—not that external things correspond with my representations (representations of this kind are just *correct* representations held by *me* as *this* [individual]). In the Idea we are not dealing with this or that—be it representations, or external things. And—yet again, *everything* that is actual is the Idea inasmuch as it is

---

a. *das Betätigende*

something-true, and it has its truth only through the Idea and in virtue of it. The singular being is some side or other of the Idea; that is why other actualities were needed for it—actualities which likewise appear to subsist distinctly on their own account. It is only in all of them together and in their relation that the Concept is realised. By itself the singular does not correspond to its concept; this restrictedness of its way of being constitutes its *finitude* and its fall.

The Idea itself is not to be taken as an idea *of something or other*, any more than the Concept is to be taken merely as determinate concept. The Absolute is the universal and One Idea, which particularises itself in the act of *judging* into the *system* of determinate ideas—whose whole being consists, nonetheless, in their returning into the One Idea, i.e., into their truth. It is because of this judgment that the Idea is *at first* just the One and universal *substance*, but its developed, authentic actuality is to be as *subject* and so as spirit.

Inasmuch as the Idea does not have an *existence* as its starting point and support, it is often mistaken for something belonging only to formal logic. We must leave this view to the standpoints for which the existing thing, and all the further determinations that have not yet penetrated to the Idea, still count as so-called *realities* and genuine *actualities*.—Equally mistaken is the notion according to which the Idea is only what is *abstract*. That the Idea is abstract is true enough in the sense that everything *untrue* is consumed in it; but in its own right the Idea is essentially *concrete*, because it is the free Concept that determines itself and in so doing makes itself real.[a] It would only be what is formally abstract, if the Concept, which is its principle, were taken to be the abstract unity, and not how it really is, i.e., as the *negative return into itself and* as *subjectivity*.

Addition. Truth is understood first to mean that I *know* how something *is*. But this is truth only in relation to consciousness; it is formal truth, mere correctness. In contrast with this, truth in the deeper sense means that objectivity is identical with the Concept. It is this deeper sense of truth which is at issue when we speak, for instance, of a "true" State or a "true" work of art. These ob-jects are "true" when they are what they *ought* to be, i.e., when their reality corresponds to their concept. Interpreted in this way, the "untrue" is the same as what is sometimes also called the "bad". A bad man is one who is "untrue", i.e., one who does not behave in accord with his concept or his destination. But without any identity at all between

---

a. *sich selbst und hiemit zur Realität bestimmende Begriff*

Concept and reality nothing can subsist. Even what is bad and untrue can only *be* because its reality conforms to some extent with its Concept. Precisely for this reason, what is thoroughly bad or contrary to its concept disintegrates inwardly. It is by virtue of the Concept alone that things in the world have their own standing—or, to use the language of religious representation, things are what they are only because of the divine and hence creative thought that dwells within them.

When we speak of the Idea, it must not be taken to mean something far away and beyond. Instead, the Idea is what is perfectly present, and it is likewise to be found in any consciousness too, however confused and impaired it may be there.—We imagine the world as a great whole which has been created by God—in such a way that God has manifested himself to us in it. In like manner, we regard the world as governed by divine Providence, and this implies that the world, in its mutual externality, is eternally led back to the unity from which it came forth, and is preserved in accordance with that unity.

The concern of philosophy has always been simply with the thinking cognition of the Idea, and everything that deserves the name of philosophy has always had at its foundation the consciousness of an absolute unity of what is valid for the understanding only in its separateness.—It is not just now that we can for the first time ask for a proof that the Idea is the truth; the whole preceding exposition and development of thinking contains this proof. The Idea is the result of this journey. But this result is not to be understood as if it were *only* mediated, i.e., mediated by something other than itself. Rather, the Idea is its own result, and, as such, it is immediate just as much as it is mediated. The stages of Being and of Essence, previously considered, and similarly those of the Concept, and of objectivity, while distinct from one another, are not something fixed and resting upon themselves; instead, they have proved to be dialectical, and their truth is only that they are moments of the Idea.

§ 214

The Idea can be grasped as *reason* (this is the proper philosophical meaning of "reason"); and further as the *Subject-Object*, as the *unity of the ideal and the real, of the finite and the infinite, of the soul and the body,*[a] as the *possibility that has its actuality in itself,* as that whose *nature* can be comprehended only as *existing,* and so forth. [It can be grasped in all these ways] because all the relationships of the understanding are contained in the Idea, but in their *infinite* self-return and self-identity.

> It is an easy task for the understanding to show that everything asserted about the Idea is self-*contradictory*. But the proof can be sent home to the understanding; or rather, that has already been brought about in the Idea: this is the work of reason, which is not

a. Leib

at all as easy as that of the understanding.—The understanding shows that the Idea contradicts itself, because the subjective, for instance, is merely subjective and the objective is really opposed to it; and being is something quite other than the concept, so that it cannot be plucked out of it;[33] likewise, the finite is merely finite and the exact opposite of the infinite, so that it is not identical with it—and so on, through all determinations, one after the other. But the Logic demonstrates the opposite instead, namely, that the subjective that is supposed to be merely subjective, the finite that is supposed to be merely finite, and the infinite that is supposed to be merely infinite, and so on, do not have any truth; they contradict themselves and pass over into their opposites.—As a result, the passing-over and the unity, in which the extremes are [present] as sublated—as a shining or as moments—reveals itself as their truth.

The understanding that applies itself to the Idea is a misunderstanding in two ways. *In the first place*, it still takes the *extremes* of the Idea (express them any way you like, as long as *they* are *in their unity*) in the sense and determination that they have when they are *not* in their concrete unity, but are only abstractions outside of it. It equally fails to recognise the *relation*, even when it has already been expressly posited. For instance, it overlooks the very nature of the *copula* in the judgment, which says that the singular, or the subject, is not just singular but universal as well.—*Secondly*, the understanding takes *its own* reflection, that the self-identical Idea contains the *negative* of itself (the contradiction), to be an *external* reflection which does not fall within the Idea itself. But, in fact, this is not a wisdom that belongs just to the understanding; rather, it is the Idea itself which is the dialectic which eternally divides and distinguishes what is self-identical from what is differentiated, the subjective from the objective, the finite from the infinite, the soul from the body. Only in this way is the Idea eternal creation, eternal vitality, and eternal Spirit. While the Idea itself is this passing-over or rather self-translation into the *abstract understanding*, it is also eternally *reason*; it is the dialectic that makes this product of the understanding, this diversity, understand its own finite nature once more, makes it see that the independence of its productions is a false semblance, and leads it all back to unity. Since this double movement is not temporal, and not in any way separate and distinct (for then it would again belong to the abstract understanding), it is the eternal intuiting of itself in the other: the Concept that *has* carried *itself* out in its objectivity, or the object that is *inner purposiveness*, essential subjectivity.

The *various ways* of interpreting the Idea—as the unity of the ideal and the real, of the *finite* and the *infinite*, of *identity* and *difference*, and so forth—are all more or less *formal*, because they designate some level or other of the *determinate Concept*. Only the Concept itself is free, and what is truly *universal*; in the Idea, therefore, its *determinacy* is at the same time only itself: an objectivity in which the Concept, as the universal, sets itself forth, and in which it has only the determinacy that is its own, [i.e.,] the total determinacy. The Idea is the *infinite judgment*, of which the sides are each the independent totality, while (precisely because it completes itself in this way) each of them has also passed over into the other. None of the concepts that are determined otherwise is this totality that is completed in both of its sides—both as the *Concept* itself and as *objectivity*.

§ 215

The Idea is essentially *process*, because its identity is only the absolute and free identity of the Concept, because this identity is the absolute negativity and hence dialectical. The Idea is the course in which the Concept (as the universality that is singularity) determines itself both to objectivity and to the antithesis against it, and in which this externality, which the Concept has with regard to its substance, leads itself back again, through its immanent dialectic, into *subjectivity*.

Since the Idea is (a) *process*, the expression of the Absolute as "the *unity* of the finite and the infinite, of thinking and being, etc." is false (as we have often said); for "unity" expresses an abstract, *quietly* persisting identity. And because the Idea is (b) *subjectivity*, that expression is equally false for another reason: "unity" there expresses the *In-itself*, the *substantial* [side] of the genuine unity. Thus, the infinite only appears to be *neutralised* with the finite, just as the subjective is neutralised with the objective, and thinking with being. But in the *negative* unity of the *Idea*, the infinite overgrasps the finite, thinking overgrasps being, subjectivity overgrasps objectivity. The unity of the Idea is subjectivity, or thinking, or infinity, and therefore it has to be essentially distinguished from the Idea as *substance*, just as this *overgrasping* subjectivity, thinking, or infinity has to be distinguished from the one-sided subjectivity, thinking, or infinity, to which it reduces itself in judging and determining.

Addition. As a process, the Idea runs through three stages in its development. The first form of the Idea is *life*, i.e., the Idea in the form of immediacy. The second form is that of mediation or difference, and this is the Idea as *cognition*, which appears in the dual shape of the *theoretical* and the *practical* Idea. The result of the process of cognition is the reestablishing of unity enriched by distinction; and this gives the third form of the (herewith) *absolute Idea*. This last stage of the logical process proves at the same time to be what is genuinely first and what is only through itself.

A. LIFE

§ 216

The *immediate* Idea is *life*. The Concept is realised as soul, in a *body*. The soul is the immediate self-relating *universality* of the body's externality; it is equally the *particularising* of the body, so that the body expresses no distinctions in itself other than the determinations of the Concept; and finally it is *singularity* as infinite negativity: the dialectic of the body's scattered[a] objectivity, which is led back into subjectivity from the semblance of independent subsistence. [This happens] in such a way that all of the body's members are reciprocally both *means* and purposes for each other from moment to moment, and that life, while it is the *initial* particularising of the members, becomes its own *result* as the *negative* unity that is *for-itself*, and in the dialectic of corporeity it con-cludes itself only with itself.—Thus, life is essentially *living being*,[b] and in its immediacy it is *This Singular* living being. In this sphere, the determination of finitude is that, because of the immediacy of the Idea, soul and body are *separable*; this constitutes the mortality of what is alive. But it is only insofar as it is dead that these two sides of the Idea are diverse *components*.

Addition. The single members of the body are what they are only through their unity and in relation to it. So, for instance, a hand that has been hewn from the body is a hand in name only, but not in actual fact, as Aristotle has already remarked.[34]—From the standpoint of the understanding life is usually considered to be a mystery, and in general as *incomprehensible*. But here the understanding only confesses its finitude and nullity. In fact, life is so far from being incomprehensible that on the contrary, we have the Concept itself before us in it, and, more precisely, the Idea that exists as the Concept, the *immediate* Idea. But this expresses

a. *auseinanderseiende*
b. Lebendiges

at once the defect of life too. The defect consists in the fact that the Concept and reality still do not genuinely correspond with one another. The concept of life is the soul, and this concept has the body for its reality. The soul is, as it were, diffused into its bodily nature, and so it is still only *sentient*, not yet free being-for-itself. Hence, the process of life consists in the overcoming of the immediacy in which life is still entangled; and this process itself, which is once more a threefold one, results in the Idea in the form of judgment, i.e., the Idea as *cognition*.

§ 217

The living being is the syllogism whose very moments are inwardly systems and syllogisms (§§ 198, 201, 207). But they are active syllogisms, or processes; and within the subjective unity of the living being they are only *One* process. Thus, the living being is the process of its own con-cluding with itself, which runs through *three processes*.

§ 218

(1) The first of them is the process of the living being *inside* itself. In this process it sunders itself and makes its corporeity into its object, or its *inorganic* nature. As what is relatively external, this inorganic nature enters on its own part into the distinction and antithesis of its moments, each of which abandons itself to the others, assimilates the others to itself, and maintains itself by self-production. But this activity of the members is just the One [activity] of the subject into which its productions return—so that in all this only the subject is produced; i.e., it simply reproduces itself.

Addition. The process of the living being inside itself has in nature the threefold form of sensibility, irritability, and reproduction.[35] As sensibility, the living being is immediately simple relation to itself, the soul, which is everywhere present in its body, so that the mutual externality of the bodily parts has no truth for it. As irritability, the living being appears sundered within itself, and, as reproduction, it is constantly reestablishing itself out of the inner distinction of its members and organs. It is only as this constantly renewed inner process that the living being *is*.

§ 219

(2) But the *judgment* of the Concept goes on, in its freedom, to release the *objective* out of itself as an independent totality; and, as *immediate* singularity, the negative relation of the living being to itself makes the *presupposition* of an inorganic nature that confronts it. Since this negative

of itself is nonetheless a conceptual moment of the living being itself, it is in the living being—which is at the same time a concrete universal—as a *want*. The dialectic, through which the object (as *in-itself* null) sublates itself, is the activity of the living being that is certain of itself; in and through *this process against an inorganic nature*, it *maintains itself, develops* itself, and *objectifies* itself.

Addition. The living being confronts an inorganic nature to which it relates as the power over it, and which it assimilates. The result of this process is not, as in the case of the chemical process, a neutral product in which the independence of the two sides that confronted one another is sublated; instead, the living being proves itself to be what overgrasps its other, which cannot resist its power. Inorganic nature, which is subdued by the living being, suffers this subjection because it is *in-itself* the same as what life is *for-itself*. So in the other the living being only comes together with itself. When the soul has fled from the body, the elementary powers of objectivity come into play. These powers are, so to speak, continually ready to pounce, to begin their process in the organic body, and life is a constant struggle against them.

§ 220

(3) The living individual, which behaves itself inwardly as subject and concept in its first process, assimilates its external objectivity to itself in the second process; and in this way it *posits* real determinacy *within itself*, so that it is now *genus in-itself*, or substantial universality. The particularising of this universality is the relation of the subject to *another subject* of the same genus, and the judgment is the relationship of the species to these individuals which are determined vis-à-vis one another in this oppositional way—the *difference of the sexes*.

§ 221

The process of the *genus*[36] brings it to its *being-for-itself*. Since life is still the immediate Idea, the product of this process falls apart into two sides: on the *one* hand, the living individual generally, which was to begin with presupposed as immediate, now emerges as something-mediated and *generated*; but on *the other* hand, the living *singularity*, which on account of its initial immediacy stands in a *negative* relationship to universality, *goes under* in this universality as what has power [over it].

Addition. The living being dies because it is the contradiction of being *in-itself* the universal, the genus, and yet existing immediately only as a singular being. In death the genus proves itself to be the power over the immediately singular being.—For the animal, the process of the genus is the highest point of its living career. But the animal does not succeed in being for-itself in its species; instead, it succumbs to the power of the latter. The immediate living being mediates itself with itself in the process of the genus; and in this way it elevates itself above its immediacy, but always just to sink back into it again. So, to start with, life simply runs its course into the spurious infinity of the infinite progress. But what, according to the Concept, is brought about through the process of Life is the sublation and overcoming of the immediacy in which as life the Idea is still entangled.

§ 222

As a result, however, the Idea of life has freed itself not just from *some one or other* (particular) immediate This, but from this initial immediacy in general. Thereby the Idea of life comes to *itself*, or to its *truth*; and therefore it enters *into existence for its own self as free genus*. The death of the merely immediate singular organism[a] is the *emergence of spirit*.

B. COGNITION

§ 223

The Idea exists freely *for-itself*, inasmuch as it has universality as the element *of its existence*, or inasmuch as objectivity itself is as the Concept; [i.e.,] inasmuch as the Idea has itself as its ob-ject. Its subjectivity, which has [now] become determined as universality, is *pure distinguishing inside* itself: an intuiting that holds itself within this identical universality. But, as determinate distinguishing, the Idea is further the judgment of repelling itself as a totality from itself, and, to be precise, of *presupposing* itself first of all as *external universe*. There are here two judgments, which, although identical *in-themselves*, are not yet *posited* as identical.

§ 224

The relation between these two Ideas, which are identical *in-themselves* or as Life, is therefore a *relative* one. This is what constitutes the determination of *finitude* in this sphere. We have here the *relationship of reflection*, because the distinguishing of the Idea within itself is just the *first*

a. *Lebendigkeit*

judgment; because the *presupposing* is not yet *a positing*; [and because], for that very reason, the objective Idea is for the subjective Idea the immediate world that is *found to be already there*, or the Idea as life is [here] in the appearance of *singular existence*. [At the same time and all in one]— inasmuch as this judgment is pure distinguishing *within* the Idea itself (see the preceding paragraph [§ 223])—the Idea is *for-itself* both itself and *its other*. In this way the Idea is the *certainty* of the *implicit*[a] identity of this objective world with it.—Reason comes to the world with absolute faith in its ability to posit this identity and to elevate its certainty into *truth*, and with the drive to *posit* the antithesis [between itself and the world], which is *in-itself* null and void *for it* as null and void.

§ 225

In general terms this process is *cognition*. In this process the antithesis, the one-sidedness of subjectivity together with the one-sidedness of objectivity, is *implicitly* sublated within *One* activity. But initially this sublating happens only *in-itself*; hence, the process as such is itself immediately affected by the finitude of this sphere, and it falls apart into the *doubled* movement of this drive, posited as two diverse movements. [To start with, there is the movement] to sublate the one-sidedness of the *subjectivity* of the Idea by means of the assumption of the world that [simply] is[b] into oneself, into subjective representing and thinking; and to fill the abstract certainty of oneself with this objectivity (which thus counts as genuine) as its *content*. And, conversely, [there is the movement] to sublate the *one-sidedness* of the objective world, which therefore counts, on the contrary, only as a *semblance*, a collection of contingencies and of shapes which are in-themselves null and void—[the movement] to determine this world through the *inwardness* of the subjective, which here counts as what is truly objective, and to in-form it with this subjectivity.[c] The first movement is the drive of knowing toward truth, or *cognition as such*—the *theoretical* activity of the Idea—the second is the drive of the *good* toward its own accomplishment—*willing*, the *practical* activity of the Idea.

(α) Cognition
§ 226

The universal finitude of cognition (the finitude that lies in the first judgment, in the *presupposition* of the antithesis [§ 224] against which its very

a. an sich *seiende*
b. *der seienden Welt*
c. *und ihr dieses einzubilden*

own agency is the built-in contradiction) determines itself more precisely, in its own Idea, by giving the moments of this Idea the form of diversity from each other; and, since these moments are nevertheless complete, they come to stand in the relationship of reflection to each other, not in that of the Concept. Hence the assimilation of the material as something-given appears as its *being taken up* into conceptual determinations which at the same time remain *external* to it, and which likewise present themselves in diversity from one another. This is reason acting as *understanding*. By the same token, therefore, the truth that is reached by this cognition is only *the finite* [truth]; the infinite truth of the Concept is fixed as a goal that is only *in-itself*, or as a *beyond* for this cognition. But in its external agency this cognition stands under the guidance of the Concept, and the determinations of the Concept constitute the inner thread of its progression.

Addition. The finitude of cognition lies in the presupposition of a world that is found to be there already, and the cognitive subject appears here as a tabula rasa.[37] People have ascribed this representation to Aristotle, although there is no one further removed from this external interpretation of cognition than Aristotle himself.[38] Finite cognition does not yet know itself as the activity of the Concept, which it is only *in-itself* but not *for-itself*. Its behaviour appears to itself as passive, but it is in fact active.

§ 227

Since finite cognition presupposes the *distinct* as something found already in being and standing over and against it—the manifold *facts* of external nature or of consciousness—it has (1) *formal identity* or the *abstraction* of universality as the form of its activity. This activity consists therefore in dissolving the concrete that is given, isolating its distinctions and bestowing the form of *abstract universality* upon them; in other words, it consists in leaving the concrete as *ground* and making a concrete universal—the *genus*, or force and law—stand out through abstraction from the particularities that seem to be inessential. This is the *analytical method*.[39]

Addition. We usually speak of the "analytic" and "synthetic" methods as if it were merely a matter of our own choice whether we follow the one or the other. But this is not at all the case; on the contrary, which of the two above-mentioned methods resulting from the Concept of finite cognition is to be applied depends on the form of the ob-jects themselves that cognition aims at. At first, cognition is analytic; the object assumes for it the shape of something isolated, and the activity of analytical cognition is directed toward tracing the singular that lies before it back to a universal. Here, thinking has the significance only of abstraction or of formal identity. This is the standpoint of Locke and of all empiricists.[40] Many say that cognition cannot go any further than this at all: to break up the given concrete ob-jects into their abstract elements and then contemplate these in their state of isolation from one another. It is apparent at once, however, that this stands things on their heads, and that any cognition that wants to take things as they *are* falls into contradiction with itself when it takes this road. For example, a chemist puts a piece of meat into his retort, tortures it in many ways, and then says that he has found that it consists of nitrogen, carbon, hydrogen, etc. But these abstract materials are no longer meat. And we have the same situation when the empirical psychologist breaks an action up into the various aspects which it presents to observation, and then holds fast to them in their separation from one another. The ob-ject that is treated analytically is regarded like an onion, so to speak, from which people strip one skin after another.

§ 228

But this *universality* is (2) also a *determinate* one; and here the activity progresses through the moments of the Concept, which in finite *cognition* is not the Concept in its infinity, [but] the *determinate concept of the understanding*. The taking up of the ob-ject into the forms of this determinate concept is the *synthetic method*.

Addition. The movement of the synthetic method is the reverse of the movement in the analytic method. Whilst the latter starts from the singular and advances to the universal, the former, on the contrary, starts with the universal (as a *definition*), and advances, through particularisation (in *division*), to the singular (in the *theorem*). Thus, the synthetic method proves to be the development of the moments of the Concept in the ob-ject.

§ 229

(aa) The ob-ject brought first into the form of the determinate Concept in general by cognition—so that its *genus* and its universal *determinacy* are thereby posited—is the *definition*. Its material and justification are provided by the analytical method (§ 227). The determinacy, however, is only supposed to be a *characteristic*; i.e., it is for the purpose of a cognition which is only subjective and external with regard to the ob-ject.

Addition. Definition itself contains the three moments of the Concept: the universal, as the proximate genus (*genus proximum*), the particular, as the determinacy of the species[41] (*qualitas specifica*), and the singular, as the defined ob-ject itself.—With regard to definition there arises, first, the question of where it comes from; and the general answer to this question is that definitions arise upon the analytic path. But then, too, this at once occasions controversy about the correctness of the definition that is set up, for it is now a question about what perceptions we started from and what points of view we had in mind at that stage. The richer the ob-ject that is to be defined, i.e.,, the more varied the aspects that it presents for consideration, the more varied do the definitions that are set up tend to be as well. Hence we have, for example, a whole mass of definitions of life, or of the State, and so on. Geometry, on the contrary, has it easy in the making of definitions, because its ob-ject, space, is so abstract.

Moreover, there is no necessity at all in the content of the ob-jects defined. We are supposed to admit that there is space, that there are plants, animals, and so on; and it is not the business of geometry, or botany, etc., to exhibit the necessity of the ob-jects in question. And for this same reason the synthetic method is just as unsuitable for philosophy as the analytic one, since philosophy must above all justify itself with regard to the necessity of its ob-jects. All the same, there have been many attempts to employ the synthetic method in philosophy, too. Spinoza, especially, begins with definitions, and says, for example, that Substance is the *causa sui*. The most speculative content is laid down in his definitions, but in the form of assurances. The same holds for Schelling as well.[42]

§ 230

(bb) The specification of the second moment of the Concept, the determinacy of the universal as *particularisation*, is its *division* according to some external aspect or other.

Addition. The requirement is that divisions should be complete; and for this there must be a principle or ground of division, which is so constituted that the division based on it embraces the entire content of the domain that is designated in general terms by the definition. More precisely, the principle of division must be taken from the nature of the very ob-ject that is to be subdivided, so that the division is made naturally and is not merely artificial, i.e., arbitrary. Hence, for example, the division of mammals in zoology is mainly based upon the teeth and the claws, and this makes sense, because the mammals distinguish themselves from one another through these parts of their bodies, and the universal type of the various classes can be traced back to them.[43]

Any division is to be considered genuine when it is determined by the Concept. So genuine division is, first of all, tripartite; and then, because particularity presents itself as doubled, the division moves on to fourfoldness as well. In the sphere of spirit trichotomy predominates, and it is one of Kant's merits to have drawn attention to this.[44]

§ 231

(cc) In its *concrete singularity*—where the determinacy (which in the definition is simple) is taken as *a relationship*—the ob-ject is a synthetic relation of *distinct* determinations: a *theorem*. Since there are diverse determinations, their identity is a *mediated* one. The bringing forward of the materials that constitute the middle terms is the *construction*; and the mediation itself, from which the necessity of that relation for cognition flows, is the *demonstration*.[a]

The way the distinction between the synthetic and the analytical methods is usually specified makes the use of one or the other appear on the whole to be optional. If the concrete [case] which is presented as a *result*, according to the synthetic method, is *presupposed*, then the abstract determinations, which constitute the *presuppositions* and the *material* for the demonstration,[b] can be analysed out of it as its *consequences*. The algebraical *definitions* of curved lines become *theorems* in the procedure of geometry. And the Pythagorean theorem, too, if it is taken as a definition of the right-angled triangle, would yield, by way of analysis, the propositions which have already been demonstrated in order to prove it in geometry. The optional character of the choice rests upon the fact that both methods equally start from something that is *externally presupposed*. According to the nature of the Concept the analytical procedure comes first, since its first task is to elevate the given, empirically concrete material into the form of universal abstractions; only after that can the abstractions be set up as the starting definitions in the synthetic method.

Although these methods are essential, and are brilliantly successful in their own field, they cannot be used for philosophical cognition. This is obvious because they have presuppositions and because cognition functions in them as understanding, and advances toward formal identity. In Spinoza, who made notable use of the geometrical method—and for *speculative* concepts at that— the formalism of this method makes itself conspicuous at once. The philosophy of Wolff, which carried this method to the height of pedantry,[45] is also a metaphysics of the understanding with regard to its content.—The misuse of this method and its formalism, in philosophy and in the sciences, has been replaced in more recent years by the misuse of what is called "construction". The

a. Beweis
b. *Beweis*

notion that mathematics *constructs* its *concepts* became current through the influence of Kant;[46] [but] this only means that mathematics does *not* deal with *concepts at all*, but with abstract determinations of *sensible intuitions*. As a result, the specification of *sensible* determinations (taken up from *perception* in a way that bypasses the Concept), along with the further formalism of a classification of philosophical and scientific ob-jects, tabulated according to a presupposed schema, but for the rest in a completely arbitrary manner—all this has been called a "construction of concepts". Admittedly there lies at the bottom of all this an obscure notion of the *Idea*, of the unity *of the Concept and objectivity*, as well as of the concreteness of the Idea. But this game of construction as it is called falls far short of presenting the *unity*, which only the *Concept* as such is; and by the same token what is sensibly concrete in intuition is not a concrete [content] of reason and the Idea.

Since *geometry* is concerned after all with the sensible (though abstract) intuition of space, it has no difficulty in fixing simple determinations of the understanding in this space; that is why geometry alone employs the synthetic method of finite cognition in its perfection. It is important to note, however, that geometry does, in its normal course, finally strike upon *incommensurabilities* and *irrationals*; at this point, it is *driven beyond* the principle of the understanding if it wants to go further in its determining. As so often happens elsewhere, so here, too, we find that terminology is stood on its head: what is called "rational" belongs to the *understanding*, while what is called "irrational" is rather the beginning and a first trace of *rationality*. When other sciences reach the limit of their advance according to the understanding (which happens to them necessarily and quite often, since they are not confined to the simplicity of space or of number), they easily find a way out. They break off their consistent advance and take up what they need (often the opposite of what preceded) from without, from representation, opinion, perception, or from any other source. Since this finite cognition is not conscious of the nature of its method or of the relationship of this method with the content, it cannot [re]cognise that it is being led on by the necessity of the *determinations of the Concept* in its progression through definitions, divisions, etc.; nor can it [re]cognise the point where it reaches its limit, and once it has transgressed this limit, it is unaware that it finds itself in a field where the determinations of the understanding (which it still continues to use in a rough and ready way) are no longer valid.

§ 232

The *necessity*, which finite cognition produces in its *demonstration*,[a] is to begin with an external one, directed only at subjective insight. But in necessity as such, finite cognition itself has abandoned its presupposition and starting point, the simple *finding* and *givenness* of its content. Necessity as such is implicitly the Concept that relates itself to itself. In this way the subjective Idea has (in-itself) arrived at what is determinate in and for itself, *not-given*, and hence *immanent* in the subject; and it passes over into the *Idea* of *willing*.

Addition. The necessity that cognition achieves through proof is the contrary of that which forms its starting point. In the latter, cognition had a given and contingent content; but at the conclusion of its movement, it knows that its content is necessary, and this necessity is mediated by subjective activity. Similarly, subjectivity was at first wholly abstract, a mere tabula rasa,[47] whereas from now on it proves to be determining. But in this lies the passage from the Idea of cognition to the Idea of willing. This passage consists, more precisely, in the fact that the universal in its truth must be interpreted as subjectivity, as the Concept that is self-moving and active, and that posits determinations.

(β) Willing
§ 233

As what is in and for itself determinate and as a *content* that is equal to itself and simple, the subjective Idea is the *good*. Its drive to realise itself has the converse relationship to that of the Idea of the *true* and aims rather to determine the world that it finds already there according to its own purpose.—On the one hand, this *willing* has the certainty that the presupposed object is *null and void*—but, at the same time on the other hand, being finite, it takes the purpose of the good to be a merely *subjective* Idea and it presupposes the *independence* of the object.

§ 234

The finitude of this activity, therefore, is the *contradiction* that the *purpose of the good* is being achieved and equally is not being achieved in the self-contradicting determinations of the objective world; that it is posited equally as an inessential purpose and an essential one, as an actual purpose and at the same time as a merely possible one. This contradiction

a. Beweis

presents itself as the *infinite progress* in the actualisation of the good, which is fixed in this progress as a mere *ought*.[48] *Formally* the vanishing of this contradiction consists in the fact that the activity sublates the subjectivity of the purpose and hence the objectivity, the antithesis that makes both finite; it does not just sublate the finitude of *this* subjectivity but subjectivity in general: *another* similar subjectivity, i.e., the *re*-production[a] of the antithesis, is not distinguished from the one that was supposed to be an earlier one. This return into itself is at the same time the *recollection*[b] of the *content* into itself—a content which is the good and the identity in-itself of both sides. It is the recollection of the presupposition of the theoretical attitude (§ 224) that the object is what is substantial and true in it.

Addition. Whereas the task of intelligence is simply to take the world as it *is*, the will, in contrast, is concerned to make the world finally into what it *ought* to be. The will holds that what is immediate, what is given, is not a fixed being, but only a semblance, something that is *in-itself* null and void. We encounter here the contradictions which, at the standpont of morality, drive us from pillar to post.[49]

This is, in general, the standpoint of Kant with regard to human action,[c] and also that of Fichte. The good ought to be realised; we have to work at this, to bring it forth, and the will is simply the good that is self-activating. But then if the world were as it ought to be, the result would be that the activity of willing would disappear. Therefore the will itself also requires that its purpose shall not be realised. This correctly expresses the finitude of willing. But we must not stop at this finitude, of course, and it is through the process of willing itself that this finitude is sublated, together with the contradiction that it contains. The reconciliation consists in the will's returning—in its result—to the presupposition of cognition; hence the reconciliation consists in the unity of the theoretical and practical Idea. The will knows the purpose as what is its own, and intelligence interprets the world as the Concept in its actuality. This is the genuine position of rational cognition.

What is null and vanishing constitutes only the surface of the world, not its genuine essence. This essence is the Concept that is in and for itself, and so the world is itself the Idea. Unsatisfied striving vanishes when we [re]cognise that the final purpose of the world is just as much accomplished as it is eternally accomplishing itself. This is, in general, the outlook of the mature person, whereas youth believes that the world is in an utterly sorry state, and that something quite different must be made of it. The religious consciousness, on the contrary, regards the world as governed by divine Providence and hence as corresponding to what it *ought* to be. This agreement between is and ought is not rigid and unmoving, however, since the final purpose of the world, the good, only *is*, because it constantly brings itself about; and there is still this distinction between the spiritual

a. *ein* neues *Erzeugen*
b. Erinnerung
c. *in praktischer Beziehung*

and the natural worlds: that, whilst the latter continues simply to return into itself, there occurs in the former certainly a progression as well.

§ 235

As a result the *truth* of the good is *posited*—as the unity of the theoretical and the practical Idea: [the truth] that the good has been reached in and for itself—that the objective world is in this way in and for itself the Idea positing itself eternally as *purpose* and at the same time bringing forth its actuality through [its] activity.—This life, which has returned to itself from the difference and finitude of cognition, and which has become identical with the Concept through the activity of the Concept, is the *speculative or absolute Idea*.

C. THE ABSOLUTE IDEA

§ 236

As unity of the subjective and the objective Idea, the Idea is the Concept of the Idea, for which the Idea as such is the ob-ject, and for which the object is itself—an object in which all determinations have come together. This unity, therefore, is the *absolute truth and all truth*, it is the Idea that thinks itself, and at this stage, moreover, it is [present] *as* thinking, i.e., as *logical* Idea.

Addition. The absolute Idea is first of all the unity of the theoretical and the practical Idea, and hence equally the unity of the Idea of life with the Idea of cognition. In cognition we had the Idea in the shape of difference; the process of cognition has shown itself to us as the overcoming of this difference, and the reestablishing of that unity which, as such and in its immediacy, is initially the Idea of life. The defect of life consists in the fact that it is still only the Idea *in-itself*; cognition, on the contrary, is the Idea only as it is *for-itself*, in the same one-sided way. The unity and the truth of these two is the Idea that is *in* and *for itself*, and hence *absolute*.—Up to this point the Idea in its development through its various stages has been *our* ob-ject; but from now on, the Idea is its own ob-ject. This is the *noēsis noēseōs*, which was already called the highest form of the Idea by Aristotle.[50]

§ 237

Since there is no passing-over within the *absolute Idea*, no presupposing, and no determinacy at all that would not be fluid and transparent, this Idea is for-itself the *pure form* of the Concept, which intuits *its content* as itself. It is its own *content*, inasmuch as it is the ideal distinguishing of itself from itself, and [because] one of the distinct [terms] is its identity with itself; but in this identity the totality of the form (as the system of the determinations of the content) is contained. This content is the system *of the logical*. All that remains here as *form* for the Idea is the *method* of this content—the determinate knowing of the currency of its moments.

Addition. When the expression "absolute Idea" is used, people may think that it is only here that we meet with what is right, that here everything must give itself up. It is certainly possible to sing the hollow praises of the absolute Idea, far and wide; in the meantime, its true content is nothing but the entire system, the development of which we have been considering so far. So it can also be said that the absolute Idea is the universal, but this universal is not merely the abstract form that confronts the particular content as something-other; on the contrary, it is the absolute form into which all determinations, the whole fullness of the content posited by it, have returned. In this perspective, the absolute Idea is to be compared with the old man who utters the same religious statements as the child, but for whom they carry the significance of his whole life. Even if the child understands the religious content, it still counts for him only as something outside of which lie the whole of life and the whole world.

And the situation is the same with human life in general and with the events that make up its content. All labour is directed only at this or that goal; and when it is attained, we are amazed to find just what we willed and nothing more. What is of interest is the whole movement. When we are carrying on with our lives, the end in view may appear very restricted, but it is the whole *decursus vitae* [course of life] that is embraced together in it. In the same way and for the same reason, the content of the absolute Idea is the whole display[a] that has passed before us up to this point. The last step is the insight that it is the whole unfolding that constitutes its content and its interest.

Moreover, this is the philosophical perspective: that everything which, taken by itself, appears to be restricted gets its value by belonging to the whole, and being a moment of the Idea. This is how we have had the content, and what we now have is the knowledge that the content is the living development of the Idea, and this simple looking back is contained in the form. Each of the stages considered so far is an image of the Absolute, but initially in a restricted way, and hence it drives itself on to the whole, whose unfolding is what we have called method.

§ 238

The moments of the speculative method[51] are (α) the *beginning*, which is *being* or the *immediate*; it is all by itself, on the simple ground that it is the

---

a. *Ausbreitung*

beginning. But from [the standpoint of] the speculative Idea it is its *self-determinating* which, as the absolute negativity or movement of the Concept, *judges* and posits itself as the negative of itself. In this way *being*, which appears as abstract affirmation for the beginning as such, is on the contrary *negation*, *positedness*, mediatedness in general, and *pre*supposedness. But as the negation of the *Concept* (which is strictly identical with itself even in its otherness and is the certainty of itself), it [i.e., being] is the Concept that is not yet posited as Concept; i.e., it is the Concept *in-itself.*— As the Concept that is still indeterminate, i.e., determined only in-itself or immediately, this being is therefore just as much the *universal*.

> The *beginning*, in the sense of immediate being, is taken from [sense-] intuition and perception: this is the beginning of the *analytical* method of finite cognition. And in the sense of universality, being is the beginning of the synthetic method of finite cognition. But since the logical is immediately both something-universal and equally something that [simply] is, or since it is both something that the Concept presupposes to itself and is equally the Concept itself in its immediacy, its beginning is equally both a synthetic and an analytical beginning.

Addition. The philosophical method is both analytic and synthetic, but not in the sense of a mere juxtaposing or a mere alternation of both these methods of finite cognition; instead, the philosophical method contains them sublated within itself, and therefore it behaves, in every one of its movements, analytically and synthetically at the same time. Philosophical thinking proceeds analytically in that it simply takes up its ob-ject, the Idea, and lets it go its own way, while it simply watches the movement and development of it, so to speak. To this extent philosophising is wholly passive. But philosophical thinking is equally synthetic as well, and it proves to be the activity of the Concept itself. But this requires the effort to beware of our own inventions and particular opinions which are forever wanting to push themselves forward.

§ 239

(β) The *progression* is the posited *judgment* of the Idea. As the Concept in-itself, the immediate universal is the dialectic of spontaneously[a] reducing its own immediacy and universality to a moment. Thus, the *negative* of the beginning, or what was first, is now posited in its *determinacy*; it is *for one*;[b] it is the *relation* of distinct [terms], or the *moment of reflection*.

a. *an ihm selbst*
b. für eines[52]

This progression is equally both *analytical*—because through the immanent dialectic only what is contained in the immediate Concept is posited—and *synthetic*, because this distinction had not yet been posited in the immediate Concept.

Addition. In the progression of the Idea the beginning proves itself to be what it already is in-itself, namely, what is posited and mediated and not what simply and immediately *is.*[a] It is only for that consciousness which is itself immediate that nature comes first or immediately, while spirit is mediated by it. For, in fact, nature is posited by spirit, and it is spirit itself that makes nature into its presupposition.

§ 240

Within Being the abstract form of the progression is an *other* and *passing-over* into an other; within Essence [it is] *shining within what is opposed*; in the *Concept* it is the distinctness of the *singular* from the *universality* which *continues* itself as such into what is distinct from it, and is [present] *as identity* with the latter.

§ 241

In the second sphere the Concept (which at first is *in*-itself) has come to *shine*, and as a result it is already *in-itself* the *Idea.*—The development of this sphere becomes a return into the first, just as the development of the first is a passage into the second. It is only through this double movement that distinction gets its due, since each of the two that are distinct consummates itself, considered in itself, into the totality and works out its unity with the other. Only this self-sublating of the one-sidedness of *both* [sides] *in themselves* prevents the unity from becoming one-sided.

§ 242

The second sphere develops the relation of the distinct [terms] into what it is initially; i.e., into the *contradiction* in these [terms] themselves—in the *infinite progress*. This contradiction resolves itself (γ) into the *end* where what is different is posited as what it is in the Concept. This is the negative of what is first, and, in its identity with that, it is the negativity of its own self; hence [it is] the unity within which both of these first [terms] are as

---

a. *nicht als das Seiende und Unmittelbare*

ideal and as moments; [they are there] as sublated, i.e., as preserved at the same time. Con-cluding itself with itself in this way from its *being-in-itself* by means of its difference and through the sublation of this difference, the Concept is the *realised* Concept; i.e., it is the Concept that contains the *positedness* of its determinations within its *being-for-itself*. It is the Idea for which, being what is absolutely first (in the method), this end is at the same time only the *vanishing* of the *semblance* that the beginning is something-immediate, and the Idea is a result. This is the cognition that the Idea is the One Totality.

§ 243

In this way, the method is not an external form, but the soul and the Concept of the content. It is distinct from the Concept only inasmuch as the moments of the *Concept, each in itself*, in its *determinacy*, reach the point where they appear as the totality of the Concept. Since this determinacy, or the content, leads itself back, along with the form, to the Idea, the latter presents itself as a *systematic* totality, which is only *One* Idea. Its particular moments are *in-themselves* this same [Idea]; and equally, through the dialectic of the Concept, they produce the simple *being-for-itself* of the Idea.—As a result the Science [of Logic] concludes by grasping the Concept of itself as the Concept of the pure Idea for which the Idea is.

§ 244

Considered according to this *unity* that it has with itself, the Idea that is *for itself* is *intuiting* and the intuiting Idea is *Nature*. But as intuiting, the Idea is posited in the one-sided determination of immediacy or negation, through external reflection. The absolute *freedom* of the Idea, however, is that it does not merely *pass over* into *life*, nor that it lets life *shine* within itself as finite cognition, but that, in the absolute truth of itself, it *resolves to release out of itself* into freedom the moment of its particularity or of the initial determining and otherness, [i.e.,] the *immediate Idea* as its reflexion,[a] or itself as *Nature*.

Addition. We have now returned to the Concept of the Idea with which we began. At the same time this return to the beginning is an advance. What we began with was being, abstract being, while now we have the *Idea* as *being*; and this Idea that *is*, is *Nature*.

---

a. *Widerschein*

NOTES

Preface to the First Edition

1. The philosophical *Manier* that "presupposes a schema" is the same "formalist" degeneration of the "Identity Philosophy" that is attacked in the Preface to the *Phenomenology* (Miller, §§ 14–16, 50–53). It is clear from his correspondence that in the *Phenomenology* Hegel's target was various friends and followers of Schelling rather than Schelling himself. See further, H. S. Harris, "The Cows in the Night."

2. Although the main attack is directed at "Schelling's school" it seems clear that Schelling himself is included here. It was others (such as H. Steffens, J. Görres, and J. J. Wagner) whom Hegel accused in the *Phenomenology* of making schematic parallels, and focusing upon curious accidents, in their philosophy of nature. But he was already remarking, during that period, that (through his continual thought-experiments) Schelling had "conducted his philosophical education in public." The "adventures of thought" here surely refer to that, just as the *Verrücktheit* refers to the case of the student invented by Jean Paul (in his novel *Titan*), who had to be confined to an asylum in consequence of his total absorption in the study of the Identity Philosophy.

3. From his critical essays of the early Jena years we know that Hegel must (minimally) have had G. E. Schulze and W. T. Krug in mind here. There were many others who belonged to the "other side" in those years, but these two fit the stereotypes of "clever scepticism" and "modest criticism" perfectly. It is probably Schulze (in his mammoth *Kritik*) who is the "schoolmaster giving lessons to the centuries." (Compare Di Giovanni and Harris, 293–362).

4. In showing this preference for the Romantics over the Common Sense school, Hegel echoes the Preface to the *Phenomenology*, written ten years earlier. "Revelling" reminds us of the claim that "Truth is the Bacchanalian revel"; and "the sunrise of the rejuvenated spirit" is in the Preface also (see Miller, §§ 47 and 11).

5. The comparatively friendly remarks about "immediate knowing" refer to Jacobi; and in 1827 Jacobi's position was used as the transition from the critical empiricism of most followers of Kant to properly speculative philosophy. But Hegel's attitude toward Schleiermacher's *theology* of immediate experience became increasingly polemical during the Berlin years.

Preface to the Second Edition

1. For the many theorists of the "facts of consciousness" in the generation of German philosophers after Kant, see first the essay of George Di Giovanni in *Between Kant and Hegel*. A fuller account of the philosophical scene will be found in Beiser's *The Fate of Reason*. But both authors are concerned with a time twenty or thirty years earlier than this Preface.

2. The great prophet of "immediate knowledge" was Jacobi. See §§ 61–78. (But Jacobi had been dead for more than ten years. The voice of immediate knowledge in Hegel's Berlin was Schleiermacher.)

3. This is a revised version of a remark of Mephistopheles: "From the Evil One they are free, but the evil ones remain" (*Faust*, pt. 1, "Witches Kitchen").

4. *Faktum*. See note 21 to the Glossary.

5. *durch Nachdenken*. Here, as well as in some other places, this is Hegel's word for the procedure of Descartes. So we have used an appropriately Cartesian word for it.

6. It is true that Tholuck characterises the monotheistic mysticism of the Sufis as "pantheistic." But he does not call the monist philosophers pantheists; and Hegel's polytheistic pantheism arises entirely from his own sophistical reading of Tholuck's argument.

7. This famous remark comes from the reports of Jacobi in his *Letters on the Teaching of Spinoza* (1785). See *Werke*, 4:i, 68. Hegel's citation is from memory. What Lessing said, according to Jacobi, was, "People always talk about Spinoza still, as if he were a dead dog."

8. J. J. Brucker, *Historia critica philosophiae*, vol. 6, 1767. Compare Hegel's criticisms in the *Lectures on the History of Philosophy*, trans. Haldane and Simson, 1:43, 112; compare also 1:51–55 with his remarks about the history of philosophy here.

9. Homer, *Iliad* 1.401, 2.813, 14.290, 20.74. In 1827 Hegel actually wrote "certain stars." He repeated this error in his review of Göschel in 1829, but by 1830 he had discovered that he was mistaken.

10. Compare Haldane and Simson, 3:197–99, or better still, *Vorlesungen*, Band 9:82. This latter volume provides us with the course of 1825–26; for the translation see the Index of References. The expression *qualirt* cannot actually be found in Boehme (who uses *qualificirt*). But Hegel is thinking of the importance of *Qual* in Boehme's speculation.

11. The "Fata Morgana" was properly a mirage in the Straits of Messina. The tradition of the English Normans was that King Arthur's sister, the enchantress Morgan le Fay, lived in Calabria (Brewer). For this and the other passages to which Hegel directly refers, Nicolin and Pöggeler have provided the relevant citations from Tholuck's essay in their notes.

12. The English newspaper report about the Unitarians was in the *Morning Chronicle*, 6 June 1825. See *Gesammelte Werke [G.W.]*, 19:491–92 (note to 14, 33–35).

13. Berlin, 1824; the emphasis is Hegel's.

14. Actually Tholuck cites Anselm in only two places, of which this is one. See Hegel, *G.W.*, 19:492–93 (note to 15, 33–36).

15. Hegel found in his edition of Boehme (Hamburg, 1715) the information (given in the "Life" by A. von Frankenburg) that Boehme's friend Balthasar Walther had conferred this title upon him.

16. Compare Haldane and Simson, 3:192–93, 198–99, 208, 214; or, better still, *Vorlesungen*, Band 9:80, 87 (Brown and Stewart, 3:119–20, 130–31).

17. Nicolin and Pöggeler cite the appreciative remarks of Franz von Baader about Hegel in the first of his six volumes of *Fermenta Cognitionis*; in the passage with which Hegel takes issue here (from the separate polemic of 1824) von Baader refers specifically to § 193 of the 1817 *Encyclopaedia*. The doctrine that he criticises will be most easily found by Anglophone readers in *Philosophy of Nature* (Petry or Miller), § 248, note. Baader replied to the aggressive defence offered by Hegel in the present note in a short essay titled "Hegel on My Doctrine in the Preface to the Second Edition of the Encyclopaedia." See his *Sämtliche Werke*, series I, 10:306–309; for the essay of 1824 see *Sämtliche Werke*, series I, 2. The *Fermenta Cognitionis* will also be found in the first two volumes.

18. *Verum norma sui et falsi* is a dictum of Spinoza's. See the *Ethics*, 2, 43, scholium. He uses the precise expression that Hegel cites here in Epistle 76 (to Albert Burgh). See *Opera*, ed. Gebhardt, 4:320.

Foreword to the Third Edition

1. In the 1829 *Jahrbuch für wissenschaftliche Kritik* Hegel promised a comprehensive review of five polemics against his philosophy. Actually he reviewed only the first two of them. See *Berliner Schriften*, 330–402.

2. The reference is to a controversy at Halle between von Hengstenberg's *Evangelischen Kirchenzeitung* and the rationalists in the theology faculty. See Hegel's *Letters*, no. 659 to Göschel, 13 December 1830 (Butler and Seiler, 543–44).

3. This is a mistake. Apart from putting one soul in Hell while the body was still alive on earth, Dante has St. Peter himself proclaim the damnation of two Popes before they are dead. (But none of his victims was alive to read what he wrote.)

4. The text (and probably Hegel's manuscript) was faulty. There is no article, a singular subject, and a plural verb. Lasson's correction "human individuals posit themselves" is the simplest. Nicolin and Pöggeler insert the definite article and singularise the verb—which gives the statement a more "philosophical" form. The sense is unchanged, and it is quite clear.

5. Hegel had planned to review Justinus Kerner's book about the medium of Prevorst (Stuttgart, 1829). But in the *Yearbook* of his school for 1830 a review by Lüders appeared instead. Her visions were regarded as evidence for the spiritual world beyond this one.

6. The polemic that Hegel is discussing was between scriptural fundamentalists and theologians inspired by the Enlightenment. Hegel thinks both parties are equally mistaken, and that the interpretation of Scripture given by both sides is equally devoid of any speculative (i.e., philosophical) content.

7. The echo is from Rom. 3:4; but quite probably the quotation itself comes from a hymn. See further note 12 to § 11 below.

8. Aristotle, *Metaphysics* 12.7.1072b24.

Introduction (§§ 1–18)

1. (§ 2 R) Schleiermacher is the probable target of this attack. Compare Hegel's Preface for H. W. F. Hinrichs' *Religion in Its Inner Relationships to Science* (Berlin, 1822). A translation by A. V. Miller will be found in F. G. Weiss (1974).

2. (§ 3) Hegel seems to distinguish three levels: (1) the content in *feeling*, etc., permeated by (nonreflective) thinking (see § 2 R); (2) the content in feeling mixed with reflective thought; and (3) the content in pure thought.

3. (§ 6 R) This is the page reference for the first edition of 1821. The references for modern editions are Hoffmeister (1955), 14; *Theorie Werkausgabe [T.W-A.]* (Suhrkamp), 7:24; Knox, 10.

4. (§ 6 R) See especially *Science of Logic*, bk. 2, pt. 3, chap. 2 (Lasson, 2:169–84; Miller, 541–53).

5. (§ 7 R) The work of Grotius was actually titled *On the Law of War and Peace* (Paris, 1625). Newton, of course, called his book *The Mathematical Principles of Natural Philosophy* (London, 1687).

6. (§ 7 note*) Thomas Thomson (1773–1852) was a distinguished professor of chemistry (see Partington, *History of Chemistry*, 4:716–21). His *Annals of Philosophy* appeared from 1813 to 1826. The *Art of Preserving the Hair* was published anonymously (London, 1825). Hegel's knowledge of it came from his reading of the *Morning Chronicle*. The note that he made at the time has been published by M. J. Petry—see *Hegel-Studien* 11 (1976):34; or *G.W.*, 19:497–98 (note to 34, 17–19).

7. (§ 7 note*) Wallace—relying on the *Times*—gives the dates of the debate and the Shipowner's dinner as 3 February and 12 February 1825. From that source he also revises the quotation ascribed to Canning: "the just and wise maxims of sound, not spurious philosophy." But Hegel's source was actually the *Morning Chronicle*; and he noted the date of the debate correctly in his excerpt (see Petry, *Hegel-Studien* 11 (1976):29–30; the relevant data can also be found in *G.W.*, 19:497–98). For the Shipowner's Society dinner excerpt see Petry, 31–32. Canning's words, as reported by the *Chronicle*, were: "But a period has lately commenced when Ministers have had it in their power to apply to the state of the country the just maxims of profound philosophy. . . . " Hegel's excerpt was word perfect, so we have translated his citation back to English in accord with his original. Hegel referred both to Thomson's *Annals* and to this excerpt in the Introduction to his course on the *History of Philosophy* (see Haldane and Simson, 1:57–58).

8. (§ 8 R) This maxim was everywhere used (correctly) as a summary of the Aristotelian position. (See especially *De Anima* 2.8.432a.) But Leibniz made the appropriate response to the tabula rasa interpretation of this tag: *Nisi intellectus ipse* ("Nothing in the intellect that was not previously in the sense—except the intellect itself!"). Jacobi drew attention to this comment in the Preface to his Collected Works (*Werke*, 2:16). For the passage in Leibniz himself see *New Essays*, 2:1, 2.

9. (§ 10 R) This became a commonplace of critical empiricism beginning with Locke's Preface for the *Essay*. But in Kant himself the most familiar echoes of it are in the *Critique of Pure Reason* [CPR] B, 7–9, 22–27; and the opening paragraphs of the *Prolegomena*.

10. (§ 10 R) Wallace refers us to the *Facetiae* ascribed to Hierocles for this and other deeds of the guileless Scholasticus. For details, see *G.W.*, 19:499 (note to 37, 1–2).

11. (§ 10 R) This criticism of K. L. Reinhold is an old hobbyhorse of Hegel's. See especially the *Difference Essay* (1801), trans. Harris and Cerf, 174–92. For a balanced account of Reinhold's work see Di Giovanni, "The Facts of Consciousness," in *Between Kant and Hegel*, eds. Di Giovanni and Harris.

12. (§ 11) Underlined because it is an intentional echo of Rom. 3:4. The conflict there is between "unbelief" and the "faith in God"—see note 5 to the 1830 foreword, above. (Hegel also used the phrase in his own translation of Aristotle, *De Anima* 3.4.429a19.)

13. (§ 11 R) Hegel probably means us to remember *Phaedo* 89c–90e. But Nicolin and Pöggeler refer also to *Laches* 188c–e and *Republic* 411d.

14. (§ 12 R) It is Schelling's own early philosophy of the Absolute Identity that is here compared with the necessarily "formal" beginning of Greek speculation. Compare Haldane and Simson, 3:529–45, especially 534, 540, and 542–45.

15. (§ 13) As Wallace has already pointed out, it would be difficult to map the history of philosophy (or even Hegel's account of it) directly onto the *Logic*. But the clue given here to what Hegel is doing should never be forgotten (compare the Remark to § 12).

16. (§ 13 R) Fichte, Schelling, and Hegel all of them habitually wrote as the mouthpieces of "Philosophy" simply. But, as Wallace pointed out, Reinhold and J. S. Beck had claimed to do this also. The attempt to stand above any "battle of the schools" begins with Kant.

17. (§ 16 R) The use of the term "anthropology" in Kant and the post-Kantian schools was quite different from ours. In Hegel's philosophy of subjective spirit, "anthropology" is the first division; it is followed by "phenomenology" and "psychology." Wallace defines "anthropology" neatly as "a study of those aspects of psychology which are most closely allied with physiological conditions." The "facts of consciousness" provided the foundation for Reinhold and other philosophers who adopted the method of Hume and his Scottish opponents. See the essay of Di Giovanni referred to in note 11.

18. (§ 16 R) Wallace thought, plausibly enough, that in this section of his Remark Hegel was referring to the scientific work of Goethe. But his own lectures on the philosophy of world history are the appropriate paradigm in the sphere of Spirit.

19. (§ 17) Wallace points out correctly that the doctrine of "spiritual circularity" is found in Proclus and in Christian neo-Platonism (especially Erigena). But the reader should note that Hegel is *not* here talking about a "procession from" and "return to" God. The neo-Platonic conception of a "procession" of the finite from the Absolute was revived by Schelling. From 1804–05 onward Hegel steadily rejects it as a mistaken view. See, for instance, *Phenomenology* (Miller, § 162).

The Science of Logic: Preliminary Conception (§§ 19–83)

1. (§ 19 A1) Wallace thought that it was Fichte who had preached the new dawn—he cites the *Wissenschaftslehre* of 1794. But that "glorious dawn" is long past now. It seems clear that the three Additions to this paragraph come from courses given at different times, and that this first one is the earliest. In that case, Hegel's polemic here is directed at the "demagogues" of the student youth movement in 1818–20. Among them, the most notable logician was J. F. Fries. He lost his professorship at Heidelberg in November 1819. (A good brief account of the political crisis in the German universities during these years can be found in A. T. B. Peperzak, *Philosophy and Politics*, 15–31.)

2. (§ 19 A1) Hegel may be playing here on "setzen": "Die Älteren setzen nun allerdings ihre Hoffnung auf die Jugend, denn sie soll die Welt und die Wissenschaften fortsetzen."

3. (§ 19 A1) Hegel's "auf der Sandbank dieser Zeitlichkeit" comes from the Eschenberg translation of Shakespeare's *Macbeth* (act I, sc. 7: "But here, upon this bank and shoal of time/ We'd jump the life to come"). He evoked the same echo in his *Philosophy of Religion* manuscript of 1820; and it was Walter Jaeschke who spotted the reference—see *Vorlesungen*, Band 3:4, line 52 (and the note on p. 375).

4. (§ 19 A3) Anaxagoras was banished from Athens (probably not long before the Peloponnesian War began, but the date is a subject of controversy); Socrates was put to death after the war (399 B.C.). Protagoras was prosecuted at Athens during the war. In all cases "impiety" was the main ground for the prosecution.

5. (§ 20 R) See *Critique of Pure Reason [CPR]* B, 131: "The 'I think' must *be able to* accompany all of my representations." As Wallace rightly commented, Hegel's reference is rather loose. It was *Fichte*'s interpretation of the formal "I think" that was crucial for the development of German idealism.

6. (§ 20 R) The doctrine of the thinking self as "the Category" is expounded in the first pages of chap. 5 of the *Phenomenology*.

7. (§ 20 A) On the history of logic after Aristotle, Hegel has more to say in his Introduction to the *Science of Logic* (Lasson, 1:32–34; Miller, 51–53).

8. (§ 21 A) Hegel is probably referring to *experiences* such as learning to distinguish *colours* (and to say, for example, "This rose is red"). He is *not* talking about the learning of grammar, the parsing of sentences, etc.

9. (§ 22 A) In 594 B.C. (approximately) Solon gave Athens a constitution (which the city accepted). Hegel's knowledge of his work was based on the "lives" of Solon in Plutarch and Diogenes Laertius.

10. (§ 23 R) The target of Hegel's irony is probably Schleiermacher. (But it was Fichte who made this a watchword, and he influenced *many* of Hegel's contemporaries.)

11. (§ 23 R) See *Metaphysics* A.2.982a2ff; and compare Haldane and Simson, 2:135–36.

12. (§ 24 A1) Apparently Schelling only used the phrase "petrified intelligence" in a poem printed in the *Zeitschrift für spekulative Physik*, 1800. See *Werke*, 4:546. (Wallace found the reference—as well as some others like it—and he quotes the poem.)

13. (§ 24 A2) See Introduction, p. xxvii.

14. (§ 24 A2) *In der Mitte . . . seine Pole zusammenschließt* "con-cludes its poles in the middle term." The "impotence" consists precisely in the shift to a spatial sense of "middle".

15. (§ 24 A2) Compare *Phenomenology* Preface (Miller, § 58).

16. (§24 A2) Compare the lecture of 1804 quoted in the Introduction above, and *Science of Logic* (Lasson, 1:9–12; Miller, 31–33).

17. (§ 24 A3) From the "Scepticism" essay of 1802 we can learn that the supreme master of "high Scepticism" was Plato in the *Parmenides*. Also that the misapplication of sceptical method to the "forms of reason" began in the school of Sextus. See the translation in Di Giovanni and Harris, 322, 325–30, 334–39. For a fuller account of the significance of the sceptical tradition (both ancient and modern) for Hegel, see M. N. Forster, *Hegel and Scepticism*.

18. (§ 24 A3) Hegel's discussion here should be compared with the interpretations offered in his *Philosophy of Religion* lectures; see Hodgson, 3:104–108, 207–11, and 300–304. (The "*Erkenntnis* of Good and Evil" is logically significant because simple Evil is *aufgehoben* in it. This would not be the case in the mere "acquaintance" of simple *Kenntnis*—or elementary *Wissen*.)

19. (§ 25 R) What follows is the authoritative statement of the relation between the *Phenomenology* and the new introductory discussion (§§ 26–78) that was first written for the 1827 edition of the *Encyclopaedia*. Compare and contrast the references in the *Science of Logic*. The description of the development as "behind the back of consciousness" is an echo of *Phenomenology* (Miller, § 87).

20. (§ 28 A) For the origin of these "questions" (and the consequent identity of the "older metaphysics") see note 25 below.

21. (§ 28 A) The source of Hegel's knowledge of this "Oriental" doctrine is probably Philo, via August Neander. See Jaeschke's note in *Vorlesungen*, 5:353, note to 202, 742–45.

22. (§ 29 R) See note 21.

23. (§ 31 R) Compare the doctrine of the "speculative proposition" in the Preface to the *Phenomenology* (Miller, §§ 58–62).

24. (§ 32 A) This use of "dogmatism" is typical in Sextus Empiricus; but Hegel means to refer both to the "Pyrrhonists" and to the "Academics." See further note 17 above.

25. (§ 33) The four branches of metaphysics discussed in §§ 33–36—ontology, cosmology, psychology, rational theology—come from the School-Metaphysics that Wolff bequeathed to a host of followers. Thus, the first *Stellung* of thought—which Hegel calls simply "Metaphysics" in his Table of Contents—is really that of Wolff and his school.

26. (§ 34 A) Where Hegel found this term, which he ascribes to the Scholastics, is not clear. But it comes either from a history of philosophy or from his reading of von Baader, Boehme, and German mysticism. In his *Philosophy of Religion* lectures Hegel used it once only (1827, Band 5:196, line 586; Hodgson, 3:271); and Jaeschke has no note on it.

27. (§ 36 R) The origins of the "eminent sense" are probably in neo-Platonism. It was an axiom of scholastic metaphysics that the "cause" must "contain" the effect. But a spiritual or intellectual "cause" (such as God, or the human mind) can only contain its *physical* effects in an *eminent* sense. Thus God as its Creator "contains" the world *eminently*. The generally accepted definition of causal eminence can be found in St. Thomas (*S.T.* 1:4, 2); but see also Descartes' Meditation III for one of the most celebrated appeals to it. The "eminence" of God's attributes *generally* (not only his causal power, but his wisdom and goodness, etc.) was the principal topic of the "negative theology." The standard authority for that is Pseudo-Dionysius *On the Divine Names*. But Hegel encountered the doctrine of God's "eminent" perfections in the *Theodicy* of Leibniz; and it is altogether more likely that he has Spinoza's attack upon it (Epistle VI) in his mind, rather than anything he may have learned during his theological education.

The doctrine was part of the Wolffian School-Metaphysics. Hence, apart from the Spinoza letter, the following references are pertinent: Wolff, *Theologia Naturalis*, pt. 1, §§ 1096, 1098, 1099, 1066, 1068; and pt. 2, chap. 2, §§ 158–59 (quoted in *G.W.*, 19:502 [note to 55, 23]). Also Leibniz, *Theodicy*, § 4, 192; *Monadology*, § 41; *Principles of Nature and Grace*, § 9. (See Hodgson, 3:75.)

28. (§ 36 A) *allerrealste Wesen*. The German would normally and naturally be rendered "Supremely Real Being", since *Wesen* corresponds to both "being" and "essence" in English, but the majority opinion favoured "essence" in order to translate *Wesen* consistently. See the Introduction, p. xviii.

29. (§ 36 A) The first "abstract" refers to the fixed separation between the determinations of the understanding; the second time "abstract" indicates the absence of all negation and hence of all determination. A useful survey of the different uses of *abstrakt* in Hegel's *Logic* is provided by Philip Grier in ed., Di Giovanni, *Essays on Hegel's Logic*; for the methodical acquisition of "concreteness," see J. Glenn Gray (1971).

30. (§ 37) Clearly—in view of his comments about Hume in § 39—Hegel means to embrace the whole movement of thought from Bacon and Locke onward. He can still call it the "second" *Stellung* of thought, because (as he explains in the lecture commentary on § 38) the "metaphysical" *Stellung* embraces the earlier tradition of mediaeval Scholasticism. But he is mainly concerned with the German followers of "Scottish Common Sense," and with "Humean" sceptics like G. E. Schulze.

31. (§ 38 A) *Faust*, pt. 1, lines 1940–41, 1938–39 (trans. David Luke, Oxford University Press, 1987). A more literal translation would read:

Chemistry calls it "The handling of Nature"
It fools itself and it knows not how.
It has the parts right in its hand,
But it lacks, alas, just the spiritual bond.

32. (§ 39 R) This is the first of four references to Hume (see §§ 47, 50, 53 for the others). In all of them Hegel takes Hume as the paradigm of the "naïve empiricism" that trusts experience and rejects "metaphysics." He understands very well that Hume is a "mitigated" Sceptic, not a "Pyrrhonian"; and he thinks the worse of him for it. But he also recognises the crucial role of Hume in the "awakening" of Kant. In § 53 he mentions the ancient Sceptics and Hume (both together) as cultural relativists about ethical principles. It seems likely that Hegel read the first *Inquiry* and the "Natural History of Religion", as well as some parts of the *History of England*. He may have read more, but he depends heavily on Schulze and on manuals of the history of philosophy. Compare further Haldane and Simson, 3:369–75, and *Vorlesungen*, 9:146–48.

33. (§ 39 R) The *Critical Journal* is reproduced as a whole in *G.W.*, Band 4. There is an English translation of the "Scepticism" essay in Di Giovanni and Harris.

34. (§ 40) See especially the Introduction to the *CPR*.

35. (§ 41) See especially *CPR* B, 2; *Prolegomena*, §§ 18–19.

36. (§ 41 A2) *Das Gedachte*. It is clear from Hegel's immediate effort to specify this "more closely" that he does not mean what anyone just happens to "think," but the result of a process of *logical* thinking, i.e., any "thought" that is valid for all, because it embodies a "category" that everyone must use.

37. (§ 42) Kant, of course, calls it the "transcendental unity of apperception"—see *CPR* B, 132ff (§ 16). For a better account of Hegel's interpretation of it see *Faith and Knowledge*, trans. Cerf and Harris, 69–75.

38. (§ 42) Kant's theory is in the "Transcendental Aesthetic" of the *CPR*.

39. (§ 42) Kant's "table" and "deduction" of twelve categories is in the "Transcendental Analytic" of the *CPR*.

40. (§ 42 R) "Fichte's contribution" was principally in the *Wissenschaftslehre* of 1794 and the two Introductions of 1797. In one of the Aphorisms from his *Wastebook* (probably late 1804/early 1805) Hegel defined it thus: "Only after the history of consciousness *does one know what one has in these abstractions*, through the Concept: *Fichte's* contribution" (*Hegel-Studien* 4 [1967]:13; *Independent Journal of Philosophy* 3 [1979]:4).

We can see from this that the *Phenomenology* itself was Hegel's "deduction of the categories" in accordance with Fichte's own project for a theory of rational *consciousness*. But we can see *here* that the *Logic* itself is the "metaphysical deduction" that Kant only pretended to supply.

41. (§ 42 A2) See *CPR* B, 352–53, 383, 593, 671, 893–94.

42. (§ 43) The reference here is to Kant's famous dictum: "Thoughts without content are empty, intuitions without concepts are blind" (*CPR* B, 75). Hegel's own logic depends on the fact that "pure thoughts" have a "content" of their own. But it is true for him, as much as for Kant, that nothing is a "pure thought" unless it has actual application in "experience." (See also Kant, *CPR* B, 102, 122–23; and *Prolegomena*, §§ 18–19.)

43. (§ 43 A note*) Hegel refers to the Philosophy of Nature and the Philosophy of Spirit as the *Realphilosophie*.

44. (§ 44 R) Kant's initial statement about the "thing-in-itself" (in the Preface to the Second Edition of the *CPR*) is as follows:

> That space and time are only forms of sensible intuition, and so only conditions of the existence of things as appearances; that, moreover, we have no concepts of understanding, and consequently no elements for the knowledge of things, save insofar as intuition can be given corresponding to these concepts; and that we can therefore have no knowledge of any object as thing-in-itself, but only insofar as it is an object of sensible intuition, that is, an appearance—all this is proved in the analytical part of the Critique. Thus it does indeed follow that all possible speculative knowledge of reason is limited to mere objects of *experience*. But our further contention must also be duly borne in mind, namely, that though we cannot *know* these objects as things-in-themselves, we must yet be in position at least to *think* them as things-in-themselves; otherwise we should be landed in the absurd conclusion that there can be appearance without anything that appears (*CPR* B, xxvi–vii; compare further B, 294ff, 313, 343).

When we do think this unknowable—and hence absolutely problematic—"thing" in a perfectly determinate way, we reach "the ideal of All of Reality (*omnitudo realitatis*)" as a "singular being":

> If, therefore, reason employs in the complete determination of things a transcendental substrate that contains, as it were, the whole store of material from which all possible predicates of things must be taken, this substrate cannot be anything else than the idea of an All of Reality (*omnitudo realitatis*). All true negations are nothing but limitations—a title which would be inapplicable, were they not thus based upon the unlimited, that is, upon the All.
>
> But the concept of what thus possesses all reality is just the concept of a *thing-in-itself* as completely determined; and since in all possible [pairs of] contradictory predicates one predicate, namely, that which belongs to being generally, is to be found in its determination, the concept of an *ens realissimum* is the concept of a singular being. It is therefore a transcendental *ideal* which serves as basis for the complete determination that necessarily belongs to all that exists (B, 603–604).

Compare further the note to § 124 R.

45. (§ 44 R) This was the alchemist's term for the "dead" precipitate that remained when all the "living spirit" had been extracted or given off.

46. (§ 44 R) See *CPR* B, 346–49.

47. (§ 45 A) As Wallace rightly pointed out, the distinction is older than Kant. But Kant's usage is the definitive starting point for Hegel's theory (see especially *CPR* B, 355–66). The "goodness of God" in creating finite things is Kant's "faculty of *rules*" by which the categories are applied to the manifold of sense to produce unities of intuition and concept. In the speculative view this unself-conscious interpretation of the world is the spontaneous activity of the productive imagination. Kant's "reason" is the "faculty of *principles*" which aims to grasp the Infinite, but falls into "dialectic." Hegel's speculative reason comprehends the dialectic of the finite concepts of understanding, and grasps *itself* as the "true Infinite."

48. (§ 47) In this paragraph Hegel gives a summary of what Kant calls the "paralogisms" of Pure Reason. For Kant's own arguments in full see *CPR*, Transcendental Dialectic, bk. 2, chap. 1 (B, 399ff).

49. (§ 48) Kant's treatment of four antinomies arising from the rational concept of the "world" is in the Transcendental Dialectic, bk. 2, chap. 2 (*CPR* B, 432ff). For the whole account of Kant's view, but especially for the antinomies, Hegel's discussion in the *History of Philosophy* should be consulted; see *T.W-A.*, 14:333–86; Haldane and Simson, 3:427–78. (See also the course of 1825 in *Vorlesungen*, 9:150–56.)

50. (§ 48 R) Compare *CPR* B, 433, 448, 452.

51. (§ 48 R) Hegel is here referring mainly to Remark 2 in bk. 1, pt. 2, chap. 1, of vol. 1 as published in 1812 (see *G.W.*, 11:113–20), 147–50. But the revised version of vol. 1 was published only a short time after the third edition of the *Encyclopaedia*. So Lasson, 1:182–93 (Miller, 190–99) contains the fullest account of Hegel's views at this time. See also pt. 2, chap. 2, sec. C, Remark 2 (Lasson, 231–36; Miller, 234–38).

52. (§ 48 A) Kant's antinomies are constructed of "theses" and "antitheses" balanced on the model of ancient scepticism; and he uses the Greek terms for the two sides. Hegel's use of *Gegensatz* derives from this model. Both *Gegensatz* and *Entgegensetzung* occur frequently in Fichte's writings, but Hegel chose to use the former to express the logical principle of *antinomy*; see note 17 to the Glossary. A Hegelian concept evolves logically into a *Gegensatz* (our "antithesis")—i.e., a contradictory unity. We should notice that *Hegel does not use the triad of "thesis/antithesis/synthesis"* (which Fichte took over from Kant); and the reason for this goes deeper than his preference for native German terms. The move to the language of the people expresses the liberation of properly speculative "reason" from the "reflective" methods of the critical "understanding."

53. (§ 49) Kant treats God as "the Ideal of Pure Reason." See the Transcendental Dialectic, bk. 2, chap. 3 (*CPR* B, 595ff, especially 604).

54. (§ 50) In the School-Metaphysics of Wolff various traditional proofs of God's existence were standardised and categorised. The fact that *Dasein Gottes* is the ordinary German usage is logically significant for Hegel. So in the translation we always render it *literally* rather than colloquially (cf. note 83). Kant discusses the "proofs" one by one; and the easiest way to find out what they were is to examine his refutations. For the "cosmological proof" see the Transcendental Dialectic, bk. 2, chap. 3, sec. 5; and for the "physico-theological proof" see the following sec. 6, *CPR* B, 631–58. (This last is more familiar as the "Argument from Design.")

55. (§ 50) See note 29 above.

56. (§ 50 R) Both here and at the beginning of the paragraph Hegel echoes remarks that he made in his review of Hinrichs. Compare Miller's translation of this review (see Index). Hegel's target there—and probably here also—was Schleiermacher. But see also Jacobi's 1816 Preface for his *David Hume* (*Werke*, 2:56).

57. (§ 50 R) See especially *Ethics*, 2, 7, scholium. Whether Hegel's statement is "inaccurate" (as Wallace claimed) is a moot point, because it is not clear that "infinite attributes" (in pt. 1, def. 6, and prop. 1) means "infinitely *many*." But since Hegel characterises the statement of Spinoza's position here as *ganz ungeschickte* it is not clear that his "correction" of it is meant to be perfectly adequate by itself. It is *Jacobi*'s interpretation of Spinoza that he is concerned to combat. (See especially the *Briefe über Spinoza*, Beilage 7, *Werke*, 4:2, 125–62; and for the explicit accusation of atheism, ibid., 216—but that was "notorious" long before Jacobi took up the cudgels—Hume learned it from Bayle.)

58. (§ 50 R) This curious "critical defence" of Spinoza was first offered by Solomon Maimon. See *G.W.*, 19:505 (note to 67, 14–15) for the relevant references.

59. (§ 50 R) Hegel's *ihre* refers to *die Vorstellung*, which is here equated with Spinoza's *imaginatio*. A study of Spinoza's use of *imaginatio* and *ratio* is very helpful for the understanding of

what Hegel means by *vorstellen* and *denken* (when they are *opposed*—for in the Cartesian sense in which it is used here, *denken includes vorstellen* and all other modes of reflective self-consciousness).

60. (§ 51) See Kant's Transcendental Dialectic, bk. 2, chap. 3, sec. 4. (The famous example of the "hundred dollars" will be found in *CPR* B, 627.)

61. (§ 51 R) Hegel put these three words in quotes (as well as italics). Probably he was thinking of the definition that he cites from Spinoza below [§ 76, note]: the *causa sui . . . non potest concipi nisi existens*. We can see here that Hegel means to defend Spinoza's ontological argument against Kant. Thus Spinoza's rationalism is not comprehended under the "metaphysics" of the "First *Stellung* of Thought." Almost certainly Leibniz is not comprehended there either, even though Wolff's position derived from him.

62. (§ 52) Compare *CPR*, Introduction, sec. 7 (B, 24–26).

63. (§ 53) Compare Kant's *Foundations of the Metaphysics of Morals*, Akad 4:413, 448 (Beck, 72–73, 103).

64. (§ 53) See note 31 above. This induction excludes the possibility of universal, "objective" rational imperatives. (For Hume's argument see especially *Enquiry Concerning the Principles of Morals*, sec. 3.)

65. (§ 54 R) Compare the first sentence of sec. 1 of Kant's *Grundlegung zur Metaphysik der Sitten*: "Nothing in the world—indeed nothing even beyond the world—can possibly be conceived which could be called good without qualification except a *good will*" (Beck, 55).

66. (§ 54 A) Hegel discussed this "Eudaemonism" at some length in the introductory pages of *Faith and Knowledge* (see Cerf and Harris, 58–66). Both the followers of Wolff and the "popular philosophers" of common sense can be counted as "Eudaemonists." So can the French Enlightenment—see *Phenomenology* (Miller, §§ 560–61, 581). For Kant, the most important opponent of this type was probably Moses Mendelssohn.

67. (§ 55) This paragraph (and the next two) are concerned with the *Critique of Judgment* [*CJ*]. For the "intuitive understanding" see especially § 77. The "Idea" (mentioned at the beginning of the Remark here) is discussed there. Kant's discussion of "inner purposiveness" is in § 66. The two parts of the *Critique* ("Aesthetic Judgment" and "Teleological Judgment") deal with the "products of art" and the "products of organic nature" respectively.

68. (§ 55 R) All of Schiller's aesthetic essays were inspired by the *Critique of Aesthetic Judgment*. But Hegel is probably thinking especially of the letters *On the Aesthetic Education of Man*. There is a magnificent critical edition of this, text and translation by E. Wilkinson and L. Willoughby (Oxford, 1967), and a good translation by R. Snell (London, Routledge, 1954). See especially Letters no. 5 and no. 6.

69. (§ 55 R) This appeal can be found in Jacobi, in Fichte, and in Schelling. But see especially Jacobi's Spinoza book, *Werke*, 4:i, 212–13.

70. (§ 55 R) For the relation of the Idea to the "Ideal" in Kant, see not only *CJ*, § 17, but *CPR* B, 596–98, 838–39. (For the "final purpose of the world" see *CJ*, § 84.)

71. (§ 56) Kant's theory of "genius" is in *CJ*, §§ 46–50; and the *Critique* begins with the theory of "judgments of taste" (§§ 1–22).

72. (§ 57) This is the main topic of the *Critique of Teleological Judgment* (§§ 61–84). See also the Introduction to the *Critique* as a whole (xxvii–xxxviii; Pluhar, 18–26).

73. (§ 58) Compare *CJ*, § 75.

74. (§ 60 note*) Hegel gives the reference for the *first edition* (1790). The quotation comes from § 88 (*Akad* 5:454–55; Pluhar, 345). It is interesting (and significant) that after giving only

paragraph (§ 54) to the *Critique of Practical Reason*, Hegel sums up Kant's ethical philosophy mainly in terms of the *Critique of Teleological Judgment* (§ 58–60).

75. (§ 60) For the "postulate of immortality" see especially *Critique of Practical Reason, Akad* 5:3–4, 121–24, 142–46 (Beck, 118–19, 225–27, 244–47). The "perpetually posited contradiction" is explored at length in the "Moral World-View" (*Phenomenology* [Miller, §§ 559–631]).

76. (§ 60 R note*) Gottfried Hermann, *Handbuch der Metrik*, Leipzig, 1790.

77. (§ 60 R) It is apparent from the argument of this Remark that the "empiricism" of §§ 37–39 is "*naïve* empiricism." This is Locke's "new way of ideas"; and it reaches its perfect form in Hume. This "naïve empiricism" is essentially *anti*-metaphysical; Kant's "critical" achievement was to do justice to the traditional metaphysics (of Wolff and his many followers) within the limits of finite experience, as those limits were clearly projected by Locke and distinctly defined by Hume. That tradition *needs* the Critical Philosophy because it cannot do justice to the a priori role played by thought in the interpretation of experience. But the empiricists also have the option of solving this problem by setting themselves against the traditional metaphysics in another way. They can have a metaphysics of their own based on the assumed absolute primacy of *external* perception. In this way "naïve empiricism" gets degraded into *materialism* and *natural determinism*. The problem of the spontaneity and freedom of thinking here vanishes by *fiat*. This was the path followed by many *French* disciples of Locke (for instance, Condillac, D'Holbach, and LaMettrie). It is they who represent *metaphysizieriender Empirismus*. ("Naïve empiricism" and "the Critical Philosophy" are historic moments in the Hegelian solution for the antinomy of necessity and freedom. "Materialism" is a simple deviation and a side issue.)

78. (§ 60 R) This is clearly *not* the authority of some external actuality (such as the Bible or the church). It is the authority of the *inner* sense. Hegel's argument here depends upon Jacobi's extension of the Humean theory of "belief" to embrace faith in God. (That extension of Hume was actually initiated by Hamann; but it is Jacobi who appears as the exemplary *Gestalt* of "immediate knowing" here.) "Metaphysical" empiricism is "consistent" in the sense that it is *monistic*. It allows only one form of true belief and makes the concept of "matter" into its "ultimate, highest content."

79. (§ 60 R note b) Hegel uses *Vorurteil*, generally rendered "prejudice". But this is a highly pejorative term. In the present context it is quite clear that Hegel is positive about *this Vorurteil*. We translate it by "assumption".

80. (§ 60 A1) *nur eine historische Beschreibung*. It seems possible that this characterisation of Kant's method is a deliberate assimilation of it to the "historical, plain method" of Locke (*Essay*, Intro., § 2, ed. Yolton, 1:5). Hegel owned a 1721 edition of Locke's *Essay* in English. But the most direct and probable source of Hegel's usage is Kant himself; see especially *CPR* B, 864. (This gives a very ironical twist to Hegel's comment here.)

81. (§ 60 A2) In Fichte's theory the *Ding-an-sich* is "thinkable" only negatively, not positively as in Kant. The Fichtean *Anstoß* is a critical heritage of enlightened Materialism, rather than of Deism, as in Kant. Thus, what Fichte says about it is:

> the principle of life and consciousness, the ground of its possibility is admittedly contained in the self; but this gives rise to no genuine self, no empirical existence in time; and any other kind, for us, is absolutely unthinkable. If such a genuine life is to be possible, we need for the purpose another and special sort of shock (*Anstoß*) to the self on the part of a not-self.
>
> According to the Science of Knowledge, then, the ultimate ground of all reality for the self is an original interaction between the self and some other thing outside it, of which nothing more can be said, save that it must be utterly opposed to the

self. In the course of this interaction, nothing is brought into the self, nothing alien is imported; everything that develops therein, even out to infinity, develops solely from itself, in accordance with its own laws; the self is merely set in motion by this opponent, in order that it may act; without such an external prime mover it would never have acted, and since its existence consists solely in acting, it would never have existed either. But this mover has no other attribute than that of being a mover, an opposing force, and is in fact only felt to be such.

Thus, in respect of its existence the self is dependent; but in the determinations of this existence it is absolutely independent. In virtue of its absolute being, it contains a law of these determinations, valid to infinity, and an intermediary power of determining its empirical existence according to this law. The point at which we find ourselves, when we first set this intermediary power of freedom in play, is not dependent on us; considered in its full extension, the series that from this point on we shall traverse to all eternity, is wholly dependent on ourselves.

The Science of Knowledge is therefore *realistic*. It shows that the consciousness of finite creatures is utterly inexplicable, save on the presumption of a force existing independently of them, and wholly opposed to them, on which they are dependent in respect of their empirical existence. Nor does it assert anything beyond this opposing force, which the finite being feels, merely, but does not apprehend. All possible determinations of this force, or not-self, which may emerge to infinity in our consciousness, the Science of Knowledge undertakes to derive from the determinant power of the self, and must indeed really be able to derive them, as surely as it is a Science of Knowledge. . . .

This fact, that the finite spirit must necessarily posit something absolute outside itself (a thing-in-itself), and yet must recognise, from the other side, that the latter exists only *for it* (as a necesary noumenon), is that circle which it is able to extend into infinity, but can never escape. A system that pays no attention at all to this circle is a dogmatic idealism; for it is indeed the aforesaid circle which alone confines us and makes us finite beings; a system which fancies itself to have escaped therefrom is a transcendent realist dogmatism (*Werke*, 1:279–81; *Science of Knowledge*, trans. P. Heath, 245–47).

82. The main representative of this "third *Stellung*" was F. H. Jacobi. There is a notable contrast between the treatment of Jacobi's view here and the much harsher treatment accorded to him in *Faith and Knowledge* (Cerf and Harris, 97–152). There is now a good discussion of this section by Kenneth Westphal (1989).

83. (§ 62 R note a) Since "existence" has to be used for translating *Existenz*, we cannot speak about the "proofs of the existence of God." *Existenz* is a much more developed logical category than *Dasein*. But neither category allows for an adequate comprehension of "God". See also note 10 to the Glossary.

84. (§ 62 R) The probable target of this polemic was the *Logic* of J. F. Fries (see *G.W.*, 19:508 [note to 77, 1–8]).

85. (§ 62 R) See *Werke*, 4:2, 127. (A translation by Di Giovanni is in preparation.)

86. (§ 62 R) This mode of reference to the *natural* sciences, though not quite concordant with *our* convention, is supported by titles like that of Newton's *Principia* ("*Mathematical* Principles of Natural Philosophy"). Hegel means to designate the inorganic sciences in which "mechanism" reigns supreme, and for which the Kantian understanding is "constitutive." (Hegel's model of "exact science" was Lagrange. But Jacobi refers to Copernicus, Kepler, Newton, and Laplace; see the 1814 Preface, *Werke*, 2:55–56.)

87. (§ 62 R) Hegel's use of *immanent* here differs from that later adopted by his followers. Since the "true Infinite" comprehends the finite within itself as a *necessary* moment of its being, almost all Hegelians came to speak of it as "immanent" in finite experience. As the paradigm of Lalande shows, what Hegel means here is that the Infinite cannot be thoughtfully *discovered* in the finite (as the force of gravity can, for example). The speculative thinker must first *transcend* the finite; then what is discovered in the "overgrasping return" is the *infinitude of what was previously called finite*. Thus, it would be more natural for Hegel himself to express his speculative view by speaking of the "immanence of the finite in the Infinite" (rather than vice versa).

88. (§ 62 R) Hegel got this story from Jacobi (*Werke*, 2:55); or possibly straight from Fries (*Populäre Vorlesungen*, 1813) who was Jacobi's source. Wallace comments: "What Lalande has actually written in the preface to his work on astronomy is that the science as he understands it has no relation to natural theology—in other words, that he is not writing a Bridgewater treatise." But it seems probable that the remark was made in lectures, and spread by word of mouth.

89. (§ 63) That "Reason is what humanity consists in," Jacobi repeats continually. Wallace quotes aptly from *Werke*, 2:343: "Reason is the true and proper life of our nature." That our reason is a *Wissen von Gott* is *more* than Jacobi usually allows. Our awareness of God is not "knowledge" for him but only a "presage" (*Ahndung*). But there is not much doubt that Hegel still has the 1814 Preface to *David Hume* in mind. See especially *Werke*, 2:7–11, 55–68. Hegel himself agreed with Jacobi's emphatic contrast between immediate *Wissen* and actual *Wissenschaft*. He differed from Jacobi in holding that *Wissenschaft* is possible.

90. (§ 63 R) This famous claim (which brought many polemical attacks upon Jacobi) was made in the *Letters on Spinoza* (1785): "Through faith we know that we have a body, and that other bodies, and other thinking beings are present outside us" (*Werke*, 4:1, 211).

91. (§ 63 R) Here Hegel reduces Jacobi's "Faith" to the "Truth of Enlightenment." Compare *Phenomenology* (Miller, §§ 574–81). (Jacobi comments on the relation of his philosophical faith to Christian faith, both in the Spinoza book, and in *David Hume*. See *Werke*, 4:212–13 and 2:144.)

92. (§ 64 R) H. G. Hotho, *De Philosophia Cartesiana* (Berlin, 1826). From Hegel's discussion of the *Cogito* here, it is evident that the rationalism of Descartes is not comprehended under the "Metaphysics" of the first *Stellung*. The great rationalists are all part of the tradition of speculative philosophy proper.

93. (§ 64 R) An examination of passages cited from Hotho's dissertation, *De Philosophia Cartesiana*, shows that their relevance is as follows:

> "Replies to the Second Objections:" The fuller context of Hegel's direct quotation is: But when we are aware that we are thinking things, this is *a certain primary concept, that is not concluded from any syllogism; and when someone says "I am thinking, therefore I am, or I exist,"* he does not deduce existence from thought by means of a syllogism, but recognises it as something self-evident by a simple intuition of the mind. This is clear from the fact that if he were deducing it by means of a syllogism, he would have to have had previous knowledge of the major premise, "Everything that thinks is, or exists"; yet in fact he learns it from experiencing in his own case that it is impossible that he should think without existing. It is in the nature of our mind to construct general propositions on the basis of our knowledge of particular ones. (Descartes, *Philosophical Writings*, trans. J. Cottingham, 3:100. Hegel's own quotation is italicised.)

The *Discourse on Method*, pt. 4, contains Descartes' argument for the certain existence of the self and of God in its briefest (and perhaps its most perspicuous) compass. But Descartes does not talk *about* the argument, or allude to its nonsyllogistic character (see the translation by D. A. Cress, 16–18). A possible reason for Hegel's reference to it here is suggested in note 94.

"*Ep.* I.118" refers to Clerselier's edition of the *Lettres de M. Descartes* in three volumes (Paris, 1657). See Letter 440 in *Oeuvres*, eds. Adam and Tannery, 4:442ff. The most pertinent passage (trans. A. Kenny in *Philosophical Letters* of Descartes, 197) is:

> I will also add that one should not require the first principle to be such that all other propositions can be reduced to it and proved by it. It is enough if it is useful for the discovery of many, and if there is no other proposition on which it depends, and none which is easier to discover. It may be that there is no principle at all to which alone all things can be reduced. They do indeed reduce other propositions to the principle that *the same thing cannot both be and not be at the same time*, but their procedure is superfluous and useless. On the other hand it is very useful indeed to convince oneself first of the existence of God, and then of the existence of all creatures, through the consideration of one's own existence (to Clerselier, June 1646).

94. (§ 64 R) This is where the reference to *Discourse on Method*, pt. 4, is probably relevant. Compare this sentence of Descartes: "And noticing that this truth—*I think therefore I am*—was so certain that the most extravagant suppositions of the sceptics were unable to shake it, I judged that I could accept it without scruple as the first principle of the philosophy I was seeking" (eds. Adam and Tannery, 6:32; Cress, 19).

95. (§ 67) In his own *Lectures on the History of Philosophy* Hegel refers to *Phaedrus* 246–51 for this (Haldane and Simson, 2:36–41). See note 97 for some other relevant references.

96. (§ 67 R) See Jacobi, *Werke*, 3:210 ("On a saying of Lichtenberg's").

97. (§ 67 A) Plato's doctrine of "Reminiscence" is typically presented in the dialogues through the myth of the soul's existence in the realm of the Ideas before birth (see, for instance, *Meno* 81, *Phaedo* 75). The Cambridge Platonists formulated Plato's theory as the view that certain fundamental concepts are "innate" in the mind; and in this form the theory was pilloried by Locke (in the first book of his *Essay*). But by the time the *Essay* was published the theory was universally familiar in the shape that it assumes in the work of Descartes. It is the Cartesian version that is defended by Leibniz (against Locke) in the *Nouveaux Essais*. The "Scottish philosophers" whom Hegel refers to here are Thomas Reid, James Oswald, and James Beattie. Reid developed a "common-sensical" version of the theory of "innate ideas." Hegel's knowledge of the Scottish School may derive partially from translations, although in his *Lectures* he relies upon compendia of the history of philosophy (see Haldane and Simson, 3:375–78; and *Vorlesungen*, 9:144–46).

98. (§ 71 R) The most obvious texts here are *De Natura Deorum* 1.43; 2.12. But the principle of *consensus* is of more general application, and older. Cicero gives Epicurean doctrine in Book 1: "For what nation or what tribe of men is there that does not have some preconception of the Gods without any teaching? This Epicurus calls *prolepsis*, that is information of a sort preconceived in the mind" (*De Natura Deorum* 1.43); and Stoic doctrine in bk. 2: "By everyone of every nation the main issue is agreed; for in all it is innate, and as it were engraved in the mind that there are Gods." But Cicero's speakers were only "rationalising" Aristotle's "What seems so to everyone, that we say *is*" (*Ethics*, 5.1173a1).

99. (§ 71 note*) The only poets who maintained monotheism were Xenophanes and Parmenides. No one treated them as "atheists"—though Xenophanes was certainly a severe critic

of the "Gods of the City." Clearly it is the philosophers who are in Hegel's mind (and the poets only come in because it was Aristophanes who portrayed Socrates proclaiming that the "Clouds" had *taken the place* of Zeus). Both Protagoras (who was an agnostic) and Anaxagoras (who was a monotheist) were accused of "impiety" before Socrates was brought to trial. (This "Greek" argument seems to be Hegel's own. The preceding discussion of idolaters—and the argument of § 72—may well owe something to Hume's *Natural History of Religion*.)

100. (§ 71 note*) Sir John Ross, *A Voyage of Discovery Etc.* (London, 1819). Hegel excerpted 128–29; see *Berliner Schriften*, ed. Hoffmeister, 710; or *G.W.*, 19:511, note to 86, 30–32. Sir W. E. Parry, *Journal of a Voyage* (London, 1821). It cannot be proved decisively that Hegel read Parry. He was a lieutenant on the Ross expedition, and Hegel may have known of him through that.

101. (§ 71 note*) See *Histories* 2:33. Hegel found the English report of Roman atheism in the *Morning Chronicle*, 16 March 1825. See Petry in *Hegel-Studien* 11 (1976):32–33 (or *Berliner Schriften*, 731; or *G.W.*, 19:512 [note to 86, 33–35]). But the "bigots" Hegel seems to have added by himself.

102. (§ 76 R) In the latest translation the section reads as follows:

> 9. *What is meant by "thought"*
> By the term "thought", I understand everything which we are aware of as happening within us, insofar as we have awareness of it. Hence, *thinking* is to be identified here not merely with understanding, willing, and imagining, but also with sensory awareness. For if I say, "I am seeing, or I am walking, therefore I exist," and take this as applying to vision or walking as bodily activities, then the conclusion is not absolutely certain. This is because, as often happens during sleep, it is possible for me to think I am seeing or walking, though my eyes are closed and I am not moving about; such thoughts might even be possible if I had no body at all. But if I take "seeing" or "walking" to apply to the actual sense or awareness of seeing or walking, then the conclusion is quite certain, since it relates to the mind, which alone has the sensation or thought that it is seeing or walking (Descartes, *Philosophical Writings*, 1:195).

103. (§ 76 R note*) Hegel refers here to *Principia* 1:17. (Our translations are from Descartes, *Philosophical Writings*, vol. 1.)

104. (§ 76 R note*) Proposition 11 of pt. 1 of the *Ethics* reads: "God, or the substances abiding in infinite attributes, of which each one expresses eternal and infinite essence, necessarily exists."

105. (§ 77 note*) The reference is to the first sentence of the first speech by the interlocutor (Boso) in *Cur Deus Homo* 1:1.

106. (§ 78 note a) Here "prejudices" is too pejorative. See also note 78 to § 60.

107. (§ 80 A) In the poem *Natur und Kunst*: "Wer Grosses will, muß sich zusammenraffen;/ In der Beschränkung zeigt sich erst der Meister,/ Und das Gesetz nur kann uns Freiheit geben" (*Werke*, Berlin edition, Aufbau Verlag, 1973, 2:121). (The same moral is preached often in *Wilhelm Meister's Apprenticeship*.)

108. (§ 80 A) This contrasts sharply with Hegel's usual characterisation of the Understanding as the death-dealing power—for which the *locus classicus* is probably the Preface to the *Phenomenology* (Miller, § 32). Hegel's *dialectical* conception of the understanding, as itself a unity of opposite values, of fixation and separation, is not generally understood. Often, indeed, it is not even *remembered*. But its importance for Hegel is shown by the way he recurs to this positive evaluation of Understanding in his commentary on § 81.

109. (§ 81 R) At this point it is worth recalling the sentence that Wallace cited from Fichte: "Yet it is not *we* who analyse: But knowledge analyses itself, and can do so, because in all its being it is a *for-self*" ("Darstellung der Wissenschaftslehre," 1801, first printed 1845, *Werke*, 2:37).

110. (§ 81 A1) Hegel is probably relying on Diogenes Laertius, 3:56, here. But he knew, and himself relied upon, the other tradition according to which Aristotle called Zeno the inventor of dialectic (Diogenes Laertius, 9:25). (Compare the remarks about the *Parmenides* below.)

111. (§ 81 A1) Hegel's memory slipped here (and his first editors failed to correct the error). It is of course Meno who is brought to this admission.

112. (§ 81 A1) Compare Hegel's comments in the "Scepticism Essay" (1801, Di Giovanni and Harris, 323–24, 328–29) and in the *History of Philosophy* (Haldane and Simson, 1:261–62, 264).

113. (§ 81 A2) Hegel's contrast between the "ancient" and the "modern" scepticism goes back to the "Scepticism Essay" of 1801, which can be read in Di Giovanni and Harris, 313–62, with the essays of Harris (on the ancient) and Di Giovanni (on the modern scepticism). It will be seen that Hegel here gives a somewhat higher evaluation of Sextus and Cicero (who are the *sources* of "ancient scepticism" for his students) than he gave them (in comparison with *their* "sources") in the essay itself. (For a very good account of Hegel's interpretation and use of the whole sceptical tradition see M. N. Forster, *Hegel and Scepticism*.)

The Doctrine of Being (§§ 84–111)

1. (§ 84 note a) See note 38 to the Glossary and note 16 to the Introduction.

2. (§ 85 note b) See the Introduction, pp. xxiii–xxiv.

3. (§ 85) Wallace gives an outline history of the term (*Logic*, 3d ed., 318). Hegel adopted it in concert with Schelling, but his logical usage is fixed by Spinoza who defines God as *ens absolute infinitum*. The "Absolute" is that which is not *bounded by* (not related to or dependent upon) anything else. What is distinctive about Hegel's usage is that, in order to be without any externally bounding "relations," that which is "absolute" must *logically* contain (or "comprehend") *all* finite relations and necessities. It cannot simply be "other" than they are—for that itself would be a "relation" *to* them.

4. (§ 86 R) *Letters on Spinoza* (2d ed., 61; repeated in Beylage, 7:398; *Werke*, 4:1, 87, and 4:2, 127). "I=I" is Fichte's first principle; and the "Absolute Indifference or Identity" is the principle of Schelling's school; the intuition of what is "absolutely certain" is the beginning of the Cartesian philosophy. Hegel's "beginning" takes us back to Parmenides of Elea; but as he emphasises at once it is directly confirmed by the School-Metaphysics (the "first *Stellung*") which is all that remains of Christian Scholasticism. Wallace refers us to a manual of Baumgarten's Metaphysics here; but Hegel probably expected his students to think of Kant's great assault on Mendelssohn's version of the Ontological Argument (Transcendental Dialectic, bk. 2, chap. 3, sec. 2–4, *CPR* B, 599–630). The definition of God as the *Inbegriff aller Realitäten* comes immediately from *CPR* B, 605–10.

5. (§ 86 A2) The closest equivalent in Parmenides' poem seems to be in fragment 6: "For 'it is' can be, but 'it is not' cannot." But Wallace is probably right in appealing to fragment 2 (though he misreads it and cites only half enough). There, the Goddess tells Parmenides that "the only ways that exist for thinking are on one side that it is and cannot not be, which is the

way of persuasion that attends upon Truth; and on the other side, that it is not, and it is necessary that it should not be, but that I tell thee is quite without persuasion. For thou could'st not know that which is not nor utter it. For thinking and being are the same" (Diels and Kranz, *Fragmente der Vorsokratiker* [D.K.], 28B, 2, 3, 6. Our reading follows that of Kirk and Raven—though not word for word—except in the last sentence [fragment 3] which we read as Hegel would have done).

6. (§ 86 A2) This was the "starting point" of *Schelling*'s Philosophy of Identity. "Ich = Ich" is the starting point of Fichte's idealism; and although many thinkers spoke of "beginning from God," the exemplar in Hegel's mind is Spinoza.

7. (§ 87) In the *Science of Logic* Hegel warns: "*Nothing* is usually opposed to *something*; but something is already something-that-is-determinate [*ein bestimmtes Seiendes*] which is distinct from another something; therefore the nothing that is opposed to the something is also the nothing of something or other, a determinate nothing. Here, however, nothing is to be taken in its indeterminate simplicity" (Lasson, 1:67–68; Miller, 83).

8. (§ 87 R) It hardly needs to be pointed out that Hegel's information about Buddhism was very inadequate. What is significant is that by offering it as the paradigm of the absoluteness of the Nothing—and ignoring the effort of Gorgias to travel the Eleatic path of "it is not" with which he was quite familiar—Hegel shows us that his *Logic* is more than a developmental theory of Western thought. He has told us that the moments of the Idea do appear in a temporal sequence in our history. But he now takes the very first available opportunity to break that sequence himself, though it should also be recorded that he probably did not regard Gorgias as a "speculative" philosopher.

9. (§ 87 R) "Freedom" as the highest form of negativity is the very principle of self-articulation, and as such it *is* absolute affirmation.

10. (§ 88 R) Wallace very sensibly refers us here to the comment of Aristotle:

> The first of those who studied science were misled in their search for truth and the nature of things by their inexperience, which as it were thrust them into another path. So they say that none of the things that are either comes to be or passes out of existence, because what comes to be must do so either from what is or from what is not, both of which are impossible. For what cannot come to be (because it is already), and from what is not nothing could have come to be (because something must be present as a substratum). So too they exaggerated the consequence of this, and went so far as to deny even the *existence* of a plurality of things, maintaining that only Being itself is (*Physics* 1.8.191a26ff).

For Hegel, the dialectic and the speculative sublation of the exclusive alternatives was the *logical* road out of this impasse. He offers us a logical theory of *development*. We should notice that this section (5)—against "pantheism"—was added only in 1830. It reflects the growing strength of the pious opposition to "speculative" theology; compare further the Foreword to the 1830 edition.

11. (§ 88 A) It is of little interest to raise the question of the mere "being" of God, precisely because God is infinitely concrete. *Welches* refers to *Sein*, but what follows explicates God's *genuine* being, not his merely abstract being. Only the question about the latter is of little interest.

12. (§ 88 A) This is the most astonishing historical misstatement in Hegel's work. He repeats it in the *History of Philosophy* lectures, so it is definitely not a mistake of transcription. (For his account of Heracleitus see Haldane and Simson, 1:278–98; compare *Vorlesungen*, 7:69–81.) The fact that his first editors let it stand seems to show that they knew it to be a considered

opinion of Hegel's, and not a simple failure of memory. For the source of the quotation was ready to hand. In the very first book of the *Metaphysics* (A.4.985b4–10) Aristotle reports that the Atomists

> Leucippus and his associate Democritus say that the full and the empty are the elements, calling the one being and the other nonbeing—the full and solid being being, the empty nonbeing (whence they say being no more is than nonbeing, because the solid no more is than the empty); and they make these the material causes of things.

Something must have convinced Hegel that he was entitled to project the saying back into the book of Heracleitus. He was, of course, convinced that Heracleitus thought and wrote after Parmenides; and the way that Plato reports the views of Heracleitus may have seemed to support his view that Heracleitus was the real origin of what Diels more plausibly ascribes to the shadowy Leucippus (*D.K.*, 67, A6). There was some excuse for dating Heracleitus according to a genetic hypothesis about his thought, because all the reports of his "life" are of doubtful worth. But this daylight robbery perpetrated against Leucippus is a striking example of a *wishful* use of his own logic on Hegel's part.

13. (§ 88 A) "das Werden . . . hat . . . sich in sich weiter zu vertiefen und zu erfüllen." With "vertiefen" here cf. § 84.

14. (§ 89 R) Hegel depends mainly on Aristotle's account in *Physics* 6.9. See further *T.W-A*, 18:295–319; Haldane and Simson, 1:261–78; compare *Vorlesungen*, 7:62–69. It is clear from the way that Hegel's account of Zeno opens there that he has the Eleatics in mind here when he speaks of "the Ancients." What he says here is paraphrased directly from his lecture manuscript. It was Parmenides and Zeno who maintained "that the One *is*."

15. (§ 91 A) This tag, which Hegel loves, is a misquotation. The nearest equivalent in Spinoza's surviving texts is in Epistle 50, "Figure is nothing else but determination, and determination is negation [*et determinatio negatio est*]."

16. (§ 91 A note c) "dies Recht." *Dies* could also be read as *das*, which is how Bourgeois (525) and Verra (273) read it.

17. (§ 92) See note 28 to the Glossary.

18. (§ 92 A) *Etwas Anderes* is naturally rendered in English as "something else", rather than "something other". Whenever it occurs we have to remember its essential relatedness to "other."

19. (§ 92 A) Hegel's students apparently copied this down as a direct quotation. Actually it is only a paraphrase of *Timaeus* 35a–b.

20. (§ 94) This "spurious infinity" is typically found in the natural philosophy of Galileo and Newton (with reference to space, time, causal chains, etc.); and the logical paradigm of it is the series of natural numbers. But the way it is deployed in the practical philosophy of Kant and Fichte is a more important ground of Hegel's antipathy. It is the "postulate of immortality" required for an "infinite progress in morality" that represents for him the absolute triumph of the "ought." This antipathy is the reason why he virtually ignores the *Critique of Practical Reason* in his own systematic outline of Kant (§§ 53–60 above). Compare the last sentences in his lecture commentary on this paragraph.

21. (§ 95) As Hegel's explanation in the following Remark shows, this is logically identical with the "Absolute." Compare note 3.

22. (§ 95 R) This is because every "genuine" philosophy interprets all finite data in the context of a "genuinely infinite" Concept. In that sense every systematic philosophy—every philosophy that operates constructively with Kant's "Ideas of Reason"—is an "Idealism" in the same

sense as Hegel's philosophy; and Hegel's philosophy is *not* "Idealism" in Berkeley's sense *at all*. As Hegel says in the *Science of Logic*: "The antithesis of idealistic and realistic philosophy is therefore without significance" (Lasson, 1:145; Miller, 155). See also Notes to the Glossary.

23. (§ 96 A) This "interpretation" was the work of Schelling. It can be found in his earliest essays on the Philosophy of Nature. Wallace refers us to the *Einleitung* of 1799 (*Werke*, 3:272). But the doctrine can be readily found in the available translations. See for instance *Ideas for a Philosophy of Nature* (1797, 1803), trans. E. E. Harris and P. Heath, 27; or *Bruno* (1801), trans. M. Vater, 158–59. The doctrine stems from Spinoza's thesis that "the order of ideas is the same as the order of things."

24. (§ 98) Hegel relies especially on Cicero. See *De Divinatione* 2.17, 40, and *De Natura Deorum* 1.8.

25. (§ 98) The reference is to the second chapter, "The Metaphysical Foundations of Dynamics" (*Akad* 4:498–517; Ellington, 40–94). What Hegel means by "muddy confusion" here is explained fully in the *Science of Logic* (1812), *G.W.*, 11:102–107. For the second edition of 1830 see Lasson, 1:170–76; Miller, 178–84.

26. (§ 98 A1) In the famous General Scholium at the end of *Principia*, Newton himself held to a "corpuscularian" theory of matter. "Corpuscles" differed from "atoms" in that they *could be divided*. This is the logically degenerate form of "atomism" which Hegel discusses in the Remark to § 98.

27. (§ 98 A1) A. G. Kästner (1719–1800) was a professor of mathematics and physics at Göttingen (and a literary essayist of considerable repute). His "warning" is probably to be found somewhere in *Angfangsgründe der höheren Mechanik*.

28. (§ 102 R) As a moment of number, *Anzahl* is "annumeration"; but as a number that is *one* of the factors of multiplication (or of squaring), it is "the annumerator".

29. (§ 103 A) This was the name that *Schelling* gave to his speculative idealism in 1801 (see especially *Bruno*). Hegel here acknowledges implicitly that his mature idealism is still a "philosophy of Identity." But he distinguishes the speculative "identity" of Nature and Spirit (or the Real and the Ideal) from the formal logical "law of identity." The philosophical champions of this formal "identity" were Reinhold and Bardili.

30. (§ 104 R) Actually the reporter is Simplicius in his commentary on the *Physics*; see *D.K.*, 29, B1.

31. (§ 104 A2) For Spinoza's distinction between the infinite of Reason and that of imagination see especially *Ethics*, 1, prop. 8, scholium; *Ethics*, 2, prop. 44; and Epistle 12 (= 29 in the Paulus edition that Hegel himself used). For Hegel's own understanding of Spinoza on this point, see *Faith and Knowledge* (Cerf and Harris, 105–13).

32. (§ 104 A2) From the poem "Über die Ewigkeit" published as "incomplete" in *Versuch schweizerischer Gedichte*, Bern, 1732. Hegel cites it in exactly the same form in the *Science of Logic* (Lasson, 1:227; Miller, 230); so perhaps Wallace's conjecture that the missing fourth line—with other variants—was added later (and published in the second edition, 1777) is correct. But one suspects that Hegel learned the poem as a boy, and never looked at the book after that. (Kant's reference to the poem as "eery" is in *CPR* B, 641.)

33. (§ 104 A3) Hegel depends upon Aristotle, *Metaphysics* A.5.985b23ff. The "story everyone knows" about the musical intervals is in Iamblichus, *Life of Pythagoras*, §§ 115ff. It is told in detail in *T.W-A.*, 18:258–59; Haldane and Simson, 1:226–28. Hegel's treatment of the Pythagorean School in his lectures is exceptionally copious.

34. (§ 106 A) *Qualität* here must be *Quantität*.

35. (§ 107 A) Protagoras said, "Of all things Man is the Measure." Plato (in *Laws* 4:716c) expressly contradicted him, by asserting that "God, not Man, is the Measure." When Hegel

speaks of *Nemesis* as Measure he may have something from Pindar or the tragedians in mind. But we should remember the "broad oath" in Empedocles, and the Furies as "ministers of Justice" in Heracleitus, who will not suffer the Sun to "overstep his measures." Cosmic "justice" is first explicit in Anaximander. (See *D.K.*, 31, B30; Aristotle, *Metaphysics* B.4.1000b12, 22B94, and 12B1.)

36. (§ 107 A) Wallace suggested Psalms 74 and 104; also Proverbs 8 and Job 38. The famous text, "Thou orderest all things in weight, number, and measure," is in the Apocrypha (Wis. 11:21).

37. (§ 108 A) The logical examples of the Sorites Paradox come from Diogenes Laertius, Cicero, and Horace. In the ancient tradition, the bald-tailed horse was a bald-headed man. According to Diogenes Laertius (2:108) it was Eubulides of Megara who first drew attention to the logical difficulty of deciding when someone is bald if one removes the hairs one by one. Horace turned the example from a man's head to a horse's tail in the first Epistle of his second book (line 65ff). The Greek *sorites* means a "heap"; and Cicero gives the original *heap of wheat* example in his *Academica* 2:92. I have not found the peasant with his overloaded donkey but it is proverbial, not original with Hegel—cf. "It's the last straw that breaks the camel's back." (The Sorites Paradox should be distinguished from the Sorites Argument, where many syllogisms are heaped together into a single chain of premises with a final conclusion that connects the first and last terms.)

38. (§ 109 A) Hegel's use of this image is not confined to natural philosophy. He used it first for the *historical* evolution of "Religion" in the *Phenomenology* (see Miller, § 681). Thus, the progressive self-determination of the Absolute Spirit in its history falls within the category of Measure.

The Doctrine of Essence (§§ 112–159)

1. (§ 112 note a) See Introduction, pp. xxv–xxvi.

2. (§ 112 R) See note 45 to § 44 R.

3. (§ 112 A) See Introduction, pp. xviii–xix.

4. (§ 112 A) We should notice that Hegel mentioned the French "Supreme Being" in the same breath between two references to the German "Supreme Essence." That the "être suprême" *is* an "essence"—and a supremely *empty* one, not a concrete "being" at all—he showed in the *Phenomenology* (see Miller, §§ 557, 574–78, 586).

5. On *Grund* as "ground" and "reason", see note 9 below. The French expression "raison d'être" comes closest to what Hegel means by *Grund*.

6. (§ 115 R) Abstraction is the method by which the understanding makes every content "absolute." For the *speculative* identity of the Absolute see the note to § 103 A above. The "contradiction" implicit in the form of any synthetic proposition is the foundation of the "speculative" proposition. Compare §§ 79–82 (and *Phenomenology*, Miller, §§ 58–63).

7. (§ 117 R) This is the so-called "Identity of Indiscernibles"; see the *Monadology*, § 9: "There is never in nature two beings [i.e., "essences" in Hegel's sense] that are perfectly like one another, and where it is impossible to find an internal difference, i.e., one based on an intrinsic character." (The story in Hegel's lecture commentary, of the courtiers searching for two identical leaves, can be found in Leibniz, *Nouveaux Essais*, bk. 2, chap. 27, § 3.)

8. (§ 119 R) Note that *every* general concept is "contradictory" because it is *both* "A and not-A" and *neither* "A or not-A." Anyone who says this in ordinary discourse is either stupid or a Sophist; but it is the key to the logical dialectic. The "polarity" of "forces" is how "real contradiction" appears in the real world. Fichte pioneered this conception of "contradiction" in logic, and Schelling in the philosophy of nature.

9. (§ 121 R) See Leibniz, "Principles of Nature and Grace," § 7–8; *Monadology*, § 32. This is ordinarily called the "principle of sufficient reason" in English; but fidelity to Hegel's categoreal structure obliges us to use the word "ground" here. "Reason" in Hegel is one name for the absolutely comprehensive category of the *Logic* (cf. § 82). As Hegel says in his commentary only "the Concept" can be "the sufficient ground." Leibniz formulated and used the principle in this sense (see especially *Monadology*, §§ 32–38). The "principle of ground" is ultimately the logical demand for a *final* cause (although the examples in the Addition show that it can be applied to efficient causes). Hegel uses its *logical* character to bend the religious quest back upon itself. Logical cognition can only comprehend *itself* as its own *end*.

10. (§ 121 A) The Sophists used the "principle of ground" dialectically, i.e., *sceptically*. It was Protagoras who formulated the principle that opposite but equal "grounds" could always be given. Socrates, in his reaction to the theory of Anaxagoras (*Phaedo* 97c), formulated the Leibnizian (or speculative) principle. No reason was *sufficient*, he argued, except a proof that the existing order was "for the best." (Hegel's own account of the "battle" is in Haldane and Simson, 1:384–89; cf. also 398–99.)

11. (§ 124 R) The thinkable but unknowable, and hence completely problematic, ground of "appearance" in Kant's critical theory (see § 44 and the note to it). In Hegel's theory of experience the *Ding an sich* is replaced by the self-knowing *Sache selbst* (see Introduction, p. xxv). In Hegel's use (following but dialectically controverting Kant) the simple *Ding* is the essence that is "truly taken" in perception (*Wahr-nehmung*). Compare *Phenomenology*, chap. 2.

12. (§ 126 R) Hegel uses the (now defunct) scientific theory of "matters" as a conceptual bridge between "perception" and "understanding." As he rightly says, no one regarded the "matters" as proper "things." In his own view (as in ours) magnetism, electricity, etc. were "forces." But the theoretical mistake was logically necessary for the development of the Concept, because in a "thing-world" the transient and variable "properties" of the real *things* have to be conceived as having a "real" foundation. (See further *Phenomenology*, chap. 2; *Science of Logic*, Miller, 491–98; *Philosophy of Nature*, § 334.)

13. (§ 130 note a) See the Introduction, pp. xxv–xxvi.

14. (§ 130 R) The theory of "pores" comes from Empedocles (see *D.K.*, 31, A86). But among the scientific thinkers of his time Hegel found it specifically in John Dalton (compare *Phenomenology*, Miller, § 136, and the note in *G.W.*, 9:495–96; also *Science of Logic*, Miller, 496–98).

15. (§ 131 A) This was published in 1801. Hegel's comments show how far he was from being a "subjective idealist," i.e., an "idealist" in the traditional sense of the term; compare the note to § 95 R above.

16. (§ 136 R) *Gott. Einige Gespräche* was first published in 1787. Hegel wrote a review of the second edition (1800); but it was never published, and is now lost. There is an English translation by F. H. Burkhardt (Indianapolis, LLA, 1940). For the place of Herder's polemic in the Spinoza controversy see Beiser, *The Fate of Reason*, chap. 5.

17. (§ 136 A2) Newton himself was, of course, a devout believer in the revealed truth of the Scriptures. But the image of him as the father of Deism was set already by Leibniz. (For Hegel's critique of Deism compare § 73–74.)

18. (§ 140 note*) Goethe's response appeared first in his *Zur Morphologie* (1820); see now *Werke*, 1:555–56. The poem of von Haller on "The Falsity of Human Virtues" appeared in his *Gedichte* (Bern, 1732); it can be found now in the Critical Edition (Frauenfeld, 1882), 61ff.

Hegel changes the *weist* ("shows") of both poets into his Swabian *weisst* (3d sing. present indicative of *wissen*). Otherwise, what he quotes here is *Goethe's* version.

19. (§ 140 A) See, for instance, *Phaedrus* 247a, *Timaeus* 29e, *Metaphysics* A.2.983a4. Compare also Haldane and Simson, 2:134–36.

20. (§ 140 A) *Maxime und Reflexionen* (from "Ottilie's Diary" in the *Wahlverwandschaften*, 1809), *Werke*, 18:479.

21. (§ 140 A) History written in order to teach lessons of morality and prudence. The concept originates in Polybius, *History* 9.2.5 and is characterised by Hegel in his Introduction to the *Philosophy of History* (Rauch, 7–9).

22. (§ 140) See "Minority Comments," above, as well as note 22 to the Glossary. *Formell*, together with "subjective", distinguishes the interests that are here referred to from the true import of the will and deeds of world-historical individuals. See Hegel's *Lectures on the Philosophy of History* (T.W-A., 12:46–48; Rauch, 32–35). (See also what Hegel says about the modern idea of "virtue" in the *Phenomenology of Spirit*, especially Miller, 234 [= Suhrkamp *Werke*, 3:290].) In the present context *formell* could be rendered with "hollow".

23. (§ 142 A) For Hegel's view of "Aristotle's polemic against Plato" in greater detail, see Haldane and Simson, 2:139–41.

24. (§ 143 R) *CPR* B, 266 (compare Hegel, *Difference*, Harris and Cerf, 80).

25. (§ 145 A) Hegel is often accused of doing this, both in the field of natural science and in that of history. But whatever mistakes he may make, it is a mistake of his interpreters to suppose that this is the basis of them. Far from being a rational determinist of some kind, he is logically concerned to demonstrate that contingency is necessary (both in the order of nature, and in the realm of spirit) and that freedom is fundamental to the existence of scientific cognition. About "chance" in Nature he is Aristotelian (rather than Kantian); and he himself says here that the view of history which is often ascribed to him is "an empty word-game and a strained sort of pedantry." None of those who suppose themselves to be his critics has ever put it more clearly.

26. (§ 147 note b) See the Introduction, p. xxv, and note 15 to the Glossary.

27. (§ 147 A) This thumbnail account of "Providence" as the rational pattern of history is explained more fully in the Introduction to the *Philosophy of History* (Rauch, 12–18). Compare (and contrast) Schelling's *System of Transcendental Idealism* (*Werke*, 3:602–604; Heath, 210–12). "Providence" is not discussed often in the *Philosophy of Religion* lectures, and Hodgson has not indexed it. The references are: 1:249 (1820); 334 (1824); 402n (1827?); 2:163n, 182–85 (1820); 198, 213, 486 (1824); 561n, 667–68 (1827); 3:75, 378 (1820).

28. (§ 147 A) For pagan "necessity" and "Fate" see especially Hodgson, 2:126–27, 141–52 (1821); 395–404, 469–70, 480–82, 499–500 (1824); 651–52, 665–67 (1827); 756–57 (1831). For Christian self-knowledge of Spirit, see Hodgson, 3:64–65, 132–62 (1820); 237–47 (1824); 266–71, 334–47 (1827); 371–74 (1831). But see also *Phenomenology*, chap. 7.

29. (§ 149) Hegel's use of the singular verb *wird* has the effect of *identifying* the "ground" with the "contingent condition." The coincidence of the two is what comes about in their "immediacy." But it is not clear whether that is all that Hegel means.

30. (§ 151 A) God as *Ding* is what we have in Deism; God as *Sache* is what we have in Spinoza's *Ethics*; God as "principle of personal individuation" is what we reach in the *Monadology*. These examples will help the comprehension of the conceptual progression (and vice versa). The "Oriental intuition" of God is the Mosaic Lawgiver. This is the *Sache selbst*, not a *person*. Only a subject for whom a community of other subjects is *logically necessary* is a "person." Thus, from the point of view of someone for whom God is a "person" Spinoza is an "atheist"; otherwise not. But we ought to say of him whatever we say of Moses—except

that because Moses is not a philosopher this logical requirement is not clear to him (or to those who read about him).

About "pantheism" (and hence about Spinoza's "acosmism") Hegel's position is (arguably) affected by the need for a definition that cannot be applied to his own (and Schelling's) idealism. For Hegel's view of Spinoza see further the *Science of Logic* (Lasson, 2:164–67; Miller, 536–40); and the *History of Philosophy* (*T.W-A.*, 20:161–97 with *Vorlesungen*, 9:103–13; Haldane and Simson, 3:256–90). See also the *Philosophy of Religion*; for the relevant discussions refer to "Pantheism" in the Index as well as "Spinoza".

31. (§ 153 R) *Werke*, 4:2, 144–46. See further *Faith and Knowledge*, Cerf and Harris, 97–116, and Haldane and Simson, 3:411–16). Wallace's explanatory note, 3d ed., 329, is also helpful.

32. (§ 158 A) See *Ethics* 5, props. 27, 32, 36, etc. This love, which is a direct participation in God's life and love, comes to us when we achieve "intuitive science."

The Doctrine of the Concept (§§ 160–244)

1. (§ 160) *indem*. The original 1830 edition reads "in dem" which is grammatically imposs-ible. Nicolin and Pöggeler suggest "Totalität, in der . . . " This would have to be translated "and [the Concept] is a *totality*, in which *each* of the moments is *the whole* that it [the Concept] is". The 1827 edition reads, " . . . and as the *totality* of this negativity, in which *each* of the moments is the *whole* that it is, and is posited as inseparable unity with it, it [the Concept] is in its identity with itself what is in and for itself determinate."

2. (§ 160 A) "der Begriff als solcher läßt sich nicht mit den Händen greifen." Hegel is probably playing here on the verbal connection between "Begriff" and "greifen".

3. (§ 161 A) Bonnet's theory of *Emboîtement* was inspired by Leibniz (who was himself reviving the Stoic and Mediaeval theory of the "seminal reasons"). Bonnet himself rejected the box analogy, claiming that each germ contained the next, in the way the plant contains the seed. Logically, the point is that no *free* development is possible. Hegel himself does not believe that there is real "evolution" in nature. But his dialectical theory of conceptual *develop-ment* provides a logical theory that is properly prepared for the possibility of natural evolu-tion. Kant's *CJ*, § 80 compares the rival theories of "epigenesis" and "preformation" in their logical aspects. Wallace provides illuminating quotations from the "Chinese box" tradition (3d ed., 329–30).

4. (§162 R) Hegel's letter to Niethammer (Letter 122, 20 May 1808, Hoffmeister, 1:229; Butler and Seiler, 175) tells us who some of the "ordinary logicians" were who fattened up their discussions in this way—Steinbart, Kiesewetter, and Mehmel.

5. (§ 163 A1) Clearly Hegel is restating Aristotle's theory of "natural slavery" in the language of post-Kantian idealism (cf. *Politics* 1:3–7.1253b1–1255b30). Aristotle was not consistent about the slave's "selfhood." For he said that, although the free man could not be friends with a slave "as a slave," there could be friendship with him "as a man" (*Ethics* 8.11.1161b5–8; cf. *Politics* 1.1255b12–15). But probably this distinction only acknowledges the empirical fact that many men of slave status were not "natural slaves."

6. (§ 163 A1) See the *Social Contract*, bk. 2, chap. 3.

7. (§ 165 R) *clear*, *distinct* [*deutliche*], and *adequate*. The classification comes from Descartes (Meditation III) and Leibniz. But when he calls it "ordinary" Hegel is referring us to the logic books of the school of Wolff. Thus Wallace's reference to Baumeister's *Institutes* of Rational

Philosophy was very apt (3d ed., 300–301). But no one reads Baumeister now, while all readers of Hegel's logic ought to be readers of Leibniz. See therefore "Meditations on Knowledge, Truth and Ideas" (*Philosophical Papers*, ed. L. E. Loemker, 1:448–50). (It is fairly clear that Hegel himself did not have Baumeister's slightly more complex classification in mind. *G.W.*, 19:515, note to 139, 18–19, supplies the appropriate reference for Kiesewetter's *Logic*.)

8. (§ 165 R) For some "ordinary logic books" in which these distinctions were made, see *G.W.*, 19:515–16, note to 139, 27–31.

9. (§ 166 A) In the early history of embryology the blood spot in a fertile egg was identified as the "salient point" from which the development of the living organism begins. See, for instance, Aristotle, *History of Animals* 6.3.

10. (§ 169 R) Compare here the *Phenomenology* Preface, Miller, § 62.

11. (§ 171 A) See *CPR* B, 95.

12. (§ 172 R) It is important to realise that Hegel's *Logic* is concerned with "relations of ideas," rather than with "matters of fact." Compare *Phenomenology* Preface, Miller, § 39–42.

13. (§ 174 A) Reading "der Begriff desselben" instead of "derselben".

14. (§ 175 A) "im *singulären* Urteil". See the Introduction, pp. xix–xx.

15. (§ 175 A) Hegel's *Logic is* concerned with the *universal* truths of scientific observation and natural law. But this example from his study of Blumenbach (see *Science of Logic*, Lasson, 2:455; Miller, 798) shows vividly that philosophical "truth" is a *value* concept. If dolphins could *talk* we should have to revise our *human* concepts radically.

16. (§ 177 A) To understand the disjunctive "necessity" here we must read this assertion as, "A *primary* colour, for painting, is either red, yellow, or blue." (But the triadic division of poetry is directly based on the moments of the concept, so it is altogether more interesting to reflect upon.)

17. (§ 182 R) The "current meaning" of the distinction between "syllogism of understanding" and "syllogism of reason" is probably that given by Kant in *CPR* B, 359 ff.

18. (§ 182 A) See further the *Philosophy of Religion*, Hodgson, 1:126–27. Pre-Kantian "Deism" seems never to be discussed in the *Lectures*; for the "Trinity" see Hodgson's index.

19. (§ 187 R) The figures (*schemata*) of the syllogism arise from the order of the terms in the two premises and the conclusion. Using S, M, and P for the three terms in any valid syllogism, valid arguments can be constructed (so Aristotle said in *Prior Analytics* 1.4.26a21) in three schematic patterns:

first figure: S-M, M-P ∴ S-P
second figure: M-S, M-P ∴ S-P
third figure: S-M, P-M ∴ S-P

But it is clear that Aristotle realized that valid syllogisms were possible in a fourth figure: P-M, M-S ∴ S-P. All valid arguments in this figure can be presented in the first figure quite easily. Theophrastus (who is supposed to have shown this) was presumably only teaching Aristotle's own doctrine.

The definite acknowledgement of a "fourth figure" was credited to Galen through a misunderstanding caused innocently by a late scholiast (see I. M. Bochenski, *A History of Formal Logic*, sec. 24.30 to sec. 24.34). Zabarella published the error in the West; see W. and M. Kneale, *Development of Logic*, 183.

Aristotle did not recognise four figures, because his theory is not based on the formal placement of the terms S and P in the conclusion. He defines S and P "according to their extension, and so not a formal definition but one dependent on their meaning" (Bochenski, *A*

History of Formal Logic, 13.21). The same is true, certainly, of Hegel's "speculative syllogistic." So, however he himself understood Aristotle's theory, he was certainly within his rights in rejecting the "fourth figure." (The fourth figure was admitted on formal grounds by a thirteenth-century Jewish logician—whose work never reached the Latin world. Leibniz was apparently the first Western logician to formalize the syllogism completely in the modern way. See Bochenski, 32.18–32.32 and 36.11.)

20. (§ 187 R) Compare further Haldane and Simson, 2:196–201.

21. (§ 190 A) We see here that "Observational Reason" (*Phenomenology*, chap. 5A) is "instinctive" for a logical reason. The scientific observer must move from a finite set of observed cases to the "intuition" of the essence. Hegel's conception of scientific method is itself still only "instinctive." But we can see, at least, that what makes an observational leap "reasonable" is the fact that it fits into the "concept" of a whole.

22. (§ 190 A) It is principally followers and allies of Schelling who have brought the philosophy of nature into discredit. The inspiration of Hegel's own philosophy of nature comes from Schelling's work. So, although Schelling was sometimes guilty of analogical reasoning, that is not all there is in his theory. We should notice that Hegel does not want his own philosophy of nature to be interpreted analogically. (Compare the note to §§ 145 A above.)

23. (§ 192 A) It is principally Kant's critical employment of this distinction in the *CPR* that makes it necessary for Hegel to attack it here. We should notice that in Hegel's *Logic* (as in Aristotle) "syllogism" is the *method* of science. The logic of Being and Essence is Hegel's "doctrine of elements"; the logic of the Concept is his "doctrine of method." The difference from the "traditional" usage (as defined, notably, in *CPR* B, 735–36) is quite striking.

24. (§ 193 R) *Proslogium*, chap. 2. Compare Descartes, Meditation III; Spinoza, *Ethics*, 1, prop. 11. What "happened to Anselm's argument long ago" was the response by Gaunilo, "On Behalf of the Fool," which (in accordance with Anselm's own decision) is always printed with the *Proslogium*. (See further Hegel's exposition of Anselm in Haldane and Simson, 3:61–67; *Vorlesungen*, 9:33–35.) The great "attempt to look down upon the so-called ontological proof" was that of Kant in *CPR* B, 625–27.

25. (§ 194 R) See the "Principles of Nature and of Grace" as well as the *Monadology*. Compare Haldane and Simson, 3:328–48; also *Vorlesungen*, 9:130–36.

26. (§ 194 A1) No one has yet found any passage that exactly bears out what Hegel claims here. Wallace points to the "First Introduction to the *Wissenschaftslehre*" (1797), *Werke*, 1:430; Heath and Lachs, 13. But this refers only to "fatalism," not to "superstition and fear." Students at Berlin in the 1820s would surely think of the *Atheismusstreit* when Hegel praised Fichte in this way; and although he did not speak of "God as Object" Fichte did characterise the position he was opposing as one of "superstition and fear." See, for example, the *Appelation an das Publikum* (1799), *Werke*, 5:209, 230. (In the main, however, Hegel is expressing what Fichte meant to him and other young Romantics in the Tübingen Seminary during the early years of the Revolution.)

27. (§ 195 R) In the *Phenomenology* Hegel presents "mechanical piety" as a necessary phase in the evolution of our culture (Miller, § 217, 228–30), just as he claims in his lecture commentary below that "mechanical memory" is a necessary moment of subjective psychology (cf. *Encyclopaedia*, §§ 461–64).

28. (§ 195 A) "der noch in sich unaufgeschlossen Materie". *unaufgeschlossenen*, from *aufschließen*, yet another play with *schließen*, on which see notes 31 and 32 below.

29. (§ 204 R) See *De Anima* 2.1.412a14: "By life we mean self-nutrition, together with growth and decay"; 2.415b15: "The soul is the final cause of its body." But Aristotle's main discussion of teleology is in *Physics* 2.8. For Kant's theory of "internal purposiveness" see *CJ*, §§ 61–66. It

was the followers of Wolff who were the chief proponents of *"finite* or *external* purposiveness."* (See Hegel's commentary on § 205 for examples of what is meant.)

30. (§ 206 A) The reference is to the thesis of Thales from which the Ionian philosophy began. But water is also the "neutral" element in Hegel's theory of the elements (see *Encyclopaedia* § 284; *Philosophy of Nature*, ed. Petry, 2:39–41; and Haldane and Simson, 1:173–82).

31. (§ 206 A) *zusammenschließen*. See Introduction, p. xxvii. Here, and in the following lines, Hegel uses various cognates of *schließen*.

32. (§ 206 A) *Beschließen* and *sich entschließen* (v.i.) both mean "to decide", but the two German expressions allow Hegel to distinguish between the two aspects of decision-making.

33. (§ 214 R) This is a deliberate echo of Kant's famous criticism of the Ontological Argument (*CPR* B, 631). See also § 51 and Remark.

34. (§ 216 A) See *Generation of Animals* 1.19.726b24.

35. (§ 218 A) This triad goes back to von Haller (and perhaps further). But it was a lecture of C. F. Kielmeyer in 1793 that focused the attention of the Romantic philosophers of nature upon it. See especially Schelling's treatise *On the World-Soul, Werke*, 2:503–69. In chap. 5 of the *Phenomenology* Hegel criticises the attempt to found an *observational* science of the living organism upon it. But he still employs it in his own "speculative" theory.

36. (§ 221) On its "objective" side *Gattung* here means what is ordinarily (but loosely) called "the human species". But spiritually (and also in the technical parlance of biological classification) "humanity" is a genus; and in Hegel's *Logic* it is *"the* Genus".

37. (§ 226 A) See note 8 to § 8 R.

38. (§ 226 A) It must have been some follower of Locke who fathered the tabula rasa off upon Aristotle. (As Hegel argued in § 8 R, it is a complete misinterpretation of the primacy of sense-experience in Aristotle's theory of knowledge.)

39. (§ 227) Both this and the synthetic method (§ 228–31) are explained much more fully in the *Science of Logic*, Miller, 786–818.

40. (§ 227 A) See above § 38 A; but also compare Haldane and Simson, 3:298–300.

41. (§ 229 A) See note 36 above.

42. (§ 229 A) The difficulty is that a properly speculative *definition* (e.g., the definition of substance as "cause of itself") is a contradiction. Schelling's most noteworthy imitation of the Spinozist method was the "Darstellung meines Systems," *Werke*, 4:104–212.

43. (§ 230 A) Hegel committed himself to this view of the classification of animals already in the *Phenomenology* (Miller, § 246). In his Berlin lectures on *Philosophy of Nature* he cites Cuvier in support of it (*Encyclopaedia*, § 370 A; Petry, 3:182). But his knowledge of Cuvier's work (1812) was necessarily later. In 1807 he was depending on Aristotle, Linnaeus, and Blumenbach.

44. (§ 230 A) *CJ*, § 9 (note). The logical explanation for fourfold division in Nature, and triadic division in Spirit, seems to be a lineal descendant of the "square" of Nature and "triangle" of Spirit in the Disputation Theses of 1800 (Thesis III, *Erste Druckschriften*, ed. Lasson, 404; trans. N. Waszek in ed. D. Lamb, *Hegel and Modern Philosophy*, 253–55).

45. (§ 231 R) For examples, see the *Science of Logic*, Miller, 815–16. Hegel also says there that Spinoza's model of "mathematical method" was "exploded by Kant and Jacobi."

46. (§ 231 R) See *Prolegomena*, §§ 4 and 7; and *CPR* B, 741. The "construction of concepts in intellectual intuition" became Schelling's official method. The "misuse" of it is mainly to be attributed to his "formalist" associates and students. Compare *Phenomenology*, Preface, Miller, §§ 50–53, and note 2 to the 1817 Preface above. But we find the method itself under attack already at the (fragmentary) beginning of the *Jena Logic*; Burbidge and Di Giovanni, 5–8.

47. (§ 232 A) See note 38 above; and note 8 to § 8 R.

48. (§ 234) See note 20 to § 94.

49. (§ 234 A) For the "contradictions" in which moral reflection goes round and round (*herumtreibt*), see further the sections of the *Phenomenology* titled "The Moral World-view" and "Dissemblance," Miller, §§ 599–631.

50. (§ 236 A) What Aristotle actually defines as *noēsis noēseōs* is God's own *noēsis*. See *Metaphysics Lambda* 9.1074b33. Hegel quotes the passage itself at the end of the *Encyclopaedia*. Hegel, on the other hand, is clearly claiming that *our* thinking has at this stage become "divine."

51. (§ 238) For a much more detailed account of the moments of the speculative method see *Science of Logic*, Lasson, 2:485ff; Miller, 825ff.

52. (§ 239 note b) *für eines*. See *Science of Logic*, Lasson, 1:149ff; Miller, 159ff. "To be for one" expresses the return of *Dasein* within the being-for-itself, or how, in its unity with the infinite, the finite is something-ideal (*Ideelles*). It is the relationship (*Verhalten*) of what is ideal to itself as ideal. Here, in § 239, this term serves to remind us of the ideal nature of all distinct terms that are produced by the progression of the Concept. All of them, even the beginning itself, are posited and mediated and not something that simply and immediately is. See the following addition.

GLOSSARY

German term	English translation	Related terms
Absicht	intention, aim	Ziel
abgesondert	separate(ly)	trennen
Abhängigkeit	dependence	Unselbständigkeit
Abwechslung	alternation	Wechsel
Affirmation	affirmation	Behauptung, Versicherung
allgemein	universal, general(ly)	
Allgemeine (das)	the universal, what is universal	
Allgemeinheit[1]	universality	
Allgemeinheiten	generalities	
Allheit[31]	allness	Inbegriff
an ihm selbst[2]	in itself, in its own right	= an sich (selbst)
an sich[2]	in-itself, implicitly	für sich
an sich (selbst)[2]	in itself, on its own part	= an ihm selbst
an und für sich[2]	in and for itself	
andere	other, else	
Andere (das)	the other	
Anderes (ein)	an other	
Anderes	another	
Anderssein	otherness	
Änderung	alteration, change	Veränderung
anerkennen	recognise	erkennen
Anerkenntnis	recognition	
Anerkennung	recognition	
Angabe	specification	Spezifikation
angemessen	adequate, appropriate	
Anlage	talent, disposition, aptitude	Gesinnung, Talent
anschauen	intuit	
Anschauung	intuition	
Ansich (das)[2]	the In-itself	
Ansichsein[2]	being-in-itself	Fürsichsein
Ansicht	view, perspective	Betrachtung
Anstoß	shock	
Antithese[17]	anti-thesis	Gegensatz
Anundfürsichsein[2]	being-in-and-for-itself	
Anzahl	annumeration, annumerator	
Arbeit	labour	
Art	kind, species, type	Gattung
auffassen	interpret, apprehend, grasp	fassen, erfassen
Auffassen (das)	interpreting, apprehending	
Auffassung	interpretation	
Auffassungweise	approach	
aufheben[3]	sublate	
Aufheben (das)[3]	the sublating	
Aufhebung[3]	sublation	

336

Aufstellung	setting-up	
aufzeigen	exhibit, show, expound, point out	
Ausbreitung	expansion	Breite
äußere	outer, outward, external	äußerlich
Äußere (das)	what is outward	
außereinander	mutually external	
Außereinander (das)	mutual externality	
äußerlich	external	äußere
Äußerlichkeit	externality, outwardness	
äußern (sich)	manifest (oneself) outwardly	
Außersichsein	self-externality	
Äußerung[4]	utterance, manifestation	Entäußerung
Band	bond	Verbindung
Bedeutung	significance, meaning, sense	Sinn
bedingen	condition	
Bedingung	condition	
Befriedigung	satisfaction, contentment	Zufriedenheit
Beglaubigung	attestation, authentication	Bewährung
begreifen[5]	comprehend	
begrenzen	limit	beschränken
Begriff[5]	concept	Vorstellung
begrifflos	conceptless, without concept, that lacks the concept	
Begründung	grounding	Berechtigung
behaupten	assert, claim, maintain	
Behauptung	assertion, claim	Affirmation, Versicherung
bei sich (sein)	(being) at home with oneself	
Bei-sich-sein (das)	being-with-oneself	
bekannt	familiar, well-known	vertraut
Bekanntschaft	familiarity, acquaintance	
Berechtigung	justification, qualification	Begründung, Rechtfertigung
Beruf	calling, profession	Bestimmung
Beschaffenheit[6]	constitution, way of being constituted, character	
beschränken	restrict	begrenzen
Beschränktheit	restrictedness	
Beschränkung	the restricting	
besondere	particular	
Besondere (das)	the particular	
Besonderheit	particularity	
Besonderung	particularisation	
Bestand	subsistence	
bestehen	subsist	
bestehen aus	consist of	
bestimmen	determine	
bestimmt	determinate, definite, precise	
Bestimmtheit[7]	determinacy	
Bestimmtsein	determinateness, determination	
Bestimmung[7]	determination, vocation	Definition, Beruf, Schicksal

betätigen (sich)	actively	
betätigend (sich)	self-actuating	
Betätigung	activation, activity, exercise	Handlung, Tätigkeit, Tun, Übung, Wirken
betrachten	regard, consider	
Betrachtung	view, examination	Ansicht
bewähren (sich)[8]	validate (itself)	sich erweisen
Bewährung[8]	validation	Beweis, Beglaubigung
beweisen	prove	
Beweis	proof, demonstration	Bewährung
Beweisen (das)	process of proof	
Bewußtsein	consciousness, mind	
Bewußtwerden	become conscious/aware of	
Beziehung[9]	relation, reference	Verhältnis
Bezogenheit	relatedness	
Bildung	education, training, culture	gebildet
Boden	soil, basis, domain, field	Grund, Grundlage
darstellen	present, display	
Darstellung	presentation, account	
Dasein[10]	being-there, thereness, what is there, way of being	Existenz
Daseiendes	that which is there	
Definition	definition	Bestimmung
Denkbestimmung[11]	thought-determination, determination of thought	Gedankenbestimmung, Kategorie
denken[12]	think	
Denken (das)	thinking, thought	Gedanke
Dialektik[13]	dialectic	
das Dialektische	the dialectical	
different	differentiated	
Differenz[14]	difference	Unterschied
Differentiierung	differentiation	
Ding[15]	thing	Sache
Diremption	sundering	Entzweiung
dirimieren	sunder	
Eigenschaft	property, feature, attribute (of God)	
eigentlich	proper, in the proper sense, authentic(ally)	
eigentümlich	peculiar	
Eigentümlichkeit	peculiarity	Partikularität
ein (Allgemeines)	something-(universal)	
Einfälle	inventions, brain waves	
eingebildet	imaginary	Phantasie
Einheit	unity, unit	[See pp. xxxviii–l.]
Einigkeit	union, harmonious unity	
Einteilung	division	
einzelne[16]	singular, single	
Einzelne (das)	the singular, single instance, singular being	Individuum
Einzelnen	single instances, single bits	
Eizelnheit[16]	singularity	
Einzelnheiten	single instances	

empfinden	feel, sense	
Empfindung	sensation, sense-experience, feeling	Gefühl
End	end	Zweck, Ziel
Endzweck	final purpose	
entäußern (sich)[4]	divest oneself	
Entäußerung[4]	uttering, self-emptying (of God)	Äußerung, Entfremdung
entfalten (sich)	unfold (itself)	
Entfalten (das)	the unfolding	
Entfremdung[4]	alienation	fremd, Entäußerung
entgegensetzen	oppose	
entgegengesetzt	opposite	
Entgegensetzung[17]	opposition	Gegensatz
Entwicklung	development	
Entzweiung	splitting in two, schism	Diremption
erfassen	apprehend, grasp, capture	fassen, auffassen
ergeben (sich)	follow from/as the result of, emerge, surrender	
erheben (sich)	raise, elevate (oneself)	
Erhebung	elevation	
erinnern (sich)[18]	recollect, be mindful of, remember	
Erinnerung	recollection, reminiscence	Gedächtnis
erkennen[19]	[re]cognise, have cognizance of, be(come) cognizant of	kennen, wissen
Erkennen (ein)	a process of cognition	
Erkenntnis	cognition	
Erörterung	explanation, discussion	
erscheinen[20]	appear	scheinen
Erscheinen (das)	the appearing	
Erscheinung[20]	appearance, phenomenon	Schein, Phänomen
erweisen (sich)	show itself, prove itself	sich bewähren
Etwas[15]	something	
Existenz[10]	existence	Dasein
Explication	explication	
Faktum[21]	*factum*	Tatsache
fassen	grasp, apprehend	erfassen, auffassen
Figur	figure	Gestalt
Form	form	
formal[22]	formal [*formal*]	
formell[22]	formal(ly), in a formal way	
Formelle (das)	the formal aspect, what is formal	
förmlich	formalistic	
Fortbestimmung	process of further determination	
Fortgang	advance, progression, course	Progress, Verlauf
Fortgehen (das)	progression	
Fortschreiten (das)	advancing	
Frage	question, quest	
fremd[4]	alien	Entfremdung
für eines	for one	

für sich	for-itself, explicit	an sich
Fürsichsein	by itself, on its own account	= an sich (selbst)
	being-for-itself	
Gang	journey, path, procedure	Verfahren, Verlauf
Ganze (das)	the whole	
Gattung	genus, kind	Art
Gebilde	[symbolic] pattern	Gestaltung
gebildet	cultivated	
Gedächtnis	memory	Erinnerung
Gedanke	thought	Denken (das)
Gedankenbestimmung[11]	determination of thought,	Denkbestimmung
	thought-determination	
gedankenlos	unthinking, thoughtless,	
	mindless	
Gedankenlosigkeit	absence of thought,	
	unthinking (mind)	
Gefühl	feeling	Empfindung
Gegensatz	antithesis	Antithesis,
		Entgegensetzung
Gegenstand[23]	ob-ject, subject matter, topic	Objekt
gegenständlich	ob-jective, of ob-jects	objektiv
Gegenteil	opposite, contrary,	entgegengesetzt
	counterpart	
Gehalt[24]	import, basic import	Inhalt
Geist[25]	spirit, mind	Gemüt
gemäß	conform, in accordance with	
Gemeinschaftlichkeit	communality	
gemeint[33]	meant	meinen
Gemüt[26]	mind (and heart)	Geist
Gesetztsein	positedness	
Gesinnung	disposition	Anlage
Gestalt	shape	Figur
Gestaltung	formation, configuration	Gebilde
Getrenntsein	separateness	trennen
Gewalt	power, violence	Macht
Glaube	faith, belief	
gleich	equal	
gleichgültig	indifferent	
Gleichgültige (das)	what is indifferent	
Gleichgültigkeit[27]	indifference	Indifferenz
Gleichheit	equality	[Cf. p. xliv.]
G. mit sich selbst	self-equivalence	
Glückseligkeit	happiness	Seligkeit
Grenze[28]	limit	Schranke
Grund	ground, reason, basis	Boden, Grundlage
Grundbestimmung	basic determination	
Grundlage	foundation, basis	Boden, Grund
Grundsatz	principle	Prinzip
Handlung	action	Betätigung,
		Tätigkeit, Tun
herabsetzen	reduce, degrade	zurückführen
herauskommen	come forth, result	
heraussetzen	set forth	

heraustreten	step out of, move out of	
herkommen	emerge	
hervorbringen	produce	
hervorgehen	emerge, go forth, issue from	
Hinausgehen (das)	progression from	
hinausschicken	project (beyond itself)	
hinausschreiten	transcend, go beyond	
hinaustreten in	emerge into	
Historie	descriptive collection	
historisch	historical, descriptive(ly), informative	
Idee[29]	idea	
Idealität[29]	ideality	
ideell[29]	ideal	
in sich[30]	inward(ly), within itself, into itself	
inadäquat	inadequate	unangemessen
Inbegriff[31]	essential sum, comprehensive sum, sum total	Allheit, Zusammenfassung
indifferent	undifferentiated	gleichgültig
Indifferenz[27]	Indifference	Gleichgültigkeit
Individuum	individual	Einzelne (das)
Inhalt	content	Gehalt
innere	inner, inward	innerlich
Innere (das)	what is inner/inward, inwardness, the inner side	
innerlich	internal	inner
Innerlichkeit	inwardness, what is inward	
Innerste (das)	what is innermost, the inmost heart	
Insichgehen (das)	going-into-itself	
insichseiend[30]	self-contained, that is within-itself	
Insichsein (das)[30]	being-within-self, self-containment	
Intelligenz	intelligence	Vernunft, Verstand
Interesse	interest, concern, point	
Irrtum	error	Täuschung
Isolierung	isolation	Vereinzelung
Kategorie[11]	category	Denkbestimmung
kennen[19]	to be aware of	erkennen, wissen
kennenlernen	to become acquainted with	
Kenntnis	awareness, acquaintance	
Kenntnisse	information, learning	
Kraft	force	
Kriterium	criterion	Maßstab
Leben	life	
Lebendiges (ein)	a living being	
Lebendigkeit	vitality, organism	
Lehrsatz	thesis, theorem	Satz
Logik (die)[32]	the Logic, logic	
Logische (das)[32]	the logical, logical thinking	

Macht	might, power	Gewalt
Mangel	defect, want	
mannigfaltig	manifold	
Mannigfaltigkeit	manifoldness, diversity, multiplicity	Verschiedenheit
Maßstab	standard, criterion	Kriterium
Material	material	Stoff
Materie	matter	Sache
meinen[33]	mean	gemeint
Meinung[33]	opinion	
Menschenverstand	common sense	Verstand
Merkmal	characteristic	
Moralität	morality	Sittlichkeit
nachdenken	think (it) over, think about (things)	
Nachdenken (das)[34]	the thinking-over, [reflective] thinking, meditation	Reflexion
Nacheinander (das)	succession	
näher	more precise(ly), more articulate	
nebeneinander	side by side, juxtaposed	
Nichts[35]	nothing	
Objekt[23]	object	Gegenstand
objektiv	objective	
Objektivität	objectivity	
partikulär	particular [partikulär]	
Partikularität	peculiarity, particularity [partikuläritat]	Besonderheit, Eigentümlichkeit
Phantasie	imagination	eingebildet
Phänomen	phenomenon	Erscheinung
Prinzip	principle	Grundsatz
Progress	progress, progression	Fortgang
Prozess	process	
prozesslos	lacking all process, without process	
Räsonnement	abstract argumentation	
räsonnieren	argue (abstractly)	
real[36]	real [real]	reell
Realität[36]	reality	Wirklichkeit
Rechtfertigung	justification, legitimation	Berechtigung
reell[36]	real	real
Reflexion[34]	reflection	Nachdenken, Widerschein
R. in sich	inward reflection	in sich
R. in sich selbst	inward self-reflection	
relativ	relational, relative(ly)	
Relativität	relationality, relativity, relative character	
Sache[15]	matter, matter [itself], thing in question, thing [Sache]	Ding, Materie

sachlich	simply factual	
Satz	proposition, statement, thesis	Lehrsatz
scheiden	divide, separate (out)	trennen, teilen
Scheidung	division, separation, severance	Einteilung, Trennung
Schein[20]	shine, semblance	Erscheinung
Scheinbarkeit	apparent character	
scheinen[20]	shine, seem	
Scheinen (das)	shining	
Schicksal	destiny, fate	Bestimmung
schlecht	bad, spurious (infinity), wrongly	
schließen[37]	conclude	zusammenschließen
Schließen (das)	syllogistic reasoning	
Schluß[37]	syllogism	
Schranke[28]	restriction	Grenze
seiend sind[38]	[simply] are	
Seiende (das)[38]	what *is*	
sein[38]	to be	
Sein (das)[38]	being	
selbständig	independent, self-standing	
Selbständige (das)	what is independent	
Seligkeit	blessedness	Glückseligkeit, Unseligkeit
setzen[39]	posit	
Setzen (das)	the positing	
Singularität	singularity	Einzelnheit
Sinn	sense, meaning, mind	Bedeutung
sinnlich	sensible, sensory	
Sinnlichkeit	sensibility	
sittlich	ethical	
Sittlichkeit	ethical life	Moralität
sollen[40]	ought, to have to be, to be supposed	
Spekulation[41]	speculation	
das Spekulative[41]	the speculative	
Spezifikationen	specifications	Angabe
Stoff	stuff, material	Material
Stoffe	stuffs	
Talent	talent	Anlage
Tat	act	
tätig	active	
Tätigkeit	activity	Betätigung, Tun
Tatsache[21]	fact	Faktum
Täuschung	illusion, deception, mistake	Irrtum
Teil	part	
teilbar	divisible	
Teilen	divide	scheiden, trennen
trennbar	separable	
trennen	separate, sever	scheiden, teilen
Trennung	separation, severance	
Trieb	drive, impulse	

Tun (das)	the doing, agency, the deed	Betätigung, Handlung, Tätigkeit
Übergang	passage (into), transition	
übergehen	pass over (into)	
Übergehen (das)	the passing-over (into)	
übergehend	in passage, transient	vorübergehend
übergreifen[42]	overgrasp	
überschreiten	overstep, exceed	
Übung	exercise	Betätigung
Umschlag	overturn	
umschlagen	overturn, turn over	
Umschlagen (das)	the overturning	
Umstände	circumstances	Verhältnisse
umstürzen	overturn, overthrow	
unangemessen	inadequate, incongruous	inadäquat
Unangemessenheit	lack of proportion	
unendlich	infinite	
Unendlichkeit	infinity	
ungetrennt	not separate	
Ungetrenntheit	unseparatedness	
unselbständig	dependent, not independent, not self-standing	
Unselbständigkeit	dependency	
Unseligkeit	damnation	Seligkeit, Verdammung
unterscheiden	distinguish	
Unterscheiden (das)	the distinguishing	
Unterscheidung	the distinguishing	
Unterschied[14]	distinction, distinctness	Differenz
unterschieden	distinct	different, verschieden
Unterschiedenheit	distinctness	Verschiedenheit
Unterschiedensein	distinctness	
Untrennbarkeit	inseparability	
unverständlich	unintelligible	
Ursache	cause	
veränderlich	alterable	
Veränderlichkeit	alterability	
Veränderung	alteration, change	Änderung, Wechsel
verändern	alter, change	verwandeln
verbinden	link, bound up, connect	verknüpfen, zusammenfassen
Verbindung	bond, association, combination	Band, Verknüpfung, Zusammenhang
Verdammung	anathema, damnation	Unseligkeit
vereinzeln	isolate	
vereinzelt	in isolation	
Vereinzelung	isolation	Isolierung
Verfahren (das)	procedure	Gang
Verhältnis[9]	relationship, ratio, perspective, situation	Beziehung
Verhältnisse	situations, circumstances	Umstände
verhalten (sich)	behave, conduct (oneself), relate	

German	English	
Verhalten (das)	attitude, conduct, behaviour	
verkehrt	inverted	
verknüpfen	connect, combine, link	verbinden, zussammenfassen
Verknüpfung	connection, combination, linkage	Verbindung, Band, Zusammenhang
Verlauf	course, journey	Gang
Vermögen	faculty	
Vernunft[43]	reason	Verstand
vernünftig[43]	rational	verständig
verschieden	diverse, various	different, unterschieden
v. sein von	diverge from	
Verschiedenheit[14]	Diversity	Mannigfaltigkeit, Unterschiedenheit
verschwinden	vanish, disappear	
Versicherung	assurance, declaration	Behauptung
Verstand[43]	understanding	Vernunft, Intelligenz
verständig[43]	that belongs to the understanding	vernünftig
verständlich	intelligible	
vertraut	familiar	bekannt
verwandeln	transform	verändern
Verwechslung	confusion	Verwirrung
Verwirrung	confusion	Verwechslung
Voraussetzung	presupposition, assumption	
Vorbegriff	preliminary conception	
vorhanden (sein)	(to be) present/given/before us	
vorstellen[5]	represent, imagine	
Vorstellung[5]	representation, notion, representational thinking, representational consciousness	Begriff
vorübergehen	pass away	übergehen
vorübergehend	passing away, transient	übergehend
Vorurteil	prejudice, assumption	
wahr	true	
Wahre (das)	what is true	
wahrhaft	genuine(ly), truly	
Wahrheit	truth	
Wechsel	exchange, variation	Abwechslung, Änderung, Veränderung
Wechselwirkung	reciprocal action	
Wert	value, worth	
Wesen[44]	essence	
Wesenheit	essentiality	Wesentlichkeit
wesentlich	essential	
Wesentlichkeit	essentiality	Wesenheit
Widerschein	reflexion	Reflexion
Widerspruch	contradiction	
Willkür	freedom of choice, arbitrariness, caprice, whim, arbitrary choice	
willkürlich	arbitrary	
Wirken (das)	effective action	Betätigung

wirklich[36] [43]	actual, effectively	
Wirklichkeit[36]	actuality	
Wirksamkeit	influence	
Wirkung	effect, operation	
wissen[19]	know	erkennen, kennen
Wissen (das)	the knowing, knowledge	
Wissenschaft	science	
Ziel	goal, aim, fulfillment	End, Zweck
zufällig	contingent, random, chance	
Zufälligkeit	contingency	
Zufall	chance	
Zufriedenheit	satisfaction	Befriedigung
zurückführen	trace back to, lead back into	herabsetzen
zusammenfallen	collapse, coincide	
zusammenfassen	combine	verbinden, verknüpfen
Zusammenfassen (das)	combination	Verknüpfung
Zusammenfassung	comprehensive whole	Inbegriff
zusammengehen	go together	
Zusammenhalt	cohesion	
Zusammenhang	connectedness, coherence	Verknüpfung
zusammenhangen	to (be) connect(ed) with, belong together	
zusammenschließen[37]	con-clude	schließen
Zweck	purpose	End, Ziel
zweckmaßig	purposive, purposeful	

NOTES TO THE GLOSSARY

1. *Allgemeinheit.* For Hegel, genuine universality is "concrete"; i.e., it represents the inward articulation of the Concept (*Begriff*) in its dialectical development. This universality is not just what individuals have in common, nor is it their exhaustive collection. Ultimately, or in its full development, the universal is the rational itself, and it can be thought only speculatively. As a logical category, universality is "abstract" if it fails to develop into particularity and singularity. The universality of a species with regard to the individuals that are subsumed under it is an abstract universality, established by the understanding.

2. *An sich* most often means that which is as yet (onto-)logically undeveloped, or implicit. Used in opposition to "posited" (*gesetzt*), it expresses the lack of mediation (or of the recognition of mediation). This is how it is typically opposed to *für sich. An sich* can also be the equivalent of *an ihm (selbst)*; it then expresses what something is (or does) in its own right without foreign intervention. In the first two cases we use "in-itself", in the third case "in itself", "in its own self" (§§ 118, 119) or "in its own right" (§ 105); and exceptionally "inner" (§ 117 A) or "spontaneously" (§ 239).

The composite *Ansichsein* is translated by "being-in-itself". Here, as elsewhere, hyphens are used to hold a German composite together visibly in English. In the Kantian perspective, *das Ansich* means the true being or nature of things. For Hegel, to stop at the mere *Ansich* means to grasp things not in their truth, but in the form of mere abstraction, i.e., in their still undeveloped state.

Für sich, as opposed to *an sich,* means what is, or rather has become "posited" (*gesezt*), or explicit, what has reached a stage of (at least relative) development. Often an element of (self-)consciousness is present. But *für sich* also expresses a certain sufficiency. Both senses can be expressed by "for-itself"; but sometimes "explicit" is preferred to convey the first meaning, "on its own account" or "by itself" to convey the second. In this last case *für sich* becomes almost identical with *an ihm selbst* and with *an und für sich* in the nonlogical, colloquial sense.

An und für sich, when used in conjunction with *an sich* and *für sich,* means a fully developed and explicit return into itself from the stage of the (supposed) self-sufficiency of distinct and even opposite terms. It expresses the complete (but irreducibly processual) self-comprehension (and being) of the Concept, of Spirit, and of the Idea. *An und für sich (selbst)* can also be used in a more colloquial (and opposite) sense, meaning "taken abstractly", or "on its own and by its own nature". (See § 88 A.) Since the choice here is a matter of interpretation, we have translated it everywhere by "in and for itself".

3. *Aufhebung.* See Hegel's own explanation in § 96 A and in the *Science of Logic,* trans. Miller, 106–107; see also the Introductions, pp. xxxi–xxxii, xlvi–xlvii.

4. *Äußerung* means manifestation, expression, utterance, saying. In the *Logic* it is used mostly in connection with *Kraft* ("force"). We translate "utterance", because this word preserves the etymological link between "utter", "outer", *äußere.*

Entäußerung means divestiture, renunciation, and, in juridical contexts, alienation. The latter word has to be reserved for translating *Entfremdung* (*fremd* = "alien"). Used in a religious context, *Entäußerung* and *sich entäußern* recall the biblical term *kenosis* which is used for the self-humbling of God in his incarnation as a man. Literally it means the emptying-out of oneself. Motion into outwardness and rendering oneself vulnerable are components of the meaning. Where the expressive movement as such prevails, we use "uttering" (§ 117), but in a religious context we translate by "self-emptying" (Hegel's note on p. 16).

347

5. *Begriff* means the logical subject itself, logical thinking as it develops through its entire movement of self-comprehension. The word "concept" is used because of its etymological link with "comprehend"—*begreifen*. Far from being the static, neatly circumscribed thought-content which we call a "definition", the Concept is the movement of comprehension itself. Where it is used in the absolute, and singularised, we write "the Concept"; where we have the plural or a particular instance, we do not use the initial capital.

Vorstellung means what is represented, pointed out, laid before (*vor*) us. *Sich vorstellen* is to picture something to oneself or to imagine it. It is the thinking of ordinary life. We translate it by "representation" or "notion". The latter word has been used, quite inappropriately, for *Begriff*. It means a general, vague, or imperfect idea of something, an opinion or subjective view. All this is often expressed by *Vorstellung*, never by *Begriff*.

Locke's "way of ideas"—and all of the "common sense" philosophising that was founded upon it—was (and is) a deliberate effort to interpret *Begriffe* in terms of *Vorstellungen*. For Hegel, philosophy consists in replacing *Vorstellungen* with *Begriffe*, without leaving the first simply behind. See also pp. lxi–lxii.

6. *Beschaffenheit* means the state or condition of a thing, its quality, its disposition or nature, but also the constitution—of a body, for example. It expresses the fact of being determined, not just in-itself, but also outwardly. Nevertheless, this outward determination is itself a part of a thing's own, immanent determination. The word "constitution" best expresses this complex notion.

7. *Bestimmtheit* is a state of being determined or fixed by the process of *Bestimmung*. Translators have usually used "determinate*ness*" for this; but "determinacy", which was designated "rare" in the *New English Dictionary*, is less cumbrous and more natural. We believe that, thanks largely to the rising fortunes of "indeterminacy", it now stands a fair chance of entering the language of philosophy and science.

Bestimmung means decision, appointment, definition, but also prescription, destination, and vocation. It is a more "dynamic" term than *Bestimmtheit*. "Determination" renders this active sense well. The entire Logic is one movement of self-determination. In the Philosophy of Spirit, it often refers to the human (rational) "vocation"; so in those contexts we translate accordingly.

8. *Bewähren* means to confirm, aver, verify, substantiate; *sich bewähren* means to prove true, to hold good. We could have translated it by "verify" and "verification" to preserve the link with *wahr*—"true" (*verum*). But *Bewährung* has little to do with verification in the ordinary sense (for instance, in the empirical sciences). "Validation" and "validate" better express the meaning of the German term which includes the ontological reference to nature and spirit.

9. *Beziehung, Verhältnis*. See the Introduction, p. xix.

10. *Dasein* often expresses the mere presence of a (finite) being. But in its most primitive logical sense, it is "determinacy" itself in all its generality or indeterminate variety. We translate it by "being-there". See further the Introductions, pp. xx–xxi, xxxvi–xxxviii.

Existenz is essential being, or essence as appearing in immediacy. It is the first (and least articulate) return of being within essence. It is here that we have to use the word "existence". See also the Introduction, pp. xx, xxxviii.

11. *Denkbestimmung* means a determination of thought; Hegel also uses *Gedankenbestimmung* for it. Especially in the *Logic* these terms stand for what we (and sometimes Hegel himself) call "the categories", i.e., those meanings that have become thoroughly independent of any particular form of reality. When these properly logical universals are meant, we speak of "the thought-determinations", just as we do of "the categories" (*Kategorien*). Every moment in the *Logic* is a *Bestimmung* of pure thought; so there are more "categories" in Hegel's *Logic* than there are in the familiar lists of Aristotle and Kant.

12. *Denken* means "thinking" in the ordinary discursive sense, too. But for Hegel it refers to that which makes all human activity properly human: the production of meaning, the "making sense" that pervades even perception, feeling, willing, etc. Genuinely philosophical, i.e., speculative, thinking is the thinking that comprehends all production of meaning *as such*. Precisely *this* universality is its peculiarity. Philosophical thinking is that form of thinking which comprehends the articulation of thinking in all its forms, including philosophy (see § 2). Thinking is "logical" inasmuch as it develops those meanings that are independent of any particular form of reality within one coherent movement of self-articulation.

13. *Dialektik, das Dialektische.* Although *Dialektik* sometimes stands for the entire movement of the self-articulation of meaning or thought, this term refers more specifically to the self-negation of the determinations of the understanding (*Verstand*), when they are thought through in their fixedness and opposition. This is "the dialectical" as the very principle of all movement, life, and cognition. (See in particular § 81, including R and A.)

14. *Differenz, Unterschied, Verschiedenheit.* See the Introductions, pp. xxiii–xxiv, xliv–xlvi.

15. *Ding, Etwas, Sache. Etwas* means a determinate and finite thought-content, "something" in general, not some "thing"; it is the opposite of the "other" in the dialectic of "Quality" (or "suchness").

Ding and *Sache* are more developed thought-determinations. *Ding* is the logical equivalent of what we call a "thing" when we are speaking of the objects in our physical environment. *Sache* involves the presupposition of conditions and activities necessary to the solution of a theoretical problem or the pursuit of a practical "cause" (see § 148); most often it is a content of meaning (which may be that of a "thing") that is recognised as such. We have generally translated *Ding* with "thing" and *Sache* with "matter". See further our remarks in the Introduction, pp. xxiv–xxv.

16. *Einzelne, Einzelnheit.* See the Introduction, pp. xix–xx.

17. *Entgegensetzung* is to be distinguished from *Gegensatz*; it is a more developed and more dynamic category (see § 119). "Opposition" is the best translation (cf. *setzen* = "to posit"). For *Gegensatz* "antithesis" is available, provided we do not interpret this term as indicating the "anti-thesis" in the Fichtean sense of the negation of the "thesis". *Antithese* in the latter sense is translated by "anti-thesis". Hegel's table of oppositions closes with *Widerspruch*, or "contradiction", as its supreme form.

18. *Erinnern* means to remind or call to mind. *Sich erinnern* means to remember. Both *erinnern* and *Erinnerung* retain in Hegel's use of them a link with their root *inner* ("inner"); it is the gathering up and recollecting of the preceding stages of a movement. "Recollect" conveys this meaning best, with a few exceptions.

19. *Erkennen, kennen, wissen,* and cognates. See the Introductions, pp. xxi–xxii, xl–lii.

20. *Erscheinen, scheinen, Erscheinung, Schein.* See the Introduction, pp. xxv–xxvi.

21. *Faktum* is to be distinguished from *Tatsache*; the latter means "fact" in the ordinary sense of the word. *Faktum* stands for a content of experience which, though it is given as already expressed, is open to further interpretation.

22. *Formal, formell. Formell* is mostly a negative term: It expresses the absence of content. Often this is made explicit by the use of the expression "merely formal". *Formal* expresses rather the presence of a form; but it also tends to get the negative connotation of "being taken separately and abstractly" (§ 19 R). These two terms are sometimes used interchangeably (the *Science of Logic* speaks of "der formale mechanische Prozeß", but already the first edition of the *Encyclopaedia* uses the term "formeller Mechanismus"). In our text *formal* occurs much less frequently. We translate *formell* by "formal", and while we use the same term for *formal* we add the German in a footnote. See also pp. xlii–xliii.

23. *Gegenstand, Objekt.* See the Introductions, pp. xxii–xxiii, xliii–xliv.

24. *Gehalt* refers to the constituents or ingredients, but more specifically to the intrinsic value of something; for instance, to the proportion of gold in an alloy (the "grade"). We have translated it by "import" or "basic import" in the sense of "meaning (content)". *Inhalt* is, of course, translated simply as "content". See also p. xliv.

25. *Geist; Subjekt, Subjektivität; Bewußtsein, Selbstbewußtsein. Geist* is the word, the notion, and the concept that constitute the highest definition of the Absolute. As finite or human, spirit is distinct from nature, but in the fullness of its meaning, spirit overgrasps nature. This does not mean that only thought or mind (in the ordinary sense) exists, but rather that Hegel conceives the Absolute as being essentially what we might call "the universe of meaning". "Spirit" expresses this universe as self-articulating, as in that sense "subjective". "Subjectivity" here transcends its correlativity with regard to "objectivity". It overgrasps objectivity; it is not relative, but it remains (inwardly) relational.

"Spirit" refers primarily to the interlocutive and interpersonal relation that underlies and activates all community. It names the concrete subject of the production of meaning, a production in which we all participate, but which none of us can claim for oneself. Ultimately, however, the process of the articulation of meaning has no other subject but meaning itself: In that sense "spirit" is nothing but the Idea "as being for-itself and coming to be in and for itself" (§ 18 R).

Bewußtsein or "consciousness" is how spirit appears: as initially a thinking subject facing a world of ob-jects. It is spirit only in-itself or implicitly. The *Phenomenology of Spirit* is the science of the experience of consciousness through which it becomes spirit conscious of itself as spirit. Self-consciousness is spirit for itself. But the result of the experience of consciousness is not just consciousness of the individual self, or of the communal self, but in and through both it is the knowledge of spirit as the ultimate Self, as the Idea itself.

26. *Gemüt* means feeling, heart (as in "good-hearted"), but also disposition and turn of mind. We translate it by "mind and heart", except where one of these words already occurs. Hegel probably took over this usage from Schiller, who used *Gemüt* to designate the integrity or "wholeness" of the human personality.

27. *Gleichgültigkeit, Indifferenz.* See the Introductions, pp. xxiv, xlv–xlvi.

28. *Grenze, Schranke. Grenze* is best translated by "limit", and *begrenzt* by "limited". *Beschränken* is stronger than *begrenzen*; "to restrict" best renders this aspect. In its relation to the "ought" (*sollen*) of its transgression, "limit" (*Grenze*) becomes "restriction" (*Schranke*).

29. *Idee, ideell, Idealität, Idealismus. Idee* is Hegel's term for the Absolute inasmuch as it is the total process of the self-articulation of meaning and of what is meaningful. We translate it as "the Idea". Where it is used in the plural or as particularised ("the idea of . . . "), we drop the initial capital. But everywhere the *Idee* is the *Begriff* as realised, or as being realised. See the *Science of Logic,* Miller, 755ff. What is recognised as a moment in the *Idee* is called *ideell*; and *Idealität* belongs to what is *ideell*. "Ideality" is the truth of what is finite, of reality; and the recognition of this ideality is "Idealism" in Hegel's sense. See § 95 R.

30. *In sich* can mean either "within itself" or "into itself". Where the choice between them is clear from the context we have used the one or the other expression. But it is often possible to interpret *Reflexion in sich* in both ways, with the reader having to decide which of the two is preferable. For this reason we quite often use "inward reflection", preserving the ambiguity of the German.

Insichseiend, Insichsein. The adjective is translated by "self-contained", the noun by "self-containment", or "being-within-self". In the dialectic of "Quality" it is the opposite of "being-for-other".

31. *Inbegriff, Allheit. Inbegriff* means more than just the sum of a multitude of things (or properties, attributes). It is not just an aggregate, but rather the comprehensive whole of an internally related network (like "the press", *das Zeitungswesen*, or "the taxation system", *das Steuerwesen*). We translate it with "essential sum", "comprehensive sum", "sum total". "Essential sum" can be said of God as *Inbegriff aller Realitäten*, or *Omnitudo realitatis*, i.e., as the eminent source and "compendium" of what makes everything that exists "real." *Allheit* means the universality of the subject term in universal judgment. Hegel takes this category from Kant's table of judgments and makes it into the first form of the syllogisms of reflection (see *Enc.* § 190). We translate it by "allness".

32. *Logik, das Logische.* We write "the Logic" wherever Hegel refers to his speculative logic, which is identical with metaphysics. Speculative logic is the metaphysics of the *logos* or of "reason." The first part of the *Encyclopaedia* is "the Logic," as distinct from the *Realphilosophie* contained in "the Philosophy of Nature" and "the Philosophy of Spirit." Sometimes *die Logik* refers to "logic" in the traditional sense, and we translate accordingly. *Das Logische* sometimes stands for the subject matter of Hegel's *Logic*, just as *die Natur* is the subject matter of the Philosophy of Nature. But it has also a more explicit and dynamic meaning, best expressed by "logical thinking", which we use together with "the logical".

33. *Meinung* refers either to a personal, subjective opinion, or to the bare intention to signify. Hegel often stresses the etymological link with *mein* ("mine"). Where appropriate, we translate it as "opinion", but sometimes as "what is (only) meant" (*meinen = "to mean"*).

34. *Nachdenken* means to reflect (on something), to think about something, to think it over. But *das Nachdenken* cannot be translated by "reflection", since this term has to be reserved for *Reflexion*. We use "thinking-over" and "to think it over" or "to think about it".

   Reflexion often refers to "reflection" in the ordinary sense of a subjective consideration of some matter or other. But Hegel frequently uses it to express the (inward) articulation of meaning or thought-content, especially in the Doctrine of Essence.

35. *Nichts*, as used by Hegel at the beginning of the *Logic*, does not mean what is "not something". Something is already a determinate being, distinct from something else. As "not something", nothing would itself be determinate. In contrast *Nichts* is to be taken in its totally indeterminate simplicity. "Nothingness" would express this better than "nothing". But Hegel uses the ordinary term *Nichts*; we translate with "nothing" while repeating Hegel's own warning. See the *Science of Logic*, Miller, 83.

36. *Real, reell, Realität; wirklich, Wirklichkeit.* Although Hegel himself says that *das Reelle* and *das Reale* are practically synonymous, and that no interest is served by distinguishing different shades of meaning here (see the *Science of Logic*, Miller, 149), we have included the German term in a footnote wherever "real" stands for *real*.

   As a logical category, *Realität* belongs to the dialectic of "Quality." It is Quality (or "suchness") inasmuch as it is opposed to the negation that is contained in it; it is *Dasein* as (a) determinacy that simply *is* (*seiende Bestimmtheit*). It means "to be such as not other". This most abstract and poor category falls far short of *Wirklichkeit*. The latter expresses the unity of *Wesen* and *Existenz*; its development, as the last part of the Doctrine of Essence, deploys the most important categories of traditional metaphysics. What is *wirklich* is rational in the Hegelian sense, i.e., "meaningful", a worthy expression of the Idea, which is "quite simply effective (*das Wirkende*) and actual (*das Wirkliche*) as well" (§ 142 A). We translate *Wirklichkeit* by "actuality". See also *Dasein* and *Existenz*.

37. *Schließen, Schluß, zusammenschließen.* See the Introductions, pp. xxvii, xlvii.

38. *Sein, das Sein, das Seiende, sind seiend.* In Hegel's *Logic*, the term "being" first refers to "pure being" understood as absolute absence of determinacy, not as the result of a process of

abstraction, but meant to be taken as strictly immediate. But the same term stands, more generally, for the entire first part of the Logic in which "immediacy" is prevalent and the movement from one category to the next is called a "passing-over" (*übergehen*). "To be *seiend*" means to be taken as immediate; we translate *sind seiend* with "[simply] are." (See §§ 80, 84, 89, 113.)

39. *Setzen* is translated by "to posit"; it most often means "to be made explicit" as a moment in the process of the self-articulation of meaning. It is thus opposed to *an sich*.

40. *Sollen* as a logical category is a moment in the dialectic of Quality; we translate it by "ought" (see note 28 above). But this term also means "ought" in the sense of obligation or duty. It further refers to what is "supposed" to be such and such. We translate it accordingly.

41. *Spekulation, das Spekulative*. The "mirroring" (*speculum* = "mirror") is for Hegel not that of reality or nature in the mind. It takes place in the thinking-together of thought-determinations that for the understanding are radically opposed, and even contradict each other. In speculative thought they "mirror" each other and only in this way can they be genuine comprehension. "The speculative" unites them as their (inwardly articulated, or "reflecting") totality. It is expressed by using one of the opposed terms which is now understood as "overgrasping" (*übergreifen*) the other. "The speculative" is the thought of what is "rational" (or "meaningful"). (See in particular § 82, including R and A.)

42. *Übergreifen*. See the Introduction, pp. xxvi–xxvii.

43. *Vernunft, vernünftig; Verstand, verständig*. A thinking that is merely *verständig* lets the determinate distinctions count as ultimate, as fixed and final. *Verstand* is precisely this way of thinking; it is not a faculty of the soul in the traditional sense. *Vernünftig* is not generally what we call "rational" in ordinary usage; it is certainly not "rationalistic". In Hegel's use it is rather that which is truly "meaningful", what exhibits the Idea. But we have to translate it with "rational", and *Vernunft* with "reason". Reason is the dialectical and speculative way of thinking that sublates (*aufheben*) the fixed distinctions of the understanding. This is why, while there can be understanding without reason, there can be no reason without understanding. But "reason" is also "objective": It is the meaningful structure of reality, that what makes it *wirklich* (or "actual"). And the proper philosophical significance of "reason" is the Idea (see § 214).

44. *Wesen*. See the Introduction, pp. xviii–xix.

INDEX OF REFERENCES

All identifiable works referred to in Hegel's text or our notes are listed here, except for classical authors. The fragments of pre-Socratic philosophy are in Diels and Kranz, or translated in Kirk and Raven; both these works are listed. Other classical authors—when not readily available in many editions—can be found in the Loeb Classical Library. The object of this index is primarily to direct the reader to the best modern editions, and especially to English translations where these are known to us. Some information about the texts used by Hegel himself has occasionally been added.

ANSELM (of Canterbury), *Cur Deus Homo* and *Proslogion* (with Gaunilo, *Apologia pro Insipiente*). In F. S. Schmitt, ed., *Opera Omnia*. Edinburgh: Nelson, 1946. The best English translations are: *Why God Became Man*, J. M. Colleran, trans. Albany: Magi Books, 1969; and *Proslogion with Gaunilo's Reply*, M. J. Charlesworth, trans. Oxford: 1965.

BAADER, Franz Xaver von, *Bemerkungen über einige antireligiöse Philosopheme unserer Zeit.* Leipzig: 1824; and *Fermenta Cognitionis*. 5 vols. Berlin: 1822–24; both in *Sämtliche Werke*.

—————, "Hegel über meine Lehre." In *Sämtliche Werke*. Vol. 10, 306–309.

—————, *Sämtliche Werke*. F. Hoffmann et al., eds. 16 vols. Leipzig: 1851–60.

BEISER, Frederick C., *The Fate of Reason: German Philosophy from Kant to Fichte*. Cambridge: Harvard Univ. Press, 1987.

BOCHENSKI, I. M., *A History of Formal Logic*. Notre Dame, IN: Univ. of Notre Dame Press, 1961.

BODAMMER, T., *Hegels Deutung der Sprache*. Hamburg: Meiner, 1969.

BOEHME, Jakob, *Theosophia Revelata*. 2 vols. [Hamburg]: 1715. (The edition used by Hegel; it includes the "Life of Boehme" by A. von Frankenburg.)

—————, *The Works of Jacob Behmen*. 4 vols. London: 1644–52; reprinted, 1909–24.

BOURGEOIS, Bernard. See HEGEL, *Encyclopédie*.

BROWN, R., and STEWART, J. M. See HEGEL, *Lectures*.

BRUCKER, J. J., *Historia critica philosophiae*. 5 vols. Leipzig: 1742–44.

BUTLER, C., and SEILER, C. See HEGEL, *Letters*.

CERF and HARRIS. See HEGEL, *Faith and Knowledge*.

CLARK, M. See Bibliography.

COOK, D., *Language in the Philosophy of Hegel*. The Hague: Nijhoff, 1969.

DE NEGRI, Enrico. See HEGEL, *Fenomenologia*.

DESCARTES, René, *Discourse on Method* and *Mediations*. D. A. Cress, trans. Indianapolis: Hackett, 1979.

—————, *Lettres de M. Descartes*. Clerselier, ed. 3 vols. Paris: 1657.

—————, *Philosophical Letters*. A. Kenny, trans. Oxford: Blackwell, 1970.

—————, *Oeuvres de Descartes*. C. Adam and P. Tannery, eds. 12 vols. Paris: 1897–1910; Index général, Paris: 1913.

—————, *The Philosophical Writings of Descartes*. J. Cottingham, R. Stoothoff, and D. Murdoch, trans. 2 vols. Cambridge: Cambridge Univ. Press, 1985.

DIELS, H., and KRANZ, W., *Fragmente der Vorsokratiker*. 7th ed., 3 vols. Berlin: Wiedmannsche Buchhandlung, 1954. (= *D.K.*)

DI GIOVANNI, George, "The Facts of Consciousness." In *Between Kant and Hegel: Texts in the Development of Post-Kantian Idealism*, 3–50. Albany: SUNY Press, 1985.

_____, and HARRIS, H. S., *Between Kant and Hegel: Texts in the Development of Post-Kantian Idealism*. Albany: SUNY Press, 1985.

[DIONYSIUS,] "On the Divine Names." In *The Works of Dionysius the Areopagite*. J. H. Parker, trans. London: 1987–99; photoreprinted, Merrick, NY: Richwood, 1976.

FICHTE, Johann Gottlieb, *Appelation an das Publikum*. 1799. In Fichte, *Sämtliche Werke*, I. H. Fichte, ed. 8 vols. Berlin: Veit, 1845/6; photoreprinted, Berlin: de Gruyter, 1971. Vol. 5.

_____, "Darstellung der Wissenschaftslehre," 1801 (first printed 1845). In *Werke*. Vol. 2.

_____, *The Science of Knowledge* (*Wissenschaftslehre*, 1794) with the Two Introductions of 1797, P. Heath and J. Lachs, trans. New York: Appleton, 1970.

FORSTER, Michael N., *Hegel and Scepticism*. Cambridge: Harvard Univ. Press, 1989.

GERAETS, Theodore F., "Les trois lectures philosophiques de l'Encyclopédie ou la realisation du concept de la philosophie chez Hegel." *Hegel-Studien* 10 (1975):231–54.

GOETHE, J. W. von, *Werke*, Berliner Ausgabe, 22 vols. Berlin: Aufbau Verlag, 1973ff. (The edition cited herein. *Faust* in Band 8.)

GRAY, J. Glenn, "Hegel's Logic: The Philosophy of the Concrete." *Virginia Quarterly Review* (Spring 1971): 175–89.

GRIER, Philip T., "Abstract and Concrete in Hegel's Logic." In G. Di Giovanni, ed. *Essays on Hegel's Logic*. Albany: SUNY Press, 1990.

GROTIUS [Hugo de Groot,] *On the Law of War and Peace*. Paris: 1625. F. W. Kelsey, trans. Oxford: Clarendon, 1925. (The *Prolegomena* is reprinted, Indianapolis: Library of Liberal Arts, 1957.)

HALDANE, E. S., and SIMSON, F. H. See HEGEL, *Lectures*.

HARRIS, H. S., "The Cows in the Night." *Dialogue* 26 (1987):627–43; and "Postscript," 665–68.

_____ and CERF. See HEGEL, *Difference*.

_____ and KNOX. See HEGEL, *System of Ethical Life*.

HEGEL, G. W. F., *Aesthetics*. T. M. Knox, trans. 2 vols. Oxford: Clarendon Press, 1975.

_____, "Aphorisms from the Wastebook" (1802–06). In Rosenkranz, supplemented by F. Nicolin, *Hegel-Studien* 4 (1967):9–19; S. Klein et al., trans. *Independent Journal of Philosophy* 3 (1979): 1–5.

_____, *Berliner Schriften*, J. Hoffmeister, ed. Hamburg: Meiner, 1956.

_____, *Briefe von und an Hegel*, J. Hoffmeister and F. Nicolin, eds. 4 vols. Hamburg: Meiner, 1952–81.

_____, *The Difference between Fichte's and Schelling's System of Philosophy*. H. S. Harris and W. Cerf, trans. and eds. Albany: SUNY Press, 1977.

_____, Disputation Theses of 1800. *Erste Druckschriften*. G. Lasson, ed. 403–404; N. Waszek, trans. In D. Lamb, ed., *Hegel and Modern Philosophy*. London: Croom Helm, 1987.

_____, *Doctrine of Reflection* (Book 2 of *Science of Logic*). W. T. Harris, trans. New York: Appleton, 1881. (Not consulted by us.)

_____, *Enciclopedia* I: *La scienza della logica* (con le aggiunte), a cura di Valerio Verra. Turin: UTET, 1981.

_____, *Encyclopédie des sciences philosophiques* I: *La science de la logique*. Traduit par B. Bourgeois. Paris: Vrin, 1970.

_____, *Encyclopédie des sciences philosophiques en abrégé*. Traduit par M. de Gandillac. Paris: Gallimard, 1970.

_____, *Encyklopädie der philosophischen Wissenschaften*. Heidelberg: Osswald, 1817; reprinted in *Werke* (Jubiläumsausgabe), Band 6.

——————, *Encyklopädie der philosophischen Wissenschaften*. 3d ed. C. F. Winter, 1830; F. Nicolin and O. Pöggeler, eds. Hamburg: Meiner, 1959.

——————, *Encyklopädie der philosophischen Wissenschaften im Grundrisse*. 2d ed. Heidelberg: Osswald, 1827; W. Bonsiepen and H.-C. Lucas, eds. In *Gesammelte Werke*, Band 19. Hamburg: Meiner, 1989.

——————, *Erste Druckschriften*. G. Lasson, ed. Leipzig: Meiner, 1928.

——————, *Faith and Knowledge*. W. Cerf and H. S. Harris, trans. and ed. Albany: SUNY Press, 1977.

——————, *Fenomenologia dello Spirito*. 2 vols. A cura di E. De Negri. Florence: La nuova Italia, 1936; 2d ed., 1960.

——————, *Gesammelte Werke*. Rheinische-westfälischen Akademie der Wissenschaften, ed. Hamburg: Meiner, 1968ff. (The *Wissenschaft der Logik* [1812–16] is in Band 11–12; the 1831 revision of volume 1 is in Band 21. The *Enzyklopädie* [1827] is in Band 19.)

——————, *Grundlinien der Philosophie des Rechts*. 4th ed. J. Hoffmeister, ed. Hamburg: Meiner, 1955.

——————, *Hegel's Doctrine of Formal Logic*. H. S. Macran, trans. Oxford: Clarendon, 1912.

——————, *Hegel's Logic of World and Idea*. H. S. Macran, trans. Oxford: Clarendon, 1929.

——————, *Introduction to the Philosophy of History*. L. Rauch, trans. Indianapolis: Hackett, 1988.

——————, *The Jena System of 1804–05: Logic and Metaphysics*. J. Burbidge et al., trans. Kingston and Montreal: McGill-Queen's Press, 1986.

——————, *Lectures on the History of Philosophy*. E. S. Haldane and F. H. Simson, trans. 3 vols. London: Kegan Paul, Trench Trübner & Co. Ltd., 1896 (latest reprint, Atlantic Highlands, NJ: Humanities Press, 1983).

——————, *Lectures on the History of Philosophy*. R. Brown and J. M. Stewart trans., with the assistance of H. S. Harris. 3 vols. Los Angeles: Univ. of Calif. Press (vol. 3, 1990; vols. 1 and 2, in preparation). (A translation of the lecture course of 1825–26 as edited in *Vorlesungen*, Band 6–9.)

——————, *Lectures on the Philosophy of Religion*. P. C. Hodgson et al., trans. 3 vols. Los Angeles: Univ. of Calif. Press, 1984–87. (Translation of *Vorlesungen*, Band 3–5.)

——————, *Letters*. C. Butler and C. Seiler, trans. Bloomington: Indiana Univ. Press, 1984.

——————, *Logic, being* Part One of the Encyclopaedia (1830). William Wallace, trans., with foreword by J. N. Findlay. Oxford: Clarendon, 1975. (This is the third edition; first edition, 1873, second 1892.)

——————, *Logique*. Traduit par A. Vera. 2 vols. Paris: Ladrange, 1859; photostatic reprint, Brussels: Culture et Civilisation, 1968.

——————, *Phenomenology of Spirit*. A. V. Miller, trans. Oxford: Clarendon, 1970.

——————, *Philosophy of Nature*. M. J. Petry, trans. 3 vols. London: Allen and Unwin, 1970.

——————, *Philosophy of Nature*. A. V. Miller, trans. Oxford: Clarendon Press, 1970.

——————, *The Philosophy of Right*. T. M. Knox, trans. and ed. Oxford: Clarendon Press, 1942.

——————, *Philosophy of Subjective Spirit*. M. J. Petry, trans. Dordrecht: Reidel, 1979.

——————, "Reason and Religious Truth." Foreword to H. F. W. Hinrichs, *Die Religion usw*, 1822. A. V. Miller, trans. In *Beyond Epistemology*, 227–46. F. G. Weiss, ed. The Hague: Nijhoff, 1974.

——————, *Science of Logic*. W. H. Johnson and L. G. Struthers, trans. 2 vols. London: Allen and Unwin, 1928.

——————, *Science of Logic*. A. V. Miller, trans. London: Allen and Unwin, 1969.

——————, *Selections*. M. Inwood, ed. New York: Macmillan, 1989.

——————, *Subjective Logic* (Book 3 of *Science of Logic*). H. Sloman and J. Wallon, trans.

London: John Chapman, 1855. (Rather loose paraphrase, but the earliest rendering of any part of Hegel's *Logic* in English. Not consulted by us.)

_____, *System der Wissenschaft: Erster Teil, die Phänomenologie des Geistes*. Bamberg and Wurzburg, 1807. (The first edition of the *Phenomenology*; see *Gesammelte Werke*, Band 9.)

_____, *System of Ethical Life and First Philosophy of Spirit*. H. S. Harris and T. M. Knox, trans. and eds. Albany: SUNY Press, 1979.

_____, *Texts and Commentary*. W. A. Kaufmann, trans. Garden City, N.Y.: Anchor, 1966.

_____, *Vorlesungen über die Geschichte der Philosophie* IV. P. Garniron and W. Jaeschke, eds. Hamburg: Meiner, 1986 (*Vorlesungen*, Band 9). (The first three volumes *Vorlesungen*, Band 6–8, are in preparation.)

_____, *Vorlesungen über die Philosophie der Religion*. W. Jaeschke, ed. Hamburg: Meiner, 1983–85 (*Vorlesungen*, Band 3–5).

_____, *Werke* (complete edition, edited by a committee of Hegel's friends). 18 vols. in 21. Berlin: 1832ff. Band 6: *Encyklopädie . . . Erster Teil: Die Logik . . . mit Zusätze*. L. Boumann, ed. Berlin: 1840.

_____, *Werke* (Jubiläumsausgabe). H. Glockner, ed. 20 vols. Stuttgart: Fromann, 1927ff (includes *Hegel-Lexikon*, 2 vols.).

_____, *Werke in 20 Bänden* (*Theorie-Werkausgabe*). E. Moldenhauer and K. M. Michel, eds. Frankfurt: Suhrkamp, 1970. Band 7: *Grundlinien der Philosophie des Rechts*; Band 8: *Enzyklopädie . . . (1830) Erster Teil. Die Wissenschaft der Logik*. Mit den mündlichen Zusätzen. (= *T.W-A.*)

_____, *Wissenschaft der Logik*. 3 vols. Nüremberg: 1812–16; reprinted in *Gesammelte Werke*, Band 11 and 12.

_____, *Wissenschaft der Logik*. 2 vols. G. Lasson, ed. Leipzig: Meiner, 1923.

_____, and SCHELLING, F. W. J., *Kritisches Journal der Philosophie*. 2 vols. Tübingen: Cotta, 1802–03; reprinted complete in *Gesammelte Werke*, Band 4.

HERDER, G. W. von, *Gott. Einige Gespräche* (1788, 1800); *God. Some Conversations*. F. H. Burkhardt, trans. Indianapolis: Library of Liberal Arts, 1940.

HERMANN, Gottfried, *Handbuch der Metrik*. Leipzig: 1790.

HIEROCLES [K. W. Ramler,] *Scherzreden*. Berlin: Aus dem Griechischen des Hierocles, 1782.

HINRICHS, H. W. F. *Die Religion im inneren Verhältnisse Zur Wissenschaft*. Heidelberg: Groos, 1822.

HOTHO, H. G., *De philosophia Cartesiana*. Berlin: 1826.

HUME, David, *History of England*. W. B. Todd, ed. 6 vols. New York: Liberty Classics, 1983.

_____, *Inquiry Concerning Human Understanding*. L. A. Selby-Bigge, ed. Oxford: Clarendon, 1902.

_____, "Natural History of Religion." In *Essays Moral, Political and Literary*. Oxford: Clarendon, 1969.

INWOOD, Michael, ed., *Hegel*. Oxford: Oxford Univ. Press, 1985. (See also HEGEL, *Selections*.)

JACOBI, F. H., *Briefe über Spinoza* (1787); reprinted in *Werke*, Vol. 4. (An abridged translation is in preparation. See the following item.)

_____, *Werke*. 6 vols. in 8, Leipzig; photographic reprint, Darmstadt: Wissenschaftliche Buchgesellschaft, 1968. (A translation of selected Jacobi texts by G. Di Giovanni is in preparation.)

JAESCHKE, W. See HEGEL, *Vorlesungen über die Philosophie*.

KANT, *Critique of Judgment* (Riga, 1790, 1793). L. W. Pluhar, trans. Indianapolis: Hackett, 1987.

_____, *Critique of Practical Reason* (Riga, 1788). L. W. Beck, trans. Chicago: Univ. of Chicago Press, 1949; reprinted, New York: Garland, 1976. (Includes also the *Foundations of the Metaphysics of Morals*; the *Critique* is also reprinted separately in the Library of Liberal Arts, 1956.)

——————, *Critique of Pure Reason* (A and B). Norman Kemp Smith, trans. London: Macmillan, 1933. (*Critik der reinen Vernunft*, Riga, 1781 [= A]; Hegel used the 2d ed., Riga, 1787 [= B]). (= *CPR*)

——————, *Gesammelte Schriften*. The Prussian Academy of Sciences, ed. 9 vols. Berlin and Leipzig: 1910–23. (= *Akad*)

——————, *Grounding for the Metaphysics of Morals* (Riga, 1785). J. W. Ellington, trans. Indianapolis: Hackett, 1981.

——————, *Prolegomena to Any Future Metaphysics*. J. W. Ellington, trans. Indianapolis: Hackett, 1977.

KASTNER, A. G., *Angfangsgründe der höheren Mechanik*. 2d ed. Leipzig: 1793.

KAUFMANN. See HEGEL, *Texts and Commentary*.

KERNER, Justinus, *Die Seherin von Prevorst*. Stuttgart and Tübingen: 1829.

KIRK, G. S., and RAVEN, J. E., *The Presocratic Philosophers*. 3d ed. Cambridge: Cambridge Univ. Press, 1989.

KNEALE, William C. and Martha, *Development of Logic*. Oxford: Clarendon Press, 1962.

KOYRÉ, Alexandre, "Note sur la langue et la terminologie hégéliennes." *Revue philosophique de la France et de l'Étranger* 112 (1931):409–39; reprinted in *Études d'histoire de la pensée philosophique*. Paris: Gallimard, 1971.

LAMB, David, ed., *Hegel and Modern Philosophy*. London: Croom Helm, 1987.

LASSON, G. See HEGEL, *Wissenschaft*.

LEIBNIZ, G. W., *Monadology and Other Essays*. P. Schrecker, trans. Indianapolis: Hackett, 1965. (Includes "Principles of Nature and of Grace.")

——————, *Nouveaux Essais* (1765). P. Remnant and J. Bennett, trans. Cambridge: Cambridge Univ. Press, 1981.

——————, *Philosophical Papers and Letters*. L. E. Loemker, trans. and ed. 2 vols. Chicago: Univ. of Chicago Press, 1956; reprinted, Dordrecht: Kluwer, 1969.

——————, *Theodicy*. A. Farrer, ed.; E. M. Huggard, trans. London: Routledge, 1952; abridged reprint, D. Allen, ed. Indianapolis: Library of Liberal Arts, 1966.

LOCKE, John, *Essay on Human Understanding*. J. Yolton, ed. New York: Dent, 1961.

MACRAN, H. S. See HEGEL, *Logic*.

McCUMBER, John, "Hegel's Philosophical Languages." *Hegel-Studien* 14 (1979):183–96.

MARX, Karl, and ENGELS, Friedrich, *Collected Works*. Vol. 1. Moscow: Progress Publishers, 1975.

MILLER, A. V. See HEGEL, *Phenomenology, Philosophy of Nature, Science of Logic*.

MUIRHEAD, J. H. "How Hegel Came to England." *Mind* 36 (1927):423–47; a revised version was published in *The Platonic Tradition in Anglo-Saxon Philosophy*. London: Allen and Unwin, 1931 (pt. 2, chap. 2, 147–73).

NEWTON, I., *Philosophiae naturalis principia mathematica*. London: 1687, trans. from the 3d ed. (1726) and F. Cajori, ed. Berkeley: Univ. of California Press, 1934 (paper, 1962). (Hegel owned the 2d ed., Amsterdam: 1714.)

NICOLIN, F., and PÖGGELER, O. See HEGEL, *Encyklopädie*.

PARTINGTON, J. R., *History of Chemistry*. 4 vols. London: Macmillan, 1960–70.

PEPERZAK, A. T. B., *Philosophy and Politics*. The Hague: Nijhoff, 1988.

PETRY, M. J., "Hegel's Excerpts from the Morning Chronicle." *Hegel-Studien* 11 (1976):11–80. See also HEGEL, *Philosophy of Nature, Philosophy of Subjective Spirit*.

RICHTER, Jean Paul Friedrich, *Titan*. 4 vols. 1800–03; C. T. Brooks, trans. Boston: Ticknor and Fields, 1862.

ROSENKRANZ, Karl, *G. W. F. Hegels Leben*. Berlin: 1844; photographic reprint, Darmstadt: Wissenschaftlifche Buchgesellschaft, 1963.

ROUSSEAU, J.-J., *The Social Contract*. G. D. H. Cole, trans. New York: Dent, 1913.

SCHELLING, F. W. J., *Bruno*. M. Vater, trans. Albany: SUNY Press, 1984.

_____, "Darstellung meines Systems" (1801); see *Sämtliche Werke*. Vol. 4, 105–212. (First published in the *Zeitschrift für spekulative Physik*, 1800–01.)

_____, "Einleitung zu dem Entwurf eines System der Naturphilosophie" (1799); reprinted in *Sämtliche Werke*. Vol. 3, 269–326.

_____, *Ideas for a Philosophy of Nature*. E. E. Harris and P. Heath, trans. Cambridge: Cambridge Univ. Press, 1988.

_____, *Sämtliche Werke*. K. F. A. Schelling, ed. 14 vols. Tübingen: Cotta, 1856–61. Selected works from this edition have been photoreprinted in 8 vols., Darmstadt: Wissenschaftliche Buchgesellschaft, 1966–68.

_____, *System of Transcendental Idealism (1800)*. P. Heath, trans. Charlottesville: Univ. Press of Virginia, 1978.

SCHILLER, J. C. F., *On the Aesthetic Education of Man*. E. M. Wilkinson and L. A. Willoughby, trans. Oxford: Clarendon, 1967.

_____, *On the Aesthetic Education of Man*. Trans. with an introduction by Reginald Snell. London: Routledge and Kegan Paul, 1954; New York: Frederick Ungar, 1965.

SIMON, Josef, *Das Problem der Sprache bei Hegel*. Stuttgart: Kohlhammer, 1976.

SPINOZA, Benedict de, *Chief Works*. R. H. M. Elwes, trans. 2 vols. New York: Dover Press, 1951.

_____, *Opera*. H. E. G. Paulus, ed. 2 vols. Jena: 1802–03 (the edition used by Hegel).

_____, *Opera*. C. Gebhardt, ed. 4 vols. Heidelberg: 1924 (the edition cited herein).

STIRLING, J. H., *The Secret of Hegel* (1865). 2d ed. Edinburgh: Oliver and Boyd, 1898; photographic reprint, Dubuque, IA: Brown, n.d. (Includes translation of "Quality" and "Quantity" from the *Science of Logic*; also of §§ 99–106 from the *Encyclopaedia Logic*.)

THOLUCK, F. A. G., *Blüthensammlung aus der morgenländischen Mystik*. Berlin: 1825.

_____, *Die Lehre von der Sünde und vom Versöhner*. 2d ed. Hamburg: 1825.

_____, *Die spekulative Trinitätslehre des späteren Orients*. Berlin: 1826.

THOMAS AQUINAS, *Summa Theologiae*, pt. 1. In *Basic Writings*. A. C. Pegis, ed. 2 vols. New York: Knopf, 1944. (= *S.T.*)

THOMSON, Thomas, ed., *Annals of Philosophy; or Magazine of Chemistry, Mineralogy, Mechanics, Natural History, Agriculture, and the Arts*. 16 vols. London: 1813–20.

VERRA, Valerio. See HEGEL, *Enciclopedia*.

WALLACE, William. See Bibliography; see also HEGEL, *Logic*.

WESTPHAL, Kenneth R., "Hegel's Attitude toward Jacobi in the 'Third Attitude of Thought towards Objectivity.'" *Southern Journal of Philosophy* 27 (1979):135–56.

ZÜFLE, Manfred, *Prosa der Welt. Die Sprache Hegels*. Einsiedeln: Johannes Verlag, 1968.

BIBLIOGRAPHY

Two especially useful sources of bibliographical information regarding Hegel are K. Steinhauer, *Hegel Bibliography* (Munich/London: Saur, 1980), and *Hegel-Studien* (Bonn: Bouvier, 1961ff), which runs regular comprehensive surveys of publications on Hegel. Regular reviews of new publications on Hegel are found in "Bulletin de littérature hégélienne" in *Archives de Philosophie*, and in *The Owl of Minerva*, the biannual journal of the Hegel Society of America.

The following lists (with just one exception) only writings on Hegel's logic as a whole, thus excluding treatments of particular themes. Within those limits the list is not meant to be exhaustive so much as useful. Naturally, in both respects there is an element of arbitrariness in what is included and what excluded. Not listed is the literature in German published during roughly the first half of nineteenth century, which can be found in Steinhauer's bibliography (cited above), or the conveniently assembled selective list in V. Verra's Italian translation of the *Encyclopaedia Logic, La Scienza della Logica di Georg Wilhelm Friedrich Hegel* (Turin: Unione Tipografico Editrice Torinese, 1981), p. 69.

BAILLIE, J. B., *The Origin and Significance of Hegel's Logic. A General Introduction to Hegel's System*. London: MacMillan, 1901; reprinted, New York: Garland, 1983. Mainly chaps. 8 and 9.

BIARD, J., BUVET, D., KERVEGAN, J.-F., KLING, J.-F., LACROIX, A., LECRIVAIN, A., and SLUBICKI, M., *Introduction à la lecture de la Science de la Logique de Hegel*. 3 vols. Paris: Aubier-Montaigne, 1981–87.

BURBIDGE, J., *On Hegel's Logic. Fragments of a Commentary*. New York: Humanities Press, 1981.

CASSIRER, E., *Das Erkenntnisproblem in der Philosophie und Wissenschaft der neueren Zeit*. Vol. 3, 328–362. (1920). 2d ed. Berlin: B. Cassirer, 1923.

CLARK, M., *Logic and System. A Study of the Transition from "Vorstellung" to Thought in the Philosophy of Hegel*. The Hague: Nijhoff, 1971.

CORETH, E., *Das Dialektische Sein in Hegels Logik*. Vienna: Herder, 1952.

DAMEROW, P., and LEFÈVRE, W., "Die wissenschaftliche Problemlage für Hegels 'Logik'." *Hegel-Jahrbuch* (1979):349–68.

DI GIOVANNI, G., ed., *Essays on Hegel's Logic*. Albany: SUNY Press, 1990.

ELEY, L., *Hegels Wissenschaft der Logik. Leitfaden und Kommentar*. Munich: Wm. Fink, 1976.

FINDLAY, J. N., *Hegel: A Re-Examination*, chaps. 6–8 (1958). 2d ed. London: George Allen and Unwin, 1964.

FISCHER, K., *Hegels Leben, Werke und Lehre* (Band 8, I Teil of Fischer's *Geschichte der neueren Philosophie*). 2d ed. Heidelberg: Carl Winter, 1911; Kraus reprint, 1973, pt. 1., bk. 2., chaps. 13–22.

FLEISCHMANN, E., *La Science universelle ou la logique de Hegel*. Paris: Plon, 1968.

FULDA, H. F., *Das Problem einer Einleitung in Hegels Wissenschaft der Logik*. (1965). 2d ed. Frankfurt/M.: V. Klostermann, 1975.

———————, HORSTMANN, R.-P., and THEUNISSEN, M., *Kritische Darstellung der Metaphysik. Eine Diskussion über Hegels Logik*. Frankfurt/M.: Suhrkamp, 1980.

GADAMER, H.-G., "The Idea of Hegel's Logic." In *Hegel's Dialectic. Five Hermeneutical Studies*, 75–99. New Haven: Yale Univ. Press, 1976.

GENTILE, G., "The Reform of the Hegelian Dialectic." A. Armstrong, trans. *Idealistic Studies* 11 (1981):187–213.

GUZZONI, U., *Werden zu Sich. Eine Untersuchung zu Hegels "Wissenschaft der Logik"*. Freiburg/Munich: Karl Alber, 1963.

HARRIS, E. E., *An Interpretation of the Logic of Hegel*. Lanham, MD: Univ. Press of America, 1983.

HARRIS, W. T., *Hegel's Logic. A Book on the Genesis of the Categories of the Mind. A Critical Exposition*, mainly chaps. 11–32. Chicago: Griggs, 1890; reprinted, New York: Garland, 1983.

HARTMANN, N., *Die Philosophie des deutschen Idealismus*. Band 2, pt. 3. Berlin: Walter de Gruyter, 1929.

HENRICH, D., ed., *Hegels Wissenschaft der Logik. Formation und Rekonstruktion*. Veröffenlichungen der Internationalen Hegel-Vereinigung, Band 16. Stuttgart: Klett-Cotta Verlag, 1986.

HIBBEN, J. G., *Hegel's Logic. An Essay in Interpretation*. New York: Scribner's Sons, 1902; reprinted New York: Garland, 1983.

HÖSLE, V., *Hegels System. Der Idealismus der Subjektivität und des Problem der Intersubjektivität*. Band 1, *Systementwicklung und Logik*. Hamburg: Felix Meiner, 1987.

HYPPOLITE, J., *Logique et existence. Essai sur la logique de Hegel*. Paris: Presses Universitaires de France, 1961.

——————, "On the *Logic* of Hegel" (1952). In J. Hyppolite, *Studies on Marx and Hegel*, 169–84. London: Heinemann, 1969.

INWOOD, M. J., *Hegel*. London: Routledge and Kegan Paul, 1983.

JOHNSON, P. E., *The Critique of Thought. A Re-Examination of Hegel's 'Science of Logic'*. Aldershot: Averbury/Gower Publishing Co., 1989.

KRONER, R., *Von Kant bis Hegel*, 2:415–502. (1924/1927). 2d ed. Tübingen: J. C. B. Mohr, 1961.

LAKEBRINK, B., *Kommentar zu Hegels "Logik" in seiner "Enzyklopädie" von 1830*. 2 vols. Freiburg/Munich: Karl Alber, 1979, 1985.

LENIN, V. I., *Philosophical Notebooks*. Vol. 38 of the *Collected Works*, esp. 85–243, 317–26. 4th ed. Moscow: Foreign Languages Publishing House, 1961.

LEONARD, A., *Commentaire littéral de la logique de Hegel*. Paris: Vrin/Louvain: Éditions de l'Institut Supérieur de Philosophie, 1974.

McTAGGART, J. M. E., *A Commentary on Hegel's Logic*. Cambridge: Cambridge Univ. Press, 1910; reprinted, New York: Russell & Russell, 1964.

MARCUSE, H., *Hegel's Ontology and the Theory of Historicity*, pt. 1 (1932). 2d ed., 1968. Cambridge, MA: MIT Press, 1987.

——————, *Reason and Revolution. Hegel and the Rise of Social Theory*, pt. 1, chap. 5 (1941). 2d ed. London: Routledge and Kegan Paul, 1955.

MARX, W., *Hegels Theorie logischer Vermittlung. Kritik der dialektischen Begriffskonstruktion in der "Wissenschaft der Logik."* Stuttgart: Frommann-Holzboog, 1972.

MURE, G. R. G., *A Study of Hegel's Logic*. Oxford: Oxford Univ. Press, 1950.

NOEL, G., *La Logique de Hegel*, mainly chaps. 2–4. Paris: Alcan, 1897.

PELLOUX, L., *La Logica di Hegel*. Milan: Vita e Pensiero, 1938.

PINKARD, T., "The Logic of Hegel's *Logic*." *Journal of the History of Philosophy* 17 (1979):417–35. Reprinted in M. Inwood, ed., *Hegel*. Oxford: Oxford Univ. Press, 1985.

——————, *Hegel's Dialectic*, chaps. 1–5. Philadelphia: Temple Univ. Press, 1988.

PIPPIN, R. B., *Hegel's Idealism. The Satisfactions of Self-Consciousness*, pt. 3. Cambridge: Cambridge Univ. Press, 1989.

RADEMAKER, H., *Hegels "Wissenschaft der Logik" Eine darstellende und erläuternde Einführung*. Wiesbaden: Franz Steiner Verlag, 1979.

ROSEN, M., *Hegel's Dialectic and its Criticism*. Cambridge: Cambridge Univ. Press, 1982.

ROSEN, S., G. W. F. Hegel. *An Introduction to the Science of Wisdom*, chaps. 3–5. New Haven: Yale Univ. Press, 1974.

ROYCE, J., "Hegel's Terminology." In J. B. Baldwin, ed., *Dictionary of Philosophy and Psychology*, 1:454–65. Rev. ed. New York: Macmillan, 1925.

SCHMIDT, J., *Hegels Wissenschaft der Logik und ihre Kritik durch Adolf Trendelenberg*. Pullacher Philosophische Forschungen, Band 13. Munich: Johannes Berchmans Verlag, 1977.

SPAVENTA, B., "Le prime categorie della logica di Hegel" (1864). In *Scritti filosofici*, 185–252. G. Gentile, ed. Naples: Morano, 1900.

STACE, W. T., *The Philosophy of Hegel. A Systematic Exposition*, pt. 2. London: Macmillan, 1924.

TAYLOR, C., *Hegel*, pt. 3. Cambridge: Cambridge Univ. Press, 1975.

THEUNISSEN, M., *Sein und Schein. Zur kritischen Funktion der Hegelschen Logik*. Frankfurt/M.: Suhrkamp, 1980.

WALLACE, W., *Prolegomena to the Study of Hegel's Philosophy and Especially of His Logic*, mainly chaps. 26–32. 2d ed. Oxford: Univ. Press, 1894.

WEISS, F. G., ed., *Beyond Epistemology. New Studies in the Philosophy of Hegel*. The Hague: Nijhoff, 1974.

BRIEF GUIDE TO THE BIBLIOGRAPHY

PRIMARILY GENERAL APPROACHES TO HEGEL'S LOGIC

GADAMER, HYPPOLITE (1969), and PINKARD (1979) are brief overall perspectives on the subject. The second may be supplemented by the author's earlier book. PINKARD (1988) regards Hegel's logical theory as an "explanation of possibility." ROYCE is a very useful guide to central concepts.

BAILLIE, W. T. HARRIS, and WALLACE are older works, written from an Absolute Idealist standpoint and thoroughly sympathetic to Hegel. CLARK is a study of Hegel's conception of the relation of ordinary language (*Vorstellung*) to thought proper (*Denken*). CORETH is on Hegel's conception of ontology (Thomist orientation). DAMEROW/LEFÈVRE situates Hegel's logic with respect to the scientific scene of the time, especially mathematics, and follows a Marxist orientation. FULDA is a detailed discussion of the question of the appropriate "entry" into the *Logic*, vis-à-vis the claims of the *Phenomenology of Spirit* and the earlier sections of the first part of the *Encyclopaedia*. GUZZONI's theme is Hegel's idea of development as realisation of the implicit. HENRICH brings together a wide range of papers on the *Logic* as a whole (especially in the first part of the book) and on particular topics, from a variety of standpoints.

HÖSLE discusses the historical background of the Hegelian philosophy, analyses the structure of his system and his method, and develops the main thesis of the work, namely, that there is no thorough-going correspondence between the *Logic* and the "Realphilosophie". INWOOD's very long book places a heavy emphasis on the introductory sections of the *Encyclopaedia Logic*; it is at once expository and critical. W. MARX and M. ROSEN are highly critical. S. ROSEN has much on the historical affiliations of the *Logic*. SCHMIDT is a Thomist-oriented response to Trendelenberg's critique of Hegel's logic.

THEUNISSEN presents a distinctive interpretation according to which Hegel's "objective" logic is an exhibition of traditional metaphysics which is simultaneously a critique of its pretension to represent the truth (*Schein*) and an unveiling of the truth (*Sein*), whilst the "subjective" logic is a presentation of the latter in the form of a theory of "communicative freedom," found in Hegel's theory of the judgment. The account is discussed in FULDA/ HORSTMANN/THEUNISSEN. SPAVENTA's essay inspired GENTILE'S "reform of the dialectic," which was very influential on the second generation of Anglo-Hegelians (especially Collingwood).

WHOLLY OR PRIMARILY STEP-BY-STEP COMMENTARIES

PARTS OF BOOKS

WALLACE, already mentioned, also belongs here. FISCHER's presentation, part of his large, nineteenth-century *Geschichte der neueren Philosophie*, is wooden, sticking closely to the original texts. CASSIRER (in his usual elegant style), HARTMANN, and KRONER present the *Logic* in the context of "classical" German idealism. STACE essentially paraphrases the *Encyclopaedia of the Philosophical Sciences*; though, like FISCHER, it is on the whole pretty wooden, Stace can often be very helpful, especially as a guide to a first reading of the *Logic*. FINDLAY was the first book to try to make Hegel accessible to "analytically" minded philosophers. TAYLOR also attempts to make sense of Hegel, and in particular the *Logic*, in a no-nonsense, "contemporary" way. It is highly recommended. LENIN presents reading notes on the *Science of Logic* made in late 1914–15; it is especially influential on Soviet writing on Hegel, and very stimulating in many ways. MARCUSE (1955) is also a Marxist treatment, emphasising the social-critical significance of the *Logic*, whilst his earlier work (1987), strongly influenced by Heidegger, is, as its title suggests, a presentation of the *Logic* from the point of view of an ontology of history.

MONOGRAPHS

BASED WHOLLY OR MAINLY ON THE *ENCYCLOPAEDIA LOGIC*

HIBBEN is a short work by one of the earlier American Hegelians, not without value as a first orientation. MURE is a solid commentary, published at a time when most Anglophone philosophers could scarcely spell Hegel's name. It emphasises Hegel's affiliations with Aristotle. E. E. HARRIS is a useful book, though his closeness to what he is commenting upon often leads to his failing to see what readers not so identified with Hegel might require to be elucidated. These works follow the general drift of the *Encyclopaedia*. LAKEBRINK and LEONARD offer sentence-by-sentence commentaries on that text though with extensive reference to the larger *Logic*. Both are Thomist in orientation, the first more explicitly so.

BASED WHOLLY OR MAINLY ON THE *SCIENCE OF LOGIC*

W. T. HARRIS, NOEL, and McTAGGART are older commentaries, all written from an Idealist standpoint. The first two are fairly brief and may be useful to the beginner. The third is an elaborate work and not recommended to the novice. (E. E. Harris's book has many polemics with McTAGGART.) PELLOUX comes from a Catholic press. FLEISCHMANN is a detailed commentary; ELEY and RADEMAKER are briefer, the former making considerable use of the resources of modern formal logic.

BIARD ET AL. is a meticulous commentary on the text of that work, one volume's being devoted to each of the three main parts. JOHNSON's book is very much looser in exegesis, its aim being mainly to bring out the significance of the *Logic* for general philosophical problems, particularly as they occur in more recent discussion. PIPPIN's account of this part of Hegel's work does not attempt a commentary on the whole of it. Rather, he is concerned to show that the general thesis of his book, namely, that Hegel was basically rethinking Kant's project in the *Critique of Pure Reason*, is confirmed and further illuminated there. BURBIDGE is a very dense commentary on the first chapter of each of the three parts of the *Logic*, plus chapters on related topics. The volume edited by G. DI GIOVANNI contains the papers given at the Conference of the Hegel Society of America (Chicago, 1988) on ''Hegel's Logic.''

ANALYTICAL INDEX
by H.S. Harris

For the most part this index aims to be as exhaustive as possible. But some entries are illustrative only, and some are incomplete because time and patience were exhausted first.

I have capitalized the headings that I take to be links in Hegel's logical chain. My decisions were taken after consulting both Wallace and Stace. I have tended to agree more with Stace, but I have not exactly followed either of them. (H stands for Hegel; and the letters U, P, S stand for Universal, Particular, Singular.)